Venezuela Before Chávez

Venezuela Before Chávez

Anatomy of an Economic Collapse

Edited by
RICARDO HAUSMANN
and FRANCISCO RODRÍGUEZ

The Pennsylvania State University Press
University Park, Pennsylvania

LIBRARY OF CONGRESS CATALOGING-IN-PUBLICATION DATA
Venezuela before Chavez : anatomy of an economic collapse /
edited by Ricardo Hausmann and Francisco Rodríguez.
    p.   cm
Summary: "A collection of essays that explore the collapse of
economic growth in Venezuela since the 1970s. Essays discuss
the relevance of public investment, labor markets, fiscal policy,
institutions, politics, and values"—Provided by publisher.
Includes bibliographical references and index.
ISBN 978-0-271-05631-9 (cloth : alk. paper)
1. Venezuela—Economic conditions—1958– .
2. Venezuela—Economic policy.
3. Financial crises—Venezuela.
I. Hausmann, Ricardo, editor of compilation.
II. Rodríguez, Francisco, 1970– , editor of compilation.

HC237.V4653 2013
330.987'0633—dc23
2013020926

Contents

PREFACE AND ACKNOWLEDGMENTS | *vii*

Introduction | *1*
Ricardo Hausmann and Francisco Rodríguez

1 Why Did Venezuelan Growth Collapse? | *15*
Ricardo Hausmann and Francisco Rodríguez

2 Venezuela After a Century of Oil Exploitation | *51*
Osmel Manzano

3 Public Investment and Productivity Growth in the Venezuelan
Manufacturing Industry | *91*
José Pineda and Francisco Rodríguez

4 The Incidence of Labor Market Reforms on Employment in the
Venezuelan Manufacturing Sector, 1995–2001 | *115*
Omar Bello and Adriana Bermúdez

5 Understanding Economic Growth in Venezuela, 1970–2005:
The Real Effects of a Financial Collapse | *157*
Matías Braun

6 Much Higher Schooling, Much Lower Wages: Human Capital
and Economic Collapse in Venezuela | *187*
Daniel Ortega and Lant Pritchett

7 Income Distribution and Redistribution in Venezuela | *207*
Samuel Freije

8 Competing for Jobs or Creating Jobs? The Impact of Immigration
on Native-Born Unemployment in Venezuela, 1980–2003 | *239*
Dan Levy and Dean Yang

9   Sleeping in the Bed One Makes: The Venezuelan Fiscal Policy Response
     to the Oil Boom | 259
     María Antonia Moreno and Cameron A. Shelton

10   Institutional Collapse: The Rise and Decline of Democratic Governance
     in Venezuela | 285
     Francisco Monaldi and Michael Penfold

11   The Political Economy of Industrial Policy in Venezuela | 321
     Jonathan Di John

12   Explaining Chavismo: The Unexpected Alliance of Radical Leftists
     and the Military in Venezuela under Hugo Chávez | 371
     Javier Corrales

13   Oil, Macro Volatility, and Crime in the Determination of Beliefs
     in Venezuela | 407
     Rafael Di Tella, Javier Donna, and Robert MacCulloch

14   Understanding the Collapse: Venezuela's Experience in Cross-National
     Perspective | 425
     Ricardo Hausmann and Francisco Rodríguez

     CONTRIBUTORS | 443
     INDEX | 445

Preface and Acknowledgments

On March 5, 2013, Venezuela's president Hugo Chávez died after a two-year struggle with cancer, putting an end to fourteen years in the presidency. Several books have already been published over the past few years trying to assess Chávez's legacy, and many more will certainly come.[1] This is not one of them. Rather, this book is about Venezuela before Chávez came to power. It tries to understand how one of the continent's most prosperous nations, which boasted a vibrant democracy at a time when much of the region was mired in authoritarianism, saw a prolonged collapse of its economic and political institutions over the last two decades of the twentieth century. While this book is not about Chávez, it *is* about how Chávez became possible.

Hugo Chávez did not come to power in a political vacuum. His radical authoritarian message was capable of striking a deep chord among Venezuelans only after they became convinced that their institutions were incapable of bringing them prosperity or stability. Chávez was only possible after two decades in which living standards fell by more than one-fourth and the country's political system imploded. In a context of continued economic deterioration and weakened political institutions, there was a clear opening for a political movement that called for radical change. This was the opportunity that Hugo Chávez saw, and took full advantage of, in 1998.

After 1998, the story of *chavismo* could have been simpler—and shorter. Hugo Chávez's policies would have wreaked economic havoc in just about any economy, except an economy that saw its terms of trade grow more than sevenfold. In real terms, Venezuelan oil prices had reached their lowest level in nearly three decades—$7.66 a barrel—in the second week of December 1998, the week during which Chávez was first elected to the presidency.[2] Between 1998 and 2011, Venezuela's terms of trade grew 6.7 times more rapidly than the regional average and 3.1 times more rapidly than Bolivia's, which had the second-highest terms-of-trade growth in the region. Even after a decline in physical production and exports of oil caused by the systematic overtaxation of the oil industry and the virtual disappearance of non-oil exports, Venezuela's exports in 2011 were 3.6 times as large as in 1998.

Despite this stroke of luck, Chávez almost lost power three years into his administration. In early 2002, the nation faced a balance of payments crisis and was forced to enact a major macroeconomic adjustment—a crisis that occurred despite the fact that oil prices had nearly doubled since Chávez had reached office. It is worth emphasizing that this economic adjustment occurred before the onset of that year's political crisis: GDP contracted by 4.4 percent and the currency slid by 21 percent in the first quarter of 2002, while the first attempt to drive Chávez from office took place in April 2002.

However, the ensuing political crisis—which included not only the coup but also a two-month-long general strike between December 2002 and January 2003—gave Chávez the extraordinary opportunity to shift the blame for poor economic performance onto the country's political opposition while he consolidated political control over key institutions. In all likelihood, these moves would have only briefly prolonged the hold on power of what was then a deeply unpopular government (Chávez's disapproval ratings stood at 67 percent in June 2002, according to the Venezuelan survey firm Datanalisis). But oil saved the day again, rising from $26 in 2003 to $91.4 in 2008 and $103 by 2012.

The resulting windfall dwarfed anything ever experienced in Venezuelan history, including the increase seen in the oil booms of the 1970s and '80s.[3] This windfall allowed the government to generate a massive increase in its size, which expanded nearly threefold in real terms during Chávez's tenure in office, growing from 28.8 percent to 41.1 percent of GDP. This enormous expansion in the activities of the state brought about an improvement in many indicators of Venezuelans' quality of life, such as per capita incomes, poverty rates, and health indicators—though it also coincided with skyrocketing homicide rates. Contrary to popular belief, it was not associated with a change in the priorities of government spending; the fraction of spending devoted to social programs, even after one takes account of off-budget funds, was remarkably stable during Chávez's administration and not very different from that of previous governments.[4]

It would have been very hard, in fact, for such a huge oil boom to *not* have brought about an improvement in Venezuelans' quality of life, as it in fact did. But the results were lackluster. Venezuela's drop in poverty rates over this period was actually similar to those of Colombia, Brazil, and Peru, while its growth performance (2.6 percent annual growth since 1998) was the lowest among Latin America's ten largest economies.[5]

Still, the fact that living standards started improving after Chávez came to office—and that they had declined steadily during the previous two decades— seemed to lend support to the idea that there was something wrong in Venezuela before Chávez came to power, and that *chavismo* had fixed it. Chávez's basic storyline for explaining what had happened to Venezuela was that it was a wealthy country whose wealth was being siphoned off by its elites, and that this state of affairs could only be reversed by firm action by the state in order to redistribute that wealth to Venezuela's poor majority. Even the turn toward authoritarianism seemed easy to justify, as some degree of firm-handedness was surely necessary to wrest away resources from the previously all-powerful oligarchy.

So while Venezuelans' living standards were improving largely because an exogenous shock had led to an increase in the resources available to the nation, Venezuelans became increasingly focused on how to redistribute the pie instead of making it bigger. They bought into the story that living standards were improving due to Chávez's management of the economy and his willingness to redistribute wealth. What emerged was a political economy that was premised on a distributive interpretation of reality—even as that reality was being affected by factors that had little to do with internal distributive dynamics.

Today, that interpretation is coming up against the harsh realities of economic constraints. Despite historically high oil prices, Venezuela has continued to overspend and erode its productive base. In 2012, the consolidated public sector reached a staggering deficit in excess of 14 percent of GDP, following a massive expansion of public spending whose main purpose was to guarantee the ailing leader's reelection. The country once again has one of the highest country risks in the world. It has adopted, for the fourth time in Venezuelan history, a multiple exchange rate regime with a huge differential between the official and the parallel rate. It has again adopted extensive price and import controls that have been pitifully unable to suppress inflation, which averaged 42 percent per year in the first four months of 2013 and have caused massive shortages across many product categories, including essential food items. It has created distortionary incentives throughout the economy that impede the efficient allocation of resources and incentives. It has created fundamental insecurity in the property rights of all Venezuelan and foreign investors, from the largest global corporations to farmers and families who rent out their homes.

There are differences and similarities between what Venezuela is undergoing at this moment and the crises that the country underwent in the past decades, which we describe in the following pages. The macro picture does look remarkably similar in some respects to those of 1983, 1989, and 1996, after long bouts of overspending and overvaluation leading to highly contradictory fiscal-cum-exchange rate adjustments. They also often happen in an economy with multiple exchange rates and extensive price and import controls. But those adjustments tended to take place in the context of low or declining oil prices, whereas this one is occurring with oil still near its historical highs.

In other respects, the setting is very different. The microeconomic distortions, electricity shortages, and insecure property rights are much greater than they have ever been. In addition, Venezuela faces the current crisis with little capacity to manage a set of potentially explosive social conflicts and with almost all relevant public institutions strongly subordinated to the government party. The systematic takeover of public arenas by pro-Chávez forces has left little space for opponents to operate within the existing framework, introducing an element of serious potential political instability if and when political preferences shift against the administration. In contrast to the situation before 1998, when a Venezuelan president could be impeached by an independent judiciary and there was frequent alternation in power between competing parties, the current array of institutions is so closely controlled by government forces that they provide very few guarantees that the changing political preferences of Venezuelans will be allowed to be expressed.

The seeds of the weakening of Venezuela's democratic institutions were sown long before Chávez came to power. As we describe in what follows, this weakening is deeply linked to the country's failure to find ways to prepare for and adjust to shifts in oil prices. Political and economic institutions worked well under increasing or even stable prices but were ill prepared to manage the strong declines in oil rents that characterized the period between 1981 and 1998. Venezuela's difficulties in diversifying its economy—in itself associated with the little scope for creating competitive alternatives to oil production—gave the economy very few buffers that would allow it to react to an adverse oil price shock. The misguided macroeconomic policies that were often adopted and that the Chávez regime reinstated, including multiple exchange rate regimes and price and import controls, aggravated the economy's inability to absorb shocks and facilitate diversification into new non-oil tradable activities.

So the improvements in living standards seen during the Chávez era are not the consequence of the country's having addressed the fundamental causes of its previous collapse. Instead, the problems that led to such a dismal performance during the last two decades of the previous century are much more severe now. They have been temporarily sidelined by the oil price boom. But if oil prices stay where they are—and even more, if they were to decline—the underlying problems that caused the previous collapse will come roaring back again, as they seem to be doing this year.

At the root of these problems is the fact that, despite its strong criticism of its predecessors, the Chávez regime replicated much of what they had done, amplifying the economy's incapacity to respond to downturns in commodities prices or even to accommodate their stabilization. It is regrettable that this occurred at a time during which the largest oil boom in the nation's history afforded it extraordinary conditions in which to carry out a process of deep structural transformation. Any future attempt to address the country's structural problems will, in all likelihood, not count on a similar set of conditions. When that time comes, we hope that the information and analysis contained in the following pages help those who take up that task.

Many people have collaborated in the elaboration of this book, and we would like to acknowledge our debt to them. Financial support from the Instituto de Estudios Superiores de Administración (IESA) and the Andean Development Corporation were vital in getting the process of reflection under way. We would particularly like to acknowledge the support of Patricia Márquez and Jonathan Coles at IESA and Luis Miguel Castilla at CAF, who became strong advocates for our project. Sandy Thatcher saw the manuscript through its initial stages at Penn State University Press and provided invaluable advice, as did two anonymous referees. Rodríguez benefited from support given by IESA, the University of Notre Dame, and Wesleyan University. Patricia Jacques, Margarita Navarro, Erinn Wattie, and Victoria Whitney at Harvard's Center for International Development helped us see the manuscript through its more advanced stages. Our wives, Ana Julia and María Eugenia, provided steadfast support. Only we, however, should be blamed for any mistakes found in this work.

Ricardo Hausmann   Francisco Rodríguez
Harvard University   *Bank of America Merrill Lynch*

NOTES

1. See Carroll (2013), Corrales and Penfold (2010), Levitsky and Roberts (2011), and Gott (2011).

2. This would be equivalent to $10.72 in 2012 dollars. It is the lowest weekly price in real terms attained since the start of Venezuela's weekly price series in 1995, and it is lower in real terms than any annual price of any year since 1920, with the exception of 1970 ($1.76 in current dollars, $10.41 in 2012 dollars).

3. Between 1970 and 1982, oil prices grew by 512% in real terms, yet the value of oil production grew only 213% because production dropped by 49%. Between 1998 and 2012, oil prices grew by 581% and production fell by 8.2%, for an increase in the value of oil production of 525%.

4. See Rodríguez (2008a, 2008b) for a detailed discussion of this issue.

5. Between 1999 and 2011, Venezuela's poverty fell from 50.4% to 31.9%, or 18.5 percentage points in a thirteen-year period. Colombia saw poverty decline by a similar magnitude (from 50% to 34%, or 16 percentage points) in the shorter nine-year period between 2002 and 2011. Brazil saw a 13.9-point decline in the ten-year period between 1999 and 2009, while Peru saw a 30.9-point decline in the seven-year period between 2004 and 2011. All data from World Bank (2013).

REFERENCES

Carroll, R. 2013. *Comandante: Hugo Chávez's Venezuela*. New York: Penguin Press.

Corrales, J., and M. Penfold. 2010. *Dragon in the Tropics: Hugo Chávez and the Political Economy of Revolution in Venezuela*. Washington, D.C.: Brookings Institution Press.

Gott, R. 2011. *Hugo Chávez and the Bolivarian Revolution*. 2nd ed. New York: Verso.

Levitsky, S., and K. Roberts. 2011. *The Resurgence of the Latin American Left*. Baltimore: Johns Hopkins University Press.

Rodríguez, F. 2008a. "An Empty Revolution: The Unfulfilled Promises of Hugo Chávez." *Foreign Affairs* 87, no. 2.

_____. 2008b. "Revolutionary Road? Debating Venezuela's Progress." *Foreign Affairs* 87, no. 4.

World Bank. 2013. *World Development Indicators Database*. http://databank.worldbank.org/data/home.aspx.

INTRODUCTION

Ricardo Hausmann and Francisco Rodríguez

On the western tip there is a fountain of an oily liquor next to the sea . . . some of those who have seen it say that it is called *stercus demonis* [devil's excrement] by the naturals.
—Gonzalo Fernández de Oviedo y Valdés (1535)

The twentieth century saw the transformation of Venezuela from one of the poorest to one of the richest economies in Latin America. Between 1900 and 1920, per capita GDP had grown at a rate of barely 1.8 percent; between 1920 and 1948, it grew at 6.8 percent per annum. By 1958, per capita GDP was 4.8 times what it would have been had Venezuela had the average growth rate of Argentina, Brazil, Chile, and Peru (calculations based on Maddison 2001). By 1970, Venezuela had become the richest country in Latin America and one of the twenty richest countries in the world, with a per capita GDP higher than Spain, Greece, and Israel and only 13 percent lower than that of the United Kingdom (Heston, Summers, and Aten 2002).

In the 1970s, the Venezuelan economy did an about-face. Per capita non-oil GDP declined by a cumulative 18.64 percent between 1978 and 2001. Because this period was associated with growth in labor force participation, the decline in per worker GDP was even higher: 35.6 percent in the twenty-three-year period. The oil sector's decline was even more pronounced: 64.9 percent in per capita terms, 49.2 percent in per worker terms from its 1970 peak.

Venezuela's development failure has made it a common illustration of the "resource curse"—the hypothesis that natural resources can be harmful for a country's development prospects. Indeed, Venezuela is one of the examples Sachs and Warner (1999, 2) use to explain the idea that resource-abundant economies have lower growth. But Venezuela's growth experience has not only been used to illustrate the deleterious effect of resource rents. Easterly (2001, 264), for example, cites the Venezuelan decline in GDP in support of the idea that inequality is harmful for growth. Becker (1996), in contrast, has argued that the same growth performance actually shows that economic freedom is essential for growth.

How much do we really know about what caused the Venezuelan growth collapse? In our view, a minimal requirement of any explanation for Venezuela's dismal growth performance must pass two basic tests. On the one hand, it must explain why Venezuela has had such a disappointing growth performance in comparison to the rest of Latin America. On the other hand, it must explain why Venezuela did so poorly after the 1970s when it had been able to do so well in the previous fifty years.

Many existing explanations do not pass these tests. For example, Venezuela's failure to grow is often attributed to its lack of progress in carrying out free-market reforms during the eighties and nineties. While Venezuela is indisputably far from a stellar reformer, existing data do not support the hypothesis that it is substantially different from many other countries in the region in this respect (at least until 1999). According to Eduardo Lora's (2001) index of economic reform, the Venezuelan economy by 1999 was more free market–oriented than were the economies of Mexico and Uruguay, and its speed of reform (in terms of proportional improvement in the index) was actually the median for the region between 1985 and 1999. Lack of reforms thus does not appear to be a promising explanation for Venezuela's lack of growth.

Alternatively, consider the hypothesis that Venezuela's growth problems are due to the exacerbated rent-seeking that was generated by the concentration of high-resource rents in the hands of the state. If this explanation is correct, then how do we account for the fact that Venezuela was the region's fastest-growing economy between 1920 and 1970, a period during which the role of oil was dominant and fiscal oil revenues were significantly higher than during the nineties? Why were corruption, patronage politics, and rent-seeking not a hindrance to development during Venezuela's golden age of growth?

The purpose of this volume is to present a critical analysis of the Venezuelan growth experience, and to attempt to offer new explanations of the enigma of the country's economic collapse. It is a collective undertaking by economists and political scientists to attempt to gain insight into the causes of Venezuela's growth performance by systematically analyzing the contribution of each potential factor. Each chapter consists of an in-depth analysis of one dimension of the growth collapse, ranging from labor markets to infrastructure provision to the political system. While each chapter reflects the vision and analysis of the authors, each is shaped by the interaction and discussion between project participants that took place in two conferences held in Caracas in 2004 and Cambridge in 2006, sponsored by the Center for International Development and the David Rockefeller Center for Latin American Studies at Harvard University, the Andean Development Corporation, and the Instituto de Estudios Superiores de Adminstración.

Toward Within-Country Growth Empirics

This project also represents an attempt to move toward systematic country-level studies of development experiences that are rigorous and informed by economic theory, but which also pay due attention to national specificities and idiosyncrasies. Since the publication of Barro's (1991) seminal contribution to the empirical growth literature, econometric studies in the field of economic growth have been concentrated on the use of cross-national data to evaluate different hypotheses of the causes of long-run growth. Despite the significant contribution of this literature to our understanding of the process of economic development, there has been a growing awareness of the limitations of cross-country economic data to help us understand why some countries are rich and others poor (Rodrik 2005). Internationally comparable country-level data are necessarily limited in their scope and depth. Many of the potential explanatory factors that could account for differential growth performances are difficult to quantify for a large number of countries. Issues of endogeneity and specification tend to plague cross-country regression work.

While many of these problems are not unique to analysis of cross-national data sets, there is a set of distinct methodological problems that do appear to be more characteristic of the study of economic development with the aid of empirical growth data. Foremost among them is the problem of dealing with real-world complexity. The workhorse linear growth regression embodies a particular vision of the world according to which there is an underlying similarity between all of the countries included in the sample, and in which all possible interactions between policies, institutions, and economic structure are assumed away.

In contrast, designing a growth strategy is somewhat like getting to the peak of a mountain that is covered by clouds. You can't see where the peak is. You may not even know in which direction to travel. All you know is that if you go up, there is some probability that you are ascending the peak. The project of cross-country growth empirics can be seen as the project of constructing a map that will allow us to get to the peak of that mountain. The problems encountered in that literature indicate that we may not have a reliable map for some time to come. So the relevant policy question becomes: What do you do if you don't have a map? Or if you have one but realize it's not very good?

One answer, recently given by Hausmann, Rodrik, and Velasco (2004), relies on exploiting local instead of global information. In the context of our metaphor, if you want to get to the peak you should try to infer where you are from, using careful observation of the vegetation, the terrain, the flow of rivers, and just about any other observable characteristic that allows you to make an inference. These authors develop this idea in the context of the design of growth strategies under radical uncertainty. They call their method "growth diagnostics" in part because it is very similar to the approach taken by medical specialists in identifying the causes of health ailments—a context in which assuming everyone has the same problem is unlikely to be very helpful. The idea is to look for clues in your immediate environment as to what may be the binding constraints on growth.

The growth diagnostics exercise consists in asking a set of basic questions to rule out possible explanations of the problem. The answer to these questions is inherently country- and time-specific, as one cannot assume that different units of observation—be they countries or persons—are always affected by the same ills. The essential idea is to identify the key problem you are interested in attacking as well as the signals that the economy would provide if a particular constraint were the cause of that problem. If the economy suffers from signs of low investment and entrepreneurship, you want to start out by asking whether this is because returns are not attractive or credit is very costly. If the latter were the cause, you would expect to see signs of high costs of finance. If, in contrast, you find that returns are not attractive, you may want to delve deeper into the issue: are the actual rates of return low, or is the problem that investors don't think they will be able to keep the returns from their activity with certainty? Is this due to political risk of expropriation, lack of enforcement of laws, or market failures? The process goes on until one identifies the constraints that are likely to give you the highest local increase in growth.

An alternative attack on the issue of complexity has been undertaken by Rodríguez (2007a), who asks whether there is an effective way of using the cross-national data to understand the potential effects of different components of reform strategies on economic growth without assuming that the world is unrealistically simple—as the linear growth regression framework invariably does. He uses nonparametric econometrics to capture the key general features of the complex reality embodied in growth relationships. The essence of those methods is that instead of asking whether a policy such as trade protectionism is good for growth—a question that simply lacks a well-defined answer in a complex world—it asks more general questions such as: Does the effect depend on other variables? Is it at least not harmful for growth? Does the "average" country benefit or lose out from trade protection?

Rodríguez's empirical analysis comes up with some interesting results. One is that growth regressions often tend to exaggerate the effects of changes in independent variables in relation to more flexible methods that do not impose unrealistic restrictions. But this exaggeration is not uniform across different types of explanatory variables. In fact, the relative importance of different variables changes dramatically when we go from the restrictive linear approach to the more flexible nonparametric approach. Policy variables become much less significant, while structural and institutional variables become much more significant in accounting for changes in growth.

A third approach to dealing with issues of real-world complexity in the empirical analysis of economic growth is to reduce the number of experiences that one tries to fit into a common framework. If the weakness of cross-country growth empirics is essentially that it attempts to bundle countries whose development processes are fundamentally different, then one natural approach is to unbundle countries and look at either groups of countries with similar characteristics or single countries at a time. Hausmann, Rodrik, and Pritchett (2004) and Hausmann, Rodríguez, and Wagner (2008) have concentrated alternatively on cases of growth accelerations and collapses in searching for common explanatory factors that can help explain why these phenomena occur and what determines variations in their evolution.

This book is an example of the unbundling strategy taken to its ultimate consequences: the exclusive concentration on understanding the phenomenon of growth in one country during a particular historical period. We make no claim to rediscovering the wheel: there is a long tradition of case study literature in economic growth (e.g., Leff 1972; Gelb 1988; Wade 1990). We believe, however, that the contribution of our approach lies in the fact that it is informed by growth theory, and does not eschew the systematic analysis of empirical evidence and the use of analytical models. Each of the chapters in this study puts forward a set of well-defined hypotheses about the relationship between its issue of interest and the country's growth experience. It uses the empirical evidence to evaluate them and to contribute a piece to the explanation of the fuller puzzle.

This chapter is also part of a broader project, in which we have undertaken similar efforts to understand the cases of growth collapses suffered since the 1970s in two other Andean economies: Bolivia and Peru.[1] The basic idea was to look at countries that were marked by similarities in some of their initial conditions—such as high levels of resource dependence and similar geographical location—and that experienced similar economic outcomes. However, we did not straitjacket the analyses into a common analytical framework, but rather decided to let researchers come up with independent explanations—an experiment that emerged with some striking similarities as well as surprising differences.[2]

In this sense, we believe it is possible to develop an analytical toolkit that allows growth economists to systematically analyze and evaluate competing hypotheses about growth at the country level. Our work is thus fully in the spirit of Rodrik's (2002) call for the elaboration or design of analytical country narratives of development experiences. We view this line of research as taking the first steps in the development of an *within-country growth empirics* that serves as a rigorous alternative to the problems of the existing empirical literature on economic growth.

Questions and Answers

The key organizing principle of this work starts from one basic question that we asked each of the project participants: to what extent is what occurred in your area of study a cause of the country's economic collapse, and to what extent is it a consequence? Authors approached this question with differing methodologies and produced different answers. Some argued for a vital causal role of their sector. Others argued that their sector was not a relevant contributing factor to the country's growth performance. And others yet argued for a mutually reinforcing set of feedback loops between growth and their area of study.

What emerges is a complex, nuanced vision of Venezuelan economic growth that goes considerably beyond the conventional wisdom. It is far from unicausal—indeed, it emphasizes several contributing factors. At the same time, however, it is far from an "anything goes" explanation: our set of contributing factors is much smaller than the set of variables we initially considered. Our collective undertaking has thus served as a mechanism that allows us to reach a solution that emulates Einstein's recommendation that theories should "make the irreducible basic elements as simple and as few as possible without having to surrender the adequate representation of a single datum of experience" (1933, 10–11).

The logical starting point for an explanation of the Venezuelan collapse is an evaluation of the country's aggregate growth performance. This is the task carried out by Hausmann and Rodríguez in "Why Did Venezuelan Growth Collapse?" That chapter starts out by quantifying the extent of the collapse and the ways in which one would attempt to account for it in the context of an aggregate growth model. The authors reach a simple conclusion: Venezuela's growth performance can be accounted for as the consequence of three forces. One is declining oil production. The second is declining non-oil productivity. The third is the incapacity of the economy to move resources into alternative industries as a response to the decline in oil rents that has occurred since the seventies. The authors then concentrate on this second factor, asking why Venezuela found it so difficult to develop an alternative export industry, in contrast to other countries that suffered declines in their traditional exports. Their answer is that Venezuela's concentration in oil puts it in a particularly difficult position because of an idiosyncratic characteristic of the oil industry: the specialized inputs, knowledge, and institutions necessary to produce oil efficiently are not very valuable for the production of other goods. Using results from recent research on the structure of the product space, the authors show that oil-abundant economies lie in a relatively sparse region of this space, where it is difficult to find new products toward which you can reallocate resources if you suffer declines in your traditional export sector.

What about the other two factors, the decline in oil production and the decline in non-oil productivity? Most of the remaining chapters in the book are concerned with providing explanations for these phenomena. Osmel Manzano's piece "Venezuela after a Century of Oil Exploitation" tackles the issue of accounting for the oil sector's performance. The key question here is why a country that boasts massive amounts of oil reserves decides not to take advantage of them and instead to maintain limits on production. Manzano argues that this policy was framed in an era in which oil was believed to be near exhaustion, so that policymakers prioritized conserving oil and diversifying the economy away from oil exports. These principles may have made sense in the sixties, but they were no longer reasonable after new exploration revealed that the country had indeed quite massive amounts of reserves, while changes in consumption patterns and greater efficiency of extraction techniques led to the oil glut of the eighties and nineties.

The issue of productivity is more complex. Moses Abramovitz (1956) aptly referred to aggregate measures of productivity as "measures of our ignorance." At a broad level, total factor productivity reflects a variety of factors that can affect how capital and labor are transformed into output in a country at a particular moment in time. These factors can range from society-wide changes in policies, institutions, and economic structure to microeconomic distortions that lead to inefficiencies in resource allocation. A collapse in financial intermediation, chronic underinvestment in public infrastructure, or the spread in social conflict could all lead to a decline in total factor productivity. The rest of the chapters in the book explore in more detail the potential explanations for the productivity decline, asking whether these were caused by the growth collapse or were a consequence of it.

"Public Investment and Productivity Growth in the Venezuelan Manufacturing Industry" by José Pineda and Francisco Rodríguez looks at this question by estimating directly the effect of public investment in a panel of Venezuelan manufacturing firms. The relationship between investment and productivity is a complex one whose estimation is clouded by the possibility of reverse causation: does public investment generate higher productivity, or does the public sector tend to invest more in localities where productivity is growing? Pineda and Rodríguez use a unique natural experiment provided by the earmarking of national revenues through the Intergovernmental Decentralization Fund to generate exogenous variation in the degree of public investment. They find that the contribution of public investment to productivity growth in the Venezuelan manufacturing sector is substantial: according to their estimates, non-oil per capita GDP would be 37 percent higher than its present value had the government not allowed the stock of public capital to decline after 1983. This explanation suggests that the misallocation of public expenditures is a substantial contributor to the Venezuelan economic collapse.

Distortions in the allocation of factors of production can also generate declines in aggregate productivity. Such is the case with labor market regulations. While minimum wages, firing restrictions, and mandated nonwage benefits often have a reasonable justification in terms of the provision of social insurance, they can also generate substantial distortions to the reallocation of labor across firms. In countries with a large unregulated economy, these can generate considerable incentives to shift to the informal sector. Indeed, between 1990 and 2001 Venezuela was the country with the highest growth rate in informal sector employment in Latin America (Bermúdez 2004). Omar Bello and Adriana Bermúdez's chapter, "The Incidence of Labor Market Reforms on Employment in the Venezuelan Manufacturing Sector, 1995–2001," attempts to estimate the cost of these increased regulations using the same panel of manufacturing firms. Since Venezuelan labor market regulations had differing effects based on firm size, and since the changes in these regulations are exogenous to the firm decision, Bello and Adriana Bermúdez can obtain an estimate of the employment effect of labor market regulations that is not contaminated by endogeneity. The authors find a substantial effect of increases in labor market regulations on firm employment, suggesting that the marked increase in labor market restrictions during the nineties may have become an impediment to the reallocation of resources toward manufacturing.

In "Understanding Economic Growth in Venezuela, 1970–2005: The Real Effects of a Financial Collapse," Matías Braun looks at another possible suspect for the collapse in aggregate productivity. Between 1989 and 1996, Venezuela suffered a series of deep credit crunches from which it never fully recovered. Therefore, even though the size of Venezuela's banking sector was consistent with what one would expect for the country's level of income up to the 1980s, by the mid-2000s the sector was between four to six times smaller than one would expect. Braun argues that this collapse had a significant effect not only on the capacity to allocate credit to the economy but also on the efficiency of the resources that were allocated.

Not all the chapters in the volume conclude that their potential explanatory variable is indeed a cause of the growth collapse. Were that the case, the sense of our exercise would be very much open to question. Attributing the collapse to everything is the same as attributing it to nothing. Thus one of the most satisfying results of our project was to find that several authors argued that their sector or area of interest was not a relevant contributor to the collapse.

The clearest example of such a response is Daniel Ortega and Lant Pritchett's "Much Higher Schooling, Much Lower Wages: Human Capital and Economic Collapse in Venezuela." This chapter looks at the hypothesis that lack of schooling may be a contributor to the collapse. The authors' answer is a resounding "no." Venezuela's growth in schooling capital was substantially higher than the median country and even faster than the median East Asian country! Even after allowing for changes in quality and restrictions to the reallocation of labor across sectors, the authors find little solid evidence of a contribution of lack of human capital to the decline in output. Indeed, if anything, Venezuela's huge increase in human capital makes the puzzle even larger, as it implies that the massive collapse in output per worker is exceeded by the collapse in output per education-adjusted units of labor.

A second "no" comes from Samuel Freije's study "Income Distribution and Redistribution in Venezuela." The increasing relevance of distributive conflict in Venezuela has fueled speculation that the growth in poverty and inequality is at the root of the implosion of Venezuela's political system. Freije finds that while Venezuelan inequality has increased, its increase is consistent with what one would expect given the collapse in capital accumulation and the growth in informalization. Further, Venezuela in the 1970s was a relatively equal economy by Latin American standards, so it is difficult to tell a story in which inequality is a causal determinant of the collapse. Obviously, however, the subsequent increase in inequality could have fueled growing social conflict and help explain part of the subsequent implosion of the political system.

A third—albeit more qualified—"no" comes from María Antonia Moreno and Cameron Shelton's study of the evolution of fiscal policy during Venezuela's economic collapse, "Sleeping in the Bed One Makes: The Venezuelan Fiscal Policy Response to the Oil Boom." In contrast to much conventional wisdom, Moreno and Shelton contest that Venezuela actually carried out significant fiscal adjustments after the onset of the debt crisis. While they do pin part of the blame on the excessive fiscal expansion of the seventies and early eighties, which made the downward adjustment all the more difficult, they argue that the post-1983 response was actually quite reasonable. Falling oil revenues were met with efforts to raise new sources of revenue and cut expenditures. Although these cuts were not sufficient to close the growing gap, this is more than anything due to the magnitude of the decline in oil revenues and not to flaws in the fiscal response— which in any case is commonly far from optimal just about everywhere.

The possibility of feedback loops illustrates the complexity of thinking about causation in the growth context. Poor fiscal policy may be a consequence instead of a cause of the collapse, but the collapse may have generated a vicious circle whereby deteriorations in fiscal policy made it even more difficult for the economy to retake a path of economic growth. A similar mechanism is illustrated in Dan Levy and Dean Yang's "Competing for Jobs or Creating Jobs? The Impact of Immigration on Native-Born Unemployment in Venezuela, 1980–2003," which looks at how changes in immigration patterns have affected patterns of job creation in Venezuela. Using exogenous shocks in income in migrant home areas to identify the effect of migration on domestic unemployment, Levy and Yang find a contrast between Colombian immigration, which tends to raise Venezuelan unemployment, and European immigration, which does not. This is consistent with the idea that European immigrants generate considerable positive externalities that offset their direct effects on labor supply and wages. It also suggests that the reversal in European migration that occurred because of the growth collapse could have generated a feedback loop in which the initial collapse caused the loss of a vibrant immigrant community and its spillover effects on the domestic population.

The Venezuelan collapse was not only economic. Up until the 1990s, Venezuela boasted a stable democratic political system that was commonly viewed as an example to follow by other developing middle-income countries. During the ensuing decade, this system collapsed, leading to the near disappearance of traditional parties and their replacement by a highly polarized politics. In "Institutional Collapse: The Rise and Decline of Democratic Governance in Venezuela," Francisco Monaldi and Michael Penfold study the causes of this collapse. Their claim is that it can be attributed to a mixture of the governance problems created by oil, the dramatic fall in per-capita oil fiscal revenues in the late eighties and nineties, and the political reforms introduced in the late eighties and early nineties, which weakened and fragmented the party system and undermined political cooperation.

Jonathan Di John's "The Political Economy of Industrial Policy in Venezuela" explores the economic consequences of the political collapse. The central question of this chapter is why the Venezuelan political system proved incapable of implementing a reasonably rational industrial policy that took advantage of oil revenues to channel them into the growth of the non-oil sector. Di John contends that this was the result of a growing *incompatibility* between the country's "big push" heavy industrialization development strategy, on the one hand, and the increasing populism, clientelism, and factionalization of the political system. Policies were becoming more factionalized and accommodating precisely at a time when the development strategy required a more unified and exclusionary pattern for the allocation of rents and subsidies.

The last two studies in the book look at another dimension of the political collapse, which is the ascendance to power of a radical leftist movement headed by Hugo Chávez in the late nineties. In "Oil, Macro Volatility, and Crime in the Determination of Beliefs in Venezuela," Rafael Di Tella, Javier Donna, and Robert MacCulloch try to explain why the Venezuelan public is so responsive to left-wing, populist, and antimarket rhetoric. They argue that the emergence of these preferences can be explained by the country's history of macro volatility, its dependence on oil, and the generalized belief that corruption and crime are high. However, the authors caution that these beliefs are often divorced from reality, and present evidence consistent with this fact. In Venezuela, the social construction of beliefs appears to play a significant role in the creation of new ideologies.

In contrast to the focus of Di Tella, Donna, and MacCulloch on the political demand for a shift to the left, Javier Corrales's "Explaining Chavismo: The Unexpected Alliance of Radical Leftists and the Military in Venezuela under Hugo Chávez" attempts to understand the characteristics of the Venezuelan political system that made possible the emergence of a radical leftist movement. Corrales's key argument is that the degree of openness of many political institutions in Venezuela, which did not subject the radical left to institutional exclusion or severe repression, allowed for the survival of cadres of extreme leftist politicians, intellectuals, and bureaucrats that were in a position to offer the supply of a radical project once the demand arose.

Most of the studies in this book have not tried to explain the economic consequences of the country's shift to a radical leftist paradigm.[3] We believe that the *consequences* (as opposed to the causes) of chavismo merit a separate study of their own. The fact that the Bolivarian revolution is a recent and ongoing process poses a set of methodological challenges that are distinct from those dealt with in this book. Revolutions, as Simón Bolívar himself pointed out, must be observed up close but are best judged from afar. Our focus has been instead to understand the causes of the economic and political collapse that started during the oil boom of the seventies and that is at the root of many of Venezuela's current predicaments. The fact that Venezuela is currently undergoing an oil boom comparable in magnitude to the one it experienced more than thirty years ago suggests that the lessons to be learned from studying the past may have their greatest relevance in understanding the present.

NOTES

1. See Hausmann, Morón, and Rodríguez 2007; and Gray, Morón, and Rodríguez 2007.

2. These are explored in more detail in Rodríguez 2007b.

3. Recent attempts at understanding the political and economic consequences of the Bolivarian revolution have been made by Miguel et al. 2011; Ortega and Rodríguez 2008; and Rodríguez 2008.

REFERENCES

Abramovitz, Moses. 1956. "Resource and Output Trends in the United States since 1870." *American Economic Review* 5 (46): 5–23.

Barro, Robert. 1991. "Economic Growth in a Cross-Section of Countries." *Quarterly Journal of Economics* 106 (2): 407–43.

Becker, Gary. 1996. "The Numbers Tell the Story: Economic Freedom Spurs Growth." *Businessweek*, May 6.

Bermúdez, A. 2004. "La legislación laboral en Venezuela y sus impactos sobre el mercado laboral." In *El desempleo en Venezuela: Causas, efectos e implicaciones de política*, edited by F. Rodríguez, C. Risopatrón, A. Bermúdez, M. E. Boza, A. Daza, S. Freije, and D. Ortega, 39–60. Caracas: Oficina de Asesoría Económica de la Asamblea Nacional.

Easterly, William. 2001. *The Elusive Quest for Growth: Economists' Adventures and Misadventures in the Tropics.* Cambridge: MIT Press.

Einstein, Albert. 1933. *On the Method of Theoretical Physics.* New York: Oxford University Press.

Gelb, A. 1988. *Oil Windfalls: Blessing or Curse?* New York: Oxford University Press for the World Bank.

Gray, George, Eduardo Morón, and Francisco Rodríguez. 2007. "Bolivian Economic Growth: 1970–2005." Reproduced by the Andean Development Fund.

Hausmann, Ricardo, Eduardo Morón, and Francisco Rodríguez. 2007. "Peruvian Economic Growth: 1970–2005." Reproduced by the Andean Development Fund.

Hausmann, R., L. Pritchett, and Dani Rodrik. 2004. "Growth Accelerations." *Journal of Economic Growth* 10 (4): 303–29.

Hausmann, R., and R. Rigobón. 2003. "An Alternative Interpretation of the 'Resource Curse': Theory and Policy Implications." In *Fiscal Policy Formulation and Implementation in Oil-Producing Countries*, edited by J. M. Davis, R. Ossowski, and A. Fedelino, 13–44. Washington, D.C.: IMF Press.

Hausmann, Ricardo, Francisco Rodríguez, and Rodrigo Wagner. 2008. "Growth Collapses." In *Money, Crises, and Transition: Essays in Honor of Guillermo Calvo*, edited by Carmen Reinhart, Andrés Velasco, and Carlos Vegh, 303–29. Cambridge: MIT Press.

Hausmann, Ricardo, Dani Rodrik, and Andrés Velasco. 2004. "Growth Diagnostics." In *The Washington Consensus Reconsidered: Towards a New Global Governance*, edited by Narcís Serra and Joseph E. Stiglitz, 324–54. New York: Oxford University Press.

Heston, Alan, Robert Summers, and Bettina Aten. 2002. "Penn World Table Version 6.1, Center for International Comparisons at the University of Pennsylvania (CICUP)." http://pwt.econ.upenn.edu/php_site/pwt61_form.php.

Leff, Nathaniel. 1972. "Economic Retardation in Nineteenth-Century Brazil." *Economic History Review* 25 (3): 489–507.

Lora, Eduardo. 2001. "Structural Reforms in Latin America: What Has Been Reformed and How to Measure It." Working Paper 466, Research Department, Inter-American Development Bank, Washington, D.C.

Maddison, Angus. 2001. *The World Economy: A Millennial Perspective*. Paris: Organisation for Economic Co-operation and Development.

Martínez, Aníbal R. 1997. "Petróleo crudo." In *Diccionario de Historia de Venezuela*, edited by Fundación Polar, 3:614–31. 4 vols. Caracas: Fundación Polar.

Miguel, Edward, Chang-Tai Hsieh, Daniel Ortega, and Francisco Rodríguez. 2011. "The Cost of Political Opposition: Evidence from Venezuela's *Maisanta* Database." *American Economic Journal: Applied Economics* 3 (2): 196–214.

Ortega, Daniel, and Francisco Rodríguez. 2008. "Freed from Illiteracy? A Closer Look at Venezuela's Robinson Literacy Campaign." *Economic Development and Cultural Change* 57 (1): 1–30.

Rodríguez, Francisco. 2007a. "Cleaning Up the Kitchen Sink: Growth Empirics When the World Is Not Simple." Working Paper 2006-004, Department of Economics, Wesleyan University, Middletown, Conn.

_____. 2007b. "An Empirical Test of the Poverty Traps Hypothesis." Wesleyan Economics Working Paper 2008-005, Department of Economics, Wesleyan University, Middletown, Conn.

_____. 2008. "An Empty Revolution: The Unfulfilled Promises of Hugo Chávez." *Foreign Affairs* 87 (2): 49–62.

Rodrik, Dani. 2002. In *Search of Prosperity*. Princeton: Princeton University Press.

_____. 2005. "Why We Learn Nothing from Regressing Economic Growth on Policies." Unpublished paper. Harvard University, Cambridge, Mass. http://www.hks.harvard .edu/fs/drodrik/Research%20papers/policy%20regressions.pdf.

Sachs, Jeffrey D., and Andrew M. Warner. 1999. "Natural Resource Intensity and Economic Growth." In *Development Policies in Natural Resource Economies*, edited by Jörg Mayer, Brian Chambers, and Ayisha Farooq, 13–77. Cheltenham, U.K., and Northampton, Mass.: Edward Elgar in association with UNCTAD.

Wade, Robert. 1990. *Governing the Market: Economic Theory and the Role of Government in East Asian Industrialization*. Princeton: Princeton University Press.

1 WHY DID VENEZUELAN GROWTH COLLAPSE?

Ricardo Hausmann and Francisco Rodríguez

Toward the end of the 1970s, Venezuelan economic growth experienced a stunning reversal. Since the beginning of the century, the country had undergone a sustained economic expansion that took it from being one of the poorest countries in the region to being the second-richest one even before the first oil boom (based on data from Bulmer-Thomas 1994, tables 9.4 and A.2). In 1979, that trend made an about-face.[1] Venezuelan non-oil per capita GDP declined at an annual rate of 0.9 percent over the ensuing twenty-three years, for a total cumulative decline of 18.6 percent. What is more striking is that this occurred despite a significant incorporation of new workers into the labor force, which should have *ceteris paribus* raised per capita income. Therefore, per worker GDP fell at an annual rate of 1.9 percent in the non-oil sector; its cumulative decline was 35.6 percent.

The causes of this collapse are not well understood. It is true that Venezuela was prey to many of the factors that characterize resource-dependent economies, such as exposure to terms of trade volatility, an appreciated exchange rate that is unfavorable to the production of tradables, and a highly inefficient public sector. But all these factors seemed able to coexist with economic growth during the more than half a century of sustained expansion that preceded the collapse. Indeed, Venezuela was widely viewed twenty-five years ago as an example of how

This project was supported by the Center for International Development at Harvard University and the David Rockefeller Center for Latin American Studies at Harvard University, the Instituto de Estudios Superiores de Administración, and the Andean Development Corporation. We thank Federico Sturzenegger as well as conference participants at IESA and Harvard for their comments and suggestions. Francisco Rodríguez thanks the Kellogg Institute of International Studies of the University of Notre Dame, the Instituto de Estudios Superiores de Administración, and Wesleyan University for their financial support. Reyes Rodríguez provided excellent research assistance.

to tackle the development process. For example, in October 1981, the American political scientist Peter Merkl wrote, "It appears that the only trail to a democratic future for developing societies may be the one followed by Venezuela. . . . Venezuela is a textbook case of step-by-step progress" (Karl 1987, 63).

Understanding the Venezuelan economic collapse has interesting implications for thinking about the development process more broadly. It is now recognized that development experiences vary widely in terms of the timing and intensity of growth episodes (Pritchett 1998; Hausmann, Pritchett, and Rodrik 2004). One of the most interesting yet understudied subclasses of growth experiences is that of countries whose failure to achieve higher living standards comes not from an incapacity of attaining high growth rates but from the incapacity to sustain them. Argentina, the Soviet Union, and Indonesia are three cases of countries that were viewed as development examples before the collapse of their economies. Indeed, out of one hundred fifty-four countries in the Penn World Tables (Heston, Summers, and Aten 2002), forty-one suffered decreases of more than 20 percent in their terms-of-trade adjusted per capita GDPs over periods of variable length, and fifteen suffered decreases of over 50 percent. If we were to understand why some economies suffer collapses in their growth rates, we would go a long way towards explaining the divergence that appears to characterize the unconditional distribution of world incomes over the past fifty years.

The Venezuelan growth experience is a common example in the by-now established literature regarding the link between poor growth performance and resource abundance (Sachs and Warner 1999; Gelb 1988; Tornell and Lane 1999; Gylfason 2001; Mehlum, Moene, and Torvik 2002; Busby, Isham, Pritchett, and Woolcock 2002; Hausmann and Rigobón 2003).[2] Generally, this literature finds that resource abundance tends to be associated with lower growth rates. Most recently, Sala-i-Martin, Doppelhofer, and Miller (2004) show that the fraction of GDP in mining is one of eighteen variables (out of sixty-seven considered) that can be shown to have robust effects on growth in Bayesian averages of classical estimates derived from cross-country growth regressions.[3]

A handful of papers have been concerned specifically with the Venezuelan growth experience, among which we count Rodríguez and Sachs (1999), Hausmann (2003), and Bello and Restuccia (2002). These papers differ with respect to the primary causal factor that is emphasized. Rodríguez and Sachs stress the decline in oil rents, Hausmann centers on the increase in credit risk, and Bello and Restuccia highlight the increase in government intervention. All papers share the common characteristic of being calibration-oriented approaches that attempt to see whether a stylized model can predict the magnitude of the decline. As pointed out by Rodríguez (2006), these results are highly sensitive to changes in the data set used for their calibration exercise. This is a result of broad disparities in existing measures of Venezuelan GDP, with different series showing discrepancies of up to three percentage points in annual growth rates for periods greater than a decade. Therefore, getting the data right is a vital component of an adequate growth diagnosis of the Venezuela economy.

In this chapter, we show how alternative explanations of the Venezuelan collapse can be integrated in a simple theoretical framework that can be used to understand the relative importance of each factor in accounting for the country's economic decline. We illustrate within a three-sector framework how the economy will display different reactions to changes in oil rents and productivity, depending on whether it falls in the region of parameters that lead to complete or incomplete specialization. We also show that this holds regardless of whether there is capital mobility. Our theoretical framework is used to trace the decline of Venezuelan growth to three primary causes: (1) the decline in per capita oil rents, (2) the fall in total factor productivity (TFP), and (3) the lack of specialization in alternative exports. We show that the decline in oil rents can be understood as the product of policy decisions and the evolution of the international oil market. We then go on to tackle the harder question of how we can account for the lack of development of an alternative export industry.

In essence, we argue that Venezuela's inability to develop an alternative export industry has to do with its starting pattern of specialization. Countries are able to enter new export markets only if the new goods are similar to those it currently produces. It is only in that way that it can take advantage of its specialized inputs, technical knowledge, and institutional configuration in producing a good that it has not produced before. The existing patterns of specialization of countries will have an effect on the emergence of new export goods. Some countries will have the luck of producing goods that are similar to many other high-value goods. They will thus have little trouble shifting production to those new goods. Other countries, in contrast, will occupy sparser regions of the product space, in which few goods are sufficiently similar to those they currently produce. Venezuela—like most oil-exporting countries—occupies such a region, a fact that significantly hinders its capacity of shifting to new export industries.

The following section deals with data problems and presents our best estimate of the magnitude and timing of the collapse. After that we introduce a simple three-sector model of the economy and show how to trace the growth collapse to the three underlying causes mentioned above: the decline in oil rents, the fall in TFP and the failure of an alternative export sector to emerge. In the following section we argue that in order to understand the decline in capital accumulation, one must understand why an alternative set of export industries failed to emerge in response to the decline in oil revenues. The two sections after that go on to examine theoretically and empirically the possible causes behind the lack of dynamism of the Venezuelan non-oil export sector. And in the final section, we provide some concluding remarks.

How Large Is the Collapse?

The main impediment to the primary task of this chapter—to elucidate the explanatory power of different theories in accounting for the Venezuelan economic collapse—comes from the substantial variation that exists between different commonly used data sets with respect to the magnitude and timing of the reversal in growth. Different indicators of GDP can give broadly different estimates of economic performance for Venezuela. As shown in table 1.1, the differences between the average annual growth rates that come out of these indicators can be as large as 3.4 percentage points over decadelong periods. Sorting out the reasons for these differences and establishing the appropriate data to be used are prerequisites of any meaningful calibration or growth accounting exercise.

Table 1.1   Growth rates according to alternative data sets

	Peak year	1950–60	1960–70	1970–80	1980–90	1990–2000
Banco Central de Venezuela (2000)	1977	3.59%	2.33%	0.62%	−1.94%	−0.15%
Rodríguez (2006)	1977	—	2.18%	0.30%	−1.93%	0.24%
Maddison (2001)	1977	2.57%	1.01%	−0.51%	−1.99%	0.94%*
Heston, Summers, and Aten (2002)	1970	2.83%	2.95%	−2.79%	−1.36%	−0.80%
World Bank (2006)	1977	—	1.46%	−0.76%	−1.75%	−0.15%
Baptista (2006)	1977	2.12%	2.22%	0.33%	−2.68%	−0.39%**
Minimum		2.12%	1.01%	−2.79%	−2.68%	−0.80%
Maximum		3.59%	2.95%	0.62%	−1.36%	0.94%
Range		1.46%	1.94%	3.41%	1.32%	1.74%

* Refers to 1990–98.
** Refers to 1990–99.

Rodríguez (2006) discusses in detail the reasons for the differences among these series. He concludes that the main source of differences comes from the different valuation that is given to the oil sector in different series. This is not a trivial matter, as per capita oil production fell by 64 percent between 1970 and 2000, so weighing it by a higher price will imply a lower growth rate for the aggregate economy. Alternative assumptions on base-year prices interact with the choice of technique for linking series originally produced for different sub-periods to produce widely disparate results. Two other sources of differences include the use of unofficial estimates of sectoral production by some authors and the treatment of the discrete jump in measured GDP that occurred with the 1984 base year change.[4]

The solution one adopts to the problem raised by an overabundance of disparate estimates of GDP growth depends on the issue one is interested in tackling. One may be interested in economic growth because of a primary interest in living standards, or because of a preoccupation with economic performance. In more formal terms, one may want to measure shifts over time in the consumption possibilities frontier or in the production possibilities frontier. If prices stay constant, then these two measures will coincide. But when relative prices experience significant changes over time, they may start showing wide differences.[5]

If one is interested in economic growth because one wants to understand the evolution of a society's capacity to sustain greater living standards (shifts in the consumption possibilities frontier), then most of the estimates in table 1.1 are unlikely to be useful. The reason is that these estimates all come from measures of GDP at constant prices, which by definition do not take into account changes in the purchasing power of exports. But a great part of the changes that occurred in Venezuela's capacity to sustain living standards during the second part of the twentieth century had to do precisely with changes in the relative price of oil. Further, those changes can be directly linked to policy decisions, in particular Venezuela's adoption of the OPEC strategy of curtailing production in order to exploit international market power. Note that this type of strategy, if successful, would tend to cause a decrease in per capita constant price GDP even while improving the country's relevant consumption possibilities. This seems counterintuitive for a measure of living standards.

A more appropriate measure of living standards should include an adjustment for the effect on consumption possibilities of changes in the terms of trade. Such a measure is reported, though often ignored, in the Penn World Tables (Heston, Summers, and Aten 2002) as the Terms-of-Trade Adjusted Real GDP per Capita. Instead of valuing net exports at constant prices (as their commonly used real chained GDP series does), this series adds net exports in current prices relative to the price index of domestic absorption. These numbers confirm the story of Venezuela's growth collapse, albeit in a more nuanced way than do some of the more commonly used data. For the last half of the twentieth century taken as a whole, Venezuela looks, in terms of consumption possibilities, like an average Latin American economy: indeed, its growth rate average is exactly that of the region (1.36 percent), which is slightly lower than the world average of 2.10 percent. However, this mixes two very distinct periods: in the first one, Venezuela's GDP growth exceeded world and Latin American growth by a substantial margin, occupying the 36th percentile of world growth rates and the 25th percentile of Latin American growth rates. In the second period, comprising the last twenty years of the twentieth century, the country fell way behind the rest of the world, dropping to the last quintile of both world and Latin American growth.

Suppose instead that we are interested in per capita GDP as a measure of economic performance (we want to estimate shifts over time in the production possibilities frontier). Then there is no compelling reason to use a terms-of-trade adjusted series. Indeed, as one would be primarily interested in decomposing these shifts in changes in technology and changes in inputs, a terms-of-trade adjustment would add unnecessary noise. But then it seems we are stuck with the broad variation in different indicators that arises as a result of using alternative base years.

A more productive route to take if attempting to understand shifts in production possibilities would be to look separately at production in the oil and non-oil sectors, thus circumventing the issue of choice of a relative price to value these two sectors. Choice of base year is relatively irrelevant when one looks at growth in these sectors separately, in contrast to what happens when one looks at aggregate growth. In essence, the problem is that a constant price indicator of GDP literally mixes apples and oranges—or, more appropriately, barrels and arepas. Separating these series allows us to see that we are looking at two distinct issues: a collapse in per capita oil production, which fell by more than two-thirds between 1957 and 2001, and a less pronounced yet significant decline in non-oil per capita GDP, which fell by approximately one-fifth between 1978 and 2001. Table 1.2 shows these numbers, as well as the per worker figures, which are less pronounced for the oil sector (45–49 percent), but more pronounced for the non-oil sector (36–40 percent). These numbers give us the magnitude of the decline that we will attempt to explain.

In sum, our argument is that the decline in oil and non-oil GDP are two separate phenomena with distinct causes, and that there is much to be gained by analyzing them separately. During the period corresponding to the decline, the Venezuelan oil industry was almost completely publicly owned, with production

Table 1.2   Magnitude and timing of decline in oil and non-oil production, alternative indicators

	1968 prices	1984 prices	Törnqvist chained
Oil sector			
Per capita			
Peak year	1957	1957	1957
Decline from peak	−67.00%	−66.65%	−68.43%
Per worker			
Peak year	1970	1970	1970
Decline from peak	−44.97%	−44.85%	−49.16%
Non-oil sector			
Per capita			
Peak year	1978	1978	1978
Decline from peak	−19.95%	−23.79%	−18.64%
Per worker			
Peak year	1978	1978	1978
Decline from peak	−36.60%	−39.65%	−35.57%

and input use the results of explicit policy decisions. The opposite is true of the non-oil sector, which was predominantly owned and operated by the private sector. This is not to say there was no relationship between the performance of both sectors—indeed, we will argue quite the contrary—but that analytically it will be useful to separate their discussion, trying to understand what the main determinants of the country's petroleum policy were and using these production decisions as an input for the study of the non-oil sector's performance. Chapter 2 by Manzano deals in detail with the performance of the oil sector; in the rest of this chapter, we concentrate on understanding the causes of the decline in non-oil GDP, touching when necessary on the role that the decline in oil fiscal revenue has played in it.

Sources of Growth

Table 1.3 presents a standard growth accounting decomposition for the Venezuelan non-oil sector covering the 1957–2001 period as well as the two pre-collapse and collapse subperiods. Our decomposition separates changes in output into the contribution of three types of capital (residential, nonresidential, and machinery and equipment), four types of labor (unschooled and classified by primary, secondary, and higher schooling attainment), and total factor productivity. The annual percentage growth rate in the non-oil sector during the period of study is −0.90 percent. This decline occurs despite a substantial growth in the

Table 1.3 Total factor productivity growth decompositions in the non-oil sector, heterogeneous capital and labor

Years	TFP growth	Non-oil GDP growth	Nonresidential capital		Residential capital		Machinery and equipment		Total capital	
	Growth	Growth	Growth	Contribution	Growth	Contribution	Growth	Contribution	Growth	Contribution
1957–2001	0.36%	1.35%	0.91%	0.10%	1.26%	0.04%	0.78%	0.31%	0.94%	0.45%
1957–78	1.78%	3.81%	3.36%	0.32%	4.26%	0.12%	3.32%	1.16%	3.55%	1.60%
1978–2001	−0.84%	−0.90%	−1.33%	−0.16%	−1.49%	−0.06%	−1.54%	−0.59%	−1.44%	−0.81%

	No schooling attained		Primary schooling attained		Secondary schooling attained		Higher schooling attained		Labor force growth	
	Growth	Contribution	Growth	Contribution	Growth	Contribution	Growth	Contribution	Growth	Contribution
1957–2001	−2.20%	−0.28%	4.48%	0.55%	−0.23%	−0.04%	6.51%	0.31%	0.74%	0.54%
1957–78	−1.57%	−0.28%	6.66%	0.87%	−1.94%	−0.37%	7.17%	0.21%	0.44%	0.43%
1978–2001	−2.77%	−0.25%	2.49%	0.49%	1.33%	0.14%	5.92%	0.38%	1.01%	0.75%

skill-adjusted rate of labor force participation, which by itself would have generated an increase of 0.75 percentage points in the growth rate. In other words, the magnitude of the decline to be accounted for corresponds to an annual fall in the per skill-adjusted worker GDP ratio of 1.65 percentage points. This decomposes almost evenly, according to our growth accounting exercise, in a contribution of TFP growth of −0.84 percentage points and a contribution of the aggregate capital stock of −0.81 percentage points.

Note that this exercise understates the effect on growth of the decline in productivity for at least two reasons. On the one hand, the stock of capital reacts endogenously to changes in the rate of TFP growth, so that part of the decline in the capital stock should be explainable as a response to the decline in productivity (Hulten 1992). Further, the benchmark against which a certain rate of TFP growth should be measured is the growth of production techniques available to the economy at a given point in time. Parente and Prescott (2000) have suggested that an appropriate benchmark is 2 percent, which is not too different from the rate of TFP growth attained by Venezuela during the pre-collapse period (1957–78) of 1.78 percent. Therefore, it appears that productivity growth played an important role in the Venezuelan economic collapse.[6]

However, the data also suggest that there is an important autonomous role for capital accumulation. In a standard one-good Ramsey economy, the capital–labor ratio will respond to changes in productivity with an elasticity of $1/(1-\alpha)$, with α denoting the capital share. But as we can see in table 1.3, the Venezuelan capital–labor ratio declines at an annual rate of 2.44 percent, significantly higher than what would be expected as a result of the decline in productivity with a capital share of $1/3$ $[\approx(3/2)\cdot(-0.84)=-1.26]$.[7] In other words, the estimates of table 1.3 imply that more than half the decline of capital's stock decline cannot be explained as a simple response to the fall in productivity.

Below we attempt to understand the collapse in the capital stock, given the economy's productivity performance, after which we return to the issue of productivity growth.

The Decline in Capital Accumulation

It seems logical that any attempt to understand an apparently unexplained collapse in capital accumulation should take as its departure point the most salient fact about the evolution of the Venezuelan economy during the past twenty-five years, which is the steep decline in oil rents from the levels they reached during the 1970s. As shown in figure 1.1, per capita fiscal oil revenues rose steadily until

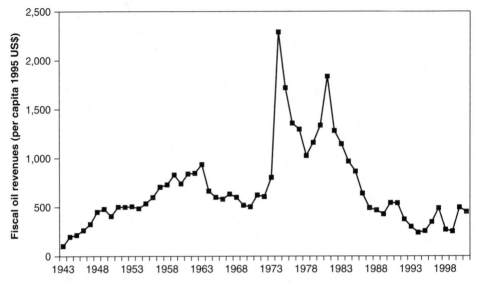

Fig. 1.1   Per capita fiscal oil revenues in constant US$, 1943–2001

the 1970s, when they started declining; by the 1990s, they had reached less than one-third of their 1970s value but were also substantially lower than any level the country had experienced since the 1940s. Intuitively, it makes sense to expect a contraction of this magnitude in the country's main source of export and fiscal revenue to produce a significant decline in capital accumulation.

However, the idea that an adverse shock to resource exports should have any effect on the non-oil-producing sector is actually quite hard to justify in an equilibrium model. The reason is that, in an open economy that is also incompletely specialized, factor prices will be determined by international prices. Since non-oil GDP must equal non-oil factor income, the fact that the domestic economy cannot affect factor prices implies that whatever happens in the oil sector will have no effect on the level of non-oil GDP.

To fix ideas, consider the following simple three-sector model proposed by Hausmann and Rigobón (2003). In that model, there are two sectors (tradables and non-tradables) that use two factors of production (capital and labor), plus a third sector that is simply modeled as an exogenous source of export revenues (the oil sector). The model also has an open capital account with an international interest rate that is given by $\bar{r}$. Let us assume for simplicity that both sectors have the same Cobb–Douglas technology, so that differences in production will be driven completely by differences in relative prices. The production functions are thus $Y_t = AK_t^{\alpha}L_t^{1-\alpha}$ and $Y_{nt} = AK_{nt}^{\alpha} L_{nt}^{1-\alpha}$. The labor force is fixed at $\bar{L}$ and per capita oil revenues are $\bar{g}$, which we take to be exogenous and spent totally on non-tradables by the government. Consumers have Cobb–Douglas preferences $U(C_t, C_{nt}) = C_t^\gamma C_{nt}^{1-\gamma}$. Consumers own all labor as well as an exogenous per capita stock of capital $\bar{k}^h$, which is unrelated to the domestic capital stock. The solution to this system, provided incomplete specialization, is given by the solution to the following system of six equations in six unknowns:

$$w = (1 - \alpha)AK_t^\alpha L_t^{-\alpha} \tag{1}$$

$$w = P_{nt}(1 - \alpha)AK_{nt}^\alpha L_{nt}^{-\alpha} \tag{2}$$

$$r = \alpha A K_t^{\alpha-1} L_t^{1-\alpha} \tag{3}$$

$$r = P_{nt}\alpha A K_{nt}^{\alpha-1} L_t^{1-\alpha} \tag{4}$$

$$L_t + L_{nt} = \bar{L} \tag{5}$$

$$P_{nt}AK_{nt}^\alpha L_{nt}^{1-\alpha} = (\gamma(w + r\bar{k}^h) + \bar{g})\bar{L}. \tag{6}$$

It is easy to note that wages and relative prices are constant in the solution to this system. Letting $k_i = \dfrac{K_i}{L_i}, i = \{t, nt\}$, equations (1)–(4) imply that $k_t = k_{nt} = \left(\dfrac{\bar{r}}{A\alpha}\right)^{\frac{1}{\alpha-1}}$. This means that the aggregate capital stock will be given by

$$K = K_t + K_{nt} = \left(\frac{\bar{r}}{A\alpha}\right)^{\frac{1}{\alpha-1}}\bar{L}, \tag{7}$$

which is invariant to the level of oil revenues. Revenue shocks are accommodated by changes in the allocation of labor, so that prices, capital stocks, and GDP remain stable. The equilibrium employment in non-tradables will be given by

$$L_{nt} = \bar{L}\left\{\gamma(1 - \alpha) + \frac{\bar{g} + \gamma\bar{r}\bar{k}^h}{A\left(\dfrac{\bar{r}}{A\alpha}\right)^{\frac{\alpha}{\alpha-1}}}\right\}. \tag{8}$$

The model with incomplete specialization has implications that are in stark contrast with the Venezuelan experience. In this model, neither the capital stock, the relative prices, nor the aggregate non-oil GDP varies with $\bar{g}$. The oil sector is simply tagged on to the rest of the economy, which functions independently of the resource sector. Changes in oil GDP do have an effect on consumption—through lower imports—but do not affect the capacity of the rest of the economy to generate revenue.

This result does not depend on the assumption of perfect capital mobility. As we show in the appendix, a model characterized by a closed capital account delivers the same results. The reason is that when the capital account is closed, the long-run rate of return is determined by the steady-state equilibrium conditions. It will depend on savings and depreciation rates as well as the parameters of the production function, but not on oil revenues. Therefore, since the steady-state return to capital is given, we can extend the above reasoning to show that the capital stock, relative prices, and aggregate non-oil GDP will still be invariant to resource earnings.

However, note what happens when oil revenues rise beyond a certain level. According to equation (7), when $\bar{g}$ reaches $g_O^* = (1 - \gamma(1 - \alpha))$ $A\left(\dfrac{\bar{r}}{A\alpha}\right)^{\frac{\alpha}{\alpha-1}} - \gamma \bar{r} \bar{k}^h$, the whole of the labor force is allocated to non-tradables production. Beyond that point, tradables production disappears and (7) and (8) no longer give us the solution. (1) and (3) now become inequalities and the aggregate capital stock is given by

$$K = K_{NT} = \frac{\alpha}{1 - \gamma(1 - \alpha)}(\bar{g} + \gamma \bar{r} \bar{k}^h)\bar{L}. \qquad (9)$$

As equation (9) indicates, the capital stock is now fully responsive to changes in the level of oil revenues. The response is illustrated in figure 1.2, which shows how the capital stock responds to different levels of oil revenues. At low levels of oil revenues, the capital stock is completely insensitive to increases in oil revenues. But after g^* is surpassed, changes in oil revenues are converted with a unit elasticity into changes in the capital stock. These effects are similar when there is no capital mobility (see the appendix for details).[8]

This exercise leads us to the conclusion that complete specialization is a necessary ingredient of an explanation of the Venezuelan economic collapse. The collapse in non-oil GDP that coincides historically with the decline in oil revenues can be explained only if we assume that Venezuela was unable to reallocate factors to the production of other tradable goods because alternative tradable sectors were nonexistent. Had there existed an alternative export sector in Venezuela in 1980, the growth of that sector would have played a stabilizing role in the country's reaction to falling oil revenues. In its absence, the domestic economy had to react to adverse oil shocks by contractions in domestic production. Theory predicts that this process will continue until (1) the fall in oil revenues is halted

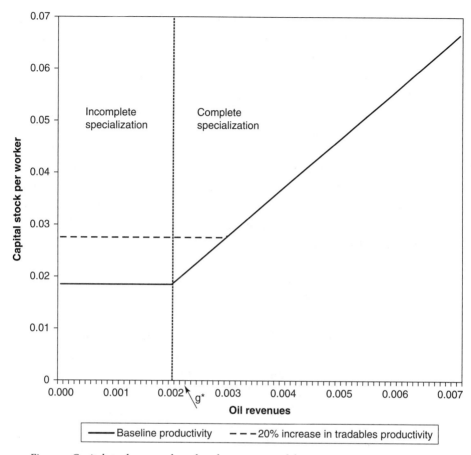

Fig. 1.2   Capital stock per worker, closed economy model

and (2) the real exchange rate falls sufficiently to make the production of non-oil tradables competitive.

The model also has very interesting policy implications. Let the levels of productivity of the tradables and non-tradables industry differ, and let the production function for the non-tradables industry now be $Y_{nt} = BK_{nt}^{\alpha} L_{nt}^{1-\alpha}$. Let us assume there is a set of government policies that can have an effect on the level of tradables productivity A. For simplicity, assume that these policies are costless. It is easy to check that the above-derived solutions for the capital stocks are not affected: under incomplete specialization $P_{nt} = \frac{A}{B}$ and thus K is still given by (9). Since the capital stock levels under complete specialization do not depend on productivity, they are also unaffected by this change.

In figure 1.2 we have also plotted the effect of an increase in tradables productivity of 20 percent. This increase makes production of tradables kick in at a much higher level of oil revenues and thus halts the decline in the capital stock generated by further decreases in oil rents. Without the policy, a decline in oil revenues from 4,000 to 1,000 in 1984 US$ leads to a decline of 50 percent in the per worker capital stock, but with the increase in productivity, it generates a decline of only 26 percent in the capital stock.

What is surprising about this result is it shows that a policy oriented toward increasing productivity in a very small (perhaps even nonexistent) sector can have a dramatic effect on the path of the capital stock and GDP. The effects go beyond the tradables sector because in equilibrium the wage rate is raised in both industries. Note that, in contrast, increases in productivity of the apparently more significant non-tradables industry have no equivalent effects on the path of capital accumulation. Any factor that increases the productivity of the tradables industry is likely to have far reaching effects on welfare and economic growth.

Why Didn't Venezuela Develop an Alternative Export Industry?

The discussion presented above has established the key role played by the non-oil export sector in attenuating the decline in capital accumulation generated by falling oil revenues. It suggests that understanding the nature of the Venezuelan export sector is vital for an analysis of Venezuela's growth prospects. The following discussion is intended to highlight certain aspects of this sector that can help us understand its performance during the decline of oil rents.

Non-oil Export Performance Since the 1980s

A first look at export performance since the 1980s seems to suggest that there has been some growth of non-oil exports during the period of collapse, as would be expected by the models discussed in the previous section (see fig. 1.3). However, the growth has been unexceptional by just about any standard. Per capita real non-oil exports (measured in 2000 US$) have grown by 42 percent since 1982. Their share of total exports grew from 7.1 to 19.7 percent of total exports, due mainly to a decline in oil exports. The annual real growth rate of per capita exports, at 2.01 percent, is the third lowest in the group of ten oil exporters that suffered important collapses in oil exports during the last twenty-one years. Even three-fifths of that growth has been in sectors, such as iron ore, petrochemicals, and aluminum, that heavily rely on the economy's comparative advantage in petroleum, natural resources, and energy. Although non-energy-intensive non-oil exports have grown at a satisfactory rate of 5.2 percent a year, this is partly due

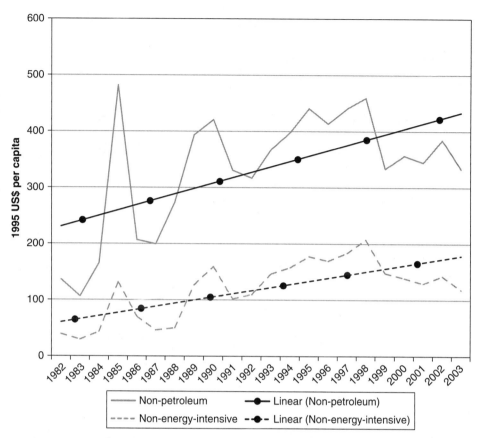

Fig. 1.3 Non-oil exports, 1982–2003

to the fact that it was an incredibly small sector, providing only thirty-nine dollars per capita in export revenue in 1982. This growth is also surprisingly weak if one views it in the light of the considerable real exchange rate depreciation that occurred between the early eighties and the late nineties: as shown in figure 1.4, the Venezuelan real exchange rate depreciated by more than 50 percent between the early eighties and the mid-nineties, before appreciating again in the late nineties under the Caldera–Chávez exchange rate bands policy. In fact, between 1983 and 1989, the country had a multiple exchange rate regime with differentials between the bottom and the top rate well in excess of 100 percent. Exports were not just stimulated by the level of the real exchange rate, but also by the possibility of arbitraging across exchange rates. In April 1989, the exchange rate regime was unified in the context of a large real depreciation. Non-oil exports stagnated after that, suggesting that arbitrage was an important component of the export performance in the 1980s.

Fig. 1.4   Real bilateral and multilateral exchange rate for Venezuela, 1970–2002

Among the oil-exporting countries that suffered significant export collapses since 1981, two (Mexico and Indonesia) were able to experience sufficiently strong growth in their non-oil export sector to compensate for the decline of oil exports and generate an overall positive export growth. (Ecuador is a third case, in which the expansion of non-oil exports appears to have exactly compensated for the decline in oil exports.) Venezuela's growth rate of non-oil exports is one-sixth that of Mexico and one-fourth that of Indonesia. A more long-run comparison of Venezuela, Indonesia, and Mexico shows striking differences in the behavior of the three countries: while in Mexico and Indonesia the collapse in oil exports was accompanied by a substantial expansion in the secondary exports sectors, this did not happen in Venezuela.

It is important to bear in mind that the period we refer to coincided with an unprecedented expansion of world trade. Figure 1.5 controls for this fact by calculating the evolution of Venezuela's median market share in non-energy-intensive sectors. Although this series does display an upward trend, it also shows that Venezuela's market participation in non-energy-intensive sectors has not increased since the early 1990s.

Figure 1.6 shows a decomposition of Venezuela's export growth by region of trade partner. By and large, the main contribution to the growth of Venezuelan non-oil exports comes from its growth in trade with members of the Andean Pact and the G3. The Andean Pact is a customs union established in 1995 that arose out of a free trade area formed two years earlier and includes Bolivia, Colombia, Ecuador, Peru, and Venezuela; the G3 is a free trade agreement (FTA) that covers Mexico, Venezuela, and Colombia. This growth has been concentrated in the Colombian market, imposing considerable limitations on market size. Figure 1.6 also shows that the impressive growth of Venezuelan non-oil exports in the mid-nineties was reversed with the trade and exchange restrictions that Venezuela imposed after 1999. Two key decisions are worth mentioning: the imposition of restrictions on cross-border transportation of merchandise by Venezuela on

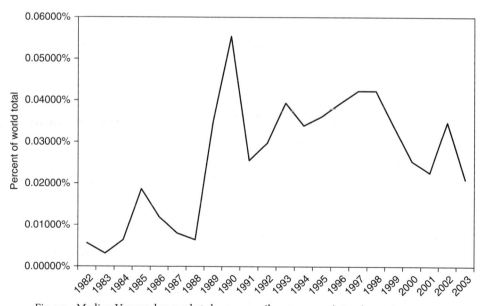

Fig. 1.5   Median Venezuelan market share, non-oil non-energy-intensive sectors

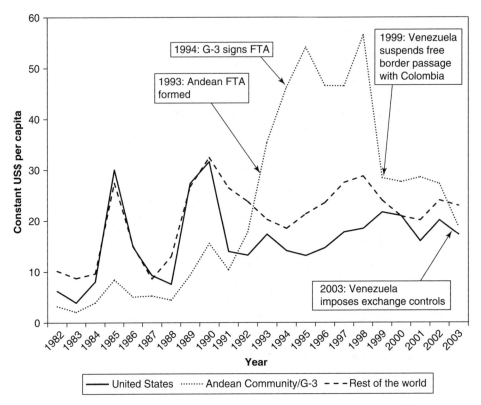

Fig. 1.6   Venezuelan non-energy-intensive exports, by region

May 12, 1999, which requires reloading merchandise at the border so that it is at all times transported by domestic operators; and the subsequent imposition of exchange controls in 2003, with the ensuing temporary paralysis of more than 80 percent of Colombian–Venezuelan trade and the cessation of private debt payments between the two countries.[9] The cross-border controls as well as restrictions by Venezuela on the imports of garlic and onions from Peru and coffee from Colombia have led the Andean Community to authorize these countries to impose retaliatory tariffs on Venezuela (Gutiérrez 2002, 15). The effect of these decisions goes beyond their direct impact on the incentives to export in particular industries, also affecting the degree of uncertainty regarding policy stability with respect to conditions for open international trade.

In sum, Venezuela has experienced positive but unexceptional non-oil export growth since the eighties. The data also suggest that (1) it is concentrated in energy-intensive products, which are just another way of exploiting Venezuela's comparative advantage in oil; (2) measured in relation to world trade, it has stagnated since the early nineties; and (3) it is concentrated in trade with the Andean Community and the G3, and thus it is limited by the small local market size in the limited set of products that Venezuela exports, and is highly sensitive to changes in trade policy like those that have occurred since 1999. With the recovery in oil revenues since 2004, Venezuela's non-oil export performance has gone in reverse. In this context, it is not obvious that a non-oil export sector exists that can buffer non-oil output from the economy-wide effects of an eventual decline in oil revenues.

Where Do New Exports Come From?

We can summarize our argument to this point as follows. There are two sources of poor Venezuelan growth in the non-oil sector: the decline in productivity and the decline in the capital stock over and above what one would expect solely from the fall in productivity. The latter cannot be explained as a response to a fall in oil revenues unless we are willing to assume that Venezuela is adequately characterized as a completely specialized economy. Complete specialization occurs when the economy lacks an alternative set of export goods to which it can move resources. The inability to develop these new goods is thus at the roots of a consistent account of Venezuela's growth problems.

While this explanation is internally consistent, it still leaves unanswered the underlying question of why Venezuela was unable to develop a set of alternative export goods to which it could shift production when it was hit by the export collapse. Many countries have seen massive changes in their patterns of specialization over time, whereby resources are shifted to previously inexistent industries. Indeed, this type of structural transformation has been at the root of the change experienced by East Asian countries during the postwar period from agricultural producers to exporters of unskilled labor-intensive manufactures and, in some cases, to exporters of high-technology products. Why was Venezuela incapable of experiencing a similar productive transformation?

Answering this question requires a theory of the evolution of comparative advantage. Regrettably, conventional models of trade and technological change have little to say about the form that this evolution can be expected to take. The Heckscher–Ohlin model explains the pattern of specialization as a consequence of changes in factor endowments but takes productivity in goods as a given. Most dominant approaches to modeling productivity growth (e.g., Aghion and Howitt 1992; Grossman and Helpman 1991) assume homogeneity across products and are thus inappropriate for studying the emergence of particular industries. What we require is a theory that will help us understand why some countries will become more productive in producing particular sets of goods, and how that depends on their existing patterns of specialization.

Such a theory has been proposed recently by Hausmann and Klinger (2006, 2007). These authors have shown that the density of the product space, in a sense that can be precisely defined, is a key determinant of the future evolution of comparative advantage. Countries are more likely to develop a comparative advantage in goods that are "closer" to the goods they currently produce. Theoretically, we would say that two goods are close to each other if the specialized inputs necessary to produce one can also be used to produce the other. The problem is that these specialized inputs may be very hard to measure, as they include not only specialized labor and capital but access to particular markets, public infrastructure provision, or the provision of specific forms of property rights protection. Therefore, Hausmann and Klinger suggest using a purely empirical measure of export similarity given by the relative frequency with which these goods are exported together. More formally, product similarity is given by the minimum of the conditional probabilities of exporting one good given that you are exporting the other one,

$$\varphi_{ijt} = \min \left\{ p(x_{it}|x_{jt}), p(x_{jt}|x_{it}) \right\}, \qquad (10)$$

where $p(x_{it}|x_{jt})$ is the probability that you have revealed comparative advantage in good i at time t given that you have revealed comparative advantage in good j at time t.

This measure of proximity can be used to build an indicator of the value of unexploited opportunities for export that can be particularly useful in our context. Hausmann and Klinger suggest precisely such a measure, which they call a country's "open forest." The idea of this measure is to capture the sophistication of the goods that an economy could produce with its productive assets. The measure is built as a weighted average of the sophistication of all potential export goods, where the weights are given by the distance between these goods and the economy's present export basket. The measure of distance in the product space is calculated based on the frequency with which particular good-pairs are exported by the same country, while the measure of sophistication is given by the average income of the countries that export that good, which we call $PRODY_{jt}$, as originally proposed by Hausmann, Hwang, and Rodrik (2006). More formally, let x_{cjt} be an indicator variable that takes the value 1 if country c has a revealed comparative advantage greater than 1 in good j at time t and 0 otherwise.

Then we can define a measure of the "option value" of a country's unexploited export opportunities as follows:

$$open\_forest_{ct} = \sum_i \sum_j \frac{\varphi_{ijt}}{\sum_i \varphi_{ijt}} (1 - x_{cjt}) x_{cit} PRODY_{jt}. \qquad (11)$$

Thus *open_forest* captures the flexibility of an economy's export basket, in that it measures the value of the goods the country could be producing with the inputs it currently devotes to its export production. *open_forest* is particularly appropriate for thinking about an economy's capacity to react to adverse export shocks. To fix ideas, suppose that an economy's exports of good i were to disappear overnight. This could happen, for example, as a result of the exhaustion of a natural resource, the emergence of a new lower-cost supplier in international markets, or the invention of a cheap substitute for that good. We know that this economy must shift resources into a new export sector. φ_{ijt} can be interpreted as our best guess of the probability that this country will shift resources into good j, and $\varphi_{ijt}(1 - x_{cjt})$ can be seen as our best guess of the probability that it will export a good j that it is not already exporting. $\varphi_{ijt}(1 - x_{cjt}) PRODY_{jt}$ is the expected value (measured in terms of the sophistication of exports) from exporting that good, making *open_forest* the weighted average of that expected value over all goods that the economy currently exports. In other words, *open_forest* reflects the expected value of an economy's next best export basket if it moved out of its current basket of exports.

As shown in figure 1.7, Venezuela's *open_forest* is remarkably low even by the standards of its neighboring countries. In 1980, at the start of Venezuela's growth collapse, the country's *open_forest* stood at just 13.8 percent of the world average and 15.7 percent of the South American average. It also had a substantially lower value of *open_forest* than its three neighbors, Colombia, Brazil, and Guyana (though it surpassed Guyana in the mid-eighties). Interestingly, it is also significantly lower than Mexico's, which may account for Mexico's much higher capacity to react to its decline in oil revenues in the eighties.

Venezuela's low *open_forest* appears to be a common characteristic of oil-exporting countries. Figure 1.8 presents the scatter plot of *open_forest* against per capita GDP in 1975. Fuel-exporting countries—countries that had a share of fuel exports in total exports greater than 80 percent in 1975—are denoted with a circle in the scatter plot. These countries have significantly lower levels of open forests than would be predicted by their level of income. Indeed, the average open forest for a fuel exporter is 2.17 log points lower than for a non-fuel exporter, even after

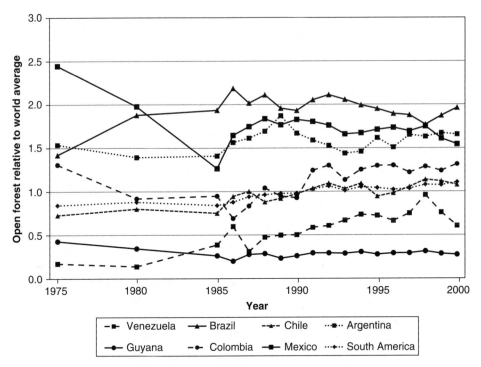

Fig. 1.7   Open forest, Venezuela and selected Latin American countries

Source: Authors' calculations based on data from Hausmann and Klinger (2007).

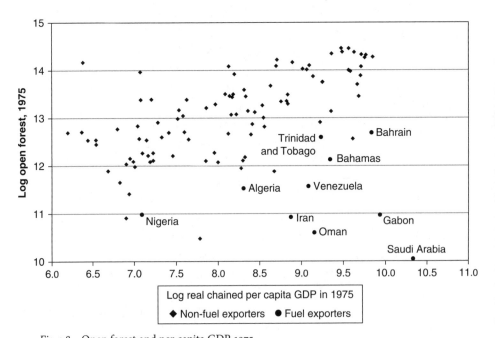

Fig. 1.8   Open forest and per capita GDP, 1975

Source: Data based on Penn World Tables 6.2 (Heston, Summers, and Aten 2002).

controlling for differences in income levels. In other words, it appears that the set of specialized inputs necessary for the production of oil are not very useful when it comes to producing other high-value goods.

Although Venezuela's low *open_forest* value is suggestive of its low export flexibility, how much do we know about the effect of export flexibility on the magnitude of growth collapses? Hausmann, Rodríguez, and Wagner (2008) have recently analyzed this issue in an empirical study of 535 episodes in which growth decelerates to negative rates. Their study analyzes both the causes for these growth decelerations as well as the determinants of the speed of recovery. Interestingly, they find that *open_forest* is a quantitatively strong and robust predictor of the probability of recovery from a recession. Their empirical exercise uses the statistical methodology of survival analysis to study the determinants of the duration of economic crises. The method of duration regressions allows them to address a problem that plagues the existing literature, which is the lack of a systematic method for dealing with the problem of censoring—crises that have not ended by the most recent year of data. If we have n countries with $t_1 \ldots t_n$ crises duration, the duration regression framework concentrates on finding the estimate of the probability density function $f(t)$ with associated survival time $S(t)$ that maximizes the likelihood function:

$$L = \prod_i f(t_i)^{\delta_i} S(t_i)^{1-\delta_i}. \tag{12}$$

Let us assume δ_i is an indicator variable that takes the value 0 if the peak per worker GDP has not been reached by the last observation in the sample. The authors study the determinants of crisis duration both under alternative parametric functional forms for $f(t)$ and by nonparametric estimation of $f(t)$, and address country-level heterogeneity by frailty adjustments and variance-corrected estimators. In table 1.4, we revisit their results. In contrast to their specification, however, we include a dummy variable for oil-exporting countries. As can be seen in column (1), the probability of recovery from a crisis is substantially lower for oil than for non-oil-exporting countries. The magnitude is substantial: the probability of recovery from a crisis (the hazard rate) in any particular year is 59.4 percent *lower* $[1-\exp(-.902)]$ on average for oil-exporting countries. Columns (2) and (3) show that this effect is robust quantitatively and statistically to controlling for initial per working-age person GDP and continent and decade dummies. As soon as we control for *open_forest* (column [4]), however, the correlation between the oil-exporting dummy and crisis duration becomes insignificant and, indeed, changes sign. In columns (5), (6), and (7) we introduce a set of alternative controls for democracy, inequality, social conflict, sudden stops, and inflation, none of which are significant. Our key result is not affected: *open_forest* is a robust predictor of crisis duration, and trumps the effect of oil exporting.

Table 1.4 Weibull duration regressions, open forest

	(1)	(2)	(3)	(4)	(5)	(6)	(7)
Oil exporter	-0.902	-1.281	-0.98	0.042	0.399	0.727	1.19
	(3.06)***	(2.87)***	(2.12)**	(0.08)	(0.63)	(0.97)	(1.58)
Log GDP per working-age person	—	0.258	-0.181	-0.275	-0.634	-0.789	-1.003
	—	(2.73)***	(1.13)	(1.29)	(2.49)*	(2.62)***	(2.85)***
Open forest	—	—	—	0.575	0.697	0.997	1.153
	—	—	—	(3.53)***	(3.39)***	(3.59)***	(3.80)***
Polity democracy index	—	—	—	—	0.035	-0.087	-0.105
	—	—	—	—	(1.53)	(0.91)	(0.95)
Inequality* (1−democracy)	—	—	—	—	—	-0.063	-0.075
	—	—	—	—	—	(1.49)	(1.55)
Inequality	—	—	—	—	—	-0.024	-0.015
	—	—	—	—	—	(0.77)	(0.44)
Sudden stop	—	—	—	—	—	—	-0.151
	—	—	—	—	—	—	(0.66)
Log of inflation	—	—	—	—	—	—	-0.049
	—	—	—	—	—	—	(0.08)
Constant	—	—	-1.804	-1.619	-1.675	-0.876	-0.909
	—	—	(4.90)***	(3.73)***	(3.45)***	(1.24)	(1.23)

	(1)	(2)	(3)	(4)	(5)	(6)	(7)
Latin America	—	—	-1.975	-1.195	-1.068	-0.05	-0.045
			(4.08)***	(1.77)*	(1.48)	(0.05)	(0.04)
Africa	—	—	-1.062	-0.887	-1.328	-1.105	-1.122
			(1.87)*	(1.30)	(1.89)*	(1.39)	(1.31)
South and Central Asia	—	—	-0.875	-0.19	-0.72	-0.426	-0.663
			(2.17)**	(0.40)	(1.25)	(0.55)	(0.80)
East Asia and Pacific	—	—	-2.411	-1.808	-1.641	-2.156	-1.773
			(5.25)***	(2.48)**	(2.12)**	(2.58)**	(1.89)*
Central and Eastern Europe	—	—	-1.024	-0.453	0.061	0.218	0.138
			(2.50)**	(0.93)	(0.10)	(0.31)	(0.19)
Middle East and North Africa	—	—	0.197	-0.72	0.362	0.07	0.147
			(0.62)	(1.16)	(1.34)	(0.08)	(0.16)
Observations	535	331	331	230	199	173	154
Number of groups	180	149	149	101	87	76	64

NOTE: Absolute value of z statistics in parentheses. Columns (3)–(7) also include a full set of decade dummies.

* Significant at 10%
** Significant at 5%
*** Significant at 1%

Table 1.5 Weibull duration regressions, density indicator

	(1)	(2)	(3)	(4)
Oil exporter	0.293	0.669	1.094	1.227
	(0.53)	(1.07)	(1.46)	(1.64)
Log GDP per working-age person	−0.245	−0.638	−0.773	−0.961
	(1.11)	(2.55)**	(2.65)***	(2.76)***
Density of product space	2.479	0.724	1.045	1.256
	(1.29)	(3.36)***	(3.63)***	(3.88)***
Open forest	−1.775	—	—	—
	(0.97)	—	—	—
Polity democracy index	—	0.04	−0.101	−0.105
	—	(1.72)*	(1.06)	(0.94)
Gini*(1–democracy)	—	—	−0.071	−0.075
	—	—	(1.70)*	(1.54)
Gini	—	—	−0.016	−0.016
	—	—	(0.52)	(0.45)
Sudden stop	—	—	—	−0.18
	—	—	—	(0.78)
Log of inflation	—	—	—	−0.112
	—	—	—	(0.17)
Latin America	−1.551	−1.592	−0.88	−0.812
	(3.47)***	(3.29)***	(1.25)	(1.09)

Africa	−1.19	−1.063	−0.097	0.141
	(1.71)*	(1.47)	(0.11)	(0.14)
South and Central Asia	−0.731	−1.285	−1.075	−0.957
	(1.02)	(1.85)*	(1.37)	(1.11)
East Asia and Pacific	−0.118	−0.687	−0.454	−0.538
	(0.24)	(1.19)	(0.59)	(0.64)
Central and Eastern Europe	−1.631	−1.577	−2.056	−1.699
	(2.14)**	(2.05)**	(2.50)**	(1.80)*
Middle East and North Africa	−0.342	0.096	0.204	0.263
	(0.66)	(0.16)	(0.29)	(0.36)
Constant	14.889	2.939	4.034	4.828
	(0.91)	(1.16)	(1.42)	(1.38)
Observations	229	198	172	154
Number of groups	100	86	75	64

NOTE: Absolute value of z statistics in parentheses. All columns also include a full set of decade dummies.

*Significant at 10%
**Significant at 5%
***Significant at 1%

Table 1.6   Probability of recovery and expected crisis duration times for alternative open forest values

Open forest level	Yearly probability of recovery	Expected duration of crisis
Venezuela historical	0.062	17.291
South America	0.154	7.326
Neighboring countries	0.200	5.711
East Asia	0.346	3.397
Venezuela oil	0.282	4.116

NOTE: Simulations capture the expected probabilities of recovery (hazard rates) and mean crisis duration in years for a country that has the same values as Bolivia of all variables except for open forest, which is set to the historical values of the selected comparison groups in 1980. Neighboring countries are Brazil, Colombia, and Guyana. East Asian countries are Hong Kong, South Korea, Singapore, and China. Venezuela oil refers to a value of open forest equal to the historical value minus the average effect of oil abundance in a regression of open forest on the log of GDP plus a dummy variable for oil-exporting countries.

Table 1.5 explores the extent to which the performance of the *open_forest* variable is determined by the measure of product sophistication *PRODY*, by presenting results for similar regressions in which the *open_forest* indicator is unweighted by any sophistication measure. This is a closer measure to the density of the space of unexploited profit opportunities. In column (1) we include both *open_forest* and the density variable, and show that the measures are so collinear that the regression cannot identify separate effects. In column (2) we drop *open_forest* and keep the density indicator, and find that its effect is indeed robust and trumps the oil-exporting dummy. Columns (3) and (4) introduce the same set of controls as the last two columns of table 1.4 and find that the robustness of the density indicator remains. Indeed, the oil-exporting dummy is now close to statistical significance ($p=0.101$), with a *positive* sign, indicating that if an oil exporter were to manage to have a similar density indicator than a comparable non-oil exporter, we may even expect it to have a faster recovery. This does not happen in general because oil exporters have lower densities.

The results of table 1.4 imply a considerable effect of *open_forest* on the probability of recovery from crises. In order to understand the magnitude of this effect, note that a coefficient of 0.575 (the estimate from column [4] of table 1.4) implies that a increase of one standard deviation in *open_forest* generates an increase of 90.5 percent in the probability of leaving the crisis: $\exp(0.557)\cdot sd(open\_forest)$. One way to understand the effect of these results is by studying how the probability of Venezuela's recovering from its growth collapse would change if it had different values of *open_forest* in 1975, holding fixed the level of all other explanatory variables at their historical values. We undertake this exercise in table 1.6. Row 1 starts by considering the model estimate for Venezuela at its historical *open_forest* value. The exercise is based on the parameter estimates of the model in column (5) of table 1.4. The probability of recovering from the crisis in any given year is estimated at 0.062, and the expected duration time of the crisis predicted by the model to be 17.29 years. In other words, the model predicts that Venezuela would be expected to take more than seventeen years in recovering its peak per worker GDP. Row 2 considers the case in which we use as a reference the average *open_forest* value for all South American countries. In this case the expected duration of crisis falls to 7.33 years. If Venezuela had instead had the *open_forest* of its three neighboring countries (Colombia, Brazil, and Guyana), we see that its expected crisis duration time falls to just 5.71 years. The next exercise shows the effect of having the *open_forest* of the set of fast-growing East Asian countries. In this case, the expected crisis duration declines to 3.39 years. In the last row, we consider the counterfactual of "Venezuela without oil"—that is, Venezuela with the historical values of all variables but with the *open_forest* of a typical non-oil-exporting country at its level of income. We see that crisis duration would have been only 4.12 years in expectation.

The key conclusion we draw from this exercise is that oil-exporting countries do not have an easy time developing new export products. Their difficulties come from the fact that there are few high-value goods that can be produced with the set of specialized inputs, technological know-how, and institutional development that are appropriate for oil production. This makes the product space relatively sparse for these countries. This may not be a problem if oil production is growing—in that case, there is no need to develop alternative export sectors. But it can become a substantial hindrance to recovering from crises if doing so requires moving into the production of new goods.

Concluding Comments

This chapter has provided a new explanation for Venezuela's growth collapse. We have argued that Venezuela's failure to recover from the recession it fell into during the late seventies is due in part to its inability to develop new export sectors. This inability can be traced to a characteristic that current Venezuelan specialization patterns share with those of most other oil-exporting countries: the specialized inputs, skills, and institutions that are appropriate for use in oil production are not easily transferable to other goods. Venezuela, in other words, inhabits a sparse area of the product space, a fact that hinders its capacity to respond to export collapses by developing alternative export industries.

We have suggested that any coherent explanation for the Venezuelan growth collapse must pass two simple tests. First, it must explain why Venezuelan economic performance differs so much from that of the rest of the region. Explanations that blame policy failures or social conflict for Venezuela's lackluster growth do not pass this test, as Venezuela is not markedly different from the rest of the region in these dimensions. Second, it must explain why Venezuelan economic performance changed so dramatically in the seventies. Explanations that blame rent-seeking or institutional quality for Venezuela's growth performance are incapable of explaining why the same institutions and the same levels of rent-seeking were compatible with the highest growth in the region for the half century starting in 1920.

Our explanation, in turn, easily passes these two tests. As we have shown above, Venezuela's export flexibility is considerably lower than that of most other Latin American nations. This is due to the simple fact that, unlike the rest of the region, Venezuela is an oil exporter that inhabits a sparse region of the product space. Further, lack of export flexibility need not be a hindrance to a country when its traditional exports are growing, as was the case for Venezuela before the seventies. If you are experiencing high export growth in traditional sectors, you have no need to move to alternative exports and export flexibility has no value. It is when traditional exports start doing poorly that you need to reallocate resources to new sectors. Venezuela's low export flexibility can thus explain why the country did not recover from the crisis it has experienced since the late seventies while at the same time being compatible with its high growth during the preceding period.

It is important to point out that our explanation is only a partial account of Venezuelan economic growth. While the lack of development of alternative export sectors can help explain the decline in capital accumulation that occurred during the growth collapse, it does not explain the collapse in total factor productivity, which, as we have shown, occurred at an annual rate of −0.84 percent between 1978 and 2001. Other chapters in this book deal directly with the causes of this decline, ranging from the decline in public infrastructure investment to growing stringency of labor market regulations to the collapse in financial intermediation.

Our explanation can shed more light in general on the vast literature concerning the "Dutch disease." As we discussed in the introduction, the observation that resource-abundant economies tend to grow more slowly, first made in the cross-country growth context by Sachs and Warner (1997), has spurred a huge literature. Our chapter suggests that what may make resource-abundant countries stand out is not necessarily their aggregate growth performance but rather their incapacity to recover from adverse shocks. It thus points to the need to examine closely asymmetries in the response of growth to external shocks and to study seriously the possibility that countries may fall into "specialization traps," whereby they end up occupying a sparse region of the product space that is difficult to exit. A fuller exploration of these ideas in the cross-national context offers an interesting avenue for future research.

APPENDIX: THE CLOSED ECONOMY MODEL

Suppose that capital accumulation occurs through domestic savings, with individuals assumed to save a constant fraction of their income s. As domestic savings finances capital accumulation, the capital stock is owned by domestic residents, who own no other capital. Equations (1)–(5) are as above, with equation (6) replaced by

$$P_{nt}AK_{nt}{}^{\alpha}L_{nt}{}^{1-\alpha} = (\gamma(1-s)(w+rk) + \bar{g})\bar{L}. \quad (A.1)$$

The capital stock will grow over time according to

$$\dot{K}_t = s(w\bar{L} + rK) - \delta K. \quad (A.2)$$

We have omitted time subscripts as we will concentrate on the steady state, which is given from equation (A.2) by

$$sw\bar{L} = (\delta - rs)K. \quad (A.3)$$

Note that as equations (1)–(5) are the same, it is still the case that K is given by (7), with r now an endogenous variable. From the steady-state condition, the steady-state rate of return is $r^{ss} = \dfrac{\delta\alpha}{s}$, so that in the steady state,

$$K = K_t + K_{nt} = \left(\frac{\delta}{As}\right)^{\frac{1}{\alpha-1}}\bar{L}, \quad (A.4)$$

which establishes that the capital stock is invariant to increases in oil revenues under incomplete specialization, just as in the model with capital mobility. Employment in non-tradables is given by

$$L_{nt} = \bar{L}\left\{\gamma(1-s) + \frac{\bar{g}}{A\left(\dfrac{\delta}{As}\right)^{\frac{\alpha}{\alpha-1}}}\right\}. \quad (A.5)$$

As before, there is a threshold $g_C^* = (1 - \gamma(1 - s))A\left(\dfrac{\delta}{As}\right)^{\frac{\alpha}{\alpha-1}}$ beyond which full specialization develops. It is easy to check that after this point the capital stock becomes

$$K = \left(\frac{\delta}{s}(1 - \gamma(1 - s))\right)^{-1}\bar{g}\bar{L}, \qquad (A.6)$$

so that the capital stock again becomes fully responsive to shifts in oil revenues.

Note that equations (8) and (A.5) are similar. The differences come from three facts: (1) Equation (14) uses the steady-state level of the interest rate instead of $\bar{r}$; (2) as the closed economy model has no domestic ownership of foreign capital, the term $\bar{r}\bar{k}^h$ disappears from all expressions; and (3) s plays the same role in the closed economy model as α does in the open economy one. This last result reflects the fact that in the open economy model α reflects the share of additional oil revenue—which are converted one by one into increases in demand for non-tradables—that international capital owners can expect to receive, and that thus call forward greater capital inflows, whereas in the closed economy model s reflects the fraction of these revenues that will ultimately be channeled toward capital accumulation.

NOTES

1. As we will discuss in further detail below, estimates of the timing and magnitude of the decline in Venezuelan GDP vary widely due primarily to differences in the valuation of the oil sector. The figures cited correspond to the Törnqvist chained index built by Rodríguez (2004) and discussed in greater detail below.

2. Lederman and Maloney 2007 gives a contrasting view.

3. Interestingly, however, the share of primary exports in GDP (Sachs and Warner's original variable) does not make it into their list, nor does a dummy for oil-exporting countries.

4. The use of unofficial estimates affects the Baptista and Maddison data. With respect to the 1984 jump in nominal GDP, the key issue is whether to treat it as genuine growth in the supply of goods and services or to assume that it corresponds to previously unmeasured goods. Readers interested in a fuller discussion of these issues are referred to Rodríguez 2006.

5. See Fisher and Shell 1998 for a full treatment of these issues.

6. It could be argued that, by not taking into account changes over time in the quality of the capital stock, we have underestimated the contribution of embodied technological change to the growth rate. Estimating embodied technological change requires price indices of quality-adjusted investment goods as calculated by Gordon (1990) or Greenwood, Hercowitz, and Krusell (1997), which are unavailable for the Venezuelan economy. It is unlikely that this could be a major contributing factor, however, as Venezuelan gross investment rates during the period of study were barely enough to cover depreciation during the 1978–2001 period. Even in the case of the United States, where the growth rate of equipment capital was 4.37 percent for the 1949–83 period, the resulting underestimation of the contribution of the capital stock to growth due to embodied technological change has been calculated at 0.3 annual percentage points (Hulten 1992).

7. If one uses the historical capital share, the predicted decline in the capital stock increases to 1.92 percent, still short of the historical decline. On why national accounts data may overestimate capital shares in developing countries, see Gollin 2002.

8. A possible approach for distinguishing between the two models would be to use (9) and (A.4) to calibrate the behavior of the economy's capital stock and to evaluate comparatively the performance of the models. Our attempts to do so have not produced satisfactory results, mainly because there is an important range of variation for oil revenues for which the models will have very similar predictions. At least from the point of view of understanding the relative magnitudes of the decline in capital accumulation, these models appear to be sufficiently close to observational equivalence to raise the question of the utility of further attempts to distinguish between them.

9. See Gutiérrez 2002 on cross-border transport.

REFERENCES

Abel, Andrew. 1983. "Optimal Investment under Uncertainty." *American Economic Review* 73 (1): 228–33.

Aghion, Philippe, and Peter Howitt. 1992. "A Model of Growth through Creative Destruction." *Econometrica* 60 (2): 323–51.

Anderson, T. W., and Cheng Hsiao. 1982. "Formulation and Estimation of Dynamic Models Using Panel Data." *Journal of Econometrics* 18 (1): 47–82.

Arellano, Manuel, and S. Bond. 1991. "Some Tests of Specification for Panel Data: Monte Carlo Evidence and an Application to Employment Equations." *Review of Economic Studies* 58 (2): 277–97.

Banco Central de Venezuela. 2000. *Series Estadísticas de Venezuela (1940–1999)*. Caracas: Banco Central de Venezuela.

———. 2007. "Reservas internacionales y tipos de cambio de referencia." http://www.bcv.org.ve/c2/indicadores.asp.

Baptista, Asdrúbal. 2006. *Bases cuantitativas de la economía venezolana, 1830–2002*. Caracas: Fundación Polar.

Bello, O. D., and D. Restuccia. 2002. "Venezuela's Growth Experience." Working Paper 431, Department of Economics, University of Toronto.

Bermúdez, A. 2004. "La legislación laboral en Venezuela y sus impactos sobre el mercado laboral." In *El desempleo en Venezuela: Causas, efectos e implicaciones de política*, edited by F. Rodríguez, C. Risopatrón, A. Bermúdez, M. E. Boza, A. Daza, S. Freije, and D. Ortega, 39–60. Caracas: Oficina de Asesoría Económica de la Asamblea Nacional.

Bernard, Andrew, and J. B. Jensen. 2004. "Why Some Firms Export." *Review of Economics and Statistics* 86 (2): 561–69.

Blades, Derek. 2000. "Maintaining Consistent Time Series of National Accounts." Paper prepared for Joint ADB/ESCAP Workshop on Rebasing and Linking of National Accounts Series, Bangkok, March 21–24.

Bulmer-Thomas, V. 1994. *The Economic History of Latin America since Independence*. New York: Cambridge University Press.

Calderón, C., and L. Servén. 2003. "Macroeconomic Dimensions of Infrastructure in Latin America." Policy Research Working Paper 5317, World Bank and Development Research Group, Washington, D.C.

Canning, D. 1999. "The Contribution of Infrastructure to Aggregate Output." Policy Research Working Paper 2246, World Bank, Washington, D.C.

Das, Sanghamitra, Mark J. Roberts, and James R. Tybout. 2007. "Entry Costs, Producer Heterogeneity, and Export Dynamics." *Econometrica* 75 (3): 837–73.

Easterly, William, and Luis Servén, eds. 2003. *The Limits of Stabilization: Infrastructure, Public Deficits, and Growth in Latin America*. Washington, D.C.: World Bank.

Fisher, F. M., and K. Shell. 1998. *Economic Analysis of Production Price Indexes*. Cambridge: Cambridge University Press.

Gelb, A. 1988. *Oil Windfalls: Blessing or Curse?* New York: Oxford University Press for the World Bank.

Gollin, Douglas. 2002. "Getting Income Shares Right." *Journal of Political Economy* 110 (2): 458–74.

Gordon, R. J. 1990. *The Measurement of Durable Goods Prices*. Chicago: University of Chicago Press.

Greenwood, J., Z. Hercowitz, and P. Krusell. 1997. "Long-Run Implications of Investment-Specific Technological Change." *American Economic Review* 87 (3): 342–62.

Grossman, Gene M., and Elhanan Helpman. 1991. "Trade, Knowledge Spillovers, and Growth." *European Economic Review* 35 (2/3): 517–26.

Gutiérrez, A. 2002. "Las trabas no arancelarias en el comercio bilateral agroalimentario entre Venezuela y Colombia." Working Paper 11, Inter-American Development Bank, Washington, D.C.

Gylfason, T. 2001. "Natural Resources, Education and Economic Development." *European Economic Review* 45 (4–6): 847–59.

Hausmann, Ricardo. 2003. "Venezuela's Growth Implosion: A Neo-Classical Story?" In *In Search of Prosperity: Analytic Narratives on Economic Growth*, edited by D. Rodrik, 244–70. Princeton: Princeton University Press.

Hausmann, Ricardo, Jason Hwang, and Dani Rodrik. 2006. "What You Export Matters." Working Paper 123, Center for International Development, Harvard Kennedy School, Cambridge, Mass.

Hausmann, Ricardo, and Bailey Klinger. 2006. "Structural Transformation and Patterns of Comparative Advantage in the Product Space." Working Paper 128, Center for International Development, Harvard Kennedy School, Cambridge, Mass.

———. 2007. "The Structure of the Product Space and the Evolution of Comparative Advantage." Working Paper 146, Center for International Development, Harvard Kennedy School, Cambridge, Mass.

Hausmann, Ricardo, Lant Pritchett, and Dani Rodrik. 2004. "Growth Accelerations." NBER Working Paper 10566, National Bureau of Economic Research, Cambridge, Mass.

Hausmann, Ricardo, and Roberto Rigobón. 2003. "An Alternative Interpretation of the 'Resource Curse': Theory and Policy Implications." In *Fiscal Policy Formulation and Implementation in Oil-Producing Countries*, edited J. M. Davis, R. Ossowski, and A. Fedelino, 13–44. Washington, D.C.: IMF Press.

Hausmann, Ricardo, Francisco Rodríguez, and Rodrigo Wagner. 2008. "Growth Collapses." In *Money, Crises, and Transition: Essays in Honor of Guillermo Calvo*, edited Carmen Reinhart, Andrés Velasco, and Carlos Vegh, 303–29. Cambridge: MIT Press.

Hausmann, Ricardo, and Dani Rodrik. 2003. "Economic Development as Self-Discovery." *Journal of Development Economics* 72 (2): 603–33.

Hausmann, Ricardo, Dani Rodrik, and Andrés Velasco. 2004. "Growth Diagnostics." In *The Washington Consensus Reconsidered: Towards a New Global Governance*, edited by Narcís Serra and Joseph E. Stiglitz, 324–54. New York: Oxford University Press.

Heckman, J., and C. Pagés. 2003. "Law and Employment: Lessons from Latin America and the Caribbean." NBER Working Paper 10129, National Bureau of Economic Research, Cambridge, Mass.

Heston, Alan, Robert Summers, and Bettina Aten. 2002. "Penn World Table Version 6.1, Center for International Comparisons at the University of Pennsylvania (CICUP)." http://pwt.econ.upenn.edu/php_site/pwt61_form.php.

Hulten, C. 1992. "Growth Accounting When Technical Change Is Embodied in Capital."
    American Economic Review 82 (4): 964–80.
———. 2001. "Total Factor Productivity: A Short Biography." In *New Developments in
    Productivity Analysis*, edited by Charles R. Hulten, Edwin R. Dean, and Michael J.
    Harper, 1–47. Chicago: University of Chicago Press.
Hulten, C., and F. C. Wykoff. 1981. "The Estimation of Economic Depreciation Using Vintage
    Asset Prices: An Application of the Box-Cox Power Transformation." *Journal of
    Econometrics* 15 (3): 367–96.
Inter-American Development Bank. 1999. *Facing Up to Inequality in Latin America*.
    Washington, D.C.
International Monetary Fund International Financial Statistics. 2007. *International Financial
    Statistics*. Washington, D.C., CD-ROM.
Isham, J., L. Pritchett, M. Woolcock, and G. Busby. 2002. "The Varieties of Resource Experience:
    How Natural Resource Export Structures Affect the Political Economy of Economic
    Growth." *World Bank Economic Review* 19 (2): 141–74.
Karl, Terry Lynn. 1987. "Petroleum and Political Pacts: The Transition to Democracy in Venezuela."
    Latin American Research Review 22 (1): 63–94.
Lederman, Daniel, and William Maloney. 2007. *Natural Resources: Neither Curse nor Destiny*.
    Washington, D.C.: World Bank.
López Obregon, Clara, and Francisco Rodríguez. 2001. "La política fiscal venezolana
    1943–2001." In *Reporte de Coyuntura Anual, 2001*, 19–38. Caracas: Oficina de Asesoría
    Económica y Financiera de la Asamblea Nacional.
Maddison, Angus. 2001. *The World Economy: A Millennial Perspective*. Paris: Organisation for
    Economic Co-operation and Development.
Maloney, W., and J. Nuñez. 2002. "Measuring the Impacts of Minimum Wages: Evidence from
    Latin America." In *Law and Employment: Lessons from Latin America and the Caribbean*,
    edited by James Heckman and Carmen Pagés, 109–30. Chicago: University of Chicago
    Press.
Manzano, Osmel. 2007. "Venezuela after a Century of Oil Exploitation." Reproduced by
    the Corporación Andina de Fomento, Caracas, and now chapter 2 of the present
    volume.
Martin, P., and C. A. Rogers. 1995. "Industrial Location and Public Infrastructure." *Journal of
    International Economics* 39 (3/4): 335–51.
Mehlum, H., K. O. Moene, and R. Torvik. 2002. "Institutions and the Resource Curse."
    Economic Journal 116 (5): 1–20.
Pagés, Carmen, and James Heckman. 2000. "The Cost of Job Security Regulation: Evidence
    from Latin American Labor Markets." *Economía* 1 (1): 109–44.
Parente, Stephen L., and Edward C. Prescott. 2000. *Barriers to Riches*. Cambridge:
    MIT Press.
Pritchett, L. 1998. "Patterns of Economic Growth: Hills, Plateaus, Mountains, and Plains."
    Policy Research Working Paper 1947, World Bank, Washington, D.C.
Rodríguez, F. 2004. "Un nuevo índice encadenado del producto interno bruto de Venezuela,
    1957–2001." *Revista BCV* 18 (2): 99–118.
———. 2006. "The Anarchy of Numbers: Understanding the Evidence on Venezuelan
    Economic Growth," *Canadian Journal of Development Studies* 27 (4): 503–29.
Rodríguez, F., and J. Sachs. 1999. "Why Do Resource-Abundant Economies Grow More
    Slowly?" *Journal of Economic Growth* 4 (3): 277–303.
Sachs, Jeffrey D., and Andrew M. Warner. 1999. "Natural Resource Intensity and Economic
    Growth." In *Development Policies in Natural Resource Economies*, edited by Jörg Mayer,
    Brian Chambers, and Ayisha Farooq, 13–77. Cheltenham, U.K., and Northampton,
    Mass.: Edward Elgar in association with UNCTAD.

Sala-i-Martin, X., G. Doppelhofer, and R. I. Miller. 2004. "Determinants of Long-Term Growth: A Bayesian Averaging of Classical Estimates (BACE) Approach." *American Economic Review* 94 (4): 813–35.

Sánchez-Robles, B. 1998. "Infrastructure Investment and Growth: Some Empirical Evidence." *Contemporary Economic Policy* 16 (1): 98–108.

Tornell, A., and P. Lane. 1999. "The Voracity Effect." *American Economic Review* 89 (1): 22–46.

United Nations. 2007. "Comtrade database." http://comtrade.un.org/.

World Bank. 2006. *World Development Indicators Database*. Washington, D.C., CD-ROM.

2 VENEZUELA AFTER A CENTURY OF OIL EXPLOITATION

Osmel Manzano

In this chapter, the Venezuelan oil sector's performance is reviewed and compared with the performance of the oil sector of similar oil-producing countries. The changes in oil fiscal revenue per capita over the last sixty years resemble those of the GDP per capita for Venezuela. After three decades of sustained growth, the oil sector collapsed in the 1980s and it has not recovered since. It is argued that to understand the behavior of the sector, it is important to divide the study into different periods, taking into account changes in both the way Venezuelan oil policy is formulated and implemented, and in the nature of international oil markets. It is further argued that the periods in which oil policy was relatively in line with international markets fundamentals were those of expansion, while the periods in which oil policy seemed to diverge from those fundamentals were those when fiscal revenue collapsed.

When analyzing Venezuela's economic performance, it is impossible not to consider the oil sector. As explained in the introduction, even now, the sector represents 80 percent of exports, thus making it the largest source of foreign

I would like to thank the following for helpful comments and suggestions: Amy B. Barrigh, Graham Davis, Ricardo Hausmann, Ana Maria Herrera, William Hogan, Francisco Monaldi, Jose Pineda, Alejandro Puente, Francisco Rodriguez, Federico Sturzenegger, Ricardo Villasmil, Ian Sue Wing, and seminar participants at IESA (Venezuela), Northeastern University, and the John F. Kennedy School of Government at Harvard University and at the LACEA conference. I also thank Federico Ortega and Vanessa Alviarez for being excellent research assistants. All errors that remain are mine. I also acknowledge the International Center for Energy and the Environment at IESA (Venezuela), which provided financial support. This chapter was completed while I was in residence at the John F. Kennedy School–Respol YPF Fellows Program. The ideas and views expressed on this chapter are solely my responsibility and do not necessarily reflect those of the Corporacion Andina de Fomento. Comments are welcome at manzanom@ alum.mit.edu.

currency. It represents more than 40 percent of government revenue, and in the past this figure was as high as 70 percent. It is thus the biggest contributor to the fiscal sector. Finally, it comprises more than 25 percent of all economic activity.

Given the foregoing, it is important to understand the performance of the oil sector as it relates to the performance of the rest of the economy. As will be shown below, a case can be made for thinking that oil fiscal revenue has had an enormous effect on changes in the GDP per capita in Venezuela. Oil has been produced commercially in Venezuela since the beginning of the twentieth century. At that time, Venezuela was one of the poorest countries in the region. The available evidence suggests that oil played an important role in making it one of the richest countries in the region during the 1970s.[1] However, the evidence also suggests that oil played a role in the collapse of the Venezuelan economy, because oil fiscal revenue started to fall at around the same time the GDP per capita fell.

There have been extensive debates about the role natural resources should play in a country's economic development, with different views supporting different recommendations for the formulation and implementation of policy. One approach proposes that oil-rich countries should focus on a diverse range of economic activities different and not related to oil production. There are a number of arguments for this diversification strategy. One is that the oil sector, along with sectors pertaining to other natural resources, has decreasing returns to scale, few links to the rest of the economy, and "stagnant" markets.[2] In addition, it has been shown in theoretical studies that resource booms have a negative effect on the industrial development of resource-rich countries.[3] These arguments led to the concept of the "resource curse," according to which resource-rich countries will have poor economic performance.[4]

A different approach holds that an oil-rich country has a comparative advantage in the oil sector and would benefit from its development. Recent research has shown that poor growth appears to result from a concentration on exports, rather than from an abundance of resources.[5] Moreover, this line of research has found that resource-rich countries that have experienced strong economic growth have benefited from their comparative advantage, by developing the sector and using the resultant benefits to develop other sectors (Blomstrom and Kokko 2003; Maloney 2002). Doubts about the "stagnant markets" argument have also been raised in the literature on the price and the market of primary products.[6] In addition, it has been argued in the literature that resource products are linked to technology and innovation, and are therefore a source of growth in productivity (Wright and Czelusta 2002).

It is not the objective of this chapter to test these two views to determine which is closer to the truth. Rather, the performance of the Venezuelan oil sector will be compared with that of the oil sectors of similar oil-producing countries. There will be a certain amount of discussion of how the sector's performance affects growth. However, the focus will be on the sector's performance per se, because the position taken will affect policy decisions regarding the oil sector.

The remainder of this chapter is organized as follows. The first section will analyze the changes in the oil fiscal revenue and provide an overview of oil policy. The middle sections (second through fifth) will each analyze a period in the history of oil exploitation in Venezuela. In each section, the reasons for viewing the period in question as an era distinct from the others will be explained. The final section concludes my argument.

The Evolution of Oil Fiscal Revenue

The chapter by Hausmann and Rodríguez in this book, "Why Did Venezuelan Growth Collapse?" describes the role oil fiscal revenue plays in explaining the collapse of the Venezuelan economy. In order to deepen our understanding, it is important to understand what drives the collapse of those revenues. The following equation shows a very simplified way of thinking about fiscal revenue: $Fiscal\ Revenue = \tau_e \cdot (p - c) \cdot q$.

Fiscal revenue is derived by applying taxation (with an effective tax rate τ_e) to the flow of taxable income. In this case, taxable income is the result of the net income $(p-c)$ multiplied by the quantity of the good sold (q). Evidently, this formulation does not take into account all the issues regarding taxation in general, and the taxation of oil in particular. These issues will be discussed below. Nevertheless, the formula offers a simple way of determining whether changes in fiscal revenue are driven by changes in tax pressure, the net revenue, or the quantity.

In table 2.1, I present the decomposition of oil fiscal revenue in changes in tax rates, net revenue, or quantity. Between 1960 and 2001, oil fiscal revenue per capita fell 7 percent. Nevertheless, we see that both the effective tax rate and the net income grew. The fall in fiscal revenue is due to the fact that production per capita fell by 67 percent. Following the peak of 1973, the revenue per capita from 1973 to 2001 fell by 47 percent; again, this is due mostly to the fall in oil production per capita.

In this regard, this work differs from the alternative views of the evolution of oil fiscal revenue in Venezuela. In particular, Mommer (2003) states that, after the nationalization of the oil industry in 1976, Petroleos de Venezuela (hereafter referred to as PDVSA) became something of a "state within a state" and that the different governments that followed failed to create a new efficient fiscal and regulatory system. Consequently, Venezuelan oil policy was put on a path toward minimization of fiscal oil revenues.

Table 2.1   Decomposition of growth in oil fiscal revenue per capita

Period	Total change			
	Oil fiscal revenue	τ_e	p–c	q
1960–2001	−7%	38%	107%	−67%
1973–2001	−47%	4%	18%	−57%
Benchmarks discussed in this chapter				
1960–73	75%	33%	75%	−25%
1973–88	−34%	60%	16%	−64%
1988–2001	−20%	−35%	2%	21%
Alternative benchmarks				
1960–75	175%	43%	296%	−51%
1975–83	−43%	−19%	18%	−41%
1983–89	−45%	12%	−46%	−9%
1989–2001	9%	7%	−17%	24%

SOURCE: Author's calculations based on Ministerio de Energía y Minas (various years); International Monetary Fund 2004.

As seen from table 2.1, the main driver of the fall in oil fiscal revenue between 1960 and 2001 was the fall in oil production. Between 1960 and 2001, both the tax rate and the net income increased. The last lines show the periods discussed by Mommer. From the table it is evident that the collapse on oil fiscal revenue took place between 1975 and 1989. In addition, the table shows that the fall in production is the main driver, and that production was falling even before nationalization.

Further, after 1983 the effective tax rates actually started to increase. According to Mommer (2003), 1983 is the year when PDVSA executives embarked on their strategy of internationalization as a first step toward the reprivatization of the industry and minimization of oil fiscal revenues. Finally, the table also shows that after 1989, oil fiscal revenue per capita actually increased, and again the main driver is production.

Consequently, in order to understand the evolution of oil fiscal revenue in Venezuela, the key variable to study is oil production. Production increased up until 1973. Right after that, production almost collapsed, and it was only after 1986 that it began to increase again. In 2002, oil production was around three million barrels a day, still below the level of 1973. Of course, this implies an important fall in oil production per capita. Oil production per capita declined from 1962 to 1985. Since then, production per capita has increased, but is still below the average of the period from 1921 to 2001. In 2002, oil production per capita was 31 percent lower than in 1976 (and 71 percent lower than the historical high in 1957). Moreover, the average oil production per capita in the 1990s was 67 percent lower than in the 1960s.

In effect, oil production per capita follows closely the changes in GDP per capita. It increased steadily until the 1970s, then declined. The particular period in which the two variables moved in opposite directions was between 1957 and 1976. However, during this period in which production was falling, fiscal income increased, due not only to prices but also to the increased fiscal pressure. Therefore, in the long run, it seems that oil production can help to explain a lot of the movement of the GDP—or, in other words, that the Venezuelan expansion and later collapse cannot be dissociated from changes in oil production.

Consequently, to understand the fall in fiscal revenue per capita it is important to study what has driven oil production in Venezuela.[7] Consideration of the resources used in oil production makes it evident that the most important factor is capital (leaving aside oil reserves). Increases in production are linked to important increases in investment in the oil sector in the immediately preceding years.

The only period in which there seems to have been an important increase in investment that was not accompanied by an expansion of production was the early 1980s. However, two factors must be taken into account when assessing this period. First, production was falling at the time and a considerable amount of investment was required merely to stabilize it.[8] In addition, OPEC imposed quotas on member countries, the result of which was that production could not increase. Hence, if we wish to consider the true effect of investment in this period, we should look at production capacity, rather than actual production. The dashed line in figure 2.1 shows that production capacity started to increase in 1980, in response to investment.[9]

Given that increases in production are linked to important increases in investment in the oil sector in the immediately preceding years, investment must be

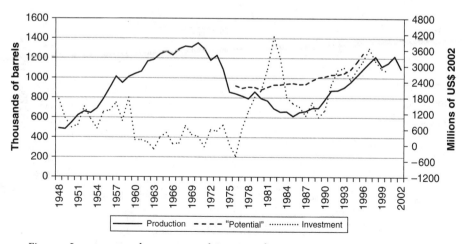

Fig. 2.1   Investment and government claim on profits

studied if the performance of oil production is to be explained. The oil sector has a number of characteristics that must be considered. As was mentioned above, it is extremely capital-intensive. Moreover, most of the investment has to be made at the beginning of the project. It is also specific to particular uses, and recovering it requires a relatively long time.[10] The fact that important amounts of capital must be committed *ex-ante* to projects with long maturity periods implies that in addition to the usual determinants of investment (cost of capital, profitability, etc.), the sector is sensitive to the stability of institutional rules that surround it—in particular, institutions regarding property rights and taxation.

The latter is important, because the sector in countries like Venezuela is prone to the presence of economic rents, and those rents are associated with the resource.[11] In Venezuela, the government is the owner of the resource. In this context, the fiscal system is used to achieve two goals: the regular function of collecting fiscal revenues, and the collection of the rents from the resource.[12]

As shown in figure 2.2, this distribution of revenues between the government and the producers seems to have played an important role in shaping investment. The figure shows that investment spikes are associated with reductions in the government's claim on profits. As will be explained later, the conditions created by the laws passed in 1944 appeared to clear the way for a significant increase in investment in the sector. After a democratic government was established in 1958, however, the government began to increase its claim on profits until the industry was nationalized in 1975. The first, and striking, impression that one gets from the graph in figure 2.2 is that the government's actions between 1958 and 1975 caused

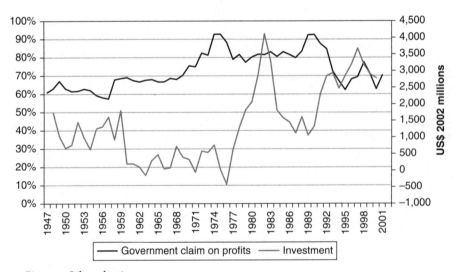

Fig. 2.2   Oil production

a collapse in investment. After nationalization, the government reduced the fiscal pressure on the sector, which allowed the new state enterprise (PDVSA) to invest. When prices collapsed in the 1980s, however, the government again started to increase its claim on profits and investment fell. Finally, the graph shows an increase in investment in the 1990s, when the government again reduced its claim on profits in the sector.

Table 2.1 and figure 2.2 have shown a broad picture of the performance of the oil sector. Nevertheless, it is clear that, within this broad view, there are differences across different periods. For example, table 2.1 shows that there are periods in which oil revenue per capita increased. Similarly, there are periods in which production per capita increased. The effective tax rate also differs across periods. Therefore, to better understand the relationship between the government and the oil producers, it is important to identify and analyze the main guidelines that underlay oil policy in Venezuela in the different periods.[13]

Table 2.2 provides a brief summary of the periods of oil production in Venezuela. Essentially, the categorization is based on two main characteristics: government administrations and developments in the international oil market.

Table 2.2   Eras of oil production in Venezuela

Period	Government administrations		Oil market
Discovery and boom	Authoritarianism	J. V. Gomez (1908–35) E. Lopez C. (1936–41) I. Medina A. (1941–45) Democratic attempt "Junta Revolucionaria" (1946–47) R. Gallegos (1948) "Junta Militar" (1949–52) M. Perez J. (1953–58)	Increasing participation of oil as an energy source
The end of the comparative advantage	Democracy	R. Betancourt (1959–63) R. Leoni (1964–68) R. Caldera (1969–73)	The Middle East established itself as the main supplier of oil (1960–73)
The change in the international context		C. A. Perez (1974–78) L. Herrera C. (1979–83) J. Lusinchi (1984–88)	Substitution of oil and "energy" as a production input (1974–86)
Unchanged policy views in a changing international context?		C. A. Perez (1989–93) R. Caldera (1994–98) H. Chavez (1998–)	OPEC's market share policy (1986–)

In the sections that follow, the taxonomy will be justified and each period will be analyzed carefully.

Discovery and Boom (1914–1958)

References to the presence of oil in Venezuela go back all the way to colonial times. In 1539, a barrel of oil was sent to Spain at the request of King Carlos V. This event is documented as the first shipping of oil for export.[14] It is in the late nineteenth and early twentieth centuries, however—when oil began to be used more widely as a source of energy—that commercial activity around the sector began to increase. The first "oil concession" was granted in 1865 and the first oil company, Petrolia del Tachira, was founded in 1878. Innumerous concessions and licenses were granted after that. But it was not until 1914, with the discovery of Mene Grande, the first giant oil field, that Venezuela clearly entered the commercial era of oil exploitation.

This period was characterized by the biggest expansion in oil production in Venezuela; see figure 2.3, where the expansion is expressed in logarithms to highlight the proportional increases in oil production. The main reasons behind this expansion were, obviously, the presence of important resources and the proximity to the main market for oil, the United States. However, it was also important that between 1908 and 1935 Juan Vicente Gomez ruled Venezuela. In the nineteenth century, Venezuela was characterized by a long civil war and a sequence of

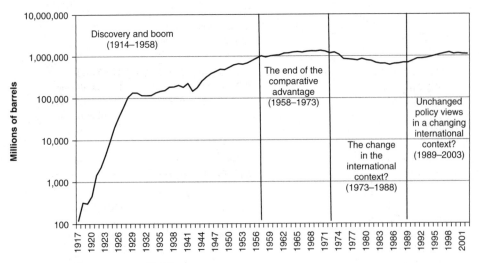

Fig. 2.3 Energy use worldwide

governments that were often unable to complete their terms of office because of rebellions and general political unrest. Gomez, though a fierce dictator, managed to pacify and stabilize the country. This offered foreign investors a relatively stable environment in which to invest.[15]

Figure 2.3 shows that between 1929 and 1943, oil production seems to have stalled. This is due to two factors: the Great Depression and political uncertainty in Venezuela. The more important of the two was the Great Depression, which clearly affected the demand negatively. Once the world started to recover, however, there was an increase in political uncertainty in Venezuela. After Gomez died, the movement for change to a democratic regime gained strength, and this was accompanied by demands for a better deal for the country with respect to the exploitation of oil. Failure to have these demands met generated increasing unrest in the population, including a strike of the oil workers in 1936. Even though, in theory, there was hydrocarbon legislation prior to 1943, it was revised constantly and, in practice, the fiscal rules for oil exploitation were set on a contract-by-contract basis. Therefore, there was a perception of an uncertain political landscape with no clear rules for the oil sector.

As argued above, this changed with the passing of the Hydrocarbons Law and the Income Tax Code in 1943. Both instruments removed the uncertainty about concessions periods and fiscal rules from oil companies. This helped to increase production further in this period, as shown in figure 2.3. Nevertheless, it is important to note that in the figure, the slope for this second expansion is not as steep. This implies a slower growth rate than in the earlier period. It is important to bear this fact in mind for the next section.

Parallel to this expansion was the relationship between the oil sector and the rest of the economy. Since its appearance at the beginning of the twentieth century, oil has been seen as a "temporary" productive sector. Most Venezuelan intellectuals of the time warned about the problems this temporary boom could cause for other productive sectors, saying that it would be impossible to restore these sectors to their former state once the supply of oil had been exhausted.[16] This perception that the productivity of the oil sector was only temporary led to one of the guiding principles of the Venezuelan oil policy: the "sowing of oil." According to this principle, given that oil is an industry that can last only for a certain period, the income from it should be invested in other sectors of the economy in the service of diversification.[17]

This principle more or less guided the administrations in the period. As argued in Urbaneja (1992), for these nondemocratic governments, the sowing of oil implied the development of infrastructure and urbanization. A low infant mortality in 1960 indicates that by then, basic services such as water sanitation were already being provided. A high number of airport flights and large amount of electricity consumed in 1970 shows that by then, Venezuela had a relatively well-developed infrastructure for transport and utilities.[18]

Although some industrial policies were implemented during this period, this does not necessarily reflect a particular orientation toward one sector. Moreover, there was no perception that oil could be a productive sector that could be integrated with the other sectors of the economy; therefore, there was no policy toward such integration. Nevertheless, it is important to note that there was a perception that Venezuela should capture a greater share of the oil market. To this end, steps were taken to increase oil production. The Hydrocarbons Law of 1943 encouraged the domestic refining of oil and was central to the development of the current refining network in Venezuela. In 1958, the installed refining capacity was 883,000 barrels a day and the total of crude oil refined in that year was ten times higher than in 1943. In addition, in 1956, the government established the Venezuelan Institute of Petrochemicals, with the idea of fostering the development of a petrochemical sector. Although the construction of a petrochemical complex began, in 1958 Marcos Perez Jimenez, the dictator of that time, was ousted and the democratic era began.[19] Though the democratic governments finalized the petrochemical complex, as it will be pointed out below, the priorities will have changed.

In summary, this first period is characterized by the development of the oil sector in Venezuela, which had important resources and was geographically proximate to the main market. These conditions, along with a relatively stable framework for oil companies, made Venezuela the third-largest producer (behind the United States and the Soviet Union) and the largest exporter of oil in the world.

The End of the Comparative Advantage (1958–1973)

Simultaneously with the beginning of the democratic era, important changes were occurring in the oil markets. As shown in table 2.3, other future producers of what would become the Organization of Petroleum Exporting Countries (OPEC) were asserting themselves in the market.[20] Moreover, as seen from the table, Venezuela was at a disadvantage relative to those countries. Venezuelan costs were higher[21] and reserves were lower (given the high rate of extraction relative to the reserve stock). In this context, the new democratic regime pushed for a second and important principle that guided oil policy: "preservation."

The preservation principle was based on the notion that oil is a scarce resource of great value and therefore Venezuela must minimize its extraction in order to save it for the future.[22] Even before they assumed government, pro-democratic

Table 2.3   State of the oil market in 1961

	1961		
	Market share	Extraction rate	Development + extraction costs
Algeria	1.6%	2.6%	0.695
Indonesia	2.1%	1.9%	1.002
Iran	5.9%	1.7%	0.279
Iraq	5.0%	1.5%	0.194
Kuwait	8.9%	1.0%	0.201
Libya	0.1%	0.2%	1.339
Nigeria	0.2%	3.0%	2.685
Qatar	2.6%	2.8%	0.195
Saudi Arabia	2.1%	1.0%	0.191
United Arab Emirates	0.0%	0.0%	0.561
Venezuela	14.5%	6.3%	2.272
Total OPEC	43.1%	1.7%	—
Non-OPEC	56.9%	5.6%	—
Mexico	1.4%	4.3%	6.984
United States	35.6%	8.3%	2.163

SOURCES: Author's calculations based on Energy Information Administration 2004; Adelman 1993.

forces accused the authoritarian governments of the first half of the twentieth century of "giving away" Venezuelan oil. This became a relatively successful political platform. Once democracy was instituted, the preservation principle became a main guideline for the different administrations.

The preservation principle motivated two types of policy. First, the government increased substantially its claim on profits from the sector, as seen in figure 2.2. The argument was that since oil is such a valuable commodity of limited availability, the government, as the owner of the resource, should maximize its share of the rents generated from it. This goal was achieved through royalties and the levying of income tax. The second course of action was the "no more concessions" policy. The concessions given after the law of 1944 were set to expire in 1983. The government announced that there would be no more concessions and that those set to expire in 1983 would not be renewed.

Traditionally, the literature credits these policies for a contraction of investment and blames them for the collapse in production after 1970.[23] However, there are two important points to be made that could weaken this hypothesis. First, investment was taking place between 1958 and 1970. As argued in the appendix, there were positive investment outlays. Moreover, the actual physical measure of the main production asset (the number of active oil wells) increased over time; and as shown in figure 2.3, production continued to increase. Second, it has been already mentioned that Venezuela had higher costs, which suggests that the Venezuelan oil sector lost its competitive edge in this period. Other measures (stated in the appendix) also suggest this. Therefore, it should have been expected that oil companies would have shifted investment from Venezuela to other, more productive oil countries. But the traditional literature has given little or no attention to this aspect of the international oil market. Therefore, the answer to the question of what would have happened if the fiscal pressure on the sector had been kept constant or increased moderately has not necessarily been answered.

The fact that the change in the net assets of oil firms in Venezuela was negative might suggest that even though oil firms were investing in the country, they were also undergoing a process of assets relocation in their world portfolio. From the importers' point of view, the United States was quickly losing market share. Other importers more or less kept their share. However, given the size of the United States, this pattern implies that a great opportunity to supply importers was opening up in the market.

Nevertheless, the important factor was action taken by other exporters of oil. Venezuela was also losing market share rapidly. Most of the loss was due to an increase in the share of countries that would become OPEC members, which were more productive than Venezuela. The Soviet Union marginally increased its share, but it is easy to argue that these were areas outside the reach of oil firms. In addition, there were relatively minor gains in terms of the total market share of smaller exporters.[24] Nevertheless, it is important to note that according to Adelman (1993), most of these smaller exporters had lower costs than did Venezuela. Consequently, Venezuela was losing market share to producers that had lower costs.

If to the previous elements we add the already mentioned fact that, even after the Hydrocarbons Law of 1943, the growth rate of the Venezuelan oil sector was slowing down,[25] it is difficult to argue that Venezuela could have kept its 1960 market share. Therefore, some asset relocation should have been expected from the oil firms' point of view. Given this context, *ex post* it seems logical that a viable strategy would have been to reduce the fiscal pressure on oil firms, in order that they might compete with other OPEC countries, hence minimizing the fall in market share.

But Venezuela followed a different strategy. It approached its main competitors and negotiated with them to form OPEC and coordinate tax policy.[26] As seen in table 2.4, all the OPEC producers increased their fiscal participation as they became members and began gaining control of their oil sector. In addition, even though concessions were not going to be renewed, foreign oil firms were

Table 2.4   Effective tax rates for the oil sector on OPEC members

	1960	1971	1972	1973	Notes
Algeria	30% (1969)	35%	47%	50%	Independence 1962. Member since 1969.
Indonesia	n/a	50%	40%	33%	Fixed amount taxes. Share in 1977: 56%.
Iran	42%	52%	54%	63%	—
Iraq	43%	63%	45%	77%	—
Kuwait	44%	35%	39%	50%	—
Libya	10% (1962)	19%	18%	16%	Member since 1962. Nationalization 1970. Share in 1975: 64%.
Nigeria	30% (1967)	54%	54%	60%	Member since 1971.
Qatar	43% (1961)	58%	60%	64%	—
Saudi Arabia	38%	50%	51%	48%	—
UAE	10% (1964)	51%	52%	50%	Member since 1967.
Venezuela	45%	62%	66%	73%	—

SOURCES: Author's calculations based on Adelman 1993; Organization of the Petroleum Exporting Countries Organization (various years).

signing investment agreements in joint ventures with the state-owned oil company (the Venezuela Oil Corporation, or CVP by its initials in Spanish). The facts described by Martinez (2005) suggest that, even though oil firms knew that concessions were not going to be renewed, they were negotiating the establishment of "service contracts" with the CVP. This was a course of action that had already been followed in other OPEC countries that had nationalized their industry.[27] These service contracts would have entailed that the oil firms stay in Venezuela, producing for the CVP.

It is difficult to appraise the complete oil policy framework (nonrenewal of concessions and increased fiscal pressure), even taking into account the information available to the policymakers at the time as an element for the analysis. On the one hand, it seems that the increase in the government take by itself, and even perhaps the policy of "no more concessions," did not necessarily deter investment. On the other hand, judging by the intended result of the move to form OPEC, it was successful. As shown in table 2.1, even though oil production was falling, oil fiscal revenue increased.

The key assumption behind this policy framework was of a finite amount of reserves. As will be shown below, the extraction rate of oil worldwide was increasing (which implies that reserves were diminishing) and the energy intensity of the world (the amount of energy required to generate a dollar of economic activity) was also increasing. Therefore, it seemed at the time that oil might indeed become a scarce commodity. Moreover, as presented in Cuddington and Moss (2001), although there was, in the late 1950s, an increase in the diffusion of technology in the oil sector, most of the new technology was derived from advances in geochemistry, stratigraphy, and fluid system sciences. These advances were useful for the logging and testing of wells and were important for reducing exploration costs. They did not facilitate the development of new sources of oil reserves. Nevertheless, as will be argued below, the key technological advances that helped to change the perception of oil reserves came in the late 1960s and early 1970s.

Further, even if knowledge was available in the late 1950s about the possibility of new reserves around the world, in particular outside OPEC, it seemed that the price in 1960 was relatively low. If we compare the return of leaving an oil barrel in the ground and extracting it later (ten, twenty, or thirty years) with the strategy of extracting it, selling it, and investing the proceeds of the sale in a U.S. Treasury bond, clearly the better strategy would have been to leave it in the ground. This is true for each of the three maturity periods and for the period between 1962 (the first year for which information is available for all the returns) and 1973. Therefore, it was optimal to reduce the extraction of oil.

The foregoing discussion is not intended to deny the role played by the progressive squeeze of profits from the oil firms in the collapse in oil production that later took place. Rather, its aim is to put that factor in context. Most probably, Venezuela would have lost market share anyway and the information available to policymakers at the time was not the same as today. Nevertheless, it is clear that the policy followed (that of increasing taxes and promoting preservation of the resource) did not help to place the country in a position to take advantage of a possible period of higher prices. Nevertheless, as shown by the figures presented in the appendix, the negative consequences of the policy of higher taxes and "no more concessions" were beginning to show in the late part of the period. In particular, 1971 is central to the understanding of the period. That year, the number of active wells decreased by 10 percent and the productivity per well decreased substantially.[28] This suggests that oil firms stopped investing even in keeping production flowing. After 1970, the relationship between oil companies and the government began to deteriorate, because the government alleged that oil companies were not charging prices that were effective for tax purposes, while the companies argued that they were.[29]

On January 1, 1971, President Rafael Caldera announced that the government would nationalize the natural gas business. Six days later, a decree was issued that regulated the price that oil firms should use for tax purposes.[30] Finally, in July, a law was passed that forbade oil firms from taking their assets out of Venezuela, in order to ensure the stability of oil production after 1983, when the concessions were set to expire. Clearly, while accepting that these events were part of a wider conflict between oil companies and oil-producing countries, we can see that they also gave a signal that induced oil firms to halt investment.[31] However, the facts described in the next section allowed policymakers to ignore these consequences.

In addition to following this principle of "conservation," the democratic era continued with the idea of "sowing oil." Nevertheless, there was an important ideological change. The priority for government expenditure would focus on social areas: health, education, and housing. According to official figures,[32] social expenditure rose from 17 percent of the budget in 1962 to 33 percent in 1973, in the context of a growing budget overall. This policy of investing in people had important effects on educational coverage, improved health conditions, and better housing conditions, among other improved social indicators.

What did not change, though, was the lack of a policy for integrating the oil sector with the rest of the economy. Even though the refining capacity continued to grow until 1965, the growth was due mostly to the completion of the refineries whose construction started after the Hydrocarbons Law of 1943. A second petrochemical complex was started, but was based mostly on state-owned firms or joint ventures in which the state had the majority of the capital. During this time, import-substitution policies were in full swing in Latin America.[33] Therefore, these attempts at industrialization around oil, rather than reflecting a "cluster vision" of the sector, were just part of a wider set of policies that had the goal of producing most of the goods imported by the country.[34]

In summary, Venezuelan oil policy in this period was guided by the perception that producing oil was a temporary activity. This perception justified a strategy that tried to derive the maximum fiscal revenue from the sector and use that revenue in other sectors, particularly the social sector. Given that production reached its peak during this period and then started to decline, in general this increased fiscal pressure is associated with the collapse of the sector. Nevertheless, as has been argued in this section, this claim must be taken in context: (1) it is difficult to prove wrong the government assumption that the amount of economically viable oil reserves was limited, given the information available at the time, and moreover, it was optimal to keep oil in the ground; (2) Venezuela seemed to be bound to lose market share anyway; (3) in terms of the goal that it wanted to attain, the government stabilized a falling fiscal revenue; and (4) there were other developments in the relationship between the Venezuelan government and oil firms that were as important as the increase in the effective tax rate.

The Change in the International Context (1973–1988)

The previous section described the conflict between oil firms and oil-rich countries that took place in the 1960s. As stated above, the conflict led the major oil-producing countries to create OPEC, increase their claim in oil income, create their own national oil companies (NOC), and, in some cases, even nationalize the oil sector. In this situation, investment was driven away from the oil sector, and therefore little effort was made to explore additional oil reserves and the market tightened. Oil extraction increased progressively from 1960 and peaked in the 1970s at around 4 percent of known reserves per year. It thus seemed as though oil reserves were only sufficient to sustain an additional twenty-five years of production.[35]

Moreover, in a context of relatively strong economic growth,[36] the demand for oil grew even faster. Figure 2.4 shows the number of barrels needed to generate a GDP of US$1,000. As the figure shows, the world was using more and more oil for the production of goods, and this trend increased until 1974. Therefore, it was not only that oil seemed to become more scarce, but also that the world was relying on it more and more.

In this context, two successive crisis in the Middle East (the Yom Kippur War and the Iran–Iraq War) created disruptions in oil supply, and prices reached a historical high. Given these circumstances, oil-importing countries took important measures to increase energy efficiency in order to reduce their dependence

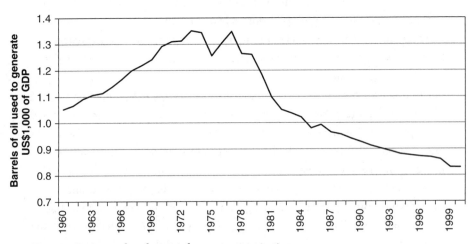

Fig. 2.4   Resource abundance and export concentration

Source: Author's calculations based on Energy Information Administration 2004 and World Bank 2004.

on oil. Figure 2.4 shows how, due to the measures taken by consuming countries, the number of barrels needed to produce a GDP of US$1,000 has fallen 30 percent from that year to the present. Most remarkably, half of that decline occurred between 1980 and 1986.

In addition, oil companies started to increase their search for oil outside OPEC. After the first price increase in the seventies, drilling activity reached the highest levels of the last thirty years. The average for active rigs in the period from 1975 to 1985 was 102 percent higher than the rest of the period. As a result, by 1986, an additional 175 billion barrels were added to world oil reserves compared to 1980. This figure represents 27 percent of the reserves available in 1980.

Of those new additions, 55 percent were outside OPEC, mostly in the North Sea. The discovery of new oil reserves increased the theoretical duration of the reserves, assuming the amount of oil extracted per year stayed the same.[37] This expansion of reserves was made possible by technological advances in the field of oil development.

According to Cuddington and Moss (2001), during the 1970s and 1980s, important technological advances were made in the area of offshore exploration, drilling, and production. This made it possible to develop the North Sea. Therefore, this period showed that, provided the expense is not too great, technology will make available reserves that were previously unreachable or not economically viable.

A similar case could be made for the demand. High prices would encourage the development of technologies that help to achieve a more efficient use of energy and motivate a search for alternatives to oil.[38] As shown in figure 2.4, after 1976 the number of barrels needed to generate a GDP of US$1,000 declined sharply. This is the result of two actions: an increase in energy efficiency and a substitution of oil as an energy source by other alternatives, such as hydroelectric and nuclear power.

As a consequence of these technological changes, the increase in oil efficiency helped to curb the demand for oil, while the increased effort in exploration led to an increase in its supply. These two phenomena were the main factors that pushed prices down. By 1985, the price of oil was 20 percent lower than in 1981. In this context, what policy was followed?

It is in the period between 1971 and 1988 that production fell, for two reasons. First, as was explained above, the policy of the previous period, in particular the actions taken at the end of that period (nationalization of the gas industry and a law that prevented oil companies from taking their assets out of the country) clearly induced a collapse of investment. In 1975, these actions were carried further, up to the point of the full nationalization of the oil industry.

Although the fall in the number of active wells (used as a proxy for investment) was reversed somewhat by 1971, and by 1973 its number had reached 12,655, after that brief recovery it continued falling to a level of 10,202 in 1977, below the number of active wells in 1962. Moreover, as argued above, the productivity of oil wells was declining and it continued to decline for a long time. Therefore, it is clear that the transition toward a NOC affected the productive capacity of the sector: there were fewer oil wells and those wells were producing less oil.

Nevertheless, at first, the results behind that the policy decision explained above seemed to support this perception. Oil fiscal revenue continued to increase until 1982. For Venezuela, this increase produced the result that even though oil production per capita was 62 percent lower in 1980 than in 1958, exports per capita were 109 percent higher and fiscal revenue 234 percent higher. Therefore, the impression was that the policy of increasing taxes was effective and so continued to be put into effect. Nevertheless, after 1981, it became evident that prices were falling. In 1982, oil fiscal revenue per capita fell by 25 percent due to a similar decline in prices.

In this context, production continued to decline all the way until 1985. As shown in figure 2.1, however, it seems that production capacity fell until 1980 and increased after that. Therefore, the effect on production of the policies followed in the previous period could explain only part of the contraction in production. The second factor explaining this contraction is the policy behind decisions taken at the OPEC level.

Behind the policy decisions to continue to increase taxes (on the part of the Venezuelan government) and to reduce production (on the part of OPEC) was the perception of what was occurring in the oil market. This perception was the idea, already mentioned above, that oil was finite and that the world was highly dependent on it. Consequently, the policy decision was to "preserve" oil. Nevertheless, these perceptions did not take into account the changes in the market described above. OPEC assumed that these circumstances were temporary and decided to establish quotas and reduce production in order to keep prices higher. Therefore, from 1982 to 1986, oil fiscal revenue per capita continued to decline, due to the reduction in output and prices that more or less remained static.

In this period, it seems from the data that policies (on the part of both the Venezuelan government and OPEC) were not necessarily in line with the events unfolding in the oil market. Even so, this misperception did not last long. In 1986, Saudi Arabia, the biggest producer in OPEC, decided to stop being the "swing" producer of the organization.[39] That year, the price of oil fell around 50 percent in nominal terms, and the Venezuelan basket barely averaged above US$10.

Given this fall in exports and fiscal revenue, an important issue arises. Would Venezuela have been better off outside OPEC and not following the policies set by the cartel? The answer to that question will depend on whether OPEC has market power. If OPEC does not have market power, we may conclude that Venezuela would have been better off remaining outside OPEC. However, although the issue is still being debated, recent evidence suggests that the answer to the question—whether OPEC has market power—might be "not always."[40] If that is so, matters become complicated. If OPEC does have market power on occasions, the issue then becomes whether Venezuela's membership was necessary for OPEC to possess and exercise that power on the occasions that it does possess it. The matter is complicated further by the issue of what the benefits would have been for Venezuela had it not been a member of OPEC. Remember that other smaller producers had lower costs. Consequently, outside of OPEC, Venezuela was not the most productive oil country. Given the above, there would seem to be no definitive answer as to whether Venezuela was right to promote OPEC and remain a member.

As in the other periods, we are not only interested in oil policy, but also in the diversification strategy that followed in the context of the oil policy. In this period, alongside the policy of trying to keep prices higher through OPEC actions, the policy of "sowing of oil" continued. Moreover, the windfall generated by the price shocks was spent in other sectors, with the intent of further diversifying the economy away from oil. Big state-owned companies were established in a variety of sectors, ranging from basic metals to tourism. Therefore, in this period, not only was the idea of diversifying the economy present, but also the idea that the state should carry out that task.

In summary, during this period, the oil policy that democratic governments followed showed signs of not being aligned with the developments in the oil market. Oil fiscal revenue per capita peaked in 1974 and GDP per capita peaked two years later. The response to the fall in oil revenues was to cut production, in the hope that prices would increase. This did not happen and oil fiscal revenue continued to fall. Under these circumstances, different oil-producing countries took different approaches. The next section will analyze the Venezuelan performance after 1988.

Unchanged Policy Views in a Changing International Context? (1989–2003)

In 1986, Venezuela was facing falling oil revenues and, as explained above, this was due to the fall in oil production. As seen in figure 2.3, in 1986, production began to increase again and continued until 1998. Nevertheless, the first increase was partly thanks to the effort made earlier that halted the decline in production capacity in 1980. The administration in place from 1984 to 1988 took advantage of this increased capacity, but little investment was made; rather, most of the investment was made in the 1990s.

In this section, I will argue that the expansion in production was not necessarily greater than the expansion in other oil-producing countries, and that this is due to the institutional setting. It is relatively evident that an increase in oil production would have increased oil fiscal revenue, and Venezuela did increase production. Nevertheless, Venezuela, in a sample of thirty-eight countries, ranks twentieth in terms of growth in oil production in the period 1986 to 2001.[41]

In this regard, in previous sections it was assumed implicitly that a variety of factors can affect growth in oil production: field productivity, discovery risk, and well pressure, among different geological factors. If we look at the productivity of active oil wells,[42] Venezuela in the same sample ranks twenty-fourth and is 0.47 standard deviations below the mean. Therefore, for a country such as Venezuela, the crucial factor is the actual decision to increase production.

To capture that decision, an index is calculated for what would be called "effort." The index is the combination of the two main activities that drive oil production: drilling and extraction.[43] If we compare Venezuela with the same sample in this index, Venezuela ranks thirtieth and is 1.02 deviations below the mean.

To put these numbers in context, consider two examples. Firstly, Norway ranks second in oil production growth. However, it ranks twenty-fifth in "effort." The reason for the growth in Norwegian oil production is that it ranks second in productivity. Given that its oil fields are extremely productive, it could increase production faster than most countries during that period without too much effort. For the second example, consider the case of Argentina. Argentina ranks sixth in oil production growth. This increase in oil production was achieved despite its ranking thirty-first in productivity. This growth is then explained by the fact that Argentina ranks tenth with respect to effort.

In this context, it seems that Venezuela did not manage to grow faster in terms of oil production because its "effort" was not in line with productivity. In other words, countries either less productive or less abundant than Venezuela but that had a higher "effort" had superior increases in production. As mentioned above, oil is a capital-intensive sector, in which an important part of the investment is made up front. It takes a long time before such investment is recovered. Therefore, the institutional setting of the host country and the fiscal rules for the sector become important factors for potential investors to consider.

In this regard, after 1986, an effort was made to increase oil production. However, fiscal income was declining and the oil industry was state-owned. This led to an ongoing conflict between the goal of increased production and fiscal needs, because any attempt to increase production would have to be financed by the state. A first approach was to let the PDVSA issue debt to finance its production plans. But this debt was considered public debt, which generated competition between the government and PDVSA in the financial markets. Moreover, interest payments and amortizations started reducing PDVSA funds available to the government and the tensions returned.[44] Therefore, there were limited debt issues made by the PDVSA.

A clear second option would have been to let private companies back into the country to develop the sector. Venezuela did that through a set of small reforms in the institutional setting. In 1991, operating agreements ("convenios operativos") were introduced, and marginal fields that under normal circumstances were not going to be exploited by the PDVSA were instead given to private companies, which would produce the oil for a certain fee per barrel. Next, in 1993, associations for the production of heavy and extra-heavy oil were introduced ("asociaciones estrategicas"). One could describe these crudes in two ways: either as low-commercial-value crudes or as those requiring a special "pre-refining" that would make them suitable for any refinery and, consequently, characterize them as high-production-cost crudes. Finally, in 1996, new areas were given over to private investors for exploration and exploitation. This was termed the "opening up" ("apertura"). Although these areas were supposed to contain light and medium crudes, little or no exploration was actually carried out.[45] All new contracts were given tax breaks to make them profitable for the private sector.

In summary, the state-owned oil firm was making a modest effort to increase production and to invest in the country (though the private sector was asked). Nevertheless, these fiscal agreements were not necessarily the most competitive. For the sample presented above, we constructed an index of fiscal regimes in the oil sector.[46] In this index, Venezuela ranks thirty-second and is 1.08 standard deviations below the mean. For comparison, Argentina ranks eighteenth. Consequently, the conditions offered were not necessarily competitive, given the productivity of the oil sector.

Further, as noted above, the areas given to the private sector were not the most productive (some were explicitly marginal, others had not been and never were explored). Manzano (2000) evaluated these reforms from the point of view of efficiency and concluded that although the reform resulted in greater efficiency, the fields selected for the reform were not those most negatively affected by the tax code. The areas in which the most gains could be made were those that remained under PDVSA control. Moreover, in these areas, a reduction in tax rates would have increased tax collection, which implies that they were overtaxed.

During this period oil production increased. Nevertheless, it seems that the increase was modest compared to increases in other oil-producing countries. As argued below, and in accordance with what was discussed above, Venezuela is less productive in the oil sector than are other countries. Given this situation, a significant amount of investment is required to expand the sector. In this regard, the institutional setting, in particular the restrictions on the state-owned oil company and the lack of attractiveness of the tax regime for private investors, seems to have played a role.

That being so, why has Venezuela not changed its institutional setting in order to make a greater effort in the oil sector? Using a framework of intergenerational accounting for fiscal burdens, Fernandez, Gomez, and Manzano (2005) found that future generations will be worse off, in the respect that their fiscal burden will be higher, with the current rate of extraction than with an optimal rate of extraction.[47] Consequently, it seems that the lower effort does not seem justified by intergenerational concerns.

Alternatively, it could be argued that Venezuela could not expand its production capacity due to its membership in OPEC. Nevertheless, as argued in the appendix, it does not appear that OPEC countries were coordinated in this period.[48] Moreover, looking at the actual eleven members in 2001, only Iran, Kuwait, Libya, and Venezuela were producing less than Venezuela in 1973. Therefore, most OPEC countries returned to the production levels prior even to the period when the conditions of the market changed, but Venezuela was not one of them.[49]

Following the argument of looking not only at oil policy but also at the diversification strategy, an additional course of action would have been to add value to oil exports. This chapter does not try to assess industrial policies. Rather, it focuses on industry that is related to the oil sector and the possibility of increasing exports value per capita by developing downstream by-products or upstream suppliers. The reason for exploring this possible strategy for increasing oil-related export is that, in most of the countries analyzed here, the oil sector is still dominated by a state-owned oil company. Therefore, the possibility of developing connected sectors depends on oil policy.

As argued by Lederman and Maloney (2003), a policy of diversification was important for countries whose exports are concentrated in only a few products. Their results support the idea that concentrating on export reduces growth. However, this concentration is not related to oil richness. In figure 2.5, an index of concentration is plotted against a measure for oil richness: reserves divided by GDP. The graph shows that there is no clear relationship between oil richness and concentration on export. Further, the diversification of exports does not imply diversification "away" from the sector. Therefore, policies might have varied according to the differing characteristics of each country.

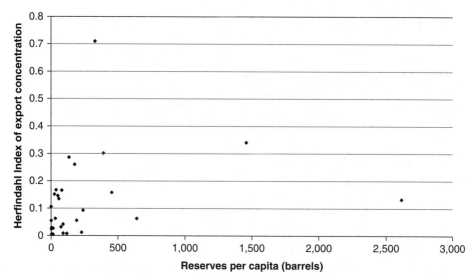

Fig. 2.5   Specialization pattern

Source: Author's calculations based on Energy Information Administration 2004; World Bank 2003; and Lederman and Maloney 2003.

To see the different strategies followed by different countries, an index for the diversification pattern is constructed for the group of countries with the greatest abundance.[50] In it, the change in net exports per capita in twenty-eight differ-ent categories of goods for each country is compared to the relationship of those sectors with the oil sector in the United States. These relationships are based on the implied multipliers of the input–output matrix of the United States.[51] Then a correlation was calculated between that multiplier and the change in net exports experienced by each country in those twenty-eight sectors for the period studied. A positive diversification index implies that the pattern followed was around sec-tors related to the oil industry. A negative index implies that the pattern followed was around sectors not related to that industry. In figure 2.6, we plot that index against relative oil richness.

At first sight, there is no clear relationship. However, the reader will note that two lines are drawn. All the countries in the upward sloping line increased their non-oil net exports per capita. All the countries in the downward sloping line decreased their non-oil net exports per capita. These relationships seem to indi-cate that, for the nine countries in this sample, which includes Venezuela, those that increased their non-oil net exports followed a pattern suited to their endow-ments. Countries with less oil reserves followed a pattern of diversification away from oil, while countries with higher reserves followed a pattern around the oil sector. By contrast, countries that followed a pattern of diversification that was

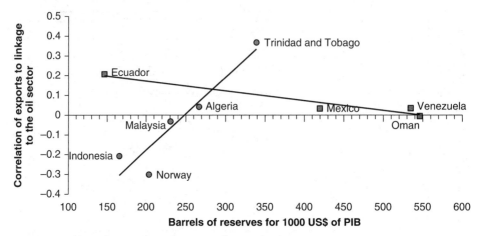

Fig. 2.6   Specialization pattern against relative oil richness

Sources: Author's calculations based on UN Commodity Trade Statistics Database 2004; World Bank 2003; and Energy Information Administration 2004.

not in accordance with their endowments were not able to increase their non-oil exports per capita. Among those countries is Venezuela.

Of course, a further issue that should be considered is whether an increase in net exports is desirable, but a resolution of this issue lies beyond the scope of this chapter.[52] The relevant issue here is why Venezuela followed a pattern not connected with oil, in contrast to, for example, Trinidad and Tobago. In the 1990s, Venezuela embarked on a program of structural reform, similar to those followed by other Latin American countries. These programs proposed the opening of the economy to the international markets, the removal of distortions, and the establishment of institutions needed to achieve macroeconomic stability (e.g., central bank independence), among other measures. In Venezuela, however, not all the reforms could be implemented.[53] Further, these programs lacked policies that nowadays are seen as necessary in the process of diversifying the economy.[54]

In a review of the effects of the oil sector on the Venezuelan economy, Clemente, Manzano, and Puente (2005) estimated whether being linked to the oil sector has an effect on productivity. The authors found that companies that use oil and oil derivatives as an input in their production process have lower productivity. This is mostly due to policy decisions. Domestic prices of oil derivatives are subsidized in Venezuela, as a result of past policies, and this is an area in which policy updates have been inhibited. As a result, domestic prices are around one quarter of international prices. This subsidy affects the productivity of consumers of oil derivatives negatively.

In addition, Clemente, Manzano, and Puente explored the effect on productivity of being a supplier to the oil sector, and found not only negative effects in productivity but also negative spillovers to other firms that use products made by firms that supply the oil sector. This is because the PDVSA's purchasing policies were not designed with a strategy of export diversification in mind. Usually, the products of local suppliers were more expensive and of lower quality, but government intervention forced the PDVSA to buy a certain amount of local wares. Hence, there were no incentives for firms to become more productive or to sell to international markets.

Subsidizing the domestic prices of oil products and obliging the PDVSA to buy a certain amount of local products were policies that deviated from the original goal of the "sowing of oil" principle.[55] However, the main point is that these instruments were not designed to increase the value of oil-related exports. Therefore, we may conclude that in the case of Venezuela there was no intention of pursuing that aim.

To summarize the period, even though production grew in Venezuela, it seems that the expansion was modest and there was no attempt made to link the oil sector with the rest of the economy. The main reason behind these problems seems to be institutional. The issue thus arises as to why Venezuela did not change its institutional setting in order to take advantage of the oil sector. Changes were made, but they were modest. It seems that the reason for making such small changes is that the whole system of institutions was still based on the policy orientation of "preservation." Because of the nationalization law, oil production, and even refining, was reserved for the state. For the private sector to participate, each contract had to be approved by Congress.

An examination of why those policy guidelines were not changed lies beyond the scope of the present investigation and would better conducted in the context of a debate on Venezuelan political economy.[56]

Concluding Remarks

Changes in the oil fiscal revenue per capita resembled those of the Venezuelan GDP per capita throughout the last century. After three decades of sustained growth, oil fiscal revenue collapsed in the 1980s and it has not recovered since.

We have argued that the collapse was due to the fall in oil exports per capita, which was driven mainly by the fall in oil production per capita. Although other factors might have played a role, such as oil prices, oil quality, and production costs, it is clear that changes in oil production per capita are correlated to those in oil exports. Therefore, to understand the reasons behind the collapse in oil fiscal revenue, it is important to study the factors that drive oil production in Venezuela.

We have argued that, overall, looking back at oil policy, the policy followed between 1914 and 1958 seemed to be on the right track. But it is difficult to argue against the policy implemented between 1958 and 1973. Probably, what seemed to be a reasonable assessment of the environment, given the information available, led to a short-run policy consistent with that assessment. However, it might have had long-term negative consequences.

Following those two periods, oil policy played a fundamental role in explaining the collapse of oil production. Oil policy was then driven by two principles: preservation and the sowing of oil. Taken together, the two principles implied (1) that oil extraction should be relatively low, in order to keep oil stored for the future; and (2) that the rents generated by the oil sector should be invested in other sectors to diversify the economy away from oil.

These principles, though apparently appropriate in the context that prevailed in the international oil markets up to 1980, became less so after changes in policies by net oil-importing countries and oil companies in response to the price crises of the seventies. After the crises, energy use became more efficient and oil was sought and found in nontraditional places. Thus 1986 is considered the year in which this new reality became apparent, at the time when oil prices collapsed.

After 1986, different oil-producing countries took different routes. From a sample of oil-producing countries that was analyzed, it emerged that countries that decided to expand their oil sectors as well as to increase their oil exports through a broader view of the sector (i.e., including suppliers and users and expanding those sectors) fared better. In this regard, Venezuela increased oil production in absolute terms, but relatively less than did the leading countries. The evidence seems to indicate that, given the nature of the oil sector in Venezuela and the institutional framework in place at the time, a better fiscal arrangement was needed in order to generate higher growth. The main reason for this is that the principles described above continued to guide oil policies, because most of the laws governing the sector had been written by that time. This does not assume that no attempts were made to pursue a different policy. We have described some efforts to do so. There was resistance, however, and it was not possible to attain the consensus required to change the relevant laws.

APPENDIX I: OIL-RELATED STATISTICS, 1960–1973

This appendix presents a series of statistics related to the oil sector with the aim of supporting the arguments of this third section of the chapter.

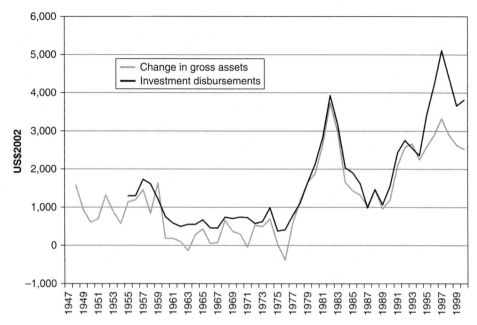

Fig. 2A.1   Difference in investment concepts

Source: Author's own calculations using Ministerio de Energía y Minas (various years).

Investment in the Venezuelan Oil Sector Between 1960 and 1973

Figure 2A.1 and Figure 2.A.2 present physical measures of investment and assets in production. As seen in the figure, in that period oil wells were completed and the number of producing wells increased.

Productivity of the Oil Sector

Here we present data on productivity in the oil sector. Figure 2A.2 presents the evolution of productivity by oil well in Venezuela. The graph shows the decline in productivity between 1960 and 1973, which shows that firms were investing even though wells were less productive.

Figure 2A.3 presents the excess return of an investment strategy on keeping a barrel of oil in the ground for ten, twenty, and thirty years as opposed to extracting it, selling it, and the investing in a financial instrument. In this case, we use U.S. Treasury bonds and the prime rate. As seen in the graph, between 1962 and 1972, the best strategy was to keep the oil in the ground.

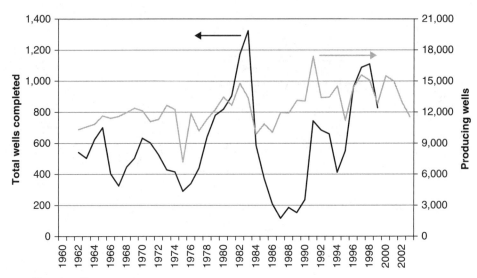

Fig. 2A.2   Investment concepts

Source: Author's own calculations using Ministerio de Energía y Minas (various years).

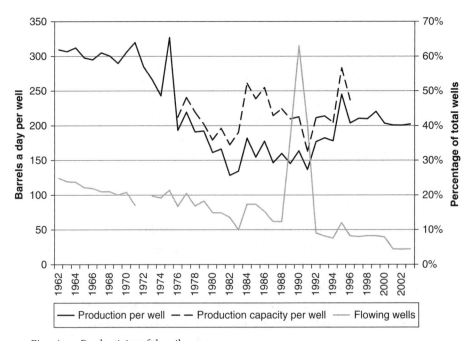

Fig. 2A.3   Productivity of the oil sector

APPENDIX II: OPEC BEHAVIOR

The next table presents the behavior of OPEC country members over time, specifically for the following periods: 1960–73, 1974–88, and 1989–2003. The correlations are made on the first difference of oil production. First differences are used because, for all countries, the production figures are I(1)—integrated of order 1. It can easily be seen that the highest correlation or joint movement corresponds to the production of the period 1974–88, with twenty-one positive and significant coefficient correlations. Therefore, the establishment of quotas from OPEC could explain the contraction of Venezuelan oil production at that time.

In contrast, for the period (1989–2001), the number of positive and significant coefficient correlations falls to sixteen. In addition, seven coefficients are negative and significant, which were not present in the previous period. This shows that OPEC countries have less coordination than before, and that the loss of market share of some countries members means an increase of market share for other OPEC countries. This situation is similar to the first period, when production quotas had yet to be established in OPEC.

Table 2A.1 Correlation matrix, OPEC countries' production

| | | | | | | 1960–2001 | | | | | |
	Algeria	Indonesia	Iran	Iraq	Kuwait	Libya	Nigeria	Qatar	Saudi Arabia	UAE	Venezuela
Algeria	1	—	—	—	—	—	—	—	—	—	—
Indonesia	0.1999	1	—	—	—	—	—	—	—	—	—
Iran	0.2590*	0.2355	1	—	—	—	—	—	—	—	—
Iraq	-0.0693	-0.0744	-0.0338	1	—	—	—	—	—	—	—
Kuwait	0.1443	-0.0883	0.1314	0.5476*	1	—	—	—	—	—	—
Libya	0.3919*	0.1162	0.1388	0.2156	0.2047	1	—	—	—	—	—
Nigeria	0.1727	0.3614*	0.2805*	0.3099*	0.3137*	0.1507	1	—	—	—	—
Qatar	0.1314	0.0672	0.0167	0.1292	0.0948	0.0693	-0.1134	1	—	—	—
Saudi Arabia	0.158	0.6471*	-0.0136	-0.1609	-0.0158	0.0556	0.4714*	0.1384	1	—	—
UAE	0.2866*	0.5350*	0.4233*	0.0251	-0.0045	0.2203	0.5637*	0.0917	0.6525*	1	—
Venezuela	0.1041	0.2541	0.0819	0.0556	0.2027	0.4195*	0.2498	0.0997	0.3465*	0.2694*	1

*10% statistical significance

Table 2A.1 continued

| | | | | | | 1960–1973 | | | | | |
	Algeria	Indonesia	Iran	Iraq	Kuwait	Libya	Nigeria	Qatar	Saudi Arabia	UAE	Venezuela
Algeria	1	—	—	—	—	—	—	—	—	—	—
Indonesia	0.237	1	—	—	—	—	—	—	—	—	—
Iran	−0.3856	0.5404*	1	—	—	—	—	—	—	—	—
Iraq	−0.421	0.2501	0.3051	1	—	—	—	—	—	—	—
Kuwait	−0.1174	−0.6593*	−0.5042*	−0.5006*	1	—	—	—	—	—	—
Libya	0.1373	−0.2932	−0.4880*	0.1816	0.0928	1	—	—	—	—	—
Nigeria	−0.3073	0.2871	0.5899*	−0.03	0.0749	−0.4930*	1	—	—	—	—
Qatar	0.0236	−0.0417	−0.1332	0.0716	−0.3019	−0.0599	−0.5287*	1	—	—	—
Saudi Arabia	−0.0874	0.6211*	0.7883*	0.326	−0.5485*	−0.6950*	0.5010*	−0.0677	1	—	—
UAE	−0.5082*	0.4275	0.8370*	0.5927*	−0.3828	−0.3861	0.5692*	−0.1403	0.8001*	1	—
Venezuela	−0.074	−0.1459	−0.2703	0.29	−0.0849	0.5361*	−0.4044	−0.1638	−0.4397	−0.2845	1

*10% statistical significance

(Continued)

Table 2A.1   continued

					1974–1988						
	Algeria	Indonesia	Iran	Iraq	Kuwait	Libya	Nigeria	Qatar	Saudi Arabia	UAE	Venezuela
Algeria	1	—	—	—	—	—	—	—	—	—	—
Indonesia	0.1748	1	—	—	—	—	—	—	—	—	—
Iran	0.3006	-0.0252	1	—	—	—	—	—	—	—	—
Iraq	0.5194*	-0.1031	-0.0117	1	—	—	—	—	—	—	—
Kuwait	0.5012*	0.1497	0.0678	0.6879*	1	—	—	—	—	—	—
Libya	0.6598*	0.1722	0.1073	0.6569*	0.5526*	1	—	—	—	—	—
Nigeria	0.3433	0.2764	-0.019	0.6610*	0.5167*	0.4898*	1	—	—	—	—
Qatar	0.383	0.4067	-0.1087	0.3977	0.5472*	0.4586*	0.4864*	1	—	—	—
Saudi Arabia	-0.112	0.7679*	-0.3666	0.0701	0.1738	0.0863	0.4384	0.4488*	1	—	—
UAE	0.3712	0.5443*	0.1977	0.4792*	0.3503	0.3757	0.5776*	0.277	0.5766*	1	—
Venezuela	0.2115	0.2442	-0.1472	0.2422	0.6349*	0.3781	0.4560*	0.5885*	0.4358	0.1141	1

*10% statistical significance

Table 2A.1 continued

1988–2001

	Algeria	Indonesia	Iran	Iraq	Kuwait	Libya	Nigeria	Qatar	Saudi Arabia	UAE	Venezuela
Algeria	1	—	—	—	—	—	—	—	—	—	—
Indonesia	-0.1409	1	—	—	—	—	—	—	—	—	—
Iran	0.5109*	0.4195	1	—	—	—	—	—	—	—	—
Iraq	-0.4659*	-0.3576	-0.3024	1	—	—	—	—	—	—	—
Kuwait	-0.1258	-0.5159*	0.0548	0.5706*	1	—	—	—	—	—	—
Libya	0.5903*	0.3445	0.4309	-0.6167*	-0.5461*	1	—	—	—	—	—
Nigeria	0.4323	0.3002	0.8326*	-0.0614	0.0085	0.2978	1	—	—	—	—
Qatar	0.2918	0.0063	0.2289	0.3714	0.1899	0.1864	0.2641	1	—	—	—
Saudi Arabia	0.5958*	0.4125	0.5336*	-0.7383*	-0.4590*	0.8569*	0.357	0.2401	1	—	—
UAE	0.6202*	0.5418*	0.7642*	-0.4510*	-0.3499	0.7624*	0.6025*	0.4228	0.7824*	1	—
Venezuela	-0.0575	0.5282*	0.2936	-0.0944	-0.1497	0.5151*	0.3307	0.21	0.4079	0.4438*	1

*10% statistical significance

NOTES

1. See Rodríguez and Sachs 1999 for a formal modeling of this relationship.

2. The word "stagnant" is used to argue that the share of primary products in world markets is decreasing, as are their relative prices. Prebisch (1950) is the most oft-quoted proponent of this idea.

3. This is what is referred to as the "Dutch disease." See Salter 1959; Krugman 1987.

4. The empirical study that demonstrated this relationship was Sachs and Warner 1995.

5. Lederman and Maloney 2003. Moreover, Manzano and Rigobón 2001; and Hausmann and Rigobón 2003 show possible channels that can explain this low growth.

6. Cuddington, Ludema, and Jayasuriya (2007) found that relative prices seem not to be declining. Chami (2003) raised some doubts that all commodities are losing market share in the United States in comparison with industrial goods.

7. Thus far, we have avoided discussing the relationship between prices and quantities, which for some authors is relevant, particularly because Venezuela is an OPEC member. The issue will be discussed below.

8. In 1975, oil production fell 23 percent, as will be documented in detail below.

9. This figure is not available at Ministerio de Energía y Minas. This information was available in an annual report from PDVSA, which is no longer produced. The author thanks former members of the Office of the Chief Economist of PDVSA for making the information available.

10. Investment specificity refers to possible alternative uses of investments made. An investment is highly specific when it can be used for only one purpose within the scope of the project in which it has been invested. For example in oil, all the exploration investment is specific to the oil fields discovered. In addition, most of the infrastructure that is set up to pump the oil out of the ground is also specific to each well.

11. Oil fields in Venezuela are more productive that the average field in the rest of the world, though there are countries that are more productive than Venezuela. Therefore, oil production could be represented in a production function where capital, labor, and natural resources are the production factors and these economic rents are the remuneration of the natural resource.

12. In the few places where the owner of the resource is a private agent, there is typically a contract between the landlord and the producing firm that stipulates a payment from the latter to the former. Separately, the producer will pay taxes.

13. A good review of the Venezuelan political system and its relationship with oil can be found in Urbaneja 1992.

14. For a detailed description of all the events surrounding oil in Venezuela, see Martinez 1986.

15. Moreover, Gomez quickly realized the importance of oil fiscal revenue and used it to consolidate power.

16. They used the Dutch disease argument. Alberto Adriani (1931) was one of the authors that issued the most warnings about the end of the "agrarian era" for Venezuela, mainly because of the presence of oil. However, other works (Mayobre 1944; Peltzer 1944) discussed the problems of an appreciated exchange rate on the industrialization of Venezuela.

17. The name of the principle came from an editorial published in 1936 by Arturo Uslar Pietri, an influential writer and intellectual.

18. Even though 1970 is twelve years after the period studied, the reader should realize that acquiring information on these variables for an international comparison is difficult. However, the statistics for the variables presented here do not change dramatically over short periods and so can be taken as representative of the period studied.

19. Further evidence of the relative lack of a comprehensive policy toward the integration of the oil sector in the Venezuelan economy is provided by the state of technical education related to oil. Most of the technical expertise in the sector had to be provided by foreigners. Geology as

a university program was not introduced until 1937 and petroleum engineering not until 1952. It is important to notice that, by that time, the government ran most of the universities in the country.

20. In this chapter, we define as OPEC producers those countries that are now members of OPEC. Ecuador and Gabon, which joined the organization for a period and then left, are not considered members.

21. Costs in Nigeria seem larger than those in Venezuela. For the period, they more or less were around the same value as the Venezuelan costs. Nevertheless, the Nigerian Ebony Light reference crude oil was of higher quality than the Venezuelan Tia Juana Light reference; accordingly, its price was around fifty cents higher.

22. Juan Pablo Perez Alfonzo is recognized as the main ideologist behind the preservation principle. See, for example, Perez Alfonzo 1962. Perez Alfonzo was one of the founders of OPEC and energy minister of the first administration of the democratic era.

23. See, for example, Tugwell 1975; Espinasa 1996; Monaldi 2002, 2006.

24. This does not imply that these were not important gains in terms of the relative size of the production of these countries. This group includes Angola, Colombia, Ecuador, Egypt, Gabon, Malaysia, Oman, Tunisia, and Trinidad and Tobago.

25. This seems to suggest that the oil sector was more or less reaching a peak in terms of potential growth.

26. In 1959, in the first Arab Petroleum Congress, prior to the foundation of OPEC, oil producers (including Venezuela) reached an informal agreement that eventually led to the creation of OPEC. This was known as the Cairo Agreement. Among other things, the participating countries agreed that the share of revenue from the oil sector to the governments should increase to around 60 percent of the income.

27. For example, in Libya, which nationalized its industry in 1970, and Algeria, which did so in 1971. In addition, in Saudi Arabia, Iran, and Iraq, the National and Independent Oil Companies started joint ventures of some form.

28. In fact, as is shown in the appendix, this was the beginning of a period that saw productivity per well fall all the way up to 1984, well past nationalization.

29. Evidently, this is also part of the distributive conflict between the government and oil firms.

30. This instrument, called "export value for fiscal reference," lasted until well after nationalization.

31. It is important to mention that private oil companies were signing service contracts with the government even after 1971.

32. Oficina Central de Presupuesto 1988.

33. See Maloney 2002.

34. According to Oficina Central de Presupuesto 1988, between 1964 and 1973, from 9 to 13 percent of the budget went on supporting productive sectors of infrastructure spending, which indicates an active intervention of government in the economy. More than 60 percent went to agriculture, however, which indicates that government priorities were in other economic sectors.

35. It has already been stated that from the point of view of returns, less oil should have been extracted.

36. According to World Bank 2004 figures, the world GDP grew at an average rate of 5.3 percent between 1960 and 1970.

37. Moreover, given the price of oil and the prevailing interest rate, this was a period in which the optimal strategy was to take oil out of the ground and invest the revenue that was derived, rather than leaving the oil in the ground. Therefore, the lower extraction rate really shows a picture different from the prevailing perception prior to 1974.

38. A review of the way economic thought evolved during the second half of the twentieth century can be found in Adelman 1993.

39. The agreement between OPEC members was that all members but Saudi Arabia would have a constant share of production and that Saudi Arabia would change its production in order to clear the market at a "fair" price. OPEC behavior has been widely studied. A review of this literature can be found in De Santis 2000.

40. The appendix contains data about OPEC behavior. For a more formal treatment, however, see Smith 2005; and Almoguera and Herrera 2005. Although the two papers have different objectives, both more or less agree that there have been different periods in which OPEC was able to behave more closely as a cartel (Smith) and to have some impact on the market (Almoguera and Herrera).

41. According to Energy Information Administration 2004, in 1986 there were oil reserves in sixty-seven countries. Of those countries, thirty-eight have a relatively complete set of statistics.

42. Productivity is measured as oil production per active oil well.

43. The index is constructed for the whole sample of oil-producing countries.

44. The government even had to eliminate the "fiscal value of exports." As explained before, this was an instrument introduced in the 1960s, when the value of oil exports was increased by 20 percent for income tax purposes.

45. These areas should be "next in line," for exploratory purposes, after the areas that the PDVSA has been exploring.

46. This index is based on Van Meurs 1997 and reflects the attractiveness of fiscal institutions for investors in the oil sector. See the appendix for details.

47. The optimal rate is derived from an extraction model estimated with the Venezuelan parameters for the oil sector based on Deacon 1993 and Medina 1997.

48. Again, the reader is referred to Smith 2005; and Almoguera and Herrera 2005, which formally test OPEC behavior.

49. If Venezuelan oil production had been the same in 2001 as in 1973, assuming that all else remained constant, oil fiscal revenue per capita would have been 4 percent higher than in 1960, instead of 7 percent lower as shown in table 2.1.

50. The criterion for abundance is based on the fact that the country is in the top 25th percentile in the ratios of reserves to GDP and reserves to population.

51. The main reason for using the U.S. matrix is that there are no matrices with a unified methodology (like those of Global Trade Analysis Project) for these countries. The United States is used instead because of its mature oil sector, where oil has been produced for more than a century. It was the largest producer until 1973 and is still the third-largest oil producer in the world. The relationship between non-oil sectors and the oil sectors is based on multipliers from an input–output matrix. See the appendix for details.

52. For instance, all the countries but Algeria in the upward-sloped line have a positive GDP per capita growth, and the average growth was 2.10 percent. Of the countries in the negative-sloped line, two have positive rates (Mexico and Oman) and two have negative rates (Ecuador and Venezuela). Their average GDP per capita growth was 0.44 percent.

53. For a complete description of reform programs in Venezuela and their successful or failed implementation, see Gonzalez et al. 2007.

54. Hausmann and Rodrik 2003. In Trinidad and Tobago, these policies were adopted in one form or another. For a review of the economic performance of Trinidad and Tobago, as well as the policy implemented, see Artana, Bour, and Navajas 2006; Barclay 2003; and Berezin, Salehizadeh, and Santana 2002.

55. Both policies were used to distribute the rents generated by the oil sector. Of course, they were not necessarily ends sought by the original proponents of the principle. Urbaneja 1992; and Gonzalez et al. 2007, among others, have claimed that since the 1970s, policy outcomes have deteriorated. Urbaneja, in particular, has argued that it was due to the perception on the part of policymakers that massive rents were being generated by the oil sector in the 1970s. These rents generated the impression that cost–benefit analysis for policymaking was less necessary.

56. One hypothesis is that for those changes to take place would require an important consensus in Congress, but that this was difficult to achieve. Although it is not clear that constitutional reform was needed in order to pursue a different oil policy, it is accepted that at least changes in "organic" laws were required. In order for them to be passed or changed, organic laws required the approval of two-thirds of the members of Congress. Some authors have proposed that after 1989 is precisely the time when political fragmentation started in Venezuela and it became more difficult to generate consensus. See Gonzalez et al. 2004; and the chapter in this book by Monaldi and Penfold, "Institutional Collapse: The Rise and Decline of Democratic Governance in Venezuela."

REFERENCES

Adelman, M. A. 1993. *The Economics of Petroleum Supply.* Cambridge: MIT Press.

Adriani, Alberto. 1931. "La Crisis, los cambios y nosotros." In *La Economía Contemporánea de Venezuela: Tomo I,* edited by Hector Valecillos and Omar Bello, 19–42. Caracas: Banco Central de Venezuela.

Almoguera, Pedro, and Ana M. Herrera. 2005. "A Study of OPEC Cartel Stability." Mimeo, Michigan State University, East Lansing.

Artana, Daniel, Juan Luis Bour, and Fernando Navajas. 2006. "Designing Fiscal Policy to Achieve Development," in Rojas-Suárez, Liliana, and Carlos Elías, editors, From Growth to Prosperity: Policy Perspectives for Trinidad and Tobago. Washington, D.C.: IDB Publications.

Baker Hughes. 2004. "Baker Hughes Rig Counts." Houston. http://investor.shareholder.com/bhi/rig_counts/rigCountArchive.cfm.

Barclay, Lou Anne. 2003. "FDI-Facilitated Development: The Case of the Natural Gas Industry of Trinidad and Tobago." UNU-INTECH Discussion Paper 2003–7, United Nations University, Tokyo.

Barro, Robert J., and Xavier Sala-i-Martin. 1995. *Economic Growth.* New York: McGraw-Hill.

Berezin, Peter, Ali Salehizadeh, and Elcior Santana. 2002. "The Challenge of Diversification in the Caribbean." Working Paper 02/196, International Monetary Fund, Washington, D.C.

Blomstrom, Magnus, and Ari Kokko. 2003. "From Natural Resources to High-Tech Production: The Evolution of Industrial Competitiveness in Sweden and Finland." Discussion Paper 3804, Center for Economic Policy Research, Washington, D.C.

Chami, Jorge. 2003. "Especialización y crecimiento de las exportaciones en América Latina: Naturaleza de las competencia de productos entre diferentes exportadores." *Perspectivas* 2 (1): 7–68. Publicaciones CAF, Caracas.

Clemente, Lino, Osmel Manzano, and Alejandro Puente. 2005. "Oil Sector Impact on Industrial Productivity in Venezuela." Mimeo, Corporación Andina de Fomento, Caracas.

Cuddington, John, Rodney Ludema, and Shamila Jayasuriya. 2007. "Prebisch–Singer Redux." In *Natural Resources and Development: Are They a Curse? Are They Destiny?* edited by Daniel Lederman and William F. Maloney, 103–40. Stanford: Stanford University Press.

Cuddington, John, and Diana L. Moss. 2001. "Technological Change, Depletion, and the U.S. Petroleum Industry: A New Approach to Measurement and Estimation." *American Economic Review* 91 (September 2001): 1135–48.

Deacon, R. T. 1993. "Taxation, Depletion, and Welfare: A Simulation Study of the U.S. Petroleum Resource." *Journal of Environmental Economics and Management* 24 (March 1993): 159–87.

De Santis, Roberto. 2000. "Crude Oil Price Fluctuations and Saudi Arabian Behavior." Kiel Working Paper 1014, Kiel Institute of World Economics, Kiel, Germany.

Energy Information Administration. 2004. *International Energy Annual Report, 2002.* Washington, D.C.

Espinasa, Ramón. 1996. "Ideología, marco institucional y desarrollo del sector petrolero." *Revista Venezolana de Economía y Ciencias Sociales* 2 (2/3): 211–13.

Fernandez, Aureliano, Juan C. Gomez, and Osmel Manzano. 2005. "Intergeneration Accounting of Oil Wealth in Venezuela." Mimeo, Corporación Andina de Fomento, Caracas.

Gonzalez, Marino, Francisco Monaldi, German Rios, and Ricardo Villasmil. 2007. "The Difficulties of Reforming and Oil based Economy: The Case of Venezuela," in Fanelli, José, Understanding Market Reforms in Latin America: Similar Reforms, Diverse Constituencies, Varied Results. Palgrave Macmillan.

Hausmann, Ricardo, and Roberto Rigobón. 2003. "An Alternative Interpretation of the 'Resource Curse': Theory and Policy Implications." Working Paper 9424, National Bureau of Economic Research, Cambridge, Mass.

Hausmann, Ricardo, and Dani Rodrik. 2003. "Economic Development as Self-Discovery." Working Paper 8952, National Bureau of Economic Research, Cambridge, Mass.

International Monetary Fund. 2004. *International Financial Statistics.* Washington, D.C.

Kaufmann, Daniel, Aart Kraay, and Massimo Mastruzzi. 2003. "Governance Matters III: Governance Indicators for 1996–2002." World Bank Policy Research Working Paper 3106, World Bank, Washington, D.C.

Kaufmann, Daniel, Aart Kraay, and Pablo Zoido-Lobaton. 1999. "Governance Matters." World Bank Policy Research Working Paper 2196, World Bank, Washington, D.C.

Krugman, Paul. 1987. "The Narrow Moving Band, the Dutch Disease, and the Competitive Consequences of Mrs. Thatcher on Trade in the Presence of Dynamic Scale Economies." *Journal of Development Economics* 27:41–55.

Leamer, Edward, Hugo Maul, Sergio Rodríguez, and Peter K. Schott. 1998. "Does Natural Resource Abundance Increase Latin American Income Inequality?" *Journal of Development Economics* 59 (1): 3–42.

Lederman, Daniel, and William Maloney. 2003. "Trade Structure and Growth." Policy Research Working Paper 3025, World Bank, Washington, D.C.

Maloney, William. 2002. "Missed Opportunities: Innovation and Resource-Based Growth in Latin America." *Economía* 3 (1): 111–51.

Manzano, Osmel. 2000. "Tax Effects upon Oil Field Development in Venezuela." Working Papers Series 2000-006, Center for Energy and Environmental Policy Research, MIT, Cambridge, Mass.

Manzano, Osmel, and Roberto Rigobón. 2001. "Resource Curse or Debt Overhang." Working Paper 8390, National Bureau of Economic Research, Washington, D.C.

Martinez, Anibal. 2005. *Cronología del petróleo Venezolano.* 5th ed. Caracas: Ediciones Petroleum World.

Mayobre, Jose Antonio. 1944. "La paridad del Bolivar." In *La Economía Contemporánea de Venezuela: Tomo I*, edited by Hector Valecillos and Omar Bello, 43–84. Caracas: Banco Central de Venezuela.

Medina, Humberto. 1997. "Evaluación de los efectos de diferentes esquemas impositivos sobre la senda exploración y producción de una empresa petrolera en el tiempo (un análisis para el caso Venezolano)." Mimeo, Petroleos de Venezuela SA, Caracas.

Ministerio de Energía y Minas. Various years. *Petróleo y otros datos estadísticos.* Caracas: Dirección de Economía e Hidrocarburos.

Mommer, Bernard. 2003. "Subversive Oil." In *Venezuelan Politics in the Chávez Era*, edited by Steve Ellner and Daniel Hellinger, 131–46. Boulder: Lynne Reiner.

Monaldi, Francisco. 2002. "Government Commitment Using External Hostages." Paper presented at the Annual Meeting of the American Political Science Association, Boston, August 28.

_____. 2006. "Inversiones inmovilizadas, instituciones y compromiso creíble: Implicaciones sobre la evolución de la inversión en la industria petrolera venezolana." In *Crecimiento Económico en Venezuela: Bajo el signo del petróleo*, edited by J. Pineda and F. Sáez, 187–217. Caracas: Banco Central de Venezuela.

Monaldi, Francisco, Rosa Amelia González de Pacheco, Richard Obuchi, and Michael Penfold. 2006. "Political Institutions, Policymaking Processes, and Policy Outcomes in Venezuela." Research Network Working Paper R-507, Inter-American Development Bank, Washington, D.C.

Oficina Central de Presupuesto. 1988. *Cuarenta Años de Presupuesto Fiscal.* Caracas.

Organization of the Petroleum Exporting Countries Organization. Various years. *Statistical Annual Bulletin.* Vienna.

Peltzer, Ernesto. 1944. "La industrialización de Venezuela y el alto tipo de cambio del Bolívar." In *La Economía Contemporánea de Venezuela: Tomo I*, edited by Hector Valecillos and Omar Bello, 85–108. Caracas: Banco Central de Venezuela.

Perez Alfonzo, Juan. 1962. *Política petrolera.* Caracas: Imprenta Nacional.

Prebisch, Raúl. 1950. *The Economic Development of Latin America and Its Principal Problems.* New York: United Nations.

Rodríguez, Francisco, and Jeffrey D. Sachs. 1999. "Why Do Resource Abundant Economies Grow More Slowly: A New Explanation and an Application to Venezuela." *Journal of Economic Growth* 4:277–303.

Sachs, Jeffrey, and Andrew Warner. 1995. "Natural Resource Abundance and Economic Growth." Working Paper 5398, National Bureau of Economic Research, Washington, D.C.

Salter, W. E. G. 1959. "Internal and External Balance: The Role of Price and Expenditure Effects. *Economic Record* 35:226–38.

Smith, James. 2005. "Inscrutable OPEC? Behavioral Tests of the Cartel Hypothesis." *Energy Journal* 26 (1): 51–82.

Tugwell, Franklin. 1975. *The Politics of Oil in Venezuela.* Stanford: Stanford University Press.

UN Commodity Trade Statistics Database. 2004. United Nations Statistics Division, New York. http://comtrade.un.org/.

Urbaneja, Diego. 1992. *Pueblo y petróleo en la política Venezolana del siglo XX.* Caracas: Ediciones CEPET.

Van Meurs and Associates Ltd. 1997. *Worldwide Fiscal Systems for Oil, 1997.* New York: Barrows Inc.

World Bank. 2004. *Global Development Indicators.* Washington, D.C.

Wright, Gavin, and Jesse Czelusta. 2002. "Resource-Based Growth Past and Present." In *Natural Resources and Development: Are They a Curse? Are They Destiny?* edited by Daniel Lederman and William F. Maloney, 183–212. Stanford: Stanford University Press.

3 PUBLIC INVESTMENT AND PRODUCTIVITY GROWTH IN THE VENEZUELAN MANUFACTURING INDUSTRY

José Pineda and Francisco Rodríguez

Between 1977 and 2001, Venezuelan per worker GDP declined by 36 percent. During the same period, the Venezuelan public sector disinvested significantly in its public assets, leading to a decline in non-oil public sector capital stock per worker of 29.1 percent. Did Venezuela's decline in public capital contribute to the collapse in economic growth? Figure 3.1 (below) shows the time series for non-oil GDP and the non-oil public capital stock, both measured in relation to the number of workers in the non-oil sector. The figure shows clearly that per worker GDP peaks in 1977 and had already declined precipitously by the time that the public capital stock starts declining after 1983. Thus it would appear implausible to explain the initial decline in GDP growth as a result of the decline in the provision of public capital. If anything, it appears that the decline in public investment may be part of a lagged response to the economy's deterioration. However, the figure also shows that after 1983 both the public capital stock and non-oil GDP continued declining steadily. If we believe that the public capital stock enters positively into the production function, it is plausible that the decline in public capital that occurs after 1983 contributed to the decline in non-oil productivity and production from the late 1980s on.[1]

Such a story would rely on the existence of a strong causal link going from public investment to productivity. The existence of such a link is far from established in the empirical literature. Although there are good theoretical reasons to expect public capital to have an effect on productivity (Arrow and Kurz 1970; Ogura and

The authors are very grateful for the excellent research assistance provided by Lenin Balza, Maria Esther Caballero, Zachary Gidwitz, Leonardo Ortega, and Reyes Rodríguez.

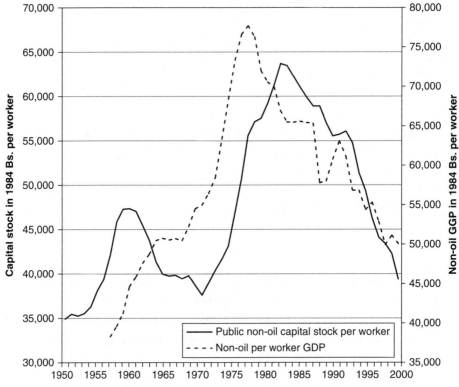

Fig. 3.1   Public capital and non-oil GDP, 1950–2001

Sources: Authors' own estimates based on BCV (various years); Baptista (2002); and Ministerio de Energía y Minas (various years).

Yohe 1977), empirical results are at best mixed. Evidence from the United States presents strong time-series and cross-state correlations between public infra-structure and productivity (Aschauer 1989; Munnell 1990). However, Hulten and Schwab (1991), Tatom (1991), and Holtz-Eakin (1994) have argued that these results disappear when the time-series data are first-differenced or when fixed effects are introduced in panel data regressions, suggesting that they were due to spurious correlations between nonstationary variables (in the time series) and endogeneity or misspecification (in the cross-section). Fernald (1999), however, found that the construction of the U.S. Interstate Highway System led to a considerable increase in the productivity of transport-intensive industries, consistent with the hypothesis of the existence of a causal link from infrastructure to productivity.

The cross-country evidence is similarly mixed. On the one hand, authors such as Easterly and Rebelo (1993) have found that public transport and com-munication investment are positively correlated with growth, but Devarajan, Swaroop, and Zou (1996) and Canning (1999) have argued that infrastructure is overprovided in many developing countries (though Esfanhani and Ramírez [2003] have contested this). Recently, Calderón and Servén (2003b) have argued that a substantial part of the growth in the output gaps between East Asia and Latin America can be traced back to the cutbacks in infrastructure spending that occurred in Latin America as a result of the fiscal adjustment programs precipitated by the debt crisis in the eighties.

All these estimates are confronted by a daunting empirical problem. Precisely because of the political forces in action to determine the allocation of investment projects, spending on infrastructure is likely to be an endogenous variable, making identification of its effect on productivity growth difficult. If governments are more likely to invest in prosperous and economically developed regions, then there will be a spurious positive correlation between investment in infrastructure and productivity growth; if policymakers try to use public investment to compensate for the backwardness of existing regions or to help out regions in crisis, in contrast, there will be a downward bias in the least squares estimate of the effect of infrastructure investment on productivity growth. It will be extremely difficult to find exogenous and excludable instruments for investment in infrastructure. For example, Calderón and Servén (2003a) have used urban population and population densities as well as lagged values of infrastructure stocks to estimate the effect of infrastructure on per worker GDP. If investment in infrastructure is endogenous, however, lagged infrastructure will be correlated with any persistent productivity shock, while population and population densities may have a direct effect on production or be correlated with omitted variables.

This chapter addresses the question of endogeneity in the estimation of the effect of public infrastructure spending on productivity by using state-level variations in infrastructure investments carried out by the Venezuelan Intergovernmental Decentralization Fund (Fondo Intergubernamental para la Descentralización, FIDES) established in 1993 to finance local infrastructure projects carried out by state and municipal governments in Venezuela. The FIDES was created simultaneously with the approval of a 1993 law establishing a national value-added tax on goods and services. The political negotiation leading to the adoption of the law led the caretaker administration of Ramón J. Velásquez (1993–94) to accept the distribution of 15 percent of collected VAT revenues directly to state and municipal governments through FIDES, with the condition that these resources be devoted to investment projects that would be cofinanced with the local government's own resources. Since its creation, the 15 percent proportion of total VAT revenues to be distributed to regions has remained constant.

FIDES establishes that each state and local government receives a fraction of total national VAT revenues that is a function of its population (45 percent), its land area (10 percent), and a compensation index designed to benefit less well-off states (45 percent). The compensation index depends on the receipts of other central government transfers (the Special Economic Allocations Fund and the Situado Constitucional),[2] from its Human Development Index (HDI) at the state level (which is between 0 and 1),[3] and its receipts from the part of FIDES that is allocated according to population and land area. The variation in a state's share of funds from FIDES actually comes from the interaction between the highly non-linear function and *national-level* fiscal revenues. Further details are provided in the appendix.[4]

Since the FIDES allocation rule is given, in practice variations in FIDES allocations over time come from variations in national-level oil and non-oil revenues. These changes have differential effects on public investment across states because the rule used to allocate FIDES allowances across states is nonlinear. Changes in national VAT revenues, for example, affect not only the total of resources to be distributed among states but also the share that each state gets of those resources. In other words, these changes generate a source of variation in public investment that is both exogenous at the state level and not collinear with a pure time effect. The source of identification is thus the interaction between a variable that is exogenous at the state level (national variation in revenues) and a rule whose parameters have been unchanged since its adoption.

Our main results from this analysis show that productivity is significantly affected by public capital investment. In fact, according to our simulations, per capita GDP would have been 37 percent higher if it had not been for the sharp decline in public investment. This striking result provides strong evidence that declining public investment contributed to Venezuela's economic collapse.

The rest of this chapter proceeds as follows. The next section describes the FIDES law. The following section discusses our empirical methodology and some issues with our estimation strategy. After that we present our results and then conclude.

The Intergovernmental Decentralization Fund and the Special Economic Assignments Law

The Intergovernmental Decentralization Fund (FIDES) was created in November 1993 as a result of the political discussion regarding the institution of the value-added tax (VAT) in Venezuela. The VAT reform, originally introduced by the Carlos Andrés Pérez administration before Congress in 1989, had met significant political opposition and was sidetracked. When Pérez was impeached in 1993, the caretaker administration of Ramón Velásquez negotiated with Congress the approval of this law, subject to the proviso that 15 percent of VAT revenues would be directly allocated to regional governments for the carrying out of public investments.

The law contemplates a broad definition of areas in which the FIDES may serve to pay the cost of public investments. Particularly important is the list of areas in which these investments can be financed by FIDES, which includes "projects of productive investment that promote the sustainable development of the community, states and municipalities," and "works of infrastructure and activities within the framework of national development plans" (FIDES 2005, Article 22). Although these provisions allow for a broad definition of the type of investment projects, the law does specifically state that these resources must only be used for "programas y proyectos" (programs and projects), a term that in Venezuelan legislation is equivalent to capital expenditures. Projects typically financed include construction of schools, repairs to roads, and acquisition of vehicles for use by the local police force.

The fact that these resources are indeed devoted to public investment projects may have to do more with the organizational details of the fund than with the letter of the law. Indeed, the 1999 Venezuelan constitution also requires states to devote at least 50 percent of their state revenues toward public investment, but no state government in Venezuela currently obeys this prescription. The FIDES law, however, requires the directory of the fund to approve the list of investment projects and to only disburse the funds after approval, and subject to co-participation of the state or local government in funding the project.

Empirical Strategy

We will use a panel of manufacturing firms derived from the Encuesta Industrial of the National Institute of Statistics to estimate the effect of FIDES-financed public investment on firm-level productivity between 1996 and 2001. We will estimate a firm level production function as follows:

$$y_{it} = \alpha_0 + \alpha_1 k_{it} + \alpha_2 l_{it} + \alpha_3 a_{it} + \omega_{it}. \qquad (1)$$

Let us assume y_{it} is the log of real value added, k_{it} is the log of the capital stock, l_{it} is employment, and a_{it} is the log of the firm's age measured in years. ω_{it} is the firm level productivity, which is determined according to

$$\omega_{it} = \eta_i + \beta p_{it} + \varepsilon_{it}, \qquad (2)$$

so that firm-level productivity is composed by a firm-specific effect, the productivity effect of the stock of public infrastructure, p_{it}, and a white-noise term.

We do not observe the stock of public infrastructure. However, we do know that it evolves according to

$$p_{it} = (1 - \delta)p_{it-1} + i_t, \qquad\qquad (3)$$

where δ is the rate of depreciation and i_t is public investment in infrastructure. Let public investment in infrastructure be the sum of FIDES and non-FIDES investment. The availability of greater resources from FIDES will affect public investment in infrastructure in two ways. First, according to the FIDES law, states must put down a minimum share of their own resources toward financing these projects. Further, the availability of FIDES may allow state governments to carry out projects that they would not otherwise have carried out with their own resources. On the other hand, states may simply use FIDES to carry out projects that they would have done anyway, so that the availability of FIDES resources may reduce non-FIDES investment. The total effect of FIDES resources on investment may thus be greater than or less than one.[5] We summarize it in the multiplier γ, so that investment in infrastructure is

$$i_{it} = \gamma f_{it} + n_{it} = \gamma f_{it} + n_{i0} + (n_{it} - n_{i0}), \qquad\qquad (4)$$

where f_{it} is FIDES (or FIDES-induced) investment, n_{it} is infrastructure investment that is unrelated to FIDES, and n_{io} is its unconditional mean $E(n_{it})$. Note that since δf_{it} includes the direct and indirect effect of FIDES expenditures, n_{it} is by definition uncorrelated with f_{it}. These steps set up the basis for the rest of our estimation technique, explained fully in the appendix.

In practice, our estimation strategy will be carried out in two steps. In the first step, we will estimate ω_{it} by the Olley and Pakes (1996) semiparametric method that allows us to obtain consistent estimates of the production function parameters that take into account the endogenous determination of firm-level capital and its likely correlation with productivity shocks arising from two forces: (1) the fact that firms that experience a positive productivity shock are likely to invest more; and (2) the fact that firms that experience a positive productivity shock are less likely to exit. When we have all the parameter estimates for (1) we can simply calculate ω_{it} and go on to estimate (B.2) and (B.3) though an Arellano and Bond (1991) or fixed-effects estimator.

One important observation about our data is that our indicator of FIDES expenditure refers to the funds allocated in yearly budgets, and not the fraction of those funds that was actually spent. We consider the budget allocations to be the correct variable for our estimation strategy because, in contrast to realized expenditures, budget allocations are strictly determined by the FIDES rule and thus truly exogenous. It is also true that the FIDES law generated an entitlement for regions to use these resources, so that the budgeted allocations were, unlike other items, in effect available to be spent by the regions provided that their projects satisfied the technical requirements imposed by the FIDES board of directors. The fact that f_{it} measures budget allocations implies that our estimate should be interpreted as the total effect on a region's productivity of providing resources to that region to spend on infrastructure. This total effect, which is captured by the product of the parameters γ and β multiplying f_{it} in (B.2) and (B.3), is different from the production function coefficient β that other studies commonly seek to estimate. That said, $\gamma\beta$ may be the more relevant parameter for policy purposes, as it captures the expected effect of providing a region with resources that must be spent on public investment projects. This is the effect that would interest a multilateral bank that finances an infrastructure project, a national government deciding whether to transfer funds to regional governments for public investment, or a voter deciding whether to support higher taxes in order to finance public investment.

Estimation Results

Table 3.1 shows the results of our estimates of equation (B.3) using autocorrelation-corrected fixed effects panel estimation. Note that we do not present random effects or cross-sectional estimates because our argument for exogeneity refers to the changes over time in FIDES allocations, which are generated by the interaction of the allocation rule and changes in national revenue, and not to the cross-sectional differences. The latter would simply be a reflection of the political choices made at the time at which the rule was originally set. All our estimates include a set of year dummies. The dependent variable is constructed as outlined in the previous section; the independent variable of interest is the log of budgeted FIDES expenditures as a fraction of gross state product. The latter is estimated using the United Nations Development Programme's (various years) estimates of state-level income.

The estimates of table 3.1 show a significant effect of FIDES investment on productivity. In the estimation with no controls, the estimate implies an elasticity of 0.4 of output to public investment. This is remarkably similar to Fernald's (1999) estimate of the elasticity of manufacturing productivity to the construction of the U.S. Interstate Highway System of 0.38. The value of the coefficient diminishes somewhat with the introduction of controls for the firm's capital share, ownership by residents, and ratio of exports to production, as well as the state share of manufacturing in gross state product: when all four controls are introduced (column 5)

Table 3.1   Fixed effects with AR(1) disturbances (all firms)

Dependent variable	Change in productivity					
	1	2	3	4	5	6
FIDES	0.3972	0.3966	0.3512	0.3412	0.315	0.0522
	(2.28)**	(2.28)**	(1.97)**	(1.91)*	(1.76)*	(0.23)
Capital share	—	−0.0214	−0.0199	−0.0224	−0.0211	−0.2295
(rK/wL+rK)		(0.18)	(0.16)	(0.19)	(0.17)	(0.81)
Development	—	—	0.0001	0.0001	0.0001	0.0007
(Manuf. VA/PIB)			(1.14)	(1.15)	(1.17)	(1.94)*
Residents	—	—	—	0.0015	0.0015	−0.0026
(Percent ownership of residents)				(2.03)**	(2.02)**	(1.49)
Export (exports/ production)	—	—	—	—	−0.099	0.1482
					(1.82)*	(1.62)
FIDES · capital share	—	—	—	—	—	0.1924
						(0.80)
FIDES · development	—	—	—	—	—	−0.0004
						(1.57)
FIDES · residents	—	—	—	—	—	0.0038
						(2.61)***
FIDES · export	—	—	—	—	—	−0.6051
						(3.31)***
Constant	−4.8788	−6.7615	−6.5284	−7.1096	−6.9898	−8.7605
	(0.87)	(1.04)	(1.05)	(1.12)	(1.08)	
N	5,675	5,669	5,669	5,668	5,668	5,668
R^2	0.0745	0.0751	0.0755	0.0765	0.0774	0.0828

NOTE: Absolute value of t-statistic in parentheses. All specifications include time dummies. Capital share is measured as the ratio of capital income over the sum of labor and capital income. Level of development is measured by the ratio of manufacturing value added to gross state product.

*Significant at 10%
**Significant at 5%
***Significant at 1%

the elasticity estimate falls to 0.32 and its statistical significance dips to 10 percent. Two of the controls are significant: the ownership share of residents and the share of exports in firm production. Interestingly, the significance of these coefficients appears to be picking up an interaction with FIDES investment: when we introduce a full set of interaction terms these are strongly significant (at 1 percent) and significance of both FIDES investment and the ownership and export variables disappears. This suggests that the effect of FIDES on productivity occurs through its effect on the productivity of nationally owned firms and firms that produce for the domestic sector (as opposed to those that produce exportables).[6]

Similar results arise from the Arellano–Bond estimation of equation (B.2), shown in table 3.2. The coefficient estimate is somewhat lower (0.32). However,

Table 3.2   Arellano–Bond (all firms)

Dependent variable	Productivity					
Lagged productivity	0.3452229 (8.82)***	0.3490881 (8.89)***	0.3461752 (8.83)***	0.344972 (8.82)***	0.3446922 (8.82)***	0.3367109 (8.71)***
FIDES	0.3233016 (3.59)***	0.3261382 (3.61)***	0.3148505 (3.49)***	0.3159334 (3.50)***	0.3141896 (3.49)***	0.1698891 (1.33)
Capital share (rK/wL+rK)	—	−0.1785324 (1.56)	−0.1747917 (1.53)	−0.1754684 (1.54)	−0.1717127 (1.51)	−0.4338046 (2.37)**
Development (manuf. VA/PIB)	—	—	0.0001271 (1.31)	0.0001299 (1.34)	0.0001318 (1.37)	0.00018 (0.91)
Residents (percent ownership of residents)	—	—	—	0.0009647 (1.51)	0.0009526 (1.49)	−0.0006611 (0.63)
Export (exports/ production)	—	—	—	—	−0.1236608 (1.34)	0.1364423 (2.16)**
FIDES · capital share	—	—	—	—	—	0.2718932 (1.95)*
FIDES · development	—	—	—	—	—	−0.0000202 (0.16)
FIDES · residents	—	—	—	—	—	0.001618 (1.78)*
FIDES · export	—	—	—	—	—	−0.6259281 (3.16)***
Constant	−0.1234322 (8.46)***	−0.1160632 (2.94)***	−0.1209379 (8.02)***	−0.1214537 (8.05)***	−0.1202148 (7.98)***	−0.1167837 (7.63)***
Sargan test of overidentifying restrictions	0.1098	0.112	0.1183	0.1205	0.1233	0.1624
Arellano–Bond test that average autocovariance in residuals of order 1 is 0	0.0000	0.0000	0.0000	0.0000	0.0000	0.0000
Arellano–Bond test that average autocovariance in residuals of order 2 is 0	0.1094	0.1296	0.1298	0.1253	0.1275	0.1975
N	5,366	5,359	5,359	5,358	5,358	5,358

NOTE: Absolute value of t-statistic in parentheses. All specifications include time dummies. Last three rows list p-values for rejection of null hypothesis in each of the three tests.

*Significant at 10%
**Significant at 5%
***Significant at 1%

note that given that the estimated specification has a lagged disturbance term, the coefficient on FIDES investment reflects the short-run elasticity, whereas the long run elasticity would be equal to 0.49 [0.323/(1−0.345)]. In the Arellano–Bond estimation, the significance of FIDES investment is much higher and remains robust to the introduction of controls. It loses statistical significance, as before, only when a full set of interaction terms is introduced. In this case, we also find a negative significant interaction with the share of exports in gross production and the share of resident ownership. The interaction with the capital share is now also significant (at 10 percent).

As noted in the previous section, implementation of the Olley–Pakes algo-rithm requires estimation of a survival probability function. In order to do this, it is necessary to have data on entry and exit of firms. However, the Encuesta Industrial is a random survey in which a firm may exit the sample because it is no longer operating or because it was no longer surveyed. When estimating survival probabilities, we take advantage of the fact that in the Encuesta Indus-trial's sample all plants of more than one hundred employees are always covered. In other words, the Encuesta becomes a census for plants with more than one hundred employees. We thus estimate the survival probability function for firms with more than one hundred employees and then use the coefficients from that function to correct for selection bias for all firms. Note that this simply makes use of the implicit assumption made when one estimates the production function (1) for the whole sample, which is that small and large firms have the same param-eters in their production function. But the doubt may naturally arise about how important is the approximation error induced by this method. In tables 3.3 and 3.4 we present the results of carrying out all three steps (instead of just the second one) of the Olley–Pakes algorithm restricted to plants of more than one hundred employees. The coefficient on FIDES is still positive and the point estimate of the regression with no controls is similar in magnitude but is now statistically insig-nificant. The interaction term between FIDES investment and domestic owner-ship does remain significant (at 5 percent), but the interaction with exports is no longer so. In the Arellano–Bond estimates (table 3.4) a similar pattern emerges: positive albeit insignificant coefficient estimates on FIDES, with two of the inter-actions significant, that with the capital share (at 5 percent) and that with exports (at 10 percent).

There are two possible ways to interpret the weakness of the coefficient when one passes to the restricted sample. One is as a signal that the application of the Olley–Pakes algorithm to the broader sample is inappropriate. The other one is as an indication that the effect of FIDES expenditure is relevant only for small firms.

Table 3.3 Fixed effects with AR(1) disturbances (large firms)

Dependent variable	Change in productivity					
FIDES	0.4515	0.4452	0.1492	0.1419	0.056	−0.2816
	(1.57)	(1.54)	(0.50)	(0.48)	(0.19)	(0.75)
Capital share	—	−0.1327	−0.1501	−0.1466	−0.1146	−0.4972
(rK/wL+rK)		(0.77)	(0.87)	(0.85)	(0.67)	(1.18)
Development	—	—	0.0007	0.0007	0.0008	0.0017
(manuf. VA/PIB)			(3.64)***	(3.65)***	(3.99)***	(2.98)***
Residents (percent	—	—	—	0.0012	0.0011	−0.0041
ownership of				(1.13)	(1.04)	(1.52)
residents)						
Export (exports/	—	—	—	—	−1.1222	−0.6622
production)					(4.77)***	(1.08)
FIDES · capital share	—	—	—	—	—	0.3488
						(0.98)
FIDES · development	—	—	—	—	—	−0.0007
						(1.64)
FIDES · residents	—	—	—	—	—	0.005
						(2.16)**
FIDES · export	—	—	—	—	—	−0.466
						(0.86)
Constant	−1.4577	−1.535	−1.8033	−1.9026	−1.9665	−1.8052
	(0.63)	(0.66)	(0.77)	(0.81)	(0.81)	(0.73)
N	2,129	2,129	2,129	2,129	2,129	2,129
R^2	0.0818	0.0822	0.0899	0.0905	0.1039	0.1095

NOTE: Absolute value of t-statistic in parentheses. All specifications include time dummies.

*Significant at 10%
**Significant at 5%
***Significant at 1%

Consistently with this hypothesis, splitting the broader sample between large and small firms (using the one hundred employees threshold) delivers significant coefficients only for the sample of small firms under both specifications.

One common criticism of the Olley–Pakes approach is that it relies on investment to proxy for unobservable shocks to productivity. Levinsohn and Petrin (2003) have argued that materials inputs may be a better proxy for unobservable shocks as they respond to the entire productivity term—instead of just to the "news" that investment may be capturing. In order to check the robustness of our approach to the method used to estimate productivity, we re-estimate our regressions of tables 3.1 and 3.2 using the Levinsohn–Petrin methodology, where we have chosen firm electricity consumption as our proxy for materials use. Results

Table 3.4   Arellano–Bond (large firms)

Dependent variable	Productivity					
Lagged productivity	0.2827831 (5.78)***	0.2828891 (5.78)***	0.287732 (5.92)***	0.2891572 (5.95)***	0.2971224 (6.14)***	0.2905152 (6.05)***
FIDES	0.229978 (1.48)	0.2347314 (1.51)	0.1763094 (1.13)	0.1786343 (1.14)	0.1754602 (1.13)	0.2206786 (0.95)
Capital share (rK/wL+rK)	—	−0.1491047 (0.95)	−0.1650096 (1.05)	−0.1611685 (1.03)	−0.1291719 (0.84)	−0.5573552 (2.15)**
Development (manuf. VA/PIB)	—	—	0.0005431 (3.32)***	0.0005481 (3.36)***	0.0006146 (4.02)***	0.0008068 (2.39)**
Residents (percent ownership of residents)	—	—	—	0.001026 (1.16)	0.0008955 (1.03)	0.0012311 (0.69)
Export (exports/ production)	—	—	—	—	−1.122256 (3.43)***	−0.6420202 (1.35)
FIDES · capital share	—	—	—	—	—	0.4084824 (1.98)**
FIDES · development	—	—	—	—	—	−0.000134 (0.64)
FIDES · residents	—	—	—	—	—	−0.0003442 (0.21)
FIDES · export	—	—	—	—	—	−0.4467807 (1.67)*
Constant	0.0056813 (0.19)	0.0022151 (0.07)	−0.0534271 (1.28)	−0.0907628 (3.82)***	−0.0787124 (3.33)***	−0.077976 (3.26)***
Sargan test of overidentifying restrictions	0.0623	0.0582	0.0689	0.0677	0.0825	0.0709
Arellano–Bond test that average autocovariance in residuals of order 1 is 0	0	0	0	0	0	0
Arellano-Bond test that average autocovariance in residuals of order 2 is 0	0.208	0.2149	0.2	0.1778	0.1448	0.1606
N	2,083	2,083	2,083	2,083	2,083	2,083

NOTE: Absolute value of t-statistic in parentheses. All specifications include time dummies. Last three rows list p-values for rejection of null hypothesis in each of the three tests.

*Significant at 10%
**Significant at 5%
***Significant at 1%

are displayed in tables 3.5 and 3.6. The correlation between the Levinsohn–Petrin and the Olley–Pakes estimates of productivity is 0.9568, so it is not surprising that our results are similar. Indeed, the elasticity estimate becomes somewhat stronger in the fixed effects specification, increasing to 0.44 (as opposed to 0.40 using Olley–Pakes) in the baseline estimation of column 1, but slightly weaker in the Arellano–Bond specification, where it falls to 0.44 (from 0.49 in the Olley–Pakes specification) of column 1, table 3.6. All the basic results are, however, unchanged: the sign on the FIDES variable remains positive and significant until the full set of interactions is introduced, when the significance is picked up by the interactions between FIDES investment and domestic ownership on the one hand and exports (with a negative sign) on the other.

Table 3.5   Levinsohn and Petrin productivity, fixed effects specification

Dependent variable	Change in productivity					
FIDES	0.4347	0.4361	0.3947	0.3869	0.3626	0.1532
	(2.52)**	(2.54)**	(2.24)**	(2.19)**	(2.05)**	(0.68)
Capital share	—	0.0238	0.0252	0.0232	0.0243	−0.1264
(rK/wL+rK)	—	(0.20)	(0.21)	(0.19)	(0.20)	(0.45)
Development	—	—	0.0001	0.0001	0.0001	0.0007
(manuf. VA/PIB)	—	—	(1.05)	(1.05)	(1.07)	(2.05)**
Residents (percent	—	—	—	0.0012	0.0012	−0.0024
ownership of	—	—	—	(1.63)	(1.62)	(1.40)
residents)						
Export (exports/	—	—	—	—	−0.0919	0.1537
production)	—	—	—	—	(1.71)*	(1.69)*
FIDES · capital	—	—	—	—	—	0.139
share	—	—	—	—	—	(0.59)
FIDES ·	—	—	—	—	—	−0.0004
development	—	—	—	—	—	(1.72)*
FIDES · residents	—	—	—	—	—	0.0034
	—	—	—	—	—	(2.33)**
FIDES · export	—	—	—	—	—	−0.6009
	—	—	—	—	—	(3.32)***
Constant	−5.5104	−8.0843	7.7791	8.2375	−8.1668	−10.2563
	(1.08)	(1.26)	(1.27)	(1.33)	(1.28)	(1.34)
N	5,684	5,678	5,678	5,677	5,677	5,677
R^2	0.0763	0.0773	0.0776	0.0783	0.079	0.0841

NOTE: Absolute value of t-statistic in parentheses. All specifications include time dummies.

*Significant at 10%
**Significant at 5%
***Significant at 1%

Table 3.6   Levinsohn and Petrin productivity, Arellano–Bond specification

Dependent variable	Productivity					
Lagged productivity	0.3334 (8.48)***	0.3386 (8.59)***	0.3369 (8.55)***	0.336 (8.55)***	0.3353 (8.54)***	0.3252 (8.37)***
FIDES	0.2937 (3.37)***	0.2955 (3.38)***	0.2876 (3.30)***	0.2886 (3.31)***	0.2872 (3.30)***	0.1521 (1.23)
Capital share (rK/wL+rK)	— —	−0.00302524 (0.03)	−0.00187732 (0.02)	−0.00181351 (0.02)	0.00174443 (0.01)	−0.16123465 (0.86)
Development (manuf. VA/ PIB)	— —	— —	0.00010596 (1.09)	0.00010666 (1.10)	0.00010854 (1.12)	0.00011153 (0.58)
Residents (percent ownership of residents)	— —	— —	— —	0.0005535 (0.89)	0.00054175 (0.87)	−0.00106351 (1.05)
Export (exports/ production)	— —	— —	— —	— —	−0.12567268 (1.35)	0.15085727 (2.39)**
FIDES · capital share	— —	— —	— —	— —	— —	0.16694076 (1.21)
FIDES · development	— —	— —	— —	— —	— —	0.00001066 (0.09)
FIDES · residents	— —	— —	— —	— —	— —	0.00159596 (1.81)
FIDES · export	— —	— —	— —	— —	— —	−0.64819021 (3.25)***
Constant	−0.09415629 (6.79)***	−0.07846667 (2.08)**	−0.0748661 (1.99)**	−0.09091817 (6.34)***	−0.08968063 (6.26)***	−0.08595909 (5.91)***
N	5,374	5,367	5,367	5,366	5,366	5,366
Sargan test of overidentifying restrictions	0.036	0.040	0.044	0.044	0.046	0.051
Arellano–Bond test that average autocovariance in residuals of order 1 is 0	0.000	0.000	0.000	0.000	0.000	0.000
Arellano–Bond test that average autocovariance in residuals of order 2 is 0	0.084	0.115	0.113	0.108	0.112	0.192

NOTE: Absolute value of t-statistics in parentheses. All specifications include time dummies. Last three rows list p-values for rejection of null hypothesis in each of the three tests.

*Significant at 10%
**Significant at 5%
***Significant at 1%

One possible explanation of our effect is that productivity-enhancing investments are migrating from areas with low infrastructure investment to areas with high infrastructure investment. While our estimate would still be appropriate as a measure of the effect on a state's productivity of undertaking higher levels of public investment, we could not use it to infer the effect of greater public investment on *national* productivity, as part of the increase in productivity enjoyed by high public investment states would be offset by declines in productivity suffered by low public investment states. In order to control for this effect, we present estimates of our baseline specification adding a control for average FIDES investment in neighboring states. The results of this exercise are shown in tables 3.7 and 3.8. While the effect of neighbors' FIDES investment on a state's productivity is not significantly positive in any of the specifications, the coefficient on home state FIDES investment remains statistically significant, with a somewhat greater elasticity than in the baseline exercise.

Concluding Comments

This chapter has used expenditures of the Venezuelan Intergovernmental Decentralization Fund to estimate the effect of public investment on the productivity of Venezuelan manufacturing firms. Because FIDES allocations are assigned to states through a rule that divides national VAT receipts according to the states' population, territorial expansion, and initial level of development, and as that rule has remained stable since the fund was created by law in 1993, changes in FIDES expenditures come from the interaction between the parameters of the allocation rule and changes in national revenues. This effect is exogenous at the state level and also generates sufficient variation over time to allow us to estimate its effect on firm-level productivity.

The estimates in tables 3.1 and 3.2 indicate an elasticity of productivity with respect to public capital investment of 0.32–0.4. Economically, this is a very significant effect. In 2001, the ratio of the stock of public capital to GDP was 0.615, so that the estimated effects would imply a short-run rate of return to infrastructure investment of 0.52–0.65 and a long-run rate of return (i.e., the partial derivative of steady-state income to changes in infrastructure spending) of 0.80. This evidence suggests that cutting investment in infrastructure does appear to be a very bad deal both from a fiscal viewpoint, since it erodes the potential growth of the tax base, as well as from the perspective of society as a whole, since infrastructure seems to be an investment with very high rate of return.[7]

In figure 3.2, we use the 0.32 elasticity estimate to simulate what the economy's path of non-oil GDP would have been, according to equations (1) and (2), if the

Table 3.7   "Voting with feet" specification, fixed effects

Dependent variable	Change in productivity					
FIDES	0.5298 (2.75)***	0.5218 (2.71)***	0.4762 (2.42)**	0.4828 (2.46)**	0.4544 (2.31)**	0.1916 −0.78
FIDES investment in neighboring states	−0.5111 −1.59	−0.4807 −1.5	−0.479 −1.49	−0.489 −1.52	−0.4833 −1.51	−0.4396 −1.37
capital share (rK/wL+rK)	— —	−0.0159 −0.13	−0.0144 −0.12	−0.0132 −0.11	−0.0122 −0.1	−0.2311 −0.81
Development (manuf. VA/PIB)	— —	— —	0.0001 −1.14	0.0001 −1.13	0.0001 −1.15	0.0007 (1.97)**
Residents (percent ownership of residents)	— —	— —	— —	0.0015 (2.03)**	0.0015 (2.02)**	−0.0024 −1.42
Export (exports/ production)	— —	— —	— —	— —	−0.0994 (1.83)*	0.1437 −1.57
FIDES · capital share	— —	— —	— —	— —	— —	0.2019 −0.84
FIDES · development	— —	— —	— —	— —	— —	−0.0004 −1.62
FIDES · residents	— —	— —	— —	— —	— —	0.0037 (2.53)**
FIDES · export	— —	— —	— —	— —	— —	−0.5956 (3.25)***
Constant	−4.3538 −0.77	−6.2092 −0.95	−6.0041 −0.96	−0.4257 −0.98	−0.3988 −0.91	−0.1632 −0.36
N	5,675	5,669	5,669	5,668	5,668	5,668
R^2	0.0751	0.0757	0.076	0.0769	0.0777	0.083

NOTE: Absolute value of t-statistic in parentheses. All specifications include time dummies.

*Significant at 10%
**Significant at 5%
***Significant at 1%

public capital stock had stayed constant at its 1983 value. The simulated capital stock is higher than the historical capital stock for two reasons: the direct effect of the increase in the public capital stock, equal to βdp_i, and an indirect effect through its effect on capital accumulation, which we take to react with an elasticity of $1/(1-\alpha)$, where α is the capital share. The effects are striking. We find that per capita GDP would be 37 percent higher than its present value if the public capital stock had not declined. It would still be less than its 1978 peak, but only by 12 percent instead of the actual 36 percent. Our exercise thus suggests that the decline in the public capital stock is an important part of the explanation for the Venezuelan economic collapse.[8]

Table 3.8 "Voting with feet" specification, Arellano–Bond

Dependent variable	Productivity					
Lagged productivity	0.3442 (8.80)***	0.348 (8.87)***	0.3453 (8.81)***	0.344 (8.80)***	0.3437 (8.80)***	0.3363 (8.70)***
FIDES	0.3152 (3.50)***	0.318 (3.52)***	0.30783885 (3.41)***	0.3083 (3.42)***	0.3063 (3.40)***	0.168 (1.32)
FIDES investment in neighboring states	-0.16492594 (0.86)	-0.1682992 (0.88)	-0.15061875 (0.79)	-0.1630877 (0.85)	-0.1694711 (0.88)	-0.09189913 (0.48)
Capital share (rK/wL+rK)	—	-0.18012674 (1.58)	-0.17633621 (1.54)	-0.17715374 (1.55)	-0.17343446 (1.52)	-0.43545166 (2.38)**
Development (manuf. VA/PIB)	—	—	0.00012318 (1.27)	0.00012577 (1.30)	0.00012741 (1.32)	0.0001788 (0.90)
Residents (percent ownership of residents)	—	—	—	0.00097897 (1.53)	0.00096736 (1.52)	-0.00062327 (0.59)
Export (exports/production)	—	—	—	—	-0.12421198 (1.35)	0.13453269 (2.11)**
FIDES · capital share	—	—	—	—	—	0.27258674 (1.96)*
FIDES · development	—	—	—	—	—	-0.00002104 (0.17)
FIDES · residents	—	—	—	—	—	0.00158699 (1.73)*
FIDES · export	—	—	—	—	—	-0.62186498 (3.14)***
Constant	-0.1017 (3.48)***	-0.1039 (3.55)***	-0.1012 (3.49)***	-0.1001 (3.45)***	-0.0981 (3.38)***	-0.1048 (3.65)***
N	5366	5359	5359	5358	5358	5358
Sargan test of overidentifying restrictions	0.110	0.112	0.118	0.120	0.123	0.161
Arellano–Bond test that average autocovariance in residuals of order 1 is 0	0.000	0.000	0.000	0.000	0.000	0.000
Arellano–Bond test that average autocovariance in residuals of order 2 is 0	0.111	0.131	0.132	0.127	0.130	0.199

NOTE: Absolute value of t-statistic in parentheses. All specifications include time dummies. Last three rows list p-values for rejection of null hypothesis in each of the three tests.

*Significant at 10%
**Significant at 5%
***Significant at 1%

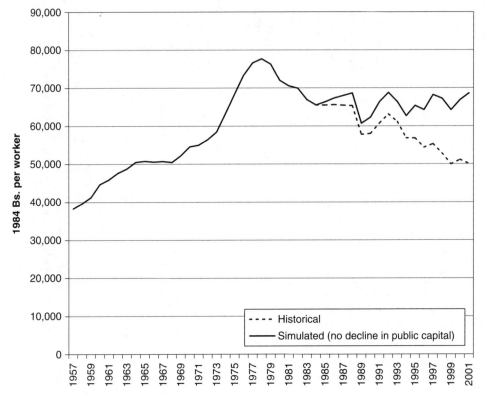

Fig. 3.2 Historical and simulated per worker GDP, scenario of no decline in infrastructure investment

APPENDIX

The Nonlinearity of the Fides Allocation Rule

The state's share of FIDES resources is allocated is calculated according to the following formulas:

$$FID_{it} = 0.15 \times VAT_t \left[0.45 \times \frac{POP_{it}}{\sum\limits_i POP_{it}} + 0.10 \times \frac{L_i}{\sum\limits_i L_i} + 0.45 \times CI_{it} \right] \quad (A.1)$$

and

$$CI_{it} = \frac{1}{\left[\dfrac{LA_{it} + S_{it} + F_{it}}{\sum\limits_{i=1}^{N} LA_{it} + S_{it} + F_{it}} \right]} + (1 - HDI_{it}). \quad (A.1')$$

Let VAT_t represent national VAT collection at time t, POP_{it} state I's population at time t, L_i state i's land area, LA_{it} its receipts of transfers from the Special Economic Allocations Fund, S_{it} its receipt of transfers from the Situado Constitucional, HDI_{it} its Human Development Index (which is between 0 and 1), and F_{it} its receipts from the part of FIDES that is allocated according to population and land area, and LA_{it} refer to resources disbursed according to the Special Economic Allocations Law of 1996.

Mathematically, thus, these allocations are disbursed according to

$$
LA_{it} = \begin{cases} 0.7 \times .25 \times ROY_{it}\left(.7\dfrac{OIL_{it}}{\sum\limits_{i\in O} OIL_{it}} + .2\dfrac{POP_{it}}{\sum\limits_{i\in O} POP_{it}} + .05\dfrac{L_i}{\sum\limits_{i\in O} L_i} + .05\dfrac{REF_{it}}{\sum\limits_{i\in O} REF_{it}} \right) & \text{if } i \in O \\[3em] 0.3 \times .25 \times ROY_{it}\left(.9\dfrac{POP_{it}}{\sum\limits_{i\notin O} POP_{it}} + .05\dfrac{L_i}{\sum\limits_{i\notin O} L_i} + .05\dfrac{REF_{it}}{\sum\limits_{i\notin O} REF_{it}} \right) & \text{if } i \notin O, \end{cases}
$$

$$\text{(A.2)}$$

with OIL_{it} and REF_{it}, respectively, denoting oil and refining production in state i at time t, and O denoting the set of oil-producing states.

Again, the mathematical expression is

$$
SIT_{it} = 0.2 \times (VAT_t + NVAT_{it})\left(0.3\frac{1}{23} + 0.7\frac{POP_{it}}{\sum\limits_{i}^{N} POP_{it}} \right).
$$

$$\text{(A.3)}$$

F_{it} is just a shorthand notation for capturing the fraction of FIDES resources that are allocated based on population and land area:

$$
F_{it} = .015 \times VAT_t\left(0.45\frac{POP_{it}}{\sum\limits_{i}^{N} POP_{it}} + 0.10\frac{L_i}{\sum\limits_{i}^{N} L_i} \right)
$$

$$\text{(A.4)}$$

To see how the bulk of the variation in a state's share actually comes from the interaction between the highly nonlinear function (A.1), denote s_{it} the share of FIDES VAT resources allocated to state i at time t. Note that

$$
\frac{ds_{it}}{dNVAT_{it}} = 0.45\left(-\frac{\left(.2\left(.3\frac{1}{23} + .7pop_{it} \right) \right)\left[\sum\limits_{i=1}^{N}(LA_{it} + S_{it} + F_{it}) \right]}{(LA_{it} + S_{it} + F_{it})^2} + \frac{\left(.2\left(.3\frac{1}{23} + .7pop_{it} \right) \right)}{(LA_{it} + S_{it} + F_{it})} \right)
$$

$$
= n(pop_{it}, l_i, oil_{it}, ref_{it}, O_i, NVAT_t, VAT_t, ROY_t),
$$

with lowercase letters denoting a state's proportional share

$$\left(pop_{it} = \frac{POP_{it}}{\sum\limits_{i=1}^{N} POP_{it}} \right).$$

This derivative differs from state to state, despite the fact that it is a response to a national-level shock. Therefore it provides us with a source of variation in public investment that is both exogenous at the state level and not collinear with a pure time effect. What is relevant for the purposes of identification is that this variation emerges from the interaction with national variation in revenues, which is exogenous at the state level, and a rule whose parameters have been unchanged since its adoption. Essentially, our variation is the result of an interaction between national-level shocks (to value-added tax revenues, non-value-added tax revenues, and oil royalties) and a nonlinear allocation rule. It is this variation between state expenditure levels as a response to national-level shocks that we will use to identify the effect of FIDES-financed increases in public expenditures on productivity. A similar reasoning applies to the derivative of s_{it} with respect to value-added tax revenues VAT_t and oil royalties ROY_t:

$$\frac{ds_{it}}{dROY_{it}} = 0.45 \left(\left(-\frac{((.7 \times .25(.7oil_{it} + .2pop_{it} + .05l_i + .05ref_{it})))\left[\sum\limits_{i=1}^{N}(LA_{it} + S_{it} + F_{it})\right]}{(LA_{it} + S_{it} + F_{it})^2} \right) + \frac{1}{LA_{it} + S_{it} + F_{it}} \left(\begin{array}{l} (.7 \times .25(.7oil_{jt} + .2pop_{jt} + .05l_j + .05ref_{jt})) \ if \ i \in O \\ + (.3 \times .25(.9pop_{jt} + .05l_j + .05ref_{jt})) \ if \ i \notin O \end{array} \right) \right) \Leftrightarrow i \in O$$

$$\frac{ds_{it}}{dROY_{it}} = 0.45 \left(\left(-\frac{((.7 \times .25(.9pop_{it} + .05l_i + .05ref_{it})))\left[\sum\limits_{i=1}^{N}(LA_{it} + S_{it} + F_{it})\right]}{(LA_{it} + S_{it} + F_{it})^2} \right) + \frac{1}{LA_{it} + S_{it} + F_{it}} \left(\begin{array}{l} (.7 \times .25(.7oil_{jt} + .2pop_{jt} + .05l_j + .05ref_{jt})) \ if \ i \in O \\ + (.3 \times .25(.9pop_{jt} + .05l_j + .05ref_{jt})) \ if \ i \notin O \end{array} \right) \right) \Leftrightarrow i \notin O$$

$$= r(pop_{it}, l_i, oil_{it}, ref_{it}, (1 - hdi)_{it}, O_i, NVAT_t, VAT_t, ROY_t)$$

$$\frac{ds_{it}}{dVAT_{it}} = 0.45\left(-\frac{\left(.2\left(.3\frac{1}{23} + .7pop_{it}\right)\right)\left[\sum_{i=1}^{N}(LA_{it} + S_{it} + F_{it})\right]}{(LA_{it} + S_{it} + F_{it})^2} + \frac{\left(.2\left(.3\frac{1}{23} + .7pop_{it}\right)\right)}{(LA_{it} + S_{it} + F_{it})}\right)$$

$$+ 0.45\left(-\frac{(.15(.45pop_{it} + .10l_i))\left[\sum_{i=1}^{N}(LA_{it} + S_{it} + F_{it})\right]}{(LA_{it} + S_{it} + F_{it})^2} + \frac{(.15(.45pop_{it} + .10l_i))}{(LA_{it} + S_{it} + F_{it})}\right)$$

$$= n(pop_{it}, l_i, oil_{it}, ref_{it}, O_i, NVAT_t, VAT_t, ROY_t).$$

More Detailed Explanation of the Empirical Strategy

The Olley–Pakes methodology consists of three steps. In the first step, we estimate the production function semiparametrically as a function of the capital stock, the number of workers and the years of the firm (k_{it}, l_{it}, a_{it}), and private investment c_{it}. The basic idea is that since investment is an increasing function of productivity, then controlling for private investment will allow us to recover a consistent estimate of the coefficient on l_{it}. In the second step we estimate the probability of survival as a nonparametric function of k_{it}, a_{it}, and c_{it}. Using this estimate of the probability of survival, we can control for selection bias effects and estimate the production function coefficients on k_{it} and a_{it} by nonlinear least squares.

Taking first differences of (2) and using (3) and (4) gives us

$$\omega_{it} - \omega_{it-1} = \beta n_{i0} - \beta\delta\eta_i - \beta\delta\omega_{it-1} + \beta\gamma f_{it} + \beta(n_{it} - n_{i0}) + \varepsilon_{it} + (1 - \beta\delta)\varepsilon_{it-1}. \quad \text{(B.1)}$$

Equation (B.1) tells us that changes in productivity are a combination of four terms: a firm-specific fixed effect $\beta n_{i0} - \beta\delta\eta_i$; a "convergence" effect $- \beta\delta\omega_{it-1}$ that depends on the initial level of productivity and is caused by the depreciation of public infrastructure; the effect of FIDES investment, captured by $\beta\gamma f_{it}$; and a linear combination of white-noise terms $\beta(n_{it} - n_0) + \varepsilon_{it} + (1 - \beta\delta)\varepsilon_{it-1}$ that can be treated as a sole disturbance. This gives rise to the specification we will present in the text,

$$\omega_{it} = a_0 + a_1\omega_{it-1} + a_2 f_{it} + \chi_i + v_{it}, \quad \text{(B.2)}$$

where the expected value of a_2 equals $\beta\gamma$ and is positive, and

$$v_{it} = \beta(n_{it} - n_0) + \varepsilon_{it} + (1 - \beta\delta)\varepsilon_{it-1}.$$

Note that f_{it} is uncorrelated with the error term v_{it}, so that a_2 can be estimated consistently by panel methods as long as the fixed effect χ_i is differenced away. Note also from the definition of v_{it} that the disturbance in this regression will be autocorrelated.

Equation (B.2) represents a dynamic panel that can be estimated by the techniques of Arellano and Bond (1991). An alternative and simpler specification arises if we are willing to assume that the depreciation rate of public infrastructure is negligible. Here (B.1) becomes

$$\omega_{it} - \omega_{it-1} = b_0 + b_2 f_{it} + \chi_i + v_{it}, \qquad \text{(B.3)}$$

which can be estimated through conventional panel estimators, provided that a correction for autocorrelation is made.

NOTES

1. This decline is not a result of asset sales to the private sector. Venezuela was one of the least aggressive privatizers in the regions during the nineties. Only two large state-owned enterprises were sold to the private sector: the state telecommunications firm, which was sold for $955 million in 1991, and the state-owned airline VIASA, which was sold for $145 million the same year, and which was later dismantled. Adjusting for these two sales makes no appreciable difference to our public capital stock series.

2. The Situado Constitucional is a rule for distributing among local and state governments one-fifth of total government revenues, 80 percent of which goes to state governments (the rest going to municipal governments). In all, 30 percent of these revenues are distributed among states in equal parts while the rest are distributed proportional to population. The Special Economic Allocations Fund (LAEE) provides for states to receive 25 percent of government revenues derived from royalties on oil production. Three oil-producing states (Anzoátegui, Monagas, and Zulia) receive 70 percent of the revenues assigned according to LAEE, whereas the remaining twenty states divide the other 30 percent. The main distinction between LAEE and FIDES is that the former is much more targeted in the type of investment projects that can be financed through it. (A second distinction is that the approval and supervision of projects occurs within the Ministry of Interior and Justice and not by an autonomously run entity like FIDES, making standards much laxer).

3. The Human Development Index is calculated at the state level by the National Institute of Statistics in collaboration with the United Nations Development Programme, using information on life expectancy, literacy, education enrollment, and per capita income (purchasing power parity adjusted).

4. Equations (A.1)–(A.3) in the appendix make clear that there are a number of sources of variation of FIDES allocations. These include state-level populations, oil royalties, oil refining and production, and the diverse components of the state's Human Development Index. In practice, the variation in population shares and state-level HDIs from year to year is minor.

5. The importance of these effects is the main reason we do not follow an IV strategy in this chapter, and prefer to estimate the reduced form coefficient of productivity on FIDES investment. Attempts to instrument realized FIDES expenditures with budgeted expenditures yielded strong evidence of non-excludability of the instrument.

6. This effect could be due to the fact that FIDES investment is allocated to more local (small) type projects decided by the state governments.

7. In this regard, it is important to mention that the very high rate of returns could be due to the fact that this was a relatively new investment program at the state level, but as this type of investment increases over time this could have reduced the very high rate of return. For example, Fernald 1999 showed that this was the case for the road investment in the United States before and after 1973.

8. There are two important caveats to this calculation. To the extent that the elasticity of productivity to the public capital stock is different in manufacturing than in the rest of the economy, this calculation may give an inaccurate estimate of the counterfactual scenario of a constant public capital stock. The second one is that this calculation takes our estimated parameters as estimates of β, which could in reality be smaller if $\gamma > 1$.

REFERENCES

Arellano, Manuel, and S. Bond. 1991. "Some Tests of Specification for Panel Data: Monte Carlo Evidence and an Application to Employment Equations." *Review of Economic Studies* 58 (2): 277–97.

Arrow, K., and M. Kurz. 1970. *Public Investment, the Rate of Return, and Optimal Fiscal Policy.* Baltimore: Johns Hopkins University Press.

Aschauer, D. A. 1989. "Does Public Capital Crowd Out Private Capital?" *Journal of Monetary Economics* 24 (2): 171–88.

Banco Central de Venezuela. Various years. *Anuario de Cunetas Nacionales.* Caracas: Banco Central de Venezuela.

Baptista, Asdrúbal. 2006. *Bases cuantitativas de la economía venezolana.* Caracas: Fundación Polar.

Calderón, César, and Luis Servén. 2003a. "Macroeconomic Dimensions of Infrastructure in Latin America." Policy Research Working Paper 5317, World Bank and Development Research Group, Washington, D.C.

———. 2003b. "The Output Cost of Latin America's Infrastructure Gap." In *The Limits of Stabilization: Infrastructure, Public Deficits, and Growth in Latin America*, edited by William Easterly and Luis Servén, 95–118. Washington, D.C.: World Bank.

Canning, D. 1999. "Infrastructure's Contribution to Aggregate Output." Policy Research Working Paper 2246, World Bank, Washington, D.C.

Devarajan, S., V. Swaroop, and H. Zou. 1996. "The Composition of Public Expenditure and Economic Growth." *Journal of Monetary Economics* 37 (2/3): 313–44.

Easterly, William. 1998. "When Is Fiscal Adjustment an Illusion?" Policy Research Working Paper 2109, World Bank, Washington, D.C.

Easterly, W., and S. Rebelo. 1993. "Fiscal Policy and Economic Growth. An Empirical Investigation." *Journal of Monetary Economics* 32 (3): 417–58.

Easterly, William, and Luis Servén, eds. 2003. *The Limits of Stabilization: Infrastructure, Public Deficits, and Growth in Latin America.* Washington, D.C.: World Bank.

Esfahani, H. S., and M. T. Ramírez. 2003. "Institutions, Infrastructure, and Economic Growth." *Journal of Development Economics* 70 (2): 443–77.

Fernald, J. G. 1999. "Roads to Prosperity? Assessing the Link between Public Capital and Productivity." *American Economic Review* 89 (3): 619–38.

FIDES (Fondo Intergubernamental para la Descentralización). 2005. "Ley que Crea el Fondo Intergubernamental para la Descentralización." http://www.oas.org/juridico/spanish/ven_res47.pdf.

Holtz-Eakin, D. 1994. "Public Sector Capital and the Productivity Puzzle." *Review of Economics and Statistics* 76 (1): 12–21.

Hulten, C., and R. A. Schwab. 1991. "Is There Too Little Public Capital?" Paper presented at the American Enterprise Institute Conference on Infrastructure and Policy Options for the 1990s, Washington, D.C., February 4.

Levinsohn, J., and A. Petrin. 2003. "Estimating Production Functions Using Inputs to Control for Unobservables." *Review of Economic Studies* 70 (2): 317–41.

Ministerio de Energía y Minas. Various years. *Petróleo y Otros Datos Estadísticos*. Caracas: Ministerio de Energía y Minas.

Munnell, A. H. 1990. "Why Has Productivity Growth Declined? Productivity and Public Investment." *New England Economic Review*, January/February, 3–22.

Ogura, S., and G. Yohe. 1977. "The Complementarity of Public and Private Capital and the Optimal Rate of Return." *Quarterly Journal of Economics* 91 (4): 651–62.

Olley, Steve, and Ariel Pakes. 1996. "The Dynamics of Productivity in the Telecommunications Equipment Industry." *Econometrica* 64 (6): 1263–98.

Programa de las Naciones Unidas para el Desarrollo. 2002. *Informe sobre Desarrollo Humano en Venezuela, 2002: Las tecnologías de la información y la comunicación al servicio del desarrollo*. Caracas: Programa de las Naciones Unidas para el Desarrollo.

Rodríguez, Francisco. 2004. "Un nuevo índice encadenado del producto interno bruto de Venezuela, 1957–2001." *Revista BCV* 18 (2): 99–118.

Tatom, J. A. 1991. "Should Government Spending on Capital Goods Be Raised?" *Federal Reserve Bank of St. Louis Review*, March/April, 3–15.

World Bank. 1988. *World Development Report*. Washington, D.C.

4 THE INCIDENCE OF LABOR MARKET REFORMS ON EMPLOYMENT IN THE VENEZUELAN MANUFACTURING SECTOR, 1995–2001

Omar Bello and Adriana Bermúdez

The Venezuelan labor market has been overregulated through time. There had been many modifications in regulations that increased labor cost in Venezuela during the period 1995–2001. Bermúdez (2006) showed the impact on labor cost of each of those regulations. In this chapter, we provide evidence on the incidence of labor regulations on employment in the manufacturing sector in Venezuela. We used a panel data set processed by Pineda and Rodríguez (2006), from the Venezuelan Manufacturing Sector Survey, for the 1995–2001 period. During the second half of 1997 important changes in labor regulations took place, which fully hit home in 1998. We studied the effect of such changes on employment in that sector. Like Gruber (1997) we averaged the variables in our data set for two periods: 1995–97 and 1998–2001. We performed that procedure for both a balanced panel of firms, and an unbalanced panel of firms. Using those averages, we estimated regression in differences for blue-collar workers, for white-collar workers, and for all workers. In order to avoid a problem of endogeneity in our estimations, we used different labor regulation cost indices calculated by Bermúdez (2006). Our results indicated that the cost of labor regulations had a negative effect between the aforementioned periods. Those effects are greater for blue-collar workers than for white-collar workers.

We are grateful to Guillermo Cruces, Ricardo Hausmann, Joyce Jacobsen, Ramon Pineda, Francisco Rodríguez, and participants in the Venezuelan Economic Growth, 1970–2005 conference held in April 2006 at the Center for International Development, Harvard University, for helpful comments.

An important feature of Venezuela's labor market is that several changes in regulations took place in the last thirty years.[1] The case of Venezuela should be interesting to labor economists worldwide because: (1) the principal indicators of performance show a significant deterioration; (2) the structural labor reforms in Venezuela have not been studied empirically; (3) some of the regulations have been changed much more frequently than in other countries;[2] and (4) some of those changes could cause distortions in the allocation of resources in the economy, since they were not applied uniformly to all sectors or firms.

During the last thirty years, Venezuela experienced disappointing labor market results. The real average wage has been declining sharply since 1980. In 2003, the real average wage was Bs. 865 (bolivars), whereas in 1980 the average real wage was Bs. 3,499.[3] Over time, minimum wages have become more binding (since the difference between the average wage and median wage has diminished with respect to the minimum wage), thus a larger portion of Venezuelan workers are earning wages at or below the level of minimum wages.[4] Despite the drop in real wages, the unemployment trend has been increasing since 1980. Another sign of the deterioration of the labor market is the sharp decrease in the formality rate since 1993.[5]

What factors caused the deterioration in the Venezuelan labor market? A potential explanation lies in the regulatory framework. There are very few studies, however, due to the limited data availability about mandatory labor cost and regulations. In this direction, Márquez and Pagés (1998) and Orlando (2001) have documented the effects of some of those regulations, in terms of the impact on labor cost at a single point in time for the Venezuelan case. Those authors show that interventions in the labor market caused a difference between wage and marginal cost of labor. Márquez and Pagés calculated that in 1994, the yearly cost of a worker earning the minimum wage was 118 percent greater than the annual wage, while for a worker earning ten minimum wages that figure was 46 percent higher than the wage. Orlando, using the 1997 labor regulatory legal framework, estimated that the yearly labor cost for a worker with five years of tenure was 73 percent higher than annual wage.

Several studies that try to create indices that capture the cost of labor regulations are done for a cross-country comparison using one or two observations by country. Generally, those indices are not a measure of the price of labor facing firms at different stages of the business cycle. Examples of such studies are Márquez and Pagés (1998), Botero et al. (2003), the World Bank (2006), and Heckman and Pagés (2000, 2003). In all these studies it is found that Venezuela has some of the most burdensome and expensive labor regulations in place when compared with Latin American countries and the rest of the world. In the first three studies, the indices of labor regulations give an ordinal instead of a cardinal measurement by assigning values between zero and one to some components of the regulations and then averaging them. The resulting indices are sensitive to the weights assigned to each component. Heckman and Pagés's studies construct a direct cost—measured as a fraction of monthly wages—of complying with the job security and social security regulations, but omit other components of labor cost.

Other studies that try to measure the costs of the labor regulations are Immervoll (2007) for the OECD countries, and Tokman and Martinez (1999) for Mexico, Colombia, Argentina, Chile, Brazil, and Peru. These papers include almost all aspects of labor cost but for a few points in time. More studies have been done to create time series indicators of the cost of labor regulations for other countries, such as Saavedra and Torero (2003) for the Peruvian case, Edwards and Edwards (2000) and Montenegro and Pagés (2003) for the Chilean case, and Cardenas and Bernal (2003) for the Colombian case. However, some of these studies focus on particular aspects of the labor costs, such as payroll taxes, job security costs, and wages, while leaving others out.

In order to understand the magnitude of the reforms in Venezuela and to generate indicators for labor regulations and labor cost, Bermúdez (2006) described, analyzed, and quantified in detail the changes in labor laws and regulations for the period 1975–2005. Those regulations include several minimum wage changes and a few mandated general wage increases for some sectors; changes in payroll taxes such as INCE (Instituto Nacional de Capacitación Educativa), social security, unemployment insurance, and national housing policy contributions; the introduction and modification different bonuses such as vacation bonus, child-care bonus, participation in the firm's profit bonus, and indexed and several non-indexed bonuses; and changes in some direct dismissal costs such as advance notice, seniority payments, and severance payments.[6] Notice that those changes in regulations are exogenous variations to firms' labor costs.

She found that all these labor regulations in Venezuela have been designed in such a way that they made the process of hiring and firing workers for large firms costlier and more difficult when compared with smaller firms. For example, as a result of all these changes in regulations, non-wage-labor costs have been increasing, especially for large firms. While in 1972 these kind of firms had to pay a total tax equivalent to 5.35 monthly wages to cover the non-wage-labor cost of a year of labor services, in 1992 that rate increased to 8.98 monthly wages, and by 2002 it was equivalent to 9.81 monthly wages. Summarizing, Bermúdez found that the Venezuelan labor market has been heavily regulated since 1974, that the reforms have increased non-wage-labor cost especially for bigger firms, that some of the changes implied drastic structural changes in labor cost, and that the mandated labor cost implied by those regulations has been increasing over time, as shown by a comprehensive labor cost index.

The rest of this chapter is organized as follows. In the next section we explain the changes in labor regulation that took place between 1995 and 2001 and construct an index that takes into account all those modifications to the legal framework. The most important change during this period was in 1997, when a reform of the Labor Law[7] took place that changed seniority and severance payments as well as the concept of wage used in the calculation of those costs. Additionally, because of that reform, some mandated bonuses started to be considered as wages, so they began to figure in the calculation of several payments and payroll taxes. Further, during this period, in 1999, a different indexed food bonus was established that has been representing about 45 percent of the minimum wage cost for firms with more than fifty workers. That bonus is used as an income-complementing mechanism that does not have any impact on other labor costs. Also during this period there were some changes in payroll taxes. Next, we will explain how to construct an index that takes into consideration all those modifications in labor regulations.

In the third part, we will review some facts on Venezuela's manufacturing sector and claim that the poor performance (in terms of declining numbers of establishments and employment) is due partially to the distortions that labor regulations have created. The differences in the cost structure between different firm sizes is so important that it is possible that these differences encouraged firm downsizing, the exiting of big firms, and the entry of new firms at suboptimal scales, or at scales of production that do not allow Venezuelan firms to keep pace internationally and nationally with foreign competitors.[8] Thus we can expect that this distortion of labor cost by firm size is encouraging job destruction and informality, hindering the creation of jobs, and hampering economic growth.

In the fourth section, we answer two questions: (1) Has the increase in labor cost during the period 1995–2001 had any impact on manufacturing sector employment in Venezuela? and (2) Has the employment effect been equal for blue- and white-collar employees?

For that purpose, we used a panel data set from the Venezuelan Manufacturing Sector Survey (VMSS) processed by Pineda and Rodríguez (2006)[9] for the 1995–2001 period.[10] Following Gruber (1997), we averaged the variables on our data set for two periods: 1995–97 and 1998–2001. We performed that procedure for both, a balanced and an unbalanced panel of firms. Using those averages, we estimated regression in differences for blue-collar workers, for white-collar workers, and for all workers, using firm employment as a dependent variable and average wages and other controls as independent variables. In order to avoid an endogeneity problem in our estimations, we used different labor regulation cost indices calculated in second section following Bermúdez (2006), which are independent of employers' choices. Our results show that (1) the labor cost regulations affected manufacturing sector employment outcome, and (2) the effect is greater for blue-collar workers. Finally, we present some concluding remarks.

Labor Market Reforms in Venezuela During the Period 1995–2001

The main features of Venezuela's labor regulation are in the Labor Law and its ruling statutes.[11] Additionally, there have been quite a bundle of other regulations such as decrees, statutes, and Supreme Court rulings that have affected labor cost throughout time. The most important elements of labor costs affected through labor regulations during the period 1995–2001 were minimum wages, mandated bonuses, and job security costs.

Minimum Wages and Non-indexed Mandated Bonuses

In Venezuela, wage setting through decrees was rarely used between 1974 and 1985, but since 1985 it has been used annually. In fact, between 1995 and 2001, every year, with the exception of 1995, the minimum wage was increased by a government decree. The minimum wage has been set at different levels for different kind of workers (e.g., apprentices, concierges), and also it has been set differently for different kind of sectors (urban vs. rural). Since 2000, it also has been differentiated by firm size, so the firms that employ up to twenty workers pay a minimum wage that is lower than the one set for firms that employ twenty-one or more workers.

Very often these annual minimum-wage increases have used the consumer price index of the previous year. During the same period, however, the average manufacturer price index has been lower than the average consumer price index; thus, for the manufacturing sector, the relative increase in real minimum wages has been more pronounced than for other sectors in the economy.[12]

The government has also increased wages progressively at some points in time. For example, in 2000, it was mandatory for employers in the private urban sector with more than twenty workers to increase wages by 15 percent for those employees who earned no more than Bs. 500,000, and to increase wages by 10 percent for those workers who earned no more than Bs. 700,000.

In order to complement wage revenues with other types of income, Venezuelan governments intensively used the policy of mandated bonuses such as transportation bonuses or food bonuses per workday, especially during those periods following sharp macroeconomic drops (i.e., the 1994 financial crisis). This policy was designed in such a way that it did not have an impact on severance payments, seniority premiums, any other payroll tax, or any other labor cost directly related to the wages (vacation bonus, workers participation in a firm's profit, etc.).

The labor statutes have regulated not only minimum wages but also the concept of wage. This is extremely important since it defines the amount to be used to calculate other labor costs, especially the seniority and severance payments. One of the most important structural changes in the reform of the Labor Law carried out during 1997 came from the definition of what should be considered as wages. Since June 1997, firms had to include other bonuses current at that time (government mandated[13] or mutually arranged) within the concept of wage, and therefore it affected other non-wage-labor costs.

Figure 4.1 shows the real minimum wage (using the manufacturing price index) for firms with between one and twenty workers and for firms with twenty-one or more workers, as well as the minimum mandated monthly payment per firm size once we add the mandated non-indexed bonuses for those workers

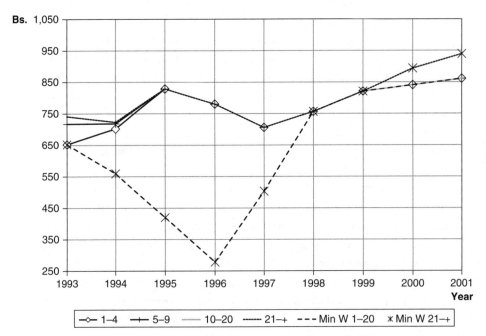

Fig. 4.1   Labor payments versus minimum wage per firm size: Real bolivars per month (MPI base 1997)

Source: Based on Bermúdez 2006.

Note: Labor payments = minimum wages + non-indexed bonuses.

earning minimum wages. Even though the change in the monthly payments between 1996 and 1998 was not very extreme, that was not the case for the jump in real minimum wages during the same period, given the fact that the government-mandated bonuses began to form an integral part of the minimum wage.[14]

To have an idea of the potential impact of this change in the definition of wage, it is important to note that on June 18, 1997, a worker earning a minimum monthly urban wage of Bs. 22,020 should have also received an additional monthly income of Bs. 52,980 from mandated bonuses.[15] So, the total monthly income earned by this worker should have been Bs. 75,000, of which only 22,020 should have been used to calculate the rest of the labor cost.[16] Taking into account that 70.6 percent of the total monthly income was previously excluded from the wage used to calculate other non-wage-labor costs and then abruptly had to be included, the effect of this change on employment should have been negative given the magnitude of the shock it created on the other labor costs, at least for those earning the minimum wage or near it.

Two other important changes relating to the wage concept were introduced with the new 1997 Labor Law. First, it established an explicit limitation of 20 percent on the percentage of additional monthly earnings that employers could pay to workers—for example, through mutually arranged bonuses—without affecting the rest of labor cost, and an amount at least equivalent to the minimum wage should always be considered completely within the concept of wage.[17] Second, it modified the concept of wage to be used for the specific calculation of severance and advance notice payments in the case of dismissal for unjustified reasons.[18]

The minimum wage has had an increasing importance in Venezuela's wage distribution. Compared to other Latin American countries, Venezuela's minimum wage has been more binding.[19] Using data from the Venezuela's Household Survey, figure 4.2 shows that the minimum wage has been more binding for blue-collar workers than it has for white-collar workers. Notice the change in those ratios since 1997.

For example, during the first half of 1996, the ratio median wage to minimum wage for blue-collar workers was 1.52 and for white-collar workers it was 2.12, which means that for the period about 50 percent of the blue-collar workers were earning wages at or below 1.52 minimum wages, whereas 50 percent of the white-collar workers were been paid wages at or below 2.12 minimum wages. After 1997, 50 percent of the blue-collar workers were earning wages at or below 1 minimum wage, and 50 percent of the white-collar workers were being paid wages at or below 1.5 minimum wages. After 1997, more workers were earning wages near the minimum wages than did so during the period 1994–97.

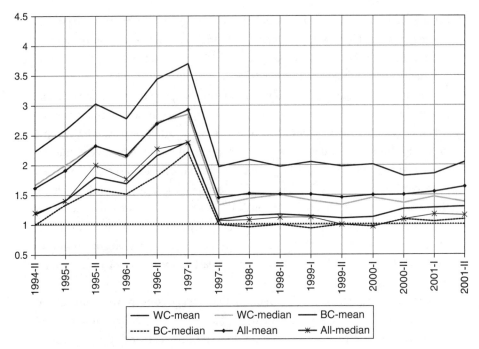

Fig. 4.2 Mean and median wage relative to minimum wage

Source: Based on authors' calculations based on Venezuelan Households Surveys.

Note: WC = white-collar worker; BC = blue-collar worker. Calculations for full-time private employees aged 15–65 and using minimum wage for a firm size 1–20 in the urban sector. I refers to the first semester and II to the second.

Binding wage floors could have a significant influence on wage distribution and the costs faced by employers. There is a broad consensus[20] that employment is likely to be reduced if minimum wages are set "too high." High wage floors could create significant employment barriers, in particular for low-productivity workers, with young people being more vulnerable. Payroll taxes and social contributions paid by the employer cannot be passed on to minimum-wage workers by lowering their remuneration with binding—and enforced—wage floors. But employers might be able to shift taxes paid for minimum-wage workers to higher-earning workers by lowering their wages.

To the extent that minimum wages could cause labor costs and worker productivity to become misaligned, then they will probably result in lower employment for the groups that initially were supposed to benefit by it. Freije (2003) found evidence of this. Using Venezuela's Household Survey, he found that workers whose initial salary was below the new minimum wage were more likely to become unemployed or leave the labor force than were workers whose initial wage was above the new minimum wage. Also, he found that workers in the formal sector had a higher probability of unemployment than did workers in the informal sector due to changes in minimum wages.[21]

Immervoll (2007) and Tokman and Martinez (1999) show that in order to alleviate the costs of employing low-productivity workers, a number of countries have implemented measures to restrain non-wage-labor costs specifically for workers whose wages are at or close to the legal minimum. However, that has not been the case for Venezuela: as we will explain, total taxes and contributions paid for minimum-wage workers have been increasing sharply, particularly after 1996.

Mandated Indexed Bonuses

During the period under analysis, Venezuela had a complex system of mandated bonuses, which was not applied to all firms in the same magnitude or at the same time. Mandated bonuses can be classified as non-indexed and indexed bonuses. The former included subsidies to specific goods and services in nominal terms, so if the government does not make further increases, the purchase capacity of those bonuses would quickly be eroded by the inflationary process. Some examples of these types of bonuses were the Decrees 617, 1240, and 1824, which in 1997 were integrated into the minimum wage.

Indexed bonuses included those that are automatically adjusted each time a new mandatory minimum wage is set, or each time that a tributary unit (TU)[22] is reset at the beginning of each year, based on the inflation of the previous year. They can have important implications for employers' expectations about labor costs in the future. Examples of such bonuses are the per-child day-care bonus—indexed using minimum wages—established in 1992, and the 1998 worker's indexed food bonus.

The latter[23] created the obligation for firms with fifty-one or more employees, and the workers who benefited from this new program were those who earned up to two minimum wages, losing the benefit when they earned at least three minimum wages. This regulation should have affected a high proportion of workers since in the second half of 1998, approximately 60 percent of workers in the formal sector earned wages at or below two minimum wages.[24]

Other indexed bonuses were already in place during the period 1995–2001 that did not go through any legal reform per se. However, the structural change in the definition of wages and the new minimum wage significantly increased the cost of labor as these bonuses were calculated as a function of wages, especially for workers earning minimum (or near minimum) wages. One of these bonuses was the child-care bonus. This regulation established a child-care bonus per child—for those between zero and five years old—whose parents earned a monthly wage that was equal or inferior to the equivalent of five times the national minimum wage, if and only if they worked at a company that hired more than twenty workers. The bonus per child would be the equivalent of 38 percent of the minimum wage. Instead of paying the child-care bonus, the affected firms had the option of establishing, financing, and maintaining a children's day-care center where the children benefited would be handled. Clearly, this regulation increased the labor cost of those workers with small children relative to those workers who did not have any.

The other two bonuses affected by the definition of wages—and in particular minimum wages—were the vacation bonus and the participation in firm's end of the year profit bonus. The vacation bonus ranged between seven to twenty-two days equivalent of daily wages depending on the worker's tenure. The participation in the firm's profit bonus fluctuated from 15 days to 120 days of daily wages depending on the firm's size and the fraction of the year that the employee actually worked at the firm.[25]

Therefore the drastic modification in minimum wages also increased these mandated bonuses that were in place in 1997, increasing the relative cost of unskilled workers, especially minimum-wage workers. This distortion was aggravated with the introduction of the indexed food bonus. On the other hand, its introduction, together with the expansion in the child-care bonus, increased the labor cost differences by firm size that might have encouraged large firms to downsize—or stop increasing the payroll—even further after 1998.

Payroll Taxes

In Venezuela, the payroll taxes are as follows: the INCE contribution,[26] social security, unemployment insurance, and the national housing program. Table 4.1 shows the main determinants of the labor cost of each of these programs. The social security statute is the most important in terms of the payroll cost, given that it has the highest nominal rate, which in turn depends on the risk of the firm.[27]

The tax rate shown in table 4.1 for social security is a contribution used to finance social insurance for labor-related accidents, maternity leave, medical care, and retirement pensions, while unemployment insurance is regulated in a separate norm. The important changes made to payroll taxes during the period 1995–2001 have to do with the nominal tax rate of the unemployment insurance and the maximum taxable wages. The interaction between the nominal tax rate and the maximum taxable wage is important, since that determines the actual effective tax rate on labor for these concepts, for different levels of wage.

Table 4.1 Payroll tax policy, 1995–2001

	From dd/mm/yy	Employer (%) rate			Employee (%) rate	Maximum taxable monthly wage
		Min. risk	Med. risk	Max. risk		
Social security						
All employers	07/01/93	9	10	11	4	5 minimum urban wages
	06/21/97	9	10	11	4	5 × 75,000 Bs.
	05/01/99	9	10	11		5 × 90,000 Bs.
By TSJ decision on 04/27/2000	04/28/00	9	10	11	4	5 × 15,000 Bs.
INCE						
Firms with five or more employees	01/08/70	2	2	2	0.5% of annual participation of profits	none
National housing program						
All employers	03/15/94	2	2	2	1	15 minimum wages
	06/21/97	2	2	2	1	15 × 75,000 Bs.
	11/05/98	2	2	2	1	none
Unemployment insurance						
All employers	07/01/93	1.70	1.70	1.70	0.50	5 minimum urban wages
	06/21/97	1.70	1.70	1.70	0.50	5 × 75,000 Bs.
	04/19/99	1.70	1.70	1.70	0.50	20 × 75,000 Bs.
	05/01/99	1.70	1.70	1.70	0.50	20 × 90,000 Bs.
	10/22/99	1.70	1.70	1.70	0.50	5 × 90,000 Bs.
By TSJ decision on 04/27/2000	04/23/00	1.70	1.70	1.70	0.50	5 × 15,000 Bs.
	07/01/00	2.00	2.00	2.00	0.50	20 × 15,000 Bs.

The provisional norm in the Labor Law reform of 1997 regarding the wage to be used for the calculation of payroll taxes affected the maximum taxable wage, returning it to a specific monetary value instead of a changing monetary norm.[28] That value was changed four times: Bs. 15,000 by the 1997 Labor Law; Bs. 75,000 and Bs. 90,000 by two "special laws" in 1997 and 1999; and Bs. 15,000 again by a TSJ decision in 2000.[29] These modifications created a divergence between the effective rates and the nominal rates during 2000–2002.[30] They also affected the maximum taxable wage for the national housing program and the unemployment insurance system.

During most of the period 1995–99, the total nominal payroll tax to be paid for workers that earned near the minimum wage was stable and equal to the total effective rate, except during 2000 and 2001 when the TSJ decided in favor of the plaintiff, and reverted to the "five times Bs. 15,000" rule (nominal), which was clearly low compared to the existent minimum urban wages during those years: Bs. 132,000 and Bs. 145,000, respectively. Thus, during the period 1995–99, the total nominal payroll tax rate for a medium-risk firm with more than five employees was 15.7 percent, and it increased to 15.85 percent and 16 percent for 2000 and 2001, respectively. However, the effective total payroll rates decreased from 15.7 percent in 1999 to 12.3 percent and 10.58 percent for 2000 and 2001, respectively, as a result of the TSJ decision.

Job Security Costs

The most important reform carried out through the modification of the Labor Law in 1997 had to do with job security costs. Venezuelan labor laws include three different employer costs in order to terminate a labor relationship: the advance notice period, the seniority fee, and an indemnity fee.

The 1997 Labor Law significantly increased the number of months to be paid for total seniority, which must be paid no matter the grounds for ending the labor relationship or who initiates it. The number of months to be paid for the concept of "indemnity" was kept the same up to five years of tenure, but it decreased sharply for higher level of tenure under the 1997 law. On the other hand, the new labor law modified the concept of wages to be used in the calculation of each of the elements of the job security cost. So in general, the 1997 law increased job security costs for workers with up to five years of tenure, but reduced them only partially for those workers with tenure levels above five years compared with the 1990 law. (See the appendix for a deeper explanation of these changes.)

Following Bermúdez (2006), we estimated the job security costs for both cases—unjustified dismissal and quitting—by firm size. Results show that the increase in the expected job security costs due to the 1997 Labor Law reform was important. Whereas in 1994, a firm with nine employees expected to pay 2.59 monthly wages for job security costs to a minimum-wage worker with one year of tenure, during 1999 that value increased to 2.94 monthly wages (a 13 percent increase). A firm with more than 101 workers expected to pay 3.2 monthly wages for job security costs in 1994 for the same worker, while in 1999 it expected to pay 3.72 monthly wages, a 16.25 percent increase.

The reform made it more difficult for firms in general to adjust to labor demand as this reform tended to increase job security costs—in particular for low levels of tenure—but it especially hindered labor demand adjustments for big firms. By avoiding worker movements from less to more productive units, this microeconomic inflexibility reduces aggregate output and slows down economic growth. Caballero, Engel, and Micco (2004) measured the microeconomic flexibility for the manufacturing sector by the speed at which establishments reduce the gap between their labor productivity and the marginal cost of such labor. The longer the persistency of the gap through time, the more inflexible the economy was at the microeconomic level. They found that Venezuela was the most inflexible among five Latin American country economies, having slightly over 53.9 percent of adjustment within a year.[31] They also found that, with the exception of Venezuela, large establishments (above the 75th percentile of workers) were substantially more flexible than small establishments (below the median number of workers).[32] Caballero and colleagues (2004) found that labor market regulations,[33] and particularly job security regulations, are among the institutional factors that reduce microeconomic flexibility by increasing adjustment costs. Job security regulations increase the costs of dismissals when firms experience negative shocks and, consequently, these regulations reduce the rate of firings during those periods. During good times, however, given the difficulties of adjusting labor demand, the optimal employment response to a positive shock is also being reduced; thus the overall effect is a reduction in the speed of adjustment to shocks.

Quantifying the Effects of Labor Reforms on Minimum Mandated Labor Cost

We have seen that in Venezuela during the period 1995–2001 there have been many changes in regulations that increased labor cost; however, we have analyzed each one partially. Thus there are important questions to answer: (1) How much has labor cost increased as a consequence of changes in regulations? (2) Has the increase in labor cost had any impact on the manufacturing sector employment level in Venezuela? (3) Has the employment effect been equal for all types of workers? In order to answer these questions, we need to have an indicator of mandated labor cost through time.

For our estimations, we use an indicator of expected mandated labor cost (IEMLC) that takes into account all aspects of the labor costs we have discussed (see Bermúdez 2006). Such an indicator is a time series quantitative index of the mandated cost for the urban sector by firm size and by worker type for the 1995–2001 period. The IEMLC is an index based on the real monetary cost of labor regulations. In order to create the index, the author chose a representative employee for empirical purposes: the urban worker[34] with one year of tenure earning a minimum wage. Notice that (1) those wages are binding in Venezuela's labor market, especially in the private sector, given that a high proportion of workers earn near minimum wages; and (2) during the period 1995–98, the median tenure ranged between one and two years for private workers. The IEMLC is different depending on firm size.

From the analysis of the labor regulations, we found that the statutes have created different costs for different firm sizes, and have also differentiated the cost of employees depending on the number of children 0–5 years old that each worker has. The total annual cost of a worker with one year of tenure is calculated as follows:

> Total annual expected cost = Gross annual minimum wages + mandated non-indexed bonuses + payroll taxes + participation in firm's profit bonus + vacation leave + vacation bonus + 0.5 total unjustified dismissal cost + 0.5 quitting cost + indexed food bonus (depending on firm size) + child-care bonus × # children under five years old (depending on firm size).

Figure 4.3 shows the IEMLC, depending on firm size, assuming that (a) the worker does not have any children under five years old, and (b) he has one child under five years old. The real values are presented using the average manufacturing price index (base 1997); however, for econometric purposes those values will vary for different subsectors within the manufacturing industry by using each subsector price index.

There is an important change in the total expected annual cost of a minimum-wage worker in 1996 for all firm sizes. During the period 1997–2001, the total real cost of a minimum wage worker increased drastically when compared with the amounts paid during the period 1993–96, especially for firms with more than twenty-one employees. On the other hand, the non-wage cost associated with regulations for those firms has significantly increased labor cost given that the vertical distances between minimum wages and total annual expected cost have been widening.

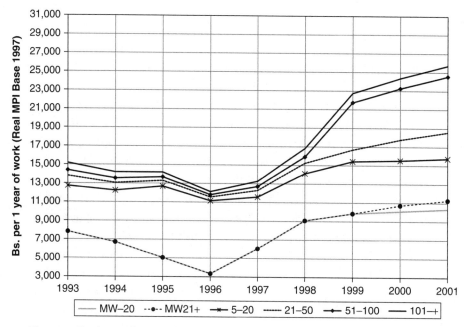

Fig. 4.3a   Total annual expected cost versus legal minimum wage for different firm sizes

Source: Based on Bermúdez 2006.

Note: The total annual expected cost is for a minimum wage urban worker who does not have any children under five years old. MW = minimum wage.

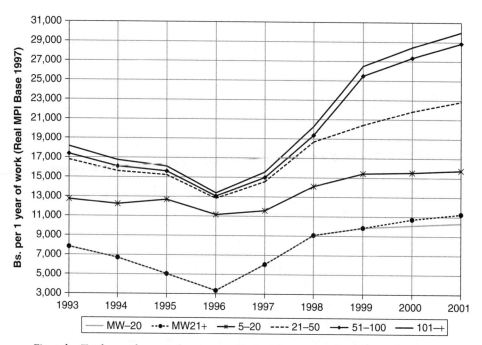

Fig. 4.3b   Total annual expected cost versus legal minimum wage for different firm sizes

Source: Based on Bermúdez 2006.

Note: The total annual expected cost is for a minimum-wage urban worker who has one child under five years old. MW = minimum wage.

Assuming that none of the workers has children under five years old, the differences in the cost structure between different firm sizes is so important that it is possible these differences are encouraging firm downsizing, the exiting of big firms, and the entry of new firms at suboptimal scales, or at scales of production that do not allow Venezuelan firms to compete internationally and nationally with foreign competitors. Thus we could expect that this distortion of labor cost by firm size encouraged job destruction and informality, and that it hindered the creation of jobs and hampered economic growth.

Further, when we compare the annual cost of hiring a worker with children under five years old, it is clear that the cost to the employer is proportional to the worker's family load for firms with more than twenty-one workers. Thus it is very possible that the child-care bonus policy creates another distortion by which employers are discouraged to hire more than twenty-one workers, workers of childbearing age, workers with a big family load, or workers who potentially could become beneficiaries of this policy (i.e., workers who earn under five minimum wages). Therefore, this policy might well end up increasing inequality and hurting those whom the laws were trying to protect.

These indicators of the effects of labor reforms on the mandated total labor cost of a minimum-wage worker by firm size, as well as the minimum wage and job security costs, will be used in the next section to estimate the impact of these reforms on labor demand in the manufacturing sector for continuing firms during the period 1995–2001.

Venezuela's Manufacturing Sector: Some Facts

In the last thirty years, the Venezuelan labor market has been characterized by a decrease in real wages, an increase in unemployment, and a relative reduction of the formal sector. Consistent with the fall in per capita GDP and productivity reported by Hausmann and Rodríguez (2006) and Bello and Restuccia (2002), the real average wage has been declining sharply since 1980. In 2003, the real average wage was Bs. 865, whereas in 1980 the average real wage was Bs. 3,499.[35] Through time, minimum wages have become more binding since the gaps between the average wage and the median wage with respect to the minimum-wage level have shortened. Therefore, a larger portion of Venezuelan workers are earning wages at or below the level of minimum wage. Despite the drop in real wages, the unemployment trend has been increasing since 1980. Another sign of the deterioration in the labor market is given by the sharp decrease in the formality rate since 1993.

Outcomes of the manufacturing sector have not been the exception, as is shown by the Venezuelan Manufacturing Sector Survey (VMSS).[36] The observational unit of this survey is the establishment in the manufacturing sector with more than five workers; thus it does not include the manufacturing firms in the informal sector. Establishments are classified in four categories depending on the number of workers they are hiring: large industry (LI) are establishments with more than one hundred workers; medium industry (MI) are establishments with fifty-one to one hundred workers; small industry (SI), those establishments that employ twenty-one to fifty workers; and very small industry (VSI), establishments are those that hire between five and twenty workers.

The VMSS interviewed all establishments that belong to the MI and LI strata. For the remaining groups, the VMSS used sampling techniques. The aggregate data of the VMSS shows that between 1991 and 2003 the employment level has been declining sharply.

Employment in the manufacturing sector in 2003 was 58.18 percent of the maximum of the period. A net job loss took place in each of the different categories when we compare the extreme points of the period under analysis. For the LI group, maximum employment was attained in 1988. In 2003, the number of workers in this category represented 57.18 percent of this period's maximum employment. For the MI group, employment grew until 1979, and the 2003 employment represented 61.49 percent of the 1979 level. For the SI, the maximum employment was achieved in 1991, and by 2003 it represented only 55.42 percent of that level. It is important to note that the group that experienced an abrupt increase in the employment level was the VSI in 1996;[37] however, this group also experienced a persistent decline in employment after that year, so that employment during 2003 was only 39.12 percent of that achieved at its 1996 peak.

Similar to employment the number of plants decreased over 1975–2003 period. In the case of the LI, the number of plants peaked in 1991, reaching 979 establishments. In 2003 it was 57 percent of that maximum; that figure was 63.14 percent for the MI. Notice that the group that concentrated the most firms is the VSI. On average, during the 1975–2003 period, 67.36 percent of the firms belonged to that sector. However, on average, the VSI produced 6.3 percent of total manufacturing production. Therefore, production per firm is very low in this sector. On the other hand, that figure for the LI was 79.78 percent. The net entering in the VSI has not compensated for the net exit of establishments in the LI, MI, and SI groups; thus the number of jobs destroyed in the manufacturing sector since 1991 has been outstanding.[38] Whereas in 1991 there were 10,539 establishments operating in the formal manufacturing sector generating 498,712 jobs, in 2003 the number of establishments was 5,970 generating only 290,171 jobs. Thus 4,569 establishments exited the market, destroying 208,541 jobs.

So, during the 1975–2004 period, the manufacturing industry job losses were related to firm destruction. Consistent with this fact, Bartelsman, Haltiwanger, and Scarpetta (2004) found that the net employment decrease in the Venezuelan manufacturing sector for the period 1995–2000 was mostly due to the exit of firms; 66.66 percent of the gross job losses were explained by firms exiting the market, and 33.33 percent were explained by continuing firms shedding jobs. Loayza, Oviedo, and Servén (2005) found evidence that strict labor regulations tend to increase informality because they generally reduce firms' ability to adjust to economic shocks and therefore distort firms' decisions about entry, exit, expansions, and downsizing, and also distort decisions related to hiring and firing. Firms might switch to the noncompliant informal sector or might decide to downsize trying to avoid these regulations, thus remaining in relatively suboptimal size, losing economies of scale and scope. On the other hand, if regulations are too binding, they could drive firms out of the market, destroying jobs in the long run. These distortions have an impact on economic growth and productivity, as seen in a cross-country study: the higher the level of labor regulation, the bigger the size of the informal sector, while the larger the size of the informal sector, the slower economic growth will be.

A potential and partial explanation for the entry–exit behavior of firms within different group sizes might lie in the distortions created by the disparities in the labor cost structures between different groups.[39] This could be illustrated by calculating the differences in the minimum-mandated total labor cost for a year of service of a minimum wage worker between different combinations of group sizes, expressed as percentages (see fig. 4.4). Thus, for example, in 2001 a firm in the LI (group I) had to pay 70 percent more for a year of service of this type of worker than what a firm in the VSI (group IV) would have had to pay to the same worker. As we can see, the minimum mandated labor cost differences between group sizes became more pronounced after 1990 and exploded after 1998.

The higher the ratio of labor cost of one group—for example, group I—with respect to the other group—group II—the stronger the incentives to downsize or to exit the market for firms in group I, ceteris paribus. These forces come from the fact that firms in group I will compete in the national and international markets with domestic firms—and possibly international firms—with labor cost structures more unfavorable than the one experienced by firms in group II. Thus, in order to survive, the firms will need to downsize or finally be driven out of the market.

As a percentage of employment in the formal sector, employment in the manufacturing sector (reported by the VMSS) decreased in importance between 1975 and 2002. In 1975 it represented 15.24 percent of total formal employment. In 2003, that figure was 6.27 percent. For 1995 and 2001, those figures were 11.28 percent and 6.88 percent, respectively.

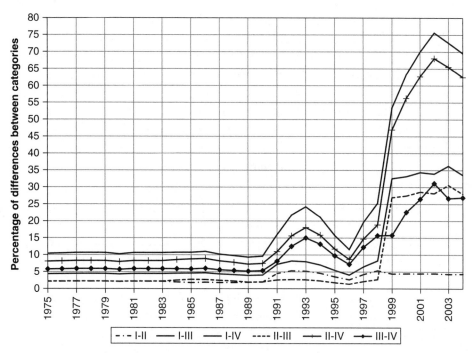

Fig. 4.4   Differences between the annual labor cost per firm size

Source: Based on Bermúdez 2006.

Note: I = firms with 101 + workers; II = firms with 51–100 workers; III = firms with 21–50 workers; IV = firms with 5–20 workers.

Between 1995 and 2001, the reduction in employment was very similar to the decrease experienced by the number of plants for all groups. When we compare the changes in employment and number of plants averages between the 1995–97 period and the 1998–2001 period, for the LI group the reduction in employment was 18.2 percent while plant reduction was 18.9 percent; for the MI group those figures were 15.3 percent and 17 percent; for SI group they were 18.5 percent and 18 percent; and for the VSI they were 23.3 percent and 23.4 percent.

Estimations

We used panel data from the VMSS processed by Pineda and Rodríguez (2006) for the period 1995–2001. From this data set, we gathered information on employment (E_{it}), production (Y_{it}), total labor cost (TLC_{it}) and its components (wage and salary) (W_{it}), other payments, (OP_{it}), and complementary costs (CC_{it}). Other payments include earnings for working overtime, profit sharing, special bonuses, provision for severance payments caused during the year, and other compensations. Complementary costs include INCE payments, and employer contribution to workers' social security and retirement funds. As mentioned before, the VMSS has information at the firm level; it does not have any information at the individual level, but it contains information for the blue-collar worker group and the white-collar worker group. An important feature of this data set is that it has information on the producer price index by sector at a three-digit level of aggregation. We use it to express labor costs and production in real terms. Using those price indices introduces an additional source of variation to the data: the industrial activity of the firm.

In addition to that, we use five variables as indicators of changes in labor regulations: (1) minimum wages, (2) seniority payments (quitting cost), (3) total unjustified dismissal cost (which includes seniority payments, advance notice, and indemnity payments for unjustified dismissal), (4) other costs, and (5) the total annual expected cost derived above.[40]

Those real annual costs (expressed as indices) were calculated on the assumption that a worker is earning the minimum wage. They reflect exogenous changes to firms' labor cost, which are based on changes in the labor regulatory framework, so they are correlated with labor costs but are not correlated with the error term. Those indices were calculated depending on the classification based on firm size from the VMSS. Therefore, they have three dimensions of variation: time, firm size, and the industrial activity of the firm.

As we discussed above, in 1997 two important changes in labor regulations took place: (1) the mandated bonuses became part of wages, and (2) the legislation related to the severance and seniority payments was modified. Notice that the former is the base for payments in (2), and for payroll taxes. Therefore (1) and (2) were two different sources of variation for severance and seniority payments. Notice also that 1998 was the first full year those changes took place.

We would like to estimate the effects of those changes on employment on the manufacturing sector. In order to do that, we implemented the following empirical strategy. We averaged each variable over the periods 1995–97 and 1998–2001.[41] We ended up with two time observations for each firm in our panel. We used two panels to average the data, a balanced one and an unbalanced one. In the first, we included only firms that were surveyed in each of the seven-year periods. This panel had 670 firms. In the other one, we used an unbalanced panel of 2,578 firms, including those with at least one observation for each of the different periods, 1995–97 and 1998–2001. We took the averages using only the years in which the firms were surveyed. Notice there is no information for at least one year for a fraction of them in our panel. A firm might not appear on the survey due to a sampling error or because it exited the market. Regarding this case, if a firm closed in 2000, we averaged the 1998 and 1999 observations, and then saw what happened with its employment decision. In other words, we processed the data in a way that the panel includes only firms that were surveyed in at least one year of the first period, 1995–97, and that were surveyed in at least one year in the period 1998–2001. We did not deal with firms' exit decisions on the understanding that this depended on a wider scope of variables than labor regulations. We dealt only with the effects of labor regulations on employment. Additionally, taking averages in this way has a potential advantage; it could help to reduce errors in variables (Wooldridge 2002), and it allows us to avoid the problem of not having data for some years for a number of firms. After that, we take first differences of the variables in our data set.

As was mentioned before, the VMSS is a census for the LI and MI strata. For the remaining groups, a random sampling technique is used. So for the SI and VSI groups, a firm might not be surveyed because it is no longer operating[42] or may be omitted due to random sampling. In the balanced panel, as we expected, firms from the LI and MI groups are overrepresented. In fact, 93.7 percent of the firms in the balanced panel belong to those strata.[43] We conducted our first set of estimations using a balanced panel.

The technique we used to process the data is similar to the work of Gruber (1997), who estimated the change in the Chilean labor market outcomes due to an exogenous decrease in employer payroll taxes caused by the privatization of Chile's social security system. His results indicate that the incidence on employment of this policy was not statistically significant, but the incidence on wages was negative and statistically significant.

We estimated the following regressions separately for all workers, for blue-collar workers, and for white-collar workers,[44] as follows:

$$\Delta\log(E_i) = \beta_0 + \beta_1 \cdot \Delta\log(W_i) + \beta_2 \cdot \Delta\log(Y_i) + \varepsilon_I \qquad (4.1)$$

$$\Delta\log(E_i) = \beta_0 + \beta_1 \cdot \Delta\log(CC_i) + \beta_2 \cdot \Delta\log(Y_i) + \varepsilon_I \qquad (4.2)$$

$$\Delta\log(E_i) = \beta_0 + \beta_1 \cdot \Delta\log(OP_i) + \beta_2 \cdot \Delta\log(Y_i) + \varepsilon_I \qquad (4.2)$$

$$\Delta\log(E_i) = \beta_0 + \beta_1 \cdot \Delta\log(TLC_i) + \beta_2 \cdot \Delta\log(Y_i) + \varepsilon_I \qquad (4.2)$$

We do not use a time subscript in (4.1)–(4.4) because after we differenced the data we end up with one observation per firm. In the context of a panel data with time dimension equal to two, a first-difference regression is equivalent to estimate a fixed effects model. Notice that any of the cost measures in equations (4.1)–(4.4) are affected by exogenous changes in labor regulations as well as endogenous decisions by the firms about employment because they depend on the number of employees, and also because they depend on the type of contract offered to new employees. If we use data on those costs from the VMSS, there is a potential endogeneity problem. Instead of those costs, therefore, we use the IEMLC derived from the changes in labor regulations that we explained above.

Using the averages from the balanced panel, we estimate separate regressions for blue-collar workers, for white-collar workers, and for all workers. Those estimations are reported in tables 4.2–4.4. For the case of all workers, the estimated coefficients for all labor regulation indices, except for "other cost index," were negative and statistically significant,[45] even in the case that we control for the difference of "real production." In the case of the blue-collar workers, all coefficients were statistically significant and they have the expected signs, with the exception of the "other cost" index. It is important to notice that the estimated coefficients for the "total labor cost index" are equal to the estimated coefficient for the "minimum wage." In the case of the white-collar workers, none of the coefficients for the labor regulation indices was statistically significant.

The regressions using the averages from the unbalanced panel are reported in tables 4.5–4.7. As is shown in table 4.6, for blue-collar workers during the two periods under consideration, each kind of labor regulation indices, except for the "other costs" index,[46] has a negative and statistically significant effect on average employment. Notice that the response for the "unjustified dismissal cost" index was greater than the response for the change of the "real minimum wage" index. When we add as a regressor—in any of those specifications—the difference of the average of "real production" in order to compensate for changes in employment due to changes in production in terms of sign and statistical significance, the parameters are very similar to the results in table 4.5. For all cases, the estimated coefficient for the "real production" variable is positive and statistically significant. In three out of five specifications, the coefficients related to labor regulations are bigger—in absolute value—in the unbalance panel than in the balance panel, while at the same time the coefficient of "real production" is smaller.

For the case of white-collar workers, the estimated coefficients for the "unjustified dismissal" and "seniority" payments are statistically significant and with the expected negative sign, whereas the estimate for the difference of "other costs" has a wrong sign (positive). As before, the slope for the "real production" is statistically significant and it shows a positive relationship. In this case, the coefficient for the difference of the "real minimum wage" is not statistically significant.

Table 4.2   Dependent variable: Δ log of number of workers (balanced panel)

Δ log of real total labor cost index	-0.14 (0.03)***	-0.12 (0.03)***	—	—	—	—	—	—	—	—
Δ log of real unjustified dismissal cost index	—	—	-0.08 (0.01)***	-0.07 (0.01)***	—	—	—	—	—	—
Δ log of real seniority cost index	—	—	—	—	-0.09 (0.01)***	-0.04 (0.01)***	—	—	—	—
Δ log of real minimum-wage cost index	—	—	—	—	—	—	-0.14 (0.02)***	-0.13 (0.02)***	—	—
Δ log of real other costs index	—	—	—	—	—	—	—	—	0.01 (0.31)	-0.001 (0.004)
Δ log of real production	—	0.14 (0.02)***	—	0.12 (0.02)***	—	0.14 (0.02)***	—	0.13 (0.02)***	—	0.14 (0.02)***
Number of observations	670	670	670	670	670	670	670	670	670	670
F p-value	0	0	0	0	0	0	0	0	0.750	0

NOTE: Standard errors in parentheses.

***Significant at 1%
**Significant at 5%
*Significant at 10%

Table 4.3 Dependent variable: Δ log of number of blue-collar workers (balanced panel)

	(1)	(2)	(3)	(4)	(5)	(6)	(7)	(8)	(9)	(10)
Δ log of real total labor cost index	-0.16 (0.08)**	-0.15 (0.08)*	—	—	—	—	—	—	—	—
Δ log of real unjustified dismissal cost index	—	—	-0.09 (0.03)***	-0.08 (0.03)***	—	—	—	—	—	—
Δ log of real seniority cost index	—	—	—	—	-0.1 (0.03)***	-0.08 (0.03)***	—	—	—	—
Δ log of real minimum-wage cost index	—	—	—	—	—	—	-0.16 (0.06)***	-0.14 (0.06)***	—	—
Δ log of real other costs index	—	—	—	—	—	—	—	—	0.053 (0.10)	0.04 (0.10)
Δ log of real production	—	0.14 (0.05)***	—	0.14 (0.05)***	—	0.14 (0.05)***	—	0.13 (0.05)***	—	0.15 (0.05)***
Number of observations	670	670	670	670	670	670	670	670	670	670
F p-value	0.043	0.002	0.026	0.001	0.002	0	0.003	0	0.596	0.01

NOTE: Standard errors in parentheses.

***Significant at 1%
**Significant at 5%
*Significant at 10%

Table 4.4 Dependent variable: Δ log of number of white-collar workers (balanced panel)

Δ log of real total labor cost index	−0.02 (0.06)	−0.01 (0.06)	—	—	—	—	—	—	—	—
Δ log of real unjustified dismissal cost index	—	—	−0.04 (0.02)*	−0.03 (0.04)	—	—	—	—	—	—
Δ log of real seniority cost index	—	—	—	—	−0.04 (0.03)	−0.04 (0.03)	—	—	—	—
Δ log of real minimum-wage cost index	—	—	—	—	—	—	−0.04 (0.04)	−0.03 (0.04)	—	—
Δ log of real other costs index	—	—	—	—	—	—	—	—	0.1 (0.07)	0.09 (0.03)
Δ log of real production	—	0.12 (0.04)***	—	0.12 (0.04)***	—	0.12 (0.04)***	—	0.12 (0.04)***	—	0.12 (0.04)***
Number of observations	670	670	670	670	670	670	670	670	670	670
F p-value	0.160	0.006	0.145	0.003	0.086	0.002	0.315	0.005	0.219	0.004

NOTE: Standard errors in parentheses.

***Significant at 1%
**Significant at 5%
*Significant at 10%

Table 4.5 Dependent variable: Δ log of number of workers (unbalanced panel)

Δ log of real total labor cost index	-0.08 (0.02)***	-0.08 (0.02)***	—	—	—	—	—	—	—	—
Δ log of real unjustified dismissal cost index	—	—	-0.15 (0.02)***	-0.13 (0.02)***	—	—	—	—	—	—
Δ log of real seniority cost index	—	—	—	—	-0.1 (0.01)***	-0.09 (0.01)***	—	—	—	—
Δ log of real minimum-wage cost index	—	—	—	—	—	—	-0.09 (0.02)***	-0.08 (0.02)***	—	—
Δ log of real other costs index	—	—	—	—	—	—	—	—	-0.05 (0.02)**	-0.01 (0.02)**
Δ log of real production	—	0.15 (0.06)***	—	0.13 (0.05)**	—	0.13 (0.05)**	—	0.08 (0.06)***	—	0.05 (0.06)**
Number of observations	2,023	2,023	1,883	1,883	1,883	1,883	2,023	2,023	2,023	2,023
F p-value	0	0	0	0	0	0	0	0	0	0

NOTE: Standard errors in parentheses.

***Significant at 1%
**Significant at 5%
*Significant at 10%

Table 4.6 Dependent variable: Δ log of number of blue-collar workers (unbalanced panel)

Δ log of real total labor cost index	-0.27 (0.00)***	-0.25 (0.00)***	—	—	—	—	—	—	—	—
Δ log of real unjustified dismissal cost index	—	—	-0.22 (0.00)***	-0.20 (0.00)***	—	—	—	—	—	—
Δ log of real seniority cost index	—	—	—	—	-0.15 (0.03)**	-0.14 (0.00)***	—	—	—	—
Δ log of real minimum-wage cost index	—	—	—	—	—	—	-0.06 (0.05)**	-0.14 (0.00)***	—	—
Δ log of real other costs index	—	—	—	—	—	—	—	—	0.01 (0.29)	-0.01 (0.86)
Δ log of real production	0.12 (0.03)***	—	—	0.06 (0.03)***	—	0.04 (0.03)***	—	0.03 (0.03)***	—	0.12 (0.03)***
Number of observations	2,578	2,578	2,578	2,578	2,578	2,578	2,578	2,578	2,578	2,578
F p-value	0.001	0	0.005	0	0.004	0	0.03	0	0.772	0.05

NOTE: Standard errors in parentheses.

***Significant at 1%
**Significant at 5%
*Significant at 10%

Table 4.7 Dependent variable: Δ log of number of white-collar workers (unbalanced panel)

	(1)	(2)	(3)	(4)	(5)	(6)	(7)	(8)	(9)	(10)
Δ log of real total labor cost index	-0.02 (0.73)	-0.05 (0.30)	—	—	—	—	—	—	—	—
Δ log of real unjustified dismissal cost index	—	—	-0.12 (0.00)***	-0.11 (0.03)**	—	—	—	—	—	—
Δ log of real seniority cost index	—	—	—	—	-0.07 (0.02)***	-0.06 (0.05)*	—	—	—	—
Δ log of real minimum-wage cost	—	—	—	—	—	—	-0.02 (0.15)	-0.03 (0.11)	—	—
Δ log of real other costs index	—	—	—	—	—	—	—	—	0.52 (0.05)**	0.04 (0.07)*
Δ log of real production	—	0.03 (0.00)***	—	0.08 (0.01)**	—	0.08 (0.02)**	—	0.03 (0.00)***	—	0.04 (0.00)***
Number of observations	2,578	2,578	2,578	2,578	2,578	2,578	2,578	2,578	2,578	2,578
F p-value	0.7303	0.008	0.013	0.006	0.02	0.008	0.149	0.006	0.002	0.007

NOTE: Standard errors in parentheses.

***Significant at 1%
**Significant at 5%
*Significant at 10%

It could indicate that wages and other labor costs for the white-collar workers are not moving similarly to the minimum-wage variation. It differs from the case of the blue-collar worker regressions, where the minimum wage was statistically significant in explaining employment changes.

Concluding Remarks

The Venezuelan labor market has been overregulated through time. In Venezuela, during the period 1995–2001 several changes in regulations increased labor cost. We show the impact on labor cost of each of those regulations. The findings in this chapter suggest that the changes in cost regulations that took place in the second half of 1997, and fully expressed in 1998 data, had a negative effect on manufacturing sector employment, especially for blue-collar workers. The estimated coefficients for the labor regulation indices for blue-collar workers regressions have the expected negative sign and were statistically significant for both the balanced and unbalanced panels. This was not the case for the white-collar regressions in the balanced panel; however, in the unbalanced panel the coefficients for seniority payments and the unjustified dismissal cost index were negative and statistically significant for this type of worker. Notice that blue-collar workers earned wages closer to the minimum wage than did white-collar workers. Bear in mind that all labor regulation indices were calculated using a worker earning the minimum wage as a representative agent. We expect that the Venezuelan labor market had been affected by those regulations, yet the generalization of our results to the whole economy must be considered with care because the data came from the manufacturing sector, and the panel data set overrepresents firms from the LI and MI strata.

APPENDIX: JOB SECURITY COST CHANGES INTRODUCED BY THE 1997 ORGANIC LABOR LAW

Venezuelan labor laws include three different employer costs in order to terminate a labor relationship: the advance notice period, the seniority fee, and an indemnity fee.[47] In general, the party wanting to end the labor relationship has to give the other party an advance notice period, which depends on a worker's tenure; if it is not given, the party that ends the relationship has to pay the other party an amount equal to the forgone wages during the advance notice period. The advance notice has been asymmetrical between workers and employers.

The advance notice period is a function of tenure that: (1) a worker who quits for unjustified reasons[48] has to give his employer; (2) an employer has to give the worker in the case of firing for economic, technological, or unjustified reasons;[49] and (3) an employer has to give to the worker in the case the firing is found by a court to be unjustifiable, or which can just paid by the employer to avoid going to court in the first place.[50]

The 1997 Labor Law significantly increased the number of months to be paid for total seniority, which has to be paid no matter the grounds for ending the labor relationship or who initiates it. The total number of monthly wages that a worker should have accumulated by the end of the labor relationship depends on tenure.

The seniority partial deposits have to be accumulated into an individual account earning an interest regulated by the central bank. Whereas the 1990 law established that partial deposits were to be made on an annual basis, the 1997 law established it on a monthly basis.

If the dismissal is unjustified, or a court qualifies it as unjustified, or if the employer dismisses a worker and wants to avoid a court procedure, the employer has to pay an indemnity fee. The number of months to be paid for the concept of "indemnity" was kept the same for up to five years of tenure, but it decreased sharply for higher level of tenure under the 1997 law. With the new law, the total number of months to be paid under unjustified dismissal increased the number of months to be paid compared with the previous regulation in place. But this simple comparative analysis is not completely satisfactory; while the total 1990 amount had to be paid using the last wage earned by the worker, under the 1997 law only a portion of it had to use the last wage.

Under the 1990 Labor Law, the wage used to calculate the total payments for seniority and the indemnity was the wage in place one month before the date in which the labor relationship ended. If the employer had made the partial annual deposits at the time of separation, he had to recalculate the principal again and pay the difference. This ruling made the cost associated with the seniority and indemnity payments very volatile, unpredictable, and uncontrollable for the employer, especially in times of high inflation, such as 1996. The main objective pursued by the labor reform of 1997 was to change the timing of the wage to be used in the calculations, reducing the unpredictability of those payments in the future.

On the other hand, the new labor law modified the concept of wages to be used in the calculation of each of the elements of the job security cost. Thus a simple comparison of monthly wages is misleading because we also have to take into account the wage used for the calculations, the timing of that wage, and the periodicity of the deposits, which in turn affects interest payments. There have been some regulatory changes in these aspects as well that make the direct comparison between the different laws more difficult. Additionally, the fact that job security payments also take into consideration the participation in the firm's profits creates a difference in the job security payments as regards different firm sizes, even if the monthly wages were the same.

In order to compare the job security costs derived from each law, our approach is to calculate the equivalent monetary value of each one for different tenure levels using a specific time series of wages, following Bermúdez (2006). We took the monthly series of minimum wage and the mandated interest rate for seniority payments for the period 1975–2005 and calculated what would have been the job security cost—for two cases, unjustified quitting (Q) and unjustified dismissing (UD)—if each regulation were kept during the whole period. We are able to calculate, for example, how much an employer would have had to pay a quitting worker, or a dismissed one, during the whole period 1975–2005 if the 1990 law (or the 1997 law) had been in place during the whole period, assuming that each month the worker was hired on a permanent basis and then quit (or was fired one year later,[51] or two years later, or three years later, and so on.

Figure 4A.1 shows the behavior of the job security payments as a proportion of the last wage and the real job security payments for a one and five years of tenure[52] for two cases: an employee who quits and another employee who is dismissed, both for an unjustified reason. We will present the results for a firm with 51–100 employees; however, we did the calculations for different firm sizes. Figure 4A.1.a shows that, while under the 1990 law an employer had to pay the equivalent of 1.25 months (using the last wage) to a quitting employee with one year of tenure in 1995, under the 1997 law he would have had to pay the equivalent of 2 months. As we can see, the job security cost for a quitting worker on average increased drastically with the 1997 law compared to the 1990 law, but the comparison of the job security cost for the case of unjustified dismissal under both laws would depend on the year of evaluation and the worker's tenure. On average, the 1997 law implied that the job security cost increased for workers with less than five years of tenure, whereas for a higher level of tenure the 1997 law tended to decrease the job security cost.

So, in general, when compared with the 1990 law, the 1997 law increased job security costs for workers with up to five years of tenure, but reduced them only partially for those workers with tenure levels above five years.

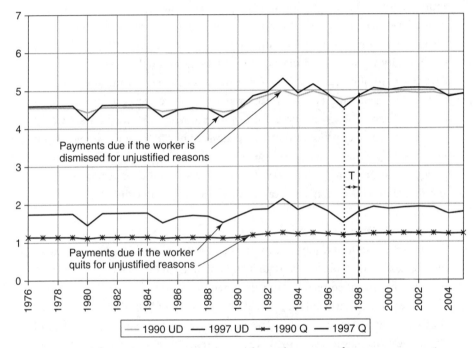

Fig. 4A.1a   Job security payments due to a worker with one year of tenure as a proportion of last wage

Source: Based on Bermúdez 2006.

Note: T = transition period.

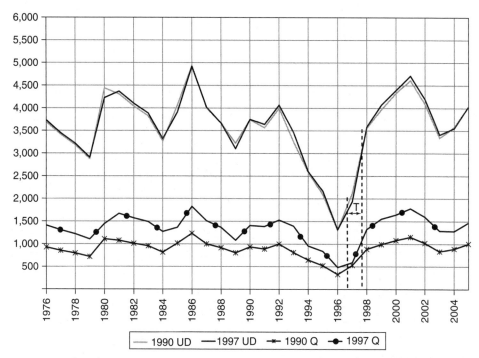

Fig. 4A.1b   Job security payments due to a worker with one year of tenure, in bolivars (real MPI base 1997)

Source: Based on Bermúdez 2006.

Note: T = transition period.

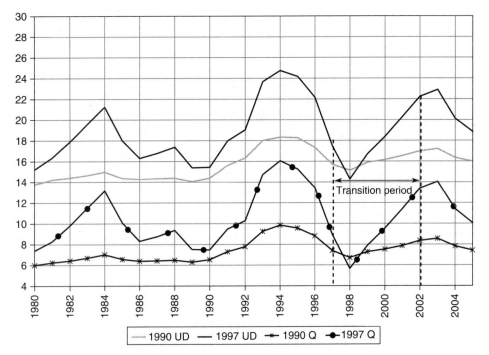

Fig. 4A.1c   Job security payments due to a worker with five years of tenure as a proportion of last wage

Source: Based on Bermúdez 2006.

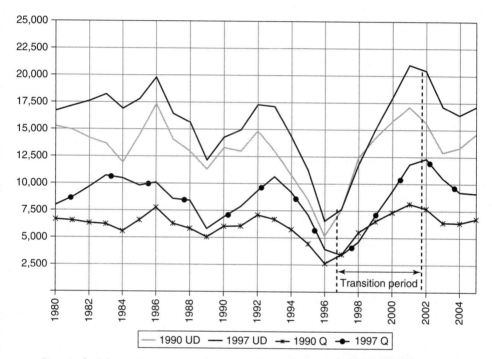

Fig. 4A.1d   Job security payments due to a worker with one year of tenure, in bolivars (real MPI base 1997)

Source: Based on Bermúdez 2006.

NOTES

1. Venezuela's labor market regulations have a long tradition. The first Venezuela Labor Law (1936) gave the government the mandate to implement a minimum wage. This occurred earlier than in the United States, where the minimum-wage legal framework, the Fair Labor Standards Act, was approved in 1938. For example, while in the United States the federal minimum wage has not been modified since 1997, in Venezuela it has been modified at least annually in that same period.

2. Lora and Pagés (1996) and Lora (2001) reported that there were very few labor reforms in Latin American countries between the mid-eighties and 1999, including Venezuela, but Bermúdez (2006) reported important and drastic structural changes in Venezuelan labor regulations in addition to the more commonly known labor reform of 1997.

3. Nominal wages deflated using the consumer price index base of 1997.

4. Evidence of this has been found by Freije (2003), Inter-American Development Bank (1999), and Kristensen and Cunningham (2006).

5. Venezuela is the country that experienced the fastest growth in the informality rate in Latin American countries during the period 1990–2001, according to the International Labor Organization.

6. In addition, there have been several dismissal freeze periods.

7. The Labor Law approved in 1997 is still in effect.

8. Bartelsman, Haltiwanger, and Scarpetta (2004) found that the net employment decrease in the Venezuelan manufacturing sector for the period 1995–2000 was mostly due to the exit of firms.

9. This panel data set from the Venezuelan Industrial Survey is available at http://frrodriguez .web.wesleyan.edu/.

10. The universe of this survey is firms in the manufacturing sector with more than five workers. Notice that under the definition used by Venezuela's National Statistics Institute, the informal sector consists of workers who have a job in firms with fewer than five employees, or who are "self-employed" nonprofessional (or independent) workers. So this survey covers only manufacturing firms in the formal sector.

11. This section is based on Bermúdez 2006, which describes in detail the principal labor market reforms from 1975 to 2005.

12. Further, some sectors within the manufacturing industry have experienced heavy competition from imported goods, such as the shoe, apparel, and textile industries, given the real appreciation of the bolivar with respect to other currencies during that period.

13. Except for the child-care bonus.

14. The magnitude of the total annual mandated non-indexed bonuses as a proportion of gross annual minimum wages began to increase sharply after 1994. Those bonuses represented on average 97.24 percent, 180.49 percent, and 40.29 percent of gross annual minimum wages for the years 1995, 1996, and 1997, respectively.

15. That is Bs. 28,600 from Decree 1240, Bs. 11,000 from Decree 617, and Bs. 13,380 from Decree 1824. See details in Bermúdez 2006. The World Bank (1998) reported that about 47.6 percent of all workers in the formal sector (28.7 percent of all workers in the economy) received the transportation and food bonuses, so almost the same percentage of people should have been receiving the income-compensating bonus.

16. Despite the fact that the 1997 Organic Labor Law had a provisional rule establishing that until a special law was published—concerning the wages to calculate payroll taxes—the monthly wage of Bs. 15,000 would replace the phrase "minimum wages" in all statutes that had defined any contribution, payroll tax, or penalty as a function of minimum wage, the very next day a new "special law" was published setting the new minimum wage at Bs. 75,000. Thus in just three days—for those earning minimum wages—the wage used to calculate the rest of labor cost

jumped from Bs. 22,020 to Bs. 75,000, an increase of 240.59 percent. In addition, on August 1, 1997, a lawsuit was filed at the TSJ (Supreme Court) against the labor minister's ruling regarding this "special law," but it was not until May 24, 2000, that the TSJ ruled in favor of the plaintiff. See Bermúdez 2006 for more on this.

17. This constraint is important when employers consider the use of the 1998 indexed food bonus as an optional wage-complementing mechanism.

18. We will explain more on this later when we review the changes in the job security costs.

19. See Freije 2003; Heckman and Pagés 2003; Inter-American Development Bank 1999; Kristensen and Cunningham 2006; and Márquez and Pagés 1998. Bermúdez 2006 found that the minimum wage has been more binding in the private sector than in the public sector. During 1998, the national urban minimum wage represented 89.3 percent of the median wage in the private sector, whereas it represented only 66.3 percent of the median wage in the public sector.

20. See Arango and Pachón 2004; Bell 1997; Maloney and Nuñez 2003; and World Bank 2006 for some LAC countries cases; and an extensive empirical review by Neumark and Wascher (2006).

21. The literature analyzing the effect of minimum wages is very extensive. Neumark and Wascher (2006) did an extensive review of the literature for the U.S. economy as well as other countries (including developing countries) since the early 1990s. They found that nearly two-thirds of 102 studies gave a relatively consistent indication of negative employment effects of minimum wages, whereas only eight gave a relatively consistent indication of positive employment effects. From the thirty-three studies they viewed as providing the most credible evidence, twenty-eight (85 percent) of them found negative employment effects. Further, when researchers focused on the least-skilled groups most likely to be adversely affected by minimum wages, they found that the evidence for disemployment effects seemed especially strong. Therefore, minimum wages may harm the least skilled workers more than is suggested by the net disemployment effects estimated in many studies.

22. A tributary unit is a measurement created in 1994 by the Tax Code in order to adjust automatically the income brackets used to establish the marginal tax rate, and consequently personal and business income tax. Also, it is used in almost all current decrees to set penalties for violations of different laws. This is a mechanism to adjust each decree automatically to inflation so that the penalties do not lose their value (or incentive) power to enforce the law. It is adjusted at the beginning of each year using the previous year's inflation as an indicator of the magnitude.

23. The decree was published on September 14, 1998, but entered into effect in January 1999.

24. The decree clearly established that the bonus should not be included for the calculation of severance payments, payroll, and so forth. The coupon was set at a minimum value of 0.25 TU/workday and a maximum value of 0.50 TU/workday. For firms with fifty-one workers or more, the lower limit of the rule implied that on average the food bonus represented approximately 45 percent of the minimum wage, while the upper limit implied approximately 90 percent of the minimum wage. For more details on this food bonus, see Bermúdez 2006.

25. For more details on these bonuses, see Bermúdez 2006.

26. National Institute for Educative Cooperation.

27. The risk of the firm is established depending on the degree to which the firm's workers are exposed to dangerous labor-related accidents. Thus a chemical firm would be more risky than an apparel firm.

28. See note 16 above for an explanation of this.

29. This stands for Tribunal Supremo de Justicia (Venezuela's Supreme Court).

30. In December 2002, the new Law of the Social Security System abolished the provisional rule of the 1997 Labor Law.

31. The authors found that even though Chile, Colombia, and Brazil were more inflexible than the United States, these countries exhibited a relatively high degree of microeconomic flexibility with 72.4 percent, 72.2 percent, and 70.1 percent, respectively, of labor adjustment taking place within a year, compared to the 90 percent for the United States, whereas Mexico ranked lower with about 58.1 percent of adjustment within a year.

32. In Brazil, small establishments closed about 67 percent of their gap within a year, while large establishments closed about 80.8 percent; in Colombia, 67.5 percent and 79 percent, respectively; in Chile, 68.5 percent and 78.3 percent; in Mexico, 56.1 percent and 60.7 percent; whereas in Venezuela the indicator was 52.9 percent for both sizes.

33. Using a sample of sixty countries for the period 1980–98, they took the indices of labor regulation created by Botero et al. 2003; and Heckman and Pagés 2000, together with different proxies for law enforcement, and through a dynamic labor demand specification estimated the effects of job security regulations. They consistently found a relatively lower speed of employment adjustment in countries with extensive legal protection against dismissal, particularly when job protection was likely to be enforced. In countries with a strong rule of law, they found that moving from the 20th to the 80th percentile of job security reduced the speed of adjustment to shocks by 35 percent and diminished annual productivity growth by 0.86 percent.

34. The urban minimum wage is the relevant wage to be applied in the manufacturing sector. We assume that this employee works only during the day shift, without overtime.

35. Nominal wages deflated using the consumer price index base 1997.

36. The VMSS is conducted by Venezuela's National Statistics Institute. Before 1975, four VMSS took place, in 1961, 1966, 1971, and 1974. Note that there was no VMSS in 1980.

37. This behavior might be explained by the downsizing and division of incumbent firms rather than new entry in the manufacturing sector, given that the differentials in labor costs between firm sizes began to grow in 1991. It takes time for firms to reduce employment levels or to reorganize because of the unions, and because labor regulations inhibit massive layoffs as they require a process of negotiations between unions, labor inspectors, and employers.

38. From the VMSS aggregate data during the 1975–2003 period, the average number of workers per establishment for a firm with more than 101 employees was 326 workers, 73 for firms with 51–100 workers, 33 for firms with 21–50, and for a firm with 5–20 employees, it was 11 workers.

39. We can calculate those disparities by knowing (1) the average number of workers per establishment per group size during that period, and (2) the minimum-mandated total annual labor cost per firm size for a worker that earns the minimum wage; and (3) assuming that all workers have a probability of 0.25 percent of having one child age under five years old.

40. Other cost = mandated non-indexed bonuses + payroll taxes + participation in firm's profit bonus + vacation leave + vacation bonus and depending on firm size (child-care bonus + indexed food bonus). Total annual expected cost = gross annual minimum wages + mandated non-indexed bonuses + payroll taxes + participation in firm's profit bonus + vacation leave + vacation bonus + 0.5 total unjustified dismissal cost + 0.5 quitting cost and depending on firm size (child-care bonus + indexed food bonus).

41. Notice that the second window is longer than the first window. In order to get windows of the same size, we re-estimated our models using a 1995–97 window and a 1998–2000 window instead of a 1998–2001 window. In terms of sign and significance there were no changes in our results.

42. We are not taking into account firms that exited the market in 1998 because we do not have any information for them between 1998 and 2001.

43. There was mobility among the different groups in the balanced panel. On average, 4 percent of the firms change groups between 1995 and 2001.

44. Workers are the summation of blue-collar workers and white-collar workers. We do not include owners or directors.

45. We additionally use dummies for the different manufacturing sectors. Those estimated coefficients are not presented.

46. When we used a pooling regression, the estimated coefficient for Δ log of real total cost, excluding seniority and severance real costs, was not statistically different from zero.

47. The 1990 and 1997 laws established that in the *unjustified* firing case, the employer had to pay additional advanced notice only for tenure levels lower than five years. Both laws established

an indemnity to be paid in the case of an unjustified firing. Thus, in order to apply the usual definition of severance payment and to compare the 1990 and 1997 laws, we added the difference between the employer's advance notice for unjustified firing and the normal employer's advance notice to the indemnity payments established in the laws to obtain an "additional indemnity" or traditional "severance payment."

48. To pursue a better job, for example. If the worker quits for justified reasons, such as sexual harassment, the worker can leave immediately and the employer would have to pay the advance notice and indemnity for the case of an unjustified dismissal.

49. The Labor Law in Venezuela has not included economic and technological reasons within the list of justifiable reasons to dismiss a worker, so it is at the court's discretion to qualify the firing.

50. When deciding to dismiss a worker, depending on the legal actions taken by the employee and the court's decisions, the employer knows *ex-ante* that he could face the following four cases depending on what he chooses to do:

(1) pay the worker the normal advance notice and the seniority payments, and the worker does not sue the employer;

(2) pay the worker the normal advance notice and the seniority payments, and the worker sues the employer but the courts decide that it was a "justified reason" in which case the employer does not have to pay anything else;

(3) pay the worker the normal advance notice and the seniority payments, and the worker sues the employer but the courts decide it was an "unjustified reason," in which case the employer would have to pay the forgone wages, from the firing up to the court decision, and reinstate the worker in his job, or pay the forgone wages, the indemnity for unjustified firing, and the difference between the advance notice under unjustified reason and the advanced notice that the employer already paid; or

(4) pay the worker the advance notice under unjustified reason, the seniority payments, and the indemnity payment, in which case the employer avoids the court procedure and the possibility of paying forgone wages, no matter the reason for dismissing the worker.

51. For example, if a permanent employee was hired on the January 1, 1999, and on December 15, 1999, he quit and gave advance notice to the employer working exactly up to the January 1, 2000, he would only receive seniority payments plus the interest on them on that date. In the case of unjustified firing, we are assuming that on January 1, 2000, the employer dismissed the worker and simultaneously paid him the advance notice for unjustified firing, the seniority payments and interests, and the indemnity payment. In both cases, the employee would have worked exactly one year. The amounts paid on January 1, 2000, will be presented in real terms, and also expressed as a ratio of the *last wage* earned by the worker on December 1, 1999. This would be the one-year tenure case paid on January 1, 2000; doing this for each month of 2000 and averaging them, we get the value for year 2000.

52. We have assumed that worker's wage is only a function of the minimum wage and tenure. See Bermúdez 2006.

REFERENCES

Arango, C., and A. Pachón. 2004. "Minimum Wages in Colombia: Holding the Middle with a Bite on the Poor." Working Paper 280, Economics, Banco de la República, Bogotá.

Bartelsman, E., J. Haltiwanger, and S. Scarpetta. 2004. "Microeconomic Evidence of Creative Destruction in Industrial and Developing Countries." Policy Research Working Paper 3464, World Bank, Washington, D.C.

Bell, L. 1997. "The Impact of Minimum Wages in Mexico and Colombia." *Journal of Labor Economics* 15 (3): 122–35.

Bello, O., and D. Restuccia. 2002. "Venezuela's Growth Experience." Working Paper 431, Department of Economics, University of Toronto.

Bermúdez, A. 2006. "Structural Changes in Labor Markets: Thirty Years of Labor Regulations in Venezuela." Working Paper, Universidad Central de Venezuela, Caracas.

Botero, J., S. Djankov, R. La Porta, F. Lopez-de-Silanes, and A. Shliefer. 2003. "The Regulation of Labor." Working Paper 9756, National Bureau of Economic Research, Cambridge, Mass.

Caballero, R., K. Cowan, E. Engel, and A. Micco. 2004. "Effective Labor Regulation and Microeconomic Flexibility." Working Paper 10744, National Bureau of Economic Research, Cambridge, Mass.

Caballero, R., E. Engel, and A. Micco. 2004. "Microeconomic Flexibility in Latin America." Working Paper 10398, National Bureau of Economic Research, Cambridge, Mass.

Cardenas, Mauricio, and Raquel Bernal. 2003. "Determinants of Labor Demand in Colombia: 1976–1996." Working Paper 10077, National Bureau of Economic Research, Cambridge, Mass.

Carneiro, A., and P. Portugal. 2004. "Wages and the Risk of Displacement." CEF.UP Working Paper 0308, Universidade do Porto, Faculdade de Economía do Porto.

Edwards, Sebastian, and Alejandra Cox Edwards. 2000. "Economic Reforms and Labor Markets: Policy Issues and Lessons from Chile." Working Paper 7646, National Bureau of Economic Research, Cambridge, Mass.

Freije, S. 2003. "Efecto del Salario Minimo sobre el empleo en Venezuela." In *El Desempleo en Venezuela*. Capitulo 5. Oficina de Asesoria Economica y Financiera de la Asamblea Nacional, Caracas, pp. 61–70.

Freije, S., K. Betancourt, and G. Márquez. 1995. "Reformas del Mercado Laboral ante la Liberalización de la economía: El caso de Venezuela." In *Reformas del Mercado Laboral ante la Liberalización de la economía en América Latina*, edited by G. Márquez. Washington, D.C.: Inter-American Development Bank.

Gruber, J. 1997. "The Incidence of Payroll Taxation: Evidence for Chile." *Journal of Labor Economics* 15 (3): 72–101.

Hamermesh, D. 1993. *Labor Demand*. Princeton: Princeton University Press.

Hausmann, R., and F. Rodriguez. 2006. "Why Did Venezuelan Growth Collapse?" CID Working Paper 181, Harvard Center for International Development, Cambridge, Mass.

Heckman, J., and C. Pagés. 2000. "The Cost of Job Security Regulation: Evidence from Latin American Labor Markets." Working Paper 7773, National Bureau of Economic Research, Cambridge, Mass.

_____. 2003. "Law and Employment: Lessons from Latin America and the Caribbean. An Introduction." Working Paper 10067, National Bureau of Economic Research, Cambridge, Mass.

Immervoll, H. 2007. "Minimum Wages, Minimum Labor Costs, and the Tax Treatment of Low-Wage Employment." Social, Employment, and Migration Working Papers 46, Organisation for Economic Co-operation and Development, Paris.

Inter-American Development Bank. 1999. *América Latina Frente a la Desigualdad*. Informe de Progreso Económico y Social, Washington, D.C.

Kristensen, N., and W. Cunningham. 2006. "Do Minimum Wages in Latin America and the Caribbean Matter? Evidence from 19 Countries." PR Working Paper 3870, World Bank, Washington, D.C.

Loayza, Norman, Ana María Oviedo, and Luis Servén. 2005. "The Impact of Regulation on Growth and Informality: Cross-Country Evidence." Working Paper 3623, World Bank, Washington, D.C.

Lora, E. 2001. "Structural Reforms in Latin America: What Has Been Reformed and How to Measure It." Working Paper 466, Inter-American Development Bank, Washington, D.C.

Lora, E., and C. Pagés. 1996. "La legislación laboral en el proceso de reformas estructurales de América Latina y el Caribe." Working Paper 343, Inter-American Development Bank, Washington, D.C.

Maloney, W., and J. Nuñez. 2003. "Measuring the Impacts of Minimum Wages: Evidence from Latin America." Working Paper 9800, National Bureau of Economic Research, Cambridge, Mass.

Márquez, G., and C. Pagés. 1998. "Ties That Bind: Employment Protection and Labor Market Outcomes in Latin America." Working Paper 373, Inter-American Development Bank, Washington, D.C.

Montenegro, Claudio, and Carmen Pagés. 2003. "Who Benefits from Labor Market Regulations? Chile, 1960–1998." Working Paper 494, Inter-American Development Bank, Washington, D.C.

Neumark, D., and W. Wascher. 2006. "Minimum Wages and Employment: A Review of Evidence from the New Minimum Wage Research." Working Paper 12663, National Bureau of Economic Research, Cambridge, Mass.

Organisation for Economic Co-operation and Development. 1995. "Job Gains and Job Losses: Recent Literature and Trends." OECD Jobs Study Working Papers 1, OECD Directorate for Employment, Labour, and Social Affairs, Paris.

Orlando, M. 2001. "El sector informal en Venezuela: Plataforma o barrera para la reducción de la pobreza." Working Paper, Universidad Católica Andrés Bello, Caracas.

Pierre, G., and S. Scarpetta. 2004. "How Labor Market Policies Can Combine Workers' Protection with Job Creation: A Partial Review of Some Key Issues and Policies Options." Social Protection Discussion Paper 0716, World Bank, Washington, D.C.

Pineda, J., and F. Rodriguez. 2006. "Public Investment in Infrastructure and Productivity Growth: Evidence from the Venezuelan Manufacturing Sector." Wesleyan Economics Working Papers 2006-010, Department of Economics, Wesleyan University, Middletown, Conn.

Saavedra, Jaime, and Máximo Torero. 2003. "Labor Market Reforms and Their Impact over Formal Labor Demand and Job Market Turnover: The Case of Peru." Research Network Working Paper R-394, Inter-American Development Bank, Washington, D.C.

Tokman, V., and D. Martinez. 1999. "Labor Costs and Competitiveness in the Latin American Manufacturing Sector, 1990–1998." *CEPAL Review* 69 (December): 51–68.

Wooldridge, J. 2002. *Econometric Analysis of Cross Section and Panel Data.* Cambridge: MIT Press.

World Bank. 1998. *Venezuela Stylized Facts and the Characteristics of the Labor Supply in Venezuela: What Can Be Done to Improve the Outcome?* Report 17901-VE, Latin America and Caribbean Region, Human Development Unit, Washington, D.C.

_____. 2006. "Minimum Wages in Latin America and the Caribbean: The Impact on Employment, Inequality, and Poverty." Working Paper, Office of the Chief Economist, Human Development Management Unit, Latin America and the Caribbean Region, World Bank, Washington, D.C.

_____. 2007. "Doing Business: Measuring Business Regulations Database." Washington, D.C. http://www.doingbusiness.org/.

5 UNDERSTANDING ECONOMIC GROWTH IN VENEZUELA, 1970–2005: THE REAL EFFECTS OF A FINANCIAL COLLAPSE

Matías Braun

Finance and Growth: The Case of Venezuela

The literature relating to the links between a country's degree of financial development and its per capita income level and rate of growth is vast.[1] Most recently it has been shown that financial development and growth are not just contemporaneously correlated, but that the first anticipates the second in a cross-section of countries.[2] The size of the effect is large: a one standard deviation higher level of financial development—as proxy primarily by measures related to the size of the banking sector and the stock market relative to the economy—implies around one percentage point higher growth rates over long periods of time. Advances have been made in addressing the potential dependence of the size of the financial system to future growth prospects; the use of legal origins as instruments for financial development has been critical.[3]

Only very recently has research focused on identifying more direct channels or mechanisms through which finance affects growth. This has been pursued in the cross-country growth regressions setting, using micro-data, and through the natural-experiment approach.[4] Still, most of the literature on the real effects of financial development to date continues to rest heavily on the comparison across countries. This is despite the fact that around one half of the variation of the traditional indicators of financial development comes from the time series within countries.[5]

I am greatly indebted to Ricardo Hausmann, Francisco Rodríguez, Michael Klein, and participants at the CID Venezuelan Economic Growth Second Conference (April 2006) for very helpful comments and suggestions.

Detailed country studies are needed to check that the main results on the literature are present in the time series, and to learn more about the specific mechanisms at work. Venezuela, in this sense, represents a great opportunity for it has seen marked changes on its degree of financial development in the last four decades.

No matter how you measure it, Venezuela's degree of financial development today is extremely low. For instance, using the traditional measure of bank credit to the private sector to GDP, the country ranks 132nd out of the 157 countries where the figure is available. This position is not related to its relatively large economy or the relevance of its oil sector, and is not peculiar to the banking system, but rather extends in a similar degree to the stock and bond markets. The system is not only small but also very inefficient: net interest margins and overhead costs are very high.

A weak legal protection of financiers and a suboptimal quality of borrower information in Venezuela are both consistent with the underdeveloped status when compared to other countries. But although these factors can form the basis for future reform, they fall short in explaining the country's sudden process of reduced development because they are quite persistent in time (as are their deeper determinants). The current state seems to be more related to the lack of consistency and the much-delayed efforts in liberalizing its financial system in the last two decades. We show that this is certainly related to the management of the late 1980s and mid-1990s crises (as we discuss below), but it also mirrors the way economic policy and the political system more generally were being conducted. Aside from partial allowance of international capital flows, as of the late 1980s Venezuela still had directed credit policies, entry barriers into the banking system, interest rate controls, and very weak financial regulation, and it had not yet engaged in banking sector privatization. In the rich world, these kinds of policies had by that time been all but abandoned. And they would be swiftly overthrown in the developing countries in the early 1990s.

Following a golden era since the mid-1970s, private credit fell abruptly in the late 1980s and again in the mid-1990s, stabilizing at around half the 1960–74 levels. This stagnation is perfectly consistent with a greatly reduced rate of growth in the non-tradable component of Venezuela's GDP. But the collapse can hardly be blamed on the evolution of income simply because, in the 1988–98 period, GDP actually grew by 23 percent (15 percent of the non-oil fraction) while real bank credit to the private sector fell by 54 percent. More formal tests of (Granger) causality are not very supportive to the hypothesis that an initial decline in growth induced the credit collapse: the positive feedback effect of growth on credit that is clearly present in the pre-crisis period—when credit was expanding quickly or stagnating—disappears during the credit-collapse years.

The evidence is much more supportive of the crowding-out story whereby a fiscal collapse increases the public sector demand for funds, thereby driving interest rates sharply higher. High rates discourage banks from lending to the private sector because of informational asymmetries (moral hazard and adverse selection), and discourage private borrowers from taking on loans. Seen by the government mainly as a source for fiscal financing, the incentives to undertake the liberalization of the financial system were likely very weak during that time. A number of facts are consistent with this hypothesis. First, both episodes of credit collapse are preceded by a couple of years of strong reversals in fiscal accounts. Second, these same episodes of increased demand for government financing coincide with periods in which foreign financing had become more stringent, leaving the domestic financial system as the only source of financing. Third, in the absence of significant changes in the supply of credit and more stringent foreign borrowing conditions, real rates were bound to rise significantly. Fourth, banks do not appear to have been unable but rather unwilling to lend to the private sector. Bank capital and assets declined far less than private credit. And fifth, banks indeed increased public sector lending substantially, explaining almost entirely the fall in real private credit.

Based on the relation of financial development and per capita income across countries and in the Venezuelan time series, the evolution of credit in other Latin American and oil-producing states during those years, and the strong persistence of financial development, one can estimate that Venezuela's financial system should be between four and six times larger than it is today. On a theoretical level, and also according to the wealth of evidence on the finance–growth nexus, this massive financial underdevelopment should have induced very poor real-economy results. Through a number of techniques and exploiting several sources of data, we show the evidence to support this having been the case.

Survey evidence indicates that, although managers do not perceive lack of financing as the most important constraint to doing business, they behave in a way quite consistent with the issue being a major problem. Not only do firms rely much more on internal and family funds for financing, but they are not particularly able to exploit their growth opportunities. Access to (the limited) bank debt appears to be as important as the existence of growth opportunities when investing, hiring, and exporting, even after controlling for other perceived constraints to doing business. Small, local, and young firms appear to be the most affected.

These perceptions are confirmed in the aggregate data for the economy. The evolution of private credit—its collapse in particular—helps predict the growth of the tradable sector that is most dependent on external financing and the one of the non-tradable sector, which is typically less able to obtain funds overseas.

A panel of manufacturing industries indicates that the collapse of credit affected more strongly those industries that are supposed to be more reliant on bank credit for financing investment, as they exhibit much larger rates of decline. Moreover, the quality of allocation of both employment and investment—as measured by their responsiveness to value-added growth—decreased significantly for these same sectors following the financial crisis. Finally, not even the largest firms in the country (the listed ones) could escape the effects of the collapse: their dependence on the availability of internal funds for investing increased significantly. The allocation of resources across sectors and firms in the economy is in all cases the most affected. Not only does it appear that the financial system ceased channeling capital to the private sector, but it also appears that the little amount they provided was not directed to the right borrowers.

The chapter follows with a section documenting Venezuela's very low degree of financial development. In the third part, we date and quantify the collapse in bank credit, and provide a brief description of the succession of events surrounding it. The fourth section documents the large, negative effects this financial underdevelopment has had on Venezuela's growth.

Venezuela's Financial System Today

When the size of its economy is taken into account, Venezuela's financial system is today one of the smallest and least developed in the world. Bank credit to the private sector amounts to just around 9 percent of GDP, ranking the country in position 132 out of the 157 countries where the figure is available for the 2000s.[6] The ratio is the lowest among the Latin American countries, and even lower than the median in sub-Saharan Africa. This is not just due to the fact that Venezuela's economy is relatively large; a figure of $400 for per capita for private credit still leaves the country well below the other major Latin American economies, and at one-seventh the value for Chile. The total stock of around $10 billion is 15 percent lower than Peru's (whose economy is half the size), and 60 percent lower than Colombia's.

These very low indicators are not easily explained with the importance of the oil sector in the economy. Even if we assume that the oil sector does not demand any domestic financial services—either directly or indirectly through the income generated—and consider only the non-oil GDP (around three quarters of the total), the stock of Venezuela's bank credit is still much lower than that of other countries. Moreover, Venezuela still ranks in the lowest decile of private credit to GDP among the thirty economies that are more dependent on oil.

Is it the low level of per capita GDP then? Figure 5.1 depicts the well-known fact that the ratio of private credit to GDP increases with (the log of) per capita GDP. Indeed, per capita GDP alone explains around half the cross-country variation in private credit. According to this relation, Venezuela's banking sector should be 5.6 times larger than it actually is.[7] In percentage terms, there is no other country with a more underdeveloped system relative to what this relation implies.

This degree of underdevelopment is not peculiar to the banking system. Out of the fifty-four countries for which data on equity markets are available, Venezuela's market capitalization to GDP of 5 percent surpasses only that of Bangladesh. With five dozen listed firms—worth on average around $100 million each—the market is only larger than that of Ecuador, Jamaica, and Trinidad and Tobago in Latin America. The relation between per capita GDP and stock market capitalization, which is again very significant, implies that Venezuela's market should be 5.4 times larger than it actually is.[8] Likewise, the number of listed firms per capita was expected to be 7.5 times larger based solely on the level of income in the country. Overall, the composition of the financial system is not particularly different in Venezuela when compared to other countries; the banking sector and the stock market appear to be similarly underdeveloped when compared to other countries.

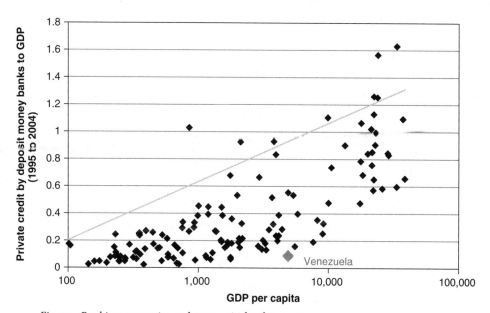

Fig. 5.1   Banking sector size and economic development

Source: Based on World Development Indicators (World Bank 2005).

The size of the private bond market in Venezuela is not even recorded by the Bank for International Settlements, the traditional source on these matters, and the total life and non-life insurance premiums are both negligible. Based on issuance data recorded in the SDC Platinum data set, the picture for the bond market is consistent with that of the rest of the system. Total issuance is extremely small even by Latin American standards. Only around 40 percent of the capital raised via bonds is raised in the local market, where the average principal ($17 million) is quite small, and the maturities (1.9 years) are extremely short.[9]

Venezuela's financial underdevelopment is not only related to the size of its financial system but is also reflected in its efficiency. Even after controlling for its small size, banks' net interest margins of 16.3 percent are about two times too high, and the highest in the entire sample of countries.[10]

These large margins have generated a virulent discussion on their determinants. A series of papers collected in Banco Central de Venezuela (2001) offer a number of possible explanations, including high transformation costs, undercapitalization of banks, high risks, and collusive practices. The conclusions reached by the different authors are not particularly consistent, and for the most part have left the question unanswered. There is even disagreement as to whether the margins are high. Nevertheless, government officials appear to have favored the market power explanation. At least since 2001 the government has put pressure on banks to reduce their interest-rate margins in order to offer loans at lower interest rates and pay higher rates to depositors. This would help consolidate the recovery by stopping the capital flight and generating employment.

Overhead costs and the level of concentration can shed light on the question. The former are extremely high and much larger than expected given the size of the banking system, while the latter is very low. Indeed, the banking sector in Venezuela has been traditionally quite dispersed and has only begun to consolidate since around 2000, following the resolution of the 1994 crisis and the authorization of foreign bank operations. This suggests that high costs, presumably due to the industry not taking advantage of the economies of scale in the sector, rather than market power, are more likely to explain high margins. One should not overstress this conclusion, however. First, it has been difficult to document the existence of economies of scale in Venezuela's banking sector. This despite the fact that economies of scale have long ago been documented in other banking markets, and that the global wave of consolidation in the industry since the late 1990s has been taken as prima facie evidence for these. Second, although concentration makes collusion more difficult, it may not preclude it. The fact that after the 2001 negotiations with the government, banks indeed reduced loan rates and increased those for deposits is consistent with this view. Finally, in a system so dependent on lending to the government, the scope for political economy explanations is wide. It is possible that an important part of banks' activity consists now in seeking rents from the government instead of lending to the public. Only around half the assets of the industry are lent to the private sector (see the following section). If rents are indeed plentiful—as it seems they have been since the government has been willing to pay very high real rates to finance its deficits—competition in private lending may not be particularly worthwhile.

Interestingly, the inefficiency in the banking industry is not found in the stock market. Turnover, although extremely low, is not lower than what the size of the market would imply.[11]

The literature has identified a series of factors that explain the cross-country differences in financial development. These can be grouped in two: those related to the laws protecting the financiers and their enforcement, and those related to the availability of the information on the borrowers. The level of Venezuela's financial development is more or less consistent with how it ranks on these measures.[12] While the degree of protection granted to both creditors and minority shareholders, and the quality of information available to shareholders are quite low, there seems to be reasonably good information about borrowers.

Although these factors can form the basis for future reform, they fall short in explaining Venezuela's low level of financial development, for the country did not have a massively underdeveloped system beforehand. Neither bank credit to the private sector nor stock market capitalization was significantly different from what was expected from its level of income per capita in the 1970s and 1980s. This is far from the usual picture, since the level of financial development is quite persistent in time. Indeed, the ranking of private credit to GDP across countries in the 1970s explains around 45 percent of the figure thirty years later, and the ranking of stock market capitalization in the early 1980s explains 65 percent of the figure today. This persistence and the initial values for Venezuela imply that the banking system and stock market should now be 4.5 and 5 times larger, respectively.

Abiad and Mody (2003) show that the time series variation in financial development can be tightly linked to specific financial sector policies. Aside from partial allowance of international capital flows, as of the late 1980s Venezuela still had directed credit policies, entry barriers into the banking system, interest rate controls, and very weak financial regulation, and had not yet engaged in banking sector privatization. Although developed countries had by that time abandoned these policies altogether, the situation in Venezuela was not very different from that of the typical developing country. As a norm, less developed countries only began liberalizing their domestic financial systems in the early 1990s. Thus the fact that up to that point Venezuela did not appear underdeveloped in relation to other countries of similar economic development is consistent with the policies being followed.

However, what is peculiar to Venezuela is that since the early 1990s (partial) reform efforts, the policies have been all but consistent in time. This mirrors what happened in the implementation of economic policy and the political system more generally. As we will see in the next section, it is also the result of the way the 1994 banking crisis was managed. The role of politics in the evolution of the financial sector cannot be overemphasized. As the lively account of the 1994 crisis by De Krivoy (2000) shows, political will is critically required to create and sustain the building blocks of a sound financial system. This "will" depends on the political economy game in which the players involved take part (Braun and Raddatz 2007, 2008).

Venezuela's Financial System Collapse

When compared to those of other countries, Venezuela's financial system looks extraordinarily small and inefficient. What is more striking is that it also looks out of line with what one would predict based on the country's income per capita and past performance, even when taking into account the importance of the oil sector and the fact that it is located in Latin America.

When Did Credit Collapse?

Figure 5.2 looks at the evolution of private credit and stock market capitalization to GDP in the time series. It is apparent that following a golden era since the mid-1970s, private credit falls abruptly in the late 1980s and again in the mid-1990s. Since then, the index has stabilized at a level of 8–9 percent, which is around half the 1960–74 levels. The stock market index follows a similar pattern, standing today at significantly lower levels than in the 1980s. This is partly due to the fall in prices and the fall in the number of listed firms. The post-stabilization booms of the early 1990s proved short-lived.

The collapse of the banking system indicator is almost entirely explained by the evolution of private credit itself, rather than by what happened to the denominator. While total GDP and non-oil GDP grew by 23 percent and 15 percent in the 1988–98 period, respectively, real bank credit to the private sector collapsed by 54 percent. Prior to 1988 real private credit shows a stable relationship with non-oil GDP, with a highly significant estimated elasticity of 1.1.[13] This elasticity is very similar to that of the average country since 1960 (1.07).[14] For the 1989–2004 period, however, the elasticity is cut in half (0.53) and is no longer significant.

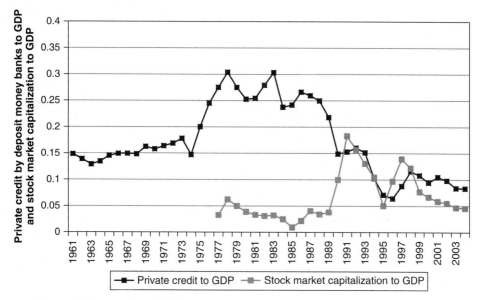

Fig. 5.2   Private credit and GDP

Source: Based on World Development Indicators (World Bank 2005).

Figure 5.3 shows this break. The break in the link between the non-oil economy and the financial sector may have started around 1978 when, despite continuing growth, real credit remained relatively constant for almost a decade.
The break may have only deepened during the 1989 recession. The statistical
tests performed are only supportive of a break in 1989,[15] however. Further, when
looked at more closely, the relation is largely driven by the evolution of the
non-tradable component of the non-oil economy. Braun and Raddatz (2007)
show that this is indeed the rule across countries: non-tradable sectors benefit much more from financial development than do tradable ones, particularly
when the economy is open to trade in goods and capital so that tradable industries have greater access to foreign financing. Thus the financial stagnation
decade is perfectly consistent with the greatly reduced rate of growth in the
non-tradable component of Venezuela's GDP. This does not establish causality,
but it lends support to the view that the break occurred in 1989 and not before.
Of course, this does not preclude the possibility that the roots of the break are
to be found in the period preceding the banking collapse (see, for instance, De
Krivoy 2000).

    The situation has not gotten back to normal since; the period 1997–2004 does
not look statistically different from 1989–96 in terms of the non-oil GDP elasticity
of real private credit. Interestingly, the elasticity of private credit with oil GDP is

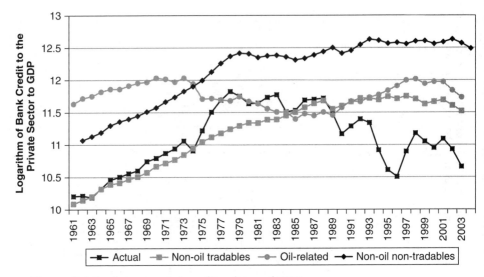

Fig. 5.3   Relation between private credit and non-oil GDP

Sources: Based on World Development Indicators (World Bank 2005) and Rodríguez 2004.

just 0.2 and not statistically significant. Oil-related growth does not seem particularly useful for the development of the domestic financial system.

It can still be the case that what happened to Venezuela's banking system can
be explained by its dependency to oil or by its Latin American location. After all,
real oil prices fell by 22 percent in the 1988–98 decade and the period includes the
Argentine and Mexican collapses.

The evolution of private credit in Venezuela is very consistent with what was
happening in these two groups prior to 1989.[16] Starting in 1989, Venezuela's banking sector parts ways with those of the comparable groups. Both series did grow
more slowly in the early 1990s when compared to the 1960s and 1970s; however,
by 2000 they had both easily surpassed their previous record levels. For Latin
America, the 1988–98 decade was in fact the best ever in term of the banking
system deepening. The link to oil does not seem particularly relevant either: although real oil prices fell, this decrease was much smaller than that of 1980–88
(60 percent) when real credit remained stable. Also, oil income actually increased
by 26 percent during the period, fueled by the surge in production.

Brief Anatomy of the Collapse

In order to explore what happened to Venezuela's banking system around the collapse we look at quarterly data for a number of indicators.[17] Figure 5.4 compares
real credit to the private sector and real assets.

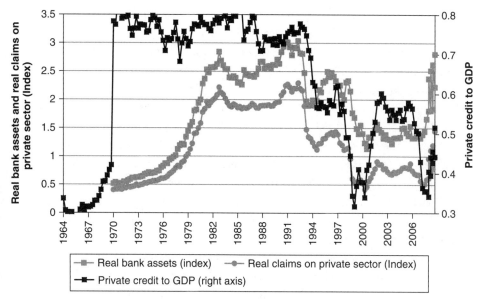

Fig. 5.4   The share of private credit in bank assets

Source: Based on International Financial Statistics, August 2009, International Monetary Fund.

Real deposits start falling sharply in mid-1987 when monetary policy turns very contractive in the face of increasing inflation. Initially the collapse in real deposits did not translate into a collapse in bank's assets. Up until December 1988 the fall in deposits was financed with foreign borrowing and capitalization. Foreign financing dries up following the balance of payments crisis of 1989. Fixed nominal lending rates and mounting inflation, and the inability to finance the loss of deposits start taking a big toll on bank profitability. Bank losses start showing up as reduced capital, so that the continuing fall in deposits finally traduces into a collapse in credit to the private sector.

Is the collapse in private credit simply the reflection of the inability of banks to extend credit? Not likely. The fall in credit went much further than what can be explained simply with the behavior of deposits, foreign financing, and capital. Even after 1991, when both real deposits and assets rebounded strongly and all but returned to their levels in the first half of the 1980s, private credit was still around 60 percent lower. The ratio of private credit to bank assets that had been very stable since the 1960s at 75 percent fell to around 55 percent in 1989 and remained there for the following three years. The banks' change in composition of assets toward Reserves and Central Bank paper—attracted by very high positive real rates following the end of the interest rate controls—fully explains the drop in the ratio of private credit to assets. Indeed, as the post-devaluation inflation receded, nominal rates remained quite high, and real rates turned positive through the 1991–93 period for the first time in more than ten years.

By mid-1993 inflation starts getting out of control again, and by mid-1994 real rates had gone back to the negative side. A huge increase in Central Bank credit to the banks—neutralizing their capital losses—and the following re-capitalization compensated the fall in deposits that at that point was pretty modest. Lack of coordination in addressing the early collapse of Banco Latino deepened the loss of trust in the system. With the Central Bank unwilling to continue lending large sums to troubled banks given the inactivity of the government, FOGAPE (Fondo de garantías para pequeños empresarios) lacking sufficient funds, and sound banks missing the incentives to come to the rescue partly due to the lack of a legal framework for mergers and acquisitions, the crisis became systemic.

Private credit collapsed once again as banks shifted toward holding Reserves and Central Bank paper. New risk-weighted adequacy ratios, enacted as part of the 1994 banking law, boosted the incentive to invest in zero-capital-requirement assets. During 1996 real deposits catch up and start falling sharply.

By mid-1996, when the crisis reaches its trough, banks were holding as much reserves as private credit. Since the recovery, total reserves have remained be-tween 20 percent and 40 percent of assets, and the behavior of real private credit has more or less mirrored that of real deposits, as was the case before the late 1980s. The ratio of private credit to assets recovered its pre-1994/95 crisis level but never again reached the level of the 1960s, 1970s, and most of 1980s. The ratio has been relatively constant at around 50 percent in the past ten years.

Why Did Credit Collapse?

A first potential generic explanation for the financial collapse is that growth caused the collapse in credit, which then amplified the initial fall in growth. We explore this story by conducting Granger causality tests for a number of yearly real activity aggregates in the last forty years (see table 5A.1 of the appendix). These tests do not establish causality in the economic sense but do help at least in determining which sectors might respond more to the fluctuations of banks' private credit and what is the sequence of events. Below we focus on establishing causality. The tests consist of checking whether past values of private credit have significant explanatory power for activity over and above what is explained by the dynamics of activity itself. Our particular specification uses real growth rates and includes two lags. We also tested with the variables in logs plus a trend obtaining very similar results.

For the entire 1963–2003 period, one cannot reject the fact that total GDP growth does not cause real private credit growth, nor that private credit does not cause GDP. While the former is true also for each subperiod (before and after the collapse), we do find some evidence that the financial deepening of the 1960s and 1970s did contribute to (or more precisely, anticipate) the rapid growth during those years. This is particularly the case for non-oil GDP, for which we cannot rule out Granger causality for that (and also the entire) period. There appears to be significant feedback into the growth of the banking system, for we can also reject the hypothesis of no causality going from non-oil GDP to private credit.

I then split non-oil GDP into the tradable and the non-tradable components. We define agriculture, mining, and manufacturing as tradable and let the rest of the non-oil economy be the non-tradable part. The ability of both components to explain future private credit is quite strong both before and after the collapse. The high degree of financial development before the collapse seems to have benefited the non-tradable sector much more clearly than the tradable one. In fact, while we easily establish causality from growth to private credit in both periods, it doesn't work the other way around. This is not surprising, for most tradable firms (importers and exporters, in particular) are much more likely to have access to both supplier and bank credit from overseas. Traded goods can be used as collateral because they can be consumed by the foreign lender, and their value does not correlate as strongly with the business cycle as that of non-tradable ones (see Braun and Raddatz 2007).

I split value added in the manufacturing sector into two components based on the natural demand for external financing of different industries. In order to do so, we split all the non-oil-related industries according to the median of Rajan and Zingales's (1998) measure of external finance dependence. The measure corresponds to the share of capital expenditure that is not financed with internal funds computed for U.S.-listed firms through the 1980s, and aggregated into ISIC-3 industries. The actual use of external finance is associated with the desired amount in view that these large firms listed in (by most measures) the most developed financial market are not very likely to be particularly constrained. If this demand is a relatively stable technological or industry characteristic, we can use this measure as an exogenous measure of the demand for external funds not only for the United States but for other countries as well.[18] Interestingly during the financial crisis period, private credit appears to Granger-cause growth in the highly external finance-dependence sectors, something that is not found for the less dependent industries. Before the collapse the opposite seems to be true.

Overall the evidence does not support the hypothesis that the growth collapse caused the credit collapse. Although growth seems to have a positive effect on credit, this is mainly driven by the pre-crisis period, when credit was either expanding very fast or stagnating. The causality from growth to credit disappears in the crisis period when using the aggregate and non-oil GDP series. The causes of the collapse, then, appear to reside more in the banking sector and not—at least primarily—in what happened to the economy.

A second potential explanation for the credit collapse is the conventional crowding-out story whereby a fiscal collapse increases the public sector demand for funds, sharply raising interest rates. High rates discourage banks from lending to the private sector because of informational asymmetries (moral hazard and adverse selection), and discourage private borrowers from taking on loans.

A number of facts—some of which we already documented—seem consistent with this hypothesis. First, both episodes of credit collapse are preceded by a couple of years of strong reversals in fiscal accounts. Second, these same episodes of increased demand for government financing coincide with periods in which foreign financing had become more stringent, leaving the domestic financial system as the only source of financing. Third, in the absence of significant changes in the supply of credit and more stringent foreign borrowing conditions, real rates were bound to rise significantly. And they certainly did. In fact, as we have seen, for the first time in many years they turned positive and remained very high throughout the 1989–94 credit collapse period. Fourth, banks do not appear to have been unable, but rather unwilling, to lend to the private sector. Bank capital and assets declined far less than did private credit. Fifth, banks indeed increased public sector lending substantially. This explains almost entirely the fall in real private credit.

How Deep Was the Collapse?

I construct three benchmarks to measure the depth of the collapse: the first one based solely on the pre-1989 relation between private credit and GDP in Venezuela (in logs, and allowing for a time trend and two lags for GDP), the second based on the pre-1989 relation between Venezuela's private credit series with those of the average Latin American and oil-dependent country (in logs and allowing for a time trend), and the third based on both relations. These benchmarks imply, respectively, that by the mid-2000s Venezuela's stock of private credit should have been 4.4, 10.6, and 2.9 times larger than it actually was. The average of these values (5.9) is not very far from the magnitudes we obtained based solely on cross-country comparisons and the persistence of the indicators (4.5 and 5.6, respectively).

Using the third benchmark, figure 5.5 asks how much of the misalignment is due to each of the major crises that form the collapse: the 1989 stabilization and the 1994 banking crisis. It turns out that each of the crises explains around half the deviation from the expected value that we see today.

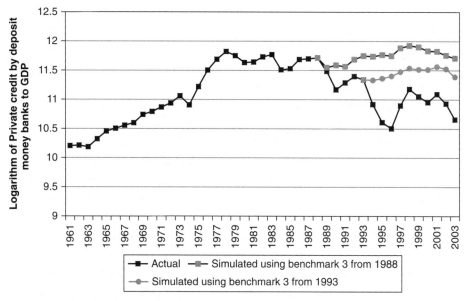

Fig. 5.5   The size of the credit collapse

Sources: Based on International Financial Statistics, August 2009, International Monetary Fund, and author's calculations.

The Real Effects of Venezuela's Financial System Collapse

Venezuela's financial system was not always as underdeveloped as it is today. A couple of big crises starting in the late 1980s took the system from a level consistent with the country's economic development to what it is now. This, the main section of the chapter, tries to determine whether the credit crunch had significant real effects on the economy. We exploit a number of different data sets to look at the issue from a number of different angles. To the time-series aggregate evidence of the last section, we add evidence from cross-sectional managers' perceptions and expectations, industry panels, and listed-firms panels.

Perceptions: Survey Evidence

The World Bank's Doing Business Survey is conducted in a large number of countries, with the goal of determining the main conditions that either enable or constrain business. In each country it asks the views of managers of around one hundred firms. In addition to recording the views on the major constraints faced in doing business, the data set includes a number of characteristics of the firms and, importantly, the expectations about future investment and growth. One of the main subjects of the survey is financing. In this section we ask whether managers' perceptions about the importance of lack of financing are consistent with what the macro-data show, and explore whether it matters for their future plans and expectations.

When compared to other problems, managers do not perceive lack of financing as a major obstacle to doing business in Venezuela.[19] Political instability, inflation, and crime seem to them much more important. Relative to other countries, both poor and rich, the position of financing in the ranking is quite low. This does not mean that financing is unimportant in Venezuela; it just means there are other major constraints. In fact, 31.3 percent of the managers surveyed responded that financing was a major constraint, a much larger figure than in the OECD. Still, when compared to those in the average country, to countries in Latin America, and to countries of similar degree of development, Venezuelan managers do not feel particularly constrained by lack of financing.

The picture that emerges from table 5.1, which shows the sources of financing used by the firms, is somewhat different. More consistent with the low ratio of private credit to GDP, bank financing accounts for a mere 15.5 percent of the total in Venezuela. This figure is 15 percentage points lower than what would be expected given the country's income level and its geographical region.[20] On the other side of the coin, internal financing, which includes retained earnings and family financing, accounts for 60 percent of the total, 22.3 points larger than expected and also very significant in statistical terms.

At least in terms of the way they actually finance their operations, managers in Venezuela behave as if they were financially constrained. Perhaps they just do not express it directly because lack of financing is overshadowed by other important factors, such as political instability and inflation uncertainty. These can certainly have an effect on growth opportunities and therefore on the demand for external

Table 5.1   Financing sources of firms

	Venezuela	All countries	Low or middle income	Latin America	OECD
Internal/family	60.1%	55.7%	64.1%	47.5%	41.4%
Bank	15.5%	17.7%	16.6%	25.9%	18.4%
Trade	7.2%	8.6%	9.3%	11.5%	8.1%
Credit/leasing	2.6%	4.7%	2.7%	3.2%	8.5%
Equity	18.2%	22.5%	19.3%	29.1%	26.9%

SOURCE: Based on Business Environment and Enterprise Performance Survey (BEEPS).

NOTE: Financing sources according to manager (percentage of total).

funds. However, the mix between the internal and external financing of the investment that is actually done is more consistent with a supply story, namely, with the banking system not being able to provide the funds—or at least not on conditions that managers are willing to accept. It is likely that (past and actual) instability increases perceived credit risk and ends up in high interest rates. In fact, when asked about the specific issues that limit their access to external finance, managers name high interest rates above everything else.

But does it matter for investment and (ultimately) for growth? In the end internal and external funds, although not always perfect, are in essence substitutes. Also, after almost two decades of working with almost no financial system on which to rely, managers might have come up with other—perhaps informal—mechanisms to finance investment. Our analysis shows that Venezuelan managers' expected future investment growth is very significantly correlated with the views of managers about what will happen to the firm's debt (see table 5A.2 in the appendix). This is true even after controlling for investment opportunities (proxy with the expected rate of growth for sales), and the perception of other factors limiting the ability to do business (proxy with the average importance of nonfinancial constraints). Expected external financing is also highly correlated with the expected growth in employment and exports.

All this suggests that external financing is perceived to be an important part of the future growth picture. But correlation does not establish causality. An important part of the story is probably investment causing increased demand for all kinds of funds, including debt. This problem is, of course, not new in the real-effects-of-finance literature. One way this has been handled is by looking at whether the financing or investment behavior differs across firms. Fazzari, Hubbard, and Petersen (1988) in particular propose looking at the sensitivity of investment to the availability of internal funds. In a world with no financial frictions—where internal and external funds are perfect substitutes—investment should not depend at all on the availability of internal funds, but only on the existence of growth opportunities. A large literature has established that these sensitivities are significantly positive, and particularly so for firms more likely to be a priori financially constrained (small, opaque, R & D intensive, etc.).

We explored the extent to which future investment can be explained with growth opportunities vis-à-vis internal cash in the context of the managers' survey in Venezuela (see table 5A.3). We measure growth opportunities with the managers' expectations of future sales growth, and the availability of internal funds with past sales growth.[21] We look at age, size, and foreign ownership. Small firms will find it harder to access external finance given the importance of fixed costs in monitoring and screening. Young firms will typically be more opaque simply because they lack a track record. These two measures have been extensively used before as proxies for the likelihood that a firm is financially constrained. To these we add foreign ownership on the assumption that the overseas owner has access to more developed financial systems. Considering the position of Venezuela in the financial development ranking, this is quite likely the case even if the owner were not from a rich country.

Overall the results show that while investment opportunities typically enter in a positive and significant way, the availability of internal funds is less robustly correlated with expected investment growth. The related literature typically finds a strong positive relation for cash flow but fails to find significance for growth opportunities. This difference is natural and goes in the same direction as the relative improvement we make in the measurement of the two variables. The importance of nonfinancial constraints is generally negative but insignificant. More to the point, when comparing the regression coefficients across the groups it is clear that relative to the availability of internal funds, investment opportunities are much important in the relatively financially unconstrained groups. In all cases, growth opportunities are more strongly related to investment in the unconstrained group, while exactly the opposite is found for the availability of internal funds. While we cannot reject the fact that both coefficients are equal in any of the constrained groups, we are able to reject the hypothesis in each of the unconstrained ones.[22]

We interpret the set of results in this section as suggesting that investment in Venezuela is today importantly determined by the availability of external funds. The limited amount of these external funds implies that small, young, and local firms cannot invest fully into their opportunities and grow as fast as they could.

Industry-Level Evidence

We already provided some evidence on the evolution of private credit (Granger) causing growth especially in the non-tradable sector, and the more dependent on external finance. In this section we take a closer look at manufacturing industry data consisting of yearly observations for twenty-six manufacturing industries for the 1963–98 period.[23]

There is by now a large literature using this methodology and similar data. The goal has been establishing that finance does matter for real outcomes and the likely mechanisms at work. Rajan and Zingales (1998) showed that, relative to less dependent ones, industries that are highly dependent on external financing grow more slowly in countries with poor financial development (measured as private credit to GDP). Braun and Larrain (2005) similarly provided evidence for the financial channel of the business cycle by showing that more dependent industries fare much worse relative to others during recessions in countries with less developed financial systems. Finally, Kroszner, Klingebiel, and Laeven (2002) showed that the growth of these same industries is the most affected during financial crises.

We start with this last piece of evidence and ask whether this was indeed the case during Venezuela's 1989–96 financial collapse. The answer is yes (see table 5A.4). The 1989–96 period is associated with an average decrease in manufacturing real value added growth of 5.4 percent per year or 36 percent in total (beyond what is predicted by mean reversion alone). The drop was not homogeneous across industries, however. The fall was increasing with the degree of external finance dependence, and very significantly so: the typical highly dependent industry saw its growth rate fall four percentage points faster a year than the typical less dependent one (−6.6 percent vs. −3.3 percent). In fact, for those industries with lower than median dependence, the credit crunch was not even associated with statistically lower growth rates. Assuming that less dependent industries are simply unaffected by credit crunches, and given that these industries represented about 60 percent of non-oil manufacturing, these results suggest that the fall in manufacturing growth could have been cut in more than half had the collapse in credit been avoided.[24]

The credit collapse indeed affected more strongly those industries that are supposed to be more reliant on bank credit for financing investment. This— together with the fact that credit appears to anticipate the growth of the highly dependent aggregate during this period—hints at a supply-side explanation, a real effect of the intermediation crunch. It also suggests that misallocation of resources across sectors is a critical piece of the mechanism through which finance affects growth. Wurgler (2000) provides some evidence on the issue by showing that in less developed settings investment is less responsive to changes in growth opportunities. He measures this by computing the responsiveness of investment to value-added growth using pooled industry data for a decade in each of a large number of countries. Less financially developed countries exhibit lower elasticities, meaning that they do not rapidly cut investment in declining sectors and increase it in booming ones. This is taken as evidence of the important allocation role of capital markets.

We checked whether the quality of allocation of resources declined following the credit crunch relative to its level when credit was plentiful, as Wurgler's cross-country analysis would imply.[25] We considered the value-added

elasticities of investment and employment growth. Both turned out to be significantly sensitive to growth opportunities when measured with real value-
added growth. The sensitivity declined after the credit collapse, especially in
the case of employment growth, and more strongly for the set of highly dependent industries.

We also explored whether the misallocation comes primarily from not directing the resources toward the right industries in a given moment of time, from not
directing the resources to a particular industry in the precise moment, or from
both. In the case of investment, most of the effect comes from cross-industry
misallocation, while for employment the problem resides in not hiring and firing
employees when it seems appropriate.

Listed-Firms Evidence

We also looked at Worldscope data on a large number of listed firms around the
world from the early 1980s through 2003 (Thomson Reuters 2003). We are interested in determining whether large, listed firms were also affected by the credit
collapse, or whether given their size and preferred access to external funds they
managed to escape from it.[26]

Consistent with Fazzari, Hubbard, and Petersen's (1988) results for the fifty-
two countries in our sample, while Tobin's q (the ratio of market to book value
of firms, a measure of investment opportunities) is not particularly useful in explaining investment, the availability of internal funds (as measured by net income
over assets) is strongly positively correlated with it (see table 5A.5). Moreover,
the importance of growth opportunities increases strongly across countries with
financial development, in particular with the level of private credit over GDP. The
role of internal funds declines with financial development, although not significantly so.

These results would lead us to expect that given the extremely low level of
Venezuela's financial development, investment there would be much more conditioned by the availability of internal funds than in other countries. This is indeed
the case, and the effect is very large, suggesting that firms there are about five
times more dependent on internal funds when investing than are firms in the
average country. This goes far beyond what one would expect given the relation
between internal funds and investment across different financial development
contexts. But it would be consistent with the fact that, as we saw in the first part,
the financial system in Venezuela is not only small but also inefficient given its
small size.

Is this higher dependence of investment on the availability of internal funds related to the 1989–96 credit collapse? We focused on the Venezuelan time series and asked whether the dependence of the firms to internal cash was higher during the credit collapse when compared to the post-collapse recovery period. The results indicate that that was indeed the case: the dependence on internal funds almost doubled during the collapse period, while the effect of growth opportunities went from positive to essentially zero. This reliance on internal cash has continued to be quite large, reflecting the fact that although private credit recovered somewhat in the late 1990s and early 2000s, it never got back to the pre-collapse levels—nor did it achieve levels more consistent with the size of the economy.

This behavior is due to a combination of both the inability to invest unless one has internal funds at the right time, and the inability to do so in the right sector. If anything, it appears that the collapse affected relatively more strongly the cross-industry allocation of funds than it did the intertemporal one.

The results for listed firms are very consistent with those found for the entire economy in the previous sections. This suggests that the strong, negative effects of the credit crunch were not limited to small firms and perhaps relatively less productive, younger, and more fragile firms, but extended through the economy and eventually reached even the largest and strongest ones. Moreover, while things improved in the late 1990s, the investment of listed firms in Venezuela remains much more dependent on the availability of internal funds and less dependent on future growth opportunities than in other countries.

Conclusions

A number of important facts are clearly present in all the different data sets we used to assess both Venezuela's actual level of financial development and its evolution through time. Venezuela's financial sector is massively underdeveloped. This is the case when compared to any benchmark: it is very small relative to the economy in terms of both banking as well as equity and bond markets—even after considering its oil dependency and being part of Latin America. Not only that, but it is also less efficient than one would expect given its size. Things were not always the same, however. Venezuela had a financial market that was consistent with its economic size until the late 1980s. A series of crunches—most likely originated in deep reversals in fiscal accounts that contributed to high real interest rates—configured a collapse between 1989 and 1996, from which bank credit to the private sector never really recovered. As of the mid-2000s, the size of the financial sector in Venezuela is between 4 and 6 times smaller than one would expect. An important part of the story is the large fall in the ratio of bank credit to the private sector to bank assets. If this ratio would just go back to its pre-collapse level (or were more similar to that of other countries), private credit would almost double.

A collapse of this magnitude was bound to have an important effect on the real economy. Survey evidence indicates that, although managers do not perceive lack of financing as the most important constraint to doing business, they behave in a way quite consistent with the issue being a major problem. Not only do they rely much more on internal and family funds for financing, but they are not particularly able to exploit their growth opportunities. Access to (the limited) bank debt appears to be as important as the existence of growth opportunities when investing, hiring, and exporting, even after controlling for other perceived constraints to doing business. Small, local, and young firms appear to be the most affected.

These perceptions are confirmed in the aggregate data for the economy. The evolution of private credit—its collapse in particular—helps predict that of the tradable sector that is most dependent on external funds and the one of the non-tradable sector, which is typically less able to obtain financing overseas. Our panel of manufacturing industries indicates that the collapse of credit indeed affected more strongly those industries that are supposed to be more reliant on bank credit for financing investment. The quality of allocation of both employment and investment decreased significantly for these same sectors following the financial crisis. Finally, not even the largest firms in the country (the listed ones) could escape the effects of the collapse: these saw their dependence on the availability of internal funds for investing increase significantly. The cross-sectional allocation of resources in the economy appears to be in all cases the most affected. It appears that the financial system ceased channeling capital to the private sector, and that the little amount they provided was not directed to the right borrowers.

This chapter has documented a number of real effects of the financial collapse using quite diverse data sets. This is useful for two reasons. First, they provide a robustness to the analysis, since the results do not seem to depend too much on the particular specification chosen or the data used. Second, the results turned out to be quite consistent, and the effects of the collapse seem to affect pretty much everyone in the economy.

APPENDIX

Table 5A.1   Ganger causality tests (p-values)

Variable	Private credit does not G-cause variable			Variable does not G-cause private credit		
	1963–2003	1963–88	1989–2003	1963–2003	1963–88	1989–2003
Total GDP	0.423	**0.017**	0.197	0.123	0.105	0.250
Non-oil GDP	**0.048**	**0.045**	0.362	**0.000**	**0.000**	0.149
Non-oil non-tradable GDP	**0.082**	**0.001**	0.502	**0.001**	**0.000**	**0.046**
Non-oil tradable GDP	0.204	0.924	0.152	**0.027**	**0.010**	**0.015**
Manufacturing value-added high external finance dependence	0.160	0.333	**0.030**	**0.087**	**0.002**	0.539
Manufacturing value-added low external finance dependence	0.531	0.641	0.394	**0.003**	0.238	**0.016**

SOURCES: Based on UNIDO 2002 and Rodríguez 2004.

NOTE: Figures in bold when significant at 10% level.

Table 5A.2   Financial constraints and real outcomes: Survey evidence

Dependent variable	Expected investment growth	Expected employment growth	Expected exports growth
Expected increase in debt	0.202***	0.345***	0.290***
	0.0745	0.087	0.100
Expected increase in sales	0.352***	0.437	0.321**
	0.114	0.134	0.153
Average importance of nonfinancial constraints	−0.146	−0.283***	−0.051
	0.106	0.124	0.141
# Obs	90	90	90
R-squared	0.19	0.29	0.15

SOURCE: Based on Business Environment and Enterprise Performance Survey (BEEPS).

NOTE: Constant included but not reported.

*10%

**5%

***1%

Table 5A.3   Financial constraints and real outcomes: Survey evidence (heterogeneity across firms)

	Dependent variable: Expected future investment growth					
	Small	Large	Local	Foreign	Young	Old
Future expected sales growth	0.271	0.397***	0.316**	0.598***	−0.072	0.612***
	0.203	0.147	0.149	0.183	0.175	0.154
Past sales growth	0.368	−0.126	0.040	−0.034	0.251	−0.194
	0.228	0.185	0.165	0.303	0.171	0.210
Average importance of nonfinancial constraints	0.095	−0.139	−0.190	0.097	−0.247	−0.086
	0.248	0.1301	0.133	0.202	0.165	0.146
#Obs	32	58	67	23	44	46
R-squared	0.16	0.14	0.09	0.36	0.10	0.28
Tests (p-value) H0: b_ futuresalesgr= b_pastsales gr	0.773	0.034	0.245	0.086	0.207	0.006

SOURCE: Based on Business Environment and Enterprise Performance Survey (BEEPS).

NOTE: Constant included but not reported.

* 10%
** 5%
*** 1%

Table 5A.4   Financial constraints and growth: Industry-panel evidence

Dependent variable: Industry real value-added growth						
Share in manuf. value-added$_{t-1}$	−0.709** 0.331	−0.620* 0.332	−3.975*** 0.874	−0.574** 0.283	−4.148** 0.760	−4.647*** 0.800
Industry external finance dependence	— —	0.104*** 0.039	— —	0.109*** 0.033	— —	— —
Private credit collapse period (1989–96)	−0.054** 0.021	−0.025 0.024	−0.033 0.024	— —	— —	— —
Industry external finance dep. · priv. credit collapse period	— —	−0.164** 0.074	−0.153** 0.074	−0.166*** 0.063	−0.155** 0.062	−0.174** 0.071
Industry tradability · priv. credit collapse period	— —	— —	— —	— —	— —	0.181** 0.081
Industry durable good · priv. credit collapse period	— —	— —	— —	— —	— —	0.007 0.057
Industry investment good · priv. credit collapse period	— —	— —	— —	— —	— —	−0.008 0.098
#Obs	777	777	777	777	777	746
R-squared2	0.01	0.02	0.07	0.32	0.40	0.37
Industry fixed effects	No	No	Yes	No	Yes	Yes
Year fixed effects	No	No	No	Yes	Yes	Yes

SOURCES: Based on Braun and Larrain 2005 and Rajan and Zingales 1998.

NOTE: Constant included but not reported.

*10%

**5%

***1%

Table 5A.5   Financial constraints and investments: Listed-firms evidence

Dependent variable: Real capital expenditure growth

	Entire Sample			Venezuela		
Tobin's q	0.001	−0.029***	0.001	0.243	−0.081	−0.077
	0.001	0.006	0.001	0.541	0.561	0.764
Net income / assets	0.714***	0.748*	0.699***	2.967***	3.262*	5.542***
	0.204	0.447	0.200	0.791	1.541	1.757
Tobin's q · private credit to GDP	—	0.160***	—	—	—	—
	—	.0320	—	—	—	—
Net income / assets · private credit to GDP	—	−0.109	—	—	—	—
	—	.3914	—	—	—	—
Tobin's q · Venezuela	—	—	0.137	—	—	—
	—	—	0.276	—	—	—
Net income / assets · Venezuela	—	—	4.181***	—	—	—
	—	—	0.507	—	—	—
Tobin's q · Credit collapse period (1989–96)	—	—	—	−0.240	0.690	−0.160
	—	—	—	0.615	0.581	0.664
Net income / assets · credit collapse period (1989–96)	—	—	—	2.834***	2.094	1.537
	—	—	—	0.874	1.555	1.391
Credit collapse period (1989–96)	—	—	—	0.189	—	0.162
	—	—	—	0.596	—	0.626
# Obs	11,655	11,655	11,655	52	52	52
R-squared	0.03	0.02	0.03	0.31	0.52	0.41
Country fixed effects	Yes	Yes	Yes	No	No	No
Year fixed effects	No	No	No	No	Yes	No
Industry fixed effects	No	No	No	No	No	Yes

SOURCE: Based on Thomson Reuters, Worldscope database.

NOTE: Constant included but not reported. Robust errors clustered at the year level.

*10%
**5%
***1%

NOTES

1. See, for instance, Bagehot 1873; Hicks 1969; Schumpeter 1912; Robinson 1952; Lucas 1988.

2. King and Levine 1993.

3. Levine and Zervos 1998; Beck, Levine, and Loayza 2000; La Porta et al. 1997, 1998.

4. Beck, Levine, and Loayza 2000; Rajan and Zingales 1998; Wurgler 2000; Love 2001; Jayaratne and Strahan 1996.

5. Braun and Raddatz 2007.

6. The cross-country data for the size and efficiency of financial systems come from Beck, Levine, and Loayza 2000. The data for GDP and other economic country variables come from World Development Indicators. All figures in this section correspond to the average of the indicator between 1995 and 2004.

7. This difference is statistically significant at p-values below 0.1 percent.

8. This difference is statistically significant at p-values below 0.1 percent.

9. See table 1 in the working paper version of this chapter.

10. This figure is statistically significant at 1 percent.

11. See figure 6 in the working paper version of this chapter.

12. See figures 7 and 8 in the working paper version.

13. This computation is done in logs and allows for a time trend.

14. This is based on variation in a yearly sample of 135 countries between 1960 and 2004.

15. The p-value here is lower than 0.1 percent.

16. See figure 15 in the working paper version.

17. These data come from IMF's International Financial Statistics.

18. Table 9 in the working paper version presents the measure for the different industries. Data on the growth of the different industries are obtained from UNIDO's Indstat data set. We have excluded the oil-related industries (petroleum refineries and miscellaneous petroleum and coal products) to make the conclusions robust to the evolution of the influential sector.

19. See tables 4 and 5 in the working paper version.

20. The p-value is lower than 0.1 percent.

21. These measures are not perfect: expectations of future sales growth are endogenous to investment, and past sales growth—although a measure of past success—might be only weakly correlated with the stock of cash. On the other hand, the approach is quite robust to the main criticism to the related literature: growth opportunities are measured with significant error that is likely to be correlated with cash or cash flows. Here we have a much more direct measure for growth opportunities (the opinions of the managers), and the cash flow proxy is much more likely to be exogenous. Also, we are not particularly interested in the absolute magnitude of the coefficient of each variable, but rather on how they compare to one another across samples of firms more or less likely to be financially constrained.

22. See the last row of table 5A.3.

23. Looking at a panel of industries has two important advantages over just considering aggregates. The first is that one is better able to control for omitted variable bias by focusing on how industries differ in a particular moment in time and not just on how each particular one evolves, since time-varying factors common to all industries can be controlled for. The second big advantage is that the endogeneity concerns are eased significantly. Although it is quite likely that the entire non-oil tradable sector affects in some way the evolution of private credit through a demand channel, it is not very likely that what happens in one particular sector that represents at most around 1 percent of GDP affects the entire banking system. This kind of data also allows being more specific about the mechanism through which the availability of finance matters for growth.

24. Notice that here we are explicitly controlling for systematic differences in the growth rate across sectors in the Venezuelan data with the inclusion of the industry's external finance dependence figure. Columns 2–4 in table 5A.4 check that the result is not driven by the omission

of either industry characteristics or what was happening each particular year by adding to the specification industry fixed effects, year fixed effects, and then both at the same time. In all cases, the financial dependence collapse interaction enters negatively and in a statistically significant way, while the coefficient is remarkably similar.

It could still be that the results are driven by other omitted industry characteristics correlated with external finance dependence that happen to be affected differently by crises. To check this, we added three industry characteristics that might matter in explaining growth in times of economic distress: the degree of tradability of the good, and whether it is durable or an investment good. The interaction for the degree of tradability enters significantly positive. This is consistent with the fact that, despite the falling trend, the 1989–96 period was one of high real exchange rate by historical standards implying higher relative prices for tradable producers (more precisely, for those that are *more* tradable since all industries belong to the manufacturing sector, which is quite tradable as a whole). Whether an industry produced a durable or investment good seemed not to matter much during the collapse in credit.

25. See tables 11 and 12 in the working paper version.

26. We focus on manufacturing for which data is more comparable across firms, and aggregate the firm-level data into ISIC-3 categories to avoid having the results depend too much on one particular firm.

REFERENCES

Abiad, Abdul, and Ashoka Mody. 2003. "Financial Reform: What Shakes It? What Shapes It?" *American Economic Review* 95 (1): 66–68.

Bagehot, W. (1873) 1999. *Lombard Street: A Description of the Money Market.* New York: Scribner, Armstrong. Reprint, New York: John Wiley & Sons.

Banco Central de Venezuela. 2001. "Las Tasas de Interés en Venezuela, Diversos Criterios." *Revista BCV* 15 (2).

Beck, T., R. Levine, and N. Loayza. 2000. "Finance and the Sources of Growth." *Journal of Financial Economics* 58:261–300.

Braun, Matías, and Borja Larrain. 2005. "Finance and the Business Cycle." *Journal of Finance* 60 (3): 1097–128.

Braun, Matías, and Claudio Raddatz. 2007. "Trade Liberalization, Capital Account Liberalization, and the Real Effects of Financial Development." *Journal of International Money and Finance* 26:730–61.

_____. 2008. "The Politics of Financial Development: Evidence from Trade Liberalization." *Journal of Finance* 63 (3): 1469–508.

Cameron, R., O. Crisp, P. Hugh, and R. Tilly, eds. 1967. *Banking in the Early Stages of Industrialization: A Study in Comparative Economic History.* New York: Oxford University Press.

De Krivoy, Ruth. 2000. *Collapse: The Venezuelan Banking Crisis of 1994.* Washington, D.C.: Group of Thirty.

Fazzari, Steven M., R. Glenn Hubbard, and Bruce C. Petersen. 1988. "Financing Constraints and Corporate Investment." Working Paper 2387, National Bureau of Economic Research, Cambridge, Mass.

Goldsmith, R. 1969. *Financial Structure and Development.* New Haven: Yale University Press.

Hicks, J. 1969. *A Theory of Economic History.* Oxford: Clarendon Press.

International Monetary Fund. 2005. "International Financial Statistics."

Jayaratne, J., and P. E. Strahan. 1996. "The Finance-Growth Nexus: Evidence from Bank Branch Deregulation." *Quarterly Journal of Economics* 111:639–70.

King, R. G., and R. Levine. 1993. "Finance and Growth: Schumpeter Might Be Right." *Quarterly Journal of Economics* 58:717–37.

Kroszner, Randy, Daniela Klingebiel, and Luc Laeven. 2002. "Financial Crises, Financial Dependence, and Industry Growth." Policy Research Working Paper Series 2855, World Bank Development Research Group, Washington, D.C.

La Porta, Rafael, Florencio Lopez-de-Silanes, Andrei Shleifer, and Robert Vishny. 1997. "Legal Determinants of External Finance." *Journal of Finance* 52:1131–50.

_____. 1998. "Law and Finance." *Journal of Political Economy* 106:1113–55.

Levine, R., and S. Zervos. 1998. "Stock Markets, Banks, and Economic Growth." *American Economic Review* 88:537–58.

Love, I. 2001. "Financial Development and Financing Constraints: International Evidence from the Structural Investment Model." Policy Research Working Paper 2694, World Bank Development Research Group, Washington, D.C.

Lucas, R. 1988. "On the Mechanisms of Economic Development." *Journal of Monetary Economics* 22:3–42.

McKinnon, R. 1973. *Money and Capital in Economic Development.* Washington, D.C.: Brookings Institution.

Rajan, R., and L. Zingales. 1998. "Financial Dependence and Growth." *American Economic Review* 88:559–86.

Robinson, J. 1952. "The Generalization of the General Theory." In *The Rate of Interest, and Other Essays,* edited by Joan Robinson, 67–139. London: Macmillan.

Rodríguez, Francisco. 2004. "Un nuevo índice encadenado del Producto Interno Bruto de Venezuela, 1957–2001." *Revista BCV* 18 (2): 99–118.

Schumpeter, J. (1912). 1934. *The Theory of Economic Development.* Cambridge: Harvard University Press.

Thomson Reuters. 2003. Worldscope Database.

UNIDO. 2002. Industrial Statistics Database (INDSTAT).

World Bank. 2005. World Development Indicators.

Wurgler, Jeffrey. 2000. "Financial Markets and the Allocation of Capital." *Journal of Financial Economic* 66:171–205.

6 MUCH HIGHER SCHOOLING, MUCH LOWER WAGES: HUMAN CAPITAL AND ECONOMIC COLLAPSE IN VENEZUELA

Daniel Ortega and Lant Pritchett

Since schooling and human capital are so widely asserted to be an integral part of development and growth, then perhaps the converse is true: a lack of human capital explains in some part the decline in Venezuela. This chapter demonstrates that this is not true: all the evidence suggests that the expansion of schooling should have led to higher output per worker and hence schooling only deepens the puzzle. First, by standard cross-national measures of schooling and schooling capital (SK), Venezuela's growth of SK was *more* rapid than the median country (and more rapid than the median of eight quickly growing East Asian countries), so no part of the Venezuelan deficit in performance can be attributed to "slow" SK growth. Second, labor force survey data on wages show that if the wage–returns relationship had been stable over time, then the additional levels of education of workers should have raised wages by 58 percent—while in fact they fell roughly by half. Even if one allows for a fall in the returns to education, the increase in wages "expected" from higher levels of schooling is 25 percent. Therefore, if one takes into account by how much higher output or wages should have been due to the increased levels of education, then whatever explains the output decline must be even larger than the observed decline. There are, however, two ways that aspects of education contributed to the economic decline. One is that quality, as measured by the test scores on higher education entrance examinations, deteriorated during the 1980s into 1990s by over 70 percent. Perhaps this quality deterioration played some role in the crisis. Perhaps puzzlingly, however, the wage premiums per year of schooling did not decline—and so "schooling capital" measures as an input into economic production are, perhaps counterintuitively, unaffected by the quality decline. Nevertheless, we attempt to assess the impact of this decline on the output decline. The final section attempts some more speculative ways in which education might be part of the collapse despite higher schooling and observed returns on schooling—if perhaps the allocation of education across sectors precluded a reallocation of output in response to the economic shock as "private" and "public" returns diverged. But while it is possible to construct coherent narratives of this type, it is difficult to construct solid evidence for this view.

The mantra of "human capital" is so deeply embedded in the growth and development literatures that one might get the impression that when we see low, or negative, growth rates over an extended period, as in the Venezuelan experience, we should also expect stagnation in education outcomes. But Venezuela apparently hasn't heard the conventional wisdom. Schooling capital (defined in a way consistent with aggregate output specifications) grew *faster* in Venezuela than in most other countries—in fact faster than in the median fast-growing East Asian countries. Now perhaps this expansion of schooling did not contribute to output because private returns to schooling, measured as the Mincer regression wage increment, collapsed. But again, no. Even taking into account the decline in the wage premiums observed using the labor force surveys over time, the increase in schooling reported should have led to wages 25 percent higher from 1975 to 2003—but in reality the average wage fell by 49 percent. While schooling quality as measured by test performance appears to have declined, this decline has not reduced the schooling premium, which is the economic valuation of schooling. Even if each schooling year is producing fewer skills, the demand for skills must be expanding sufficiently to maintain the observed wage premium—which is to schooling years, not measured skills.

All this deepens the puzzle for others attempting to explain Venezuela's decline. That is, one might set out to explain the large "raw" output and wage decline in Venezuela—but if one finds a factor capable of explaining the decline, not only does it have to explain why output and wages fell, it has to explain why output and wages fell even as the *expected* output and wages were rising due to increased schooling. That is, if our task were to help explain the output decline in Venezuela, our examination of schooling and wages is of less than zero help.

But there might be some narrative (or even theory) that can reconcile the increase in schooling and the steady observed returns to schooling in the labor market, and yet still attribute some part of the decline to schooling. In order for this to be true, however, there would have to be a large *negative* externality to schooling. Perhaps education is allocated to rent-seeking, and perhaps even a negative economic shock raises the returns to rent-seeking (and so the gap between public and private returns) sufficiently that the subsequent increase in schooling actually contributes to output decline (even while the wage-schooling profile remains upward-sloping). However, while it is possible to tell this story in a consistent and coherent way, we cannot find any empirical evidence for this view.

Higher Schooling and Lower Output per Worker

Many posit the accumulation of human capital as a major driving force behind economic growth. The converse therefore might also be expected, that a country with major decline in output per capita must have somehow failed to accumulate human capital. Or at the very least, that small investments in schooling or accumulation of human capital helps explain the growth difference between Venezuela and other countries. But this is not the case. By the standard measures of the raw accumulation of schooling years, Venezuela was not a laggard. Years of schooling grew rapidly during the entire period. Moreover, by nearly every measure of the growth of "schooling capital," Venezuela outperformed other countries.

Figure 6.1 shows the evolution of the total years of schooling of the labor force–aged population from the Barro–Lee data (right-hand scale) and the evolution of real GDP per worker from the Penn World Tables 6.1 data. Years of schooling more than doubled from 2.9 to 6.6.[1] Output per worker fell by 40 percent from a peak of P\$10,500 to P\$6,400 (P\$ is PPP adjusted) in 2000 (and this was before

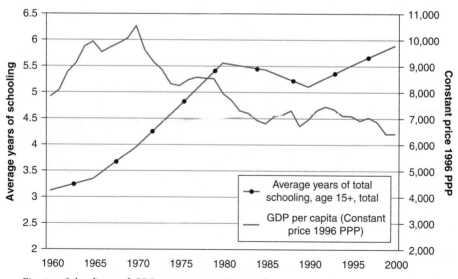

Fig. 6.1   Schooling and GDP per person in Venezuela

Sources: Based on "Penn World Table Version 6.1" (Heston, Summers, and Aten 2002) and Robert J. Barro and Jong-Wha Lee, http://www.barrolee.com.

the more recent crises). Moreover, when the growth collapse began in the 1970s, the labor force was experiencing a period of extremely rapid gains in education. Clearly nothing about the fall in output can be directly attributed to a decline in years of schooling.

But even though schooling rose absolutely, perhaps it rose at a slower pace than in other countries, so that some part of the less rapid growth can be attributed to this factor. In fact, according to the standard, if flawed, Barro–Lee data set on the average years of schooling of the labor force–aged (15–64) population, schooling expanded more quickly in Venezuela than in the median country. Table 6.1 reports the per annum growth rates of schooling using the available data for countries between 1960 and 1999 in both percentage changes and the absolute (the reason for using both becomes clearer below). Venezuela grew at 2.1 ppa (percentage per annum or purchased power adjustment) versus medians of 1.8 ppa for all countries, 1.5 ppa for LAC (Latin American and Caribbean) countries, and only 0.9 ppa for OECD countries. Using the absolute change in schooling relative Venezuela's growth was even more impressive, adding a tenth of a year of schooling each year, which is above the 75th percentile for all countries.

As suggested by figure 6.1, in which an acceleration of schooling growth is seen after 1970, if one takes just the post-1970 period, in which growth was negative, Venezuela's relative performance is even larger. From 1970 to 1999 schooling years grew at 2.5 ppa versus a median of 1.7 ppa in the eight rapidly growing East Asian economies.

Suppose we want to know how much the difference of Venezuela's growth performance differential versus some reference group (the average country,

Table 6.1   Growth rates of years of schooling, in percentage and absolute per year, for Venezuela compared with the medians of other regions

	Percentage per annum*	Absolute change per year**
Venezuela	0.021	0.096
Tigers (eight high-performing East Asian economies)	0.018	0.094
LAC	0.015	0.063
OECD (n=22; old definition, not including recent entrants)	0.009	0.070
All (n=105)	0.018	0.070

*Calculated as compound annual growth rate from initial to final estimate; for example, for Venezuela it is $(6.64/2.90) \cdot (1/39) - 1 = 0.021$.
**Calculated as total difference divided by years; for example, for Venezuela it is $(6.64 - 2.90)/39 = 0.096$.

East Asian countries, etc.) was due to various factors. It is quite common to specify an empirical growth equation that allows a decomposition of growth differentials into known correlates and residuals. One example is an equation of the type

$$(y_{t+n}^V - y_t^V) - (y_{t+n}^R - y_t^R) \equiv \alpha + \lambda(y_t^V - y_t^R) + \beta'(X_{t?}^V - X_{t?}^R)$$
$$+ (\varepsilon_{t+n,t}^V - \varepsilon_{t+n,t}^V), \tag{1}$$

where V is Venezuela and R is a reference group, the Xs are various growth correlates, the coefficients α, λ, and β (a K by 1 vector) are estimated or imputed, and the ε is a residual term that balances the accounting identity.[2] In some of the standard growth decomposition approaches, the term for "schooling" is treated in a fast and loose way that would give ad hoc a heart attack.[3]

If we think about a pure "factor accumulation" decomposition of growth into its proximate determinants of K, H, L, and a residual, then there are two key and related steps. First, just as with physical capital one has to move from physical units to value units (e.g., tractors and factories to the value of physical capital). Second, one has to specify how the appropriately specified term capturing schooling capital enters the production function.

Bils and Klenow (2000) present a general formulation in which the production function provides output as a function of units of effective labor, $H(t)$. The current stock of $H(t)$ is the result of integrating the quality-adjusted labor force over all ages

$$H(t) = \int_a^T h(a,t)L(a,t)\,da, \tag{2}$$

where the quality adjustment for a person of age a with schooling s (and hence experience of $a-s$), is given by

$$h(a,t) = h(a + n)^\varphi e^{f(s)+g(a-s)}. \tag{3}$$

The first term allows the quality of human capital of those aged a to depend on the quality of human capital of previous cohorts (those aged n years older than a) as "parents/teachers" (i.e., human capital contributes to the accumulation of human capital). They also posit a general function, $f(s)$, to map from schooling to quality and they allow for experience effects $g(a-s)$.

If $f(s) = rs$ and $g(a - s) = \gamma_1(a - s) + \gamma_2(a - s)^2$ and $\varphi = 0$, then this is the exact aggregate equivalent of the standard Mincer wage equation, assuming returns are constant across countries as $f'(s) = r$. If one also ignores the age terms, then schooling capital per worker[4] is

$$SK = e^{rs}. \qquad\qquad (4)$$

A major problem with that approach is that there does seem to be a very strong cross-sectional relationship between the level of S and r, which makes assuming a constant r across all countries in aggregating schooling into schooling capital empirically suspect.

Bils and Klenow (2000) allow for a more general function form for $f(s)$ that allows the returns to schooling to decline with additional schooling—$f(s) = \dfrac{\theta}{1-\psi}s^{1-\psi}$—and hence $f'(s) = \theta/s^{\psi}$, with θ chosen so that the mean of θ/s^{ψ} is equal to the mean Mincerian return across countries. The parameter ψ captures the inverse relationship between s and r. At the higher (absolute value) level ψ, each year of schooling contributes more to schooling capital at low levels of schooling when r is, on average, high than at high levels of schooling when r is, on average, low. Bils and Klenow (2000) and Pritchett (2006) estimate ψ empirically using collections of estimates of the wage premium and schooling, producing estimates of 0.58 and 0.66, respectively. Given the precision of these estimates, the value of $\psi=0$ can be soundly rejected.[5]

While the choice of ψ in constructing schooling capital (SK) from schooling (S) may seem a minor detail, Pritchett (2006) shows that the choice of ψ makes all the difference in empirical estimates of the association of the growth of schooling capital and growth in output per worker. All previous results (which tended to use simple expedients, like either the absolute change in S or the percentage change in S) are parametrically encompassed by variations in ψ. Using a value of zero for ψ is similar to using the level of S and its changes as a specification, while higher values of ψ are correlated with percentage change measures. By varying ψ one can produce associations of output per worker growth and SK growth that are negative, zero, or positive. So all existing growth decompositions make dubious assumptions about the relationship between schooling and schooling capital (often without emphasizing the embedded assumptions) or dubious assumptions about the empirical/output relationship (often not very clear whether it is a standard factor accumulation decomposition, a reduced form decomposition, or some strange mix)—or, in most of the literature, both sources of dubious assumptions are combined.

Fortunately, deciding among the variations across the different possible models of schooling capital is not necessary as, across the variations in the parametric form, Venezuela growth in schooling capital is well above the cross-national median and outperforms all regions. Across the range of plausible parameter values, Venezuela shows higher growth in schooling capital than does the median country, or even the East Asian high-growth countries.

The conclusion of this first section is that no part of the negative growth of the Venezuelan economy can be directly attributed to the country's failure to expand the years of schooling of the labor force.

- Growth in schooling years was rapid before, and persisted well after, the turnaround in growth.
- In the standard cross-national data, growth in schooling years was more rapid in Venezuela than in the typical country—even in the high-performing East Asian economies.
- With a measure of schooling capital that is consistent with microeconomic foundations, and a coherent specification of an aggregate production function, growth in measured schooling capital is even more rapid in Venezuela than in comparison countries.

Bringing schooling into the picture in some ways deepens the puzzle. If one tries to decompose the growth into that due to factor accumulation (or potentially factor de-accumulation) and a "residual," then—since the growth of schooling capital was rapid and positive—this makes the "residual" component of growth even larger (in absolute value, that is, more negative). Venezuela's negative growth rate of −0.75 over the period 1960 to 1990 puts it in the bottom of the growth distribution; to some extent, the similar contraction of "physical capital" of −0.48 (also toward the bottom of the cross-national distribution) helps explain this, but clearly the more rapid than average growth in schooling capital creates more puzzles than it solves.

What Has Happened to Returns to Schooling in the Labor Market?

The first question that arises given these facts is whether these investments in schooling were worthless for the economy, and maybe even for the individuals acquiring such capital. That is, perhaps the individually observed returns to schooling in the labor market collapsed during the crisis so that schooling no longer added to wages, and so the increments to schooling *years* observed above would not create any schooling *capital* valued at its "market" price. Using the labor force surveys from 1975 to 2003, however, this does not appear to be the case.

Figure 6.2 shows the evolution of the wage premium in logs for primary, secondary, and tertiary schooling from 1975 to 2003. Between 1978 (the approximate

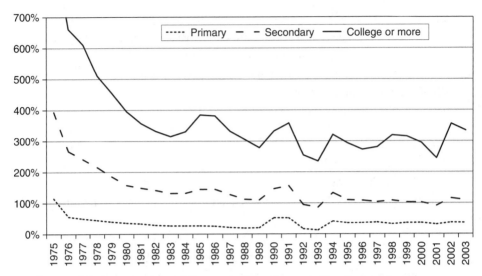

Fig. 6.2   Wage premiums from Mincer equations after controlling for experience

beginning of the collapse) and 2003, the wage premium associated with having a college education or higher fell by approximately 34 percent. But this fall occurred mostly before 1982; since then, wage premiums show remarkable stability, and even a slight increase for primary schooling. In 1981, a worker who had completed primary school earned a wage that was on average 33 percent higher than that earned by a worker with no schooling, one who had completed high school earned a wage 149 percent larger, and one who had earned a college education commanded a wage premium of 357 percent over workers without formal schooling. By 2003, this picture was not very different: the premium for primary school was 37 percent, for secondary school 110 percent, and for a tertiary degree it was 334 percent. Moreover, while the observed wage differentials fell substantially from 1975 to 1982, they did not fall to "low" levels by international standards— rather, they fell from very high levels to levels of the wage premiums that are similar to other countries in the region.

Despite this fact, over this period the labor force (and potential labor force, population aged fifteen or older) accumulated increasing amounts of schooling, consistent with the data reported above. In 1976 only 7 percent of the labor force had completed high school, and by 2003 this figure had risen to 27 percent; similarly, the fraction of the labor force with no schooling fell from 65 to 20 percent over this twenty-seven-year span. So, even though the economy was in free fall since 1978, wage premiums remained large and stable enough to sustain significant investments in schooling capital, both private and public.

These facts seem to suggest that the shock that set off the Venezuelan decline was (roughly) skill-neutral, so that pre-existing incentives to accumulate human capital were not eliminated when real wages began to fall significantly. These incentives to accumulate formal schooling were bolstered by the rapid expansion of the public school system, beginning in the early 1970s, which lowered individual costs of acquiring a secondary education (see fig. 6.3), although possibly at a significant cost in terms of quality (see below).

The modest drop in returns to schooling from the late 1970s onward, combined with the dramatic increase in the average schooling of the labor force, suggests that the fall in real wages was mostly due to a fall in everyone's wages, and not that of any particular education attainment group. We can decompose the log of the average real wage as the sum of the (log of) unskilled wage plus the share of the labor force with each schooling level times their (log) wage premium as follows:

$$\ln w = w_u + s_p \alpha_p + s_s \alpha_s + s_c \alpha_c. \tag{5}$$

Since both the shares in the labor force and the skill premiums change over time, we can ask, "If the skill premiums had remained at their 1981 (or 1978) levels and the labor force shares had changed as they actually did, what would the evolution of the real wage have been?" Alternatively we can ask, "If the skill premiums had

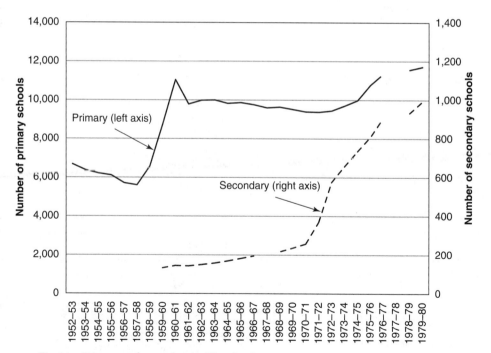

Fig. 6.3   Primary and secondary public schools

Source: Based on Ministry of Education official statistics from several years.

always been that which was observed in 2003, then how big must the fall in the intercept (the unskilled wage) have been in order for the overall average wage to have fallen as much as it did, despite the observed evolution of the skill premiums and schooling of the labor force?"

Figure 6.4 shows the evolution of the average wage. The real wage has fallen by about 67 percent from its peak in 1980. We use the (the exponential of) the decomposition in equation (5)[6] to construct two counterfactual real wage series: one that maintains the unskilled wage and the skill premiums at their 1975 levels, while the other fixes the unskilled wage at its 1975 level but uses the 2003 skill premiums. If the skill premiums had remained at their 1975 levels, and the schooling capital accumulation had occurred as it did, the real wage should have *risen* by over 58 percent instead of falling by 50 percent. While many are rightly skeptical of growth decompositions with GDP per capita like those above, this is much simpler as it is all done in wages—but the finding is the same: the increase in the years of schooling "should have" contributed to much higher real wages, so rather than "human capital" being part of the explanation of Venezuela's collapse, introducing schooling means that whatever explains the fall in output (or wages) has to account for an even larger fall.

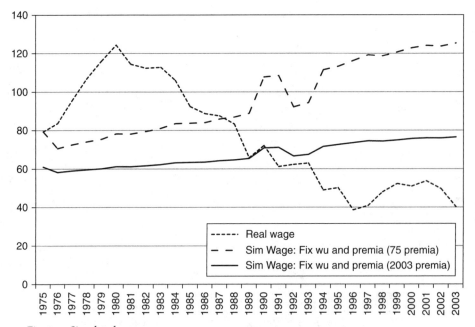

Fig. 6.4   Simulated wages

Source: Based on authors' calculations, drawing on several years of Official Household Surveys.

Perhaps returns fell. But figure 6.4 shows that even if the skill premiums had always been at their 2003 levels, then the average wage should have been about 90 percent higher than it actually was, suggesting a huge drop in the unskilled wage. That is, in order to match the 2003 real wage, keeping the returns to skilled wages fixed at their 2003 levels, the unskilled wage would have had to fall by nearly 48 percent.

The one striking fact that emerges from this analysis is that although the wage premiums fell mostly in the late 1970s, they remained fairly stable thereafter and thus have never been low enough for a significant slowdown in schooling accumulation. However, average wages plunged by around 50 percent from 1975 and by over 67 percent if compared to their peak in 1980. Figure 6.5 shows the evolution of real wages and the simulated series normalized to equal 100 at the peak of the real wage in 1980. It illustrates that from that year up to 2003, the 1975 wage premiums combined with the observed accumulation of schooling should have generated a 60 percent increase in real wages; even allowing for the observed fall in the skill premiums up until 2003, wages *should* have risen by 25 percent.

The main lesson of this section is that the basic shock was to labor as a whole and not so much to the price of skills.

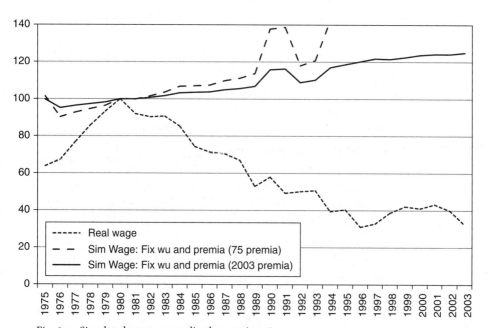

Fig. 6.5   Simulated wages normalized to 100 in 1980

Source: Based on authors' calculations, drawing on several years of Official Household Surveys.

"Kids Today": Did Schooling Quality Play a Role?

Although the previous section demonstrates that the decline in wages was not driven by a decline in the market value of skills, especially after 1982, it is useful to have an idea about the evolution of schooling quality. Although the private returns to schooling may have remained constant over time, possibly the public or social return was significantly affected by changes in quality.

Between 1984 and 2007, Venezuela performed a mandatory standardized aptitude test on every graduating high school student. The test is centrally administered (at one point it was even proctored by the National Guard), and public universities use it as one of the college admission criteria. We have data from 1987 onward on the results of these exams for the verbal and mathematics sections, as well as other information such as high school GPA and socioeconomic information. Between 1972 and 1980, the number of public secondary schools increased from around two hundred to more than one thousand nationwide. This was partly in response to a previous increase in primary public schools during the early 1960s, which later increased the demand for secondary schools.

The average test scores in math and verbal sections from 1987 to 2003[7] fell by over 60 percent, which suggests that the quality of the education system's output has deteriorated dramatically over the period. This may have been a consequence of a fall in the quality of inputs (worse-quality students as the number of exam takers expands) or a deterioration of the effectiveness of the school system itself. There is probably some truth to both effects, as would be expected during a period of rapid expansion of the school system.

The role this decline in quality played in economic growth is a difficult question, and we examine three issues.

First, did the timing of the decline in quality coincide with the onset of the growth collapse? Perhaps the quality deterioration is the result of a sustained decline rather than its cause. Unfortunately, we have direct observations on quality only since 1987. But perhaps this process is not specific to the late 1980s and 1990s. Although we don't have test score data for previous periods, we can use a proximate measure of the quality of inputs in the schooling process such as teacher wage premiums. Figure 6.6 shows the coefficients (and 95 percent confidence interval) on teacher dummies in Mincer regressions that control for the level of schooling (primary, secondary, and college or more) and experience (and its square). After controlling for schooling and experience, teachers commanded an hourly wage premium of over 60 percent in the mid-1970s, and by 1996 (the low point in the series) this had fallen to −12 percent. Only in 2001 did the premium become positive again.

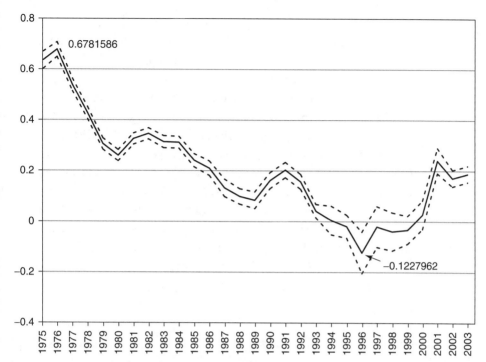

Fig. 6.6 Teacher dummy in Mincer regressions, where schooling enters via level dummies

Source: Based on authors' calculations, drawing on several years of Official Household Surveys.

This is, however, at best a very crude proxy, as one would not expect the effects of changes in the wage premiums on the quality of schooling to be instantaneous but rather to operate with long and uncertain lags. After all, since learning is a cumulative process, if the wage premiums began to decline in 1976 (even if the decline caused teaching quality to fall instantly), a typical graduate in 1977 would have been exposed to only one year of the decline, as his previous schooling was already completed. Moreover, one might expect that the main impact of declining teacher premiums would be the quality of the people recruited into the profession rather than the amount of effort put forth by those employed. This would also take some years to have an impact, as the teaching force would be a mix of those recruited with high premiums and those with lower premiums. Finally, the quality of new labor force entrants has only a small impact on the overall quality of the labor force. Even if one dates the fall in teacher premiums to 1976, the impact on quality of the labor force would come much later: when the cumulative impact of the mix of high- and low-quality teachers is seen on new entrants, the quality composition of the teaching force deteriorates, and the post-1976 entrants constitute a substantial portion of the labor force.

That the lag between teacher premiums and quality is long and variable is suggested by the comparison of the evolution of the teacher premiums and the test scores during the period in which we have observations on both. Figure 6.7 shows an adjustment of schooling capital (SK) for quality using the teacher premiums for the entire period, and also adjusting using the average SAT (PAA) scores in math (probably a better measure) from 1987 onward. This alternative adjustment exhibits, over the post-1987 period, less volatility and consistent decline, as opposed to the dramatic up and down in the wage premiums. Moreover, if one assumed that the decline in quality began early and played a major role in the collapse, one would have to extrapolate backward the decline in quality. This would imply that scores in the 1970s were astronomically higher than those today—math scores fell in eleven years, from 1991 to 2002, by about fifteen points. If one extrapolates backward a similar magnitude of decline from around thirty in 1987 to 1976, then the score would have been forty-five in 1976, compared to less than ten in 2003.

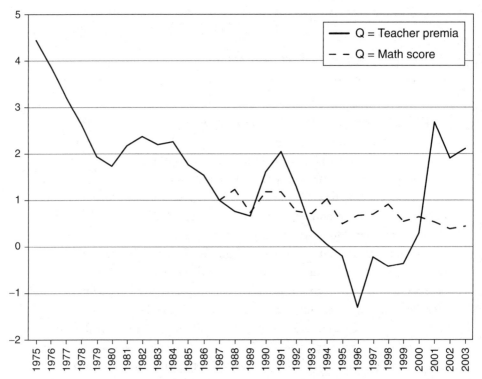

Fig. 6.7   Quality-adjusted SK using teacher premiums and test scores as quality measures (1987=1)

Source: Based on authors' calculations, drawing on several years of Official Household Surveys.

A second issue with explaining output declines based on declining test scores is that, as detailed above, the wage premiums per year of schooling did not in fact fall by very much. Hence, schooling capital measures constructed using the *valuation* of school years, which take into account the wage premiums per year of schooling, already reflect the market price of a year of schooling. If we think the test scores are reflecting some overall cognitive ability q that is augmented by schooling s, so that $q=q(s)$, then a fall in q per unit s (which is what the data about learning achievement imply). If the wage premiums are exclusively driven by q and demand for q is static, then one would expect the wage premiums per year of schooling to fall, as each year embodies less q. But we have no independent observations on the price of q—declines in supply should make it scarcer and increase the price, whereas it is also not implausible that the technical changes and policy changes would have increased the returns to cognitive skill, both of which would cause the premiums to q to have increased, such that even if q per unit s declined the wage premiums to s remained stable.

Quality has deteriorated dramatically in Venezuela in the period for which we have the data. This can potentially explain the output decline, because if cognitive skills and unskilled labor are complements in the production function, then a reduction in "skill capital" could contribute to falls in the unskilled wage by reducing its marginal product. Almost certainly a deterioration in schooling quality of the magnitude observed plays some role in reducing output and the unskilled wage. But there are two empirical questions to be resolved before we could know how important this was. First, the timing issue—while we observe a decline since 1987, and even though we show there was a decline in the wage premiums for teachers beginning in 1976, we do not know when quality began its decline. *We feel the combination of factors described above suggests it is unlikely that the declining quality explains the timing of the decline in output and unskilled wage.* The second puzzle is the contrast between the observed decline in measured cognitive skills of those completing schooling, and the wage premiums on secondary schooling completion, which is very stable over this same period. Without some ability to disentangle wage premiums to skills directly it is hard to say whether "human capital" even declined.

Is There an HK Dog That Did Not Bark?

One possibility from the previous two sections is that HK really played no particular role in the collapse—didn't start it, didn't exacerbate it (though with the caveat that falling cognitive skills may have played a role), but didn't reverse it either.

But there are, perhaps, some more complicated ways in which human capital didn't bark, but should have, or perhaps is barking but in silent ways. That is, the basic problem is that, due to a shock, the productivity factors in Venezuela (both skilled labor and physical capital) fell. This led to a decline in physical capital (eventually), but since the price of skills did not fall if the choice was between unskilled or skilled labor in Venezuela, it still paid to be skilled. But what was needed was a reallocation of factors away from existing uses toward new uses that responded to the shock, and hence changed relative prices. There are two related literatures. One is the paper of Murphy, Shleifer, and Vishny (1991) on the "allocation of talent," in which they show that the types of activities chosen by highly talented people, prototypically "rent-seeking" versus "innovation," affects long-run economic growth. This is consistent with Pritchett (2001), who argues for varying gaps between private wage returns and growth impacts, depending on the country context.

The second related literature is the game-theoretical views of "delayed stabilization," in which contests over the allocation of losses cause the delay of necessary adjustments to cope with negative shocks, and hence some shocks cause large output losses (as stabilization is delayed) while others are accommodated with smaller output losses. The best empirical evidence for these types of mechanisms for adjusting to shocks is in Rodrik (1999), which shows that growth slowdowns are associated with the *interaction* of negative shocks (e.g., terms of trade) and weak "social capability" for coping with shocks.

To reconcile the observed facts—(1) schooling increased rapidly, (2) wage premiums fell only modestly, and (3) real wages and output per capita fell dramatically, with a view where human capital played some role in the "anatomy of the crisis"—we would need a model of the type in which HK somehow delays efforts and economic transformation. For instance, one possibility would be a simple model in which there are two ways for people with HK to make money: innovation (engineers, MBAs) or rent allocation (lawyers). The relative allocation of people with HK across these two activities determines output—as the former have positive spillovers and the latter negative spillovers, so that both types of HK in equilibrium have a private return in the form of a wage premium (consistent with Mincer), but A (the general productivity term) is a function of the allocation of HK across the two types of activities. Therefore, the derivative of output with regard to HK can be negative (if the allocation is into rent-seeking), very high (if HK goes into innovation that reverses the decline in A), or zero (some mix). Moreover, one can imagine that shocks to the economy alter the relative returns— so a negative shock could raise the returns to rent-seeking, which would cause the wage premiums to be stable or to rise, but more HK flows into rent-seeking, causing the output impact of HK to be increasingly negative.

This heuristic puts forward two key empirical questions. First, did the shock cause a reallocation of talent from one type of activity to the other? This is a hard question because even if the shock reduced the total rent, does it not mean that the returns to HK investments in the rent-seeking fell? Perhaps it is even more important to have high HK to grab the rent as it shrinks. This would be the analogy with the "delayed stabilization" literature: in each period people make HK allocation decisions between rent-seeking and innovation and then total production is revealed, which is conditioned on both past HK and shocks. We conjecture that one could build a model in which the allocation of HK into rent-seeking is the privately optimal decision, even as wages decline (inclusive of skill), as the returns to engineers fall even more than for lawyers. But the average return did not go down, so the returns to at least one activity were maintained—the shock cannot have reduced the returns to both activities.

The second question, therefore, is whether there is any evidence about the allocation of educated people across occupations over time in a way that would allow us to say anything—for example, did the proportions of lawyers versus science/engineers change over time? A quick and dirty exercise of using the labor force surveys to allocate highly skilled labor into these categories does not reveal any "smoking gun" of increased allocation into "rent-seeking" over the period. We classify high school graduate workers into five categories: "innovators," "rent-seekers," "production," "science," and "other," according to their self-reported occupation.

Figure 6.8 shows the shares of high school graduates working in "innovation," "rent-seeking," and "science" occupations, and does not reveal a particularly striking break of trend at any point in the series.

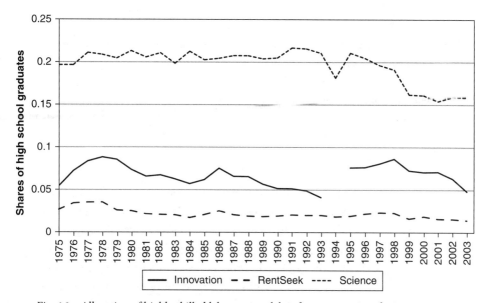

Fig. 6.8   Allocation of highly skilled labor among labor force categories of science, innovation, and rent-seeking

Source: Based on authors' calculations, drawing on several years of Official Household Surveys.

Looked at from the point of view of wages, one does not see any particular shifts in the relative wages of these categories over time. Real wages fell for all groups, and the relative movements among the groups are quite small.

Of course, narratives (we won't grace them with the name "theories" yet) like this might be correct and we just have not found the right empirical counterparts of the "rent-seekers" or "innovators."

A second class of narratives is even less precise. In the Hausmann and Rigobon (2002) model of "corner solutions," the problem is that the unskilled wage never falls low enough to make non-resource exportables competitive. So the economy remains specialized even as it gets poorer and poorer. So presumably the question is something like: why has India been able to attract "high-talent" service industries, and not the much more educated (on average) Venezuela? Or, if we go back to the model, there is "innovation" and "rent-seeking," and then "innovation" could be in tradables or non-tradables.

So if one thinks of a three-activity model—comprising engineers, architects/doctors, and lawyers—is it the case that the real problem was that the real wage for unskilled/semiskilled labor never went low enough so that HK would optimally apply itself to the "capacity to import" problem? (as it did in India, for instance, after the 1991 shock).

Conclusion

Unfortunately for Venezuelans, but fortunately for researchers, most of the trends observed here are so large it is doubtful that the methodological concerns can overturn several basic facts:

- Schooling of the labor force increased *a lot*—in fact, it more than doubled.
- The observed wage premiums for schooling remained quite robust for most of the period, at levels similar to those of other countries.
- Real wages fell *a lot*—roughly in half.

It is quite difficult to put those facts together in a way that makes "schooling" a major part of Venezuela's decline. While quality did decline, it did so (at least that can be documented) well into the decline. More important, since the wage increment per year of schooling remained roughly constant, suggesting that even if a year of schooling conveyed fewer skills, the increases in demand for skills must have increased so that growth decompositions, in terms of years and wage increments to years, are not invalidated by data about quality.

In the end, we also do know that human capital did not save the day when it might have—the decline was not checked by innovations or reallocations of factors. It might be the case that human capital allocated to rent-seeking, or more neutrally non-tradables, delayed policy changes or reforms that could have stemmed the crisis—but we must admit there is no empirical evidence for that view at this stage.

NOTES

1. This is not exactly the same increases one gets from the Venezuelan labor force data (see below), but to ensure cross-national consistency we use the Barro-Lee data in this section.

2. Note that this description is both general, in allowing for any type of growth model (exogenous, endogenous) or set of Xs (standard growth accounting into factor inputs, reduced form growth correlates), and agnostic about whether this represents a valid causal model (note "correlates" not "determinants" and "coefficients" not "parameters").

3. For instance, these often use "enrollments" as the variable to capture the growth association of schooling—but with no very good rationale, as "enrollments" are only weakly, or even negatively, correlated with the growth of schooling over any given period. Further, it is not at all clear why a proxy of the flow rather than direct estimates of the change of the stock would be appropriate. Moreover, many follow the extraordinarily dubious practice of using only *secondary* enrollment, even though there is not an empirical basis for this in observed labor market returns at the micro level. One supposes that this use of enrollment as a proxy is done with the justification that it "works" in the crudest, data-mining sense of giving the "right" sign and a t-statistic above 2.

4. This is the simple functional form that has been used (explicitly or implicitly) in much of the growth/output regression decompositions and growth accounting (Hall and Jones 1999).

5. The other parameter, φ, which captures the possible influence of previous stock on current S, is assumed to be zero for reasons explained in Pritchett 2006.

6. The Mincer coefficients are estimated from regressions that control for experience and its square; these decompositions ignore these terms. The estimated shift in the unskilled wage does not consider potentially relevant changes in the returns to experience. Between 1978 and 2003, returns to experience fell by about 40 percent and became less concave. When combined with the drop in average (potential) experience in the labor market, this may account for a non-negligible fraction of the fall in real wages.

7. Conversations with test administration officials suggest that the test has not changed significantly over time and scoring scales have remained the same throughout the period, making the reported scores roughly comparable over time. Even if it were not possible to guarantee that the tests are exactly parallel (psychometrically equivalent) year after year, any differences between them would not have a trend.

REFERENCES

Barro, R., and Jong-Wha Lee. 1993. "International Comparisons of the Educational Attainment." *Journal of Monetary Economics* 32 (3): 363–94.

Bils, Mark, and Peter J. Klenow. 2000. "Does Schooling Cause Growth?" *American Economic Review* 90 (5): 1160–83.

Gundlach, Erich, and Ludwig Wössmann. 2002. "Second Thoughts on Development Accounting." *Applied Economics* 34 (11): 1359–69.

Hall, Robert E., and Charles I. Jones. 1999. "Why Do Some Countries Produce So Much More Output per Worker Than Others?" *Quarterly Journal of Economics* 114 (1): 83–116.

Hausmann, Ricardo, and Roberto Rigobon. 2002. "An Alternative Interpretation of the 'Resource Curse': Theory and Policy Implications." NBER Working Paper 9424, National Bureau of Economic Research, Cambridge, Mass.

Heston, Alan, Robert Summers, and Bettina Aten. 2002. "Penn World Table Version 6.1, Center for International Comparisons at the University of Pennsylvania (CICUP)." http://pwt.econ.upenn.edu/php_site/pwt61_form.php.

Ludger, Wobmann. 2002. *Schooling and the Quality of Human Capital.* Berlin: Springer.

Murphy, Kevin M., Andrei Shleifer, and Robert W. Vishny. 1991. "Allocation of Talent: Implications for Growth." *Quarterly Journal of Economics* 106 (2): 503–30.

Pritchett, Lant. 2001. "Where Has All the Education Gone?" *World Bank Economic Review* 15 (3): 367–91.

———. 2006. "Does Learning to Add Up Add Up? The Returns to Schooling in Aggregate Data." In *Handbook of the Economics of Education*, edited by Eric Hanushek and Finis Welch, 635–95. Amsterdam: North Holland.

Rodrik, Dani. 1999. "Where Did All the Growth Go? External Shocks, Social Conflict, and Growth Collapses." *Journal of Economic Growth* 4 (4): 385–412.

Young, Alwyn. 1998. "Growth without Scale Effects." *Journal of Political Economy* 106 (1): 41–63.

7 INCOME DISTRIBUTION AND REDISTRIBUTION IN VENEZUELA

Samuel Freije

The Venezuelan growth experience is dismal in the sense that the country has performed poorly. During the last three decades of the twentieth century it did not experience sustained growth. Actually, by some accounts, Venezuela stagnated such that GDP per capita levels in the early years of this new century were lower than thirty years before. Barro and Sala-i-Martin (2003) in their famous book on economic growth classify Venezuela together with sub-Saharan African countries and Nicaragua as the worst performers in the period 1960–90. At the end of this growth collapse, during the late 1990s and early 2000s, the country faced social unrest and significant political changes (see McCoy and Myers 2005; Nelson 2009). Further, Venezuela is usually described as an unequal society, although not more so than other Latin American countries (see, for instance, Inter-American Development Bank 1999). A question that can be asked, then, is whether this dire economic performance is somehow related to income distribution and redistribution. In other words, has the collapse of the Venezuelan economy been due to an unequal distribution of income, or conversely, has the collapse of the economy led to worsening inequality and distributive conflict?

This is an updated version of an article originally published in Spanish as "Distribución y Redistribución del Ingreso en Venezuela," *America Latina Hoy* 48 (2008): 83–107. By then the author was associate professor of Universidad de las Americas, Puebla, Mexico. Currently the author is lead economist for the Latin American and Caribbean Region at the World Bank. The findings, interpretations, and conclusions expressed in this work do not necessarily reflect the views of the World Bank, its Board of Executive Directors, or the governments they represent. The World Bank does not guarantee the accuracy of the data included in this work. The author thanks Gabriela Zepeda, José E. Sánchez, and Melissa Rodríguez-Segura for outstanding research assistance. All the remaining errors remain the author's sole responsibility.

The relationship between inequality and growth has been a subject of intense debate and research in the Economics literature. Kuznets's (1955) is the seminal work on this subject, in which a link between these two variables is postulated. According to Kuznets, inequality first grows and then declines over the course of economic growth. This hypothesis sparked a series of empirical studies trying to corroborate the so-called Kuznets inverted U-curve for different countries and different periods. These empirical studies do not agree in confirming the Kuznet's hypothesis for every country and every period, so the link between growth and inequality varies by economic circumstances.[1]

The lack of agreement in the empirical literature has led to an equally abundant theoretical literature that aims to explain the different relationships that can be found between growth and inequality. The theoretical literature can be grouped into three general strands: first, models which state that growth affects inequality; second, models where inequality affects growth; and third, models with market imperfections where both factors fully interact.[2]

This chapter provides a description of income distribution and redistribution in Venezuela for the period 1975–2005. It analyzes the main inequality and poverty indexes over a long period in order to characterize the evolution of income distribution for this country over the course of its economic growth experience. Then it explains how the government redistributes income, and the evolution of this process. These results provide traces of the relationship between income distribution and the economic performance of this country.

The chapter draws information from several sources, both primary and secondary, for making this description. I use aggregate data from the Banco Central de Venezuela (BCV), the International Monetary Fund, and the Ministry of Finance of Venezuela, as well as micro-data from Households Surveys conducted by the National Institute of Statistics (INE). Additionally, I rely on several studies that precede this and provide useful insights on the issues dealt with here.

The evidence collected in this study shows that poverty and inequality in Venezuela was higher in year 2000 than in the early seventies. That means that the country experienced a quarter century of decline in economic growth accompanied by rising poverty and inequality. I argue that this process is associated with a sustained decline of capital investment, which involved a long-run fall in labor productivity and formal employment. Given that Venezuela was not a high-inequality country in the seventies and early eighties (at least compared to other Latin American countries), it is difficult to argue that the decline in growth and capital investment is due to early distributive conflict. What, then, was the cause of declining productive investment?

When exploring how the Venezuelan government redistributes income through its tax and expenditure policy, it is shown that heavier taxation was not among the instruments adopted for financing social expenditures. Not until the mid-nineties was a value-added tax introduced, and for the whole period under consideration, taxes from oil industry are the main source of fiscal revenues. Whenever oil prices tumbled debt (or reserves) financing of the deficit was adopted instead of a thorough fiscal reform. Consequently, social expenditures per head have been financed during the last three decades of the twentieth century mainly through oil-industry fiscal proceeds. This lack of modernization and sustainability of fiscal finances, in the face of growing instability of oil prices, may have affected investments in infrastructure, law enforcement, and more physical capital in oil and non-oil sectors, hindering the long-run growth of productivity in the country—which, as it was argued before, led to growing poverty and inequality.

Evidence from official sources indicates a rapid reduction of poverty and inequality since 2000. However, this evidence is based on surveys with serious problems of missing data and, more recently, on micro-data that are not publicly available. It can be deduced, as is shown in this chapter, that most of this poverty reduction is due to redistribution of oil-related fiscal proceeds and not to an overhaul of labor productivity.

Given the high levels of inequality that the country faced in 2000, redistributive pressure became much more intense than in the 1970s. If the rents from oil production were to stagger, as they did in the mid-eighties and nineties, redistributive policies will require new funding. Foreseeable alternatives to oil-related fiscal proceeds, such as nationalization of other industries, higher income or consumption taxes, and larger collection of social security contributions, may all be detrimental for capital accumulation. It is now that the redistributive conflicts may harshly affect future economic prospects for Venezuela.

The chapter proceeds as follows. The following section describes income distribution. It first deals with the general issue of factorial distribution and then describes several dimensions of earnings distribution. The section after that depicts the main channels of redistribution via social expenditures and taxes. The final section concludes my argument.

Income Distribution

This section first addresses the distribution of gross national income into factors of production (e.g., capital and labor), and then personal distribution of labor earnings is studied in order to determine the evolution of inequality and poverty.

Factorial Income Distribution

In Venezuela, the oil industry represents nearly one quarter of total GDP, but its output is mainly produced for exports (between 70 percent and 80 percent of its output is sent to foreign markets). In addition, given its capital intensity, the oil industry absorbs less than 5 percent of total employment. Given this, we may assume that the aggregate production function of this economy has three inputs (i.e., labor, capital in non-oil activities, and capital in oil activities), and hence income is distributed into three factors.

The factorial distribution of income in Venezuela is characterized by two main phenomena. First, the oil industry takes a sizable share of national income. Between 1957 and 2003, this share oscillates between a minimum of 6.3 percent in 1998 and a maximum of 40.8 percent in 1974. These wide oscillations depend mainly on international oil prices. In fact, the highest peaks in the share of capital income from oil activities coincide with oil-price boom years (e.g., 1974, 1980, 1990, and 2006) and the troughs with bust years (e.g., 1986, 1998, and 2009).[3] The share of labor within disposable income also shows a fluctuating pattern, but in the opposite direction.

But this is misleading. The second characteristic of this factorial distribution of income is that the share of labor is steadily falling. The share of labor within disposable income, excluding the proceeds from oil, has declined from around 70 percent in the late fifties, to less than 50 percent since the mid-eighties (see fig. 7.1). What may have caused such a shrinking of the labor lot?

The observed decline in the share of labor may be partly explained by changes in the social accounting system in Venezuela. Four different base years, as well as social accounting procedures, have been in use over the period of study. Hence, the data used in this chapter come from four series of national accounts with base years in 1957 (for the period 1950–68), 1968 (for the period 1968–84), 1984 (for the period 1984–97) and 1997 (since 1997). The relevance of these changes is apparent in figure 7.1, where it can be seen that the share of labor within national disposable income has downward breaks in years 1968 and 1984 as well as a slight upward break in 1997. There are two interpretations for these trends. On the one hand, the breaks are mere artifacts of the accounting conventions adopted in each period. On the other hand, they represent changes in the factorial income distribution that are belatedly incorporated in the national accounting. In any case, there are some changes within periods, and some more fundamental cause ought to be driving these.

The accumulation of physical capital may affect this evolution of the labor share. An increase in the use of capital relative to labor may increase or decrease

Fig. 7.1   Share of labor within non-oil national income

Note: Labor share corresponds to total compensation of employees (account D.1 in the the Systems of National Accounts) as a proportion net operating surplus (accounts B.2n and B.3n) in non-oil activities plus total compensation of employees. That is, $D.1/(D.1+B.2n+B.3n)$, where $B.2n$ and $B.3n$ are derived from non-oil industries alone. Based on Antivero 1992; and Banco Central de Venezuela (various years), Sistema de Cuentas Nacionales. Year base 1997.

the share of capital within total income, depending on the rates of substitution between these two factors of production. A falling share of labor within disposable income during a period known for declining total investment and growing population and labor force suggests that, as labor becomes relatively cheaper, given its relative abundance, it substitutes capital but in a proportion that causes a decline in the share of labor within total income.

The evolution of capital accumulation is always difficult to measure. Three different measures for Venezuela are shown in figure 7.2. This includes data developed by Hofman (2000) as well as a measure of ten-year accumulated gross investment according to Venezuelan national accounts, which I developed by making use of data from Baptista (1997), Oficina Central de Estadística e Informática (1998),

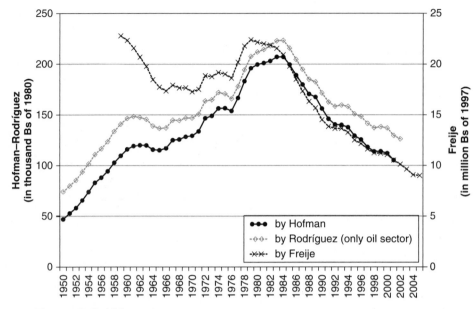

Fig. 7.2   Capital/labor ratio

Sources: Based on Hofman 2000 and author's own calculations.

and Instituto Nacional de Estadística (various years).[4] The trends are quite similar, though, showing a stable capital/labor ratio in the late sixties, a rising trend in the seventies, and a declining trend since the mid-eighties. The ratios differ only in the late fifties and early sixties, although all show a declining trend.

An econometric evaluation of the relation between labor share of income and the capital/labor ratio by Freije (2008) finds an elasticity of substitution below unity (0.8 to be precise).[5] This confirms that, after controlling for trends and changes in accounting systems, the fall in the share of labor is associated with the decline in the Venezuelan capital stock. In other words, the shrinking of the labor lot within national income is associated with lack of investment.

The fall of investment in Venezuela concentrates in the private sector. The proportion of private gross fixed capital formation has declined since the late seventies and is below 15 percent of private aggregate demand since the early eighties. This decline also affects total national investment, which is only partly compensated by public sector investment in both oil- and non-oil-related activities.[6]

In summary, factorial income distribution in Venezuela shows a picture of an economy that receives an important inflow of income via the returns to capital in the oil industry. The return to capital from the oil industry averages 20 percent of disposable income, but it registers wide variations. The rest of the economy distributes income between capital and labor in a manner that has been detrimental to labor because of the decline in investment since the mid-eighties. Given that the state has owned the oil industry since 1975, the personal distribution of income in Venezuela will depend crucially on how the returns to capital in the oil industry are distributed through taxes and public expenditures. We will study the redistribution of income in the third section. Below I describe other aspects of the income distribution in the country.

Labor Earnings Distribution

The distribution of the returns to capital and labor among different individuals is the personal or size distribution of income. It depends on the personal distribution of productive assets and the prices that such assets receive in the markets. The main problem for studying personal distribution of income is the availability of data. Usually, censuses and surveys provide information on only some productive assets and their return. In the case of Venezuela, there is no comprehensive database with information on every source of income. The Encuesta de Presupuestos Familiares (Family Budget Survey) is perhaps the most complete survey on income and expenditures, but it has been done three times over the last two decades and with different methodologies and coverage, which makes it less useful for inter-period comparisons. The Encuesta de Hogares por Muestreo (Households Sample Survey) has been done twice a year since the late sixties and is the usual source of data for income distribution studies in the country. It has the drawback of being a labor survey and reports only information on monthly labor income.[7] In what follows, I use these surveys and, hence, refer only to the size distribution of labor earnings.

The distribution of earnings has many facets. Researchers can be interested in the relationship between the earnings across different levels (inequality) or the distance of different earners with respect to a given parameter (poverty).[8] We will gauge each of these concepts in the following subsections.

INEQUALITY

There are numerous indexes for measuring inequality.[9] In addition to choosing the adequate index, it is necessary to clarify inequality of *what* and *among whom* is being studied. Labor income, consumption, and total income are usual measures of what is being distributed. Families or individuals are the usual recipient units under consideration. Figure 7.3 shows the evolution of the Gini coefficient of monthly labor earnings per capita among Venezuelan families and the Gini coefficient of hourly wages among employed workers. The difference between these two measures may be affected by demographics (family size and dependency

Fig. 7.3   Earnings distribution (as measured by Gini coefficient)

Source: Author's calculation using INE (various years), Encuesta de Hogares por Muestro.

rates) as well as economics (labor market activity rates, human capital distribution and returns to it, unemployment rates and hours of work). However, it can
be seen that the trends of the two indexes are very similar, so it can be said that
the evolution of earnings inequality in Venezuela is driven by the evolution of
inequality of hourly wages.[10]

If we concentrate on the Gini coefficient of hourly wages, we can identify
several periods in the evolution of wages inequality in Venezuela. Inequality first
declines between 1975 and 1983 and, after a sudden jump in 1984, it declines again
until 1993. It rises between 1994 and 1998, and levels off since then. These trends
are misleading, however, because of the nature of the data used to compute them.
The sudden jump in 1984 can be associated with a change in the way earnings units
were introduced in the questionnaire, so it may well be an artifact of the data.[11] In
addition, due to the high rates of inflation that characterized the second half of
the eighties, the number of top-coded observations grew steadily, which makes
one wonder whether the downward trend in inequality between 1984 and 1992 is
also data-driven. Finally, from the mid-nineties, and particularly since 2000, the
number of missing observations (because of not reporting either hours of work
or monthly earnings) grows to levels never seen before. This is a serious problem
for studying earnings inequality. A usual response is to estimate the wages for
those with missing data, but these "earnings equations" usually underestimate the

dispersion of wages. If different specifications are adopted in different years, the inequality figures may not be comparable over time. If, in addition to the previous caveats, the methods adopted are not fully transparent to the general public, then the estimation of inequality is highly unreliable.[12]

In order to avoid making conclusions from questionable data or methods, I choose to study indexes from selected periods with similar missing data percentages. For these selected periods (all of them with 9 percent of missing observations), I compute some decompositions that allow us to identify the sources of these changes in inequality.[13] Therefore, we can safely say that wage inequality (as measured by the Gini) was nearly 0.40 in the late seventies (first half of 1977), declined to 0.33 in early nineties (second half of 1992), and rose again to 0.40 in 2000 (first half of 2000).

The first decomposition consists of separating total inequality into two categories: inequality between population groups (e.g., people living in the capital versus people living in the rest of the country) and inequality that exists within a given population group. Table 7.1 shows that the proportion of inequality between groups in total inequality has declined for most groups under consideration between 1977, 1992, and 2000. Differences according to gender and age have declined in both periods. However, differences according to function (i.e., salaried worker vs. self-employed), activity (e.g., industry, utilities, commerce), and location (i.e., federal states) first declined and then rose, but to levels equal or lower than in 1977. The most important change, though, refers to changes in schooling.

Table 7.1   Wage inequality decomposition by groups

	1977	1992	2000
Total*	0.3199	0.2265	0.3445
Gender	1.1%	0.4%	0.1%
Age	5.5%	3.8%	2.9%
Education	24.7%	14.4%	15.9%
Occupation	27.8%	16.7%	17.9%
Function	9.2%	6.5%	9.1%
Activity	6.4%	3.1%	4.8%
Sector	0.2%	0.7%	1.8%
Location	5.6%	3.0%	5.1%

SOURCE: Based on author's calculations using micro-data from Instituto Nacional de Estadística (various years), Encuesta de Hogares por Muestreo.

*Given the additive decomposition $G=Gb+Gw$, each entry represents Gb/G, where G is the generalized entropy index, Gb is the between-groups component, and Gw is the within-groups component.

In 1977, differences in average wages among different groups of workers according to their education (i.e., workers with no schooling, those with primary schooling, high school, and college) represented one quarter of total inequality, whereas in 1992 and 2000 it represented around 15 percent. Inequality by type of occupation, being very much related to education, shows a similar pattern.

From this, one can conclude that the decline in wage inequality between 1977 and 1992 is somehow associated with less inequality due to education. This leads to two additional questions. First, is education less important in explaining inequality between 1977 and 1992 because of a more equitable distribution of human capital accumulation, or because the returns to education have declined? And second, what explains the rise in inequality between 1992 and 2000?

Table 7.2 shows the decomposition of several inequality indexes into a portion due to changes in observable characteristics of the workers (e.g., age, education, occupation, economic activity), a portion due to changes in the returns to these characteristics in labor markets, and a residual due to unobservable phenomena. The decline in inequality between 1977 and 1992 is largely due to a decline in the price of some productive characteristics (e.g., more than 65 percent of the decline in inequality can be explained by changes in the price of characteristics). This is compatible with the fall of inequality according to groups of education reported above. An econometric analysis of labor earnings in Venezuela for the years under study indicates that individuals with some college education, after controlling for other characteristics, earned on average 70 percent more than did individuals with some primary education in 1977, whereas in 1992 this gap declined to 50 percent. Other productive characteristics such as prime age (i.e., between forty-five and fifty-four), which can be associated with accumulated human capital through work experience, also registers a decline in its price in the labor market.[14] The cause of the rise in inequality between 1992 and 2000 is more difficult to establish. In table 7.2, one can see that unobservable variables account for most of the increase.[15]

The fall in the returns to education and experience has two plausible explanations: It may be that the fall in capital accumulation reported in the previous section led to a decline in the demand for skilled labor and hence a fall in the price paid for human capital accumulation.[16] It may also be that the quality of education has worsened, and so has the productivity of having additional schooling.[17] Of course, both phenomena may have occurred simultaneously.

The growing effect of unobservable variables on wage inequality may also have two conceivable reasons. On the one hand, it may be that the labor market in the late nineties demands different characteristics not necessarily associated with accumulated human capital. It is usually claimed that informal employment does

Table 7.2   Wage inequality decomposition by productive characteristics and their returns

	Indexes					Differences				
	1977	1992	Total		Due to characteristics		Due to prices		Due to unobservables	
Gini	0.391	0.328	−0.063	100.0%	0.007	−11.8%	−0.046	73.4%	−0.024	38.4%
90/10 percentile ratio	6.649	4.651	−1.998	100.0%	−0.278	13.9%	−1.328	66.5%	−0.392	19.6%
90/50 percentile ratio	2.750	2.273	−0.477	100.0%	−0.069	14.5%	−0.313	65.6%	−0.095	20.0%
50/10 percentile ratio	2.415	2.047	−0.369	100.0%	−0.040	10.9%	−0.248	67.1%	−0.081	22.0%
	<u>1992</u>	<u>2000</u>								
Gini	0.328	0.396	0.067	100.0%	−0.014	−20.1%	0.012	17.8%	0.069	102.3%
90/10 percentile ratio	4.651	6.818	2.167	100.0%	−0.259	−12.0%	0.284	13.1%	2.142	98.9%
90/50 percentile ratio	2.273	2.727	0.455	100.0%	−0.160	−35.1%	0.183	40.3%	0.431	94.9%
50/10 percentile ratio	2.047	2.500	0.453	100.0%	0.032	7.1%	−0.042	−9.3%	0.463	102.2%

SOURCE: Author's calculations using micro-data from Instituto Nacional de Estadística (various years), Encuesta de Hogares por Muestreo.

NOTE: Decomposition according to Juhn, Murphy, and Pierce 1993.

not pay for observable/conventional productive characteristics of the workers, because activities in this sector are characterized by low capital/labor ratios and mainly serve as a survival strategy for unemployed urban workers. On the other hand, it may be that there is more instability in wages, which could be associated with a more difficult job search process in the Venezuelan labor market. Indirect evidence for both points is shown in figure 7.4, where it can be seen that unemployment and informal employment rates are higher in 2000 (14.6 percent and 52.6 percent, respectively) than in 1992 (7.1 percent and 39.9 percent) and 1977 (5.5 percent and 33.3 percent).[18] More recent data show that unemployment and informality rates have declined from their peaks in 2000 but are still higher than the records for 1977 and 1990.[19]

In conclusion, it can be said that earnings inequality in Venezuela declined between the late seventies and the early nineties and rose again in the year 2000 to levels similar to those in the seventies. The initial decline in inequality is associated with a fall in the return to human capital accumulation represented by schooling and work experience. This fall in the returns to human capital would have led to a further decline in wage inequality had it not been for unobservable factors, perhaps associated with unstable labor markets, that increased informal employment

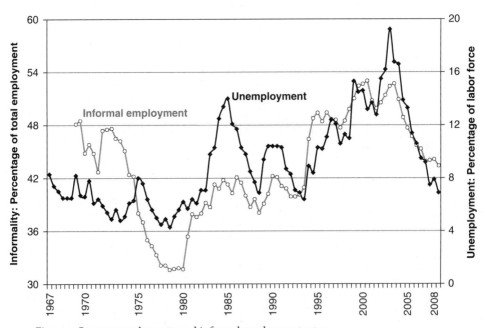

Fig. 7.4   Open unemployment and informal employment rates

Source: Author's calculation using Instituto Nacional de Estadística (various years), Encuesta de Hogares por Muestreo, and Oficina Central de Estadística e Informática 1998.

and the dispersion of wages in 2000. An analysis of earnings inequality for more recent periods is critically hindered by the growing unreliability of Household Surveys, which by year 2005 were missing information about wages and hours of work for more than 20 percent of the labor force.

SIZE DISTRIBUTION OF INCOME

Given the results on factorial income and labor earnings distribution from the two former sections, we now know that the share of labor within national income has declined since the late seventies and, in addition, labor income inequality declined from the late seventies until the mid-nineties and then rose again. Is there something that can be said about size distribution of income? I advance here two answers: one empirical and the other theoretical.

The empirical answer consists of measuring personal income inequality with an index that does not require information on all sources of income for all individuals in the society. Assuming that individuals in the bottom of the earnings distribution do not have any capital income enables us to compute the income share of the poorest 20 percent of the population with data from the Venezuelan Household Survey and the system of national accounts. These figures suggest that inequality has increased from the early seventies to the early 2000s because the share of the poorest quintile of the population has declined from 2.7 percent in 1977 to 2.3 in 1992, and to 1 percent of national disposable income in 2000.[20]

These results have two drawbacks, though. First, reported labor earnings in the Household Surveys do not include all labor costs but only what is known as take-home pay. So total accumulated labor take-home pay represents less than total labor payments to the poorest quintile. Second, the share of the bottom of the distribution is a limited measure for comparing the evolution of inequality over time.[21]

The theoretical answer stems from the decomposition properties of some inequality indexes. For instance, it can be proved that if capital and labor incomes are perfectly correlated (i.e., those who earn higher salaries are those with larger capital rents), then changes in inequality can be explained by changes in the share of labor within national income and changes in the inequality of labor earnings. Namely, it can be shown that total income inequality declines with a rise in the share of labor (assuming, as usual, that labor income is less unequally distributed than is capital income) and rises with a rise in labor income inequality.[22] Therefore, given that between the late seventies and the mid-nineties both the share of labor and labor income inequality fell, the former effects move in opposite directions so that one may compensate the other and no unambiguous answer can be given. On the other hand, since the mid-nineties labor share has continued to decline and labor income has become more unequal. These two facts lead to the conclusion than personal distribution of income has become more unequal between the early nineties and the year 2000.

Despite their limitations, both tentative answers hint in the same direction. The size distribution of income in Venezuela seems to have been stable from the late seventies to the mid-nineties but has become more unequal from the early nineties to the early 2000s.[23]

POVERTY

Another measure of interest regarding the distribution of income is poverty, which for some researchers is of more relevance than inequality. Measuring poverty requires a careful selection of indexes, recipient units, and welfare indicators.[24] These technical aspects, together with the political implications of the subject, make discussions on poverty levels very contentious anywhere.

There is a wide consensus that the Venezuelan economy experienced an alarming increase in poverty from the early eighties to the late nineties.[25] The main difference among studies was the level of poverty, given the different poverty lines that were used. Analytically, however, there was no doubt that poverty had increased in the period because average wages, labor productivity, and output per capita all registered a persistent decline during the eighties and nineties.

The record of poverty since the late nineties, however, is more contentious. The Venezuelan economy underwent a severe political crisis in year 2002, producing a GDP decline of more than 15 percent. However, it has since enjoyed a new upsurge of oil prices, propelling the economy to rates of growth above 7 percent yearly. The INE has developed a new series of poverty lines since 1997 and, according to these figures, poverty indeed rose during the years 2002 and 2003, but then declined to levels below 10 percent for 2008.[26]

The problem with these figures is that, as we explained in the above section, a large percentage of workers do not report their wages in recent Household Surveys. In order to deal with this problem, the INE imputes earnings for those who do not declare them, using fitted values from earnings equations. Even though this is a legitimate and common procedure, it has the shortcoming that imputations are always controversial.[27] In order to prevent such controversy, a full disclosure of the methods and micro-data adjustments adopted by official institutions is warranted, but that has not been the case so far in Venezuela.[28] A second problem with recent poverty figures by INE is that the welfare unit considered includes not only labor income, but also transfers and other sources of income. Using as encompassing as possible a measure of income is commendable, but this approach has the drawback that questions on nonlabor income have been included in the sample questionnaire only since 1997, which impedes long-run comparisons.

In figure 7.5, I include a series of poverty headcount measures for the period 1980–2005 using reported monthly family labor earnings per capita along with official INE figures since 1997.[29] The differences in levels among indexes for the period 1997–2005 are due to the inclusion of other sources of income and to imputation, but the trends are the same. In order to make as robust as possible a long-run comparison of poverty we choose the same three years used in the above section on earnings inequality.[30] This enables us to examine the evolution of poverty independent of concerns about missing data. In addition, it allows us to study the trends in poverty as a result of labor market performance only. We refer to this headcount as the "working poor": the percentage of the population whose family labor income is below the poverty line.

According to figure 7.5, poverty headcount in Venezuela doubled each decade between 1980 and 2000. It was 7.0 percent in 1980, 15.1 percent in 1992, and 29.9 percent in 2000. What is the origin of this dire outcome? One could first hypothesize that the increase in poverty is due to a growth in a vulnerable population group. In other words, poverty rose because of the growth of a group of

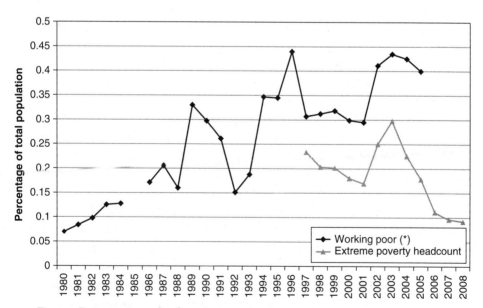

Fig. 7.5   Extreme poverty headcount

Sources: Data for working poor come from author's calculations using micro-data from INE's Encuesta de Hogares por Muestreo (various years). Data for extreme poverty rates come from INE, *Reporte Social* (various years).

individuals whose demographic or economic characteristics make them more likely to suffer poverty.[31] The share of some vulnerable groups within total population, such as female-headed households and households with unemployed heads, did go up, but the proportion of other vulnerable groups, such as of households with unschooled heads, went down or stayed constant (e.g., the proportion living in impoverished areas like the Andes and the Plains). In contrast, the poverty incidence of every group went up remarkably. Therefore, national poverty increased because poverty incidence grew for every population group. Does this mean that the fall of income affected everybody the same? In other words, is this growth in poverty due only to the collapse of national income, or is there a distributive cause as well?[32]

Table 7.3 shows a decomposition of the change in poverty headcounts by growth and inequality components, for the periods under consideration.[33] For the period 1980–1992, the increase in poverty is totally due to the fall in average labor income. Actually, the decline in wage inequality for this period (reported in the above section) would have made poverty 31.4 percent lower (i.e., 2.6 percentage points lower). On the other hand, for the period 1992–2000, the growth in poverty is due in almost equal parts to the fall in average labor income and the rise in wage inequality. For the entire period (i.e., 1980–2000), the fall in average labor income explains nearly three-fourths (73 percent) of the growth in poverty, while the remainder (27 percent) is explained by a larger wage inequality.[34]

This analysis, being restricted to labor income, fails to take into account other sources of income and transfers that do affect welfare levels and poverty. However, it does indicate in what measure families and individuals are able to lift themselves out of poverty with the most common source of income: their own labor. In this sense it can safely be said that poverty in Venezuela has increased mainly because of the persistent decline in average wages and labor productivity observed in Venezuela for the period under study.

Figure 7.6 shows the decline in labor productivity (i.e., GDP per worker) and national income accrued to labor per worker. Both trends register their lowest levels in 2003 but also show an important rebound since. However, the current levels are still well below the levels in 1980 and 1992 and barely above the marks in 2000. This suggests that the decline in poverty in recent years reported by official sources must be mostly due to a redistribution of income from sources other than labor.[35] This fact, together with the formerly reported large size of the share of the state-owned oil industry within national income, calls for a close study of the redistribution of income in Venezuela.

Table 7.3   Poverty headcount decomposition into growth and inequality components

	Indexes				Differences			
	1980	1992	Total		Due to growth		Due to inequality	
Poverty headcount*	7.0%	15.1%	0.081	100.0%	0.107	131.4%	−0.026	−31.4%
	1992	2000						
Poverty headcount	15.1%	29.9%	0.148	100.0%	0.076	51.2%	0.072	48.8%
	1980	2000						
Poverty headcount	7.0%	29.9%	0.229	100.0%	0.17	73.0%	0.06	27.0%

SOURCE: Author's calculations using micro-data from Instituto Nacional de Estadística (various years), Encuesta de Hogares por Muestreo.

NOTE: Decomposition according to Datt and Ravallion 1992.

*Refers to percentage of individuals whose family monthly labor income per head is below a nationally representative poverty line.

Redistribution of Income

Given the structure of the factorial distribution of income explained above, it is natural to think that government intervention is paramount in determining the after net-tax distribution of income in an oil-rich economy, particularly since nationalization of the oil industry in 1975. The massive size of the capital share

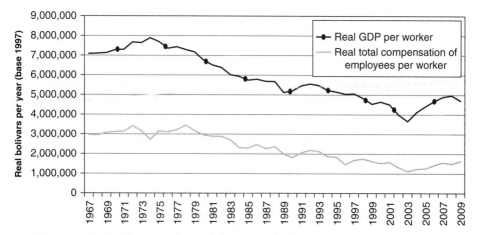

Fig. 7.6   Labor productivity in Venezuela

Source: Author's calculations using Banco Central de Venezuela (various years), Sistema de Cuentas Nacionales, and micro-data from Instituto Nacional de Estadística (various years), Encuesta De Hogares por Muestreo.

from oil production ascribed to the government implies that the personal distribution of income will very much depend on how the government spends its disposable income.

A detailed analysis of the redistribution of income requires micro-data with information not only of incomes but also of taxes paid and subsidies received by individuals and families.[36] Such data are not yet available in Venezuela, but a simulation exercise could shed some light on the distributional effect of taxes and government expenditures. Seijas, Moreno, and González (2003) do such an exercise for Venezuela. They allocate different percentages of tax incidence to families across the income distribution based on various assumptions of tax incidence by type of tax and by income and consumption patterns among families in different income strata. Similarly, they distribute social expenditures across the income distribution according to the income and consumption patterns of families in a living standards survey.

The authors find that the Venezuelan fiscal system is slightly progressive, almost proportional. They report that taxes range from very progressive (such as the corporate and personal income tax) and progressive (such as the social security contributions) to mildly regressive (such as the value-added tax). The total system is slightly progressive (a Suits index between 0.02 and 0.08).[37] Social expenditure, however, is found to be progressive: "The lowest income group (bottom twentieth quintile), which concentrates 0.65 percent of total income, receives 8.2 percent of total social expenditure, whereas the highest income group (top twentieth quintile), which gets 28.48 percent of total income, receives 1.2 percent of total social expenditure" (Seijas et al. 2003, 65).[38]

In fact, these authors compute Gini coefficients for the distribution of income among Venezuelan families, before taxes and social expenditures, after taxes, and after taxes and expenditures. According to their calculations, the tax system reduces inequality of income between 1 percent and 5 percent, depending on method, and social expenditures reduce inequality a further 20 percent.

The Seijas, Moreno, and González study has some limitations. First, it makes use of a consumption survey from 1997, and several modifications to the Venezuelan tax system have taken place since then. Hence, no evolution of the redistribution can be traced. Second, their assumptions on incidence are extreme (e.g., 100 percent of payroll tax is borne by employees). Third, they omit oil-related taxes such as taxes on income for oil companies and royalties, which, as will be explained further on, represent the largest share of government revenues. Fourth, and perhaps most important, the growing weight of the value-added tax within total government income since the mid-nineties may have made the Venezuelan tax system more regressive than accounted for in the study. However,

I think the study makes the valid point that most income redistribution in Venezuela takes place mainly through social expenditures. If we accept that the tax income is almost neutral, this redistribution is mostly financed with revenues from the oil industry, and thus the evolution of redistribution of income depends critically on how the budget is spent and on the collection of these revenues.

As an alternative to a full-incidence study, in the following sections I describe the evolution of social expenditures over a thirty-five-year period and how this evolution is related to the collection of taxes and the growth of the Venezuelan economy.

Social Expenditures

A measure of the redistributive activity of the government is social expenditure per head. This refers to government expenses per capita for activities that enhance social development such as education, health, sanitation, housing, and pensions. Social expenditure per head is the product of output per head and social expenditure per unit of output. The latter depends on the priority that the government gives to social expenditure within its total budget (also known as fiscal priority, FP) and the size of government outlays in the whole economy (also known as budgetary pressure, BP).[39] Hence, there are three components: the share of social expenditure within total government expenditure, the share of total government expenditure as a percentage of total GDP, and the GDP per head. Formally

$$
\frac{SX}{POP} = \left(\frac{SX}{GDP} \right)\left(\frac{GDP}{POP} \right)
$$

$$
= \left(\frac{SX}{TX} \right)\left(\frac{TX}{GDP} \right)\left(\frac{GDP}{POP} \right) = FP \times BP \times G,
$$

where SX corresponds to social expenditure, TX to total government expenditure, GDP to gross domestic product, and POP to total population. This formula implies that the capacity of the government to redistribute income through public spending depends on the priority it gives to social expenditure in contrast to other public expenses, such as defense and security, public administration, or economic development.[40] It also depends on the size of the public budget within the whole economy and on the affluence of the economy. The larger the size of any of these components, holding the others fixed, the larger the magnitude of public funding for social development. Hence, the evolution of social expenditure per head depends on the joint evolution of these three components.

Figure 7.7 shows the evolution of GDP per head as well as total and social public expenditure per capita since 1970. A very clear pattern emerges. After the decade of expansion in the seventies, the Venezuelan economy has undergone a permanent decline since 1979, interrupted only by two bouts of growth in the mid-eighties into the early nineties and the ongoing period that started in 2003. On the other hand, total government expenditure per head has remained stable in real terms since 1970, with the exception of two spurs that coincide with the oil booms of the years 1973 and 1980. More surprisingly, social expenditure per head has remained quite stable for the whole period.[41] This can occur only through an increase in the share of social expenditure within GDP. But, as explained above, the evolution of this share depends on changes in fiscal priority and budgetary pressure.

Figure 7.8 shows how the budgetary pressure and fiscal priority have evolved over time. The former (i.e., total government expenditure as a percentage of GDP) has remained around 22 percent from 1970 to 2000, with two sudden increases as a consequence of the oil booms already mentioned. In both cases, four years after the oil shock, budgetary pressure returned to where it was before. Since the year 2000, however, this rate has increased more than five percentage points, due to both more fiscal pressure and higher oil prices (see below).

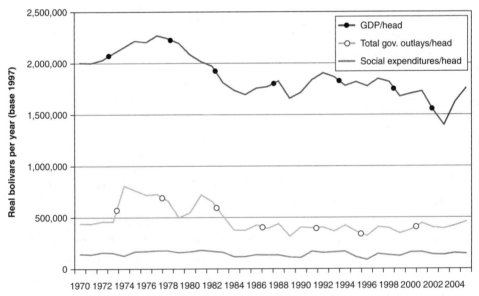

Fig. 7.7   Total and social expenditures per head

Note: Author's calculations using Banco Central de Venezuela (various years), Sistema de Cuentas Nacionales, Year Base 1997; and International Monetary Fund (various years), *Government Financial Statistics*.

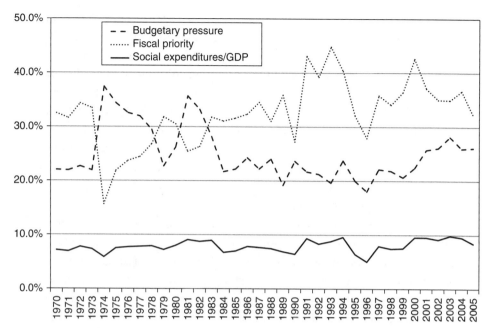

Fig. 7.8 Budgetary pressure and fiscal priority

On the other hand, fiscal priority (i.e., the share of social expenditure within total public expenses) remained around 32 percent for the period under study. It also registered two sudden declines in 1974 and 1980 that are the reverse image of the upsurges in the budgetary pressure. From 1991 to 1994, social expenditures reached the 40 percent level. Despite the steady budgetary pressure around 22 percent, this effort made it possible for the share of social expenditure within GDP to reach nearly the 10 percent mark. For the years 1995 onward, social expenditure has been below the 40 percent mark with the exception of year 2000. Consequently, social expenditures have hovered around the 10 percent mark since 1999, mostly because of growing budgetary pressure since 1999.

Is the social expenditure more volatile than other aggregate magnitudes in Venezuela? The stability of real social expenditure per head over the thirty-year period (shown in figure 7.7) indicates that it is more stable than GDP per capita and total expenditure per capita. In addition, Puente (2004) argues that the coefficient of vulnerability for social expenditure in Venezuela is 0.34, which means that social expenditure variations are two-thirds smaller than variations in total government expenditure.[42] Further, following Ravallion (2002), I have estimated the elasticity of changes in social expenditure to changes in total expenditure.[43] The results are quite stable, too, and show elasticity not significantly different from one in recessions and not significantly different from zero in expansions.

This means changes in social expenditure are affected by reductions in total government expenditure, but do not benefit from expansions in total outlays. But this is just a contemporaneous, short-term elasticity. I also find that, after a two-period adjustment, social expenditures are restored to previous levels. This implies that social expenditures are protected in the medium term: after two years, they grow in expansions and decline in recessions less than total expenditures do.

In conclusion, social expenditure in Venezuela is remarkably stable in the long run. There are noticeable short-term changes as a consequence of its dependence on GDP performance. However, unfavorable shocks have been compensated by increases in budgetary pressure and fiscal priority, which have sustained the social expenditure per head over time.

This stable social expenditure, however, may mask serious development problems. First, a stable expenditure may hide problems in the quality of social services. It has been indicated in several studies that the quality of education and health-related services in Venezuela have eroded lately. Second, the stability of social expenditure may have occurred at the expense of other much-needed investments in areas such as infrastructure or public administration (think, for example, of the need for a competent judiciary or a well-maintained roads network).[44] Third, a stable social expenditure is not necessarily good news, because developing countries require a growing social expenditure in order to attain higher standards of living. In other words, it can be said that Venezuela has stagnated in terms of social expenditures to the levels of the early seventies. Further accumulation of human capital requires more expenditure for social issues.

Taxation

After studying the redistributive activity of the government through social expenditure it is natural to ask how this is funded. Obviously, this is financed with government revenues and debt. Hence, the net redistributive effect of the government will also depend on the distributive incidence of government revenues, especially taxes. As explained above, however, no micro-data are available in this study for a detailed exploration of tax incidence across the income distribution among families in Venezuela.

Government revenues for financing total expenditure between 1970 and 2005 evolved from many different sources. Taxes on income had the largest share up until the mid-nineties, when non-taxes come to represent 30 percent or more of fiscal revenues. This is the result of a change in the tax policy of the Venezuelan government toward oil firms. This new policy relies more on taxes on oil exploitation than it does on income taxes.

The other interesting change is the surge of taxes on consumption of goods and services. Since its introduction in 1993, and after several changes, the value-added tax has come to represent the largest component of taxes on consumption, making this group rise from an average 5 percent of total government expenditures in the seventies and eighties to 20–30 percent since the mid-nineties. This change, considering that value-added taxes are usually regressive, could make us think that the tax collection in Venezuela has become less progressive, but as explained by Seijas, Moreno, and González (2003), in this case the VAT is full of exemptions and differential tariffs that make it less regressive.[45]

Income taxes largely comprise taxes on the oil industry, which is why these taxes show remarkable peaks in the boom years for oil prices: 1974, 1980, and 1990. Non-taxes are also highly connected to the oil industry because they include royalties on oil production. Hence, the relevant classification of funding of government expenditures is by oil- and non-oil-related activities. In periods of sudden rise of oil prices, the share of oil revenues stays above 60 percent of total expenditures; for instance, this includes 1974, 1980, 1990, and 2000. When oil revenues fall below the 60 percent mark, the government registers a deficit that has been financed mostly with foreign debt (1976–78), international reserves (1986–88), or domestic debt (1998–2004).

Notwithstanding this high volatility, social expenditure has been remarkably stable over the thirty-year period. This has been because of an increase in the fiscal priority that several administrations have given to social expenditure and, since 1995, to a rise in budgetary pressure. Using a decomposition exercise, we can gauge the sources of the changes in budgetary pressure that were documented in previously.[46] Table 7.4 shows that the oil-related revenues have declined period after period, with the exception of the most recent (i.e., 1999–2003).

Examining aggregate expenditure and its sources of funding in real terms by political period, it can be seen that, until 1994, half of total expenditure is funded by taxes

Table 7.4   Decomposition of budgetary pressure by political period

	Change in fiscal revenues from . . .			
	. . . oil sources/GDP	. . . non-oil sources/GDP	. . . debt financing/GDP	Change in budgetary pressure
(comparing end-year to end-year)				
1973–78	−4.0%	13.0%	25.4%	34.4%
1979–83	−1.5%	5.9%	−8.7%	−4.3%
1984–88	−9.1%	−17.5%	11.6%	−15.0%
1989–94	−3.0%	−4.7%	−10.4%	−18.0%
1994–98	−10.5%	13.9%	7.8%	11.2%
1999–2003	32.1%	−4.1%	−16.2%	11.8%

SOURCE: Author's calculations using International Monetary Fund (various years), *Government Financial Statistics.*

on income from the oil industry. Since 1994, the introduction of the VAT has caused taxes on consumption to represent one-third of total expenditure. Non-taxes, which include taxes on oil exploitation (royalties), have also increased their share of total expenditure, especially since 1998. According to IMF figures, financing of the deficit through public debt has come to represent 13 percent of total real expenditure.[47]

In summary, it can be said that the rise in budgetary pressure relates to a combination of two factors. First, since the mid-nineties, the introduction of the value-added tax as well as the domestic financing of increasing budget deficits offset the recurrent fall in oil-related fiscal revenues. Second, since 1999, an increase in international oil prices has produced a new rise in oil-related fiscal revenues that have allowed the Venezuelan government to revamp its expenditures without additional fiscal efforts.

Social Security Contributions

Social security is one of the most important mechanisms for redistribution in advanced societies. By collecting contributions from the workforce and distributing pensions and health services to pensioners, social security may effectively distribute income over time, among generations, or over income strata.[48] The Instituto Venezolano de los Seguros Sociales was created in the mid-forties and provides social insurance for retirement, job accidents, unemployment, and health services to the contributing workers and their families. Its finances depend on contributions paid by workers and their employers, as well as by transfers from the central government. As can be seen in table 7.5, the latter source became a predominant component of its total expenditure. From the mid-nineties, Venezuelan social security is unable to cover at least one-third of its outlays. This is the consequence, among other things, of the decline in the percentage of the labor force that contributes (which fell from 35 percent in the mid-seventies to less than 25 percent in 2003) and a rise in the number of beneficiaries per contributor (from 2.6 to 4.0 in the same period). By year 2003, the system is collecting from a smaller share of the population (less than 9 percent) and taking care of larger share (36 percent).

Since the mid-nineties, several proposals for reforming the system have been launched, but none was adopted. Consequently, given the decline in contributions and growing population needs, the central government is financing a larger share of social security. In other words, it is turning a social insurance system into a social assistance system. It is doing so through sources of revenue other than contributions and, hence, is making the system more progressive. As was explained above, this redistribution hinges not on collecting proportionately more from better-off workers but on the availability of oil-related fiscal revenues, value-added taxes, and public debt.[49]

Table 7.5   Balance account of the Venezuelan social security

| | Revenues | | | | Share of deficit/ |
	Total	Extra	Expenditure	Balance	surplus
1980	4.6	—	3.4	1.2	35.3%
1981	5.2	1.5	3.9	1.3	33.3%
1982	5.5	1.6	4.1	1.4	34.1%
1983	5.1	1.6	4.5	0.6	13.3%
1984	5.4	1.8	4.4	1.0	22.7%
1985	5.8	2.1	5.0	0.8	16.0%
1986	7.2	2.9	6.4	0.8	12.5%
1987	8.4	2.6	7.5	0.9	12.0%
1988	11.4	3.2	9.2	2.2	23.9%
1989	15.0	7.3	14.9	0.1	0.7%
1990	26.5	6.4	27.5	−1.0	−3.6%
1991	33.3	9.4	33.4	−0.1	−0.3%
1992	56.3	18.9	38.8	17.5	45.1%
1993	99.1	57.2	103.4	−4.3	−4.2%
1994	127.8	55.8	127.8	0.0	0.0%
1995	122.3	27.9	126.8	−4.5	−3.5%
1996	187.5	87.9	274.3	−86.8	−31.6%
1997	228.1	65.6	476.3	−248.2	−52.1%
1998	910.4	534.6	910.4	0.0	0.0%
1999	756.4	277.1	1,184.2	−427.8	−36.1%
2000	829.8	—	1,436.7	(606.9)	−42.2%
2001	1,192.1	—	1,858.4	(666.3)	−35.9%
2002	1,296.9	—	2,295.0	(998.1)	−43.5%
2003	1,953.0	—	3,216.0	(1,263.0)	−39.3%

SOURCES: Based on Ministerio del Trabajo 2001; Oficina Central de Estadística e Informática (various years); Institute Venezolano de los Seguros Sociales 1997.

NOTE: Figures in billions of current bolivars.

Conclusions

The above analysis of income distribution and redistribution in Venezuelan over the last three decades of the twentieth century can be summarized with three general statements. First, income distribution in Venezuela was more unequal and poorer in 2000 than in the mid-seventies. Second, this unfavorable evolution is associated with the fall in capital accumulation, which, in turn, is the cause of the growth collapse that has been documented here and elsewhere. Third, the decline in capital formation does not seem to be associated with initial inequality, but it is related to consequent redistributive policies. Hence, it can be said that the Venezuelan growth collapse has led to more inequality and poverty, and that recent redistributive efforts will affect economic growth. Let us elaborate each of these conclusions.

The factorial distribution of income has registered a persistent decline in the share of labor within gross national income. This decline coincides with a falling capital/labor ratio, which may be interpreted as a case where relatively cheaper labor substitutes for capital but in a less than proportionate manner, thus increasing the share of capital returns within national income. In addition, labor earnings inequality declined during the eighties because of a fall in the returns to human capital, but increased again during the nineties because of informalization of the labor market. Both phenomena can be associated with the dearth of capital investment, which lowers demand for skilled labor and entails the creation of self-employment activities as last-resort survival strategies for urban families. The combination of a smaller labor share within national income with labor earnings as unequal in 2000 as in the late seventies most likely implies that the size distribution of income is more unequal at the end of the century than it was thirty years before.

The increasingly higher levels of poverty that have been recorded since the late seventies are mainly associated with the decline in labor productivity. Three-quarters of the growth in the poverty headcount can be ascribed to the decline in average wages, and the remaining quarter to the more unequal distribution of wages. Again, the fall in labor productivity that drives the rise in poverty must be associated with the lack of productive investment, so both worsening inequality and poverty can be associated with falling capital accumulation.

Did the initial distribution of income or subsequent redistributive policies affect capital accumulation? This question may elicit two answers. On the one hand, it could be argued that capital accumulation was not affected by distributive matters. First, poverty and inequality in Venezuela in the mid-seventies were much lower than in many other Latin American countries that did not suffer a growth collapse (see Inter-American Development Bank 1999). Second, fiscal proceeds have relied heavily on taxing the oil industry, not the private sector. It was not until the mid-nineties that a neutral or mildly regressive value-added tax was introduced—which does not necessarily affect investment, but if it had, the economy had already been falling for almost two decades.

On the other hand, it could be argued that redistributive policies did affect capital accumulation. Social expenditures by the government have remained remarkably stable over the thirty-year period under study. This stability, in periods of falling oil-related fiscal proceeds, may have affected investment in other growth-related areas such as infrastructure and law enforcement, which are complementary inputs for capital formation. Similarly, the heavy reliance of the government on oil-industry fiscal proceeds may have affected the expansion of the oil industry and so forestalled the development of complementary private investments.

In any case, the theoretical literature warns us that the high poverty and inequality situation of Venezuela toward the end of the century may hinder future economic growth in Venezuela. Further redistributive policies to ameliorate this situation may be counterproductive for growth. With the exception of the nationalization of the oil industry in 1975 and the introduction of the value-added tax in 1993, no fundamental changes in the mechanisms of income distribution and redistribution have been put in place. Despite these two changes, the country still depends on the oil rent for financing social expenditures, the tax system is just moderately progressive, and the social security system is mildly regressive but unfunded.

Preliminary evidence from official sources indicates a rapid reduction of poverty and inequality since 2000. Two things must be said about this recent evidence. First, a growing problem of missing data in Household Surveys since 2000 and a lack of general public availability of micro-data since 2006 makes it difficult to evaluate the sources of poverty and inequality reduction in recent years. Second, the decline in poverty that has been registered by official sources appears to have more to do with spreading of the proceeds from a new oil-price boom than with a recovery of labor productivity. If the rents from oil production were to stagger, as they did in the mid-eighties and nineties, social policies will require new funding. Foreseeable alternatives to oil-related fiscal proceeds such as nationalization of other industries, higher income or consumption taxes, and larger collection of social security contributions may all be detrimental for capital accumulation. It is now that redistributive conflicts may harshly affect future economic prospects for Venezuela.

NOTES

1. For a review of the empirical literature on the Kuznets hypothesis, see Adelman and Robinson 1989; Fields 2001.

2. For a review of this literature, see Bertola, Foellmi, and Zweimuller 2006.

3. By the time of the writing of this chapter, data for share of oil industry within total national income is available only through 2006. See Freije 2008.

4. INE is the Spanish acronym of the Venezuelan Statistics Office (Instituto Nacional de Estadistica). The same institute was previously known as OCEI (Oficina Central de Estadística e Informática). National accounts are compiled by Banco Central de Venezuela and can be found on its website, http://www.bcv.org.ve. I also make use of estimates of capital stock made by Francisco Rodríguez, who extends Hofman's data until 2002 and separates it into oil and non-oil sectors. I thank Francisco Rodríguez for providing these data.

5. The elasticity of substitution is the rate of change of a factor of production for another. These results correspond to the capital/labor ratio computed by Freije. Results using Hofman or Rodríguez are qualitatively similar. Econometric results are available from the author upon request. For an explanation of the concepts and methods used, see Freije 2008.

6. Data for private sector investment includes capital formation in oil-related activities until 1975, when the industry was nationalized. However, the national trend follows the private sector trend closely.

7. Since 1997, the Encuesta de Hogares por Muestreo includes questions on sources of income other than labor earnings, but there is agreement among different researchers that these sources of income are seriously misreported in this type of survey in the region.

8. Other aspects of the distribution of income are polarization and mobility. For recent conceptual reviews of these topics, see Fields 2001; Wang and Tsui 2000.

9. See, for example, Cowell 2000.

10. Other indexes have been computed and show similar trends. Results are available from the author upon request.

11. Until 1983, monthly earnings were recorded in bolivars (the national currency), but from 1984 onward they were recorded in units of ten bolivars. It is plausible that many interviewers or interviewees misrecorded monthly earnings in the first waves of this change in the sample questionnaire.

12. Top coded observations represent less than 0.5 percent of the labor force until 1986, but by 1992 these reached almost 9 percent. From 1994 onward, earnings data are not top coded but the problem of unreported earnings and hours of work surges. Between 1995 and 2000, non-reported wages oscillate between 5 and 10 percent of the labor force. Since 2000 the problem grows year after year, and by 2005 18 percent of the labor force doesn't report wages and nearly 22 percent report neither wages nor hours of work. These estimates are based on author's calculations using micro-data from INE (various years), Encuesta de Hogares por Muestreo. These concerns are even more serious in the case of poverty estimates, as examined in the following section.

13. The decompositions are by population groups and by productive characteristics of individuals. For an explanation of these decompositions, see Cowell 2000; and Juhn, Murphy, and Pierce 1993, respectively.

14. These results are derived from earnings equations estimated with micro-data from INE (various years), Encuesta de Hogares por Muestreo, for the selected years using an ordinary least squares method. Results are available from the author upon request.

15. Actually, unobservables represent more than 100 percent of the change in the Gini between 1992 and 2000. On the other hand, changes in price represent another 17.8 percent and changes in characteristics −20.1 percent. This means that if productive characteristics of workers had not changed between 1992 and 2000, the increase in the Gini coefficient would have been 20.1 percent larger than it actually was.

16. There is abundant evidence that capital and skilled labor are complementary factors of production, so that a fall in investment should be associated with a fall in the demand for skilled labor. See, for instance, Hammermesh 1993.

17. The chapter by Pritchett and Ortega in this book, "Much Higher Schooling, Much Lower Wages," shows some evidence in this direction. For a vivid recounting of the problems of public education in Venezuela, see Bruni-Celli 2003.

18. In fact, search models predict that a more inefficient job market, due to severe information asymmetries that make job matching between job-seekers and firms difficult, would entail longer unemployment duration and higher unemployment rates (see, for instance, Mortensen and Pissarides 1999). Márquez and Ruiz-Tagle 2004 find evidence that the job search in Venezuela has become more difficult for individuals without previous experience.

19. Official data from INE indicate that unemployment and informality rates were 7.9 percent and 43.4 percent, respectively, in the first half of 2008. See INE (various years), *Indicadores de la fuerza de trabajo*.

20. Author's calculations using INE (various years), Encuesta de Hogares por Muestreo; and Banco Central De Venezuela (various years), Sistema de Cuentas Nacionales. Year base 1997.

21. If, in addition, one thinks that the reporting of take-home pay varies over the years, the results may be less informative. I assume that this is not the case. A final caveat against these measures is that the income share of a poorest quintile group of the population is not a Lorenz

consistent inequality measure, and thus it might not provide a unique ranking of inequality between several periods. For a formal explanation, see Cowell 2000; or Fields 2001.

22. For a proof, see Cowell 2000; or our own derivation in Freije 2008. A similar result can be obtained from the factor decomposition of the Gini coefficient by Fei, Ranis, and Kuo (1980), if assuming also that the correlation between labor income and capital income stays very high. If one is not willing to assume high correlations of income, the subject of decomposing inequality into inequality of factor components becomes intricate (see Lerman 1999). In this case, the evolution of total income inequality depends on the evolution of inequality in each factor, the evolution of factor shares, and the evolution of the relationship between each factor and income ranks.

23. It should be noted that a recent official publication (INE's *Reporte Social*) indicates that the share of the bottom quintile rose from 4.0 percent to 5.4 percent of total income between 2000 and 2008. These numbers, although indicative of an improvement in size distribution, could also show a imprecise picture of the recent evolution of the size distribution of income for two reasons: first, the usual underreporting of nonlabor income in Household Surveys, which overstates the share of the bottom quintile within national income; and second, the already reported unreliability of recent Household Surveys due to a large share of missing observations.

24. For a thorough discussion on the methodology of measuring poverty, see Ravallion 1994.

25. See, for instance, World Bank 1991; Márquez 1995; Riutort 1999.

26. See INE (various years) *Reporte Social*. In addition to poverty measures according to poverty line methods, INE has also computed poverty measures according to "basic needs" methodology as well as the Human Development Index for the country. The United Nations Development Programme as well as other institutions such as the Universidad Católica Andrés Bello have also computed different poverty indexes. In this chapter, I concentrate on poverty line measures. Admittedly, this is a restricted view of poverty but it has the advantage of allowing us to relate economic growth and productivity performance to distributional concerns, which is my main concern here.

27. In addition, there may be several doubts on the suitability of the specification as well as the estimation techniques used for these imputations. Additionally, one may question whether the specification of the earnings equation used is the same over time.

28. An interesting example is the case of the Consejo Nacional de Evaluacion de la Political de Desarrollo Social (CONEVAL) in Mexico, which discloses to the general public (through its website) both the micro-data from household surveys and the programs used for computing official poverty figures. This allows for full transparency in the methods adopted.

29. The poverty line used for computing the headcount is the same used by the INE since 1997, called "canasta básica alimentaria" (basic needs food basket). For the period 1980–97, I use a poverty line devised by the Venezuelan National Institute for Nutrition (INN) and the OCEI (former name of the INE), which was used for other studies such as Márquez 1995. Both lines are very close in U.S. dollar terms to the World Bank's one dollar a day poverty line. No adult equivalent scales are used in either measure.

30. Actually, I use year 1980 as the oldest year (instead of 1977), because no official poverty line is available before that year. The percentage of missing observations in 1980 is ever lower than in 1977.

31. The poverty headcount, being a member of the Foster–Greer–Thorbecke class of poverty indexes, can be exactly decomposed into a population-weighted mean of subgroup poverty measures. See Ravallion 1994.

32. The change in a poverty measure of the Foster–Greer–Thorbecke class can be decomposed into a change due to changes in income growth, assuming constant income inequality, and a change in income inequality assuming constant income. In this case, we follow the methodology developed by Datt and Ravallion (1992).

33. For details, see Freije 2008, 96.

34. In figure 7.3, it can be seen that wage inequality grew between 1980 and 2000.

35. The importance of redistribution in poverty reduction during the recent decade has also been highlighted in other studies. See, for instance, Ferreira, Leite, and Ravallion 2006; Leon 2008.

36. For examples of studies on the evolution of redistribution, see, for instance, Atkinson 1999; Zandvakili 1994. For a text on the techniques for measuring tax incidence and redistribution, see Lambert 2002.

37. The Suits index is a measure of the progressivity of a tax. It ranges from −1 to +1. The tax is more progressive (regressive) the closer the Suits index is to +1 (−1). A proportional tax has a Suits index equal to zero. See Suits 1977.

38. Translation by the author.

39. The terms budgetary pressure and fiscal priority are adopted from Economic Commission for Latin America and the Caribbean 2001.

40. It could be argued that there is also income redistribution through these other expenditures, but I will concentrate on social expenditures as the foremost channel of income redistribution.

41. In this study, I limit the definition of social expenditure to government outlays in education, health, and social security. These items usually represent the largest share of social expenditure and there is little disagreement about their social development nature. Other researchers include expenditures in housing cultural activities. I do not have regular data on these items and prefer to restrict the analysis to the aforementioned sectors.

42. The coefficient of vulnerability is the ratio between the percentage change in expenditures for a certain area to the percentage change in total expenditure. See Puente 2004.

43. Econometric results available upon request.

44. The chapter by Pineda and Rodríguez in this book, "Public Investment and Productivity Growth in the Venezuelan Manufacturing Industry," highlights the problems of lacking infrastructure in Venezuela. Jaén 2003; and Monteferrante 2003 provide a summary of the decay in health and public security services in Venezuela.

45. As mentioned above, there may be some doubts on the neutrality of the tax system in Venezuela, particularly since the introduction of the VAT in the mid-nineties. In any case, Venezuela has one of the lowest incidences of this tax in the region. The revenue productivity (i.e., the ratio of effective tax rate to statutory tax rate) by the year 2000 is 0.31, which is similar to that of Mexico (0.30) but lower than that of Chile (0.58) or the average for the Latin American region (0.38) or the OECD (0.54). The VAT revenue as a percent of total consumption is 4.5 percent, again similar to Mexico (4.5 percent) but lower than Chile (10.5 percent), the Latin American average (6.7 percent), and the OECD average (9.3 percent). See Singh et al. 2005, 34.

46. This decomposition is based on the property that the percentage change of a sum is the sum of the percentage changes.

47. IMF figures for the years 2003–5. No more recent data are available from the IMF (various years), *Government Financial Statistics*. See Freije 2008, table VII, for details.

48. For a textbook reference on the economics of social security see Barr 2004, chap. 9.

49. In fact, the share of social security contribution within total government expenditure fell from 6 percent in 1970 to 2.4 percent in 2005. Interestingly, according to the simulations in Seijas, Moreno, and González 2003, the contributions to the Venezuelan social security system are only slightly regressive. The Suits index for payroll taxes and contributions is around −0.10.

REFERENCES

Adelman, I., and S. Robinson. 1989. "Income Distribution and Development." In *Handbook of Development Economics*, edited by H. Chenery and T. N. Srinivasan, 949–1003. Amsterdam: North Holland.

Antivero, I. 1992. "Series estadísticas de Venezuela de los últimos 50 años." *Colección cincuentenaria*, no. 8. Banco Central de Venezuela, Caracas.

Atkinson, A. 1999. "The Distribution of Income in the UK and OECD Countries in the Twentieth Century." *Oxford Review of Economic Policy* 15:56–75.

Baptista, A. 1997. *Bases Cuantitativas de la Economía Venezolana: 1830–1995*. Caracas: Fundación Polar.

Barr, N. *The Economics of the Welfare State*. 4th ed. Oxford: Oxford University Press, 2004.

Barro, R., and X. Sala-i-Martin. 2003. *Economic Growth*. 2nd ed. Cambridge: MIT Press.

Bertola, G., R. Foellmi, and J. Zweimuller. 2006. *Income Distribution in Macroeconomic Models*. Princeton: Princeton University Press.

Bourguignon, F. 1981. "Pareto Superiority of Unegalitarian Equilibria in Stiglitz's Model of Wealth Distribution with Convex Savings Functions." *Econometrica* 49 (6): 1469–75.

Bruni-Celli, J. 2003. "Historia de la otra ciudad: La educación pública en Venezuela." In *En esta Venezuela: Reliadades y nuevos caminos*, edited by P. Márquez and R. Piñango. Caracas: Ediciones IESA.

Champernowne, D. G., and F. A. Cowell. 1998. *Economic Inequality and Income Distribution*. Cambridge: Cambridge University Press.

Cowell, Frank. 2000. "Measuring Inequality." In *LSE Handbooks in Economics Series*. 3rd ed. London: Prentice Hall/Harvester Wheatsheaf.

Datt, G., and M. Ravallion. 1992. "Growth and Redistribution Components of Changes in Poverty Measures: A Decomposition with Applications to Brazil and India in the 1980s." *Journal of Development Economics* 38:275–95.

Economic Commission for Latin America and the Caribbean. 2001. *Social Panorama of Latin America, 2000–2001*. Santiago: ECLAC.

Ferreira, F., P. Leite, and M. Ravallion. 2006. "Poverty Reduction without Economic Growth? Explaining Brazil Poverty Dynamics, 1985–2004." Policy Research Working Paper 4431, World Bank, Washington, D.C.

Fei, John C. H., Gustav Ranis, and Shirley Kuo. 1978. "Growth and the Family Distribution of Income by Factor Components." *Quarterly Journal of Economics* (February): 17–53.

Fields, Gary S. 2001. *Distribution and Development: A New Look at the Developing World*. Cambridge: MIT Press.

Freije, S. 2008. "Distribución y redistribución del ingreso en Venezuela." *América Latina Hoy* 48:83–107.

García-Verdú, R. 2006. "An Evaluation of the Impact of the Misión Barrio Adentro on Mortality in Venezuela." Paper presented at the Meeting of the Latin American and Caribbean Economics Association, Mexico City, November 2–4.

Gómez, Irey, and Luis Alarcón. 2003. "Los nudos críticos de la política social Venezolana de 1989 a 2001." *Revista Venezolana de Economía Ciencias Sociales* 9 (2): 13–35.

Hammermesh, D. S. 1993. *Labor Demand*. Princeton: Princeton University Press.

Hofman, A. 2000. "Standardised Capital Stock Estimates in Latin America: A 1950–1994 Update." *Cambridge Journal of Economics* 24 (1): 45–86.

Instituto Nacional de Estadística. Various years. *Indicadores de la fuerza de trabajo*. Caracas.

———. Various years. *Reporte Social*. Caracas.

Institute Venezolano de los Seguros Sociales. 1997. "Memoria y Cuenta, 1997." Caracas.

Inter-American Development Bank. 1999. *Facing Up to Inequality*. Washington, D.C.

International Monetary Fund. Various years. *Government Financial Statistics*. Washington, D.C.

Jaén, M. E. 2003. "El mal estado de la salud y sus remedios." In *En esta Venezuela: Reliadades y nuevos caminos*, edited by P. Márquez and R. Piñango, 241–68. Caracas: Ediciones IESA.

Juhn, C., K. M. Murphy, and B. Pierce. 1993. "Wage Inequality and the Rise in Returns to Skill." *Journal of Political Economy* 101:410–42.

Kuznets, Simon. 1955. "Economic Growth and Income Inequality." *American Economic Review* 45 (1): 1–28.

Lambert, Peter. 2002. *The Distribution and Redistribution of Income*. 3rd ed. Manchester: Manchester University Press.

Leon, A. 2008. *Progresos en la reduccion de la pobreza extrema en America Latina*. Santiago: Project of la Agencia Española de Cooperación Internacional para el Desarrollo and la Comisión Económica para América Latina y el Caribe.

Lerman, R. I. 1999. "How Do Income Sources Affect Inequality?" In *Handbook of Income Inequality Measurement*, edited by J. Silber, 341–62. Norwell, Mass.: Kluwer Academic Publishers.

Maingon, Thais. 2004. "Política social en Venezuela." *Cuadernos del CENDES* 55:7–73.

Márquez, Gustavo. 1995. "Venezuela: Poverty and Social Policies in the 1980s." In *Coping with Austerity and Inequality in Latin America*, edited by N. Lustig, 400–452. Washington, D.C.: Brookings Institute.

Márquez, Gustavo, and C. Ruiz-Tagle. 2004. "Search Methods and Outcomes in Developing Countries: The Case of Venezuela." Working Paper 519, Research Department, Inter-American Development Bank, Washington, D.C.

McCoy, J., and D. Myers. 2005. *The Unraveling of Representative Democracy in Venezuela*. Baltimore: Johns Hopkins University Press.

Ministerio del Trabajo. 2001. "Memoria." Caracas.

Monteferrante, P. 2003. "La cotidianeidad del venezolano: Entre el miedo y la violencia." In *En esta Venezuela: Reliadades y nuevos caminos*, edited by P. Márquez and R. Piñango, 269–88. Caracas: Ediciones IESA.

Mortensen, Dale T., and Christopher A. Pissarides. 1999. "New Developments in Models of Search in the Labor Market." In *Handbook of Labor Economics*, 1st ed., vol. 3, edited by O. Ashenfelter and D. Card, 2567–2627. Amsterdam: Elsevier.

Nelson, B. A. 2009. *The Silence and the Scorpion: The Coup against Chávez and the Making of Modern Venezuela*. New York: Nation Books.

Oficina Central de Estadística e Informática. 1998. *Treinta años de la encuesta de hogares por muestreo*. Caracas: Oficina Central de Estadística e Informática.

———. Various years. "Anuario estadístico." Caracas.

Persson, T., and G. Tabellini. 1996. "Political Economics and Macroeconomic Policy." In *Handbook of Macroeconomics, Volume 1*, edited by J. Taylor and M. Woodford, 1397–482. Amsterdam: Elsevier.

Puente, José Manuel. 2004. *Revista* 18 (1). Caracas: Banco Central de Venezuela.

Ravallion, Martin. 1994. *Poverty Comparisons*. Newark: Hardwood Academic Publishers.

———. 2002. "Are the Poor Protected from Budget Cuts? Evidence from Argentina." *Journal of Applied Economics* 5 (1): 95–121.

Riutort, Matías. 1999. *Pobreza, desigualdad crecimiento económico en Venezuela*. Caracas: Universidad Católica Andrés Bello, Instituto de Investigaciones Económicas y Sociales.

Seijas, Lizbeth, María Antonia Moreno, and Wilfredo González. 2003. "La incidencia fiscal neta en Venezuela." Working Paper 48, Banco Central de Venezuela, Caracas.

Singh, A., A. Belaisch, C. Collyns, P. De Masi, R. Krieger, G. Meredith, and R. Rennhack. 2005. "Stabilization and Reform in Latin America: A Macroeconomic Perspective on the Experience since the Early 1990s." Occasional Paper 238, International Monetary Fund, Washington, D.C.

Stiglitz, J. 1969. "Distribution of Income and Wealth among Individuals." *Econometrica* 37 (3): 382–97.

Suits, D. B. 1977. "Measurement of Tax Progressivity." *American Economic Review* 67:747–52.

Uhlig, H., and Y. N. Yanagawa. 1996. "Increasing the Capital Income Tax May Lead to Faster Growth." *European Economic Review* 40:1521–40.

Wang, Y. Q., and K. Y. Tsui. 2000. "Polarization Orderings and New Classes of Polarization Indices." *Journal of Public Economic Theory* 2 (3): 349–63.

World Bank. 1991. "Venezuela Poverty Study." Mimeo, World Bank, Washington, D.C.

Zandvakili, Sourushe. 1994. "Income Distribution and Redistribution through Taxation: An International Comparison." *Empirical Economics* 19 (3): 473–91.

8 COMPETING FOR JOBS OR CREATING JOBS? THE IMPACT OF IMMIGRATION ON NATIVE-BORN UNEMPLOYMENT IN VENEZUELA, 1980–2003

Dan Levy and Dean Yang

Between 1965 and 2000, the fraction of individuals living outside their countries of birth grew from 2.2 percent to 2.9 percent of world population, reaching 175 million people in the latter year.[1] What effects do migrant inflows have on the labor market outcomes of natives in host countries? This question is of great interest to officials in charge of immigration policy in both developed and developing countries, but the empirical work on the topic has provided unclear guidance. Card's (1990) study of the impact of the Mariel boatlift on the Miami labor market found no effect of a large influx of Cuban refugees on the wages of potentially affected (lower-skilled and Cuban) workers. Friedberg and Hunt's (1995) survey of the literature concludes that immigration has only a small effect on the labor market outcomes of native workers, a finding echoed by Smith and Edmondston (1997). In contrast, in an analysis of labor supply shifts across education/experience groups in the United States, Borjas (2003) found relatively large negative effects of immigration on the wages of competing workers.

Venezuela is unique among Andean nations in having experienced dramatic migrant inflows and outflows in the post–World War II period. The question naturally arises: how have these migrant inflows and outflows affected the labor market performance of Venezuelan natives?

In this chapter, we characterize the history of international migration in Venezuela in the 1975–2003 period, and assess the link that migrant flows may

We thank Miguel Almunia-Candela, Todd Pugatch, and Ariel Sznajder for excellent research assistance, and Ricardo Hausmann, Francisco Rodríguez, and an anonymous reviewer for helpful comments.

have had with the country's growth collapse. We characterize international migration in Venezuela by examining three questions: (1) How has the stock of immigrants evolved over time? (2) How has the composition of immigrants evolved over time? and (3) How do immigrants differ from Venezuelan natives in their entrepreneurship and their human capital?

Our key findings related to migration patterns are as follows: (1) the percentage of foreign-born living in Venezuela decreased from about 5 percent to about 4 percent in the period 1975–2003, (2) there was a big shift in the composition of foreign-born from mostly Europeans to mostly Colombians, and (3) the foreign-born are much more likely than Venezuelans to be entrepreneurs, although they do not differ markedly from Venezuelans in terms of educational attainment.

We assess the link between international migration and growth by investigating the extent to which changes in the presence of foreign-born people in Venezuelan industries affected unemployment among Venezuelan natives. A standard prediction from a basic labor market model is that exogenous increases in foreign-born labor supply in a given industry leads to higher native-born unemployment, known as a "job competition" effect. This presumes wage stickiness, as well as an imperfect ability of existing workers to shift from one industry to another in response to an influx of new workers from overseas. On the other hand, it is also possible that inflows of foreign labor might *create* jobs for native workers, if the new foreign workers establish new enterprises that employ natives.

Our empirical analysis tests which effect dominates on average, looking separately at the effect of inflows of Colombians on the one hand, and Europeans on the other. To identify the causal effect of net migrant inflows on native labor market outcomes, we exploit exogenous variation in migrant inflows driven by economic shocks in migrant source areas. We find that increases in Colombian presence in Venezuelan industries have led to increases in native-born unemployment, as Colombians compete directly with Venezuelans for jobs. Native-born unemployment appears to rise roughly one-for-one with increases in Colombian presence in Venezuelan industries. In contrast, declines in European presence have had no apparent effect on Venezuelan unemployment. Declines in European presence in Venezuelan industries have not led to declines in native-born unemployment rates. Again, this is perhaps because European presence has a "job creating" effect that on average offsets any competition for jobs between Europeans and Venezuelans.

The next section of this chapter provides a brief history of immigration to Venezuela. We then describe the data used in this chapter's empirical analyses in the following section. After that, we describe major trends in immigration to Venezuela in the last three decades. We then shed light on the impact of migrant inflows to Venezuela on the unemployment rates among natives before concluding our analyses.

A Brief History of Immigration to Venezuela

Large migrant inflows to Venezuela started in 1922 with the beginning of the full exploitation of the country's oil resources. In 1936, the Venezuelan government passed the Law on Immigration and Settlement, which would set guidelines for the more than one million skilled immigrants that arrived from 1948 to 1958. Substantial Colombian immigration came at this time due to the petroleum boom. A period in Colombia's history between 1948 and 1966, known as La Violencia, led to massive internal migrations into the land bordering Venezuela, Ecuador, and Panama.

The majority of immigrants to Venezuela in the post–World War II period came from Europe. Many immigrants stayed in ethnic enclaves in Caracas and specialized in certain industries: Italians focused on construction, arts, and crafts and were often employed as mechanics. Spaniards were more diversified, working as plumbers, carpenters, and managers of cafés and restaurants. Portuguese usually worked in foodstuffs retail. Colombian immigrants in the 1960s usually worked in the manufacturing, agricultural, and construction sectors.

In 1958 and 1959, the government began to discourage immigration, but immigration was already in sharp decline and Venezuela began a period of negative net migration flows (Blutstein et al. 1985). Postwar European immigration to the cities had dominated the 1950s, while immigration in the 1960s came mainly from undocumented immigrants from Colombia and other Latin American countries who worked in the rural sector (Sassen-Koob 1979, 478).

In 1965, European immigrants in Venezuela numbered roughly 300,000 (Mille 1965). In that year, 54.9 percent of immigrants lived in the Caracas metropolitan area, whereas Colombian immigrants were concentrated in the bordering states of Táchira (8.6 percent), Zulia (10.3 percent), Aragua and Carabobo (8.6 percent), and other states (17 percent) (Chen 1968).

In 1973, following a 250 percent increase in government revenue due to the rise in international oil prices, the Venezuelan government instituted a selective policy to encourage immigration to respond to the spike in labor demand (Sassen-Koob 1979, 456). Following the 1980 economic downturn, immigrant populations began to arrive from the Dominican Republic, Guyana, and Haiti (Gonzalez, Torales, and Vichich 2003, 35). By 1990, more than half of foreign residents in Venezuela came from Colombia, with the majority living in the Venezuelan border states of Zulia and Táchira. In 1999, violence was a major catalyst for Colombian migration to Venezuela, with the U.S. Plan Colombia causing refugee flows into Venezuela. Specifically, in the Colombian border provinces of Arauca and Norte de Santander, 1.51 percent and 3.52 percent of the population, respectively, had been displaced into Venezuela.

Data

The main data source used in this study is the Venezuelan Encuesta de Hogares, a semiannual survey conducted since 1975 on representative samples of households living in Venezuela. For every year in which the survey was conducted, we have information on the year of birth and place of birth of the person interviewed. This allows us to construct a history of the number of foreign-born people living in Venezuela and of the net flows of foreign-born.

The survey has information on whether the individual was an employer, and we code all employers as entrepreneurs for the purpose of the study. It also has information on the years of schooling of each person, which allows us to look at whether there are large differences in levels of schooling between migrants from different countries.

The survey has two main limitations for the purposes of our study. First, it began in 1975, which means we cannot rely on it to characterize migration before then, and we can assess the link between international migration and the growth collapse only from 1975 onward.[2] Second, because it only samples people living in Venezuela, we do not know how many foreign-born left the country and how many came into the country from one year to another—that is, we can only infer net flows of foreign-born people living in Venezuela.

Large-Scale Trends in International Migration to Venezuela

The number of foreign-born living in Venezuela increased from about 600,000 in 1975 to about 1,000,000 in 2003. Most of the increase occurred in the first five years of this period. Since 1980, the number of foreign-born living in Venezuela oscillated between 800,000 and 1,000,000. Given that the overall population in Venezuela grew during the 1975–2003 period, this pattern in the evolution in the number of foreign-born meant that the proportion of foreign-born living in Venezuela increased in the 1975–80 period (from about 5 percent to 6 percent), and declined consistently since then (to about 4 percent in 2003).

Foreign-born people are much more likely to be entrepreneurs than are Venezuelans. In fact, the fraction of foreign-born people living in Venezuela who are entrepreneurs ranged between 14 percent and 31 percent in the 1975–2003 period, whereas the fraction of Venezuelans who are entrepreneurs ranged between 4 percent and 6 percent in this same period. Among the foreign-born living in Venezuela, the Europeans are much more likely than are the Colombians to be entrepreneurs (fig. 8.1). There was a big shift in the

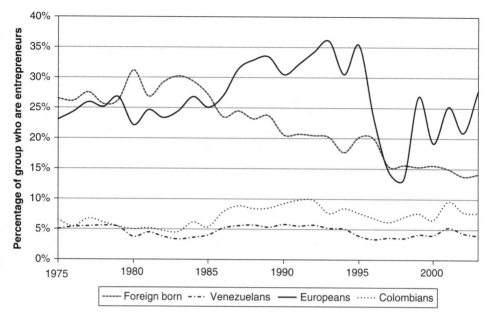

Fig. 8.1   Prevalence of entrepreneurship

Source: Authors' calculations from Venezuela's Encuesta de Hogares (1975–2003).

composition of foreign-born from mostly Europeans to mostly Colombians in the period 1975–2003. The fraction of Colombians went up from about one-third to two-thirds, whereas the fraction of Europeans went down from about 50 percent to about 15 percent. The fraction of foreign-born not born in either Colombia or Europe stayed relatively constant throughout the period.[3]

This shift in composition of foreign-born changed entrepreneurship in Venezuela. As the fraction of Europeans, among people living in Venezuela, has decreased over time, so has the fraction of entrepreneurs who are foreign-born. Indeed, this latter fraction decreased from about 27 percent in 1975 to about 14 percent in 2003. European entrepreneurs, who represented almost 20 percent of all entrepreneurs in Venezuela in 1975, now represent less than 4 percent (appendix table 8A.1). The number of foreign-born entrepreneurs living in Venezuela started at about 65,000 in 1975, reached its peak (around 120,000) in the period 1987–92, and then declined to about 75,000 in 2003.

While there are some modest differences between Europeans and Venezuelans in terms of average years of schooling, these are very small among the subset of entrepreneurs (appendix table 8A.2). European entrepreneurs and Venezuelan entrepreneurs have, on average, about the same level of schooling (seven years).

In summary, the main findings on the history of international migration in Venezuela that are relevant to this chapter are the following: (1) the percentage of foreign-born living in Venezuela has decreased from about 5 percent to about 4 percent in the period 1975–2003, (2) there has been a big shift in the composition of foreign-born from mostly Europeans to mostly Colombians, (3) the foreign-born are much more likely than are Venezuelans to be entrepreneurs, but the fraction of foreign-born entrepreneurs decreased over time, and (4) foreign-born individuals do not differ markedly from locals in terms of educational attainment. The next section describes how these factors may have been related to the growth collapse in Venezuela.

Impact of Foreign-Born Presence on Native-Born Unemployment

The dramatic declines in European presence and the increases in Colombian presence in Venezuela over the last three decades prompts the question: how have these changes affected the labor market performance of Venezuelan natives?

The standard prediction from a basic labor market model is that increases in foreign-born labor supply in a given industry would lead to higher native-born unemployment, a "job competition" effect. This presumes wage stickiness, as well as imperfect or delayed ability of existing workers to shift from one industry to another in response to an influx of new workers from overseas. One might intuit that this "job competition" effect would be more important if the new incoming workers are similar to existing native-born workers.

However, a less widely considered possibility is that inflows of foreign labor might *create* jobs for native workers, which can happen if the new foreign workers establish new enterprises that employ natives. We might expect that this "job creation" effect would be more likely for inflows of workers with entrepreneurial skills, available financial capital, or higher education levels.

In principle, the impact of new inflows of the foreign-born into Venezuelan industries could have either a negative or positive effect on native unemployment. The empirical analysis will test which effect dominates on average, looking separately at inflows of Colombians on the one hand, and Europeans on the other. This will be done by estimating the causal effect of the fraction of foreign-born workers in a particular industry and in a particular year, and the unemployment rate of native workers in that same industry and year. A positive relationship between these two variables would be supportive of the "job competition" hypothesis; a negative relationship would support the "job creation" hypothesis.

In order to estimate the causal effect of the fraction of foreign-born workers on native unemployment, there are two key empirical challenges. First, there may be reverse causation—that is, inflows of native-born workers into certain industries may lead foreign-born workers to exit the industry. Second, there may be some factors that are not accounted for and that may affect both foreign-born inflows and native unemployment. For example, if a certain industry suddenly becomes more attractive (because of government subsidies, technological advancements, or other factors), we may observe inflows of both native and foreign-born workers into this industry, suggesting a negative association between the fraction of foreign-born workers on native unemployment in that industry.

For these two reasons, using a standard OLS regression in our analysis is unlikely to capture the true causal effect of the fraction of foreign-born workers on native unemployment. To address these two key empirical challenges, we use an econometric technique called *instrumental variables*. The idea is to estimate the effect of the fraction of foreign-born workers on native unemployment with the help of a third variable (called an *instrument*) that affects native unemployment, but only through the presence of foreign-born in a given industry—in other words, this third variable should not affect native unemployment directly or through any channel other than the presence of foreign-born workers.[4] The instrument we used is based on economic fluctuations taking place outside Venezuela, in migrant source countries. The idea is that these economic fluctuations affect foreign-born inflows into Venezuela, but do not affect native unemployment directly. For example, if there is an economic crisis in Portugal, this may lead to a net inflow of Portuguese people into Venezuela, but should not have a direct effect on the unemployment rate of natives. The technical appendix to this chapter describes in detail the empirical estimation strategy, the choice of the instrument, and the full set of empirical results. Below we present the key results from our analyses.

In table 8.1, columns (1) and (2) present the outcomes from two regressions (using the instrumental variable technique mentioned above), estimating the effect on the native unemployment rate of Colombian presence and European presence, respectively. Column (1) suggests that an increase of 1 percentage point in the fraction of Colombian workers in a Venezuelan industry leads to a rise of 1.17 percentage points in the unemployment rate of native workers in that industry. The effect is statistically significant at the 1 percent level and reasonably large in magnitude. This result is supportive of the "job competition" hypothesis—the idea that an inflow of Colombian workers into a Venezuelan industry is displacing Venezuelan workers from that industry.

Column (2), on the other hand, suggests that an increase of 1 percentage point in the fraction of European workers in a Venezuelan industry does not have a statistically significant effect in the unemployment rate of native workers in this industry. The magnitude of the effect (0.45) is moderate, but it is not statistically

Table 8.1   Effect of Colombian and European presence on unemployment rate
of native-born workers

Dependent variable: Native-born unemployment rate		
	(1)	(2)
Colombian presence	1.17	—
	(0.24)***	—
European presence	—	0.46
	—	(0.66)
Year fixed effects	Yes	Yes
Industry fixed effects	Y	Y
Observations	570	570

SOURCE: Based on Venezuela's semiannual Encuesta de Hogares (1980–2003).

NOTE: "Colombian presence" is the fraction of individuals in an industry who were born in
Colombia. The "European presence" variable is defined analogously. Standard errors in parentheses,
clustered by industry. Unit of observation is industry-year. Results are based on instrumental
variable regressions. See the technical appendix for details.

* Significant at 10%
** Significant at 5%
*** Significant at 1%

significant. This result is not supportive of the "job competition" hypothesis, and
in fact is suggestive that the "job creation" hypothesis may be at play.

Conclusion

We document in this chapter that the Venezuelan economic collapse since 1980
has been associated with very large inflows of Colombians and even larger
outflows of Europeans in the past three decades. We shed light on the likely
impact that these large migrant inflows and outflows have had on the labor market
performance of native-born Venezuelans.

Our analysis of Venezuelan labor market data from 1980 to 2003 reveals that
increases in Colombian presence in Venezuelan industries has led to increases in
native-born unemployment, as Colombians compete directly with Venezuelans
for jobs. Our estimates indicate that native-born unemployment rises roughly
one-for-one with increases in Colombian presence in Venezuelan industries. In
contrast, declines in European presence are likely to have been somewhat neutral in their effect on Venezuelan unemployment. Declines in European presence
in Venezuelan industries have not led to declines in native-born unemployment
rates. This is, perhaps, because European presence has a "job creating" effect that,
on average, offsets any competition for jobs between Europeans and Venezuelans.

APPENDIX

This technical appendix describes in detail the identification strategy, the construction of the data set, and the full set of empirical results. We assume that the reader is familiar with the econometric techniques used.

Identification Strategy

Consider the following regression equation for the unemployment rate U_{it} for native-born Venezuelans in industry i in year t:

$$U_{it} = \alpha F^j_{it} + \mu_i + \gamma_t + \varepsilon_{it}. \qquad (A.1)$$

In equation (A.1), F^j_{it} is the presence in industry i of individuals born in location j in year t. The variable μ_i is a fixed effect for industry i, γ_t is a year fixed effect, and ε_{it} is a mean-zero error term.

A problem with estimating this regression equation via ordinary least squares is that the coefficient on foreign-born presence in the industry α need not represent the causal effect on native-born unemployment. For example, there may be reverse causation: if net inflows of native-born workers into the industry stimulate net exit by the foreign-born, thus leading to negative bias in the regression coefficient. Omitted variable concerns also arise, such as third factors (e.g., technology-driven improvements in worker productivity) that stimulate inflows of both native and foreign-born workers. This latter case would lead the regression coefficient on F^j_{it} to be positively biased.

It is therefore important to isolate a source of variation in foreign-born industry presence that is exogenous with respect to native-born outcomes in the industry. We therefore focus on variation in foreign-born industry presence that is driven by economic fluctuations taking place *outside* Venezuela, in migrant *source countries*. To the extent that migrant flows to Venezuela are in part driven by economic conditions in migrant source areas, improvements in economic conditions overseas should reduce net migration (inflows minus outflows) to Venezuela.

Economic conditions outside Venezuela should help predict net migration to the country as a whole, but how then does one predict the allocation of these migrants across Venezuelan industries? We assume that when migrants arrive, they are more likely to seek employment in industries where migrants from the same source areas are already employed. This makes sense if the existence of intra-industry migrant networks lower the costs of job search (as in Munshi 2003).

To make this idea more concrete, consider the foreign-born presence (Europeans and Colombians separately) by industry in Venezuela for three time periods (1975–79, 1980–91, and 1992–2003). In the earliest period, European-born industry presence was highest in international organizations (39.49 percent), wholesale trade (13.22 percent), real estate and services to firms (12.50 percent), and restaurants and hotels (11.89 percent); and lowest in hydraulic works and water supply (1.26 percent), public administration and defense (0.92 percent), and wood extraction (0.21 percent). In the same period, Colombian-born presence showed different patterns, being highest in professional services including housekeeping (9.19 percent), wood industry and furniture (5.15 percent), restaurants and hotels (5.01 percent), and clothing and leather (4.50 percent); and lowest in fishing (0.40 percent), and oil and natural gas production (0.19 percent).

If existing migrant networks lower job search costs for newly arrived migrants, we should expect that new migrant inflows into Venezuela should lead to larger percentage-point increases in migrant presence in those industries where migrant presence is already high. Conversely, when net migrant outflows occur, we should expect larger percentage-point declines in industries where the migrants were initially well represented.

As documented earlier in this chapter, the past three decades have seen dramatic increases in Colombian immigration to Venezuela. We would then expect that Colombian presence by industry rises more (in percentage-point terms) within industries where Colombians were initially well represented. This prediction receives some support in table 8A.1. The largest percentage-point increases in Colombian industry presence from 1975–79 to 1992–2003 were in two industries that had nearly the highest initial Colombian presence: wood and furniture (initial share 5.15 percent, rising to 9.82 percent), and clothing and leather (initial share 4.50 percent, rising to 9.82 percent).

With the large declines in net migration by European-born into Venezuela, we see an analogous pattern but with the opposite sign: the largest percentage-point declines in European-born industry presence occur in industries where Europeans were initially well represented. Most dramatically among the larger industries, European presence in wholesale trade declines from 13.22 percent to 2.44 percent, and in real estate and services to firms from 12.50 percent to 2.28 percent. (The decline in European presence in international organizations is even larger, from 39.49 percent to 10.06 percent, but this is a minor employment classification.)

Motivated by these considerations, we construct an instrumental variable for foreign-born industry presence F_{it}^j, which lags overseas economic conditions in location j (Y_{it-1}^j), and *interacts* with initial industry presence of those born in location j (F_{i0}^j). (We lag overseas economic conditions by one year because

Table 8A.1 Summary statistics for analysis of effect of foreign-born presence on native unemployment

Variable	Mean	Std. Dev.	Minimum	Median	Maximum	Num. Obs.
European presence	0.025	0.025	0.000	0.017	0.177	570
Colombian presence	0.035	0.031	0.000	0.029	0.318	570
Initial European presence (1975–79)	0.055	0.034	0.002	0.050	0.132	570
Initial Colombian presence (1975–79)	0.027	0.019	0.000	0.024	0.092	570
Log per capita GDP (t–1), southern Europe	9.517	0.173	9.280	9.553	9.780	570
Log per capita GDP (t–1), Colombia	7.651	0.105	7.515	7.678	7.799	570
Instrument for European-born presence	0.523	0.323	0.019	0.479	1.293	570
Instrument for Colombian-born presence	0.210	0.143	0.000	0.188	0.717	570
Native-born unemployment rate	0.206	0.085	0.000	0.196	0.486	570

SOURCE: Based on Venezuela's semiannual Encuesta de Hogares (1980–2003).

NOTE: "Colombian presence" is the fraction of individuals in an industry who were born in Colombia. The "European presence" variable is defined analogously. Log per capita GDP in southern Europe is weighted average across Spain, Italy, and Portugal (weights are 0.46, 0.28, and 0.26, respectively). Instrument for European- or Colombian-born presence is respective initial presence interacted with respective log per capita GDP (in year t–1).

migration does not typically occur immediately, and should require some advance planning.) The first-stage regression predicting foreign-born industry presence F_{it}^j is therefore simply

$$F_{it}^j = \alpha(F_{i0}^j {}^* Y_{it-1}^j) + \delta_i + \lambda_t + v_{it}, \qquad (A.2)$$

where δ_i is a fixed effect for industry i, λ_t is a year fixed effect, and v_{it} is a mean-zero error term.

Our strategy, then, is to examine whether and how these instrumented changes in foreign presence are associated with changes in native-born unemployment. The predicted value of foreign presence from the first stage $\hat{F}_{it}^j$ is used instead of F_{it}^j in the second-stage instrumental variables regression

$$U_{it} = \alpha \hat{F}_{it}^j + \mu_i + \gamma_t + \varepsilon_{it}. \qquad (A.3)$$

In panel data contexts, positive correlation in the error terms across observations in different time periods but within the same unit of analysis (in this case, two-digit industries) biases standard errors downward (Bertrand, Duflo, and Mullainathan 2004). We therefore report standard errors that account for arbitrary covariance structures among observations from the same industry (standard errors are clustered by industry).

It is desirable to have the regression estimates represent the impact of foreign-born presence for the typical Venezuelan worker. But industries vary considerably in total size, and so simple unweighted regressions would give equal weight in the analyses to smaller as well as larger industries. We therefore run weighted regressions, where we weigh each industry–year observation by its size (total number of workers) in the initial (1975–79) period.

Construction of the Data Set for Analysis

Data for the empirical analysis comes from the Venezuelan Encuesta de Hogares (described above) from 1975 to 2003. Data are aggregated at the industry–year level to calculate European-born presence, Colombian-born presence, and the native-born unemployment rate. The European and Colombian presence variables are simply the fraction of workers in the industry who were born in either Europe or Colombia. We do not break out Europeans by exact country of birth because, unfortunately, for most years of data (all years prior to 1994) the exact country of birth within Europe is not reported in the survey. All industries that are represented in the data for twenty-five or more years are included in the analysis (some minor industries appear in the survey only for a few years over the time period). To eliminate outliers that are likely to be due to inconsistencies in data collection over time, we apply a data-cleaning screen to all key independent and dependent variables used in the analyses: we replace the value of a variable with "missing" if its value is more than three standard deviations away from the mean value of the variable across all years.

In constructing the instrumental variables for both Colombian- and European-born industry presence, the first component is Colombian- and European-born industry presence in an initial period, which we take to be 1975–79. The measure of economic conditions is simply log per capita GDP (lagged one year) in the place of origin from World Development Indicators, 2004. Log per capita GDP is clearly defined for Colombia, but what about the analogous measure for European migrants?

While the Encuesta de Hogares records the exact country origins of Europeans in 1975–79, we do know that most Europeans in Venezuela during that period would have been from southern European countries. The 1971 Venezuelan census (which was somewhat better at recording exact country of birth) found that among the roughly 600,000 foreign-born individuals in the country, 30 percent were born in Colombia, 25 percent in Spain, 15 percent in Italy, 14 percent in Portugal, and the remaining 16 percent in other locations (including other Latin American countries) (Blutstein et al. 1985). Therefore, the measure we use for economic conditions in European source areas is the weighted average of log per capita GDP among the three most highly represented southern European countries: Spain, Italy, and Portugal. We use weights that are proportional to relative presence of migrants from these countries in the 1971 Venezuelan census (0.46, 0.28, and 0.26, respectively).

Summary statistics for the key variables used in the analysis are presented in 8A.1. The unit of observation is the industry–year, across thirty-three industries and twenty-four years (1980–2003). The first year of data we use is 1980 because the initial years of data (1975–79) are used to estimate the initial foreign-born presence by industry, and therefore cannot be used in the main empirical analysis. The mean values of European and Colombian presence across industries and periods are 0.025 and 0.35, respectively. The native-born (Venezuelan) unemployment rate has a mean of 0.206, with a standard deviation of 0.085 and a range of [0.000, 0.486].

First-Stage Estimates

Coefficient estimates on the foreign presence instruments from estimation of the first-stage equation (A.2) are presented in table 8A.2. The first two columns present coefficient estimates in regressions where the dependent variable

Table 8A.2   Impact of source-country economic shocks on foreign-born presence in Venezuelan industries, 1980–2003

First stage of instrumental variables estimates

Dependent variable	(1) Colombian presence	(2) Colombian presence	(3) European presence	(4) European presence
(Colombian presence, 1975–1979) · (log per capita GDP in Colombia, year t–1)	–2.243 (0.685)***	–2.245 (0.689)***	—	–0.047 (0.114)***
(European presence, 1975–1979) · (log per capita GDP in southern Europe, year t–1)	—	0.014 (0.340)	–1.276 (0.110)***	–1.267 (0.099)***
Year fixed effects	Yes	Yes	Yes	Yes
Industry fixed effects	Yes	Yes	Yes	Yes
F-stat.: significance of source-country instrument	10.72	10.62	134.65	82.65
p-value	0.0026	0.0027	0.0000	0.0000
F-stat.: joint significance of both instruments	—	5.65	—	163.78
p-value		0.0081		0.0000

SOURCE: Based on Venezuela's semiannual Encuesta de Hogares (1980–2003).

NOTE: Standard errors in parentheses, clustered by industry. Industry is at two-digit level. Unit of observation is industry–year.

*Significant at 10%
**Significant at 5%
***Significant at 1%

is Colombian-born presence in the industry, while in the latter two columns the dependent variable is European-born presence.

In column (1), the coefficient on the instrument for Colombian presence is negative and statistically significantly different from zero at the 1 percent level. Improvements in Colombian economic performance (with a one-year lag) led to greater declines in Colombian presence in industries where Colombians have greater presence to begin with. The regression in column (2) is identical to that in column (1), except that the instrument for European presence is included as an independent variable. The instrument for European presence is comparatively small in magnitude and is not statistically significantly different from zero. This is sensible: shocks in Europe do not affect Colombian presence in Venezuelan industries. Inclusion of the European instrument does not materially affect the coefficient on the Colombian instrument.

The magnitude of the coefficient on the Colombian instrument in both columns (1) and (2) indicates that, for an industry with initial Colombian presence of 0.05 (5 percent), a 0.02 decline in log per capita GDP in Colombia leads to a 0.0022 (0.22 percent) increase in Colombian industry presence.

Results for European presence are quite similar. The coefficient on the European presence instrument in column (3) is negative and statistically significantly different from zero at the 1 percent level. Inclusion of the Colombian presence instrument in column (4) does not materially change the coefficient on the European presence instrument. Improvements in European economic performance lead to greater declines in European presence in industries with greater initial European presence, with a one-year lag. Somewhat surprisingly, the coefficient on the Colombian presence instrument is also negative and statistically significantly different from zero at the 1 percent level, and in magnitude is nearly two-fifths the size of the European presence instrument. One possibility is that European-born migrants currently residing *in Colombia* consider the Colombian and Venezuelan labor markets to be relatively close substitutes and decide where to locate based on Colombian economic conditions. The European-born who enter Venezuela via Colombia may distribute themselves across industries in a manner more similar to the Colombian-born than do the European-born. This would mean that the Colombian presence instrument is correlated with their propensity to locate across Venezuelan industries.

The magnitude of the coefficients on the European instruments in columns (3) and (4) indicates that for an industry with an initial European presence of 0.05 (5 percent), a 0.02 decline in weighted-average southern European log per capita GDP leads to a 0.0013 (0.13 percent) increase in European industry presence.

Both the Colombian and European instruments are quite strong, as exhibited by the F-statistics at the bottom of table 8A.2. By themselves, F-statistics for each respective source-country instrument exceed the rule-of-thumb level of 10 recommended by Bound, Jaeger, and Baker (1995). When the other migrant source location's instrument is included in the regression, the F-stat. increases in the regression for European presence (column [4]), but declines somewhat in the regression for Colombian presence (column [2]).

Second-Stage Estimates (Ordinary Least Squares and Instrumental Variables)

Table 8A.3 presents regression estimates of the impact of Colombian and European presence on native-born unemployment in Venezuelan industries. Panel A presents ordinary least squares estimates from the estimation of equation (A.1), while panel B presents instrumental variables estimations. The Instrumental Variables regressions exhibit predicted values of Colombian and European presence from the first-stage regressions of table 8A.2. All regressions include fixed effects for industry and year. In both panels, the regression in column (1) additionally includes only the Colombian presence variable as an explanatory variable; the regression in column (2) includes only the European presence variable as an explanatory variable; and the regression in column (3) includes both Colombian and European presence separately as explanatory variables.

The ordinary least squares results in panel A indicate that increases in Colombian presence in Venezuelan industries are associated with increases in Venezuelan unemployment. The coefficients on Colombian presence in both columns (1) and (3) are statistically significantly different from zero at the 5 percent level. By contrast, European presence is not strongly associated with Venezuelan unemployment by industry: the coefficients on European presence are small in magnitude (and actually negative in sign) and are very far from being statistically significantly different from zero at conventional levels.

The ordinary least squares results cannot be given a causal interpretation, so we now turn to the instrumental variables results in panel B. As it turns out, these results confirm the patterns found in the ordinary least squares regressions. The coefficient on instrumented Colombian presence is large in magnitude (ranging from 1.05 to 1.167 across specifications) and is statistically significantly different from zero at the 1 percent level in both columns (1) and (3). By contrast, the coefficient on instrumented European presence (here positively signed, in contrast to the ordinary least squares results) is smaller in magnitude and is not statistically significantly different from zero at conventional levels.

Table 8A.3   Impact of foreign-born presence on Venezuelan unemployment rate
by industry, 1980–2003

Panel A: Ordinary least-squares estimates			
Dependent variable: native-born unemployment rate			
	(1)	(2)	(3)
Colombian presence	0.658	—	0.668
	(0.270)**	—	(0.289)**
European presence	—	−0.064	−0.125
	—	(0.343)	(0.353)
Year fixed effects	Yes	Yes	Yes
Industry fixed effects	Yes	Yes	Yes
Observations	570	570	570
R-squared	0.84	0.84	0.84
Panel B: Instrumental variables estimates			
Dependent variable: native-born unemployment rate			
	(1)	(2)	(3)
Colombian presence	1.167	—	1.050
	(0.244)***	—	(0.229)***
European presence	—	0.460	0.439
	—	(0.663)	(0.600)
Year fixed effects	Y	Y	Y
Industry fixed effects	Y	Y	Y
Observations	570	570	570

SOURCE: Based on Venezuela's semiannual Encuesta de Hogares (1980–2003).

NOTE: Standard errors in parentheses, clustered by industry. Industry is at two-digit level. Unit of observation is industry-year. First-stage regressions for Instrumental Variables are in previous table.

*Significant at 10%
**Significant at 5%
***Significant at 1%

In sum, exogenous increases in Colombian presence in Venezuelan industries cause increases in Venezuelan unemployment. When it comes to Colombian-born presence in Venezuelan industries, the "job competition" effect would appear to dominate any "job creating" effect. The negative effect of Colombian presence is large: the coefficient estimates on instrumented Colombian presence—from 1.050 to 1.167—indicate that the native-born unemployment rate rises roughly one-for-one with Colombian presence in the industry. By contrast, there is no statistically significant effect of exogenous increases in European presence—perhaps because some fraction of European entry into Venezuelan industries is "job creating" and therefore offsets, to some extent, any "job competition" effect. This may be due to Europeans' greater likelihood of being entrepreneurs. On net, we cannot distinguish the effect of European presence on Venezuelan unemployment from zero.

NOTES

1. Estimates of the number of individuals living outside their countries of birth are from United Nations 2002, while data on world population are from United States Bureau of the Census 2002.

2. The survey collected data on year of arrival to Venezuela, but only for the period 1994–2003.

3. The age trends are consistent with a higher influx of Colombians than Europeans. The average age of Colombians increased from thirty-one to forty-four in the period 1975–2003, whereas the average age of Europeans increased from about forty to about sixty in that same period.

4. Technically, it could affect native unemployment through some other channel if we can control (i.e., account for) this channel in our analysis.

REFERENCES

Bertrand, Marianne, Esther Duflo, and Sendhil Mullainathan. 2004. "How Much Should We Trust Differences-in-Differences Estimates?" *Quarterly Journal of Economics* 119:249–75.

Blutstein, Howard, J. David Edwards, Kathryn Therese Johnston, David McMorris, and James Rudolph. 1985. *Venezuela: A Country Study*. Washington, D.C.: American University and United States Army.

Borjas, George. 2003. "The Labor Demand Curve Is Downward Sloping: Reexamining the Impact of Immigration on the Labor Market." *Quarterly Journal of Economics* 118 (4): 1335–74.

Bound, John, David Jaeger, and Regina Baker. 1995. "Problems with Instrumental Variables Estimation When the Correlation between the Instruments and the Endogenous Explanatory Variables Is Weak." *Journal of the American Statistical Association* 90:443–50.

Card, David. 1990. "The Impact of the Mariel Boatlift on the Miami Labor Market." *Industrial and Labor Relations Review* 43:245–57.

Chen, Chi-Yi. 1968. *Movimientos migratorios en Venezuela*. Caracas: Universidad Católica Andres Bello.

Duflo, Esther, Marianne Bertrand, and Sendhil Mullainathan. "How Much Should We Trust Difference-in-Difference Estimates?" *Quarterly Journal of Economics* 119:249–75.

Friedberg, Rachel M., and Jennifer Hunt. 1995. "The Impact of Immigration on Host Country Wages, Employment, and Growth." *Journal of Economic Perspectives* 9:23–44.

Gonzalez, Estela M., Ponciano Torales, and Nora Pérez Vichich. 2003. "Migraciones laborales en Sudamérica: La Comunidad Andina." *Estudios Sobre Migraciones Internacionales*, no. 60. Report available at http://www.ilo.org/public/english/protection/migrant/download/imp/imp60s.pdf.

Mille, Nicolas. 1965. *20 años de musiues: Aspectos históricos sociológicos y jurídicos de la inmigración Europea en Venezuela, 1945-1965*. Caracas: Editorial Sucre.

Munshi, Kaivan. 2003. "Networks in the Modern Economy: Mexican Migrants in the U.S. Labor Market." *Quarterly Journal of Economics* 18 (2): 549–97.

Pellegrino, Adela. 1984. "Venezuela: Illegal Immigration from Colombia." *International Migration Review* 18 (3): 748–66.

_____. 2004. "Migration from Latin America to Europe: Trends and Policy Challenges." *IOM Migration Research Series*, no. 16. Report available at http://www.oas.org/atip/migration/iom%20report%20migration%20lac%20to%20eu.pdf.

Sandoval, Alvarez. 2003. *Integración y fronteras en América Latina.* Mérida: Universidad de Los Andes Editorial Venezuela.

Sassen-Koob, Saskia. 1979. "Economic Growth and Migration in Venezuela." *International Migration Review* 13 (3): 455–74.

Smith, James P., and Barry Edmonston. 1997. *The New Americans: Economic, Demographic, and Fiscal Effects of Immigration.* Washington, D.C.: National Academy Press.

Suarez Sarmiento, Gitanjali. 2000. *Diagnostico sobre las migraciones Caribeñas hacia Venezuela.* Buenos Aires: International Organization for Migration.

Torrealba, Ricardo. 1987. "International Migration Data: Their Problems and Usefulness in Venezuela." *International Migration Review* 21 (4): 1270–76.

United Nations. 2002. *International Migration Report, 2002.* New York.

United States Bureau of the Census. 2002. *International Data Base.* Washington, D.C.: Government Printing Office.

Van Roy, Ralph. "Undocumented Migration to Venezuela." *International Migration Review* 18 (3): 541–57.

9 SLEEPING IN THE BED ONE MAKES: THE VENEZUELAN FISCAL POLICY RESPONSE TO THE OIL BOOM

María Antonia Moreno and Cameron A. Shelton

At the broadest level, Venezuelan fiscal accounts went through three phases between the democratic consolidation of 1958 and the constitutional reform of 1999. A pre-boom period of remarkable calm existed from 1962 to 1973 during which per capita oil revenues were relatively stable and so, too, were fiscal accounts. This was followed by a pair of incomprehensibly massive spikes in per capita oil revenues—peaking first in 1974, receding, then peaking again in 1981—which gradually eroded to pre-boom levels by 1985. This period witnessed massive increases in spending during the first peak, adjustment as the peak subsided, a resurgence during the second peak, and renewed adjustment as the second peak subsided. But the pre-boom calm was never restored: from 1986 through the 1990s, per capita oil revenues continued to decline significantly below their pre-boom levels, necessitating continued fiscal adjustment. During this period, fiscal policy was in considerable turmoil: oil revenues volatile and declining, new sources of non-oil revenues developing, and both the magnitude and composition of expenditures fluctuating significantly from year to year.[1]

The story of Venezuelan fiscal policy is the reaction to these massive, exogenous shocks to revenues. In this chapter, we will document this reaction, compare it to theoretical prescriptions for optimal fiscal policy when faced with such shocks, and assess the degree to which suboptimal fiscal policy in the face of these shocks is responsible for the sustained contraction in non-oil per capita GDP that Venezuela suffered from 1979 to 2003.

There are essential questions. First, was the windfall of the oil booms spent wisely? The answer here is pretty clearly "no," though it must be qualified by a realistic appraisal of the political feasibility of optimal fiscal policy. Second, to what extent did excesses during the boom years saddle the economy with a crippling legacy that can account for the continued decline? Or to restate: Why didn't the squandering of the boom simply represent a missed opportunity, after which the economy could resume its original growth path? Was the aftermath of the boom entirely to blame, was post-boom fiscal policy also at fault, or were non-fiscal factors to blame? This second question must be addressed to judge the degree to which the *sustained* growth collapse can be laid at the door of improvident fiscal policy.

Optimal Fiscal Policy in the Face of a Deluge

Fluctuations in Venezuelan fiscal accounts, and indeed in the economy as a whole, are driven primarily by fluctuations in the international market for crude oil. Oil revenues averaged 66 percent of total central government revenues during the period leading up to the collapse, 1962–79. Moreover, oil revenues had a coefficient of variation 2.3 times as high as non-oil revenues over the same period. Before the collapse and the ensuing volatility in GDP and instruments of taxation, fluctuations in total revenues were driven almost entirely by fluctuations in oil revenues. As we will see, expenditures roughly follow revenues, with negligible inter-temporal smoothing.

The magnitude of the shock to revenues resulting from the oil price hikes of 1973–74 is staggering. The increase in central government revenues between 1973 and 1974 due to the oil sector was 34.5 percent of 1973 GDP. Over the entire period of high oil prices from 1974 to 1985, the increase of oil prices above their 1960–73 average contributed an additional 523 percent of 1973 GDP to a government that traditionally occupied 18–20 percent of the economy. These figures do not account for the additional profits retained by the oil sector, which then had an indirect impact on government revenues through spending in the non-oil sector. To deliver an equivalent shock to the present-day U.S. economy would require the addition of $87 trillion (constant 2012 dollars) over the next eleven years *to government revenues alone.* A boom of this magnitude simply has no precedent in the developed world and had few precedents anywhere in 1974.

What constitutes optimal fiscal policy in the face of such a colossal influx of revenues? If we view the government as a unitary, benevolent social planner facing an inter-temporal optimization problem, consumption of this windfall ought to be smoothed by investing the vast majority of it. But there are several obstacles to such an increase in the investment rate.

First, it is difficult to believe that the domestic economy could find efficient use for this much new capital in such a short span of time. Neoclassical growth models assume diminishing returns to capital, implying that developing countries earn higher raw rates of return on investments than do advanced economies. These models further assume that the productivity of investments is independent of the speed with which they are undertaken: there exists a set of investments ready to be undertaken whenever the economy can raise the capital. From the perspective of growth models, it follows that all investment ought to be domestic.

This assumes that the proper growth path and associated investments are costlessly and instantly identifiable. But the profitability of an investment depends on the future stream of profits, which depend in turn on the future state of the marketplace. The required projection of the marketplace becomes far more elusive in a climate of ultra-rapid growth and sectoral change. Moreover, easy liquidity often results in laxity of due diligence. The resulting combination has historically led to devastating excesses in developing and advanced economies alike. The overinvestment in Internet infrastructure and the spate of barely planned dot-coms in the United States in the late 1990s is one recent and widely publicized example in a long history. A future of potentially exciting but poorly understood opportunities acts like soapy water: all that is required is a puff of easy credit to produce a raft of bubbles.

In essence, most growth models assume there is no horizon to the growth path. On the contrary, identification of profitable investments requires knowledge of current prices and the ability to project future prices. If individual investments are sufficiently small and are taken in sequence, such that each subsequent investment may observe the previous one, then investments are likely to proceed along an efficient path. When one's stride is short compared to the horizon, one can keep to the path. But if investment is undertaken all at once, even by a single social planner who can solve coordination problems, it seems unlikely that such a planner would be capable of anticipating the complex web of interactions between the various investments to be undertaken simultaneously. During such a rapid flow of funds, the economic landscape may change too quickly for price signals to adjust and be noticed, and for the implications to be processed. This is especially true if allocations are no longer governed by prices but by an industrial planning ministry. If one takes a stride many times longer than the horizon, one may find that the path of development has turned aside and one has stridden blindly into a quagmire.

The traditional solution in developing countries is state-planned industrialization. Central coordination may ease some, though not all, of the difficulties with directing massive investment. Certainly the direction of capital by a single social planner makes possible projects exhibiting increasing returns to scale, requiring broad technical expertise or the coordination of many firms, or requiring long gestation periods. The perils of planning a large step all at once are somewhat alleviated by the existence of developed countries further along the growth path, whose histories may provide some guide to successful industrialization. Nonetheless, the past forty years have made it abundantly clear that there is no one-size-fits-all development strategy. Moreover, even if the broad brushstrokes are correctly painted, successful implementation is fraught with unforeseen, country-specific perils.

Drawing on sixteen case studies of natural-resource booms, Ascher (1999) details the unforeseen difficulties governments face trying to pursue centrally planned investment strategies for such windfalls: low accountability of state-owned enterprises (SOEs), unwise investments within the sector, mispricing of inputs and outputs, failure to minimize costs, underexploitation and inefficient exploitation due to undercapitalization. His cases highlight the difficulty in sustainably extracting revenues from the natural-resource sector. As both Ascher and many contributions to this volume (Di John, Manzano, and Hausmann and Rodríguez) detail, Venezuela struggled to extract revenues without crippling the development of the oil industry.

Perhaps as worrying is the likelihood that a rapid and massive investment, even if properly directed, would result in a divergence of aggregate supply and demand. In the long run, spending the boom on productive investments (as opposed to consumption or projects with poor returns) ought to increase aggregate supply as well as aggregate demand. In practice, increases in the former lag behind increases in the latter, as investments take time to produce returns. Moreover, proper coordination of centrally directed industrialization is nontrivial and can easily result in disappointing productivity gains. This is especially true of the kind of "big push" policies to which Venezuela turned in 1974. Di John (in this volume) writes:

> "Big push" natural-resource-based industrialization (NRBI) strategies commit large sums of state resources to long-gestating, technologically demanding investment projects, which require complementary investment and state-business conglomerate coordination. … As it turned out, the Achilles' heel of Venezuelan industrialization strategy was to be a growing inefficiency in the implementation of such big-push strategies. The greater learning costs and gestation periods of such investments bring greater economic and political challenges and risks that distinguish this type of economic strategy from the small-scale and simple technology of the easy ISI (import-substitution industrialization) stage.

Di John then explains how failures in the coordination, monitoring, and discipline of the state-owned enterprises and private businesses receiving government loans—due largely to populist, clientele politics—led to a failure of the investments to lead to productivity gains.

Absent productivity gains and export earnings, a huge increase in government investment produces an imbalance between domestic aggregate supply and demand, leading to too many dollars chasing too few goods. This kind of imbalance may regularly result from investments that are unproductive or whose returns are delayed. Given the enormity of the Venezuelan oil boom, the associated imbalances were a sizeable fraction of GDP, resulting in considerable overheating and the attendant misallocations: in short, dire consequences for the non-oil sector. A smoother growth path of government expenditure would have served to prevent domestic aggregate demand from outstripping so completely domestic aggregate supply, thus preventing runaway inflation.

Di John describes the difficulties in selecting the proper firms, coordinating complementary investments, monitoring the use of funds, and effectively conditioning government loans and transfers on performance. The question often glossed over concerns the ability of the central government to identify the proper growth path. Di John submits that Venezuela invested in exactly the same mix of heavy manufacturing industries—such as steel and chemicals—as the countries that industrialized successfully through big push policies. While this signals that such an industrial mix is not fatally flawed, it does not necessarily follow that this was the correct mix for Venezuela or the most efficient mix overall.

The clear prescription would be to establish a sovereign wealth fund to smooth the domestic absorption of the windfall. The fund would buy foreign securities—in effect, lending the money overseas to larger markets with a larger pool of credible investment opportunities—to be repatriated in the future. In the meantime, a smaller, more manageable fraction of the money would be steadily invested in the proven domestic enterprises whose rate of return exceeded that available overseas. Reducing the ratio of new investment to the size of the established economy would have two effects. First, breaking the windfall into several moderate strides rather than one long one would enable institutional learning-by-doing, enabling the economy to adjust to and address mistakes in the initial approach. Second, it would reduce the magnitude of the inevitable momentary divergences of demand and supply. And third, lengthening the period over which the windfall is invested would smooth the windfall beyond the point in time when reversion of oil prices turned off the fiscal tap, making the transition from oil to non-oil economy smoother.

During the sample period, Venezuela failed to put into practice a functioning oil development fund to smooth the use of the windfall.[2] Practically the entirety of the boom was domestically invested as soon as it was accrued: net foreign loans never constituted more than 1 percent of total expenditures in any year, and averaged just over one-third of 1 percent during the boom years from 1974 to 1985.

The fiscal balance averaged a deficit of 0.6 percent of total GDP during the period 1974–85. We will show that this unwillingness to smooth the entry of oil revenues into the economy contributed to an overheating of the economy, which undermined growth. In effect, there was neither inter-temporal smoothing of the surplus nor rationing of domestic credit. The fiscal authority failed to control the taps, so the economy was deluged.

The Venezuelan Growth Spiral

During the period 1972–94, the Venezuelan economy underwent four repetitions of a distressing cycle (see fig. 9.1). Driven by a surge in the price of oil, a boom in per capita oil revenues led to a surge in growth of the non-oil sector.[3] As the initial boost to revenues (and expenditures) subsided, the growth surge continued a few years longer before the economy slid into recession. The next oil price spike rescued the economy from recession briefly, only to lead to a new cycle. But the cycle is not closed: as we progress from one to the next, the economy gradually spirals downward. Each new cycle begins with some combination of higher inflation, more debt, and slower growth than the previous cycle. The last two frames of figure 9.1 compare the pre-spiral era to the post-spiral era to show the cumulative effect on the economy. The average annual growth rate of real per capita non-oil GDP has declined from 3.3 percent in the pre-boom era to −2.8 percent in the post-boom era. Moreover, growth is far more volatile in the post-boom era. True, oil revenues are on average 16.7 percent lower in the post-spiral era and are more volatile, but the differences in both the average growth rate and its volatility seem out of proportion to this decline. One imagines that, had the economy gone directly from the oil revenues of the pre-spiral period to those of the post-spiral period, skipping the volatile years, the consequences would not have been so dire. The Venezuelan economy has exhibited significant hysteresis in response to the oil shocks.

Is fiscal policy responsible for this hysteresis? Part of the answer comes from the efficiency of fiscal policy during the boom. Did an increase in government spending or transfers to enterprise (whether publicly or privately operated) actually stimulate output growth? Figure 9.1 strongly suggests not! But figure 9.1 does not separate the effects of discretionary fiscal policy from other concurrent effects of the oil boom. To do this requires more sophisticated econometric techniques to untangle the complex knot of macroeconomic causality.

Increased government spending ought to increase GDP both now and in the future. Increased transfer payments to households—in the form of more generous education subsidies or unemployment insurance—ought to stimulate consumer spending. Increases in public sector wages should do likewise. Meanwhile,

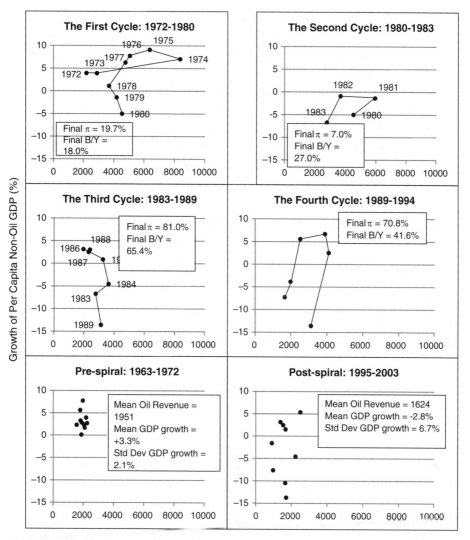

Fig. 9.1 Per Capita Fiscal Oil Revenues (constant 2006 dollars).

Successive shocks to per capita oil revenues generate bursts of growth which eventually overheat the economy, leading to inflation (π). As the revenue burst subsides, spending adjusts with a slight lag, leading to an increase in debt. The ratio of debt to GDP (B/Y) is exacerbated by the output decline of the overheated economy. The economy is never allowed to cool off fully before a new influx of revenues is added. As a result, each new cycle begins from a more dangerous position: higher inflation and a greater debt burden. Post-boom economic performance is dramatically worse than pre-boom performance: per capita GDP growth in the non-oil sector is lower and more volatile. A temporary boom has had permanent effects.

Source: Authors' calculations based on oil price data from Lopez-Obragon and Rodríguez (2001), and GDP data from Rodríguez (2004).

channeling government money into state-owned enterprises as part of an industrial development policy should lead to expenditure on capital equipment, the creation of jobs, and thus payment of salaries, and so on. All these lead to an increase in aggregate output (i.e., GDP). Moreover, the creation of new jobs and new businesses through effective investment should increase the productive capacity of the economy in the future, meaning that even a one-time increase in government spending should have a *dynamic* effect on output lasting for many years. The more efficient and better directed is the spending, the larger this long-term effect ought to be.

But it can be difficult to separate this effect from other simultaneous factors affecting both GDP and fiscal accounts. For instance, there is also a causal effect running in the opposite direction from GDP to fiscal accounts. When GDP rises, governments collect more revenues, thus enabling greater expenditures. And third factors can have an influence on both GDP and fiscal spending. For example, an increase in oil prices both increases government revenues available to be spent, and increases the revenues, and thus spending, of private agents connected to the oil sector. We are interested only in the causal effect of government spending on aggregate output. But the co-evolution of the two is governed not only by this causal mechanism but also by all the other causal channels between those two variables operating simultaneously. Thus a measurement of simple correlation between fiscal revenues and GDP does not correctly estimate the causal impact of increased fiscal expenditures on GDP because it includes the effects of these other causal channels.

To correctly isolate the effects of fiscal spending on the GDP, we estimate a three-variable VAR (vector autoregression)—net transfers, government consumption, and output growth—with oil revenues as an exogenous forcing process. This econometric work enables us to correctly isolate the dynamic causal effect of Venezuelan fiscal policy on GDP during and after the oil boom, having accounted for the other causal channels, especially the effect of oil prices. We can then answer the question, "When the government increased spending by 1 percent, what was the causal effect on GDP over the next five years?" These results are presented in table 9.3 below. The econometric details of the exercise, including the identification strategy, are included in the appendices. But first we discuss the evolution of fiscal accounts to lay out the basic facts.

Driven by Oil

Throughout this chapter, we take these oil revenues as largely exogenous to fiscal policy decisions for two main reasons. Like a producer in any market, a country may perhaps raise the price of its own oil, depending on its market share, substitutability between its oil and that of other producers, and other factors. However, given the limited government control over quantity before nationalization, its limited vote in the OPEC cartel, and its limited market share in all periods, it is unclear exactly how much market power Venezuela as an individual country, distinct from its membership in OPEC, has been historically able to exercise over periods longer than a few quarters.[4] Nonetheless, even if the Venezuelan oil industry is considered a price-taker, oil revenues may still be considered endogenous for a second reason. The strategy of exploration and extraction determines the time path of the quantity of oil produced, and thus the time path of revenues, given a price. Thus oil revenues can be considered exogenous only to the extent that the oil development strategy remains stationary.

As Manzano explains in his contribution to this volume, "Venezuela after a Century of Oil Exploitation," Venezuelan oil development policy is characterized by three broad philosophies during our sample. These philosophies broadly coincide with three different eras in the price of Venezuelan oil (see fig. 9.1 and table 9.1). In the first era (1962–73), oil prices are low and relatively stable. The Venezuelan policy is one of conservation leading to high taxation and low investment. During the second period (1974–85), prices are high and moderately volatile. Nonetheless, production and revenues per capita are falling in Venezuela due to low investment in previous years and the OPEC strategy of further limiting production to keep prices high. In the third period (1986–99), prices are middling and highly volatile. Meanwhile, conservation and total nationalization are deemed unsuitable, and a relaxation of taxes and limited return of private investment lead to a modest expansion in production. As the development strategy shifts, the data-generating process for revenues changes. But within an era, shifts in revenues are driven mainly by exogenous factors that affect the world oil market, with one crucially important exception. As oil revenues fell and adjustment was sometimes incomplete or delayed, the fiscal authority often faced serious deficits. Several times during the sample period, Venezuela devalued the official exchange rate to

Table 9.1   The average level and volatility of oil prices during the three distinct eras

	Average	Standard deviation	Coefficient of variation	Average *absolute* rate of growth	Characterization of the era
Period 1 (1962–73)	11.22	1.77	0.158	8.39	Low level, low volatility
Period 2 (1974–85)	44.96	8.31	0.185	10.18	High level, moderate volatility
Period 3 (1986–99)	19.77	4.17	0.211	19.80	Moderate level, high volatility

SOURCE: Authors' calculations on data from López-Obregon and Rodríguez 2001.

increase oil fiscal revenues to shore up fiscal accounts. Thus we have divided the sample into these three periods for analysis—1962–73, 1974–85, and 1986–99—but we measure oil prices variously in either bolivars or dollars. In our descriptive analysis, we refer to prices in constant bolivars. In the structural VAR, we enter oil prices in constant dollars to keep it from including exchange rate policy.

Spending the Windfall

Figure 9.2 shows that the first peak in oil revenues (1973–74) initiated an increase in government consumption, which continued to grow even as the peak in revenues subsided (1974–78) and was sustained through the upswing of the second peak (1979–81).[5] Additional revenues went initially to the Venezuelan Investment Fund (Fondo de Inversiones de Venezuela, FIV), through which the government would finance its development strategy contained in the Fifth National Plan: investment in large-scale industrial development projects (steel, petrochemicals, aluminum, electricity). In the fiscal area, funding was mainly vested in autonomous entities, which included hospitals, highways, a hydroelectric consortium, shipbuilding firms, a national steamship company, and an airline, among others; in the classification by sector, the spending first favored expenditures directed to productive activities (especially agriculture), and second, social items. In part, this represented a continuation of the policy of "sowing oil": continued investment in education, health, electricity, potable water, and other basic projects. But it also represented a significant foray into large-scale industrial development.

Government accounts show that the deluge was initially directed mostly toward investment rather than government consumption. Looking at figure 9.2, one can see that the composition starts out well enough, with much more of the windfall in the first few years earmarked for investment categories than for government consumption. Table 9.2 shows that the mixture of loans, grants, and outright public investment varied from year to year. For the first few years after an increase in oil revenues, most of the additional investment takes place as a boost in loans to public and private firms, after which there is a transition to direct government investment or outright transfers to SOEs.

As we shall demonstrate below, government expenditures overall are only mildly hysteretic during the boom—responding marginally less quickly to decreases than to increases in revenues. But this is not true of each individual component of expenditures. As each of the revenue booms subsided, the increases to government consumption stubbornly persisted while most of the burden of fiscal adjustment fell on investment. As a result, the composition of the additional spending fueled by the rise in oil prices shifted from investment to consumption (see table 9.2).

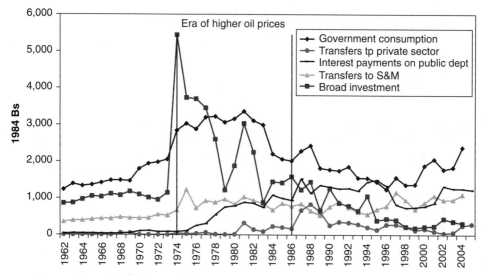

Fig. 9.2   Per capita fiscal expenditures

Source: Authors' calculations on data from Lopez-Obragon and Rodríguez 2001.

Note: The lion's share of the initial boom in 1974 goes to broad investment: government investment, net loans, and transfers to SOEs. But the increases in government consumption are more persistent and as the boom in revenues recedes, they gradually claim a greater share of government expenditures leading to an increase in debt. Explicit transfers to the private sector are not a large part of government finances. Transfers to state and municipal governments gradually increase over the period but remain relatively small.

Eventually, government consumption does respond to declines in revenues. For example, real per capita government consumption declines by 38.7 percent between 1981 and 1985, to return in 1985 to almost exactly its level in 1969, the year before the first big increase. In 1985, real per capita non-oil GDP is still 33 percent higher than it was in 1969: the contraction of the last six years has not yet completely eroded the gains of the previous decade. Thus government consumption actually occupies a smaller fraction of GDP at this point than it did before the boom. Government consumption would continue to decline over the next decade during the sustained growth collapse.

Unfortunately, with revenue fluctuations of this magnitude, even modest hysteresis delivered deficits that were a non-negligible fraction of GDP. The ratio of debt to GDP declined at the beginning of the boom (1972–75) due to GDP growth. But despite continued strong GDP growth, indebtedness soared from less than 7 percent to almost 35 percent of GDP between 1975 and 1978 as government spending receded more slowly than revenues from the high-water mark of 1974. While the second oil peak improved public finances between 1979 and 1982, the growth collapse meant that the debt-to-GDP ratio merely paused at 40 percent during these years. As the oil peak subsided, the debt ratio ballooned to 64 percent over the next two years. It would eventually grow to 74 percent in 1989 before starting a decadelong decline.

Table 9.2   Spending the boom: Consumption and investment increase over historical average (1962–1973) as a fraction of excess oil revenues

	Government consumption	Government investment	Transfers to SOEs	Net loans, domestic	Total investment	Interest payments	Phase
	(1)	(2)	(3)	(4)	(2)+(3)+(4)	(5)	
1974	21.3%	0.9%	23.2%	50.1%	51.0%	0.2%	Net loans
1975	32.5%	3.5%	23.1%	33.8%	37.3%	0.6%	
1976	37.2%	23.9%	50.1%	2.1%	26.0%	3.0%	SOEs + GI
1977	48.5%	11.7%	28.4%	32.5%	44.1%	4.0%	
1978	66.5%	23.6%	27.7%	12.3%	35.9%	10.7%	
1979	48.8%	10.9%	−9.3%	4.5%	15.4%	12.6%	
1980	43.5%	−0.3%	−1.3%	24.9%	24.5%	11.0%	Net loans
1981	36.9%	−0.4%	13.7%	28.2%	27.8%	9.4%	
1982	53.4%	17.0%	−3.0%	28.5%	45.5%	15.4%	
1983	68.6%	−1.3%	−25.2%	19.1%	17.7%	18.4%	
1984	22.9%	−8.5%	10.1%	13.5%	32.9%	20.6%	SOEs + NL
1985	20.1%	11.5%	14.4%	13.2%	28.8%	21.5%	
1974–85	39.2%	5.5%	14.9%	24.8%	45.2%	8.9%	Net loans

SOURCE: Authors' calculations on data from the Central Bank of Venezuela.

NOTE: These figures give the increase in a spending category over its pre-boom (1962–73) average as a percentage of the excess oil revenues. Excess oil revenues are calculated as that fraction of oil revenues that is due to the increase in the current oil price over its pre-boom average. Notice the different phases during the first and second oil spikes. An initial increase in net loans is eventually crowded out by consumption as the wave of excess revenues subsides. Columns (1)–(5) need not add up to 100 percent due to changes in non-oil revenues or the deficit.

There are two other trends worthy of comment. Gavin and Perotti (1997) have previously noted a mild tendency toward decentralization in Latin America as a whole. In Venezuela, however, transfers to state and municipal governments as a fraction of GDP are not statistically significantly different in the second half of the sample than in the first. Direct transfers to private individuals remain small throughout the period, peaking at 3.6 percent of GDP in 1987 and averaging less than 1 percent of GDP over the entire sample from 1962 to 1999. As in most Latin American countries, the Venezuelan government is not a significant manager of entitlement programs during the sample period.[6]

The Bang for the Buck

Of course, the total economic return on a spending item is not always in line with its classification as either consumption or investment. Our category for government consumption includes spending on education, transportation, law enforcement, health care, and other goods that may improve human capital or be classified as public infrastructure and therefore be expected to have significant returns. Similarly, not all investment is productive.

To get a measure of the effectiveness of these spending categories, we estimate a three-variable VAR of GDP, government spending on public goods, and net transfers to the private-goods sector using oil revenues as an exogenous forcing process. The identification strategy (described in appendix A) follows Blanchard and Perotti (2002), which allows distinguishing between changes in fiscal variables induced by fiscal policy shocks and those coming from the business cycle and other policy shocks. The exercise requires using quarterly data, but due to difficulty acquiring historical quarterly GDP data, our sample is somewhat truncated, running from 1976:1 to 1999:4. All variables are seasonally adjusted using the X12 process and are measured in log of per capita real values using the 1984 base year. Oil revenues have been converted to US$ to net out Venezuelan devaluations. Appendix A also details the construction of these variables from fiscal accounts as well as the construction of the elasticities required for the identification strategy.

Our decomposition of fiscal accounts separates government purchases and investments in public goods (G) from net transfers to private actors and SOEs (T).[7] The intent is to identify separately the effectiveness of direct public sector stimulus from that of transfers to the private sector.

The impulse response of output to increases of 1 percent of GDP in transfers to the private goods sector and government expenditures exhibits shocks that are expected to be expansionary, with permanent effects that are almost fully realized

Table 9.3   The response of GDP to government spending

Response of GDP to a 1% increase in net transfers

Sample	2	4	8	12	20	Max.	Quarter	Min.	Quarter
1976–99	0.15	0.08	0.08	0.07	0.07	0.16	1	−0.16	3
1976–85	−0.06	−0.01	−0.06	−0.01	−0.01	0.19	3	−0.19	6
1986–99	0.05	−0.04	−0.09	−0.07	−0.08	0.05	2	−0.05	6

Response of GDP to a 1% increase in public spending

Sample	2	4	8	12	20	Max.	Quarter	Min.	Quarter
1976–99	0.80	0.51	0.69	0.68	0.67	0.86	1	0.51	4
1976–85	0.36	−0.07	0.30	0.48	0.34	0.67	7	−0.07	4
1986–99	0.91	1.25	0.96	1.06	1.04	1.25	4	0.91	2

NOTE: The columns display the elasticity of GDP to a change in the relevant category of government spending within the listed number of quarters. For example, during the oil-boom era, a 1 percent increase in government spending would boost GDP by 0.36 percent over the first two quarters, and this effect would increase to 0.48 percent by the twelfth quarter after the increase, but would then gradually decline to 0.34 percent by five years (twenty quarters) after the initial increase. The minimal and maximal values of the response, and the quarters in which these values are obtained, are reported on the right.

within six quarters. As we discussed in the previous sections, however, both oil prices and Venezuelan fiscal policy are characterized by three distinct eras. Thus we have re-estimated the VAR for the subperiods corresponding to the different eras of the oil sector.[8] From the results, displayed in table 9.3, we can draw four important conclusions:

(1) Government spending and investment in public goods are much less effective during the oil boom (1976–85) than after it (1986–99): further evidence that the economy was already at full employment during this period.
(2) The minimal and maximal responses of GDP to an increase in transfers indicate that the initial effect is positive, but that after perhaps a year the effect becomes negative.
(3) In both subperiods, government spending on public goods is far more effective at stimulating the economy than are government transfers to SOEs and the private sector.
(4) Items (2) and (3) are true in both subperiods, but while the effect of direct government spending is stronger in the post-boom, the effect of transfers is stronger during the boom.

The response to government spending peaks at four quarters, with a medium-run multiplier of roughly one in the post-boom period but only one-third during the boom. This is strong evidence of an economy that was saturated and over-heating during the boom. The results on transfers to the private sector might be interpreted in two (or more) ways. At first glance, the general weakness suggests that government transfers—including transfers to SOEs for producing private goods—are not nearly as effective stimuli as government spending on public goods. On the other hand, in an investigation of six OECD countries, Perotti (2004) found a wide variety in the output response of a similarly defined net transfer category. As Blanchard (2006, 64) notes concerning these results, "This may tell us something about the weakness of structural VARs (vector auto-regressions), as well as something about fiscal policy. I think it would be wrong to say the fault is entirely with the structural VARs. The results may be the effects of the methodology, but they may also reflect something real."

Blanchard and Perotti have somewhat different aims than we do. They are primarily interested in stimulus from income-tax cuts in industrialized countries. On the contrary, we are interested in transfers to SOEs in a developing country. Nonetheless, this is more evidence that the macroeconomic effects of transfers are somewhat more complex than current theory predicts. For our immediate purposes, the evidence suggests that transfers to SOEs failed to deliver the expected stimulus to output within five years.

Into the Strait of Messina

The first cycle dumped a staggering amount of money into the economy. Between 1974 and 1978, the increase in oil prices above their 1960–73 average contributed 143.6 percent of 1973 GDP to government revenues. Most of this first windfall was government-directed investment, though a significant fraction went to an increase in government purchases and the public wage bill. But the economy clearly overheated. Inflation began to rise and GDP first halted in 1978 and then fell in 1979, despite the rebound of oil prices to even greater heights.

In fact, the second oil price spike contributed a second influx of easy money, which was, as a fraction of the economy before the spike, similar in magnitude to the first. Between 1979 and 1985, the increase in oil prices above their 1960–73 average contributed 164.4 percent of 1978 GDP to government revenues. But the economy was already overheated and not capable of domestically processing this second influx of cash. Inflation, which had spiked from a historical average of 3 percent in 1972 to almost 12 percent in 1974, hovered at just under 8 percent in 1978. The second influx of cash sent it soaring immediately to 20 percent in 1979.

Throughout the second cycle, the economy suffered a deep contraction to work off the inflationary excesses that followed the boom. By the end of the cycle, inflation had been reduced from a peak of 20 percent to a more manageable 7 percent. In 1983, debt was a reasonable 27 percent of GDP and the budget was close to balanced: the deficit was 1.6 percent of GDP, down from 4.7 percent the previous year, despite a one-year decline in per capita oil revenues of 24.4 percent. But non-oil GDP had contracted by a tragic 6.7 percent in 1983—the fifth consecutive year of outright decline.

At this point, the government was entering the fiscal equivalent of Odysseus's tricky voyage through the narrow, turbulent Strait of Messina. Contraction in both the oil and non-oil sectors meant GDP was declining. Meanwhile, public finances were in deficit, leading to further accumulation of debt. Faced with an increasing debt to GDP ratio, the government could choose to do nothing and suffer a rising level of debt with consequences for interest rates and future access to capital, or devalue the bolivar, increasing the domestic value of fiscal oil revenues and thus balancing the budget. Unfortunately, the latter approach is tantamount to printing money, with predictable consequences for inflation. The administration was caught between twin hazards, the Scylla of inflation and the Charybdis of debt.

Naturally, the sustainable option in such a dilemma is to improve the deficit, leading to a reduction in the debt ratio, by reducing expenditures. Unfortunately, the short-term effect of a fiscal adjustment would be a contraction, which would temporarily exacerbate the debt ratio. The trick is to properly gauge the speed of adjustment. Go too fast and the strait will constrict so much in the short run that the economy will fall prey to one peril or the other before realizing the benefits of fiscal adjustment. Go too slow and the stagnation is prolonged. A number of events combined to make the Venezuelan adjustment a long and tricky one. Chief among these was the continued decline in per capita oil revenues between 1986 and 1999, after they had already returned to pre-boom levels. Further, budgetary planning was made more difficult by the greater volatility of oil prices during this decline. Venezuelan fiscal accounts did adjust to each new contraction in revenues, but they did so with a lag. The lag meant that each contraction resulted in further accumulation of debt—a further narrowing of the strait.

Entry into the strait was prompted by the deep recession of 1978–84, during which per capita non-oil GDP fell by 20 percent in six years. At the same time, real per capita oil revenues in 1983 were less than half their peak in 1981. The government did decrease expenditures, mainly by reducing both direct government investment and transfers to SOEs, but also partly by reducing government consumption. Thus the deficit never spiraled out of control and was a relatively modest 1.6 percent of GDP in 1983. Nonetheless, the incredible decline in GDP meant that the deficits run during the adjustment grew relatively larger as the economy shrank. The debt-to-GDP ratio, having held stable near 40 percent since 1979, grew to 47 percent in 1983 and then leaped to 64 percent in 1984. To keep debt under control, the government devalued the currency in 1984 and again in

1986 (in response to the dramatic fall in world oil prices that year) to boost temporarily the domestic value of its oil earnings, thus earning breathing room from debt at the cost of inflation.

The fiscal authority was to face this same dilemma repeatedly for the next fifteen years. A decline in oil revenues would force a decline in spending and lead to slow growth. This would threaten to increase the debt-to-GDP ratio through either higher deficits or outright contraction of the economy. Contractions initiated by non-oil triggers would equally threaten an explosion of the debt ratio, producing the same dilemma. Should we devalue to avoid debt, knowing that this sets a course toward higher inflation?

Before considering whether the strait was well navigated, it is worth asking whether the necessary adjustment in the face of declining fiscal revenues was swift or slow. To that end, we have estimated a two-variable VAR, including total revenues and total expenditure (using that Cholesky ordering, expenditures responding to revenues) on quarterly data. We have estimated the VAR separately for each era to get a sense of how the responsiveness of the government to revenues shocks changed as a result of the oil boom. Finally, suspecting that expenditures are more easily and swiftly increased than they are decreased, we have allowed the response to depend on the sign of the change in revenues; hence we have two curves, one for the response of expenditures to an increase in revenues (expansion) and one for the response to a decline in revenues (contraction).

In the pre-boom period, expenditures were pretty well insulated from revenues. Expenditure is reduced in response to a decline in revenue somewhat more swiftly than it is increased when revenues rise. During this period, revenues were fairly stable in both trend and volatility around the trend, so there was little reason to respond strongly to annual variation. During the oil boom, when shocks to revenues were immense, expenditures responded rapidly to changes. There is little evidence that stabilizations were delayed—the impulse response of expenditures to revenue declines mirrors the response to revenue growth. As we noted earlier, however, the *composition* does display significant hysteresis, in that increases in investment are reversed more swiftly than are increases in consumption. It is a different story in the post-boom era. Here expenditures declined more slowly and less completely than they increased. But it would be premature to conclude that adjustment was incomplete. Adjustments to falling revenue during this period were partly solved on the revenue side by the introduction of new forms of taxation. For example, income taxes were revamped and collection improved following an IMF agreement in 1989, the VAT was introduced in 1994, and taxes were indexed to inflation starting in 1994.[9]

The swiftest adjustment to an adverse shock to oil revenues comes via a reduction in expenditures: 75 percent of the total adjustment of expenditures takes place within the first two years. These results come from a three-variable VAR of oil revenues, non-oil revenues, and total expenditures (with that Cholesky ordering) estimated for the post-boom period. Adjustment by non-oil revenues takes more time: only 30 percent of the full adjustment takes place within the first two years, and the 75 percent mark is not surpassed until the twenty-second quarter. Increases in non-oil revenues and reduction in expenditures contribute almost identical amounts to the full adjustment over ten years, and the total adjustment is a respectable 0.85, statistically indistinguishable from 1.[10]

Nonetheless, while the adjustment is comprehensive and impressive, it is clear that nonzero delay results in transitory deficits, making the central dilemma more acute with each contraction in revenues. In essence, even these moderate delays lead to a narrowing of the strait, making successful adjustment less likely. Hence, we can see that the continued decline in per capita oil revenues greatly complicated the adjustment process. Every time revenues declined, painful political battles had to be fought over how to reduce spending. Even small delays in resolving these conflicts added to the debt burden.[11]

Conclusion

Our analysis suggests that government spending on public goods was effective fiscal stimulus in the post-boom era, but that the use of such stimulus was constrained by continued high levels of inflation and debt. The length of the post-boom fiscal crisis is due in large part to two proximate causes: the exceptionally poor state in which the economy exited the period of higher oil prices, and the continued decline of per capita oil revenues.

Taking as given the state of the economy in 1983 and the subsequent decline in oil revenues, Venezuelan fiscal policy coped reasonably well with the predicament. Expenditures were reined in and new sources of non-oil revenue were raised. When fiscal accounts could not adjust sufficiently swiftly, devaluation was used to buy time, albeit at the cost of increased inflation. The fault does not lie in the process of adjustment.

In 1978, on the eve of the second oil boom, per capita non-oil GDP grew at 1.1 percent and the year's inflation was 7.3 percent.[12] Comparing these figures to their pre-boom (1962–73) averages of 3.3 percent and 2.4 percent, respectively, makes it clear that at this point the economy was seriously overheated. Ball's (1994) estimate of sacrifice ratios suggests that among OECD countries, trimming each point of inflation requires the loss of between 1.8 and 3.3 percentage points of GDP. Studies using U.S. data, including Mankiw (1991) and Cecchetti and Rich (1999), find values in a similar range.[13] Applying these values to the

Venezuelan economy in 1978, a return to historical rates of inflation would have required a loss of nine to fifteen percentage points of GDP.[14] As the gush of oil money slowed, the economy seemed to have entered this period in 1977–78, as evidenced by the decline in non-oil output growth and inflation. Whether such loss would manifest as a protracted period of slower growth or a swift outright contraction would depend on the speed with which the growth of credit was reversed. Given that most of the excess credit sprung from the oil boom, and given the swift reversal of the hike in oil revenues, it seems likely that the lost output would have come as a rather sharp contraction. Indeed, the outright contraction of the economy between 1979 and 1980, despite renewed oil-driven spending, supports this hypothesis.

It was at this moment that the second oil shock brought a second enormous boost of oil revenues. Unfortunately, instead of accepting a growth slowdown as the price of cooling off the overheated economy, thereby enabling the oil revenues to be put to productive use later, the fiscal authority chose to once again dump the entire surplus into the economy as it was accrued.

A more detailed picture of how the first and second gluts of funds first damaged and then wrecked the economy at the sectoral level is a subject for another paper. One suspects that the story is familiar: the deluge of cheap credit frequently redirected labor and capital from truly productive endeavors to activity whose productivity was an illusion that held only so long as the spigot remained open.

While imprudent and optimistic, it is perhaps understandable that the initial boom was invested entirely concurrently. The political pressure to invest domestically must have been immense, and the possible drawbacks probably seemed distant and theoretical. How could such manna from heaven be bad? By 1978, however, the clear overheating of the economy should have provided stark evidence that productivity growth could not keep pace with the growth in demand and that a different, measured approach was required. Perhaps the second oil boom simply came a few years too early, when the negative side effects of keeping an open spigot where not yet fully evident. Alas, the warning was ignored and the second batch of manna from heaven was simply shoveled onto the flames lit by the first.

This misuse left the economy in a crippled condition, facing a difficult adjustment process. The continued decline in oil revenues below their pre-boom levels presented the fiscal authority with a serious and repeated short-run dilemma: a choice between the Scylla of inflation and the Charybdis of debt. Post-boom fiscal policy did not make it through these fiscal Strait of Messina unscathed. Further, fiscal accounts continued to adjust to the repeated decline in oil revenues by raising new revenues and reining in expenditures. As the saying goes, you sleep in the bed you make.

Fiscal policy has a mixed record during the period from 1962 to 1999. On the one hand, spending the entire amount of the boom concurrently was a clear mistake, given the size of the boom relative to the economy and thus the doubts about the ability of the economy to absorb the windfall so quickly. The failure to smooth these revenues doubtless contributed to the dire position of the economy in 1983, and thus the difficulty of the subsequent adjustments process.

It may be conceded that the problem was exacerbated by the failure of these investments to produce significant productivity gains, which meant that as oil revenues, and thus government spending, receded to historic levels, there was little to take its place. This is a failure distinct from the macroeconomic fiscal decisions considered in this chapter. Nonetheless, given the deliberate strategy of investing in projects with lengthy gestation periods, it should have been obvious that increases in productivity—and thus in aggregate supply and foreign exchange—would lag behind the massive influxes of capital. These were grave oversights: to expect that such a massive windfall could be absorbed without temporary divergence of aggregate supply and demand, and not to realize that, given the size of the windfall, these disparities could crash the economy. The failure to adopt an oil investment fund to smooth the absorption of the windfall is a serious policy mistake. Fiscal policy is responsible to a considerable degree for the dismal macroeconomic position of 1983.

From this point on, the fiscal authority seems to have responded reasonably to a string of exceptionally difficult challenges. As oil revenues continued to fall, new sources of revenue were raised, and expenditures were cut. Unfortunately, budget cuts are never instantaneous and the lag between revenue fall and the adjustment of expenditures contributed to a mounting debt.

The initial reversal of the steady six-decade growth path was due to the excessive haste with which the windfall was spent, exacerbated by the inefficiency of the resulting industrialization. The prolonged nature of the crisis is due partly to the poor position with which the economy exited the boom years—for which fiscal policy is partly to blame—and partly to the prolonged decline in oil fiscal revenues.

APPENDIX A

The Identification Strategy

The specification of the VAR is

$$X_t = A(L)X_{t-1} + B(L)O_t + u_t,$$

where $X_t = [T_t\ G_t\ Y_t]'$ is the vector of net transfers to the private goods sector, government expenditures on consumption and public investment, and output growth, O_t is the exogenous variable oil revenues, and u_t represents the VAR disturbances. The VAR is estimated with four lags of each endogenous variable, four lags of the exogenous variable, plus a constant term and quarterly dummies (not shown). The number of lags was chosen using Wald lag-exclusion statistics. The quarterly dummies are excluded from the calculation of impulse responses, so the impulse response functions correspond to a shock in quarter 1. In practice, the differences in responses by quarter are minuscule. Dickey-Fuller and Phillips-Perron tests strongly indicate that all variables are I(1), thus the VAR is estimated on first differences. The reported impulse responses are for the original un-differenced variables.

Identification is achieved via the strategy detailed in Blanchard and Perotti (2002) and Perotti (2004). Without loss of generality, the VAR innovations are written as functions of the structural shocks, e. For shocks e and u, the subscript refers to the quarter, the superscript to the endogenous variable:

$$u_t^t = \alpha_{ty}\, u_t^y + \beta_{tg}\, e_t^g + e_t^t$$
$$u_t^g = \alpha_{gy}\, u_t^y + \beta_{gt}\, e_t^t + e_t^g.$$

This identification strategy is based on the assumption that discretionary fiscal policy cannot respond to output within the same quarter, thus α_{TY} and α_{GY} consist only of the automatic policy responses of T and G to Y.[15] These can be calculated (with effort) prior to the VAR using information on the tax codes and spending rules (see appendix B). In general, they will be time-varying as tax codes and other fiscal rules change. Cyclically adjusted shocks can then be calculated using these estimates:

$$\pi_t^t = u_t^t - \hat{\alpha}_{ty}\, u_t^y = \beta_{tg}\, e_t^g + e_t^t$$
$$\pi_t^g = u_t^g - \hat{\alpha}_{gy}\, u_t^y = \beta_{gt}\, e_t^t + e_t^g.$$

Assuming a particular Cholesky ordering of T and G allows one to restrict either β_{tg} or $\beta_{gt} = 0$.[16] This system can then be solved for the structural shocks e^g and e^t. These can be used as instruments for the VAR innovations to estimate the structural parameters for output, α_{yt} and α_{yg}, as follows:

$$u_t^y = \hat{\alpha}_{yt}\, u_t^t + \hat{\alpha}_{yg}\, u_t^g + e_t^y.$$

Thus the structural parameters are identified.[17]

The Fiscal Variables

The coefficients α_{TY} and α_{GY} are weighted averages of the output elasticities of each of the components of net transfers (T) and government spending (G), respectively. Net transfers and government spending are each built from several components of the quarterly fiscal accounts data. Classification was made based on whether the expenditures were spent on the production of public or private goods. Data come from the Central Bank of Venezuela.

Net transfers (T) =
   Non-oil income taxes (NOIT) (includes both corporate and household)
   + Value-added tax (VAT)
   + Customs (CUST)
   + Central Bank profits (CBV)
   + Liquor, cigarette, and gasoline taxes (LIQ, CIG, GAS)
   − Transfers to private individuals (PRIV)
   − Transfers to state-owned enterprises (PE)

Government spending (G) =
   Wages and salaries (SAL)
   + Purchases of goods and services (GS)
   + Government investment (GI)
   + Transfers to state and municipal government (SM)
   + Transfers to administrative entities (AE)

APPENDIX B

Construction of the output elasticity for each component is as follows below.

Non-oil Income Taxes

Income tax withholding for a given year is based on an *ex-ante* estimate of annual income filed in December of the previous year. Revision based on shock occurs later, at least three months after the event. Hence, except for new hires, income tax payments do not vary within the same quarter when income has been hit by a shock. Hence, the output elasticity of income tax revenues is equal to the output elasticity of employment (see Perotti 2004). Following Perotti, we have taken our estimate of $\partial e_t / \partial y_t$ to be $\hat{\beta}_0$ from the following regression,

$$e_t = \sum_{j=-1}^{4} \beta_j y_{t-j},$$

where e and y are logged values of employment and real output. This is estimated via the regression and found to be 0.22.

Firms usually adjust their tax payments for windfalls but individuals do not. We have assumed 0.2 across the entire category.

Customs, Cigarettes, Liquor, VAT

Estimate the elasticity by again taking $\hat{\beta}_0$ from the following regression over the longest recent period during which tax rates are constant,

$$\tau_t = \sum_{j=-1}^{4} \beta_j y_{t-j},$$

where τ are logged tax revenues.

Not surprisingly, the results are mostly very close to 1. Gasoline is more complex because the economy is driven by oil prices.

Transfers to Administrative Entities and SOEs

These are completely discretionary, so elasticity is assumed to be equal to zero.

Transfers to State and Municipal Governments

Transfers to subnational governments are a mandated percentage of revenues, so the output elasticity of transfers is equal to the output elasticity of revenues. This elasticity is estimated using a regression of the same form as that used for excise taxes. The point estimate is 1.14.

Other Components of G

The rest of the components of G seem to be completely discretionary and therefore have an output elasticity of zero.

NOTES

1. The period since 2000 could be characterized as a fourth distinct time frame due to both rejuvenated oil prices and the adoption in December 1999 of a new and dramatically different constitution, replacing the previous one of 1961. This period will remain outside our analysis as largely irrelevant to the question of whether Venezuelan fiscal policy has contributed to the growth collapse of 1979–2003. It remains to be seen whether the Venezuelan economy will accrue more lasting benefits from the current boom in oil prices than it did from the first boom.

2. An oil stabilization fund was enacted in a reform to the Central Bank Law in 1960, but it was eliminated in 1974. More than two decades later, in 1998, an Investment Fund for Macroeconomic Stabilization (Spanish acronym FIEM) was created, but its law underwent several reforms (1999, 2001, 2002, and 2003). In 2003, a new law was approved (the Macroeconomic Stabilization Fund Law), but it had not become operative as of the writing of this chapter.

3. The first cycle is driven by the first oil price hikes in 1973–74. The second cycle is driven by the second oil price hikes in 1979–81. The fourth cycle is driven by the mild oil price spike accompanying the Persian Gulf War. Unlike the others, the third cycle is driven not by an increase in the international price of crude oil, but by a 25 percent devaluation of the Venezuelan nominal exchange rate in 1984. Because a large fraction of Venezuela's fiscal revenues come from the export of oil, devaluation adjusts the relative price of oil exports and public goods, balancing the fiscal accounts. This was a trick the Venezuelan government was to resort to again in 1986, when the price of oil finally collapsed from the abnormally high levels that prevailed from 1974 to 1985. In effect, one could actually split the third cycle into two sub-cycles: one from 1984 to 1986, driven by the first devaluation; and another from 1986 to 1989, driven by the second devaluation. Taken together, these sub-cycles were weaker than the others and resulted in a more dire final downturn, because they were the result not of an oil boom but rather of a devaluation in the face of a revenue decline.

4. Ascher (1999) describes an incident in 1982 when the minister of hydrocarbons and mines raised the price of Venezuelan heavy crude to offset the loss of revenues from OPEC's decision to reduce prices on light crude by stating, "It was clear to oil experts that the price increase would soon reduce demand for Venezuelan heavy crude." Though not a formal estimate of elasticity, this incident illustrates that Venezuela did retain control over some prices under OPEC, but that demand exhibited significant elasticity on a timescale of a few quarters.

5. Government consumption is taken to be the sum of wages and salaries, purchases of goods and services, and transfers, both current and capital, to administrative entities. Administrative entities are the central government's autonomous agencies that provide public services in a variety of areas, including education, health care, utilities, transportation and communication, justice, housing, and environmental protection. In fact, the first big increase in government consumption comes between 1969 and 1971, *before* the oil boom. This pre-boom increase is spent mainly on an expansion of public sector programs on education and health care (goods and services +105%) and the additional salaries to government workers (+33%) to administer these programs.

6. This more limited role for government accounts for the majority of the difference in government size between Latin American governments and European governments. The fraction devoted to provision of public goods is roughly the same in both sets of countries.

7. We have tried other two-variable decompositions of fiscal accounts, which more closely match the spirit of the discussion in the above section. However, these decompositions fail to give consistently coherent results. Perhaps this indicates that such groupings are less useful than this more traditional grouping.

8. Because quarterly GDP data begins only in 1976, we cannot conduct the exercise for the pre-boom era.

9. The administration of Jaime Lusinchi (1983–88) implemented a heterodox stabilization program that included strong cuts in government spending between 1984 and 1985, a multi-tier exchange-rate system, import protection, stimulus to agriculture, extended producer and consumer subsidies, and the external debt renegotiation. Although these measures stimulated growth from 1985 to 1988, the government could no longer support the subsidies and the high debt burden, particularly after the 1986 fall in oil prices. Carlos Andres Perez (1988–93) launched a neoliberal shock therapy program (known as the Great Turn, or El Gran Viraje) with the support of the International Monetary Fund and the World Bank, which pursued the reduction of the government's role in the economy through a large-scale privatization, a tax reform, a free-market orientation in economic activities, the correction of macroeconomic imbalances and fiscal deficits, the reform of the financial sector, the liberalization of prices, exchange rates, and trade, the renegotiation of the external debt payments, and subsidies for the poor. Its implementation, which faced strong political opposition and popular rejection, was incomplete, distorted, and even interrupted during periods of unexpected oil price increases. A decentralization process that had been proposed years back and delayed by the traditional political parties (AD and COPEI) was legally approved in 1989, just after a big riot (El Caracazo) exploded as a reaction against those measures; from a fiscal point of view, however, its impact would start to be felt in 1996. Rafael Caldera (1993–98) condemned the neoliberal program of the preceding administration and started by reversing some of the previous measures, but a huge financial crisis (1994–95) and the failures of implemented heterodox measures led to a new IMF agreement in 1996 (Agenda Venezuela). Under this program, social initiatives were given big publicity, but in practice they were very similar to the neoliberal projects of Carlos Andres Perez.

10. Oil revenues here are measured in constant bolivars, so we have not separated out the effects of devaluation.

11. Manzano in this volume suggests that the decline in Venezuelan per capita oil production is not entirely due to the external factors contributing to the oil price boom of the 1970s, but may also be fueled by Venezuela's pre-boom oil development and extraction strategy. Thus it is not clear that Venezuela could have escaped adjustment even had oil prices continued to evolve smoothly. How pronounced and difficult the adjustment process would have been without the initial volatility is an open question.

12. Inflation figures throughout this chapter are punctual inflation—that is, the change in price measured from year beginning to year end—rather than average annualized rate of inflation.

13. Cecchetti and Rich do caution that their point estimates come with rather large standard errors, and further caution that one model they estimated gave much larger estimates of the sacrifice ratio.

14. It may be a stretch to apply these values to a developing economy, but recall that before the boom, the Venezuelan economy was extremely high performing, with consistently low inflation and stable growth.

15. We include contemporaneous oil revenues on the right-hand side to allow for an intra-quarter response of fiscal accounts to oil revenues.

16. In their studies of the United States and other OECD countries, Blanchard and Perotti suggest there is little theoretical or empirical guidance for the choice of ordering between G and T, and note that it makes little difference due to the low correlation between the cyclically adjusted residuals for G and T. In our case, however, there is clear anecdotal and empirical evidence that spending decisions respond to revenues rather than the other way around. Hence, we choose to order net transfers before spending.

17. For a careful response to several of the major criticisms of this method, including the timing of fiscal shocks, whether VAR innovations simply reflect the delivery schedule of fiscal programs, whether VAR innovations simply reflect accounting principles, and whether fiscal shocks are anticipated and therefore misidentified by the structural VAR, we refer you to Perotti 2004.

REFERENCES

Alesina, Alberto, and Allan Drazen. 1991. "Why Are Stabilizations Delayed?" *American Economic Review* 81:1170–88.

Ascher, William. 1999. *Why Governments Waste Natural Resources.* Baltimore: Johns Hopkins University Press.

Ball, Laurence. 1994. "What Determines the Sacrifice Ratio?" In *Monetary Policy*, edited by N. G. Mankiw. Chicago: University of Chicago Press.

Blanchard, Olivier. 2006. "Comments on Blinder's 'The Case against the Case against Discretionary Fiscal Policy.'" In *The Macroeconomics of Fiscal Policy*, edited Richard Kopcke, Geoffrey Tootell, and Robert Triest. Cambridge: MIT Press.

Blanchard, Olivier, and Roberto Perotti. 2002. "An Empirical Characterization of the Dynamic Effects of Changes in Government Spending and Taxes on Output." *Quarterly Journal of Economics* 117:1329–68.

Cecchetti, Stephen G., and Robert W. Rich. 1999. *Structural Estimates of the U.S. Sacrifice Ratio.* Staff Reports 71, Federal Reserve Bank of New York.

Gavin, Michael, and Roberto Perotti. 1997. "Fiscal Policy in Latin America." *NBER Macroeconomics Annual:* 11–61.

Hausmann, Ricardo. 1997. "Adoption, Management, and Abandonment of Multiple Exchange Rate Regimes in Countries with Import Controls: The Case of Venezuela." In *Parallel Exchange Rates in Developing Countries*, edited by Miguel Kiguel, J. Saul Lizondo, and Stephen A. O'Connell. Basingstroke, U.K.: Palgrave Macmillan.

———. 2003. "Venezuela's Growth Implosion: A Neoclassical Story?" In *In Search of Prosperity: Analytic Narratives on Economic Growth*, edited by Dani Rodrik. Princeton: Princeton University Press.

López-Obregon, Clara, and Francisco Rodríguez. 2001. "La política fiscal venezolana 1943–2001." *Reporte de Coyuntura Annual, 2001.* Caracas: Oficina de Asesoría Económica y Financiera de la Asamblea Nacional.

Mankiw, N. Gregory. 1991. *Macroeconomics.* New York: Worth.

Perotti, Roberto. 2004. "Estimating the Effects of Fiscal Policy in OECD Countries." Working Paper 276, Innocenzo Gasparini Institute for Economic Research, Milan.

Rodríguez, Francisco. 2004. "Un nuevo índice encadenado del Producto Interno Bruto de Venezuela, 1957–2001." *Revista BCV* 18 (2): 99–118.

Talvi, Ernesto, and Carlos Vègh. 2005. "Tax Base Variability and Pro-cyclical Fiscal Policy." *Journal of Development Economics* 78 (1): 156–90.

Tornell, Aaron, and Phillip Lane. 1999a. "Are Windfalls a Curse?" *Journal of International Economics* 44:88–112.

———. 1999b. "The Voracity Effect." *American Economic Review* 89 (1): 22–46.

10 INSTITUTIONAL COLLAPSE: THE RISE AND DECLINE OF DEMOCRATIC GOVERNANCE IN VENEZUELA

Francisco Monaldi and Michael Penfold

In the quarter century from 1978 to 2003, Venezuela had the worst economic performance in Latin America (with the exception of Nicaragua). Starting in 2004, the growth spike, fueled by the oil price boom, barely served to catch up to the average regional growth during the current decade. In contrast, during the previous thirty years, the country had a remarkable economic and social performance, and was considered a model democracy in the region (starting in 1958). This chapter argues that *political economy* variables—the weakening of democratic governance, the poor and declining institutional quality, and the increase in political instability—are key determinants in explaining the poor economic performance in the period under study, particularly since 1989. Even though the initial fall in growth in the ten years after per capita GDP peaked in 1978 can primarily be attributed to the dramatic reduction in per capita oil income, the debt acquired during the oil boom, and the increasing volatility of oil prices (Hausmann and Rigobón 2002; Manzano and Rigobón 2001; Rodríguez and Sachs 1999), institutional and political variables are crucial to explain why Venezuela has not been able to return to a sustainable growth trajectory in the last two decades.

We claim that the decline in institutions and democratic governance in the last two decades can be largely attributed to four factors: (1) *oil dependence and oil income volatility*, which has induced poor institutional quality and created significant challenges for governance and economic management;[1] (2) the dramatic

The authors wish to acknowledge useful comments from Ricardo Hausmann, Francisco Rodriguez, Mariano Tommasi, Jim Robinson, Javier Corrales, and seminar participants at the Harvard Kennedy School, IESA, and CAF. Stefania Vitale provided effective research assistance.

fall in per capita oil fiscal revenues in the late eighties and nineties, which contributed to the decline in the cooperative political equilibrium that prevailed in the 1958–88 period and fueled social polarization; (3) the *political reforms* introduced in the late eighties and early nineties, which weakened and fragmented the party system, further undermining political cooperation; and (4) the *institutional changes* implemented by President Chávez, which dramatically increased the stakes of power and radicalized the political system, producing a complete breakdown in political cooperation.

This chapter mainly analyzes the evolution of institutions and their effect on democratic governance, but it also highlights the role of oil dependence and oil income decline, without which it is difficult to understand the extent of the decay in democratic governance and institutional quality. In turn, it argues that the decline in governance and the low quality of institutions in Venezuela has translated into low-quality policymaking: that is, high policy volatility, incapacity to sustain inter-temporal commitments, difficulty in implementing sustainable policy reforms, and early reversal of economic reforms.

For example, Venezuela has been incapable of effectively implementing macroeconomic stabilization mechanisms, while fiscal policies have been highly procyclical and deficit-prone. Similarly, a volatile and often overvalued real exchange rate made economic diversification highly unlikely. To compound the perverse effect of these problems, trade policy was also unpredictable and inconsistent. These policy features are particularly problematic in an oil-dependent country, which requires strong institutions to manage the challenges arising from the *resource curse*. The lack of credibility of the economic and public policies, rather than the content of the policies, has been one of the key sources of the country's underperformance. Purely economic explanations for Venezuela's economic decline become puzzled by the lack of a coherent economic policy response to the decline in oil income; this chapter suggests an institutional origin to explain this conundrum.

The fall in oil income in the eighties and nineties contributed to eroding democratic governance by increasing redistributive conflicts, political polarization, and the decline in support for political parties. The interaction between oil and institutions hampered the ability of politicians to change and sustain policies conducive to economic growth. The structural limitations of institutions (partly the result of oil dependence) and the implementation of institutional reforms weakened the quality of democratic governance, making it difficult to reestablish economic growth in the period 1989–2003. The deconsolidation of the political system produced political instability, reflected in three military coups, massive riots and protests, a significant change of constitutional rules, and the collapse of traditional political parties.

The governance story of Venezuela is analyzed in three differentiated periods: (1) an initial period (1958–88), which began with a power-sharing pact, creating an institutional framework with low stakes of power, characterized by a relatively high degree of political cooperation; (2) a second period, after the fall in oil revenues, in which significant political reforms (decentralization and electoral reform) were implemented, characterized by a decline in political cooperation and party-system deconsolidation (1989–98); and (3) a third period, the Chávez revolution (1999–present), in which institutional rules were completely reshaped, producing a complete breakdown in cooperation.

The chapter structure is as follows: the next section discusses the literature on oil, institutions, governance, and growth, and presents some comparative measures of institutional quality; the following section analyzes the period of democratic consolidation under the Punto Fijo Pact; after that, we analyze the effects of oil decline and political reforms in inducing democratic deconsolidation in the nineties; the following section analyzes the recent institutional reforms of the Chávez administration and their effects on democratic governance; and in the final section we offer some concluding comments.

Institutions and Governance

There is an extensive theoretical and empirical literature arguing that institutions and governance constitute key determinants of long-run economic growth (Kauffman, Kray, and Mastruzzi 2003).[2] Following the Inter-American Development Bank (2005), this chapter focuses on the role that political institutions play in delivering policies that have positive generic attributes, such as stability, adaptability, coherence, and sustainability, which are necessary conditions for long-run economic growth. Having what might be considered the normatively "right" policies, without these generic attributes, is unlikely to yield good economic performance. The chapter takes advantage of the analytical framework developed by Spiller and Tommasi (2003) to explore the conditions in which democratic governance generates long-term cooperation between political actors capable of sustaining inter-temporal commitments. Institutional environments in which there are few key players, repeated interaction among them, and small discount rates would tend to produce long-term political cooperation among the key players. First-best policies would tend to be stable across administrations and only change significantly in response to economic shocks. According to such a framework, cooperative policymaking processes would tend to produce policies with good features such as stability, coherence, and adaptability. By contrast, institutional settings that induce a larger number of players, few repeated interactions, and high discount rates promote a policymaking environment that is less conducive to stable, adaptable, and coherent policies.

In addition, following Przeworski (1991), the chapter discusses how political institutions determine the "stakes of power"—that is, the value that key political actors place on being in power as opposed to being in the opposition. Limited stakes of power are necessary for democratic governance and inter-temporal policy cooperation. If the stakes are too high, those in power would do whatever they can to remain in power, because losing it would be too costly. Similarly, those out of power would have no incentives to respect democratic rules; they face the possibility of annihilation. This point is particularly relevant in the case of oil-dependent economies, especially during boom periods, in which the state receives a significant share of its fiscal revenues directly from the oil rents it controls, thereby increasing the stakes of power (Monaldi et al. 2005; Dunning 2008). Thus democratic governance, especially in an oil-dependent polity, requires a limitation of the stakes of holding power; otherwise, political instability, polarization, or authoritarianism can arise.

Oil and Governance

There exists also a significant empirical literature showing that oil (and mineral) dependence, as well as the external volatility that comes with it, may have a negative impact on institutional quality and on democratic governance (Subramanian and Sala-i-Martin 2003; Isham et al. 2003).[3] The proposed channels by which mineral dependence affects institutional quality are not well established, but some of the hypotheses include fiscal voracity (incentives to increase expenditures and patronage during the boom that are difficult to reverse during the bust), rent-seeking (producing misallocation of resources), corruption, and inequality.

The causal mechanisms that produce the proposed negative effect of resource dependence on democratic governance are also still highly debated. Some hypotheses are that (1) the stakes of power are very high in oil-dependent societies, and control of the oil revenue generates a high value of holding onto power, increasing the likelihood of incumbent abuse of power and democratic breakdown; (2) oil dependence allows for low levels of non-oil taxation, which leads to a lack of accountability in the use of fiscal revenue and weakens the state's administrative capacity; (3) oil rents can be spent on patronage, weakening the opposition and the rise of democratic pressures, (4) oil rents can be used for repression; (5) since the state controls most resources, civil society and private entrepreneurs are less autonomous from the government; and (6) oil rents generate a tendency toward high levels of corruption, which undermines democratic institutions (Karl 1997; Ross 2001; Dunning 2008; Haber and Menaldo 2009).

In contrast, Dunning (2008) presents a theoretical model and empirical cross-sectional results showing that, even though mineral revenues generally have an authoritarian effect, in highly unequal societies mineral revenues may contribute to democratic governance by reducing the pressures for non-oil income redistribution and therefore the potential for social conflict or elite obstruction/subversion of democracy. His model fits well with the literature on Venezuela's democracy, which has generally argued that oil revenues helped to establish democratic governance by easing political conflict while the region was generally authoritarian (Rey 1989; Karl 1997). We concur with Dunning in arguing that the dramatic decline in oil revenues has been a key determinant in the deconsolidation of the Venezuelan party system and the weakening of democratic governance; however, we propose that political institutions have a crucial role in lowering or increasing the negative effects of oil dependence over democratic governance. More recently, Haber and Mernaldo (2009), in the most sophisticated econometric analysis of this issue to date, questioned the empirical validity of the authoritarian effect of oil revenues, showing that the effect disappears once fixed effects are included in the panel regression. Such a result implies that there is no significant effect in countries across time. In other words, increasing the amount of oil revenues does not make a particular country more authoritarian. One possibility is that the negative and positive effects of oil revenues on democracy cancel each other out. Another possibility is that the cross-sectional effect in other econometric studies is caused by omitted variables and that oil revenues have no effect.

Measuring Institutions and Governance

Put simply, "good" governance involves the capacity to design and implement effective public policies, which are socially and institutionally legitimate, in a stable political environment. The institutional framework in place, in turn, significantly influences the quality of governance. The institutional framework encompasses the formal and informal rules that govern economic, political, and social behavior—for example, the constitution, the laws, the property rights, as well as informal cultural practices.[4]

The incentives generated by political institutions have a significant impact on the stability, legitimacy, and efficiency of democracy. Political institutions such as regime type, electoral system, party structure, budget procedures, and federal structures are critical determinants of the degree of political cooperation, government commitment, policy stability, and effectiveness—in other words, the key features of good governance (Haggard and McCubbins 2001; Spiller and Tommasi 2003).

There are significant difficulties in measuring institutions. In particular, most of the recently developed measures of institutional quality are more precisely measures of the outcomes of institutions, including the quality of governance, rather than the root permanent features or constraints of the institutional framework. In addition, most measures are based on perceptions rather than objective variables. Given the lack of a better alternative, the subjective measures of institutional quality developed by multilateral agencies such as the World Bank are shown as evidence that the political framework of Venezuela has been generating low-quality governance and poor public policies, at least during the last fifteen years.

The World Bank Institute (WBI) defines *governance* as "the exercise of authority through formal and informal traditions and institutions for the common good, thus encompassing: (1) the process of selecting, monitoring, and replacing governments; (2) the capacity to formulate and implement sound policies and deliver public services; and (3) the respect of citizens and the state for the institutions that govern economic and social interactions among them" (Kaufman, Kraay, and Mastruzzi 2003, 5). For measurement and analysis the WBI has translated these three dimensions into six concepts with their corresponding measure.[5]

As can be seen in figure 10.1, Venezuela fared extremely poorly in all the WBI indexes.[6] In 2004, the country was well below the Latin American average in all six indicators, and except for voice and accountability, it was ranked between the lowest 10th and the 16th percentile among all the countries in the world. In contrast, the Latin American average for the six indicators is generally between the 40th percentile and the world's median. Venezuela is among the last two countries in five indicators, and among the last three in the other indicator. Using the average of the six indicators, Venezuela is also the last in the region. Moreover, Venezuela fares even worse if compared with the average of countries in the same

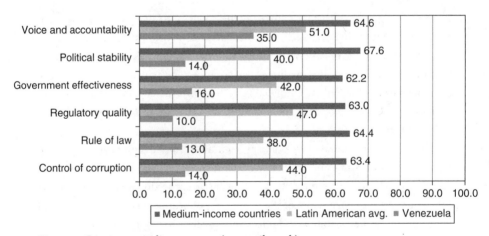

Fig. 10.1   Governance indicators, 2004 (percentile rank)

Source: Based on World Bank Institute 2005.

level of income per capita, which have ranks around the 65th percentile. This fact is particularly significant given that there is a very high correlation between income per capita and governance indicators. In the last data available (from 2008), Venezuela declined in all governance variables.[7]

In 2004, Venezuela was in the 14th percentile in terms of political stability and second to last in Latin America. This represents a dramatic contrast with the 1958–88 period, when Venezuela was considered among the most stable democracies in the region. Venezuela's index has declined in the last ten years (these indexes were first calculated in 1996). Compare the Venezuelan ratings (1996–2003) with the ones for countries such as Costa Rica (84 percent) or Uruguay (79.1 percent), and the new reality of Venezuela looks even more dramatic. Three military coups (two in 1992 and one in 2002), a major nationwide riot in 1989, and a dramatic increase in the number and size of political protests attest to the objective decline in political stability (Monaldi 2003).

Other variables that have been shown to be good predictors of economic growth are rule of law and control of corruption. Venezuela fared very poorly in both, being second to last in the region with ranks of 12.6 percent and 14.3 percent, respectively. Similarly, in the perception of corruption index of Transparency International (2005), Venezuela was second to last in the region, only above Paraguay.[8] If one accepts these indicators as valid, the differences in institutional quality between Venezuela and the median in Latin America would explain a large portion of the economic underperformance of Venezuela with respect to the regional median in the last two decades.

It is important to notice that, although Venezuela's indicators have significantly declined since the beginning of the Chávez administration in 1999, the levels of most indicators before Chávez (with the exception of voice and accountability) were also well below the regional average and even lower than the average of countries with similar income per capita. This means that the low levels of democratic governance and institutional quality can only be partially attributed to Chávez. This is consistent with our argument that governance started to decline in the late eighties, after the dramatic rise and decline in oil revenues.[9]

The Inter-American Development Bank (2005) developed a set of indexes to measure the generic qualities (features) of public policies in the region.[10] As can be seen in figure 10.2, Venezuela fares very poorly in these indexes as well. In the index of policy stability, Venezuela is last in the region.[11] As additional evidence of lack of stability, Venezuela has also one of the most volatile values for Lora's index of structural reform. Venezuela has also had one the poorest performances in the region in terms of the advancement of market reforms, being below the Latin American average during the period 1985–2002 (Villasmil et al. 2007).

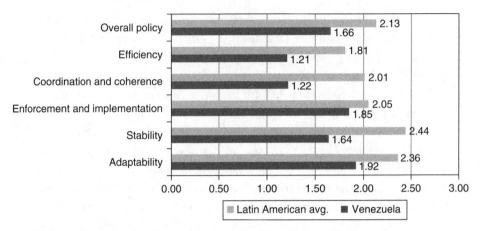

Fig. 10.2   Inter-American Development Bank public policies indicators, 2005

Source: Inter-American Development Bank 2005.

There has been also a significant decline in cabinet stability in the last two decades. In the 1958–88 period, cabinet members lasted an average of 2.13 years in their positions (in a five-year term). Equivalently, there were 2.3 ministers per cabinet position per term. In contrast, from 1989 to 1993, ministers lasted only 1.4 years, increasing to 1.8 years from 1994 to 1999, and declining again to 1.3 years in the 1999–2004 period. That dramatic change in cabinet stability correlates with political instability and induces volatile policies (Monaldi et al. 2005).

In the index of adaptability, Venezuela is among the last three countries, reflecting the perception among policy experts that the nation does not adapt quickly to significant changes in economic conditions. In the case of the index of policy coordination and coherence, Venezuela is again last in the region. Lack of coordination and coherence often also reflects lack of cooperation. In the index of enforcement and implementation based on GCR and SCS questions, Venezuela is also below the regional average.[12] Finally, in the efficiency index, Venezuela is again last in the region, which is also the case for the overall policy index. These low indicators for policy quality are consistent, under the Spiller and Tommasi (2003) and Inter-American Development Bank (2005) frameworks, with low levels of political cooperation in Venezuela.

The Consolidation of Democratic Governance in Venezuela, 1958–1988

This section analyzes the institutional foundations of governance and the key characteristics of the policymaking process during the period of democratic consolidation between 1958 and 1988. The transition to democracy in 1958–61 was consolidated under a set of institutional arrangements based on a multiparty elite agreement called the Punto Fijo Pact.[13] The pact had an enduring impact on the type of presidential system adopted by the 1961 constitution, which was aimed at limiting presidential powers, diminishing political polarization, restricting electoral competition, and creating political institutions that would foster consensus for conflict resolution (Rey 1972; Karl 1986). The learning experience from the breakdown of Venezuela's democracy in 1948 allowed the political parties to understand the importance of designing institutions to limit the stakes of power (Rey 1989). The rules, reflected formally in the 1961 constitution, were aimed at creating trust among the different political actors so that even in the case of a unified government in which a political party had control of both the presidency and Congress, formal political institutions would not allow governments to pursue one-sided policies based on this dominant position (Corrales 2003).[14]

Several specific features of Venezuela's presidential system helped to lower the stakes of power and to induce cooperative behavior among competing politicians. Some key institutional features strengthened parties over presidents: (1) a constitutionally weak presidency, with limited legislative prerogatives;[15] (2) the ban on immediate presidential re-election, forcing incumbents to wait ten years before being able to run again;[16] (3) the absence of term limits for legislators, allowing long-term careers for party leaders in Congress; (4) the setting of fully concurrent elections between presidents and the legislature, inducing cooperation between presidents and their partisan ranks and reducing party fragmentation;[17] (5) and the establishing of a proportional representation system to elect the legislature.[18] All these rules, along with the existence of centralized and disciplined political parties, such as AD and COPEI, helped consolidate Venezuela's party system throughout the 1960s and 1970s. Presidents enjoyed parliamentary majorities during most of this period, more than the average government in the region.[19]

The existence of centralized and disciplined political parties was the direct result of a proportional electoral system with closed lists.[20] This system granted party leaders extreme powers to control and discipline their party ranks. The features of Venezuela's political system in this period led some authors to typify it as a "partyarchy," given that party leaders had supreme command over all party and public affairs (Coppedge 1994).

Finally, the constitution limited electoral competition by temporarily restricting the direct election of governors and mayors. The objective of limiting Venezuela's federalism—provisionally, since the 1961 constitution established that a law (enacted by two-thirds of Congress) could activate Venezuela's federalism, as later occurred in 1989—was to reduce electoral competition by restricting the number of arenas open to contestation. The dominant political parties believed that increasing electoral competition at a moment of democratic transition would intensify political polarization and fragmentation, and reduce cooperation among political actors. By limiting political competition, the Punto Fijo Pact and the constitution planted the roots of a democracy characterized by its centralization and exclusion. In fact, as will be shown, when Venezuela's federalism was activated, it contributed to the decline of the traditional party structure (Penfold 2001).

In addition to institutional design, party leaders used the distribution of oil fiscal resources as a key element for inducing political cooperation. Various authors have discussed the relationship between oil revenue and its effect on the party system (Rey 1989; Penfold 2001; Monaldi 2003; Dunning 2008). For example, Karl (1986) argued that oil was the key economic factor creating the modern social conditions for the formation of a cohesive party system and explaining the continued support for the pact that solidified the democratic transition. According to this argument, without oil there would have been little chance for democracy in Venezuela at the time. Other works have given relatively less importance to oil revenue, emphasizing the institutional aspects of Venezuela's democratic process (Rey 1989). Oil revenue alone cannot explain the origin of institutional arrangements such as the Punto Fijo Pact. Instead, political leaders strategically used oil income distribution as a utilitarian mechanism to obtain support for the democratic system. According to both viewpoints, it should not be a surprise that the decline of the Punto Fijo party system coincided with a general decline in oil fiscal income during the 1980s and 1990s.

Policymaking Process in the Punto Fijo Democracy

The first period can be generally characterized as having conditions highly conducive to political cooperation: a small number of key political actors, repeated play, and low stakes of power (Spiller and Tommasi 2003). These characteristics were largely the direct result of the institutional framework.

The policymaking process included relatively few key players, primarily the president, the national leaders of the two major parties (AD and COPEI), and the leaders of the two peak corporatist interest groups (CTV and Fedecamaras). The existence of a highly centralized, disciplined, and non-fragmented party system, and the fact that the concerns of interest groups were channeled through corporatist arrangements with the peak labor and business associations, allowed the president to conduct policy consultation with a very limited number of actors.[21] Policy agreements were usually negotiated between the presidents, the national party leaders, and the peak corporatist groups, and then, if required, they were *rubber-stamped* into law by the disciplined party delegations in the legislature.[22]

The six presidential administrations in this thirty-year period were represented by only two parties: AD (four times) and COPEI (two times). The same parties generally controlled the leadership of Congress. With a few exceptions, the two parties controlled or heavily influenced the leading corporatist groups. Parties were typically governed by a president, a secretary general, and a national committee. Party leaders were very stable. In AD, six fundamental leaders, four of whom became presidents, led the party from 1958 to 1988. In COPEI, three fundamental leaders, two of whom became presidents, led the party. National party leaders had relatively long tenures and almost all were members of Congress with long legislative careers. National party leaders decided how the party voted in Congress, and the congressional delegation dutifully voted according to the party line. Similarly, national party leaders had significant control over congressional nominations.

Inter-temporal linkages among key political actors were strong. It was very costly for an individual politician to deviate from the cooperative equilibrium of the two-party rule.[23] As can be seen in figure 10.3, the party system had relatively low fragmentation compared to the deconsolidation period of the nineties. Fragmentation was also low by regional standards.[24] In addition, in this period, as can be seen in figure 10.4, the volatility of the party share of seats (and votes) was also relatively low and declining, particularly if compared the period of deconsolidation. Similarly, volatility was below the regional average.[25] The rate of turnover of legislators also tended to decline over this period, and was on average below the regional mean (Monaldi et al. 2005).[26]

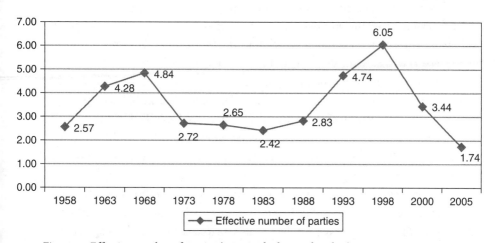

Fig. 10.3   Effective number of parties (seats in the lower chamber)

Sources: Based on data from Consejo Nacional Electoral and authors' own calculations.

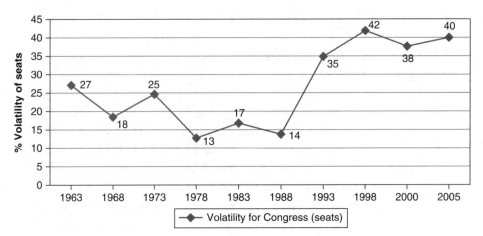

Fig. 10.4   Volatility in the number of seats in the lower chamber (percentage)

Sources: Based on data from Consejo Nacional Electoral and authors' own calculations.

While in equilibrium the Venezuelan president seemed powerful, having the leading policy role, his powers were in fact significantly restricted by the 1961 constitution. The framers, who were the leaders of the parties, set those restrictions deliberately to limit potential deviations. Largely the behavioral appearance of power was the result of the partial delegation by the national party leaders of strong and disciplined parties in a cooperative environment. As will be explained below, in the 1990s, once the president's partisan powers (strong party backing) and other formal (appointment of governors) and informal powers (discretionary use of large oil rents) declined, the president began to look relatively weak. Eventually, the 1999 constitution and further institutional reforms made by President Chávez increased the presidential powers dramatically, changing the policymaking process and increasing the stakes of power (Monaldi et al. 2005).

The low-stakes institutional framework developed by the Punto Fijo Pact allowed the country to avoid the authoritarian fate of most other oil exporters by inducing cooperation among politicians. Oil income was distributed to key political actors regardless of who was in control of the presidency. In addition, rising oil income allowed for increasing spending on public goods that promoted growth and reduced the redistributive pressures that generated the breakdown of other democracies in the region.

Before the oil boom of the 1970s, the high levels of both democratic governance and cooperation resulted in effective, stable, adaptable, and coherent public policies. Fiscal policy in 1958–73 had some remarkable features that suggest intertemporal cooperation among political actors. There were no episodes of significant fiscal deficit, and public debt remained at very low levels. Macroeconomic policy was quite effective, and public expenditure was geared toward infrastructure, health, and education (Hausmann 1992).

The oil boom and bust of the seventies and eighties marked the beginning of macroeconomic instability. Expenditures grew uncontrollably, the government nationalized key sectors of the economy, and indirect subsidies proliferated. Still, some policies remained quite cooperative and oriented toward the long term. For example, the nationalized oil industry and the Central Bank were left highly autonomous and efficient. By the end of 1988, however, ten years of economic decline presaged difficulties for the thirty-year-old democracy, which appeared highly consolidated.

The Deconsolidation of the Venezuelan Political System, 1989–1998

This section analyzes the political reforms implemented in the late eighties and early nineties and their impact on policymaking. In contrast to the previous period, this one was characterized by multiple actors, high electoral volatility, and institutional instability.

The dramatic economic decline suffered by the country during the previous decade (1978–88), largely attributable to oil income decline, set the stage for an increase in redistributive conflicts and a realignment of electoral preferences away from traditional parties. The collapse of the party system cannot be understood without realizing that a country that for decades had the best economic performance in the region suddenly became the one with the worst record. The riots of 1989, the two military coups of 1992, and the dramatic rise in social and political protests are symptomatic of the context in which political reforms were implemented. But the decline in democratic governance in the last two decades has significant roots in the institutional reforms, which contributed to the collapse of the cooperative framework that had consolidated Venezuela's democracy.

The most significant institutional changes that occurred at the beginning of this period were (1) the activation of federalism (i.e., the introduction of direct elections for governors and mayors in 1989) and (2) the modification of the legislature's electoral system from pure proportional representation to a mixed-member system with personalized proportional representation.[27] As will be argued, these changes helped to significantly weaken the power of traditional parties and national party leaders. Also, in the context of a change in electoral preferences away from traditional parties, these institutional transformations contributed to increased party fragmentation, volatility, and legislator turnover, thereby reducing the cooperative nature of the policymaking process.

On the Origins of the Political Reforms

The continued economic decay generated significant political disenchantment and a decline in the satisfaction with democracy. In the eighties, several social actors, minority parties, intellectuals, business groups, and NGOs demanded deeper democratization as a means of increasing accountability and improving government performance. These demands were a natural reaction to a regime in which political parties had pervasively controlled most spheres of social life.[28]

To address these demands, President Lusinchi (1984–89) created a Presidential Commission for the Reform of the State (COPRE) consisting of professionals linked to the political parties as well as a group of nonpartisan academics. This panel was enlisted to study the introduction a series of institutional reforms to help solve Venezuela's political accountability problems. The COPRE proposed a significant set of political reforms, including the direct election of governors and mayors, electoral reform to elect a portion of the legislators by plurality, and the democratization of party structures. These propositions met with immediate resistance from AD (the president's party), which had an absolute majority in the legislature; the leaders of the party thought that the COPRE recommendations were too radical.[29] AD was not willing to withdraw its control over the patronage network that regional and local bureaucracies offered the party. AD's national party leaders perceived the COPRE propositions to be directly aimed at undermining their political power. As a result, the reforms were not even discussed in Congress (Penfold 2004a–b).

It was only during the 1988 presidential campaign that AD's national party leaders were forced to pass some of these reforms due to the attention the presidential candidates Eduardo Fernández of COPEI and Carlos Andrés Pérez of AD paid to these issues. Pérez had won the party nomination against the fierce opposition of AD's national party leaders, and he wanted to weaken their centralized control of the party. Fernández used the reforms as a campaign tool against AD, which had been publicly opposed to any opening of the political process, possibly expecting that AD would continue blocking the reforms. Pérez's campaign in favor of the reforms forced AD to approve some of them in Congress: the election of mayors and the electoral reform to be implemented in 1993. But the election of governors, which AD feared the most, did not pass (Penfold 2004a).

Eventually, AD was prompted to support the election of governors as a consequence of massive riots that occurred one month after Perez's inauguration. The outburst took place in eight major cities and began as spontaneous protests against an increase in public transportation fares, which were brought about by a hike in the price of gasoline (Rodríguez 1996). The country was left in absolute despair after this social commotion. Although most of the blame was placed on

Pérez's adjustment program, public opinion surveys also suggested that citizens had increasingly become alienated from the democratic regime, and this was violently expressed in the streets (Penfold 2001, 2004a).

The Activation of Federalism

Although Venezuela was formally federal for more than a century, it was only in 1989, after the initiation of the direct elections of governors and mayors, that the dormant federal system was activated. There are two key institutional elements of Venezuela's federalism that transformed its party politics: the increasing competition and higher number of electoral arenas at the subnational level, and the possibility of re-election for governors and mayors, combined with the nonconcurrency between regional and presidential elections. These institutional features provided the new regional political actors with an opportunity to gain independence vis-à-vis the national authorities (Penfold 2004a–b).

During the 1958–88 period, entry barriers were relatively high, since presidential and congressional elections were held concurrently, maximizing presidential coattails. Moreover, entry into Congress was decided by national party leaders, who had control over the nominations. Instead, with the introduction of the direct election of governors and mayors, traditional political parties—characterized by hierarchical and inflexible organizations—had to present individual candidates in more than twenty states and more than three hundred municipalities. This meant that party leaders had to loosen centralized control over the nomination of candidates in order to compete effectively in these contests. Increasing the number of electoral arenas also implied reducing the entry barriers to competition. Minority parties attempting to win elections at the national level could now compete more effectively at the regional and local levels. These parties could build their organization at the national level based on their success at the regional level.

Several new political parties, such as La Causa R, Proyecto Venezuela, Convergencia-LAPI, Patria para Todos, Un Nuevo Tiempo, and Primero Justicia, used federalism as a springboard to enter the political system and attempt to build a national party organization. However, some survived just as regional parties with some representation in the national legislature. In the first election for governors in 1989, AD and COPEI largely dominated the electoral market (90 percent of the governorships). During the following elections, however, their dominance waned as new political organizations emerged and decentralized parties such as MAS obtained significant power for the first time. By 1998, AD controlled only 35 percent of the governorships, COPEI 22 percent, MAS 13 percent, MVR 17 percent, and other regional parties 13 percent (Penfold 2004a–b; Monaldi et al. 2005).

One illustrative example of how political careers were built in this period is the rise of Andrés Velásquez and his party, Causa R, which had been a marginal party in the previous period with a small representation in Congress. He was able to build the party starting with his victory as governor of the state of Bolívar in 1989. His effective performance allowed Velásquez to compete in the presidential elections of 1993 and receive 22 percent of the vote. Causa R continued its success by later winning the mayoralty of Caracas in 1992 and the governorship of Zulia in 1996. Another example is Henrique Salas Römer, the governor of Carabobo, Venezuela's largest industrial state: he first won the governorship with the support of the COPEI in 1989, though he later abandoned the party due to internal disputes with its national leadership and created a regional party in 1995 called Proyecto Carabobo, which was later relabeled Proyecto Venezuela when he decided to run for the presidency in 1998. Meanwhile, Primero Justicia entered the political scene by winning in the well-off municipalities of eastern Caracas and has remained the leading party in that state (Miranda). Un Nuevo Tiempo surged as a splinter from AD in Zulia, where it has been the most significant party ever since (Penfold 2004a–b; Monaldi et al. 2005).

The multiplication of electoral arenas not only provided an incentive for some political parties to pursue an electoral strategy aligned with regional interests, it also forced national parties to use alliances with other political organizations to compete effectively in these different arenas. National political parties became increasingly dependent on party alliances.[30] One important consequence of the emergence of these alliances is that incumbent governors could shift partners more easily to assure re-election. As the importance of the alliances increased, the independence of incumbent governors also increased, allowing them to break with the party that initially supported them or to negotiate more favorable terms with national party leaders (Penfold 2004a–b; Monaldi et al. 2005).

The opportunity of one consecutive re-election for governors and mayors in contests that were organized separately from national elections also increased the independence of these political actors. Presidents, in contrast, could be re-elected only after ten years (until 2000). Governors and mayors running for re-election had greater opportunity to distance themselves from national party leaders and even disassociate themselves from the party structure. The fact that their re-election depended largely on their performance—and not on coattails from presidential candidates backed by centralized parties—created incentives for governors to behave more autonomously. In fact, governors quickly used their fiscal and administrative resources to control and expand existing local party machinery.[31]

In sum, the introduction of re-election for governors and mayors, and the fact that they were elected on a separate basis from their national counterparts, created incentives for these new political actors to gain independence and challenge their party bosses. The federalization of Venezuelan politics also implied that these governors, in the context of a decaying party system and the deepening of the decentralization process, could build their own political organizations to support their careers. The re-election rule also fostered internal conflicts between party authorities at the national level and new party leaders at the regional and local levels. These tensions remained unresolved and on occasion forced regional players to separate themselves from their parties. In this sense, federalism enacted a dual dynamic: the formation of new regional political parties and the split from hierarchical political parties such as the AD, COPEI, and MVR (Penfold 2004a–b; Monaldi et al. 2005).

In addition, the new mixed electoral system diminished the presidential coattails, promoting fragmentation and weakening party discipline. An increasing proportion of legislators began to be elected by plurality instead of proportional representation. Moreover, the previous ballot system that maximized the connection between the presidential vote and a single party vote for all legislative positions was changed for a system with separate votes, including a personalized vote to elect a majority of the legislators (Monaldi et al. 2005).

Policymaking in a Deconsolidating Political System

The policymaking process in this period was characterized by several prominent factors. It was marked by the existence of many and volatile key players. The fragmentation and volatility of the party system significantly increased. Party discipline weakened. Governors became very powerful political actors.[32] Second, the legislature and the judiciary became relatively more relevant policy arenas, as a result of the declining role of parties and the weakening of presidents. The legislative agenda began to be influenced and negotiated with regional authorities, who were also increasingly able to influence the legislators' careers. Finally, in this period there was a declining in influence of corporatist groups and an increasing political role of the military.

The transformation of the policymaking process, along with the multiplication of relevant policy actors at the national and regional levels, implied that transaction costs increased substantially, making it more difficult for political players to commit credibly to inter-temporal policy deals. Unlike the first period, in which political exchanges were conducted at low transaction costs in small groups, in this period transactions were negotiated among a larger number of ever-changing players in more open and conflictive arenas. Paradoxically, because of the decline of party elite agreements, the legislature played a much more significant role, though this did not necessarily improve the quality of public policies. National party leaders could not easily broker deals outside of Congress, as was done before. While in the first period legislators initiated on average just 13 percent of all the laws approved, in the second period the figure doubled to 26 percent. In the case of ordinary laws, the change was also dramatic, increasing from an average of 34 percent in the first period to 62 percent in the second (Monaldi et al. 2005).

Between 1989 and 1998, legislators became more autonomous and specialized.[33] Factions within parties and individual representatives were able to undermine the power of party barons on specific policy issues. Key legislation approved at the national level (either by Congress or by executive decree) needed to be negotiated with regional actors. Proponents of legislation had to introduce regional considerations to gain the support of governors and mayors. For example, legislators were able to push reforms to deepen fiscal transfers to the regions despite the opposition from national party authorities and the national executive. Regional leaders have powerful incentives to extract more resources from the center, especially since Venezuela has the largest vertical fiscal imbalance in Latin America and the rules of the distribution of fiscal resources have become more discretionary. The indiscipline of legislators was not only expressed in the increasing independence on policy issues vis-à-vis the party leader, but also by splitting from the parties that had nominated them. Factions within national political parties such as the AD, COPEI, MVR, and MAS went their separate ways, creating their own independent legislative groups (Monaldi et al. 2005).

Institutional instability created weaker inter-temporal linkages among politicians and policymakers. These linkages were also debilitated by continuous changes in the basic institutional rules (such as the constitution and the electoral system), as well as by the increased political uncertainty due to the risk of breakdown of the democratic regime. The rules of the political game have been in permanent flux since 1989. After decades without significant modifications, electoral rules have been changed five times, considerably modifying the incentives of political actors; in fact, different versions of a mixed electoral system were used for the legislative elections of 1993, 1998, 2000, 2005, and 2010. The Constitutional Assembly of 1999, the attempt at constitutional reform in 2007, and the constitutional amendment of 2009 (granting re-election to all executive officials) have made impossible any systematic development of a political strategy. The electoral reforms contributed to the erosion of the strict control that party leaders exercised over nomination procedures. This in turn weakened party discipline in the legislature. In addition, the lack of a stable electoral system did not help to consolidate electoral incentives, thereby increasing the levels of uncertainty politicians faced when building their careers.

In 1989–98, presidents were weaker than in the past. The 1961 constitution was characterized by formally weak presidents, but this weakness had been compensated by three factors: (1) the high level of oil rents controlled by the president, (2) the partisan control of the legislature, and (3) the national executive's control over the regions. In 1989, presidential powers were substantially reduced with the introduction of the direct election of governors and mayors. Presidents lost control over part of the budget (the constitutional revenue-sharing with the regions) and over the discretionary appointment and dismissal of governors, which had been a potent negotiating tool.

In addition, the decline in oil fiscal income during the eighties and nineties and the market-oriented reforms initiated in 1989, which limited discretionary subsidies and reduced rent-seeking opportunities, also reduced the political currency of presidents and party leaders (Villasmil et al. 2007). Due to the decline in presidential power, the executive branch in the 1990s enjoyed less influence in the legislative process. In the previous period, close to 80 percent of ordinary legislation was initiated by the executive. In contrast, in this second period the figure declined to 38 percent (Monaldi et al. 2005).

Changes in the party system, particularly its fragmentation and the emergence of less cohesive and disciplined parties, undermined the partisan powers of the president. In the previous period, three of the six presidents had a partisan majority in the lower house. Four out of six had majorities in coalition with other parties. In contrast, in 1988–98, presidents did not have a majority in the legislature. This situation increased the confrontations between the legislature and the executive branch.

In 1998, Congress for the first time approved the separation of legislative and presidential elections.[34] As a result, the legislative elections that year generated the largest political fragmentation in Venezuela's history (more than six effective parties).[35] The political system had deconsolidated and the stage was set for a move toward concentration of power or political anarchy. Venezuela managed to get both in the following decade.

The Difficulties of Policymaking in the Nineties

The period 1989–98 was characterized by high volatility in public policies.[36] An ambitious market reform program was started by President Pérez's second administration. He was able to advance rapidly in the areas where he did not require congressional approval such as exchange rate liberalization, trade liberalization, and elimination of price controls, but he was not able to pass key legislation. In particular, he faced an adversarial Congress that did not pass his fiscal reform, the cornerstone of the program. The proposals for a valued-added tax, the reform of the income tax to increase collection, and the fiscal stabilization fund were not approved. The lack of presidential support in Congress, sometimes even by his own party members, combined with an oil price hike due to the Gulf War to derail any possibility of success in this and other crucial areas. The government also faced high political instability: the riots of 1989 and two military coup attempts. Pérez was impeached in 1993 by an increasingly autonomous Supreme Court, with the support of his party (AD) in the legislature (Villasmil et al. 2007).

An interim administration in 1993 led by Ramón J. Velázquez was able to pass some additional reforms, including the VAT. In order to obtain the legislative support necessary to pass the law, however, a large share of the VAT revenue had to be earmarked for a special fund to finance the investments of regional governments. For the first time in Venezuela's history, governors and mayors had become a powerful force in the national legislature, a sign of the times to come (Monaldi et al. 2005).

In his first year in office, President Caldera (1994–99) reduced the VAT while maintaining the FIDES. By 1996, the extreme adversity of the fiscal and economic problems (due to a banking crisis) forced the executive to adopt another program of adjustment, which included increases in non-oil taxes and the domestic price of gasoline, as well as the partial opening of the oil sector to foreign investment. Once again, an increase in oil prices in 1996 allowed the government to increase fiscal expenditure and halt other reforms. The favorable conditions in the oil market did not last long, however, and by late 1997 and early 1998 fiscal conditions were again deteriorating (Villasmil et al. 2007; Manzano et al. 2009).

State governors continued to influence fiscal policy during these years. In particular, in late 1996, new legislation established a minimum level of transfers (about 15–20 percent) from the VAT revenue to FIDES. At the beginning of 1998, the legislature approved a law in which a share of oil royalties had to be transferred to the states. Even though effective tax reform was elusive, tax policy was very volatile. Since 1992, the income tax law has been reformed six times, the value-added tax nine times, and the tax on banking transactions has been "temporarily" established five times (Briceño 2002). Similarly, Puente (2003b) found that the activity of Congress in the budgetary process, measured by the average absolute difference of congressional changes to the executive's budget for each year, increases substantially from 1986 onward.[37]

The volatile and incoherent policies of the nineties were followed by the full reversal of all policy reforms attempted in the previous decade. Venezuela stands out as the country with the most radical reversal of public policy in the region.[38] These regrettable features of public policy appear to be primary causes of the lack of a coherent and effective response to the challenges posed both by the decline of oil revenues and later by the recent oil boom of 2003–9.

The Chavista Revolution: The Breakdown of Cooperation, 1999–2005

In 1998, Hugo Chávez was elected president of Venezuela as an outsider, under an electoral platform that promised to dismantle what was widely perceived to be a corrupt and dysfunctional political system.[39] In the 1998 presidential election, Chávez constantly accused the old democratic regime of having used oil income to favor the political and economic elite and exclude the largest and poorest sectors of the population. Chávez's prescription to solve this problem was to create a more participatory and socially inclusive democratic system through the activation of a Constitutional Assembly with full powers to transform institutional arrangements in Venezuela.

In 1999, after being elected president, Chávez with the support of the Supreme Court successfully summoned a Constitutional Assembly to craft a new constitution.[40] With just 56 percent of the vote, the chavistas obtained 95 percent of the seats (Penfold 2002; Monaldi 2003). These disproportional results were the result of the adoption of a majoritarian system, contrary to what was established by the prevailing constitution of 1961 (requiring a proportional system).[41]

The Constitutional Assembly created the political conditions for Chávez to modify key institutional rules and substantially increase his presidential powers. First, the presidential term was expanded from five to six years with one immediate re-election. Second, the president was provided complete control over the promotions within the armed forces, without the need for approval from the legislature.[42] Third, the new constitution eliminated the Senate and therefore the equal representation of the states within the legislature. Fourth, according to the new constitution, the president could activate any kind of referendum (including one to summon a Constitutional Assembly with full powers) without any support from the legislature. Fifth, the constitution eliminated any public financing for political parties. Finally, the constitution introduced the possibility of recalling the mandate for mayors, governors, or the president, contingent on the approval of a stringent set of conditions (Penfold 2002; Monaldi 2003; Monaldi et al. 2005).

As a result of the constitutional reforms, presidentialism was reinforced and federalism weakened.[43] The political regime that emerged was drastically different from the Punto Fijo system, and different from the one prevailing in 1989–98. In the Punto Fijo period, the center of the democratic system revolved around the political parties; in the chavista era, the center of gravity of the system is the president. Given the constitutional powers provided the president under the 1999 constitution, most political actors have no choice but to subordinate their political careers to the executive branch.

The elimination of public financing for political parties and the lack of regulation of the electoral use of the executive have weakened the ability of opposition movements to compete on an equal footing with a president seeking re-election. In addition, the president's control over the legislature allowed the executive to pack the Supreme Court with supporters and appoint the attorney general and comptroller. Moreover, control over the legislature and the Court enabled the president to steer the Electoral Council. The concentration of power that has resulted dramatically increased the stakes. The 1999 constitution did open some avenues for political participation, including the recall referendum, which was later used by the opposition in 2004 to try to revoke the president's mandate; however, the strong grasp of the democratic institutions exercised by the chavismo has significantly increased the costs of participation for the opposition (Kornblith 2005).

The political regime that has emerged is a hegemonic system, in which the president (and his party) exert political control over all formal institutions. In the 2000 election for the new unicameral National Assembly, the chavismo obtained a majority of the seats for the first time (in the elections of 1998 before the Constitutional Assembly, it had a minority). In 2005, after the opposition parties decided to withdraw from the elections, claiming a lack of fair conditions, the chavismo was able to control all the seats in Congress, further increasing the stakes of power. More generally, the increasing disproportionality of the electoral system has raised the stakes.[44]

The hegemonic rule initially was not exercised in a traditional authoritarian manner (i.e., restricting freedom of press), but it has slowly evolved toward a more openly authoritarian government. In particular, the government's powers have been used to limit the participation of opposition groups in public affairs. Moreover, the president has deliberately promoted a process of political and social polarization.[45] This polarization has led to three general strikes, including one that ended in a short-lived coup against President Chávez in April 2002.

The dominance of the chavismo over legislative and judicial affairs continued to erode what was already a weak rule of law. During the Punto Fijo period, the Supreme Court was heavily influenced by partisan considerations, but it did set limits on the power of the president. Even though investors or citizens did not see the judicial system as independent, it provided some checks to executive authority. The weak rule of law has dramatically worsened and the courts at this point do not offer any restraint against the hegemonic abuse of power. According to the

World Bank's rule of law indicator, in 2008 Venezuela occupied the lowest rank in the Latin American region. In fact, Venezuela ranked above only 2.9 percent of all the countries studied. This figure indicates a dramatic deterioration compared to 1996, when Venezuela was ranked in the 30th percentile.

Due to the lack of institutional constraints from the legislative and judicial branches, the executive has been able to set up administrative procedures to bypass formal budget institutions and spend without any type of oversight. The government has created a series of special spending funds that weakened fiscal transparency and fueled off-budget spending.[46] As of today, it is impossible to estimate accurately the amount of resources that are being spent outside the formal budget and through these special vehicles. These changes in the fiscal rules were made possible thanks to the direct control the presidency has exercised since 2003 over the oil income of Venezuela's national oil company (PDVSA).[47] This unprecedented discretionary control of oil revenues dramatically strengthens the effect of the high stakes of power that exist in all oil-dependent nations.

Under Chávez, Venezuela has experienced yet another transformation of its policymaking process. In this era, there are very few key actors, a declining role of political parties, a more prevalent presence of the armed forces, and a significant dominance of the president over the policymaking process. The degree of political polarization and conflict in the country between the chavismo and the opposition is so deep that discount rates are high and policies are rarely negotiated in institutionalized arenas. Policies are usually crafted as an attempt to maximize political power rather than on efficiency considerations. Cooperation has completely broken down.

As explained before, this change in the policymaking process, which has made the president the hegemonic actor of the system, is to some extent a direct consequence of the 1999 constitution, which significantly increased presidential powers. For example, the president was given the power to call for popular referenda to approve or eliminate laws, approve constitutional reforms, or call for a Constitutional Assembly with plenipotentiary powers, all of which significantly strengthened the executive's bargaining power. As a by-product, the constitution is now extremely easy to change if the executive is willing to do so and has the necessary popular support. In addition, the presidential term was increased to six years (from five) and re-election was permitted (for one consecutive term). As a result, a Venezuelan president could rule for a longer continuous period (twelve years) than could any other Latin American president (the regional median was five years) (Monaldi 2003). In 2009, a constitutional amendment approved in a referendum gave the president unlimited re-election, increasing the stakes of power even further.

Constitutional changes have radically increased the stakes of power and therefore have promoted a less stable democracy. The consolidation of democracy requires the institutionalization of uncertainty, which is better induced by institutional arrangements that promote low stakes of power. In Venezuela, the opposition movement, albeit fragmented, claims that there are few benefits from participating, and perceive electoral outcomes as biased and not institutionalized. As a result, a significant part of the opposition has incentives to exclude itself from the regular democratic political process, and instead to invest resources in trying to overturn the regime by nondemocratic means (as observed in the April 2002 coup and the 2002–3 oil strike). This has led to a process of radical political polarization as well as a politicization of the armed forces.

The winner-take-all dynamic embedded in the 1999 constitution and the more recent institutional reforms, combined with the high personal support of President Chávez during most of his presidency, can help to explain why Venezuela has experienced in the last five years more than three general strikes, a failed military coup, and massive street protests. The differences with the previous two periods are very significant. Although the federalist arrangement has not been fully muted (governors and mayors are still elected), decentralization has been significantly reversed (Manzano et al. 2009). In addition, the elimination of the Senate has implied that states have lost some representation in the national legislature. Policies are now rarely negotiated with governors and mayors; instead, these actors tend to approach the presidency on a loyalty basis to gain access to needed resources. In this new system, the policymaking process is thus centered on a single arena—the presidency—and the presidential power does not arise from limited delegation by political parties, as was the case in the Punto Fijo era, but rather is the direct consequence of the constitutional design.

Concluding Remarks

The collapse in per capita oil income during the 1980s and 1990s was so significant that it can largely explain the crisis faced by Venezuela's political system. But why were politicians unable to re-establish a policy framework capable of sustaining policies to restore growth once the collapse had taken place? This chapter provides a stylized story of governance to explain how the dramatic decline in oil income interacted with institutional variables, which in turn affected the ability of politicians to implement and sustain policies capable of re-establishing long-term economic growth. The initial institutional arrangements adopted by the Punto Fijo Pact in the early 1960s generated low stakes of power, induced a generally cooperative policymaking process, and produced relatively good policy features. The system privileged stability over flexibility or efficiency. The distribution of oil revenues was a key element to sustain these institutional settings. Economic performance was good, in part due to the mildly favorable external environment (stability, progressively increasing oil revenue, etc.). Despite these initial conditions, in 1973–82 the oil booms created significant distortions in the political system and the economy. Abundance increased incentives for inefficiency, patronage, and corruption. Cooperation declined and the quality of policy suffered.

The dramatic oil price fall in the 1980s induced rapid economic deterioration, redistributive conflicts, and popular dissatisfaction. Political reforms were thus initiated in 1989 as a result of these outcomes. Combined with the popular disenchantment generated by the drop in oil income, these reforms resulted in the deconsolidation of the political system. Political fragmentation and volatility became the norm. Policymaking became noncooperative and politicians did not have the incentive to sustain policy reforms. The outer features of public policy further eroded, and instability decreased the likelihood of establishing a new cooperative arrangement.

Finally, the Chávez revolution prompted the total deconsolidation of the party system and political cooperation broke down completely. The new institutions increased the stakes of power and made cooperation very costly, furthering the deterioration of policymaking.

To clarify the argument presented here, it helps to address a series of questions. How is the Venezuelan case different from other Latin American countries in which the political system also deconsolidated, such as Colombia and Peru? Why does oil dependency play a key role in the decline of the political system if it is not prevalent in other cases with similar evolution? First, it is important to establish the extent of the decline of Venezuela's political system and economy. Venezuela had one of the strongest, most stable, and institutionalized party systems in the region, and one of the few democracies that survived during the sixties and seventies. It now has one of the most volatile and deinstitutionalized party systems and the worst levels of democratic governance in the region. There is no other example in the region of such dramatic decline. In most other countries in the region, there was not a consolidated party system for any significant period. Peru never had a party system like that of Venezuela. In the countries where there has been a consolidated party system, such as Venezuela's, the decline has not been as significant (e.g., in Costa Rica, Chile, and even Uruguay). Colombian parties have not deteriorated as noticeably, and were never as strong and disciplined as were Venezuelan parties.

Moreover, in the last two decades the quality of policymaking in Venezuela has been well below the regional average, with very high volatility and low effectiveness. For example, Venezuela was the country with the earliest and most extreme reversal of market reforms.

Similarly, the degree of economic decline in Venezuela during the last quarter of a century is rivaled in the region only by Nicaragua's, and inflation has been on average the highest in the region for two decades. Oil dependence and oil income decline seem critical to understand the extent of the deterioration of democratic governance.

Why then is a story linking institutional decay only to oil income decline not sufficient? Are institutional reforms relevant? Oil income decline helps to explain the increasing redistributive conflicts and the loss in support of the traditional parties. But why was the result not simply the rise of new political actors under the same governance framework? Why were AD and COPEI incapable of sustaining policy reforms after obtaining more than 80 percent of the vote in 1988? Why did fragmentation and volatility increase so dramatically after the political reforms of 1989? Why didn't a new democratic cooperative equilibrium arise? Why did cooperation break down completely after President Chávez's institutional reforms? We believe that the institutional reforms are crucial to understand why the political system deconsolidated so rapidly and dramatically, and why effective democratic governance was not re-established. The initial political reforms induced a decline in cooperation by increasing fragmentation and volatility and weakening discipline. The Chávez institutional reforms further weakened democratic governance by noticeably increasing the stakes of power.

Why did political decentralization have a deconsolidating effect? Is this true in other countries? The argument presented here is that the combination of the loss in support for traditional political parties, produced by oil-induced economic decay with rapid political decentralization had this effect. If decentralization had been introduced progressively in a situation of favorable economic conditions, the effects of fragmentation and volatility would have probably been quite limited. Still, in Argentina and Brazil, the two traditional federal countries in the region, political decentralization has produced party systems that are less cohesive and cooperative than that of Venezuela. In fact, the role of regional politicians has been significant in creating governance and economic difficulties in those two countries. There is an extensive literature showing the potential negative effects of decentralization, under certain contexts, over democratic governance (Spiller and Tommasi 2003; Monaldi 2010).[48] Mexico, the other federal country in Latin

America, which activated federalism recently, has not experienced a significant increase in fragmentation, a surge of regional parties, or volatility.[49] This can be attributed partly to the fact that Mexico's long-powerful PRI party was able to reform the economy and obtain relatively good economic performance before the opposition parties (PAN and PRD) won regional offices and the transition to competitive democracy occurred. In that sense, it has been argued that the sequence of reform—first the economy, then the political system—was accomplished in an effective order in Mexico and China. In Venezuela and Russia, however, the reverse order of reforms has had destabilizing effects. But as with the Venezuelan case, the Mexican case shows how a strongly partisan presidential system may get into governance problems once those partisan powers diminish. The difficulties of implementing policy reforms in Mexico today are similar to Venezuela's in the nineties.

It is important to emphasize that the argument presented here is not against political decentralization. Decentralization has contributed to improving the provision of public goods in Venezuela and other countries of the region. Moreover, political decentralization has many advantages in terms of democratic representativeness. In fact, during the attempts at power-grabbing experienced by Venezuela, the existence of decentralization provided a source of democratic legitimacy, unrelated to the national executive, which has been a limit to the rise of authoritarianism. But political decentralization in this context contributed to the deconsolidation of the political system and the weakening of cooperation and democratic governance.

If oil decline explains institutional decline, why does the recent oil price increase not translate into stronger democratic governance? The potential decline in redistributive conflicts can be a potential enhancer of democratic governance (Dunning 2008). As has been explained, however, the institutional framework is a key interactive factor. If the institutional framework increases the stakes of power and inhibits political cooperation, oil income increases will not necessarily enhance democratic governance. In fact, they can have the opposite effect by further increasing the stakes of power.

Moreover, the accumulated institutional decline reflected in the indicators discussed in this chapter—attributable to oil dependence, oil decline, and the institutional reforms implemented—makes it particularly difficult to manage the oil boom. In fact, the current oil boom seems to be generating, in most respects, a more extreme version of what we witnessed in the seventies. The weakened institutional framework provides fewer limits to the worst political and economic effects of the resource curse.

NOTES

1. The combination of oil dependence with poor institutional quality has particularly negative consequences for development (Sala-i-Martin and Subramanian 2003).

2. However, there still exists some debate over the causality of the phenomena, with some authors proposing that it may run in the opposite direction. The channels by which good governance and high-quality institutions translate into higher growth, which have been proposed by the literature, include the protection of property rights and its effect over the incentives for investment and human capital accumulation; the capacity to resolve conflicts and maintain political stability when major policy changes are required; the perverse effect of institutions designed for extractive purposes; and the capacity for implementing stable and coherent policies.

3. In fact, part of this literature goes a step further by claiming that the resource curse—the proposition that mineral dependence causes slower economic growth—actually works through the negative effect of resource dependence on institutional quality, which in turn hurts growth. As was the case with the institutions and growth literature, this literature has some critics, who argue that resource dependence (as opposed to abundance) is also endogenous to institutions— and as a result, that causality cannot be properly assessed. In addition, some authors argue that it is the interaction of resource dependence with low-quality institutions that causes poor growth performance. This literature has also highlighted that countries with strong institutions have been able to manage the resource booms, minimizing the perverse economic effects of resource rents (e.g., Chile, Norway, and Botswana).

4. Institutions have generally been analyzed as constraints or as equilibrium outcomes.

5. (1) Voice and accountability includes indicators related to political participation and civil liberties; (2) political stability refers to indicators measuring the perception that a government might be overthrown and the relative prevalence of political violence and terrorism; (3) government effectiveness covers indicators related to the quality of bureaucracy, political independence of the civil service, and credibility of the government's commitment to public policies (including the ability to pass legislation and stay in office); (4) regulatory quality refers to indicators of the quality of the public policies themselves (excessive regulation, unpredictability, etc.); (5) rule of law measures the extent to which agents have confidence and abide by the rules (the degree of protection of property rights, judicial independence, and crime are some of the elements included); and (6) control of corruption measures perceptions of the prevalence of corruption. See Kaufmann, Kraay, and Mastruzzi 2003.

6. Figures are shown in percentile rank, with the highest scores being in the 100th percentile.

7. For 2008, the percentile ranks are as follows: voice and accountability, 30.3 percent; political stability, 12.4 percent; government effectiveness, 17.1 percent; regulatory quality, 4.8 percent; rule of law, 2.9 percent; and control of corruption, 9.2 percent.

8. According to this index, Venezuela does perform better than some oil-rich countries such as Indonesia, Iraq, and Nigeria, but worse than other oil economies such as Russia, Kazakhstan, Iran, Saudi Arabia, Kuwait, and United Arab Emirates.

9. For 1996, the percentile ranks were as follows: voice and accountability, 51.7 percent; political stability, 21.1 percent; government effectiveness, 19.4 percent; regulatory quality, 36.1 percent; rule of law, 30 percent; and control of corruption, 22.8 percent.

10. These indexes also use subjective measures from a variety of data sets but mostly from two sources: the average, for all years available between 1996 and 2005, of some combination of perception variables from the Global Competitiveness Report (GCR) and a State Capabilities Survey (SCS) of policy experts made by the Inter-American Development Bank.

11. This index aggregates different measures, including the standard deviation of the de-trended Fraser index of economic freedom and a variety of GCR survey questions (Inter-American Development Bank 2005). Having stability does not mean that policies do not change, but that the changes respond mostly to changing economic conditions and not to political trends. Venezuela,

in the period 1988–2005, had high policy volatility in most cases originating in political changes (elections, coups, impeachment of a president, regional elections). This instability reflects low levels of political cooperation among key political actors.

12. This reflects the perceived levels of enforcement of taxes, minimum wage, and environmental legislation.

13. The pact was agreed on by the leaders of the three main political parties, Rómulo Betancourt of the social democratic AD, Rafael Caldera of the Christian democratic COPEI, and Jóvito Villalba of the center-left-nationalist URD. The pact included arrangements for power sharing, such as the distribution of cabinet positions among competing parties, and the implementation of basic common social and economic policies regardless of the presidential and legislative electoral outcomes. In addition, the pact stipulated the need to create corporatist mechanisms that guaranteed that labor unions and business interests, through umbrella organizations such as CTV and Fedecamaras, respectively, would be consulted and incorporated into the policymaking process. See Karl 1986; Corrales 2003; Monaldi et al. 2005.

14. The nature and consequences of the two democratic constitutional moments, of 1947 and 1961, reveal the different correlation of forces that prevailed, and the learning process that occurred between them (Corrales 2003). In 1947, the AD took advantage of its overwhelming popular majority to call for an elected Constitutional Assembly. It received 78 percent of the vote and 86 percent of the seats, and used its absolute dominance to impose a constitution very close to its preferences, alienating many relevant actors. But by 1958, AD's dominance had declined. Betancourt (AD) won the presidency, but this time the party received 49.5 percent of the votes and 55 percent of the seats in Congress (chamber of deputies). Based on the spirit of pact-making, the 1961 constitution was crafted by a special congressional committee cochaired by Raul Leoni (AD) and Rafael Caldera (COPEI). Party leaders decided that regardless of the electoral outcome of the congressional elections, the committee would be balanced. It included eight representatives from the AD (36.4 percent), four from the COPEI, four from the URD, three from the Communist Party (PCV), and three independents. AD leaders agreed that the composition of the constitutional committee would overrepresent the opposition. As Corrales (2003) argues, the result of this decision was "a constitution designed to prevent single-party hegemony."

15. Under the constitution of 1961 (derogated in 1999), the Venezuelan president had very limited legislative powers, especially compared with other governments in the Latin American region. Venezuela had the lowest value in the index of legislative powers developed by Shugart and Carey (1992).

16. Until 1999, Venezuelan presidents had non-immediate re-election (i.e., they could run again only when two presidential periods had elapsed, after the end of their presidency). Coppedge (1994) gives a prominent role to this institutional feature. He argues that it made all presidents "lame ducks," at the same time promoting party factionalism by maintaining former presidents as powerful actors that could eventually become presidents a second time (as did Caldera and Pérez). The lack of immediate presidential re-election combined with the absence of term limits for legislators provided an advantage for party leaders (Monaldi et al. 2005).

17. Presidents were elected by plurality for five-year terms in direct elections concurrent with the legislative elections (for all seats). Until 1993, the voter had just one ballot to vote for both the president and the legislature. One card with the color and symbol of the party (and since the 1970s, the photo of the presidential candidate) had to be marked to vote for the president, and next to it a smaller identical card had to be marked to vote for both chambers of the legislature. Voters could not split their vote between chambers. The combination of plurality (as opposed to runoff) with concurrency, and the structure of the ballot maximized presidential coattails. The presidential election—due to its winner-take-all nature—tended to produce a strategically concentrated vote, and combined with high coattails, produced high party concentration. An additional element promoting concentration was the absence of regional elections. The evidence seems to point to the significance of coattails and vote concentration. The difference between the vote for the top two presidential candidates and the vote for their parties (in the period

1958–88) was always below ten percentage points, with the exception of the 1988 election, when dissatisfaction with the AD and COPEI began to increase (Monaldi et al. 2005).

18. This feature guaranteed that minority parties would gain access to seats in Congress. The pure proportional representation system did not generate a large party fragmentation, due to the powerful coattails generated by the presidential elections (as explained above) (Monaldi et al. 2005).

19. Presidents enjoyed relatively high partisan powers in this period. They never faced a majority opposition and had very strong disciplined parties backing them. Between 1958 and 1988, three of the six presidents had a partisan majority in the lower house. Four out of six had majorities in coalition with other parties. In contrast, of the four administrations in 1988–2005, none had a single party majority in the lower house, and only one—Chávez between 2000 and 2005—had a majority in coalition with other parties. Since 2005, Chávez has had a strong majority in the legislature. The Latin American regional average, for the period 1978–2002, was 30.2 percent (percentage of time the presidential administration had a presidential party majority in the lower house) and 54.1 percent (majority coalition). See Monaldi et al. 2005.

20. The single, closed, blocked list electoral system constituted a powerful disciplinarian tool in the hands of the party leadership. The Venezuelan system allowed the party leadership to control the nominations (who gets on the list) and the order of election (who gets elected first), pooling the votes of party candidates (no intra-party rivalry), and limiting internal competition. Shugart and Carey's (1992) index of party leadership strength due to the electoral system gives Venezuela a value of eight, above the regional average of six. Only three countries in the region have a higher index. See also Monaldi et al. 2005.

21. In terms of the participation of interest groups in the policymaking process, very few democracies in the region had so few (and stable) players participating. In Venezuela, there existed single peak associations of labor and business, which were incorporated formally into the policy process. According to Crisp 2000, only Chile and Mexico had similar single peak associations, and only in Mexico were they formally incorporated as often as in Venezuela.

22. Party discipline was extremely high in this period. Virtually all votes were counted with raised hands, since perfect discipline was assumed (roll calls were almost never used). In the few instances in which a member did not want to follow the party line, his alternate member replaced him and voted as expected.

23. Minority parties such as the MAS did not have a major policymaking role, but were guaranteed access to small prerogatives in order to keep them "inside" the system (e.g., large autonomous budgets for universities and cultural projects controlled by the left). See Monaldi et al. 2005.

24. In the first elections of 1958, the effective number of parties (ENP) represented in the chamber of deputies was 2.57. In the next two elections the ENP rose significantly (to an average of 4.56), mostly due to two significant splits in the AD (the largest party). But the system consolidated again into a two-party system in the next four elections from 1973 to 1988. The ENP in that period was on average 2.65. In the elections of 1983, the ENP reached a low point of 2.42. In this period, Venezuela's party fragmentation was slightly below the Latin American average. The Latin American regional ENP average was 2.84, while the Venezuelan average was 2.63 (Monaldi et al. 2005). These figures are for the years for which we have comparative data, 1978–89. Regional averages were calculated using data from Payne et al. 2002.

25. In the Chamber of Deputies, the volatility index, measuring the change in party share, was 18.9 percent in the period 1958–88, below the Latin American average of 22.1 percent. Moreover, volatility tended to decline until 1988 (to 13.8 percent). Volatility increased dramatically in the period 1989–2000 to an average of 38.1 percent, compared to a regional average of 23 percent. Volatility in the presidential vote was even lower in the Punto Fijo period (13.9 percent), almost half the regional average of 23.9 percent. It increased dramatically afterward (52 percent) compared to a regional average of 28 percent. After 1989, Venezuela has had the largest presidential vote volatility in the region. See Monaldi et al. 2005.

26. The percentage of new legislators (turnover) tended to decline in the first period. In the first three terms from 1963–73, it was on average 71 percent, whereas in 1963–73 it declined significantly to 55 percent as the two-party system consolidated. In the second period, the percentage of new legislators rises again to an average of 78 percent (82 percent in the current legislature). Compared to other presidential countries for which there are data for turnover, the figure for the first period (63 percent) is not extremely high. In Argentina about 80 percent of the legislators are not re-elected. In Brazil the figure is 57 percent, in Ecuador 73 percent, in Chile 41 percent, and in the United States 17 percent. In contrast, in the second period, turnover reached Argentinean levels (78 percent). See Monaldi et al. 2005.

27. Overall, the electoral system continued being globally proportional; however, portions of the legislators began to be elected by plurality, establishing a personal electoral connection and increasing the system's disproportionality (Monaldi et al. 2005).

28. As explained, national party leaders had a monopoly on the nominations of candidates to the national legislature as well as the state and municipal assemblies; they appointed judges according to party loyalty; and they exercised strong discipline over their members (Coppedge 1994). More important, until 1989, regional and local politics had been absent. Presidents had the right to appoint governors, and the mayoral position did not previously exist. Governorships were assigned to members of the political party in power and were used as instruments to foster patronage (Penfold 2004a–b; Monaldi et al. 2005).

29. Gonzalo Barrios, AD's president, publicly rejected the reforms, particularly the direct election of governors, "because the country is not historically prepared for this type of reform" (Penfold 2004a).

30. AD established alliances with an average of 2.2 parties in the regions where it was able to win in the 1989 gubernatorial elections (and won 55 percent of the total). By the year 2000, AD had to establish alliances with an average of six parties to win just 12.5 percent of the governorships. But AD's reliance on these alliances, in terms of the average percentage of votes these parties added for their candidates, was relatively low. In contrast, COPEI was very dependent on these alliances to win. The average percentage of votes contributed by other parties supporting the COPEI's gubernatorial candidates increased from 7.1 percent in 1989 to 40.3 percent in 2000. See Penfold 2004a–b; Monaldi et al. 2005.

31. During the 1992 gubernatorial contests, eighteen incumbents ran for re-election and eight managed to win. In 1995, only three governors could run as incumbents and two of them were re-elected. In 1998, seventeen incumbents out of twenty-one governors were re-elected. In 2000, fifteen governors were up for re-election and five of them won. Intra-party politics in this period revolved around the conflict between the new regional leaders and the old party leadership. In 1993, regional leaders were able to win the presidential nominations in the AD (Claudio Fermín, mayor of Caracas) and the COPEI (Oswaldo Alvarez Paz, governor of Zulia), in confrontation with the traditional leadership. Again in 1998, Irene Saéz, the independent mayor of Chacao, won COPEI's nomination. See Penfold 2004a–b; Monaldi et al. 2005.

32. The effective number of parties in the chamber of deputies increased dramatically. In the previous period of two-party dominance (1973–88), the ENP was on average just 2.6. As shown in figure 10.3, it surged to 4.7 in 1993, and in 1998 it rose again to a peak of 6.1. The average ENP of the second period (4.74) is significantly higher than the regional average in the period (3.5). Venezuela went from being one of the least fragmented party systems to the third most fragmented in Latin America. Volatility has also dramatically increased in the second period. In terms of lower chamber seats, the average volatility in 1990–2000 was 38.12 percent, way above the Latin American average of 23 percent. Venezuela again moved from being one of the least volatile countries in the region to the second most volatile. Compared to the first period, average volatility more than doubled (see fig. 10.4). In terms of volatility in presidential party vote, the increase is even more dramatic. It reached 52.8 percent and 59.5 percent in the 1993 and 1998 elections, respectively. On average, Venezuela has had the highest volatility in presidential voting in the region in the last ten years. In terms of fragmentation and volatility, Venezuela became increasingly similar to countries such as Ecuador and Peru (Monaldi et al. 2005).

33. Paravisini (1998) and Crisp (2001) found some evidence of the increased specialization of legislators, in issues relevant to their constituents, as a result of the closer electoral connection provided by the election in plurality districts of a significant proportion of the legislature.

34. Congressional elections were set to coincide instead with regional and local elections, held a few weeks before the presidential elections. This modification was designed by the traditional parties to reduce the coattail effects that a potential landslide victory by Chávez might have on the legislature. Instead, the parties planned to build their support in Congress based on the strength of their regional governments (and the regional authorities' coattails).

35. The separation of legislative and presidential elections will be the norm in the future, since the 1999 constitution set a five-year legislative term and a six-year presidential term.

36. We focus on fiscal policy because it is one of the main economic policy dimensions and very illustrative of the crucial problems faced by policymakers.

37. In the period 1973–85, Congress usually approved the budget presented by the government with relatively few changes. In the period between 1986 and 1998, however, only three annual appropriations involved changes of less than 5 percent, six involved changes of more than 26 percent, and one a change of more than 36 percent. In this sense, it is possible to identify two different patterns of congressional activity in the period: one characterized by a low level of congressional involvement in the budget process (1973–85), and another with a high level of involvement (1986–99). See Puente 2003b.

38. Only Bolivia, and to a lesser extent Argentina, had policy reversals of significant magnitude.

39. In the early 1990s, Lieutenant Colonel Chávez managed to capture the electorate's attention and emerge on the political scene as a failed coup plotter, blaming corruption and market reforms as the causes for increasing poverty rates in Venezuela.

40. The prevailing constitution did not address this mechanism. To reform the constitution, a super-majority in Congress, which President Chávez did not have, was required. Nonetheless, the Supreme Court allowed the Constitutional Assembly to go forward.

41. The electoral system was originally devised by the Presidential Committee for the Constitutional Assembly and was paradoxically supported by a significant sector of civil society, which sought to promote a complete personalization of the vote and thereby reduce the influence of political parties.

42. For a more detailed examination of how civilian control over the armed forces has been relaxed in Venezuela, see Trinkunas 2002.

43. Using the Shugart and Carey index (updated later by Payne et al.), the Venezuelan president has now legislative powers close to the regional average (Payne et al. 2002), compared to the lowest in the region before 1999. Still, other factors not captured in the index make the Venezuela president formally the most powerful in the region.

44. The electoral rules approved by the Electoral Council do not enforce the proportionality principle incorporated again in the 1999 constitution, by allowing majority parties to take all the plurality seats plus an additional proportional share of the proportional seats. This violates the logic of the mixed-member electoral system. As a result, with a 56–60 percent projected vote, the chavismo would have gotten over 80 percent of the assembly seats. In 2009, a reform of the electoral system made it even more disproportional and opened the door for gerrymandering of the voting districts, making the rules highly uneven for the opposition.

45. In fact, the concentration of power has been abused as a political instrument to implement targeted political prosecutions against NGOs or politicians that have been outspokenly critical of the government, or to disenfranchise citizens from public benefits (scholarships, social benefits, jobs, etc.) if they are believed to have supported the opposition—particularly in their effort to activate the 2004 recall referendum against the president.

46. For example, instead of the expenditure in education being centralized in the ministry of the sector, it is dispersed among the central government, the National Development Bank (BANDES), and the special funds (especially FONDEN). In 2006, an estimated 10 percent of GDP was spent using off-budget mechanisms (authors' calculations).

47. This is in significant contrast to the period 1976–98, when PDVSA was financially and operationally autonomous. This radically changed after the oil strike of 2002–3, when the government fired close to twenty thousand oil company workers and eliminated the company's autonomy.

48. The case of Russia has been also studied as a case where political decentralization represented a challenge for democratic deconsolidation, even though decentralization was one of the few limits to the surge in authoritarianism.

49. Countries such as Chile, Costa Rica, and Uruguay, with more institutionalized political systems, have had limited political decentralization. Even though this does not imply causality, it is interesting to notice that politicians have deliberatively avoided political decentralization in order to maintain strong national political parties. See Monaldi 2010.

REFERENCES

Brewer-Carías, A. 1985. *Instituciones políticas y constitucionales*. San Cristóbal: Universidad Católica del Táchira.

———. 1994. *Informe sobre la Descentralización en Venezuela*. Caracas: Editorial Arte.

Calcaño, L., and M. López. 1990. *El tejido de Penélope: La reforma del estado en Venezuela*. Caracas, Venezuela: CENDES.

Combellas, R. 1999. "La inserción de los grupos de intereses en el estado venezolano." In *Doce textos fundamentales de la ciencia política venezolana*, 197–224. Caracas: Instituto de Estudios Políticos, Universidad Central de Venezuela.

Comisión Presidencial para la Reforma del Estado. 1986. *Documentos para la Reforma del Estado*. Caracas.

———. 1989. *La Reforma Administrativa*. Caracas.

———. 1990. *Antecedentes de la Reforma del Estado*. Caracas.

Coppedge, M. 1994. *Strong Parties and Lame Ducks: Presidential Patriarchy and Factionalism in Venezuela*. Stanford: Stanford University Press.

Corrales, J. 2002. *Presidents without Parties: The Politics of Economic Reform in Argentina and Venezuela in the 1990s*. University Park: Pennsylvania State University Press.

———. 2003. "Power Asymmetries and Post-pact Stability: Revisiting and Updating the Venezuelan Case." Paper presented at the Annual Meeting of the American Political Science Association, Philadelphia, August 29.

Crisp, B. 1997. "Presidential Behavior in Systems with Strong Parties." In *Presidentialism and Democracy in Latin America*, edited S. Mainwaring and M. Shugart, 160–97. Cambridge: Cambridge University Press.

———. 1998. "Presidential Decree Authority in Venezuela." In *Executive Decree Authority*, edited by J. Carey and M. Shugart, 142–74. Cambridge: Cambridge University Press.

———. 2000. *Democratic Institutional Design: The Powers and Incentives of Venezuelan Politicians and Interest Groups*. Stanford: Stanford University Press.

———. 2001. "Candidate Selection in Venezuela." Paper presented at the Latin American Studies Association XXIII International Congress, Washington, D.C., September 6–8.

Crisp, B., and J. Rey. 2001. "The Sources of Electoral Reform in Venezuela." In *Mixed-Member Electoral Systems*, edited M. Shugart and M. Wattenberg, 173–94. New York: Oxford University Press.

De la Cruz, R. 1998. *Descentralización en perspectiva*. Caracas: Ediciones IESA/Fundación Escuela de Gerencia Social.

Dunning, T. 2008. *Crude Democracy*. Cambridge: Cambridge University Press.

Haber, S., and V. Menaldo. 2009. "Do Natural Resources Fuel Authoritarianism?" Mimeo, Stanford University President's Fund for Innovation in International Studies." http://scid.stanford.edu/system/files/shared/Haber-Menaldo_5-4-09.pdf.

Haggard, S., and M. McCubbins. 2001. *Presidents, Parliaments, and Policy.* Cambridge: Cambridge University Press.

Hausmann, R. 1992. "Sobre la crisis económica Venezolana." In *América Latina: Alternativas para la Democracia*, edited J. Rey, J. Barragán, and R. Hausmann, 87–113. Caracas: Monte Avila Editores.

Hausmann, R., and R. Rigobón. 2002. "An Alternative Interpretation of the 'Resource Curse': Theory and Policy Implications." Working Paper 9424, National Bureau of Economic Research, Cambridge, Mass.

Inter-American Development Bank. 2005. *The Politics of Policies.* Cambridge: Harvard University Press.

Isham, J., M. Woolcock, L. Pritchett, and G. Busby. 2003. "The Varieties of Resource Experience: How Natural Resources Export Structures Affect the Political Economy of Growth." Economics Discussion Paper 03-08, Middlebury College, Middlebury, Vt.

Karl, T. 1986. "Petroleum and Political Pacts: The Transition to Democracy in Venezuela." In *Transitions from Authoritarian Rule*, edited by G. O'Donnell, P. Schmitter, and L. Whitehead, 196–220. Baltimore: Johns Hopkins University Press.

———. 1997. *The Paradox of Plenty: Oil Booms and Petro-States.* Berkeley: University of California Press.

Kaufmann, D., A. Kraay, and M. Mastruzzi. 2003. "Governance Matters III: Governance Indicators for 1996–2002." Policy Research Working Paper 3106, World Bank, Washington, D.C.

Kornblith, M. 1991. "The Politics of Constitution Making: Constitutions and Democracy in Venezuela." *Journal of Latin American Studies* 23:61–89.

———. 1998. *Venezuela en los noventa: Las crisis de la democracia.* Caracas: Ediciones IESA.

———. 2005. "The Referendum in Venezuela: Elections vs. Democracy." *Journal of Democracy* 16 (1): 124–37.

Mainwaring, S., and M. Shugart, eds. 1997. *Presidentialism and Democracy in Latin America.* Cambridge: Cambridge University Press.

Manzano, O., F. Monaldi, J. Puente, and S. Vitale. 2009. "Oil-Fueled Centralization: The Case of Venezuela's Federalism." Mimeo, Forum on Federations, Ottawa.

Manzano, O., and R. Rigobón. 2001. "Resource Curse or Debt Overhang?" Working Paper 8390, National Bureau of Economic Research, Cambridge, Mass.

Molina, J. 1991. *El sistema electoral Venezolano y sus consecuencias políticas.* Caracas: Vadell Hermanos.

Molina, J., and C. Pérez. 1996. "Los procesos electorales y la evolución del sistema de partidos en Venezuela." In *El sistema político venezolano: Crisis y transformaciones*, edited by A. Álvarez, 193–238. Caracas: Universidad Central de Venezuela.

Monaldi, F. 2002. "The Political Economy of Expropriation in High Sunk Cost Sectors: The Case of the Venezuelan Oil Industry." Paper presented at the Annual Meeting of the American Political Science Association, Boston, August 29–September 1.

———. 2003. "Governance, Institutions, and Development in Venezuela." Manuscript, World Bank, Washington, D.C.

———. 2005. "The Role of Sub-national Authorities in the National Policymaking Process: A Comparative Perspective of Latin American Cases." Discussion Paper S-301, Inter-American Development Bank, Washington, D.C.

———. 2010. "Decentralizing Power in Latin America: The Role of the Governors in the National Arena." In *How Democracy Works: Political Institutions, Actors, and Arenas in Latin American Policymaking*, edited by C. Scartascini, E. Stein, and M. Tommasi, 177–216. Cambridge: Harvard University Press.

Monaldi, F., R. A. González, R. Obuchi, and M. Penfold. 2005. "Political Institutions, Policy-making Processes, and Policy Outcomes in Venezuela." Research Network Working Paper R-507, Inter-American Bank Development Bank, Washington, D.C.

————. 2007. "Political Institutions and Policymaking in Venezuela: The Rise and Decline of Cooperation." In *Policymaking in Latin America: How Politics Shapes Policies*, edited by Ernesto Stein and Mariano Tommasi, 371–418. Cambridge: Harvard University Press.

Naim, M. 1993. *Paper Tigers and Minotaurs: The Politics of Venezuela's Economic Reform.* Washington, D.C.: Carnegie Endowment for International Peace.

Naim, M., and R. Piñango. 1988. *El caso Venezuela: Una ilusión de armonía.* Caracas: Ediciones IESA.

Paravisini, D. 1998. "Transformaciones en el Parlamento Venezolano (1984–1996): Especialización y representación de los intereses de los electores." Paper presented at the XXI International Congress of the Latin American Studies Association, Chicago, September 24–26.

Payne, M., D. Zovatto, F. Carrillo, et al. 2002. *Democracies in Development.* Washington, D.C.: Inter-American Development Bank.

Penfold, M. 2001. "El colapso del sistema de partidos en Venezuela: Una muerte anunciada." In *Venezuela en transición*, edited by J. Carrasquero, T. Maingon, and F. Welsch, 36–51. Caracas: CDB Publicaciones–RedPol.

————, ed. 2002. *El Costo Venezuela: Opciones de política para mejorar la competitividad.* Caracas: CONAPRI.

————. 2004a. "Electoral Dynamics and Decentralization in Venezuela." In *Decentralization and Democracy in Latin America*, edited by A. Montero and D. Samuels, 35–66. Notre Dame: University of Notre Dame Press.

————. 2004b. "Federalism and Institutional Change in Venezuela." In *Federalism and Democracy in Latin America*, edited by E. Gibson, 197–225. Baltimore: Johns Hopkins University Press.

Przeworski, A. 1988. "Democracy as a Contingent Outcome of Conflicts." In *Constitutionalism and Democracy*, edited by J. Elster and R. Slagstad, 59–80. Cambridge: Cambridge University Press.

————. 1991. *Democracy and the Market: Political and Economic Reforms in Eastern Europe and Latin America.* Cambridge: Cambridge University Press.

Puente, J. 2003a. "The Political Economy of Social Spending in Venezuela." Simposio de Investigación Económica, Oficina de Asesoría Económica de la Asamblea Nacional, Caracas, July 15.

————. 2003b. "The Political Economy of Budget Allocation in Venezuela." Unpublished manuscript, IESA, Caracas.

Puente, J., A. Daza, G. Rios, and A. Rodriguez. 2006. "The Political Economy of the Budget Process in Venezuela." Research Network Working Paper RF3-06-007, Inter-American Development Bank, Washington, D.C.

Rey, J. 1972. "El sistema de partidos Venezolano." *Politeia* 1:224–28.

————. 1989. *El Futuro de la democracia en Venezuela.* Caracas: Colección IDEA.

Rodríguez, F. 1996. "Understanding Resistance to Reform: Conflict and Agency in the Venezuela Experience." Unpublished manuscript, Department of Economics, Harvard University, Cambridge, Mass.

Rodríguez, F., and J. Sachs. 1999. "Why Do Resource-Rich Economies Have Slower Growth Rates? A New Explanation and an Application to Venezuela." *Journal of Economic Growth* 4 (3): 277–303.

Ross, M. 2001. "Does Oil Hinder Democracy?" *World Politics* 53 (3): 325–61.

Sala-i-Martin, X., and A. Subramanian. 2003. "Addressing the Natural Resource Curse: An Illustration from Nigeria." Working Paper No 9804, National Bureau of Economic Research, Cambridge, Mass.

Shugart, M., and J. Carey. 1992. *Presidents and Assemblies: Constitutional Design and Electoral Dynamics.* Cambridge: Cambridge University Press.

Spiller, P., E. Stein, and M. Tommasi. 2003. "Political Institutions, Policymaking Processes, and Policy Outcomes: An Intertemporal Transactions Framework." Working Paper 59, Economics Department, Universidad de San Andres, Buenos Aires.

Spiller, P., and M. Tommasi. 2003. "The Institutional Determinants of Public Policy: A Transaction Approach with Application to Argentina." *Journal of Law, Economics, and Organization* 19 (2): 281–306.

Trinkunas, H. 2002. "The Crisis in Venezuelan Civil–Military Relations: From Punto Fijo to the Fifth Republic." *Latin American Research Review* 37 (1): 41–76.

Villasmil, R., F. Monaldi, G. Rios, and M. González. 2007. "The Difficulties of Reforming an Oil-Dependent Economy." In *Understanding Market Reforms in Latin America*, edited by J. Fanelli, 266–318. New York: Palgrave Macmillan.

World Bank Institute. 1996–2008. "Governance Data." http://info.worldbank.org/governance/wgi/index.asp.

11 THE POLITICAL ECONOMY OF INDUSTRIAL POLICY IN VENEZUELA

Jonathan Di John

This chapter examines the political economy of industrial policy and economic growth in Venezuela in the period 1920–2003. Soon after the discovery of oil in Venezuela during the 1920s, the idea of "sowing the oil"—that is, diversifying the production and export structure—was an important organizing concept among economic and political elites (Baptista and Mommer 1987). Since the early 1950s, the industrialization process became increasingly state-led. The role of the state was marked by a purposeful policy of import substitution that coincided with the transition to democracy in 1958. Moreover, political leaders set Venezuela on the path of a more pronounced, "big push," natural-resource-based heavy industrialization that focused on the development of state-owned enterprises in steel, aluminum, petrochemicals, and hydroelectric power. This policy was not dissimilar in intent, ambition, and scope from state-led industrial strategies in South Korea, Taiwan, Malaysia, and Brazil, as well as those in some other oil-exporting developing economies.

There are several perplexing characteristics of Venezuela's growth trends. Venezuela was among the fastest-growing economies in Latin America in the period 1920–80, and its manufacturing growth rate was among the most rapid until the mid-1970s. In the period 1980–98, however, non-oil and manufacturing growth rates experienced long-run stagnation; in the period 1998–2003, manufacturing growth collapsed.[1] Table 11.1 traces Venezuela's non-oil and manufacturing growth trends.

In contrast to the literature that studies crises in authoritarian rule, and those that consider *transitions* to democracy, the Venezuelan case provides an opportunity to examine the tensions and processes of *late development* within a *long-standing* democracy.

Table 11.1   Growth trends in the Venezuelan economy, 1920–2003

	Non-oil GDP	Manufacturing
1920–30	10.2	—
1930–40	2.7	—
1940–50	9.6	6.6
1950–57	9.1	15.0
1957–70	7.1	7.7
1970–80	5.7	9.7
1980–90	1.1	2.8
1990–98	2.7	1.2
1998–2003	−3.5	−5.1

SOURCES: Based on Baptista 1997 for the period 1920–1957 and Banco Central de Venezuela, *Annual Reports* (various years), for the period 1957–2003.

NOTE: Table presents average annual growth rates. All output series in 1984 bolivars.

The dramatic slowdown in growth was paradoxical since Venezuela seemed to be a likely candidate to maintain its rapid growth. First, in the period 1974–85, Venezuela received an enormous increase in resource availability as a result of oil windfalls. Second, Venezuela maintained *relatively* high levels of physical and human capital investment in the context of a *relatively* accountable long-standing democratic polity. In the Latin American context, Venezuela has also maintained among the least inequitable distributions of income. In sum, Venezuela appeared to possess many favorable "initial conditions" and "social capabilities" (Abramowitz 1986) for rapid catch-up. (See Di John [2009, 24–32] for evidence of Venezuela's relatively favorable initial conditions in the 1970s.) Was the failure due to policy errors or inappropriate institutions? Did oil windfalls themselves become a "curse" by crowding out the development of non-oil sectors such as manufacturing? Or were there other factors that explain the slowdown in growth?

Oil windfalls are generally considered more of a curse than a blessing, an idea known as the "resource curse." Analysts posit that oil abundance harms the prospects of economic growth. There is a vast resource curse literature in economics, political science, and political economy that attempts to explain the *negative* effects oil windfalls and busts can have on the structure of the economy and on patterns of governance (see, e.g., Karl 1997). The main problem with these arguments is that they cannot explain why oil abundance has been compatible with cycles of growth *and* stagnation in Venezuela over the period 1920–2005. This chapter does much more than simply point out that oil abundance *coincided* with dramatic variations in Venezuelan economic performance; it also attempts to explain *why* the use of oil rents has been more *and* less growth- and productivity-enhancing over time. It offers a new political economy framework for explaining the dramatic variations in Venezuelan industrial growth in the post-1973 period.

The first section critically examines different *economic* versions of the resource curse arguments, notably "Dutch disease models" that focus on the potentially negative effect an oil boom can have on the manufacturing sector. The following section examines explanations that emphasize the failures in policy and institutional design, particularly arguments that stress the importance of an overly centralized, interventionist state. It discusses the extent to which the slowdown was due to excessive public enterprise investment or "inward-looking" protectionist policies, both of which supposedly generated industrial concentration. I find that both Dutch disease and policy failure arguments are problematic in light of historical and comparative evidence.

I then provide an alternative framework for understanding long-run cycles of growth in Venezuela, in order to explain why centralized rent deployment has become increasingly more inefficient over time. Advocates of laissez-faire policies and proponents of more dirigiste policies do *not* take into account the extent to which development strategies affect the nature of political conflicts. I suggest that the nature of the technology that accompanies a development strategy requires different levels of *selectivity, or concentration of economic and political power*, to be initiated and consolidated. The possibility then arises that the historically specific nature of political settlements may not be compatible with the successful implementation of a given development strategy. For the post-1980 period, I argue that the industrial slowdown in Venezuela was the result of a growing *incompatibility* between the "big push" heavy industrialization development strategy, on the one hand, and political strategies and contests, on the other. In this period, the political science literature establishes that the Venezuelan political system became increasingly populist, clientelist, and factionalized. The basic incompatibility I identify is that politics became increasingly more factionalized and accommodating precisely at a time when the development strategy required a more unified and exclusionary rent/subsidy deployment pattern. The coordination failures of the big-push industrialization strategy were manifested in the low monitoring of state-created rents and subsidies, excessive entry of private sector firms in protected sectors, and massive proliferation of public sector employment and state-owned enterprises in the decentralized public sector.

Economic Explanations of the Resource Paradox in Venezuela: A Critical Analysis of Dutch Disease Models

The relationship between natural resource wealth and economic development has been the subject of intense debates over the past century.[2] The main purpose of this section is to examine the extent to which the reigning economic explanations of the slowdown in Venezuelan manufacturing growth are defensible. I examine different economic versions of the resource curse arguments, including the Dutch disease models, and related open economy macro models focusing on the effects of high oil-determined wages. A common theme in these models is that oil booms produce exchange rate revaluations, which supposedly reduce the incentives to invest in manufacturing and generally makes manufacturing production uncompetitive.

In the Venezuelan context, Mayobre (1944) was one of the earliest to argue that an expensive exchange rate, as a result of the expanding oil industry, rendered nascent industries uncompetitive and retarded industrialization (see also Rangel 1968; Hausmann 1990, 23–54). The common theme in these arguments is that natural resource booms have adverse effects on the economic structure of the economy.

The logic of the simple Dutch disease theories can be described as follows. In an economy in full employment equilibrium, a permanent increase in the inflow of external funds results in a change in relative prices in favor of non-traded goods (services and construction) and against non-oil traded goods (manufacturing and agriculture), leading to the crowding out of the non-oil tradables by non-tradables. That is, an appreciation of the exchange rate leads to a decline in the competitiveness and hence production and employment of the traded goods sector. The mechanism through which this change takes place follows directly from the assumptions of full employment equilibrium and static technology. With these assumptions, the external funds (from an oil boom) can be translated into real domestic expenditure only if the flow of imports increases. Since non-traded goods cannot be imported easily (or only at prohibitive costs), however, a relative contraction of the traded goods sector is inevitable, otherwise the resources needed to enhance the growth of the non-traded sector would not be available. Thus the model predicts that de-industrialization is the inevitable structural change that occurs as a result of oil booms.[3] It is important to note that, even without the restrictive assumptions of full employment, oil booms can induce more investment in non-traded investments and thus discourage manufacturing investment, simply because non-traded goods prices rise relative to non-oil traded goods as a result of exchange rate appreciation. A second mechanism through which manufacturing can become less competitive in this model is through the increase in manufacturing wage rates that results from increases in the aggregate demand for labor that the oil booms can generate. In the short run, when productivity levels are fixed, unit labor costs in manufacturing rise, which can, in the absence of compensating policies, lead to a loss in manufacturing competitiveness.

The association of "de-industrialization" as a "disease" stems from the unique growth-enhancing characteristics the manufacturing sector can potentially embody. Primary products (as well as services) were not believed to possess the "external dynamic economies" (Young 1928) observed in manufacturing industries, where faster growth apparently led to increasing productivity, manifested ultimately in the dynamic specialization of employment (Verdoorn 1949; Kaldor 1966).

The potential for dynamic externalities of manufacturing to develop opens an important role for policy in affecting the growth outcomes of oil booms. Since a late-developing country faces a technological gap, additional export revenues, if channeled by an appropriate industrial policy, can play an important part, since the additional foreign exchange can accelerate the process of importing advanced technology and the machines that embody them. Additionally, if the industrial strategy promotes "learning," the additional revenues can theoretically accelerate the growth process. For instance, during the boom, the government could promote industry by channeling resources to toward that sector through, say, protection, subsidies or financial incentives. This can serve to modernize the manufacturing capital stock, which, in turn, can improve productivity. This means the structural change against non-oil tradables, such as manufacturing, is not inevitable; rather, the outcomes on which resource booms depend come from state policy responses (Neary and van Wijnbergen 1986; Gelb 1988).

Can Dutch disease models contribute to an adequate explanation of the slowdown of manufacturing growth in Venezuela? In terms of investment, there is also no evidence that oil booms in Venezuela have been associated with *declines* in investment in manufacturing. In fact, the experience of Venezuela shows that rapid growth of oil revenues is normally associated with high investment in economic activity in the traded goods, and in particular the manufacturing sector, and paradoxically the periods of downturn in oil revenues are associated with slower growth and investment in industry. In the Venezuelan case, if we compare the evolution of oil export revenues in Figure 11.1 with manufacturing investment rates in Figure 11.2, we see there is a broadly *positive* correlation between oil export revenues and manufacturing investment over the period 1960–98.

The role of state policy had a decisive impact on the use of oil windfalls. In the case of manufacturing investment, public sector manufacturing investment in natural-resource-based industries (petrochemicals, steel, and aluminum) was important in maintaining the high levels of total manufacturing investment during the oil booms of the 1970s.

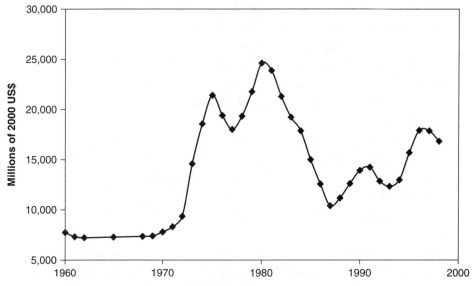

Fig. 11.1   Venezuela: Real oil exports, 1960–1998

Sources: Based on Ministerio de Energía y Minas (various years), Petróleo y otros datos estadísticos; Banco Central de Venezuela, *Statistical Series* (various years); International Monetary Fund (various years).

Note: Real retained export, three-year moving average. Real retained oil exports is the sum of the value of oil export revenues deposited in the central bank, the value of oil sector salaries and purchases of domestic products by oil companies operating in Venezuela. This sum is converted into dollars and deflated by U.S. producer prices at U.S. 2000 dollars.

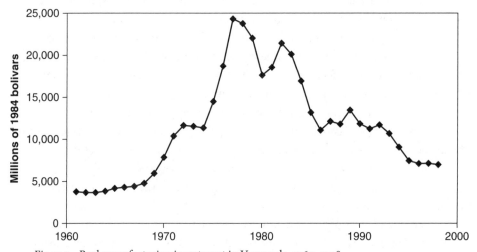

Fig. 11.2   Real manufacturing investment in Venezuela, 1960–1998

Sources: Based on Oficina Central de Estadística e Informática (various years); Banco Central de Venezuela, *Statistical Series* (various years).

Note: Three-year moving average.

The problem of an "overvalued" or "expensive" exchange rate should manifest itself in higher than average wage costs in Venezuela than elsewhere. Is it then the case that comparative manufacturing wage costs or an excessive wage share (and hence low profitability) explains the comparative performance of the Venezuelan manufacturing sector?

The cross-country and historical evidence, however, suggests that the core problems of the Venezuelan manufacturing sector lie not necessarily in excessively high wages or relatively low profitability, but rather in the inability of these sectors to catch up with the advanced economies by sustaining rapid *productivity* growth (see Appendix). Over the period 1975–96, all manufacturing sectors in Venezuela experienced substantial declines in growth rates (Di John 2009, 57).

But these declines in growth rates and accompanying declines in productivity occur in the context of a *wage collapse* in all these sectors in the period 1985–96. Moreover, some more successful late developers, both resource-rich (Malaysia and Chile) *and* resource-poor (South Korea), experienced increases in productivity growth across a range of manufacturing sectors vis-à-vis the United States, despite the fact that wages relative to the U.S. wage level *increased* in all these economies. Stagnant and declining Venezuelan industrial performance does not seem to be only or necessarily due to low investment in (and "crowding out" of) the industrial sector during and following oil boom periods, but rather has more to do with the type and productivity of industrial *investment*, which has been relatively poor. This, in turn, is related to ineffective economic management of the state, particularly industrial strategy, state-owned enterprise policy, and macroeconomic policy.

Critiques of State Intervention in Venezuela: Inefficient Public Investment and Protectionist Policies as Causes of Slowdown?

There are a series of analysts who attempt to locate the problem of allocation of investment as the result of "excessive" *public investment*, on the one hand, and excessive *industrial concentration* as a result of state-led industrial policies, on the other. This section critically examines these arguments.

Some analysts have attributed the slowdown in manufacturing growth to increases in the scale and scope of public enterprise manufacturing investment and the inefficiencies surrounding such investment in the period 1974–88. Indeed, there was a considerable increase in public manufacturing investment and production in this time frame. In 1970, state-owned enterprises accounted for 5 percent of manufacturing value added (excluding oil refining). This share rises to 8 percent in 1980 and reaches 18 percent by 1986.

While there is substantial evidence of growing inefficiencies in public manufacturing enterprises, the main issue is why these inefficiencies persist. Even if
public enterprise performance was poor, the collapse in growth in Venezuela is
primarily a result of a collapse in private investment (Hausmann 2003), which
implies that the growth of an inefficient public enterprise sector cannot plausibly
explain the growth collapse. Moreover, the areas where the public sector dominates (nonferrous metals, petrochemicals, and steel) were those where long-run
productivity performance was relatively *better* than other sectors, which were
predominately privately owned (see Di John 2009, 48–64, for evidence).

A second assertion is that state protectionism and excessive regulation stifle
the emergence of a competitive private sector. Many analyses argues that centralized, interventionist, and discretionary industrial policies have led to corruption and cronyism, which has, in turn, hindered growth-enhancing competition
(Naím 1993; Naím and Francés 1995). These analyses posit that protectionism
generated excessive industrial concentration, and that such concentration was associated with the decline in competitive pressure facing oligopolistic or monopo-
listic firms. Naím (1993) argues that, in Venezuela, "profound structural changes
were urgently needed to alleviate problems caused by the *highly concentrated,
oligopolistic industrial structure,* low overall productivity growth and significant
obstacles to non-oil exports that had been cultivated over many years of government mismanagement" (41, emphasis added). While there is clear evidence
of growing concentration in production in Venezuela over time, the comparative and historical evidence and conventional economic theory point to several
problems with the claim that protectionist policy causes dynamic inefficiency by
creating a concentrated industrial sector. The comparative evidence suggests that
the Venezuelan manufacturing sector is *not* unusually concentrated compared to
countries with much faster rates of industrial growth.

Models of oligopoly are indeterminate in terms of the dynamic efficiency of
the firms. This is because the regulatory structure of an industry (e.g., antitrust
laws) plays an important role in determining the competitive pressures facing
firm owners. Second, a greater number of firms does not necessarily assure a
greater intensity of competitive effort (Demsetz 1997, 137–42). In aerospace, for
example, the competition between just two firms, Boeing and Airbus, has not
hindered rapid innovation and intense jockeying for position. In the presence
of increasing returns, industrial concentration may be crucial to achieving the
scale economies to compete with "best practice" firms (World Bank 1993, 92–102;
Chandler and Hikino 1997, 29–34). Moreover, industrial concentration may play
the functional role of creating learning rents that compensate for both the risk
and uncertainty of undertaking investment in the context of imperfect capital

markets and the challenges of late development more generally (Amsden and Hikino 1994). The problem of industrial competitiveness in latecomers is not too high a concentration level, but rather an overdiversified conglomerate structure and below-minimum efficient plant size.[4] If the successful late developers are a useful reference, then competitiveness will more likely be improved in Venezuelan manufacturing through a purposeful industrial strategy that ensures minimum plant efficient plant size and ensures that firms receiving subsidization and protection are subject to explicit performance criteria. The identification of industrial concentration per se does not take us far in explaining poor economic performance.

The discussion in the first two sections found that the reigning economic explanations of slowdown in Venezuela have important theoretical and empirical shortcomings. Neither oil windfalls nor the level of state intervention can explain, in isolation, the Venezuelan growth slowdown in light of the historical and comparative evidence. One common lacuna in the explanations discussed is the failure to explain *why* policy failures in managing investment funds have persisted in Venezuela in the period 1973–2003.

The Compatibility of Development Strategy and Politics Matters

Advocates of laissez-faire suggest that state intervention distorts markets, stifles competition, and generates corruption, all of which creates obstacles to potentially growth-enhancing investments (e.g., World Bank 1997). In recent times, this view has dominated, as manifested in the adoption of widespread economic liberalization, particularly within Latin America. Yet the outcome of such reforms in Venezuela as well as in most of the region has been disappointing (Di John 2005). Economic liberalization has failed to revive investment and growth to the levels of 1950s and 1960s, when more interventionist policies were followed.

Proponents of economic liberalization might argue that reform policies were not followed consistently or that the reforms were not carried far enough. They would point to the fact that growth was very rapid in 1990 and 1991, and was derailed because the reforms failed to be deepened, particularly in the area of banking reform and labor regulations. There are at least two problems with this argument. First, there is little cross-country evidence that accelerations in the growth trajectory of countries were *preceded* by wide-ranging economic liberalization. Second, *comparative* regional evidence suggests that Latin American reforms were the most profound, yet the region's growth was among the lowest among less developed regions (Rodrik 2004). This brings into question the extent to which further liberalization is necessarily growth-enhancing. While the state in Venezuela and many other less developed economies have failed to generate and implement growth-enhancing regulatory structures, market liberalization does not eliminate the market failures and risks of late development that justified state intervention in the first place.

The developmental state theorists, on the other hand, have pointed to the benefits that industrial policy can have in inducing the acquisition of learning and technology (Amsden 1989, 2001; Chang 1994; Aoki, Murdock, and Okuno-Fujiwara 1997). This literature has contributed important research on the salience of targeted subsidization, or rent creation in driving the late industrialization process. While the purely economic arguments for the benefits of state intervention may be accepted, little attention is paid to where the power to implement policies and where the policy goals come from in the first place. As a result, the developmental state analysis does not explain why similar types of industrial policy *fail* in many contexts. Given the *contingent* nature of political institutions and contests, there is no reason to expect that the appropriate institutional structure and politics will emerge to accommodate a country's stage of development and changing technological challenges.

The historiography of economic analyses on Venezuela has identified changes in stages of development and development strategies. Economic histories (Hausmann 1981; Baptista 1995) have pointed to the *change in development strategy* from a smaller-scale, import-substituting industrialization toward a more large-scale, capital-intensive industrial strategy that began tentatively in the late 1950s but became a central focus of policy after 1973. In this process, the state's role as a producer increased significantly. The value of these analyses is that there is an identification of a *periodization* of development strategies as a process that is *not homogenous* in its *technological or structural characteristics*. But these analyses have not explored what a policy-induced switch in the technological nature of development strategy implies in terms of the political economy of property rights allocation and legitimacy.

An Alternative Perspective on the Political Economy of Industrial Policy

"Big push" natural-resource-based industrialization (NRBI) strategies commit large sums of state resources to long-gestating, technologically demanding investment projects, which require complementary investment and state-business conglomerate coordination (Amsden 1989, 2001; Aoki, Murdock, and Okuno-Fujiwara 1997; Chandler and Hikino 1997). This strategy also requires "extensive government support and quality competition with foreign suppliers" (Fitzgerald

2000, 64). Finally, the promotion and nurturing of *large firms* was crucial to competitiveness and learning in late developers given the centrality *of scale economies* in intermediate technology sectors (Amsden 2001, 194–99).

Big-push strategies involve a high degree of risk in acquiring technology and capturing new markets, including, most importantly, export markets. Thus state-led initiatives to socialize risk need to be undertaken by targeting firms and sectors to persuade new industrialists to invest in or upgrade new technology and improve productivity. The Fourth and Fifth Plan of the Nation encapsulated the intention to transform the industrial structure of Venezuela through a big-push industrial strategy. The emphasis the Venezuelan government placed on chemicals and basic metals as leading sectors was indeed similar to the industries targeted in all successful late developers (Amsden 2001, 138–39). As it turned out, the Achilles' heel of Venezuelan industrialization strategy was to be a growing inefficiency in the implementation of such big-push strategies.

The greater learning costs and gestation periods of such investments bring greater economic and political challenges and risks that distinguish this type of economic strategy from the small-scale and simple technology of the easy ISI (import-substitution industrialization) stage. There remains considerable debate as to whether Venezuela moved too quickly toward the development of heavy industrial sectors. While the move to the more complicated stage was not obviously necessary or desirable in 1974, the challenges of executing such a strategy certainly increased vis-à-vis the easier stage of ISI. The institutional challenges center on the need for the state to maintain *continuity* of centralized investment *coordination*, effective *monitoring* of public enterprises, *selectivity* in subsidizing investment through rent creation, *discipline* of rent recipients, and *collective action capacities* of business associations. I will consider each of these factors below.

The theoretical justification for centralized investment planning is well-known. The "big push" or "balanced growth" models (Rosenstein-Rodan 1943; Scitovsky 1954) stressed the demand complementarity between different industries, which needed *ex-ante* investment coordination by the state.[5] In the context of underdeveloped capital markets and a small internal market demand, spontaneous coordination of decentralized market actors is unlikely, since an investor in a sector characterized by increasing returns to scale (e.g., in steel) may not judge the investment profitable on the assumption that demand will not increase significantly elsewhere in the economy. This will be the case even if the investor has access to sufficient levels of skilled workers. Because of scale economies, only a large-scale and simultaneous movement is guaranteed to be profitable. The creation of demand sufficient to make large-scale investments in poor countries profitable is the crux of the coordination problem.

The coordination problem in large-scale late manufacturing development is one of the main factors behind the greater use of public enterprises in the advanced stage of ISI. Public enterprises, for example, were particularly important in the heavy industrial sectors during the critical "takeoff" years of the 1960s in both Taiwan and South Korea (Rodrik 1995). Jones and Sakong (1980) examined the development of public enterprises in South Korea in the sixties and seventies and found that the Korean policymakers had developed a coherent set of preferences with respect to where public enterprises should be established. They summarize their results as follows: "The industries chosen for the public enterprise sector [were] characterized by high forward linkages, high capital intensity, large size, output-market concentration, and production of non-tradables or import-substitutes rather than exports" (quoted in Rodrik 1995, 90). These are precisely the characteristics associated with the coordination failure that occurs during big-push industrialization efforts.

The greater presence of public enterprises does, however, increase the administrative and political challenges that the central government faces in coordinating and monitoring public sector investment. The greater the level of public sector investment implies that the failure of the central government to impose "hard budget constraints" on public sector managers will generate loss-making public enterprises. This, in turn, can generate fiscal drains and reduce the productivity of investments over time in the big-push phase.

Because big-push industrialization drives generate a large "investment hunger," the macroeconomic challenges of industrial policy are formidable. The dangers of overexpansion with such a strategy are typically occur with the buildup of unsustainable and destabilizing external debt positions that would occur if the investment does not lead to productivity improvements, thereby increasing competitiveness and export earnings. As Amsden (2001, 252) notes, "That conditions of 'lateness' are inherently conducive to overexpansion is suggested by the fact that when a debt crisis occurs, it almost always occurs in a latecomer country. This is because ... diversification in the presence of already well-established global industries involves moving from labor-intensive to capital-intensive sectors characterized by economies of scale" (252). The scale of big-push investments were, indeed, instrumental in the debt crises in Latin America in 1982 and in East Asia in 1997, as both were preceded by a *surge in investment* (253).[6]

The exigencies of "big push" industrial strategies also present significant political and economic challenges to state–business relations. Big-push investment programs entail complementary investments that have significant spillover effects in pecuniary and production terms (e.g., steel and electricity). Given the larger size of such complementary investments in big-push strategies, the *failure* of the state and business associations to *coordinate* investments may result in larger *costs* than in the earlier stage of ISI, where the scale of investments are generally lower. For example, the costs of failure to coordinate investments can lead to severe spare capacity, which has large negative effects on investment returns. Even when abstracting from the problem of coordinating investments, the failure of the state or business associations to effectively monitor investments in a single large-scale manufacturing sector can be costly. For instance, the inability of the state to impose conditional rents/subsidies or it permitting *excessive entry* (e.g., fifteen car assemblers in Venezuela since the mid-1970s) are more costly for industries exhibiting increasing returns to scale compared to small-scale manufacturing operations. Moreover, excessive entry may lead to the development of firms with too small an average plant size to compete with imports or in export markets, especially in the industries characterized by increasing returns. Where proprietary knowledge and product development, and hence research and development, are important to competitive success, large numbers of small, inefficient producers constrain the capacity to compete for latecomer industries. Small firms do not generate the turnover to direct sufficient amounts of resources to R & D (Kim and Ma 1997, 122–23; Amsden 2001, 277–81).

For large-scale, resource-based, and other heavy industrialization, *selectivity* in the subsidization process is one of the salient characteristics of industrial policies (Lindbeck 1981). This is especially the case where increasing returns to scale are relevant. The failure of the state to be selective will negatively affect productivity performance.

Selectivity needs to be complemented with state capacity to *discipline* rent recipients. The scale of the subsidization implies that big-push strategies require states to make rents conditional on performance criteria (Kim and Ma 1997). Hence, there has been significant emphasis on state *discipline* of producers as one key to the efficiency of industrial policy (Amsden 1989).

The complementary nature of big-push strategies means that decision-making and actions are interdependent. The greater the interdependence of investments, the more an institutional design that assures *reliability, predictability, and discipline* is required (Demsetz 1997, 30–34). This generally means that a legitimate and powerful centralized authority is required. An outstanding example of the importance of reliability and discipline that centralized authority provides is a military unit during war. In this perspective, it is not surprising that states which have faced internal and external *threats* have used such exigencies to increase bargaining power vis-à-vis business groups, to mobilize resources, to convince or force industrial producers to forsake short-run profits, and to make subsidies conditional on performance criteria. For instance, the willingness of business groups to cooperate with state initiatives occurs because perceived and real threats raise the price of failure (Vartianen 1999, 224).

Finally, the great risks entailed in "big push" or "second stage" industrialization strategies tend to necessitate a greater degree of cooperation and collective action *among business associations and conglomerates.* Effective collective action can help socialize the risks of developing export markets, acquiring technology, managing firm entry and exit, and negotiating with the state to provide services that are in the collective interests of a given sector (see Wade 1990; Evans 1995; Maxfield and Schneider 1997; Haggard, Maxfield, and Schneider 1997). Therefore, *fragmentation* of business associations can also lead to more costly coordination failures as the scale and scope of investments increase. This is because fragmentation can lead to *particularistic* demands and bargaining that hinders the competitiveness of the sector as a whole, when, for example, there is a level of bargaining with the state for firm entry that leads to the creation of too many firms at substandard scale.

In light of the exigencies of large-scale subsidization and interdependence, it is not surprising that big-push development strategies have enjoyed success in a very few late-developing countries such as Japan, Taiwan, South Korea, Singapore, Brazil, and Malaysia. Moreover, these late developers have been characterized by a relatively legitimate, secure, *centralized* state both in terms of political and economic organization (Woo-Cummings 1999). Relatively centralized business associations and links between the state and big business tended to accompany more complex and risky industrial strategies (Maxfield and Schneider 1997). This implies that fragmented or highly factionalized political contestation may lead to significant coordination failures in both industrial policy and macroeconomic instability.

Neither the neoliberal nor the developmental state theorists systematically consider the different political challenges that particular development strategies generate, nor do they examine the interaction of economic and politics in any more general manner. The failure of dominant paradigms on state intervention to consider the changing nature of political conflict implies that such models will fail to map the extent to which contingent political settlements are compatible with different economic challenges of catching up over time.

Periodization of Industrialization Stages and Strategies in Venezuela

This section attempts to periodize the changing nature of the development strategies and the nature of scale economies and technological complexity in the Venezuelan manufacturing sector. It is not my intention to focus on the details of economic policymaking, since there is already a substantial literature in this field (Hausmann 1995; Astorga 2000; Rodríguez 2002).

In the economic-history analyses of Venezuelan industrialization, it is generally agreed that there was an important increase in the capital-intensity and scale economies of industrial output and composition beginning in the *early 1960s* (Hausmann 1981; Astorga 2000). The development of the state steel mill, SIDOR, in 1962 and the state-led attempt to promote the metal-transforming and transport sectors, particularly the automobile and auto parts sectors from the early 1960s onward, were notable examples. The capital-intensity and scale economy of many leading industrial sectors increase further with the Fifth Economic Plan, outlined below. In the period 1973–82, the industrial strategy switches to a natural-resource-based "big push" strategy. Further, traditional ISI begins to develop protectionism for more technologically challenging sectors such as autos.

It is possible to identify transitions in development strategy by examining the structure of manufacturing. Table 11.2 includes information about the structure of output,

Table 11.2   Venezuela: Shares of selected sectors in manufacturing value added (excluding oil refining), 1936–1998 (percentages)

		F., B., & T.	Textiles	Paper	Chemicals	Non-met.	Bas. met.	Met. trans.
Output	1936	52.3	10.6	0.1	4.5	3.8	0.3	2.4
	1953	41.6	8.1	1.2	8.5	9.7	0.4	3.7
	1961	41.0	15.6	3.3	8.3	6.5	0.9	11.1
	1971	29.2	12.1	4.3	10.2	6.7	6.0	17.7
	1981	27.2	8.1	3.9	10.8	6.8	7.0	19.6
	1988	32.2	4.7	3.5	10.0	4.5	10.3	18.6
	1998	36.0	5.2	2.3	9.8	5.2	10.4	18.0
Labor	1936	59.3	11.9	0.2	2.5	4.9	0.2	1.9
	1953	48.9	8.4	1.0	4.1	6.8	0.3	3.8
	1961	27.2	23.0	2.8	5.0	6.6	1.2	14.8
	1971	24.7	15.4	3.4	7.5	6.9	4.6	16.8
	1981	18.1	11.2	2.9	7.6	6.6	7.2	18.4
	1988	25.6	7.3	0.8	7.9	6.6	9.8	13.7
	1998	22.8	4.9	0.7	9.1	7.4	6.7	12.1
Capital	1936	43.2	9.6	1.3	—	—	—	—
	1953	53.0	9.0	1.4	5.9	12.7	0.5	2.3
	1961	28.2	9.1	3.2	10.6	7.5	26.5	6.5
	1971	23.7	9.4	4.8	7.9	9.5	23.3	10.8
	1981	18.8	3.8	2.8	6.0	10.4	34.7	13.9
	1988	16.6	3.9	2.2	8.0	8.1	45.7	13.6
	1998	18.2	3.4	3.4	17.7	9.7	31.0	10.3

SOURCES: Based on Astorga 2000, 214; Oficina Central de Estadística e Informática 1988, 1998; Banco Central de Venezuela, *Statistical Series* (various years).

NOTE: All figures above are percentages. Output = value added; labor = number of employees; capital = fixed assets. The brackets in the following are the corresponding numbers of the International Standard Industrial Classification—F., B., & T.: food, beverages, and tobacco (311–14); textiles (321); paper: paper and paper products (341); chemicals: chemical industry (351); non-met: non-metallic minerals (361, 362, 369); bas. met.: basic metals (371, 372); met. trans: metal-transforming industries (381–84). The figures used to obtain the percentages of capital and value added in 1936 and 1953 are in current bolivars, and thereafter are in Bs. at 1968 prices.

employment, and capital assets in manufacturing, excluding oil refining—where indeed significant development had taken place (see Karlsson 1975 on the development of the oil refining industry). Traditional industries of food and textile comprised over 63 percent of manufacturing output. By 1971, the share of traditional industries declines to approximately 40 percent, a share that is maintained through 1996. The decline in the share of traditional industries in capital assets is also notable. While the traditional industries comprised, respectively, 52.8 percent and 62 percent of all manufacturing assets in 1936 and 1953, their share declines to 37.3 percent and 21.6 percent in 1961 and 1996, respectively. The traditional industries also show a steady though more gradual decline in the share of employment over the whole period.

While the traditional industries were declining in their share of output, capital, and employment, we see a marked increase in the shares of heavier, large-scale industrial sectors (chemicals, non-metallic minerals, basic metals, and metal-transforming industries) over time. It is telling that the relative increase of these industries is seen most in terms of the increase of their share of total manufacturing capital assets. This is due to the combination of the increased capital intensity and scale of these industries, and their relatively disappointing growth performance. The share of fixed assets of the basic metals sectors (as a proportion of all manufacturing fixed assets) increased from 0.5 percent in 1953 to 26.5 percent in 1961, and then increased as dramatically to reach a peak share of 45.7 percent in 1988. The increase in the relative share of fixed capital assets of the basic metals sector was the most pronounced of any sector in the period 1961–88. The relative share of the metal-transforming sector (which includes capital goods and transport) increased significantly, from 2.3 percent in 1953 to 6.5 percent in 1961, and reached a peak share of 13.9 percent in 1981. In aggregate terms, the share in total assets of the four sectors increased from 20.9 in 1953 to 51.1 in 1961, to 54.6 in 1971, to 65.0 in 1981, and finally reaching a peak of 75.4 in 1988. Given that the largest increase in the aggregate share of capital assets of the heavy industrial sectors occurred between 1953 and 1961, the period 1965–73 can plausibly be seen as marking a period of transition in development strategy. An important caveat would be that the dramatic increase in 1981 of the share of basic metals was owed to the state-led "big push" program in steel and aluminum.

The general economic history of Venezuela corroborates the transformation in the development strategy between 1965 and 1973. While the period 1920–58 was characterized by a relatively liberal trade policy (Di John 2009, 169–78), the role of state-created rents increases significantly from 1960 onward. The most important mechanism of promoting industrialization through state-created rents was the system of protectionism via tariff and nontariff barriers.[7] A differentiated tariff regime was set up to make some imports more expensive than others.

Differentiated tariffs allow the government to raise the import prices of goods that can be produced at home. This discourages domestic consumers from importing these goods, and at the same time encourages them to buy domestic products whose higher prices or lower quality may have prevented them from competing with foreign products at the early stage of industrialization. From the mid-1960s to the late 1989, average tariffs in the manufacturing industry were 60 percent for consumer goods, 30 percent for intermediate goods, and 27 percent for capital goods (World Bank 1990, 16–18). The average level of tariff protection and effective rates of protection as well as the tariff dispersion was broadly similar to many Latin American countries (Edwards 1995, 198–203).

A second component of the protection policy was the use various forms of nontariff protection such as import licenses and foreign exchange rationing, the latter used most extensively in the era of multiple exchange rates (1983–88). In the period 1968–89, the average share of manufactured goods subject to nontariff barrier coverage—that is, import licenses and prohibitions—oscillated between 40 percent and 50 percent (World Bank 1990, 16).[8] Comparative data for Latin America in the 1980s indicate that Venezuela's share of nontariff barrier coverage was similar to the regional average (Edwards 1995, 200).

Apart from state-led promotion of private industry, the Pérez administration (1974–79) envisioned a national project called La Gran Venezuela. The cornerstone of this vision was the heralded Fifth National Plan (1976–80), which was to set Venezuela on a path of a more pronounced state-owned, enterprise-led, natural-resource-based "big push" heavy industrialization policy. In addition to the nationalization of the oil and iron ore industries in 1976, numerous public enterprises were expanded in heavy industries (steel, aluminum, bauxite, petrochemicals, oil refining, and hydroelectric power) to provide inputs for domestic industry, in an attempt to vertically integrate the import-substitution process and to accelerate the technological capacity and diversification of the industrial and export structure (Karl 1982, 194–208). The industrial state holding, Corporación Venezuelona de Guyana, was responsible for managing natural-resource-based industrialization, and the national oil company, Petróleos de Venezuela, was responsible for the expansion and modernization of oil refining.

The big-push (NRBI) project marked a purposeful effort to expand the role of the state in direct production.[9] With the nationalization of oil in 1976 and the development of non-oil state-owned enterprises, the state became the main producer in the economy, the largest generator of foreign exchange, and the largest employer. The main objective of the NRBI was to diversify the export structure of the economy and to "deepen" the manufacturing sector by increasing the share of intermediate and capital goods production.

The other important trend to note over this period is the dominance of the public sector as the main exporter. While the nationalization of oil and iron ore had established the state as the main exporter in the economy in 1976, state-owned enterprises were also significant in the generation of aluminum, steel, and chemical exports (state-owned enterprises accounted for 95 percent of aluminum exports, 45 percent of steel exports, and 20 percent of chemical exports). By the period 1993–95, the public sector was responsible for 83 percent of total exports and 36 percent of non-oil exports. Thus the gradual shift toward large-scale, high-value-added technology was also a shift toward technology that was more state-owned.

In sum, the evidence broadly supports the notion that a big-push development strategy occurred over the period 1965–73. Continued growth became more challenging in that the industries with import-substitution possibilities—namely, intermediate and capital goods—are characterized by increasing scale economies. Further industrialization involved greater risks and required more selective targeting of capital for longer periods as new expertise had to be acquired and new markets captured. This would be especially true for the traditional industries. Conquering export markets in consumer goods is a risky and long-gestating project that requires marketing, investment in distribution channels, and increases in scale economies. The declining import coefficients in traditional industries meant that further growth there would require export-led growth. At the same time, this section has also established that the relative share of large-scale, heavy-industrial investments dominated the industrial strategy from 1973 onward.

A Revisionist Political Economy of Manufacturing Performance in Venezuela, 1958–2003

The historiography of economic analyses on Venezuela has identified changes in development strategies in the period 1965–73. Yet some of these analyses assume that the growing centralization of the state and the development of state-led big-push strategies necessarily produce, on the one hand, dysfunctional rent-seeking, cronyism, and corruption; and on the other hand, an increase in dynamic inefficiency of the economy. Venezuelan policymakers in the 1970s can be accused of switching development strategies too early by adopting an unrealistically complicated and ambitious industrial strategy in the context of a relatively underdeveloped manufacturing sector in 1970. While this may explain the increases in both capital intensity and inefficiency of investment for at most a decade, it does not explain why Venezuela's growth rate continued to decline for *more than two decades after* the early 1980s, when the big-push investments had been largely completed. The coincidence of a change in development strategy with a decline in growth is thus not inevitable, but rather a *historically specific* feature of the Venezuelan political economy in the period 1980–2003.

Convincing explanations of relative performance have to identify which features *distinguish* Venezuela from more rapid growing latecomers with similar institutional interventions, or similar or greater levels of corruption; and why rapid growth in the period 1920–80 in Venezuela evolved into slower growth and prolonged stagnation over most of the period 1980–2003. What distinguishes Venezuela from more successful cases of big-push industrialization in the period 1980–2003 is not principally the degree or scale of corruption or industrial concentration, but the nature of political strategies and settlements that underpinned the transition and consolidation of its democratic regime. The rich political science literature on Venezuela emphasizes that the Venezuelan party system formed the focal point of democratic transition and consolidation in the period 1958–98. It is well-known that this party system mobilized support through purposeful pacts and clientelist patronage that mobilized and accommodated a growing urban populist alliance (Levine 1973; Karl 1986).

I suggest an alternative explanation to the reigning approaches, one that incorporates the *economic* consequences of the growing and increasingly *factionalized political* contests between and within political parties attempting to build political clienteles and accommodate middle-class groups, emerging and established family-run conglomerates, and labor unions competing for access to centrally allocated state resources. In particular, I argue that the slowdown in growth and productivity has been caused by the *incompatibility* of populist clientelist accommodation with the requisites of a "big push" development strategy. The nature of the incompatibility was a growing political fragmentation and discontinuity in coalitions underpinning the state at precisely the time when the development strategy called for more centralized state control and continuity in policy orientation. While there is no doubt the suddenness with which Venezuela switched strategies in 1973 contributed to the pressure placed on state and private sector capacities, the *prolonged* stagnation of the Venezuelan economy still requires explanation.

Populist and clientelist accommodation has been manifested in Venezuela through well-known patterns of excessive entry into industry, excessive white-collar employment patronage in state enterprises, contradictory and rapid changes in regulations, and volatile and (politically) aggressive competition among factions of capital allied to different political patrons. The political rationale of maintaining populist support negatively affected the ability of the state to be selective in the disbursement of rents and to discipline rent recipients. Massive levels of capital flight in the 1970s and 1980s and the proliferation of unviable and contradictory subsidies and price controls were an important manifestation of the political failure of the party system to contain conflicts.

Periodization of Political Settlements and the Development of Populist Clientelism in Venezuela

The nature of the political settlement changes dramatically in the post-1958 period. The most important change that occurs is the transition to and consolidation of democracy. The purpose of this section is to suggest how the political nature of the democratization process was to affect the efficiency of rent-deployment processes and macroeconomic management. While centralized rent deployment is maintained during the democratic period, the motivations of the leadership changes dramatically as the social support base of the state and the grounds for what becomes a legitimate distribution of rents changed. The changing nature of the state will come to affect negatively the ability of state leaders to manage the rent-deployment process in line with the economic challenges that come with the switch to big-push NRBI. In particular, the nature and logic of the Venezuelan polity as it evolved disrupted the ability of the state to maintain *selectivity* in industrial promotion and made *disciplining* rent recipients (particularly capitalists in the private manufacturing sector, public enterprise managers, and public sector labor unions) difficult. Moreover, the increasing intensity of electoral rivalry further damaged *continuity* in policy and implementation, which had devastating consequences for economic efficiency. One of the principal processes accompanying electoral rivalry was a growing factionalism within and between the main two political parties. As result, both state–business relations assumed a growing factionalism and cronyism that undermined collective efforts at industrial restructuring.

   According to the vast political science literature, the Venezuelan party system and the types of broad state–society relations that developed in relation to the political parties fall into four distinct periods. The first is the period 1928–48, which saw the development of a radical populist mobilization of peasant leagues, labor unions, and middle-class groups challenging the dominant military, landed, and commercial elites. The second period refers to the era of pacted democracy in the period 1958–73, when the system of radical populist mobilization evolves into a more conciliatory and consensus-based system—or what Rey (1991) refers to as the system of elite conciliation. In the period, 1973–93, the system of pacted democracy breaks down as right-wing and left-wing threats to democratic regime fade and are replaced by a system of two-party populist electoral rivalry, one where factionalism and particularistic clientelism become the dominant forms of political competition. The period 1993–98 witnesses the decline in legitimacy of the two leading political parties, AD and COPEI, and is thus characterized by the increase in electoral rivalries. The emergence of multiparty coalitions supporting candidates independent of the two previously hegemonic parties characterize this period, which results in the election of Hugo Chávez in 1998. The period 1999–2003 marks the rise of antiparty politics, polarization of political contestation, and collapse in state–business cooperation.

The origin of the system of populist mobilization and conciliation that brought to power a brief, radical, democratic junta in the period 1945–48 and formed the multiclass, populist basis of democratic transition was a long-gestating historical process (Rey, 1991). The battle cries of the Venezuelan populist mobilization were democratization, economic nationalism, and social justice (Powell 1971, 28; Levine 1973, 1978; Karl 1986; Ellner 1999), which generated significant *populist political inclusion* not uncommon in Latin America (Di Tella 1970; Cardoso and Faletto 1979).[10]

Accíon Democrática was the most successful political party leading the mobilization of the populist clientelism. AD's defined itself as a multiclass nationalist coalition whose mission was to unite the "masses" against the landed oligarchy and the foreign oil companies. The organizational strength of AD and other political parties forced the creation of a military–civilian junta in 1945 that introduced electoral politics to Venezuela. The ensuing three-year period, known as El Trienio Adeco, marked the decisive introduction of mass politics into national life. The trienio period brought long-lasting changes. Suffrage was significantly expanded from 5 percent of the population to 36 percent in 1945 (Kornblith and Levine 1995, 42). Elections in 1946 brought AD to power with a landslide electoral victory. In three years, AD raised the number of organized peasant members from 3,959 to 43,302 while increasing the number of labor unions from 252 to 1,014 (Powell 1971, 79). AD legislated wage raises and subsidies for consumer goods. Real wages (in 1957 bolivars) increased from 7.15 Bs. in 1944 to 11.71 Bs. in 1948 (Hausmann 1981, 323). Labor union mobilization increased, as witnessed in the increase in the number of labor dispute petitions and strikes, which increased from 15 and 4 respectively in the period 1936–45 to 203 and 70 respectively in the period 1945–48! State spending in education, health, water, and communications were extended for the first time to poor, socially excluded groups and regions (ibid., 313–56).

The greatest legacy of the trienio period, however, was the bitter conflicts that ensued over the radical reforms attempted by AD. As Levine (1989, 252) notes,

"It is hard to overstate the depth of the changes *trienio* politics brought." Radical labor reforms and an extensive program of agrarian reform were introduced by an AD elite that did not perceive the need, given its electoral dominance, to consult other organized groups on its plans. Economic and social elites began to fear that the radical politics introduced would destroy long-standing privileges and the previous social order. Opposition gathered on the right, represented by the Catholic Church, the new Christian democratic party COPEI (Committee for the Political Organization and Independent Election), conservative elements in the military, U.S. oil companies, domestic business groups, and the U.S. embassy (Karl 1986, 205–6; Kornblith and Levine 1995, 42–43).

The three-year experiment with democracy gave way to a decade of repressive authoritarian rule. Under the leadership of General Marcos Pérez Jiménez, AD was banned. Labor, agrarian, and educational reforms were revoked, labor unions were repressed, and more concession-friendly policies toward oil companies were instituted. Political opposition in the period 1948–57 was crushed violently (Kornblith and Levine 1995, 43–44). The experience of the trienio was to have a profound effect on the nature of political strategy in the post-1958 era of democratic transition and consolidation.

THE ERA OF PACTED DEMOCRACY, 1958–1968

The focal point of democratic transition was the 1958 Punto Fijo Pact, which provided the institutional mechanisms of consensus building and cooperation between the dominant political party, AD, and the leading opposition party, COPEI. These two leading political parties' dominance of economic, social, and cultural aspects of Venezuelan society in the democratic era have led some to characterize the Venezuelan polity as a "partidocracia"—that is, a "partyarchy" or "party system" (Coppedge 1994; Kornblith and Levine 1995, 37–38).

The transition to a consolidated democratic system in 1958 was accompanied by significant changes in the nature of the political settlements and economic policymaking in Venezuela. Political change in 1958 was driven by the lessons political actors perceived from the failed attempt at democracy during the trienio. The main lesson most leaders of AD, COPEI, and Unión Republicana Democrática (Democratic Republican Union Party, or URD) drew from the trienio was that polarization (*acting without building consensus*) and the alienation of powerful minorities would lead to the return of authoritarian rule. Accompanying the willingness of AD to reach compromise, there was substantial public pressure among powerful interest groups to *limit the power of AD* in the likely event of new elections.

The *preservation of democratic rule* became the *primary political objective* of political party leaders. The perception among party cadres, unions, and business groups that there was a need to *secure the fragile alliance* for democracy profoundly shaped the actions of political leaders. The recognition that the army, the oil companies, and traditional dominant business groups were capable of unraveling democracy produced what Rey (1986) has called their "obsessive preoccupation" with appeasement and accommodation. This concern with fragility was met through both formal and informal negotiated compromises.

Political science and historical studies on Venezuela have emphasized that the democratic regime has been maintained by a series of political pacts and clientelist links that were an important part of building multiclass and (largely) urban populist alliances (Karl 1986; Levine 1973; Rey 1991). AD emerged as the fundamental party.[11] This party system may be characterized as a polity where processes of contestation, conflict resolution, and corruption have been accommodated through populist clientelism.

The viability of the populist and clientelist pact depended on balancing co-optation and accommodation of middle- and working-class demands. A telling indication of the change in balance of political power that the pacts sustained can be seen in the patterns of social spending in the three decades following 1958. One of the key strategies of the political parties to build middle- and working-class clientele was to increase the scope of social spending. The increase in social spending became one of the main areas for delivering jobs and services to the middle- and lower-income groups, and was important for pre-empting more radical demands for distribution. The shifts in the composition of public spending are dramatic when compared with the era of authoritarian rule in the twentieth century. As Kornblith and Maignon (1985, 205) demonstrate, social spending (which includes health, education, water and sanitation, and housing) as a percentage of total state spending grew from an annual average of 11.4 percent under Pérez Jiménez to 28.1 percent in the period 1958–73. Between 1969 and 1973, the years immediately preceding the oil boom of the 1973, it averaged 31.4 percent of total spending.

The main legacy of the pact was to institutionalize a centralized form of political clientelism where the political parties were the main channels of patronage. In terms of rent deployment, the pact re-enforced the central role of the executive in setting agendas, making policy, and implementing both. A key component of the pact was that regardless of who won the elections, each party was guaranteed some access to state jobs and contracts, a partitioning of the ministries, and a complicated spoils systems that would ensure the political and economic survival of all signatories, which included the main labor unions federations, Condeferación de Trabajadores de Venezuela (CTV) and the main umbrella business association, Federación Venezolana de Cámaras y Asociaciones de Comercio y Producción (FEDECAMARAS).[12]

In effect, the decision to divvy up ministerial posts and deploy resources to meet *political criteria laid the seeds of politicizing the public administration and allocating rents because of political rather than economic criteria.* The consolidation of populist support was to depend on tangible patronage, which AD (and eventually COPEI, its main rival after 1958) was to provide. For this reason, clienetelism took the form of material benefits provided by a political patron in exchange for political support and loyalty on the part of a client, where such support can take the form of campaign financing, campaigning, but more usually just voting for the party the patron represents. The patronage has taken many forms, both legal and corrupt. These include cheap investment credit, tariff protections, import licenses, employment opportunities in the public sector, housing and mortgage credits, and price controls on basic consumer goods.

The era of pacted democracy did not eliminate regime *fragility.* Many left-wing groups, including the Communist Party and radical elements within AD, were demanding a radical social program. Ideological disputes over the "exclusionary" nature of the pacts had two major political costs. One was that AD suffered three damaging splits in 1960, 1962, and 1967, which cut deeply into its electoral strength (Coppedge 1994, 54–56, 98–103) and was to underlie the factionalism and divisions that were to plague AD in the three decades after 1958 (Ellner 1999, 104). Second, the left turned to armed political insurgency in the period 1960–67. While the exclusion of the left reassured business and the military, "the success of the Pacto de Punto Fijo cost Venezuela the largest guerrilla movement in Latin America" (Przeworski 1991, 91).

While the basis of political clientelism and the dominance of *political* criteria in distributing rent deployment were laid with pact making, the threats from right-wing and particularly left-wing groups re-enforced, in the first decade after 1958, the need to use resource rents to build political clientele through centralized and disciplined and centralized party structures. The threats to regime survival were, according to political analysts, the main factor behind the avoidance of factionalism and tension inherent in the alliance of populist clientelism and the proliferation of subsidies and rules that were to plague the polity in the post-1968 era (Karl 1986; Kornblith and Levine 1995). As Levine (1978, 98) points out, "More than any other single factor, the development of a leftist strategy of insurrection in the early 1960s consolidated democracy by unifying centre and right around AD in response to a common threat." The maintenance of stable macroeconomic rules (e.g., stable fixed exchange rates, low inflation, and fiscal balance) and generally rapid (though slowing) economic growth was a manifestation of the stable and legitimate central public authority in this period.

FACTIONALISM AND ELECTORAL RIVALRY, 1973–1998

The nature of populist clientelism changes gradually after 1973. The *pactismo* of the first decade gave way to electoral party rivalry and factionalism between and within parties. Several political observers note that the very consolidation of the regime, the defeat of the guerrilla movement, and thus the decline in threats to the regime reduced the urgency for reaching consensus in the pact-making process (Rey 1991, 557–67; Kornblith and Levine 1995, 48–58; Levine and Crisp 1995, 227–32). The growing importance of factions and factionalism between and within political parties is well documented in Venezuela for the period of 1968 through the mid-1990s (Rey 1991; Coppedge 1994).

Several distributive conflicts accompanied the growing factionalism of the pacted democracy. The first concerned increases in labor conflicts. The AD-dominated Congress initiated more radical labor laws and encouraged a more combative labor movement. As a result, both COPEI administrations (1969–74, 1979–84) were plagued by large-scale labor conflict, which increased the polarization and political instability in the country (Gelb 1988, 289–325; Coppedge 1994, 34).

The second important distributive conflicts occurred within business conglomerate groups tied to different political factions. The nature of the AD splits in the 1970s were based on the growing rift between the old guard of AD led by its founder, Rómulo Betancourt, who favored links with the traditional family conglomerates and a more limited state role in production; and Carlos Andres Pérez, who led a faction demanding a more radical state program based on more public enterprise production, and most important, the financing of an emerging set of smaller-scale entrepreneurs to challenge the economic dominance of the more established family conglomerates. These rifts within AD can indeed be traced back to some of the same groups that led the split from AD in the early 1960s (Ellner 1999).

Rapid changes in patronage and policy, and contestations to those changes, were most evident in the first administration of Carlos Andres Pérez (1974–79). In this period, growing factionalism within AD—between the old guard headed by the former president Betancourt, and the new guard headed by Pérez—came to the fore as Pérez used the massive state resources to provide subsidies to and procurement for projects for an emerging set of family groups who were well-known campaign contributors to the president (Coppedge 2000). The economic groups close to the Perez administration were popularly known as the "twelve apostles," many of whom came, like Pérez, from the Andean region.

The ties between Pérez and the apostles were forged largely during his acrimonious power struggle to assume the AD presidential candidacy, when Pérez's own isolation in AD and lack of control over the party hierarchy convinced him of the necessity of establishing a power and financial base outside the party machinery. For Pérez and his faction of AD, the apostles represented an attempt to democratize capital by breaking the hegemony of traditional large family business groups.

The third dramatic conflict that characterized the post-1968 era concerned the increasing rejection from important factions of the big business community and the rival political party, COPEI, over growing role of state production in the economy. As noted elsewhere, the Perez administration sought to make state-owned enterprises the focal point of the big-push natural-resource-based industrialization strategy. The increased role of the state in the "strategic" sectors of the economy (oil, iron ore, steel, petrochemicals, hydroelectric power, bauxite, aluminum) represented an important disruption one of the main political rules of the game, which specified that the state should facilitate private sector investment in industry through tariff protection and subsidized long-run credit. The post-1973 era saw the state challenging the private sector in industrial production (Araujo 1975).

Overall, factionalism led to an increased contestation over patronage, which in turn fueled a greater degree of politicization and political polarization in the era of two-party electoral rivalry. If the Pérez faction of AD has wanted to redress the dominance of the old oligarchy, many other factions within AD and COPEI and within the business associations challenged the rise of new oligarchies in the private sector (e.g., the twelve apostles) and the rise of the state enterprise oligarchy within the state. As such, it is not surprising that Ellner (1985, 38–66) finds a breakdown of interparty agreement in the period 1976–80 compared with the period 1967–71. Moreover, other political analysts have argued that the increase in political factionalism was accompanied by an increase in whistle-blowing and the use of the corruption scandal in the 1980s and 1990s as a weapon of political competition (Capriles 1991; Pérez Perdomo 1995; Karl 1997, 138–85).

It is worth noting that the *coincidence* of oil nationalization in 1976 and the very large increase in fiscal resources due to the oil booms undoubtedly upset the political balance in the country. In particular, it could be argued that this disrupted interparty relations, and thus fueled increasing factionalism, as competing interest groups vied to capture power in an increasingly state-centered economy. The political pacts were formed and consolidated in the 1960s, a period of relatively stable (and even declining) oil export earnings. As a result, the state was more dependent on private sector investment (including foreign) to achieve economic growth. The oil nationalization likely lessened the counterweights (i.e., checks and balances) to the state, and thus perhaps lessened the "sense of limits" as to the use of discretionary centralized authority. This reduction in the sense of limits probably increased the abuse of power and made corruption less predictable and more contentious as a result.

Finally, the divisive manner in which economic liberalization was introduced in 1989 further fueled factionalism within AD and between AD and other parties (see Di John 2005). The decline in economic growth and increase in poverty led to a further decline in the legitimacy of political parties, and the emergence of "outsider" politicians running on anti-establishment political party platforms. This led to the formation of unstable multiparty coalitions in the period 1993–98, which contributed to a further decline in the continuity of policymaking.

THE EMERGENCE OF MULTIPARTY ELECTORAL CONTESTATION, 1993–1998

The subperiod 1993–98 represents a decline in the two-party hegemony, as economic decline and the divisiveness of economic liberalization led to dissatisfaction with the two main parties. Several factors contributed to this. The first (and perhaps most important) factor was the decisions of the two most popular and influential leaders of Venezuela's two main parties—Carlos Andres Perez (AD) in 1989, and Rafael Caldera (COPEI) in 1993—to distance themselves from their parties. Both leaders seized on crises to re-invent themselves as political outsiders. They did so with political messages and platforms that were the opposite of what they and their respective parties had established over the previous forty years. Dramatic policy switches have been shown to be a destabilizing event for fragile democracies (Stokes 1999). The decision of Perez, leader of AD, to implement neoliberal reforms using nonparty technocrats was detrimental in two ways. First, Perez's party-neglecting strategy (Corrales 2002) accentuated factionalism within AD, and made implementing reforms politically contentious. Many AD party members blocked reforms in Congress and ultimately supported the impeachment of Perez. Many AD members of Congress and of the Central Electoral Committee of AD considered Perez's actions a betrayal on two fronts: one for implementing neoliberal policies, and two for naming very few AD party members to the cabinet. Second, the launching of a neoliberal economic system went against the set of policies and symbols that defined AD's legitimacy for decades. AD became the fundamental party as a champion of the working class and peasants, and built its reputation (however tarnished it had become) by advocating and implementing state-led developmentalism, anti-imperialist struggles, and economic nationalism. Neoliberal reforms launched by AD's most established politician divided what AD stood for in the minds of their militants and sympathizers. The loss of AD's party identity most likely contributed to the significant decline in party identification through the 1990s.

Rafael Caldera lost the nomination of the party he founded, COPEI, in 1993, to Oswaldo Alvarez Paz, one of the emerging regional politicians created by decentralization and direct state elections (legislated in 1989). Caldera runs and wins with a loose coalition of small left-wing parties under the umbrella of the new "party" Caldera founds, Convergencia. Convergencia's main ally in government would be the Movimiento al Socialismo (MAS), which was an established, though small, left-wing party.

The short rise of Convergencia had serious consequences for the cohesion and legitimacy of the party system, hitherto controlled by AD and COPEI. First, Caldera's victory served an important signaling effect, making it clear that the presidency can be obtained by running outside traditional party affiliation. Second, Caldera split the COPEI vote, and thus divided what was a solid center–right organized alternative to AD and civil society. COPEI did not survive this fracture of its middle-class and business support. Third, this period sees a growing proliferation of political parties competing for the presidency and Congress. With the rise of Convergencia and the Causa R (a labor union alternative to AD), representation of the center–left vote becomes divided between these two "parties" at both the national and regional elections. In the period 1973–88, the number of effective parties averaged 2.5 for the presidency and 3.3 for the Congress. In 1993, the number of effective parties competing for the presidency rises to 5.6 and the number of effective parties in Congress rises to 5.6 as well, though AD and COPEI remain the two largest parties in both chambers.

The very negative and disappointing experience of government in the Caldera administration (1994–98) further undermined the legitimacy of the party system. Caldera *was*, after all, trying to govern with political party input (including a rapprochement with AD), as opposed to Perez, who was convinced that AD, and the party system generally, was moribund. First, Caldera inherited one of the worst banking crises in 1994 (see Di John 2004) and exacerbated the situation by shutting down the largest bank, Banco Latino, which was owned by an economic group close to the previous Perez administration (see Rodríguez 2002). Second, there was a growing incoherence in state ministries as Caldera tried to accommodate the fractious coalition. There was no clear and coherent economic strategy. For example, there were *four* economic plans initiated in Caldera's government and a large rotation of ministers (De Krivoy 2002).

Third, introduction of political decentralization and fiscal federalism in the early 1990s also contributed to the fragmentation and loss of party discipline in the two main parties in the democratic pact, AD and COPEI. According to Penfold-Becerra (2002), the post-1989 reforms that initiated direct election of mayors and governors and led to the devolution of state spending to states and municipalities, lowered the barrier to entry of marginal and emerging parties and encouraged politicians within the two main parties to develop local alliances and assert autonomy from national party bosses. Decentralization, in the context of rapid economic reforms and economic crisis, along with relentless media coverage of corruption scandals concerning the state and political parties, provided opportunities for marginal but strong parties such as MAS, but more importantly, embryonic and structurally weak political "parties" such as Causa R and Proyecto Venezuela, and later MBR-200, to compete electorally at the state level.

The emergence of federalism drastically changes the alliance strategies followed by political parties. AD, COPEI, and MAS all developed alliance-bloc systems as a strategy to protect their regional leaderships (Penfold-Becerra 2002). In 1989, AD established alliances with an average of 2.18 parties per state for the twenty-two gubernatorial elections. By 1998, AD allied with an average of 7.5 parties per state. In 1989, COPEI established an average of 5.57 alliances with parties, and 9.0 by 1998. The electoral premium COPEI obtained from these alliances rose from an average of 7 percent in 1989 to 20.6 percent in 1998. In 1998, Chávez's party, Movimiento Quinta Republica (MVR), was gaining strength at the regional level and by 1998, on the coattails of Chávez's victory, won 17.7 percent of the governorships. What is telling about these regionally based parties is that their growth never expanded to the national level in terms of party organization. In sum, this period is characterized by a growth of multiparty completion and the fragmentation of the party system, which reduced the possibility of effective coordination of government policies.

THE RISE OF ANTIPARTY POLITICS AND GROWING POLARIZATION
OF POLITICS, 1999–2003

The failure of the political parties to meet economic challenges, along with the growing polarization that neoliberal reforms unleashed, opened the space for the emergence of a political outsider. During the electoral campaign of 1998, Hugo Chávez and the MVR campaigned on an anti-corruption, anti-neoliberal, anti-political establishment discourse that called for the transformation of the political system and the constitution. The promise for a Constituent Assembly provided the focal point of Chávez's electoral pledge. Growing levels of poverty, and the policy switch to a neoliberal agenda (in the form of the Agenda Venezuela) during the Caldera administration, severely reduced the popularity and legitimacy of the traditional political parties. The MVR refused to make any alliances with traditional parties; instead, the MVR constructed a broad alliance with new and alternative movements, which together became known as the Polo Patriótico (Patriotic Pole, PP). The MVR was the electoral organization of Movimiento

Bolivariano Revolucionario-200 (Bolivarian Revolutionary Movement 200), or MBR-200, which was the political and social movement that Hugo Chávez founded in 1982 and represented the core set of political leaders and decision-makers. The MVR was designed to protect the fragile structure of the MBR-200 from the unpredictability of the electoral process (López Maya 2003). MBR-200 leaders did not want their ideological orientation compromised by the real politics of constructing electoral alliances. The fragility of anti-politics originates here in the divorce of economic and political programs from economic and political organizations.

The rise of Chávez owes much to the effectiveness of his radical anti-party, anti-corruption, and anti-oligarchy discourse. The rise of this radical anti-party politics has generated several important tendencies that have weakened the capacity of the state to revive economic growth. First, the radical nature of the political discourse has led to a growing polarization of politics. The period 2002–3 saw numerous massive street demonstrations both supporting and resisting the Chávez administration, highlighted by a two-month national strike, which included the nearly complete shutdown of the oil industry. Relations between the state and big business have been more antagonistic than at any time in the democratic era. Second, there has been a deinstitutionalization of political organizations. The 1999 constitution banned financing of political parties, which limits the organizational strength of the opposition. Moreover, the administration has limited the organizational development of its own party, which is itself subject to intense factionalization. These factors lessen the possibility of consensus building and cooperation (Monaldi et al. 2004).[13] Third, there has been a purposeful strategy to circumvent state institutions in the delivery of social services.[14] The administration has set up several government missions to improve education, health, and housing in shantytowns. But these missions, funded by resources from the state oil company, are executive-led and bypass state ministries in their planning and implementation phases. This has created a dual state structure that has led to further fragmentation, despite an increase in the centralization of power. Fourth, there is a lack of any coherent production or export strategy. Much of this has to do with the antagonistic relationship Chávez has maintained vis-à-vis many big business groups (though relations have improved as Chávez has consolidated power after the 2004 referendum). Another important factor is the ideology of chavismo, however, which is focused on supporting small-scale businesses and cooperatives through micro-credit schemes and, most important, an emphasis on social programs as the cornerstone of government policy. This strategy makes Venezuela more dependent on oil. The next section examines the economic effects of the changes in political settlements and strategies in the period 1958–2003.

*The Economic Effects of Populist Clientelist Pacts and Factionalism
in the Context of "Big Push" Development Strategies, 1973–2003*

The implications of these historical patterns of state–society relations characterized by the populist clientelism, pact making, and, increasingly, factionalism and political polarization, have been profound. The priority of preserving democracy meant that political party and state leaders needed to accommodate the growing factions of the populist coalition in the pacted democratic era. The viability and long-run weakness of the political pacts were that they provide economic rents to those groups in return for political support. While pacts are offered to protect embryonic democratic institutions from pressures to which they may not respond, the feasibility of pacts depend on partners extracting private benefits, or rents from democracy (Przeworski 1991, 87–94). In effect, pacts were to generate monopoly privileges for the recipients of rents. Extensive rents were awarded to the family conglomerate capitalists in the form of subsidies and protection (Naím and Francés 1995). The strategy of "excessive avoidance of conflict" and the need to keep the "insider" groups quiescent meant that selectivity in rent deployment and the discipline of rent recipients declined significantly.

The first effect of clientelist and populist spending can be seen in the dramatic increase in state employment. The capital-intensive nature of industrialization in Venezuela meant that, in the context or rapid urbanization, high urban unemployment could be destabilizing for the regime. The number of nonfinancial public enterprises grew from less than thirty in 1958 to more than four hundred by 1985 (Segarra 1985, 132). Since 1941, when the political parties began to establish their power, the use of employment patronage becomes an important vehicle for building political clientele.

The growth of state salaried employees increases in absolute terms throughout the period 1941–94. Further, the share of state salaried employees in total salaried employment increases from just 7.1 percent in 1941 to 31.1 percent in 1971, and peaks at 39.2 percent in 1981 (Di John 2009, 243). The strength of the clientelist patterns of patronage are also evident in the first four years of the economic liberalization period (1989–94), when retrenchment of a bloated state bureaucracy was one of the goals of the economic reforms. This period does not see any retrenchment at all; rather, there is an increase in the absolute number of state employees from 1.14 million in 1998 to 1.17 million in 1994, and the share of state salaried employees increases from 30.4 percent to 32.0 in 1994 (ibid., 243).

The development of patronage networks to build middle-class clientele can also be seen in the significant increase in real current public spending. As indicated in table 11.3, the share of public investment in total government spending declines steadily in the period 1950–98.

Table 11.3   Growth and composition of real public spending in Venezuela, 1950–1998

	Total real public spending (annual average, 1984 Bs., billions)	Composition of public spending (investment as share of total, percentage)
1950–57	22.7	46.8
1958–73	54.5	34.5
1974–88	113.5	21.3
1988–98	119.5	17.7

SOURCES: Based on OCEPRE (various years); Banco Central de Venezuela, *Statistical Series* (various years).

The decline in the share of public investment in total public spending from a peak of 46.8 percent in the period 1950–57 to a low of 17.7 percent in the period 1989–98 owes principally to the growth in personnel expenditure in state enterprises (Karl 1997, 104) and to interest payments on the external debt. In the period 1958–73, the share of interest payments averaged less than 1 percent of total current spending. In the period 1974–88, that share increased to nearly 20 percent, and rose to an average of 25 percent in the period 1999–98. The main negative economic consequence of the increase in current spending is that the public investment rate could have been much higher given the increase in real public spending over the period 1950–98.[15]

A second important economic effect of populist–clientelist politics on industrial performance was the lack of state disciplining of private or public sector rent recipients in the post-1958 period. Despite the centralizing and legitimating effect the threats to the regime played, the splits within AD were to have a longer-lasting negative effect on the ability of the state to deploy rents efficiently. The splintering of AD weakened the support base of the natural governing party and its allies in the state. As a result, state decision-makers could not afford to antagonize the core supporters of the regime, which were the political party cadres, the main business groups, and the labor unions. It is thus not surprising that there was little evidence of the state using selective targeting in subsidization and protection policy; nor was there much evidence of effective monitoring and disciplining of those firms that received state support (World Bank 1990; Naím and Francés 1995). Poorly performing firms never had their subsidies removed. This indicates that the state was not placing any sort of performance criteria as a condition for state support. ISI was as much a political project of buying in support of business groups and employment creation for the urban middle class, as it was an economic project to diversify the production and export composition of the economy.

A third effect of the populist clientelism was the lack of selectivity in the deployment of rents to emerging conglomerate groups. The proliferation of subsidies was a by-product of the politics of state–business relations. The division of business groups along shifting factional lines was to characterize the politics of big business from the early 1970s onward (Naím 1989). This factionalism affected the dynamics of state–business relationships in several ways. First, there was a noticeable increase in the fragmentation of business associations, not only between large-scale and smaller firms but also between the larger firms within the same sector (Corrales and Cisneros 1999; Coppedge 2000). As a result, industrial restructuring and state–business consultative groups were ineffective in the post-1968 era (Naím and Francés 1995).[16] A corollary result of this fragmentation was a growth in particularistic bargaining between business leaders and political party leaders and ministers in charge of dispensing licenses and subsidies. One of the main channels of influencing was through campaign financing, which became decisive to electoral victory as Venezuelan elections in the era 1973–93 were among the most expensive in the developing world (Coppedge 2000). The growing reliance on campaign financing and personal favors in the context of fluid factional changes meant there was little collective action among business groups, no performance criteria imposed by the state, a growth in the proliferation of licenses and subsidies based on political rather than economic criteria, and a growth in the insecurity and risk in the business environment. In an environment where there was insecurity in the policy of government and little export activity, rapid diversification of factories and products became the most effective means to spread risk among conglomerates in order to achieve long-run survival (Naím 1989). Thus overdiversification was generated both from political party strategies to build clientele and from business group defensive strategies to diversify risk in a rapidly changing and uncertain policy environment.

Some evidence to indicate the lack of selectivity in industrial policy can be seen in the level of firm entry in the Venezuelan manufacturing sector. Despite the widespread knowledge of the growing relative saturation of the internal market, the period 1961–98 witnesses a relatively high level of excessive entry into manufacturing.

Without an explicit export policy, the increase in the granting of protection licenses and subsidies led to overdiversification of products, which in turn generated suboptimal scale economies in plants. Nevertheless, the number of large-scale firms—which made up the vast majority of manufacturing investment and assets, and which appropriated most of state credits—increased 131 percent from 1961 to 1971 and 68 percent from 1971 to 1982! (Di John 2009, 249). More remarkable, the number of large firms increased 26 percent despite declines in medium-sized firms. The number of large-scale firms declined by 28 percent, the largest drop of any firm category in the liberalization period (1989–98), indicating the unviable nature of many of these enterprises, which in turn suggested that credits and licenses were awarded more on political than economic criteria (Di John 2009, 248–54). What is also notable is that the increasing polarization and instability of politics in the period 1999–2003 has led to a significant reduction in the number of firms of all sizes, and particularly small enterprises.

Another indicator of the lack of selectivity can be seen in the proliferation of protectionist policies. Historically, import restrictions have played a more important role in protecting domestic manufacturing sectors in Venezuela. There is clear evidence that there has been a significant proliferation of import licenses within subsectors over time. Between 1939 and 1960, 35 tariffs were subject to import licensing. By 1969, the number of tariff items subject to import licenses reached 599 (World Bank 1973, 24). By 1989, the number of tariff items subject to import restrictions increased to 5,749! (World Bank 1990, 16). In historical perspective, the period 1920–58 is characterized by a much more limited extent of protectionism in manufacturing than is in the period 1958–89. (See Di John 2009 for a discussion of the political economy factors behind more liberal trade policies in the period 1940–57).

The drop in the number of large-scale firms in the era of economic liberalization is an indication of the inefficiency of state policies in the disbursement of rents in the period 1971–88—in other words, the weakness of the private sector to invest productively. Too many large-scale firms with suboptimal scale and over-diversification of products were subsidized. Table 11.4 traces the evolution of the decline in the number of firms as classified by firm size and industrial sector in the period 1988–98.

The sectors are ordered according to the percentage decline in number of *large-scale firms* in the period, beginning with the sector where that percentage decline is smallest.

In the period 1988–96, the overall percentage fall in the number of large-scale firms was 28 percent. The decline in the number of firms is least pronounced among the state-controlled capital-intensive sectors (steel, aluminum, and industrial chemicals), which are also the sectors where productivity levels dropped the least in the 1990s (table 11A.3 in the appendix). This reflects the higher political costs of closing down state-run firms in a clientelist polity, but also the greater potential viability of these sectors. Aluminum and steel became the second- and fourth-largest exports in the country in the 1990s. But there was a much larger drop in sectors controlled by the *private* owners, reflecting the weakness of private sector productive capacity. The intermediate capital-intensity sectors (transport equipment, metal products, and electrical machinery) that were more prominently promoted in the "big push" phase dropped 36.7 percent, 40.9 percent, and

Table 11.4   Evolution in number and scale of firms in selected Venezuelan manufacturing sectors, 1988–1998

| Sector | Total | Firm size | | | |
		Large	Medium–large	Medium–small	Small
All manufacturing	9.4	−28.1	−20.6	−3.4	21.0
Iron and steel (371)	34.9	−6.7	14.3	25.0	63.2
Nonferrous metals (372)	−23.3	−14.3	57.1	−50.0	−28.6
Printing/publishing (342)	−11.1	−25.7	−55.9	−4.3	−8.3
Chemical products (352)	12.5	−26.2	11.1	−12.5	61.0
Plastics (356)	−27.5	−29.3	−16.3	−28.8	−29.1
Transport equipment (384)	33.3	−36.7	−33.3	−63.1	92.1
Metal products (381)	−1.5	−40.9	−32.6	−5.6	4.2
Textiles (321)	17.1	−44.8	0.0	8.3	65.6
Electrical machinery (383)	1.7	−52.6	−25.8	6.1	46.9
Other manufacturing (390)	−0.6	−56.3	0.0	−44.4	28.0
Wearing and Apparel (322)	−19.0	−64.9	−48.6	−33.8	−6.5
Wood products (331)	66.0	−73.3	−62.5	−4.5	102.8

SOURCE: Based on Oficina Central de Estadística e Informática (various years).

NOTE: Figures in the table represent percentage change in number of firms, 1988–1996. "Large" refers to firms with more than 100 employees; "medium–large" refers to firms with 51–100 employees; "medium–small" refers to firms with 21–50 employees; "small" refers to firms with 5–20 employees.

52.6 percent, respectively. The clothing sector, a labor-intensive activity, which has experienced some of the most fractious relations among producers in the textile business association, also experienced a dramatic decline of 64.9 percent in the number of firms.

It is plausible to argue that the decline in the number of firms could be due to other factors beyond those posited in this section. The fact that many large firms failed after liberalization can be symptomatic of excessive protection or simply of the fact that they had been set up under expectations of economic growth that were not realized. The latter explanation is relevant but not inconsistent with my analysis. The creation of firms under very protectionist conditions in the period 1974–88 was the result of an explicit policy of patronage. The number of large firms actually *increased* (for reasons of political patronage) in the 1980s *despite* the slowdown in manufacturing growth compared to the 1970s. Second, the non-oil growth rate of the economy in the period 1990–98 is actually *greater* than in the 1980s (see table 11.1), so the dramatic reduction in the number of large firms cannot necessarily be attributed to declines in growth rates alone. What is true is that the reduction in tariff and non-tariff protection in the 1990s (a policy that challenged patronage patterns) weeded out many of these unviable firms, though high real interest rates and the banking crisis of 1994 clearly affected the ability of many large firms to survive, particularly in the context of less protection.

The decline in the number of large firms is also consistent with the hypothesis advanced by Bello and Bermúdez (in this volume, "The Incidence of Labor Market Reforms on Employment in the Venezuelan Manufacturing Sector, 1995–2001") that labor legislation became significantly biased against large firms. This explanation is not inconsistent with the analysis presented here. While economic liberalization challenged traditional clientelist patronage patterns, not all the influencing of the state was eliminated in the 1990s. It is well-known that the banking sector was still influential in preventing financial deregulation (De Krivoy 2002). Similarly, labor unions and their allies (particularly in AD and in Convergencia) remained sufficiently influential to enact labor legislation that increased the labor costs of firms. It is no accident that these laws affected the large firms more in the 1990s, since the bulk of the formal sector facing increased international competition resided in large firms. This resulted, as Bermudez and Bello argue, in both downsizing and closure of plants. What is not explained (and remains and interesting research topic) is why owners of industrial assets were unable to prevent this unfavorable legislation, or more generally, why the financial sector seemed able to protect its interests to a greater degree than did the large-scale manufacturing sector. This trend has extended well into the Chávez period.

One of the more damaging effects of the proliferation of unviable firms is the very high and increasing levels of excess capacity in industry maintained throughout the post-1968 period. Sustained levels of excess capacity represent dynamic inefficiencies in capital allocation and use. For the years when excess capacity data is available, there has been a noticeable decline in aggregate capacity utilization from 67 percent in 1966 to 60 percent in the period 1985–88, reaching a low of 44 percent in 1988 and increasing to 55 percent in 1991—still very low considering that year saw the fastest growth rate in manufacturing growth (12.2 percent) of any year in the period 1980–98 (Di John 2009, 252–54).

The sectoral breakdown of excess capacity in large-scale firms is also very revealing of the great costs of the failure of industrial policy under big-push industrial strategies. Many of the intermediate and capital goods sectors had higher levels of excess capacity than the overall level in manufacturing. For instance, in the period 1985–88, average manufacturing capacity utilization was 60 percent whereas many heavy and industrial sectors—such as chemical products (44 percent), metal products (51 percent), nonelectrical machinery (39 percent), electrical machinery (54 percent), and transport equipment (38 percent)—were considerably lower. In the liberalization period, all these sectors remained below overall capacity utilization rates, with transport equipment falling to 12 percent and 22 percent capacity utilization in 1990 and 1991. Again, the capacity utilization of the state-dominated sectors (iron, steel, and aluminum), while nowhere near full capacity, is better than the overall average. In 1985–88, 1990, and 1991, capacity utilization in iron and steel was 71 percent, 62 percent, and 67 percent, respectively while capacity utilization in aluminum was 71 percent, 70 percent, and 69 percent, respectively. Again, exporting in these sectors has been instrumental in keeping utilization rates higher than the average for the manufacturing sector.

The inefficiency of overdiversification can also be seen in the number of unviable small- and medium-sized firms that were created in the period 1971–88.[17] The average capacity utilization rates of the small- and medium-sized firms were lower than large firms for all the years under consideration: 48 percent in 1966, 45 percent in 1985–88, 34 percent in 1989, and 38 percent in 1990–91. Capacity utilization rates within many of the heavy industrial sectors, such as iron and steel (35 percent), nonferrous metals (48 percent), metal products (35 percent), nonelectrical machinery (26 percent), electrical machinery (35), and transport equipment (27 percent), were either near or far below an already low small- and medium-sized firm average. In the liberalization period, all these sectors, except for nonferrous metals, remained below overall capacity utilization rates in 1990 and 1991.

Finally, the overdiversification of products and firms in a range of industrial sectors have played an important part in the weakness of technological capacity of firms. For an infant industry characterized by economies of scale, large volumes of sales and output are necessary to spread fixed costs and accumulate learning (Kim and Ma 1997, 122). As a result, unrestricted or excessive entry leads to the development of too many firms and too small a plant size. Overdiversification becomes a constraint on the development of research and development activities, since suboptimal size results in an annual turnover per firm too small to undertake the risks and costs involved in directing resources to R & D. For Venezuela, Viana (1994, 128–29) suggests that the period 1975–90 is marked by relatively low levels of R & D spending in the manufacturing industry in comparison with other Latin American economies, which, on average, direct fewer resource to R & D than do late industrializers in other regions.[18]

In a survey of six hundred large-scale manufacturing firms (defined as having one hundred employees or more) conducted in 1992 and 1993, only 19 percent reported that they dedicate any resources to "innovative activity" (which in the survey includes R & D spending, production process assessment, changes in machine design, and product innovation) in the period 1980–92, compared to the Latin American average of 27.9 over the same period. Viana also noted that the limited degree of endogenous technological capacity owes mainly to the small size of firms, which limits the possibility of most to assume the costs and risks of R & D spending. The effect of political fragmentation and uncertainty also has inhibited the development of long-run technical cooperation, or cooperation in issues related to the "supply chain," between firms in the same sector. As a result, there is no evidence of significant cooperation between firms and state-run technology institutes (ibid., 175, 165–68).[19]

A fourth negative effect of factionalism is the increase in the perception of risk of industrial investors. The increasing risk that accompanied factionalism thus saw a long-run reduction within the private banking system of commercial loans to industry. The share of commercial loans to industry as a percentage of loans to all sectors declines steadily over the period 1963–98. That share averaged 29.6 percent in the period 1963–73; declining to an average share of 19.0 percent in the period 1974–88; only to fall further to an average share of 16.8 percent in the period 1989–98 (Di John 2009, 240). The longer gestation and thus higher risk of industrial ventures was becoming less attractive over time. This result is consistent with the general collapse of private sector investment in the non-oil economy in the period 1980–98. Here again, economic liberalization has not arrested the long-run increase in factionalism and related distributive conflicts.

The main contention of this section is that the failure of the state to impose conditions and selectivity in rent deployment and coordinate investment efforts will be more costly in the big-push and advanced stage of ISI. The growing mismatch between political and economic strategies in the period 1958–98 had broad economic effects.

The negative effect of populist clientelism on state efficiency in rent deployment is reflected in the productivity performance of the manufacturing sector over time. Productivity growth lies at the heart of dynamic and competitive growth. The *incompatibility* of the populist clientelism with more demanding development strategies ultimately were reflected in declines in manufacturing growth from 1980, and varying percentage declines in productivity levels of all Venezuelan manufacturing sectors compared with the United States and other more successful late developers from the mid-1980s (see Appendix).

Conclusion

The inefficiency of centralized rent deployment in Venezuela in the period 1980–2003 owes less to natural resource abundance per se than to an incompatibility of economic and political strategies. The argument does not deny that sudden and large inflows of oil revenues in the 1970s had a negative effect on economic management in Venezuela; rather, it claims that a longer-run view of Venezuelan economic history suggests that oil abundance has been compatible with cycles of growth *and* stagnation.

Due to the abundance of oil, Venezuela was long considered an "exceptional" case in the context of twentieth-century Latin American development. This chapter revises that conclusion. First, while Venezuela did not manage the sudden inflows efficiently in the 1970s, no Latin American economy has been able to manage sudden capital inflows without undergoing substantial macroeconomic destabilization (Palma 1998). The slowdown in Venezuela's manufacturing growth in the period 1980–2003 is part of a wider slowdown in growth throughout Latin America in the same period. The wider Latin American experience, as well as the fact that a very small set of latecomers have actually sustained catching-up with advanced industrial economies, suggests that patterns of failure in Venezuela may not be so "exceptional" after all.

Explaining the growth slowdown as a mismatch of economic strategy and historically specific political strategies improves on existing explanations that emphasize political institutions or distributive struggles as the source of Venezuela's poor economic performance. The political science literature focuses on the extent to which Venezuela's political party system and state institutions became more factionalized, exclusionary, rigid, and corrupt over time. However, the focus on political institutions is unable to explain why some more authoritarian/exclusionary (and similarly corrupt) regimes grew faster than did Venezuela in the period 1980–2003. The focus placed in the Venezuelan political science literature on the level of political competition and the extent to which demands are channeled through democratic procedures may be less important issue than who is capturing the state and for what ends.

The political analyses on the party system do not examine whether maintaining legitimate rule is affected by the changing nature of the economic development strategy. If different strategies require different levels of selectivity and concentration of economic and political power to be initiated and consolidated, then the problem of legitimacy and inclusiveness cannot be adequately examined as isolated from economic strategy. If economists often fail to incorporate politics when examining the state intervention, then political scientists often fail to examine the political challenges that different technologies and stages of development generate. The growing factionalism of the Venezuelan polity, I argued, was particularly costly in terms of the efficiency of investment *because* it occurred in the context of the more advanced stage of development, which requires a greater centralization and coordination of investment. The growing proliferation of subsidies and licenses to Venezuelan firms in the period 1965–98 also suggested that the Venezuelan state, far from being exclusionary, was *too inclusionary and unselective* in its patronage patterns for it to produce an effective industrial strategy in the more advanced stage of ISI. Without examining the mechanisms through which conflict emerges, there is little scope for identifying which changes in either economic strategy or political settlements are needed to bring the polity closer to a less conflict-ridden bargaining outcome among relevant political actors.

APPENDIX: VENEZUELAN WAGES, PROFITABILITY, AND PRODUCTIVITY IN COMPARATIVE AND HISTORICAL PERSPECTIVE

Tables 11A.1, 11A.2, and 11A.3 provide comparative and time series evidence on wage levels relative to the U.S. level, productivity levels relative to the U.S. level, and profitability in Norway, Venezuela, Colombia, Chile, South Korea, and Malaysia for nine manufacturing sectors of varying degrees of capital intensity over the period 1970–97 (or the latest year for which comparative data is available). Following data on the capital intensity of different manufacturing sectors in the United States during the 1980s provided by Chandler and Hikino (1997, 46–50), I have divided the nine manufacturing sectors into three categories: (1) labor-intensive sectors (textiles, clothing, and footwear), which are presented in table 11A.1; (2) intermediate capital-intensive sectors (nonelectrical machinery, electrical machinery, and transport equipment), which are presented in table 11A.2; and (3) capital-intensive sectors (iron and steel, nonferrous metals, and industrial chemicals), which are presented in table 11A.3.

The comparative and disaggregated evidence in tables 11A.1–3 illuminate some important tendencies in the Venezuelan manufacturing sector in the period 1970–97, but do not provide much support for the expensive exchange rate/wage argument. The period 1970–85 does indeed indicate that Venezuela was a *relatively high-wage economy*. Venezuelan wages in all sectors were higher than were all the developing countries in this period, and indeed closer to the level of Norwegian wages than to the levels of the East Asian economies.

Table 11A.1 Relative wages, productivity, and profitability in labor-intensive manufacturing sectors: Venezuela in comparative and historical perspective, 1975–1995

	Textiles						Clothing						Footwear					
	1970	1975	1980	1985	1990	1995	1970	1975	1980	1985	1990	1996	1970	1975	1980	1985	1990	1996
Wages (annual wage per employee)																		
Norway	0.58	1.00	1.09	0.81	1.27	1.29	0.63	1.48	1.35	0.88	1.50	1.56	0.62	1.11	1.23	0.84	1.34	1.43
Venezuela	0.45	0.58	0.64	0.54	0.21	0.11	0.37	0.76	0.68	0.54	0.20	0.13	0.36	0.43	0.64	0.46	0.16	0.13
Colombia	0.18	0.16	0.23	0.18	0.11	0.18	0.13	0.15	0.19	0.16	0.10	0.17	0.12	0.12	0.20	0.18	0.11	0.16
Chile	0.24	0.14	0.37	0.19	0.19	0.34	0.26	0.22	0.45	0.23	0.22	0.89	0.30	0.17	0.38	0.22	0.20	0.40
South Korea	0.07	0.10	0.21	0.19	0.43	0.62	0.09	0.13	0.31	0.23	0.49	0.74	0.10	0.12	0.24	0.24	0.48	0.69
Malaysia	0.07	0.10	0.15	0.16	0.15	0.23	0.07	0.13	0.15	0.16	0.16	0.24	0.10	0.14	0.17	0.17	0.14	0.25
Productivity (value added per employee)																		
Norway	0.61	0.77	0.77	0.50	1.01	0.79	0.57	0.83	0.88	0.55	0.88	0.82	0.52	0.77	0.85	0.50	0.78	0.75
Venezuela	0.61	0.82	0.67	0.26	0.27	0.26	0.61	0.68	0.67	0.48	0.18	0.36	0.29	0.41	0.51	0.39	0.16	0.20
Colombia	0.34	0.30	0.48	0.40	0.37	0.36	0.20	0.17	0.29	0.20	0.15	0.21	0.15	0.16	0.25	0.24	0.19	0.27
Chile	0.46	0.34	0.57	0.38	0.30	0.38	0.49	0.33	0.72	0.43	0.30	0.55	0.55	0.41	0.83	0.35	0.31	0.40
South Korea	0.12	0.20	0.29	0.28	0.46	0.80	0.12	0.14	0.28	0.23	0.47	0.84	0.14	0.15	0.24	0.27	0.60	0.81
Malaysia	0.10	0.16	0.21	0.18	0.19	0.31	0.10	0.12	0.16	0.13	0.14	0.18	0.09	0.22	0.17	0.10	0.12	0.22
Profitability (1 minus wages in value added, percent)																		
Norway	47.8	32.6	31.7	30.7	30.4	32.5	41.0	27.2	25.2	29.2	28.0	27.2	36.0	24.4	35.8	26.3	26.9	22.5
Venezuela	59.8	62.8	54.3	60.3	66.4	82.2	66.9	55.5	50.8	50.7	65.3	85.7	32.2	45.2	44.4	48.7	57.1	74.1
Colombia	70.6	73.5	77.2	77.9	86.5	79.9	66.9	64.4	67.1	64.8	70.3	69.8	56.5	61.7	56.7	67.0	75.4	75.5
Chile	77.8	77.8	68.8	75.8	72.5	63.5	70.2	73.5	69.0	75.8	69.2	37.4	70.9	78.1	40.7	72.2	72.9	59.3
South Korea	64.7	71.4	64.7	66.8	60.0	68.1	60.9	60.5	60.1	56.6	55.8	66.2	56.2	54.6	62.2	60.7	65.9	65.3
Malaysia	57.6	65.4	63.7	58.0	65.8	70.1	59.1	54.0	53.8	43.8	48.9	49.3	40.2	66.5	66.5	57.8	50.0	53.3

SOURCE: Based on United Nations Industrial Organization (various years).

NOTE: Wages and productivity relative to U.S. level.

Table 11A.2　Relative wages, productivity, and profitability in intermediate capital-intensive manufacturing sectors: Venezuela in comparative and historical perspective, 1975–1997

	Nonelectrical machinery						Electrical machinery						Transport equipment					
	1970	1975	1980	1985	1990	1997	1970	1975	1980	1985	1990	1996	1970	1975	1980	1985	1990	1997
Wages (annual wage per employee)																		
Norway	0.51	0.94	1.03	0.69	1.15	1.01	0.56	0.94	1.07	0.70	1.12	1.13	0.46	0.79	0.79	0.49	0.86	0.89
Venezuela	0.22	0.35	0.37	0.31	0.12	0.08	0.32	0.40	0.46	0.35	0.15	0.12	0.35	0.40	0.47	0.32	0.13	0.06
Colombia	0.13	0.10	0.13	0.10	0.06	0.11	0.12	0.10	0.16	0.14	0.09	0.14	0.11	0.09	0.13	0.12	0.08	0.12
Chile	0.21	0.12	0.42	0.30	0.24	0.42	0.26	0.15	0.48	0.30	0.24	0.35	0.21	0.12	0.25	0.15	0.12	0.24
South Korea	0.06	0.09	0.18	0.16	0.34	0.48	0.06	0.08	0.16	0.14	0.32	0.45	0.08	0.11	0.18	0.16	0.39	0.40
Malaysia	0.08	0.10	0.13	0.14	0.12	0.17	0.11	0.10	0.11	0.12	0.10	0.17	0.09	0.09	0.13	0.13	0.11	0.15
Productivity (value added per employee)																		
Norway	0.46	0.72	0.72	0.49	0.69	0.57	0.52	0.77	0.68	0.45	0.63	0.53	0.41	0.54	0.52	0.28	0.54	0.42
Venezuela	0.50	0.41	0.45	0.38	0.18	0.18	0.50	0.52	0.49	0.41	0.20	0.17	0.50	0.57	0.58	0.35	0.15	0.36
Colombia	0.21	0.16	0.20	0.17	0.11	0.14	0.25	0.21	0.34	0.26	0.20	0.16	0.22	0.29	0.25	0.20	0.22	0.19
Chile	0.28	0.24	0.37	0.18	0.19	0.33	0.58	0.53	0.55	0.45	0.44	0.41	0.33	0.26	0.54	0.27	0.22	0.35
South Korea	0.07	0.11	0.20	0.22	0.48	0.60	0.12	0.14	0.19	0.24	0.46	0.68	0.14	0.16	0.23	0.24	0.52	0.66
Malaysia	0.08	0.16	0.18	0.17	0.19	0.23	0.22	0.18	0.16	0.17	0.12	0.17	0.13	0.13	0.19	0.18	0.24	0.24
Profitability (1 minus wages in value added, percent)																		
Norway	42.7	38.0	27.5	34.9	28.8	36.2	43.0	50.2	30.8	55.7	30.8	40.4	39.0	49.5	23.2	19.5	30.1	28.2
Venezuela	76.4	59.5	73.5	63.0	72.2	84.4	66.5	61.5	58.9	61.8	70.9	80.6	62.1	64.0	58.2	58.7	63.0	94.2
Colombia	68.1	71.5	77.0	73.0	76.9	73.2	73.6	76.3	79.0	76.3	82.6	75.9	74.8	83.5	72.7	72.6	84.6	79.3
Chile	62.0	75.0	25.5	24.6	46.3	54.0	76.5	85.7	61.2	71.0	78.9	76.4	65.3	77.5	76.4	74.4	76.5	76.4
South Korea	59.8	60.2	65.7	66.5	69.3	71.0	69.7	72.6	63.7	74.1	72.9	81.2	67.5	63.7	60.3	69.3	67.8	79.3
Malaysia	54.1	66.8	73.2	62.4	72.5	72.8	74.3	71.9	68.7	68.4	69.2	73.4	62.3	60.1	66.0	67.1	81.2	78.1

SOURCE: Based on United Nations Industrial Organization (various years).

NOTE: Wages and productivity relative to U.S. level.

Table 11A.3 Relative wages, productivity, and profitability in capital-intensive manufacturing sectors: Venezuela in comparative and historical perspective, 1975–1996

	Iron and steel						Nonferrous Metals						Industrial chemicals					
	1970	1975	1980	1985	1990	1996	1970	1975	1980	1985	1990	1996	1970	1975	1980	1985	1990	1995
Wages (annual wage per employee)																		
Norway	0.48	0.80	0.80	0.58	0.96	0.95	0.54	0.93	1.51	0.75	1.20	1.27	0.47	0.86	0.88	0.56	0.97	0.93
Venezuela	0.43	0.38	0.37	0.42	0.23	0.25	0.39	0.46	0.46	0.41	0.20	0.20	0.25	0.45	0.52	0.36	0.16	0.18
Colombia	0.12	0.10	0.14	0.15	0.08	0.15	0.13	0.11	0.13	0.17	0.09	0.16	0.16	0.14	0.20	0.17	0.11	0.16
Chile	0.32	0.13	0.27	0.26	0.22	0.41	0.35	0.15	0.42	0.37	0.30	0.63	0.24	0.12	0.39	0.23	0.22	0.33
South Korea	0.08	0.10	0.31	0.18	0.46	0.51	0.08	0.10	0.17	0.20	0.48	0.53	0.09	0.12	0.20	0.17	0.36	0.52
Malaysia	0.10	0.11	0.13	0.13	0.13	0.17	0.14	0.18	0.16	0.12	0.13	0.20	—	—	0.15	0.12	0.19	—
Productivity (value added per employee)																		
Norway	0.55	0.90	0.70	0.52	0.61	0.52	0.79	0.83	1.11	0.92	1.12	0.99	0.40	0.49	0.56	0.43	0.54	1.49
Venezuela	0.56	0.49	0.41	0.53	0.24	0.44	0.59	0.63	0.47	0.98	0.74	0.72	0.32	0.32	0.38	0.45	0.20	0.39
Colombia	0.22	0.20	0.37	0.41	0.39	0.34	0.25	0.16	0.29	0.45	0.36	0.25	0.23	0.24	0.31	0.26	0.17	0.25
Chile	0.68	0.51	0.73	0.66	0.47	0.56	5.70	0.16	2.79	3.13	3.00	0.81	0.23	0.26	0.36	0.36	0.37	0.41
South Korea	0.14	0.32	0.81	0.54	0.91	1.13	0.10	0.14	0.26	0.10	0.52	0.27	0.15	0.18	0.29	0.32	0.44	0.57
Malaysia	0.20	0.20	0.21	0.22	0.27	0.60	0.17	0.14	0.25	0.09	0.18	0.27	—	—	0.20	0.21	—	—
Profitability (1 minus wages in value added, percent)																		
Norway	51.7%	54.1	45.0	41.4	31.0	31.9	68.0	50.9	71.5	61.0	54.5	55.1	63.3	56.4	57.8	62.8	62.6	88.5
Venezuela	57.0	60.0	37.1	64.3	58.7	79.0	69.4	68.8	74.8	80.0	88.7	90.2	74.8	64.4	80.1	77.2	83.3	91.4
Colombia	68.6	71.9	79.1	80.9	90.7	82.6	75.2	69.3	88.9	81.9	89.3	77.8	77.9	85.1	87.2	81.7	86.9	88.0
Chile	74.0	87.0	79.4	79.1	79.3	72.5	97.1	97.6	95.9	94.3	95.8	99.1	67.7	88.5	89.9	81.6	87.7	85.0
South Korea	70.8	84.3	78.0	82.6	77.7	82.7	64.3	73.3	71.5	67.9	61.2	77.1	82.3	83.4	77.6	84.7	82.8	82.9
Malaysia	71.4	71.4	66.7	69.0	79.0	89.0	62.3	42.7	70.4	71.7	71.0	74.1	—	—	91.6	—	—	—

SOURCE: Based on United Nations Industrial Organization (various years).

NOTE: Wages and productivity relative to U.S. level.

After 1985, *wages collapse in all nine sectors in Venezuela*, while either increasing or nearly maintaining their levels in all the other countries in 1990 and 1996. Profitability in all nine sectors in Venezuela was higher than in the comparator countries throughout the period and *increased* over time. This implies that the problem of industrial stagnation in Venezuela has not been one of low profitability.

In latecomers, catching up with more productive incumbent producers requires rapid reductions in production costs relative to "best practice" producers (Amsden 2001). In this perspective, a central problem of the Venezuelan manufacturing performance in all nine sectors lies not necessarily in excessively high wages or relatively low profitability, but rather in the inability of these sectors to catch up with the advanced economies by sustaining rapid *productivity* growth (measured by growth in value added per employee). Productivity levels in Venezuela fall in all nine sectors relative to all countries in the sample after 1985. The distinguishing aspect of the Venezuelan capital-intensive sectors (table 11A.3) is that their long-run productivity performance is superior to the less capital-intensive sectors (tables 11A.1 and 11A.2), despite the fact that all three types of sectors experienced wage-level collapses, and experienced similar trends in profitability. The productivity levels of the capital-intensive sectors, while falling after 1985, fall *less* than do the other two types of sectors in Venezuela, and their relative productivity levels compare more favorably vis-à-vis the other late developers in the sample. Despite the relatively more dynamic performance of the Venezuelan capital-intensive sectors, the expensive exchange rate/wage argument cannot explain the comparative evidence on the capital-intensive sectors, since some of the countries, such as Norway, South Korea, and Chile, had even more rapid "catch-up" with the U.S. level despite the fact that Venezuelan wages were falling more rapidly than those in countries and that Venezuelan capital-intensive sectors had similar level of profitability to these latecomers and considerably higher profitability than Norway for the period 1970–96.

NOTES

1. The importance of presenting non-oil growth data cannot be overstated in the Venezuelan case. By presenting non-oil growth data, it is possible to identify that the slowdown in Venezuelan growth was an economy-wide phenomenon and not limited to well-known stagnation in oil production and investment in the post-1965 period. In the period 1957–70, oil production steadily increased and reached a peak of 3.4 million barrels per day in 1970. By 1975, as a result of sustained multinational disinvestment in the period 1957–70, production declined dramatically to 2.4 million barrels per day despite price increases. See Espinasa and Mommer 1992, 112. After 1975, production was restricted since Venezuela, a founding member of OPEC, adheres to the cartel's policy of limiting oil export volumes and production. Oil production stagnated in the period 1975–95, though investment in exploration increased after nationalization in 1976.

2. Findlay and Lundahl (1999) find a generally growth-enhancing role of natural-resource-rich countries in the period 1870–1914. Sachs and Warner (1995) find, in the period 1971–89, that mineral exporters, on average, grow more slowly than the average growth of non-mineral exporters.

3. Dutch disease models are summarized in Corden and Neary 1982; and Neary and van Wijnbergen 1986.

4. According to a World Bank study of the Venezuelan industrial sector, fragmentation of production is viewed as a more serious problem than is concentration. In the automotive sector, for example, as of 1989, there were fifteen assemblers in the market, which fell from 163,000 units in 1982 to 26,000 units in 1989 (World Bank 1990, 52). International standards of efficiency normally require a minimum of 100,000 units per plant, which indicates the degree to which Venezuelan auto plants are suboptimal in size. Other works by Naím (1989; Naím and Francés 1995) do in fact identify the problem of overdiversification and firm size as an important problem for the competitiveness of the Venezuelan industrial sector.

5. For a recent exposition of the "big push" argument, see Murphy, Shleifer, and Vishny 1989. See Rodrik 1995 for an analysis of how specific state policies such as control over credit allocation, tax incentives, trade policy, and "administrative guidance" helped to solve coordination failures in South Korea and Taiwan in the sixties and seventies.

6. Of course, the *duration* of a crisis will depend on the capacity of the state to effectively change institutions, in order to revive investment, growth, competitiveness, and exports. In this respect, East Asian developmental states were more successful than were their Latin America counterparts (Amsden 2001, 253).

7. It is important to note that protectionism becomes more pronounced with the elimination of the trade agreement with the United States in 1972. This treaty prohibited tariffs on imports from the United States.

8. Import licenses were used most heavily for processed food, consumer goods, and transport equipment. Import monopoly licenses were also instrumental in establishing state-owned enterprises in steel, aluminum, and petrochemicals (World Bank 1990, 15).

9. In 1970, state-owned enterprises accounted for 5 percent of manufacturing value added (excluding oil refining). This share rises to 8 percent in 1980, and reaches 18 percent by 1986. When oil refining is included, the corresponding figures are 4 percent, 36 percent, and 42 percent. In 1987, public firms were concentrated in nonferrous metals (largely aluminum), where the state sector accounted for 91 percent of production; iron and steel, where it accounted for 61 percent; and chemicals and petrochemicals products, where it accounted for 45 percent (World Bank 1990, 30). In investment, the public manufacturing investment share (excluding oil refining) accounted for 24 percent of total manufacturing investment in the period 1968–71. In the period 1972–80, the public share rises to 41 percent. Calculations are based on data from Banco Central de Venezuela (various years); and Oficina Central de Estadística e Informática (various years).

10. See Di John 2009 for an analysis of the political-economy processes behind the construction of populist mobilization in Venezuela in the period 1936–48.

11. A fundamental party (a term coined by Gutiérrez Sanín 2003) can be viewed as the natural governing party (in terms of electoral success) as well as the party whose mobilizations and strategies were central to regime founding. The justification for referring to Acción Democrática as a fundamental party in the period 1958–93 is based on the following: (1) AD never yielded its position in this period as the single biggest party in the either the House of Representatives or the Senate; and (2) AD won five of the seven presidential elections.

12. Levine (1973) and Karl (1986) discuss the pact in detail. Pact making was indeed a feature of many Andean countries in the 1950s and 1960s.

13. The factionalization of Chávez's own support base can be seen in the high degree of cabinet instability. In the period 1958–88, cabinet members lasted an average of 2.13 years in their position (in a five-year term). In 1989–93, ministers lasted only 1.4 years, in 1994–99 it increased to 1.8 years, and in 1999–2004 it declined to 1.3 years (Monaldi et al. 2004, 34).

14. Moreover, the Chávez administration does not draw on bureaucratic personnel associated with AD and COPEI, and thus misses some talented pools of labor.

15. As a result, public investment in infrastructure declines from 0.48 percent of GDP in the period 1981–85 to 0.1 percent of GDP in the period 1996–2000 (Rodríguez 2002).

16. Pharmaceuticals, textiles, and auto parts are three sectors where factionalism hindered the development of coherent policies (Naím and Francés 1995, 178). See Coronil 1998, 237–85, for a detailed discussion of factionalism in the auto parts sector.

17. The extent to which an entrepreneur or sector is overdiversified is difficult to identify *ex-ante*. I am defining the term broadly to mean the persistence of a significant portion of plants across manufacturing sectors, operating at suboptimal levels of scale economy during *both* periods of recession and full employment. The widespread occurrence of spare capacity across sectors, which does occur in the context of downturns in demand (i.e., during recessions), does not qualify as overdiversification.

18. Amsden (2001, 277–80) identifies four main problems of manufacturing competitiveness in Latin America in comparison to East Asian economies and India: relatively low levels of scientific research and patenting, a relatively low share of gross national product accounted for by science and technology, and a relatively low share of R & D spending by the private sector and the manufacturing sectors in general.

19. Only ten out of six hundred firms reported that they maintained long-run relations with state-run technology institutes. See Viana 1994, 149.

REFERENCES

Abramowitz, M. 1986. "Catching Up, Forging Ahead, and Falling Behind." *Journal of Economic History* 46 (2): 385–406.

Amsden, A. 1989. *Asia's Next Giant.* Oxford: Oxford University Press.

_____. 2001. *The Rise of "the Rest."* Oxford: Oxford University Press.

Amsden, A., and T. Hikino. 1994. "Staying Behind, Stumbling Back, Sneaking Up, and Soaring Ahead: Late Industrialization in Historical Perspective." In *Convergence of Productivity*, edited by W. Baumol, R. Nelson, and E. Wolff, 285–315. Oxford: Oxford University Press.

Aoki, M., K. Murdock, and M. Okuno-Fujiwara. 1997. "Beyond the East Asian Miracle: Introducing the Market-Enhancing View." In *The Role of Government in East Asian Economic Development*, edited by M. Aoki, H. K. Kim, and M. Okuno-Fujiwara, 1–40. Oxford: Clarendon Press.

Araujo, O. 1975. *Situación industrial en Venezuela.* Caracas: Universidad Central de Venezuela.

Astorga, P. 2000. "Industrialization in Venezuela, 1936–1983: The Problem of Abundance." In *An Economic History of Twentieth-Century Latin America*, edited by E. Cárdenas, J. A. Ocampo, and R. Thorp, 3:205–38. Oxford: Palgrave/St. Anthony's College.

Banco Central de Venezuela. Various years. *Annual Reports.* Caracas.

_____. Various years. *Statistical Series.* Caracas.

_____. 1992. *Statistical Series in Venezuela in the Last Fifty Years.* Caracas.

_____. 1993. *Socio-Labor Statistics of Venezuela, 1936–1990.* Caracas.

Baptista, A. 1995. *Teoría económica del capitalismo rentístico.* Caracas: Ediciones IESA.

_____. 1997. *Bases cuantitativas de la economía venezolana, 1830–1995.* Caracas: Fundación Polar.

Baptista, A., and B. Mommer. 1987. *El petróleo en el pensamiento económico venezolano: Un ensayo.* Caracas: Ediciones IESA.

Betancourt, K., S. Feije, and G. Márquez. 1995. *Mercado laboral.* Caracas: Ediciones IESA.

Capriles, R. 1991. "La corrupción al servicio de un proyecto politico." In *Corrupción y control*, edited by R. Pérez Perdomo and R. Capriles, 29–47. Caracas: Ediciones IESA.

Cardoso, Fernando Henrique, and Enzo Faletto. 1979. *Dependency and Development in Latin America*. Berkeley: University of California Press.

Chandler, A., and T. Hikino. 1997. "The Large Industrial Enterprise and the Dynamics of Modern Economic Growth." In *Big Business and the Wealth of Nations*, edited by A. Chandler, F. Amatori, and T. Hikino, 24–62. Cambridge: Cambridge University Press.

Chang, H. J. 1994. *The Political Economy of Industrial Policy*. London: Macmillan.

Coppedge, M. 1994. *Strong Parties and Lame Ducks: Presidential Partyarchy and Factionalism in Venezuela*. Stanford: Stanford University Press.

———. 2000. "Venezuelan Parties and the Representation of Elite Interests." In *Conservative Parties, the Right, and Democracy in Latin America*, edited by K. J. Middlebrook, 110–38. Baltimore: Johns Hopkins University Press.

Corden, M., and J. P. Neary. 1982. "Booming Sector and De-industrialisation in a Small Open Economy." *Economic Journal* 92 (December): 825–48.

Coronil, F. 1998. *The Magical State*. Chicago: University of Chicago Press.

Corrales, J. 2002. *Presidents without Parties*. University Park: Pennsylvania State University Press.

Corrales, J., and I. Cisneros. 1999. "Corporatism, Trade Liberalization, and Sectoral Responses: The Case of Venezuela, 1989–1999." *World Development* 27 (12): 2090–122.

De Krivoy, R. 2002. *Colapso del sistema bancaria venezolana de 1994*. Caracas: Ediciones IESA.

Demsetz, H. 1997. *The Economics of the Business Firm*. Cambridge: Cambridge University Press.

Di John, J. 2005. "Economic Liberalization, Political Instability, and State Capacity in Venezuela." *International Political Science Review* 26 (1): 107–24.

———. 2009. *From Windfall to Curse? Oil and Industrialization in Venezuela, 1920 to the Present*. University Park: Pennsylvania State University Press.

Di Tella, T. 1970. "Populism and Reform in Latin America." In *Obstacles to Change in Latin America*, edited by C. Veliz, 47–74. Cambridge: Cambridge University Press.

Edwards, S. 1995. "Trade and Industrial Policy Reform in Latin America." In *Policies for Growth: The Latin American Experience*, edited by A. L. Resende, 182–250. Washington, D.C.: International Monetary Fund.

Ellner, S. 1985. "Inter-Party Agreement and Rivalry in Venezuela: A Comparative Perspective." *Studies in Comparative International Development* 19 (4): 38–66.

———. 1999. "The Heyday of Radical Populism in Venezuela and Its Aftermath." In *Populism in Latin America*, edited by M. Conniff, 117–37. Tuscaloosa: University of Alabama Press.

Espinasa, R., and B. Mommer. 1992. "Venezuelan Oil Policy in the Long Run." In *International Issues in Energy Policy, Development, and Economics*, edited by J. Dorian and F. Fereidum, 45–74. Boulder: Westview Press.

Evans, P. 1995. *Embedded Autonomy: States and Industrial Transformation*. Princeton: Princeton University Press.

Findlay, R., and M. Lundhal. 1999. "Resource-Led Growth: A Long-Term Perspective." WIDER Working Paper 162, United Nations University/World Institute of Development Economics Research, Helsinki.

Fitzgerald, E. V. K. 2000. "ECLA and the Theory of Import-Substituting Industrialization in Latin America." In *An Economic History of Twentieth-Century Latin America*, edited by E. Cárdenas, J. A. Ocampo, and R. Thorp, 3:58–97. Oxford: Palgrave/St. Anthony's College.

Gelb, A., and Associates. 1988. *Oil Windfalls: Blessing or Curse?* Oxford: Oxford University Press.

Gutiérrez Sanín, F. 2003. "Fragile Democracy and Schizophrenic Liberalism: Exit, Voice, and Loyalty in the Andes." Draft paper presented to the Crisis States Programme Workshop, Johannesburg, July.

Haggard, S., S. Maxfield, and B. R. Schneider. 1997. "Theories of Business and Business–State Relations." In *Business and the State in Developing Countries*, edited by S. Maxfield and B. R. Schneider, 36–62. Ithaca: Cornell University Press.

Hausmann, R. 1981. "State Landed Property, Oil Rent, and Accumulation in the Venezuelan Economy." Ph.D. diss., Cornell University, Ithaca.

———. 1990. *Shocks externos y ajuste macroeconómica.* Caracas: Banco Central de Venezuela.

———. 1995. "Quitting Populism Cold Turkey." In *Lessons from the Venezuelan Experience*, edited by L. Goodman, J. Forman, M. Naím, J. Tulchin, and G. Bland, 252–82. Baltimore: Johns Hopkins University Press.

———. 2003. "Venezuela's Growth Implosion: A Neo-Classical Story?" In *In Search of Prosperity: Analytical Narratives on Economic Growth*, edited by D. Rodrik, 244–70. Princeton: Princeton University Press.

International Monetary Fund. Various years. *International Financial Statistics.* Washington, D.C.

Jones, L., and I. Sakong. 1980. *Government, Business, and Entrepreneurship in Economic Development.* Cambridge: Harvard University Press.

Kaldor, N. 1966. *Causes of Slow Rate of Economic Growth in the United Kingdom.* Cambridge: Cambridge University Press.

Karl, T. L. 1982. "The Political Economy of Petrodollars: Oil and Democracy in Venezuela." Ph.D. diss., Department of Political Science, Stanford University.

———. 1986. "Petroleum and Political Pacts: The Transition to Democracy in Venezuela." In *Transitions from Authoritarian Rule*, edited by G. O'Donnell, P. C. Schmitter, and L. Whitehead, 196–220. Baltimore: Johns Hopkins University Press.

———. 1997. *The Paradox of Plenty: Oil Booms and Petro-States.* Berkeley: University of California Press.

Karlsson, W. 1975. *Manufacturing in Venezuela.* Stockholm: Almquist and Wiksell International.

Kim, H. K., and J. Ma. 1997. "The Role of Government in Acquiring Technological Capability: The Case of the Petrochemical Industry in East Asia." In *The Role of Government in East Asian Economic Development*, edited by M. Aoki, H. K. Kim, and M. Okuno-Fujiwara, 101–33. Oxford: Clarendon Press.

Kornblith, M., and D. Levine. 1995. "Venezuela: The Life and Times of the Party System." In *Building Democratic Institutions*, edited by S. Mainwaring and T. Scully, 37–71. Stanford: Stanford University Press.

Kornblith, M., and T. Maignon. 1985. *Estado y gasto público en Venezuela, 1936–1980.* Caracas: Universidad Central de Venezuela.

Levine, D. 1973. *Conflict and Political Change in Venezuela.* Princeton: Princeton University Press.

———. 1978. "Venezuela since 1978: The Consolidation of Democratic Politics." In *The Breakdown of Democratic Regimes*, edited by J. Linz and A. Stepan, 26–42. Baltimore: Johns Hopkins University Press.

———. 1989. "Venezuela: The Nature, Sources, and Prospects of Democracy." In *Democracy in Developing Countries: Latin America*, edited by L. Diamond, J. J. Linz, and S. M. Lipset, 88–102. Boulder: Lynne Rienner.

Levine, D., and B. Crisp. 1995. "Legitimacy, Governability, and Reform in Venezuela." In *Lessons from the Venezuelan Experience*, edited by L. Goodman, J. Forman, M. Naím, J. Tulchin, and G. Bland, 247–386. Baltimore: Johns Hopkins University Press.

Lindbeck, A. 1981. "Industrial Policy as an Issue in the Economic Environment." *World Economy* 4 (4): 391–406.

López Maya, M. 2003. "Hugo Chávez Frías: His Movement and His Presidency." In *Venezuelan Politics in the Chávez Era: Class, Polarization, and Conflict*, edited by S. Ellner and D. Hellinger, 73–92. Boulder: Lynne Rienner.

Maxfield, S., and B. R. Schneider. 1997. "Business, the State, and Economic Performance in Developing Countries." In *Business and the State in Developing Countries*, edited by S. Maxfield and B. R. Schneider, 3–35. Ithaca: Cornell University Press.

Mayobre, J. (1944) 1990. "La paridad del bolívar." In *Ensayos escojidos, Volume 1*, edited by Hector Vallecillos and Omar Bello Rodríguez, 43–84. Caracas: Banco Central de Venezuela.

Ministerio de Energía y Minas. Various years. *Petróleo y otros datos estadísticos*. Caracas: Dirección de Economía e Hidrocarburos.

Ministry of Finance. Various years. "Superintendency of Banks, Data Base." Caracas.

Monaldi, F., R. A. González, R. Obuchi, and M. Penfold. 2004. "Political Institutions, Policymaking Processes, and Policy Outcomes in Venezuela." Latin American Research Network Working Paper R-507, Inter-American Development Bank, Washington, D.C.

Murphy, R., A. Shleifer, and R. Vishny. 1989. "Industrialization and the Big Push." *Journal of Political Economy* 97 (5): 1003–26.

Naím, M. 1989. "El crecimiento de las empresas privadas en Venezuela." In *Las Empresas Venezolanas*, edited by M. Naím, 17–55. Caracas: Ediciones IESA.

———. 1993. *Paper Tigers and Minotaurs: The Politics of Venezuela's Economic Reforms*. Washington, D.C.: Carnegie Endowment Book.

Naím, M., and A. Francés. 1995. "The Venezuelan Private Sector: From Courting the State to Courting the Market." In *Lessons from the Venezuelan Experience*, edited by L. Goodman, J. Forman, M. Naím, J. Tulchin, and G. Bland, 165–92. Baltimore: Johns Hopkins University Press.

Neary, P. J., and P. J. van Wijnbergen. 1986. *Natural Resources and the Macro Economy*. Cambridge: MIT Press.

Oficina Central de Estadística e Informática. Various years. *Encuesta industrial (Industrial Survey)*. Caracas.

OCEPRE (Oficina Central del Presupuesto). Various years. *Annual Fiscal Budget*. Caracas.

Palma, J. G. 1998. "Three and a Half Cycles of 'Mania, Panic, and [Asymmetric] Crash': East Asia and Latin America Compared." *Cambridge Journal of Economics* 22 (6): 789–808.

Penfold-Becerra, M. 2002. "Federalism and Institutional Change in Venezuela." Paper presented at the American Political Science Annual Meeting, Boston, August 28.

Pérez Perdomo, R. 1995. "Corruption and Political Crisis." In *Lessons from the Venezuelan Experience*, edited by L. Goodman, J. Forman, M. Naím, J. Tulchin, and G. Bland, 311–42. Baltimore: Johns Hopkins University Press.

Powell, J. 1971. *Political Mobilization of the Venezuelan Peasant*. Cambridge: Harvard University Press.

Przeworski, A. 1991. *Democracy and the Market*. Cambridge: Cambridge University Press.

Rangel. D. A. (1968) 1990. "Una económia parasitaria." *Ensayos escojidos, Volume 2*, edited by Hector Vallecillos and Omar Bello Rodríguez, 53–72. Caracas: Banco Central de Venezuela.

Rey, R. C. 1986. "Los veinticinco años de la Constitución y la reforma del Estado." *Venezuela* 86 (2): 26–34.

———. 1991. "La democracia Venezolana y la crisis del sistema populista de conciliación." *Revista de Estudios Políticos* 74 (October–December): 533–78.

Rodríguez, F., and María A. Moreno. 2009. "Plenty of Room? Fiscal Space in a Resource-Abundant Economy." In *Fiscal Space: Policy Options for Financing Human Development*, edited by Rathin Roy and Antoine Heuty, 399–482. New York: United Nations Development Programme.

Rodríguez, M. A. 2002. *El impacto de la política económica en el proceso de desearollo venezolano*. Caracas: Universidad Santa Maria.

Rodrik, D. 1995. "Getting Interventions Right: How South Korea and Taiwan Grew Rich." *Economic Policy* 10 (20): 53–107.

————. 2004. "Rethinking Growth Strategies." WIDER Annual Lecture 8, World Institute for Development Economics Research, Stockholm School of Economics, Helsinki, November 5.

Rosenstein-Rodan, P. 1943. "Problems of Industrialisation in Eastern and South-Eastern Europe." *Economic Journal* 53 (210/211): 202–11.

Sachs, J., and A. Warner. 1995. "Natural Resource Abundance and Economic Growth." NBER Working Paper 5398, National Bureau of Economic Research, Cambridge, Mass.

Segarra, N. 1985. "Como evaluar la gestión de la empresas públicas venezolanas." In *Empresas del Estado en América Latina*, edited by J. Kelly de Escobar, 131–54. Caracas: Ediciones IESA.

Scitovsky, T. 1954. "Two Concepts of External Economies." *Journal of Political Economy* 62 (April): 143–51.

Stokes, S. 1999. "What Do Policy Switches Tell Us about Democracy?" In *Democracy, Accountability, and Representation*, edited by A. Przeworski, S. Stokes, and B. Manin, 98–130. Cambridge: Cambridge University Press.

United Nations Industrial Organization. Various issues. *Handbook of Industrial Statistics.* Vienna.

————. Various issues. *International Yearbook of Industrial Statistics.* Vienna.

Vartianen, J. 1999. "The Economics of Successful State Intervention in Industrial Transformation." In *The Developmental State*, edited by M. Woo-Cumings, 200–234. Ithaca: Cornell University Press.

Verdoorn, P. J. 1949. "On the Factors Determining the Growth of Labor Productivity." In *Italian Economic Papers, Volume 2*, edited by L. Pasinetti, 59–68. Oxford: Oxford University Press. Originally published as "Fattori che regolano lo sviluppo della produttiva de lavoro." *L'industria* 1:45–53.

Viana, H. 1994. *Estudio de la capacidad tecnologica de la industria manufacturera Venezolana.* Caracas: Ediciones IESA.

Wade, Robert. 1990. *Governing the Market.* Princeton: Princeton University Press.

Woo-Cummings, M. 1999. "Introduction." In *The Developmental State*, edited by M. Woo-Cumings, 1–31. Ithaca: Cornell University Press.

World Bank. 1973. *Current Economic Position and Prospects of Venezuela.* Washington, D.C.

————. 1990. *Venezuela: Industrial Sector Report.* Washington, D.C.

————. 1993. *The East Asian Miracle.* New York: Oxford University Press.

————. 1997. *World Development Report: The State in a Changing World.* Oxford: Oxford University Press.

Young, A. 1928. "Increasing Returns and Economic Progress." *Economic Journal* 38 (152): 527–42.

12 EXPLAINING CHAVISMO: THE UNEXPECTED ALLIANCE OF RADICAL LEFTISTS AND THE MILITARY IN VENEZUELA UNDER HUGO CHÁVEZ

Javier Corrales

Venezuela under Hugo Chávez experienced a profound change in political regime. Knowing that a severe episode of growth collapse preceded Chávez is perhaps enough to understand why this change occurred: most political scientists agree with Przeworski and colleagues (2000) that severe economic crises jeopardize not just the incumbents, but also the very continuity of democratic regimes in non-rich countries. But knowledge of Venezuela's growth collapse is not sufficient to understand why political change went in the direction of chavismo.

By chavismo, I mean the features that characterize the political regime established by Hugo Chávez Frías after 1999. Scholars who study Venezuelan politics disagree about the best label to describe the Hugo Chávez administration (1999–2013): personalistic, popular, populist, pro-poor, revolutionary, participatory, socialist, Castroite, fascist, competitive authoritarian, soft authoritarian, third-world-oriented, hybrid, statist, polarizing, oil-addicted, Caesaristic, counterhegemonic, an "archipelago in himself," a sort of Latin American Milošević, even a political "carnivore." But there is nonetheless agreement that, at the very least, chavismo consists not simply of a "civilian–military alliance," to quote the man himself (Chávez, Harnecker, and Boudin 2005, 81), but an alliance of radical–leftist civilians and the military (Ellner 2001, 9). Chávez has received most political advice from, and staffed his government with, individuals with an extreme leftist past, a military background, or both. The Chávez movement is, if nothing else, a marriage of radicals and officers. And while there is no agreement on how undemocratic the regime has become, there is a consensus that chavismo is far from liberal democracy. By 2003, it was clear that chavismo, as a political regime, occupied a "gray zone" between democracy and authoritarianism (Coppedge 2003; McCoy 2004).

This chapter focuses on why growth collapse in Venezuela resulted in the rise of a radical leftist–military regime in Venezuela after 1998. As Hellinger (2003) points out, there was nothing predetermined about this outcome. Regime collapse could have resulted in a number of new regimes led by any number of different "contenders."

That growth collapse would lead to the rise and consolidation of a leftist–military ruling alliance seemed hard to predict based on trends in Latin America and even Venezuela at the time. There is no question that leftist–military ruling alliances are not new in Latin America (Remmer 1991), dating back to Cuba in the 1930s, when a young sergeant, Fulgencio Batista, sought to dominate Cuban politics by courting radical leftist civilians (first, student leaders, and then communists). However, since the Omar Torrijos administration in Panama (1968–78), no major episode of electorally successful leftist–civilian–military alliances occurred in Latin America until Chávez. While the economic crises in the 1960s and 1970s led to military regimes in South America, the military thereafter has tended to distance itself from the political sphere (Bustamante 1998), and the left has distanced itself from the military. In the early 1990s, the common response to the economic woes of the region was the emergence of market-oriented administrations. While few of these administrations actually campaigned on a market-oriented platform, they responded to growth collapse by introducing more economic liberalization rather than less. And despite a leftward regional trend in the 2000s, only a few governments (mostly in Bolivia, Ecuador, and Nicaragua) have been as radically leftist as that of Chávez, and even fewer as militaristic.

This chapter argues that to understand the rise of the leftist-civilian military coalition that Chávez cobbled together in 1998–99, one has to understand the story of incorporation of non-dominant political groups in Venezuelan politics starting in the 1960s. Most of the scholarship seeking to explain chavismo argues that the previous regime, the "Fourth Republic" or the "Punto Fijo regime," suffered from excessively exclusionary politics: political institutions became too rigid to give entry to new, smaller, nondominant political forces, which led to accumulated resentment, inability to implement necessary reforms, and, in the end, a strong anti–status quo sentiment by an increasingly large unincorporated sector. The old regime benefited two parties, AD and COPEI, and no one else. According to this view, chavismo was, at its core, a movement designed to break down institutional barriers, propelled by a mushrooming civil society that felt shackled by non-accommodating institutions.

In this chapter, I seek to modify the view of pre-existing institutional rigidity and closure. While some institutions did remain closed and even ossified, the most important story is how many other political institutions actually offered shelter to a number of nondominant forces, which I will call small opposition forces (SOFs). Many of these SOFs were ideologically on the far left. And while most of them were not governing Venezuela, they were not entirely homeless, and in fact often found themselves in propitious institutional environments for growth. These institutional homes were the universities (starting in the late 1960s), the military (starting in the late 1970s), institutions of civil society such as small parties and neighborhood associations (starting in the 1980s), and national and subnational executive and legislative branches of government (starting in the 1990s). It was this degree of institutional sheltering, together with two decades of growth collapse, that explains why leftist SOFs grew in numbers large enough to sustain a new ruling coalition and learned to work with the military to a degree that had few parallels in the region.

This chapter thus applies the argument I develop in Corrales (2008, 2012), following Cleary (2006) and Schamis (2006), that the rise of the left in Latin America in the 2000s is the result of both gripes (i.e., complaints about the socioeconomic status quo) and institutional opportunities. I agree with scholars on Venezuela, who almost unanimously argue that citizens by the late 1990s had ample reasons to vote for an anti–status quo option, but I disagree with those who underplay the institutional openings of the Punto Fijo era.

The second question I address is how the chavista coalition evolved over time. That Chávez succeeded in putting together a leftist–military coalition does not mean it was easy to keep it together for fourteen years. Friction has always existed within the coalition, both between and within civilians and the military, yet Chávez was always able to form cabinets in which leftist civilians and the military worked side by side. While the non-leftist military (the rebels of the Plaza de Altamira, the participants of the 2002 coup, and the many "dados de baja") as well as the nonauthoritarian left (e.g., the MAS) have abandoned the government, the leftist–military alliance survived Venezuela's biggest political crisis ever (the showdown with the opposition between 2001 and 2004) (see McCoy and Diez 2011). Table 12.1 provides just one indicator of the continuity of military influence: the number of military officials in high-level positions in the cabinet remained quite significant through 2008.

Understanding the survival of this coalition requires looking at what some scholars often call coalition-building "toolbox" (Raile, Pereira, and Power 2006). Specifically, presidential coalitions depend on the system of incentives

Table 12.1 Military officers (active and retired) in Venezuelan public office

	Circa 2005	Mid-2008
Governors	9	8
Deputies	8	N/A
Ministers	6	9*
Vice ministers	3	N/A
Directorships within ministries	16	N/A
Directorships of autonomous institutes	15	N/A

SOURCES: 2005 figures from Súmate 2005; 2008 figures obtained by author's review of newspaper articles and *Gaceta Oficial*.

*Includes the vice president.

"N/A" indicates data not available.

and penalties that the executive branch deploys to neutralize dissenters and co-opt allies. These tools give the president the "political glue" to keep allies together (Power 2010).

To glue together a leftist–military alliance, Chávez has had to deal with two different sources of tensions within his initial coalition: (1) the defection of moderate leftists, and (2) divisions within the military. To deal with these cracks, Chávez has deployed both tangible and intangible political resources. Most scholars understand the role that tangible state-based resources (e.g., fiscal spending) play in sealing these cracks. Here, drawing from previous work (Corrales and Penfold 2011), I want to stress that intangible political resources have been just as important in holding Chávez's radical civilian–military alliance together, namely, the deliberate use of (1) polarization, (2) corruption and impunity for supporters, and (3) job discrimination and other legal abuses for opponents. These three political resources are part of the glue that held Chávez's radical–military alliance in place. There were other toolkits in addition to these, mostly in the realm of foreign policy. Because of space constraints, however, I will discuss only the domestic toolkits. (For more on international politics, see Corrales 2009; Corrales and Romero 2013.)

This chapter, therefore, aims to move the debate about the origins of chavismo away from demand-side theories, which treat Chávez's radicalism as responses to what the majorities presumably want. Invoking the demand side is insufficient; it explains the desire for a change in 1999, but not why the change supplied was as radical, as militaristic, and as reliant on polarization, corruption, and discrimination as chavismo has been. To answer these questions, one has to look at the supply side of the coalition partner, and the president's choices of coalition-building tools.

A Look at the First Chavistas

How should one study the composition of the chavista coalition, and especially that of its leadership? What circles of Venezuelan society did Chávez draw from in order to appoint his first round of leaders? To answer these questions, I decided to look at the socioeconomic profile of the first set of leaders who ran under the Movimiento Quinta República (MVR), the party formed by Chávez to run for office in 1998. In an innovative study of the origins of Peronism in Argentina, Aelo (2004) follows a similar research strategy. He looks at the political background of the first set of candidates in the province of Buenos Aires running under the Peronist banner for the general elections of 1946. This exercise allows Aelo to determine the exact origin of Argentina's new "élite dirigente"—whether they were mostly newcomers, conservative, socialist, radicals, renovators, or laborites. Looking at the profile of the first set of leaders in an election provides a window into both the groups that support a new leader and the sectors from which the new leader draws allies.

Following Aelo, table 12.2 provides the political/professional background of every delegate who participated in the 1999 Constituent Assembly. This information has never been reported elsewhere. Because the chavista candidates were very carefully and strategically selected by the incumbent, and more specifically, the executive branch (Penfold 1999; Hawkins 2003; Kornblith 2003), the list offers one look at the sectors that were supporting Chávez, and vice versa. The table reveals, first, that the three largest professions represented were political activists (these are people who had a history of professional political activism) (46.72 percent), those with a military background (15.57 percent), and university professors (19.67 percent). If one includes the professional politicians who also taught part-time at the university, the total percentage for university professors is 32.78 percent.

Second, there were two careers that were significantly underrepresented: labor leaders and economists. In fact, among the chavistas, there were more former guerrillas (three) than economists (two).

The oversupply of university professors, military individuals, and career politicians is striking. It suggests that Chávez drew from a pool of Venezuelan citizens that was not entirely composed of newcomers (given the large number of career politicians) or nonelites (given the large number of attorneys, university professors, and high-ranking soldiers).

I will show that this particular pool—anti–status quo politicians, intellectuals, and soldiers—was large in Venezuela by the late 1990s. And rather than being marginalized and excluded, these groups were well protected by some of the most privileged institutions of the Punto Fijo regime. But before developing these points, I briefly review some of the alternative theories that seek to explain the rise of chavismo.

Table 12.2   Professional profile of delegates to the 1999 Constituent Assembly

	Pro-incumbent		Opposition forces		Indigenous	
	No.	%	No.	%	No.	%
Political activist	57	46.72	4	66.67	2	66.67
Lawyer	10	8.20	2	33.33	—	—
Economist	—	—	1	16.67	—	—
Union activist	3	2.46	—	—	—	—
Misc.	23	18.85	1	16.67	1	33.33
Professor	16	13.11	—	—	—	—
Teacher	1	0.82	—	—	1	33.33
Union leader	1	0.82	—	—	—	—
Former guerrilla	3	2.46	—	—	—	—
Professor	24	19.67	1	16.67	0	0.00
Economics	1	0.82	—	—	—	—
Other	22	18.03	1	16.67	—	—
Chávez's brother	1	0.82	—	—	—	—
Civilian professional	21	17.21	1	16.67	1	33.33
Lawyer	2	1.64	—	—	1	33.33
Singer	1	0.82	—	—	—	—
Business	1	0.82	—	—	—	—
Economist	1	0.82	—	—	—	—
Medical doctor	3	2.46	—	—	—	—
Sociologist	3	2.46	—	—	—	—
Others	9	7.38	1	16.67	—	—
Chávez's wife	1	0.82	—	—	—	—
Military	19	15.57	0	0.00	0	0.00
Military in the 1960s	1	0.82	—	—	—	—
Military in the 1990s	2	1.64	—	—	—	—
"who participated in 1992 coup attempts"	9	7.38	—	—	—	—
Active	5	4.10	—	—	—	—
Retired	2	1.64	—	—	—	—
Data not available	1	0.82	—	—	—	—
Total	122	—	6	—	3	—

SOURCE: Based on author's online searches of Venezuela's dailies, such as *El Universal* and *El Nacional*, with the assistance of Daniel Mogollón.

Rival Explanations

Social Immiseration

The simplest explanation for the rise of chavismo focuses on social immiseration: the idea that chavismo is the natural outgrowth of poverty expansion following growth collapse. According to this view, Chávez is "the vehicle for implementing a more just social order that had been called for by average citizens for decades" (Gibbs 2006, 276). Kenneth Roberts (2003) does a terrific job conceptualizing the grave social deterioration that took place in Venezuela since 1982, encompassing (1) economic immiseration, (2) income inequality, (3) expansion of informality in labor markets, and (4) declining capacity of labor unions to represent workers. Economic hardship combined with a labor representation crisis led to protest politics, and thus to the rise of a leftist replacement. According to this school, the popular sectors wanted a government that addressed the "root causes" of economic poverty—namely, the prevailing "social apartheid"—rather than merely the institutional imperfections of the political system (Lander 2005). Chávez is therefore seen as a response to this demand—the first leader to "talk about pueblo" (Lander 2005) and to "prioritize the demands of the popular sectors" rather than the middle and upper classes, which wanted to focus only on institutional imperfections (García-Guadilla 2005, 114).

The problem with a strictly structural–sociological account as an explanation for chavismo, even supplemented with a focus on labor politics, is not that it is wrong, but that it is indeterminate. It focuses mostly on the demand side (why were citizens willing to vote for messianic politics), but not on the supply side (why was the solution delivered of the leftist–military, semi-authoritarian variety). To be sure, a surplus of poor people explains the Chávez election in 1998, but also the election of (at least) the two previous presidents, Raphael Caldera and Carlos Andrés Pérez—each ideologically different. Since Venezuela has had surplus poverty since the 1980s, all presidents by necessity must have obtained much of the vote of the poor to beat their rivals. Roberts's characterization of Venezuela in 1998 could very well apply to Venezuela ten years before, or for that matter, Latin America as a whole in the late 1980s and early 1990s. Yet it was only in Venezuela in the late 1990s that there was an electoral rise of a radical leftist–military government. Another problem with a demand-based account is that salient policies of chavismo—such as discrimination against dissenters, special privileges to the military and other elites, anti-Americanism, inefficient management of the state sector, and corruption—are not exactly automatic outgrowths of social immiseration.

Institutional Closure

Other scholars explain chavismo by looking at the political institutions of the preceding regime and argue that Chávez mobilized groups that felt unrepresented by existing institutions. The idea that Latin America's democracies were too shallow, unrepresentative, and institutionally exclusionary of new actors became a common complaint of many scholars and citizens across the region in the 1990s. In Venezuela, there is no question that the most significant political institutions— the two large parties, AD and COPEI, and labor unions—were emblematic of what has come to be known as institutions facing a "crisis of representation," losing voters in large numbers since the 1980s (Hagopian 2005; Carothers 2002; Domínguez and Giraldo 1996). A key question to ask about the traditional parties is why they ceased being an option in the mid-1990s, whereas the radical left managed to fill this vacuum by first aligning itself with an old establishment figure such as Rafael Caldera (1994–99) and then with the military under Chávez.

The answer in the literature goes something like this. Venezuela, like the rest of the region, experienced the typical collapse of its statist economic model in the early 1980s (Naim and Piñango 1984). Because the political parties were unable to renew themselves in terms of leadership and ideas (Corrales 2002; Ellner 2003; Molina 2004; Myers 2004), they were unable to provide appropriate policy responses to the economic crises (Kelly and Palma 2004) and to let go of their special privileges (Hellinger 2003). Voters responded as they have elsewhere in the region when macroeconomic conditions collapsed dramatically: they blamed the incumbent parties and existing political institutions (see Remmer 2003 for the region; Gil Yepes 2004 for Venezuela; and Myers 2007), defected toward smaller parties, which in Venezuela were all on the left (Molina 2004), increasingly antiestablishment, and intensely disdainful of the traditional parties (see Schedler 1996 for a definition of anti-establishment). Those who did not find these parties appealing formed or joined institutions of civil society (García-Guadilla 2002; Canache 2004; Salamanca 2004).

The rise of chavismo may thus be explained as the result of two different institutional developments—the rise of extreme, formerly marginal parties at the expense of traditional parties, and the momentous rise of new civic organizations that were more anti-partisan than non-partisan (see Alvarez 2006). By promising to displace the existing parties—in collaboration with the military—Chávez was able to win the support of these two societal blocks.

It may very well be, as some theories argue, that political exclusion breeds radicalism and anti–status quo sentiments. But it does not follow that political inclusion is necessarily an antidote against radicalism. Below I show that in Venezuela, institutions provided refuge to, and actually served as an incubator of, the anti–status quo activists.

The question remains as to why traditional parties failed to offer appropriate policy responses to economic crises in the 1990s. Elsewhere I have argued that the lack of democratic, competitive primaries within the traditional parties, especially AD, created party oligarchies that were unable to adapt and incorporate new knowledge and new blood in the early 1990s (Corrales 2002). What is harder to answer is why the Caldera administration, which was supported by presumably more internally democratic parties such as the MAS, also failed. The explanation could very well be a different variable altogether: the post-1992 rise of party fragmentation—or more broadly, an expansion in the number of veto players, as Monaldi and colleagues (2005) well argue. Party fragmentation and the multiplication of veto players are known to hinder economic governance (World Bank 2002; Inter-American Development Bank 2005). A more adept leader, perhaps one less tied to Venezuela's former bipartisanship, might have been able to better manage party fragmentation (Di John 2004). My contribution to this debate is that the non-adaptability of Venezuela's traditional parties also has to do with their deficit in technical expertise.

Extreme or Aborted Neoliberalism?

Another argument about the rise of the left in Venezuela focuses on the aftershocks of neoliberalism in the 1990s. Students of neoliberalism from different ideological perspectives (e.g., Przeworski 1991; Green 2003; Easterly 2006) recognize that market reforms generate losers, at least in the short term. The losers can mobilize and even stop the reforms. A good example of this argument applied to Venezuela is that of Buxton (2003) (see also Lander 2005). In Buxton's account, Venezuela suffered the ravages of orthodox neoliberal adjustment, first under Carlos Andrés Pérez between 1989 and 1992 and then under Rafael Caldera between 1996 and 1998. She echoes the typical view on the left that market reforms aggravate poverty. The evidence relies on the uncontested findings that the 1990s was characterized by de-industrialization, mostly the result of trade opening, which in turn led to "growing fragmentation and informalisation" of labor markets, which in turn produced the breeding ground for "populist/outsider strategies" (see Di John 2004).

Yet the blame-neoliberalism argument seems overstated, in part because it is not clear that neoliberalism was overwhelmingly applied in Venezuela (Corrales 2002). In terms of fiscal adjustment (i.e., efforts to reduce spending to restore macroeconomic balance), the Venezuelan state did make aggressive attempts on at least three occasions since 1981. But in terms of actual implementation of market-oriented structural reforms, Venezuela was an under-achiever. In virtually no serious index of neoliberalism does Venezuela appear as a far-reaching case. Compared with the most sweeping liberalizers in the region (Argentina, Chile, Bolivia, Peru, Mexico), Venezuela's reforms were haphazard, incoherent, and incomplete. There was trade liberalization, but not banking liberalization. There were privatizations, but only in a few sectors. There were fiscal cutbacks, but not sustained in time to kill inflation. There were no serious pension, labor, fiscal, and education reforms. There might have been prevailing "anti-business" sentiment in the late 1990s, but this was not exactly anti-neoliberal: anger was mostly directed at corrupt or uncaring business elites, rather than at a particular set of policies. (See Gates 2010 for the distinction between anti-business versus anti-neoliberal sentiment.)

More so than neoliberalism per se, it's the "decline" of private sector investment since its peak in the early 1980s and the "instability and inefficiency" of public sector investment that generated high unemployment, and thus poverty (Freije 2003, 172). And this decline was probably the result of factors other than neoliberalism, namely, political instability in 1989 and 1992–93, persistent inflation, the banking crisis of 1994–96, and the exogenous shocks of 1997–99. To be sure, Pérez and Caldera achieved trade opening and a few grand privatizations, but crucial elements of the old statist model (heavy dependence on state investments and oil, labor market rigidities, fiscal volatility, inflation, and rent-seeking) survived through the 1990s. Venezuela's level of private investment in 1998, although greater than in 1989, was still far below that of its neighbors. Nelson Ortiz (2004) adds that, as a result of the 1994–96 banking crisis and the state-heavy response to it, the private sector actually became weaker and smaller than ever. It is thus hard to make the case that neoliberal barons dominated Venezuela in the 1990s. Venezuela's political economy in the 1990s is best described instead as a case of lingering statism, policy volatility, financial collapse, and inability to stabilize oil income streams.

A different version of the blame-neoliberalism argument is to stress precisely the negative effects of erratic (as opposed to full) implementation of market reforms. Venezuela between 1983 and 1998 found itself in a vicious cycle of aborted market reforms. Governments would launch a relatively severe adjustment package only to relax implementation a few years, sometimes months, later, culminating in yet another economic collapse and prompting the subsequent administration to start again. I have called this the ax–relax–collapse cycle (Corrales 2000, 2010). It started with Herrera Campíns, and was repeated by every administration since. The result of erratic neoliberalism from 1983 to 1998 was that Venezuela ended with the worst of both worlds: the adjustment periods produced the negative impact on low-income groups that is typical of adjustment programs at first (unemployment, declines in social spending), and the subsequent abandoning of the reforms precluded any of the economic gains that could have helped low-income groups (sustained growth, greater private investment, lower inflation and thus greater purchasing power for low-income groups). One consequence of aborted reforms was the high level of volatility of public spending as well as real investments per person in the workforce between the 1980s and early 2000s—the general direction of spending and investment was downward, but there were substantial ups-and-downs along the way. This is typical of countries struggling with multiple reform attempts. It is not surprising, therefore, that poverty rates (estimated as the percentage of the population with incomes below the poverty line) ballooned during the 1980s (from 24.3 percent in 1980 to 69.80 percent in 1991) and stayed high throughout the 1990s (see Riutort and Balza Guanipa 2001).

Yet, blaming neoliberalism—even if stated in terms of cycles of aborted reforms—provides only a partial answer to the question of the origins of chavismo. It can explain the overwhelming demand across sectors for a change in politics, but it does not explain the actual change provided. Why did the solution that emerged in 1999 come in the form of a radical leftist–military alliance, as opposed to a social–market leftist government (à la Concertación in Chile), a moderate leftist–labor alliance (à la Lula in Brazil), a moderate leftist–urban alliance (à la Tabaré Vásquez in Uruguay), a center–right alliance (à la Vicente Fox in Mexico or Alvaro Uribe in Colombia), or a right-wing civilian-military alliance (à la Fujimori in Peru). We still need an explanation for the strength of the supply of the radical left and its ties to the military in Venezuela.

Punto Fijo 2.0: The Incorporation of SOFs since the 1970s

To understand the leftist–military alliance cobbled together by Chávez, it is necessary to revisit the story of how the Venezuelan radical left, a small and insubordinate actor in the 1960s, became integrated and sheltered by the institutions of the Punto Fijo regime.

It's well-known that the Punto Fijo regime's founding documents (both the set of pacts and the constitution of 1961) did little to include the Venezuelan radical left. This occurred for two reasons. First, the radical left in the late 1950s and early 1960s was tiny (gathering less than 4 percent of the electorate) and thus had no bargaining leverage vis-à-vis the three larger parties (AD, COPEI, and the URD)

(Corrales 2001). Second, at least one fundamental demand of the radical left was completely objectionable to each of the three larger parties. AD objected to the radical left's pro-Soviet/Cuban foreign policy; the opposition parties—COPEI and the URD—objected to the radical left's call for centralization of power in the executive; and all three parties objected to the radical left's call for banning the private sector. The resulting exclusion of the radical left prompted sectors of the radical left to turn violent, plunging Venezuela into an armed struggle that lasted until 1968.

After 1968, however, SOFs and the radical left were gradually incorporated. Unlike other Latin American countries, where the radical left was repressed, in Venezuela the radical left and the democratic state came to a tacit pact in the late 1960s, according to which the regime opened up opportunities of incorporation in return for the left's abandoning the armed struggle. Landmarks in the political incorporation of the radical left included the legalization of the Communist Party in 1969, a change in Venezuela's foreign policy under Caldera in favor of "reinserting" rather than excluding Cuba from the inter-American community (Romero 2006), the legalization of Movimiento de Izquierda Revolucionaria in 1973, and the founding of the Movimiento al Socialismo (MAS) by former guerrilla leader Teodoro Petkoff in 1971 (a spin-off of the Communist Party). Even in the leading parties, leftist factions found homes. By 1973, for instance, COPEI was internally divided between a more centrist force (the "Araguatos"), a left-leaning faction (the "Avanzados"), and an even more radical wing (the "Astronauts"). President Luis Herrera Campíns came from the leftist Avanzado faction of COPEI (Ellner 2008, 64–71).

By the early 1970s, therefore, the Punto Fijo regime was very different from the Punto Fijo regime of a decade ago. This Punto Fijo regime 2.0 became institutionally hospitable to SOFs. The combination of economic growth and government-sponsored institutional openings after the 1960s encouraged a shift in radical left attitudes in the 1970s from insurrection to integration-seeking (Ellner 1993, 140–43). The MAS developed an official policy of "occasional support for AD and COPEI," intended to gain converts from those parties (Ellner 1986, 93). Both the MAS and the PCV supported Pérez's economic policies during his first administration. Leaders of the radical left even became players at the highest levels of politics in the Punto Fijo republic: the number of presidential candidates doubled from 1968 to 1973, mostly with candidates from the left. The left's role in Congress also increased. When Carlos Andrés Pérez faced charges of corruption, important leftist legislators (e.g., José Vicente Rangel, then from the PCV and eventually Chávez's right hand) argued that the accusations were rightist-inspired reprisals for progressive policies (Ellner 2008).

The MAS was the official ruling party under Caldera's second term, and two of his closest economic officials, Teodoro Petkoff and Luis Raúl Matos Azócar, were self-proclaimed "men of the left."

In short, while Venezuela's top political offices (e.g., the presidency, management positions in state-owned enterprises, leadership positions in labor federations, seats on advisory boards to the president) remained off-limits to the radical left and reserved for the large parties (Coppedge 1994) and large interest groups (Crisp 2000; Gates 2010), by the 1970s a growing number of secondary institutions became accessible. Small parties, small unions, small neighborhood associations, some media venues, some regions, and even the military had become institutional homes where radical leftist politicians and groups could function openly (Ellner 1993).

Universities

Another crucial Venezuelan institution that SOFs were able to populate was the university system. Institutions of higher education were direct offspring of the Punto Fijo regime and became one of the largest, most resource-endowed, anti–status quo,[1] autonomous institutions in Venezuela, all courtesy of the Punto Fijo state.

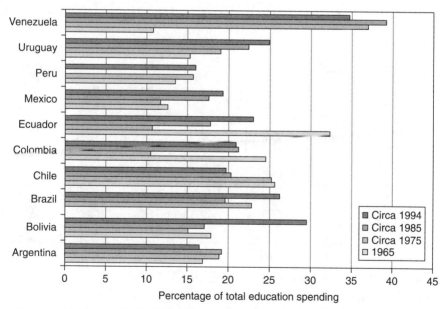

Fig. 12.1   Spending on higher education

Source: Based on United Nations Educational, Scientific and Cultural Organization (various years).

A good indicator of the importance of this institution in the Punto Fijo era is the level of resources devoted to it. The Punto Fijo regime 2.0 conducted one of the largest expansions in spending on higher education in the region (fig. 12.2). Between 1969 and 1974, public university enrollment expanded by a phenomenal 72 percent, compared to a 38 percent and a 23 percent expansion in secondary and primary education (Albornoz 1977). Between 1965 and 1998, tertiary education expanded almost fourfold whereas secondary education only doubled. Even in the economically depressed mid-1990s, Venezuela still devoted 6.8 percent of its national budget to higher education—the highest in Latin America, whose average was 3.4 percent (De Moura Castro and Levy 2000). In the 1980s and 1990s, university education absorbed 38 percent of the budget of the Ministry of Education (World Bank 2001). Although total enrollment increased by 60 percent from 1986 to 1996, total spending was still high relative to enrollment levels. By the end of the 1990s, there were 144 institutions of higher learning, of which 41 were universities. Further, abundant state subsidies made it so that most services in the university system were free or highly subsidized.[2]

The university system itself was organized in a way that made it easy for political groups to gain access. First, the system did not have strict academic

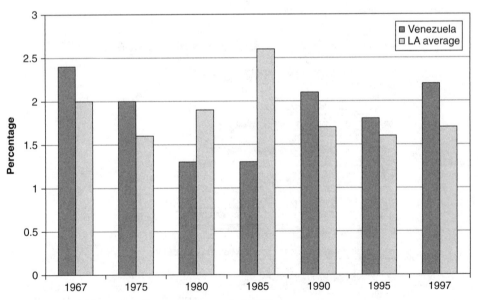

Fig. 12.2   Military spending as a percentage of GNP

Sources: Based on U.S. Arms Control and Disarmament Agency (1961–98); Department of State, Office of the Under Secretary of State for Arms Control and International Security (1994–present); World Military Expenditures and Arms Transfers (WMEAT) data files (various years), all available at the National Archives, http://arcweb.archives.gov.

requirements for faculty appointments. In the early 2000s, only 6.6 percent of faculty had doctoral degrees, compared to 19 percent in Brazil. Second, the pension system ensured that older professors could stick around. Although faculty could retire after only twenty-five years of service at a 100 percent salary, tax-free, many were then rehired by either their own institutions or some other academic center. This allowed some "retired" faculty to collect both a salary and a pension. In 1999, almost 24 percent of the personnel at the universities was "retired" (Albornoz 2003, 125). Third, at the student level, the universities did not impose restrictions on times in residence, so political activists could prolong their stay on campus beyond the average time it took to complete a degree. Of the students who enrolled at the university in 1989, only 40.5 percent graduated within five years (World Bank 2001).[3]

SOFs on the left took advantage of this institutional bigness, openness, and hospitality. Leftist activists, including former insurgents, gravitated toward the university system as students or as faculty. In the Universidad Central de Venezuela since the 1970s, the degree of representation of the radical left (PCV, MIR, URD, MEP, Bandera Roja) was greater than in the country at large. The University of Zulia in Maracaibo and the University of Oriente—with campuses in Puerto La Cruz, Cumaná, and Ciudad Bolívar, originally bastions of AD—became dominated by MAS and Marxist radicals (see Hillman 2004, 118–19). Whereas universities in Latin America (with the exception of Mexico, Costa Rica, and Colombia) during the Cold War were often purged of leftists and squeezed financially, in Venezuela they remained privileged and autonomous, offering safe harbor for leftist SOFs.

The Military

By the 1980s, the military emerged, paradoxically, as yet another state-based institution offering a haven for the radical left. After successfully demilitarizing Venezuela and asserting civilian control over the military between the 1960s and the 1970s, the Punto Fijo regime made a turnaround and became a protector of a very well-taken-care-of military institution. In this Punto Fijo regime 2.0, the military got an agreeable mission (containment and defense against Colombia), autonomy in the conduct of security affairs, and healthy military budgets. This allowed the military provided ample opportunities for social mobility (Trinkunas 2005).

The contrast in military spending between the 1960s and the 1980s reveals the extent to which Punto Fijo regime 2.0 protected the military as an institution. After an initial contraction between 1967 and 1980, military expenditures declined

as a percentage of GDP, going from above to below the Latin American average as a percentage of central government expenditure. After 1980, Venezuela's
demilitarization trend was reversed (fig. 12.3). Military expenditure, both as
a percentage of GDP and as a percentage of central government expenditure,
expanded between 1980 and 1997. The size of the armed forces went from 49,000
in 1985 to 56,000 in 1998, a 14 percent increase (IISS 2000). Table 12.3 also shows
the relative stability of Venezuela's military spending as percentage of central
government expenditures over the three decades since the 1970s. The point is
that, while other areas of government spending were being cut, the Venezuelan
military remained relatively protected.

Despite this protection, by the 1990s, members of the military had a number of
grievances that resonated with SOF anti-system ideologies, including discontent
with party-based military promotions, as well as resentment by junior officers
of the higher income enjoyed by generals (Trinkunas 2002). One reason for this
resentment had to do with the uneven distribution of resources within the military. Although Venezuela did not have a large military relative to its population
(in terms of military expenditures per capita in 1996, Venezuela ranked ninth
among twenty countries in the region; see Arcenaux 1999), by the 1990s, Venezuela
had 103 brigadier generals and 30 generals; Brazil, with a military five times as
large, had only 116 generals (Hellinger 2003). It seems that most of the economic

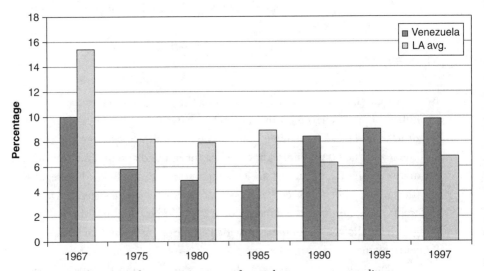

Fig. 12.3   Military spending as a percentage of central government expenditure

Sources: Based on U.S. Arms Control and Disarmament Agency (1961–98); Department of State,
Office of the Under Secretary of State for Arms Control and International Security (1994–present);
World Military Expenditures and Arms Transfers (WMEAT) data files (various years), all available
at the National Archives, http://arcweb.archives.gov.

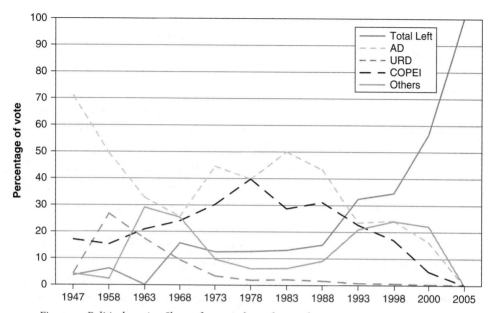

Fig. 12.4 Political parties: Share of votes in lower house elections, 1947–2005

Source: Based on Alvarez 2006.

Note: "Total left" includes the following parties. For 1947: PCV (Partido Comunista de Venezuela); 1958: PCV; 1968: PCV, MEP (Movimiento Electoral del Pueblo); 1973: PCV, MIR (Movimiento de Izquierda Revolucionaria), MAS (Movimiento al Socialismo), MEP; 1978: PCV, VUC (Vanguardia Unida Comunista), MIR, MAS, MEP; 1983: PCV, NA (Nueva Alternativa), LCR (La Causa R), LS (Liga Socialista), MIR, MAS, MEP; 1988: PCV, LCR, LS, MAS, MEP; 1993: PCV, LCR, MAS, MEP; 1998: PCV, PPT (Patria Para Todos), MVR (Movimiento Quinta República), LCR, MAS, MEP; 2000: PCV, PPT, MVR, LCR, MAS, MEP; 2005: MVR.

Table 12.3 Military expenditure as a percentage of central government spending, annual averages by decades, 1970–1999

	1970–79	1980–89	1990–99
Latin America	12.8	7.6	6.5
Argentina	12.8	17.0	11.7
Bolivia	11.5	22.4	10.7
Brazil	14.5	3.4	4.1
Chile	12.0	12.9	14.8
Colombia	11.3	10.3	17.8
Ecuador	15.3	14.0	20.7
Mexico	5.1	2.2	3.9
Peru	23.2	33.3	11.5
Venezuela	7.6	7.1	6.6

SOURCES: Based on U.S. Arms Control and Disarmament Agency (1961–98); Department of State, Office of the Under Secretary of State for Arms Control and International Security (1994–present); World Military Expenditures and Arms Transfers (WMEAT) data files (various years), all available at the National Archives, http://arcweb.archives.gov.

subsidies channeled to the military staff ended up in the hands of the upper echelons of the hierarchy, while low-ranking staff suffered declining relative wages and conditions.

One way to gauge this skewed protection is to examine the proportion of the military budget devoted to weapons acquisition. The average value of arms imports as a percentage of military expenditures expanded in the 1980s, from an average of 11.1 percent in the 1967–79 period to 38.5 percent in the 1980–89 period (U.S. Arms Control and Disarmament Agency, various years). How much of this budget was diverted to corruption is a matter of speculation. But it seems safe to assume that very little went to junior officers and non-ranking troops. Inequality between the top officers was rampant and bred discontent among the junior ranks.

There is no question that there was little room at the top of the military for anti-establishment sentiment. Promotions required Senate approval, so high-ranking officers were necessarily agreeable to the large parties. But throughout the rest of the military, soldiers enjoyed broader political autonomy from parties. Further, there are studies that show that the intelligence institutions of the military were not terribly repressive, neither across society nor within the military (Myers 2003), which would explain the ability of anti–status quo groups in the military to survive. This "complacency" seems to explain why Chávez's faction within the military, the MBR-200, was allowed to operate unencumbered for almost ten years before the 1992 coup (Ellner 2007, 149). Venezuela's intelligence framework was designed in 1958 to avoid the abuses of the Pérez Jiménez administration and remained "fragmented," lacking "horizontal linkages among its important institutions." SECONSEDE (created in 1976), the only institution with the potential to coordinate Punto Fijo national intelligence, remained on the sidelines (ibid., 88). In the 1980s, the focus on communist infiltration gave way to a focus on terrorism and drug enforcement. Further, there is evidence of underuse: during his second term, President Carlos Andrés Pérez was warned by intelligence sources of contacts between radical civilian political leaders based in Caracas slums and alienated junior army officers, but Pérez dismissed these reports. Caldera also did not use the reports.

The paradox of state–military affairs prior to Chávez is that the system was breeding anti–status quo sentiment in the military, even though that sector was relatively well treated by the state. As most analysts argue, the discontent stemmed from both politics and economics. The military came to share the views of most elites in Venezuela in the 1990s that the country's problem was the stranglehold of the party system. The upper echelons resented party-based promotions and the lower echelons resented economic inequalities within the armed forces.

The military thus became simultaneously a protégé and a victim of "partyarachy." Because it was so well protected and simultaneously abused, the military acted as both a sponge for and a breeding ground of radical anti–status quo sentiment. And because the state did not monitor too much the activity of junior officers, discontent could grow unchecked.

Subnational Politics and Voluntary Organizations

After 1989, the other institutional arena that became open and hospitable to small opposition forces of the left was subnational political office (Ellner 1993; Penfold 2002). A series of reforms, which included the remarkable 1989 decentralization measures (which decentralized spending and allowed for the direct election of governors and mayors), the shortening of municipal and congressional terms, and the institution of nominal elections, was responsible for this institutional opening. By the late 1990s, the Venezuelan state was devoting a far larger sum of money (23 percent of total spending, or 5 percent of GDP) to its regions than was the average Latin American country; most of this spending was earmarked for employment on the state and municipal levels (López Obregón and Rodríguez 2002). The index of decentralization, which ranks Latin American countries in terms of the ratio of subnational expenditures to national expenditures, places Venezuela fifth among seventeen countries. This combination of political and economic decentralization represented a form of "diffusion of power" (Ellner 2003, 14) that "lowered the cost of entry" for new actors (Levine 1998, 198; see also Crisp and Levine 1998, and Levine and Crisp 1999). Some even referred to decentralization in the 1990s as a "semi-suicide" of traditional parties (Lalander 2006), which "undermined the fundamental pillars of the partidocratic model" (Buxton 2001, 47).

Institutional openness made available new avenues of political participation. The two most important SOFs—MAS and Causa R—were the main beneficiaries. By 1992, leaders of small opposition parties of the left held four state governorships and multiple mayoralties and were making headway in Congress (figure 12.5). By 1993, leftist parties achieved control of the executive branch (the Convergencia–MAS alliance) and the lower house. These small opposition forces, no longer that small, remained intensely divided on most policy and electoral issues, but united on one theme: their scorn for the *adecopeyanismo*, a sentiment now shared not just by the urban poor (Canache 2004), but also by economic elites, sectors of the military, and the bulk of intellectuals (Hillman 2004; Morgan 2007). By 1998, only thirteen of twenty-three governorships were in the hands of the traditional parties, AD and COPEI. Penfold (2002) thus concludes that the increase in gubernatorial electoral "opportunities" permitted both "emerging parties" (LCR, PV, and MBR-200) and established leftist parties (MAS) to become "important players" in Venezuelan politics in the 1990s. In short, the marginal left was thus not governing, but it was not homeless.

The other form of mobilization was the rise of civil society (see Crisp and Levine 1998). Studies trying to quantify the rise of civic associations suggest that the total number went from approximately 10,000 in the early 1990s to as many as 24,628 or perhaps even 54,266 by the 2000s (Salamanca 2004, 100). As in the rest of Latin America (Hellman 1992), these groups tended to overrepresent the antiparty left. Some have argued that social movements were united along one cleavage (opposition to partyarchy) but divided along a socioeconomic cleavage: popular sector movements defended a more radical democracy emphasizing social justice, while movements from upper classes emphasized more liberal democracy and private property. Either way, the combined pressure of this expansion of civics led to a "deepening of democracy" in the 1980s and 1990s (García-Guadilla 2005, 113).

In short, the political position of SOFs, including the radical left, improved, even though (or perhaps because) the regime was collapsing economically. As the number of impoverished low-income groups and defectors from traditional parties increased (see Morgan 2007), the political opportunities for small opposition parties and radical left parties increased. By 1992, this combination of economic shrinking and political opening led to the decline of the traditional parties, AD and COPEI, in favor of new or previously blocked parties: Convergencia, MAS, the PCV, Causa R, and later, in 1998, the MVR. Institutional opening, rather than (or together with) institutional decay, is thus the most powerful explanation for regime change in the direction of leftist militarism.

The Nonadaptation of Parties, Including the Radical Left

I have provided an institutional explanation for the prospering of the left in Venezuela, but what about the endurance of radicalism? While not everyone in Venezuela's large left was radical—and the moderate left was unquestionably the largest electoral bloc—the radicals were not a tiny minority. More precisely, it seems that there was a large section of the left that, while embracing up-to-date ideas of democracy such as the need for more participatory mechanisms, was nonetheless still clamoring for ideas that are more aptly described as "sesensitas." These were ideas more in vogue in the left in the 1960s, such as "endogenous development," the chavista term of import-substitution industrialization;

tolerance for concentration of power in the hands of the executive; disdain for liberal democracy and private firms and property; preference for "popular power" and strong anti-imperialism; and admiration for the Cuban Revolution. Most of the left in Latin America in the 1980s and 1990s moved in the direction of greater acceptance of private market forces and definite rejection of concentration of power in the hands of the executive or military (Angell 1996; Castañeda 1993). But in Venezuela, in contrast, large sectors of the left continued to romanticize revolutionary politics—a strategy that in the 1990s generated problems for leftist parties elsewhere, either at the moment of elections or when governing (Roberts 1998). Even the MAS, the most self-democratizing party of the left, when it became the ruling party, rejected its very own planning minister, Teodoro Petkoff, for "selling his soul to" neoliberalism. What explains the ideological "non-adaptation" of so many sectors of the Venezuelan left? (see Katz and Mair 1994; Burgess and Levitsky 2003).[4]

One-Way Globalization

Part of the answer is what could be termed as "one-way globalization." The Venezuelan left was exposed to international currents, but these were mostly inwardly rather than outwardly flowing, and this biased the sector's ideological evolution. A comparison with other Latin American leftists makes this point clear.

Most Latin American leaders of the left abandoned their countries in the 1960s–70s period, fleeing right-wing dictatorships. The majority went to the United States, Canada, and Europe. This international contact contributed to the ideological moderation of the Latin American left, in tandem with the moderation of the left in the West (on how this process operated in Chile, see Angell 2001). Even those Latin American leftists who sought asylum in communist Eastern Europe underwent moderation, as they became disenchanted with Marxism in practice. In the words of Frances Hagopian (2005, 323), exile "tamed their passions" for socialism. As these exiles returned to their countries starting in the early 1980s, they served as carriers of the new, more moderate left-wing ideology they adopted while abroad. A good example was Ricardo Lagos, president of Chile from 2000 to 2006. Lagos was a hard-core supporter of Salvador Allende's Socialist government in the 1970s, and he was about to be confirmed as Chile's ambassador to the Soviet Union when Pinochet carried out his coup in 1973. He sought asylum in Argentina, and then in the United States, where he taught economics at the University of North Carolina. Upon his return, Lagos became a main advocate of the Concertación's more moderate stands, serving first as education minister and then as infrastructure minister (Navia 2006).

The Lagos style of ideological adaptation was rare in Venezuela because leftists had few political reasons to leave Venezuela involuntarily. Institutional comfort at home precluded exodus, which in turn precluded international exposure, which in part precluded ideological adaptation.

If anything, the Venezuelan radical left interacted mostly with its own kind. Precisely because Venezuela was a safe haven for the radical left, Venezuela experienced a massive inflow of exiles from the Southern Cone between 1960 and 1981. South American leftist leaders in the 1960s migrated not just to the United States, Canada, Mexico, and western European countries, but also to Venezuela and Mexico because these countries remained free of anticommunist dictatorships and institutionally open. Venezuela in particular offered generous legal opportunities for Southern Cone refugees. For instance, starting with President Caldera in 1973, and throughout the duration of the Pinochet regime in Chile in 1990, the Venezuelan government actively provided political asylum to Chileans, including the establishment of special funds for refugees (Yáñez 2004). The combined population of Argentine, Chilean, and Uruguayan nationals in Venezuela increased by almost 800 percent between 1961 and 1981. There is also evidence that these exiles became assimilated into Venezuelan society. Most of them were professionals, and 42.5 percent of them held jobs (mostly in professional fields). As further proof that these Southern Cone immigrants in Venezuela were mostly political in kind (leaving for political rather than economic reasons), immigration from Argentina and Uruguay turned negative in the 1980–84 precisely when these dictatorships expired.

In short, the Venezuelan left in the 1960s–1980s period was peculiar relative to the rest of Latin America (except Mexico) in that it remained at home. Rather than going into exile, it welcomed radical exiles from elsewhere in the region. This one-way form of ideological globalization reinforced rather than challenged groupthink, and is a key reason for the survival of ideas that many leftists elsewhere in Latin American considered outmoded by the 1990s.

The Parties' Technocratic Deficit

Just like the left, Venezuela's traditional parties, AD and COPEI, suffered their own case of non-adaptation. Elsewhere in Latin American, most postwar parties that became electorally successful in the 1990s (e.g., the Peronists in Argentina, the PRI in Mexico, the Colorados in Uruguay, the Christian Democrats and Socialists in Chile, the Liberals in Colombia, the Social Democrats in Brazil) did so after undergoing a process of internal renovation. One crucial component of that renovation was the incorporation of more *técnicos* within their ranks.

These técnicos updated their party's ideologies, and more important, gave them policy tools to deal with the crisis of the 1980s. This did not happen with AD and COPEI, which remained fairly closed to technical expertise.

The best study on the relationship between Venezuelan parties and técnicos, grouped into *colegios* (or professional associations and boards), indicates that parties and colegios always had a strong working relationship, which is not surprising for a democracy, especially one with a large, rent-granting public sector (Martz and Myers 1994; see also Crisp 2000). Until the 1970s, professionals felt that they played an important part "in creating and consolidating" Venezuelan democracy and influencing politicians (Martz and Myers 2004, 21). Over time, however, this relationship eroded and they started to feel it was politicians that influence the colegios, a clear change in the direction of influence that led to resentment by professionals toward parties.

But this is only one side of the technocratic crisis. If one looks at the ways in which técnicos, or technical expertise for that matter, entered party leadership—rather than merely the working relationship between the groups—the disconnect appears even larger.

There are two ways in which technical knowledge can penetrate parties, neither of which operated well in Venezuela after the 1970s. The first is entrance through the executive branch, a model exemplified by Mexico under PRI rule. Mexican presidents since the 1960s appointed technical experts throughout the federal bureaucracy, and these técnicos joined the ruling party leadership, and even made it to the presidency. In Venezuela, this process of técnico incorporation was never all that strong—top party positions remained in the hands of traditional politicians—and it completely collapsed under Perez (1989–2003), with AD's famous campaign against Pérez's technical cabinet (Corrales 2002).

The other entry route for technical expertise is through specialized service in the legislature: the more time a legislator spends in the legislature, the greater incentive he or she has to develop technical expertise (Jones et al. 2002). I counted the re-election rates for legislators in Venezuela, and the numbers are very low: of the 1,590 legislators who served in Venezuela between 1958 and 1998, 64.6 percent stayed for just one term; 15.3 percent stayed for two terms (see also Monaldi et al. 2005). In fact, the re-election rate for Venezuelan legislators was one of the lowest in the region (Inter-American Development Bank 2005). In addition, the productivity of the legislature, measured in terms of the number of bills approved per year, was shockingly low. At the end of the 1990s, with financial support from the Inter-American Development Bank, a major initiative was launched to bolster the technical expertise of the legislature with the creation of an office of technical advice for exclusive use by the legislature. But this office was effectively undermined by Chávez by 2001 and completely disbanded by 2003. In short, before 1999, Venezuelan legislators did not last in their posts and the legislature produced little, all of which lessened incentives for professional party-based politicians to acquire expertise.

In short, Venezuelan traditional parties suffered from what Hagopian (2005, 359) argues are two major causes of party crisis: a representational deficit (i.e., a disconnect between party leadership and civil society) and a technical-expertise deficit (a disconnect with policy wonks). The representational deficit engendered party defections by both the "new right" and "new left" (see Molina 2000; Morgan 2007; Myers 2007). Each wing felt unrepresented by ideologically paralyzed party leadership. The social democrats and Christian democrats remained attached to the old rentier–populist model, which was increasingly unappealing to the new right; and the MAS was too attached to anticapitalism, which was unappealing to the new left. At the same time, the technical-expertise deficit deprived parties of ideas, made them hesitant to experiment, and led to unimaginative responses to economic crises. This deficit has not been emphasized enough by scholars, and yet it was perhaps as serious as, and maybe even a cause of, the representational deficit that ended up decimating Venezuela's traditional parties.

Venezuela and Latin American Countries Compared circa 1998

I have argued that sociological explanations for the rise of Chávez, which emphasize the population's unaddressed economic needs and widespread desire for change in the 1990s, are insufficient to understand the political coalition built by Chávez. At best, these theories account for only the demand side, not the supply side: they cannot explain easily the availability of such a large pool of radical leftist civilians and nationalist military personnel willing to collaborate to form a government since 1999.

Table 12.4 summarizes the key factors that I have argued led to a strong radical left sector across civil society and the military: (1) institutional sheltering of the radical left; (2) feeding mechanisms; and (3) institutional protections for the military. Together with the erosion of traditional parties in the 1990s, which further lowered barriers to entry of new political groups, these factors created conditions for the rise of radical leftism in Venezuela by the late 1990s.

Table 12.4 also shows that these conditions were not replicated to the same extent elsewhere in the region. The discrepancy in these conditions explains why, elsewhere in the region, the radical left was not as large, radical, or willing to accept military involvement in politics as it was in Venezuela. If Chávez had tried

Table 12.4 Venezuela on the eve of chavismo compared to other Latin American cases, circa 1998

	Ven.	Arg.	Bol.	Bra.	Chi.	Col.	Ecu.	Mex.	Nic.	Per.
Institutional sheltering of the radical left										
Legalization of the left, 1970s	Yes	—	—	—	—	—	—	Yes	—	—
Large, open universities (i.e., purges were rare), 1960s–80s	Yes	—	—	—	—	Yes	—	Yes	—	—
Political decentralization, 1990s	Yes	Yes	Yes	—	—	Yes	—	Yes	—	Yes
Collapse of large, traditional parties, 1990s	Yes	—	Yes	—	—	—	—	—	—	Yes
Feeding mechanisms										
Immigration laws (favorable to leftists), 1960s–80s	Yes	—	—	—	—	Yes	—	Yes	—	—
Failed/aborted first-generation market reforms, 1980s–90s	Yes	—	—	—	—	—	Yes	—	—	—
Institutional protection of the military										
Relatively stable budgets (no drastic cuts since 1970s)	Yes	—	—	—	Yes	Yes	Yes	—	—	—
Military expansion in the 1980s	Yes	—	—	—	Yes	Yes	—	—	Yes	—
Declining civilian oversight of the military	Yes	—	—	—	—	Yes	—	—	—	Yes
Lack of right-wing purges in the military	Yes	—	—	—	—	—	—	Yes	—	—

Source: Author's elaboration based on Domínguez and Giraldo (1996), Hagopian (2005), and other references in the text.

to build a coalition of radical leftists and left-leaning military officers in another Latin America country in the late 1990s, he would not have been as successful. Analysts conventionally divide the political spectrum in most countries into four broad categories: extreme left, center–left, center–right, and extreme right. The exceptionality for Venezuela in 1998 was that the proportion of voters and leaders within each category differed in significant ways from the rest of Latin America (see Corrales 2011).

For one, the size of the right was not that large in Venezuela. The two forces that fed the right in Latin America were not strong in Venezuela—these being a Cold War–influenced military-fighting insurgency all the way through the early 1980s; and neoliberalism in the 1990s, which would have given rise to large pro-market political forces. The best evidence for the weakness of the right was the minimal share of the vote obtained by the two conservative candidates in the 1998 presidential elections, Miguel Rodríguez and Irene Saénz: 3.12 percent between them.

Further, within the Venezuelan left, the extreme left was strong and becoming stronger. Institutions sheltering and promoting radical thought were well protected from adjustment and were expanding as a result of decentralization and the collapse of traditional parties.

Three groups were trying to rise against the rentier model defended by parties in Venezuela—the radical left since the 1970s, and the new left and the new right in the 1990s. But the radical left enjoyed the most institutional opportunities. It had a strong presence over the university, the military, social movements, and, increasingly, the new political parties that were displacing the traditional parties. The radical left was thus best positioned to take advantage of the "unraveling" of the Punto Fijo regime. By the 1998 presidential elections, Venezuela faced an array of propitious conditions for an assault against the traditional political actors of the regime: almost twenty years of continuous economic decline, divisions within the traditional parties (which stayed impermeable to technical experts and plagued by voter detachment), and non-modernized, small opposition forces that were enjoying new allies and safe political spaces. Hugo Chávez emerged as the leader of such an assault. His task was to unite the radicals at the university and in SOFs, the suffering low-income groups, and the military.

The paradox of the origins of chavismo is that it is a movement of anti–status quo personalities that emerged because these forces experienced institutional protection. The rise of Chávez in 1998 thus represents not the sudden triumph of historically excluded groups, but rather the culmination of years in which malcontents were able to use the institutions of democracy to climb to the top. More than revolution, it was ladder climbing.

Chavismo in Office: Coalition Toolkits

The survival of Chávez's left radical–military alliance over the years did not occur automatically. There were many tensions within and between each group. To keep this coalition together, it was necessary for Chávez to deploy a variety of tactics over time.

A most prominent tactic has been the use of radicalism for political gain. Initially, except for his antiparty stance, the Chávez administration was not all that radical. At the level of economics, Chávez hardly proposed any major policy departures (at least not more than Caldera during his honeymoon). But starting in 2001, he began to take increasingly radical stands in economics and politics. Since then, Chávez's party has competed in each electoral process (2004, 2005, 2006, 2007, 2009, 2010, 2012) on a platform and a record that was far more radical than in the previous electoral contest.

There are two schools of thought on the possible origin of radicalization. One suggests that radicalization is a response to the intransigence of the status quo. The state tries to introduce structural reforms, usually in the form of distributive politics, only to confront the veto power of certain class interests. This argument is famously associated with Karl Marx, for whom revolution (rather than reform) is the only realistic path to true change, but contemporary non-Marxists have also accepted it. For instance, Easterly (2001) and Acemoglu and Robinson (2006, 321–22) argue that development produces a stalemate between elites who fear redistribution, and the masses who, mobilized by democracy, demand redistribution. In these accounts, radicalization is a consequence of unbending structures.

An alternative view of radicalization is to see it as a deliberate, and not necessarily inevitable, policy of the state. Radicalization does not occur because change necessitates it but because state elites, more so than the masses, prefer it due to its potential electoral rewards (Cohen 1994; Bermeo 2003). In "Why Polarize?" (Corrales 2011), I demonstrate how this electoral reward can happen. Essentially, radicalization caters to the most radical of government's supporters while simultaneously splitting the least ideologized sectors (i.e., the uncommitted voters or those in the ideological center) into at least three groups: moderate supporters of the government, ambivalent groups, and opponents. Depending on the ideological distribution, this societal response to radicalism can generate winning majorities for incumbents.

Yet radicalization can be politically risky. While it can increase the number of supporters, it yields a new group—the ambivalent groups. These voters do not identify openly with either pole. Ambivalent voters are risky for the government. These groups can be large and electorally decisive. Insofar as their loyalties remain in flux, ambivalent voters can at any point gravitate toward the opposition since, by definition, they have non-fixed loyalties.

Most polls provide evidence of the rise of ambivalent groups soon after Chávez begins to radicalize in office. By July 2001, for example, one reputable poll was already beginning to classify some voters as "repented chavistas." The size of repented chavistas swelled from 8.9 percent in February 2001 to 14.7 percent to 32.8 percent in December 2001 (Gil Yepes 2004). By June 2002, these repented chavistas turned into "light chavistas," "light anti-chavistas," and "hard anti-chavistas," confirming the argument that radicalization results in a loss of moderate support for the incumbent, and that these losses could easily turn anti-incumbent. In addition, defections in the military and the cabinet increased. By mid-2002, the government found itself confronting the largest amount of opposition since coming to office.

The key point is that even in situations of polarization, the size of the swing group grows to nontrivial levels. Thus even radical leftist governments need to develop strategies to deal with ambivalent groups.

What has the Chávez administration done to address these groups? In the case of the Chávez administration, three other elements of the coalition toolkit come into place: clientelism, impunity, and job discrimination (see Corrales and Penfold 2007 and 2011; Corrales 2011).

Clientelism refers to the distribution of state resources from a strong political actor (in this case, the state) to a less powerful actor (in this case, ordinary citizens and small civil society organizations). In the context of a radical–leftist government, clientelism is likely to work mostly among the less ideological sectors of the population: the extreme left does not need clientelism to support a radical–leftist government, and the extreme right won't be swayed by it either. Clientelism's only hope is thus with the non-ideologized sectors.

The other strategy that Chávez has deployed is cronyism, which differs from clientelism in that benefits pass from strong actors to other strong actors (e.g., the military, business groups, financial sectors). Like clientelism, cronyism is also a policy targeted toward the non-ideologized sectors, especially elites. Because strong actors can act as major veto groups, not just of policy but also of the administration's tenure in office, it is important for governments in unstable political settings to deploy significant resources to deal with powerful actors. One of the key reasons that corruption is so rampant (or why Chávez did little to contain it) is precisely because of the need to keep certain groups from defecting, and to keep as many elites as possible from siding with the opposition.

The final strategy to deal with ambivalent groups is job discrimination. The Chávez administration, in no uncertain terms, repeated that the largest benefits of his administration (government jobs, contracts, subsidies, etc.) were reserved for supporters, which the government in 2006 called the "rojo, rojitos" (the red ones, very red ones). The Chávez administration thus likes to portray itself as a watchful government that rewarded supporters and punished opponents through exclusion from clientelism, corruption, and government jobs. This conveyed that that there were large gains from staying loyal and large losses from dissenting. Again, this strategy targeted mostly the non-ideologized, ambivalent groups.

It is also a strategy intended to promote electoral abstentionism on the party of anti-chavistas. And more fundamentally, it is a strategy that has been intensely applied to the military through purges of non-loyal officers.

In sum, the administration offers clientelism, cronyism or impunity, and job discrimination to keep as many ambivalent voters from totally switching to the other side or capturing key institutions of the state. These policies increase the number of supporters beyond those the extreme left bloc provides.

Consequently, the coalition of leaders and voters who support Chávez by the end of 2000s had morphed in relation to the initial one. It is radical—in that it continues to support ideas that were popular among the radical left in the 1960s— but now also conservative, in that it is keen on preserving newly gained state sinecures. Chávez's supporters by 2009 included not just the extreme left, but also new and old winners: welfare recipients, actors with ties to the state, and those who profit from corruption. Although these winners come from different income groups (welfare recipients are mostly poor, state employees come from the lower middle classes, and corrupt folks are wealthier), they share the same electoral objective—to preserve their gains. These gains are access to social programs, state jobs and contracts, and impunity. What unites these groups is a fear that the opposition will take away their gains.

We can now understand why the Chávez administration relies on radicalism and intense clientelism/impunity/discrimination. The former maximizes the number of supporters relative to defectors (due to the large, albeit non-majoritarian, status of the extreme left), but it also increases the number of ambivalent groups. The latter policies target ambivalent groups. Combined, both sets of policies give rise to winning coalitions that, paradoxically, include an odd combo: committed revolutionaries and less ideologized, state-dependent actors, many of whom are social elites.

Conclusion

Explaining chavismo, both its rise and consolidation in power, requires invoking both demand-side as well as supply-side factors. A focus on the demand side (which stresses widespread discontent in the late 1990s) can explain why a majority of voters would support political change in the late 1990s, but it cannot explain why the leftist alternative that prevailed proved so radical, so compatible with the military, and so reliant on clientelism, impunity, and intimidation. To explain these questions, this chapter has offered a supply-side argument.

In deciding to form a radical–military government, Chávez could count on a large pool of voters and political leaders willing to construct this project. The initial institutional arrangements of Venezuela's democracy (the Punto Fijo regime) was not open to the radical left. But by the late 1970s, the regime had developed a set of institutions—legalization of leftist parties, universities, the military, civil society, and decentralization—that served to incubate and insulate these groups. This Punto Fijo regime 2.0, as I have called it, offered significant institutional incubation and insulation for radical left-wing groups. Incubation explains these groups' growth since the 1970s; insulation explains their modest ideological evolution. Combined with the non-adaptation of the traditional parties, together with the growth collapse of the 1980s, it is easy to understand why it was the radical left group that was the most important beneficiary of voter discontent in the late 1990s.

This analysis has implications for several key debates in comparative politics of Latin America: (1) the rise of the left in the 2000s, (2) regime evolution in general, (3) ideological adaptation of parties, and (4) the supply side of extremism.

First, on the rise of the left in Latin America, this chapter has argued that this phenomenon was driven mostly by both gripe and institutional facilities, more so than by institutional closure. The radical left in Venezuela, as elsewhere in Latin America, had strong grievances against the status quo, and these grievances intensified as inequality rose in the 1980s and as market reforms failed to deliver in the 1990s. Yet it is important to understand the extent of institutional protection in Venezuela. Whereas in the rest of the region the radical left was severely repressed, imprisoned, or exiled between the 1960s and the 1980s, in Venezuela democratic institutions since 1968 offered protections, opportunities for integration and, ultimately, access to state office in the 1990s. These institutions not only subsidized the left, but also insulated them from exposures to global forces that would have triggered ideological adaptation.

Second, on the question of regime change and democratization, this chapter has highlighted a process that seems to defy Acemoglu and Robinson's (2006) theory that democratization occurs when nonelites maximize both their de jure and de facto power vis-à-vis the state. In Venezuela, the radical left obtained a substantial "reparations" package not when it was strong and threatening, but rather when it was at its weakest—that is, when it was politically and militarily defeated in the late 1960s.

Third, on the notion of party adaptation, this chapter has emphasized the notion of one-way globalization and exclusion of technical expertise. Immigration of like-minded cohorts surpassed emigration rates, creating a relatively insular and self-reinforcing idea pool in Venezuela. Economists are used to differentiating the effects of inward versus outward economic influences in a given country. This chapter suggests that, in terms of political ideas, this dichotomy is relevant as well. The Venezuelan left's one-way globalization limited adaptation of large segments of the left. In addition, the enormous barriers that parties erected against the incorporation of technical expertise hindered party adaptation. In Venezuela, these barriers existed because of the low level of circulation of party leadership and the parties' low levels of investments in legislative affairs.

Finally, this chapter has offered an explanation for radicalism that combines both the supply side with the inherent logic of radicalism in generating loyalties based on asymmetries in the distribution of voters along the ideological spectrum. Majority pressures per se did not necessarily push Chávez to turn radical once in office. This desire to become more radical was instead the result of the personal preferences of Chávez, the large dominance of radical leaders who surrounded and cheered him, and the good supply of military officers willing to tolerate, even sympathize, with this project. This supply-side explanation for radicalism must also be supplemented with an understanding of the political logic of pursuing extremism in politics. Radicalism has a clear political payoff in situations in which the radical left is large. But radicalization also carries the risk of enlarging ambivalent groups. Deploying supplementary policies to co-opt these groups is indispensable. Chávez's supplemented his radical policies with reactionary policies such as clientelism, impunity, and intimidation to target to everyone in the least ideologized sectors.

Thus, to focus exclusively on the demand side to explain the combination of radical–military politics and corruption/impunity/intimidation is insufficient. Radical–military policies represent a break from the status quo, while corruption/impunity/intimidation represents an accentuation of, rather than a break from, the pre-Chávez status quo. The same demand force could not possibly explain the rise of such dissimilar outcomes. Combining demand-side argument with supply-side explanations, and invoking the logic of extremism, helps explain the odd combination of radicalism and conservatism at the core of chavismo.

NOTES

1. For an account of leftist (and right-wing) intellectuals at Venezuelan universities publishing attacks of the Punto Fijo regime prior to 1999, see Hillman 2004. Leftists at national universities were heavily divided between those who supported the small radical left (i.e., the "organized left") and those who supported independent leftists. See Ellner 1986, 98.

2. Food, for instance, is almost free; the cost of three meals for every weekday of the academic year was less than a dollar. Many of these subsidies were targeted to the middle classes: parking a car under a covered lot costs US$1 per month, whereas the average for a similar parking garage elsewhere in Caracas was US$1 for two hours (Albornoz 2003, 67).

3. Another culture-based avenue through which the left was subsidized was through the arts. Governments during the Punto Fijo regime devoted far more investments in the area of "culture, recreation, and religion" (6 percent of total spending) than did the rest of Latin America (less than 1 percent). See López Obregón and Rodríguez 2002. A significant portion of the culture budget went to artists and art groups associated with the left.

4. Burgess and Levitsky (2003, 883), following Katz and Mair (1994), define party adaptation as "changes in strategy and/or structure, undertaken in response to changing environmental conditions that improve a party's capacity to gain or maintain electoral office." An important component of party adaptation is changes in platforms, affiliates, and coalition partners, to reflect new economic realities.

REFERENCES

Acemoglu, Daron, and James A. Robinson. 2006. *Economic Origins of Dictatorship and Democracy*. Cambridge: Cambridge University Press.

Aelo, Oscar H. 2004. "Apogeo y ocaso de un equipo dirigente: El peronismo en la provincia de Buenos Aires, 1947–1951." *Desarrollo Económico* 44 (173): 85–107.

Albornoz, Orlando. 2003. *Higher Education Strategies in Venezuela*. Caracas: Bibliotechnology Ediciones in association with the Facultad de Ciencias Económicas y Sociales, Universidad Central de Venezuela.

Alvarez, Angel E. 2006. "Social Cleavages, Political Polarization, and Democratic Breakdown in Venezuela." *Stockholm Review of Latin American Studies* 1:18–28.

Angell, Alan. 2001. "International Support for the Chilean Opposition, 1973–1989: Political Parties and the Role of Exiles." In *The International Dimensions of Democratization: Europe and the Americas*, edited by Laurence Whitehead, 175–200. New York: Oxford University Press.

Arcenaux, Craig L. 1999. "The Military in Latin America: Defining the Road Ahead." In *Developments in Latin American Political Economy: States, Markets, and Actors*, edited by Julia Buxton and Nicola Phillips, 93–111. Manchester: Manchester University Press.

Bermeo, Nancy. 2003. *Ordinary People in Extraordinary Times: The Citizenry and the Breakdown of Democracy*. Princeton: Princeton University Press.

Burgess, Katrina, and Steve Levitsky. 2003. "Explaining Populist Party Adaptation in Latin America: Environmental and Organizational Determinants of Party Change in Argentina, Mexico, Peru, and Venezuela." *Comparative Political Studies* 36 (8): 881–911.

Bustamante, Fernando. 1998. "Democracy, Civilizational Change, and the Latin American Military." In *Fault Lines of Democracy in Post-transition Latin America*, edited by Felipe Agüero and Jeffrey Stark, 345–70. Miami: North-South Center Press.

Buxton, Julia. 2001. *The Failure of Political Reform in Venezuela*. Aldershot, U.K.: Ashgate.

———. 2003. "Economic Policy and the Rise of Hugo Chávez." In *Venezuelan Politics in the Chávez Era*, edited by Steve Ellner and Daniel Hellinger, 113–30. Boulder, Colo.: Lynne Rienner.

Canache, Damarys. 2004. "Urban Poor and Political Order." In *The Unraveling of Representative Democracy in Venezuela*, edited by Jennifer L. McCoy and David J. Myers, 33–49. Baltimore: Johns Hopkins University Press.

Carothers, Thomas. 2002. "The End of the Transition Paradigm." *Journal of Democracy* 13 (1): 5–21.

Castañeda, Jorge G. 2003. *Utopia Unarmed: The Latin American Left after the Cold War*. New York: Vintage.

Chávez, Hugo, Marta Harnecker, and Chesa Boudin. 2005. *Understanding the Venezuelan Revolution: Hugo Chávez Talks to Marta Harnecker*. Translated by Chesa Boudin. New York: Monthly Review Press.

Cleary, Matthew R. 2006. "Explaining the Left's Resurgence." *Journal of Democracy* 17 (4): 35–49.

Cohen, Youssef. 1994. *Radicals, Reformers, and Reactionaries: The Prisoner's Dilemma and the Collapse of Democracy in Latin America*. Chicago: University of Chicago Press.

Coppedge, Michael. 1994. *Strong Parties and Lame Ducks: Presidential Patriarchy and Factionalism in Venezuela*. Stanford: Stanford University Press.

———. 2003. "Venezuela: Popular Sovereignty versus Liberal Democracy." In *Constructing Democratic Governance in Latin America*, 2nd ed., edited by Jorge Domínguez and Michael Shifter, 165–92. Baltimore: Johns Hopkins University Press.

Corrales, Javier. 2000. "Reform-Lagging States and the Question of Devaluation: Venezuela's Response to the Exogenous Shocks of 1997–98." In *Exchange Rate Politics in Latin America*, edited by Carol Wise and Riordan Roett, 123–58. Washington, D.C.: Brookings Institution Press.

———. 2001. "Strong Societies, Weak Parties: Regime Change in Cuba and Venezuela in the 1950s and Today." *Latin American Politics and Society* 43 (2): 81–114.

———. 2002. *Presidents without Parties: The Politics of Economic Reform in Argentina and Venezuela in the 1990s*. University Park: Pennsylvania State University Press.

———. 2008. "The Backlash against Market Reforms in Latin America." In *Constructing Democratic Governance*, 3rd ed., edited by Jorge I. Domínguez and Michael Shifter, 39–71. Baltimore: Johns Hopkins University Press.

———. 2009. "Using Social Power to Balance Soft Power: Venezuela's Foreign Policy." *Washington Quarterly* 32 (4): 97–114.

———. 2010. "The Repeating Revolution." In *Leftist Governments in Latin America*, edited by Kurt Weyland, Raúl Madrid, and Wendy Hunter, 28–56. Cambridge: Cambridge University Press.

———. 2011. "Why Polarize? Advantages and Disadvantages of a Rational-Choice Analysis of Government-Opposition Relations under Hugo Chávez." In *The Revolution in Venezuela: Social and Political Change under Chávez*, edited by T. Ponniah and J. Eastwood, 67–98. Cambridge: Harvard University Press.

———. 2012. "Neoliberalism and Its Alternatives." In *Routledge Handbook of Latin American Politics*, edited by Peter R. Kingstone and Deborah Yashar, 133–57. New York: Routledge.

Corrales, Javier, and Michael Penfold. 2007. "Venezuela: Crowding Out the Opposition." *Journal of Democracy* 18 (2): 99–113.

———. 2011. Dragon in the Tropics: Hugo Chávez and the Political Economy of Revolution in Venezuela. Washington, D.C.: Brookings.

Corrales, Javier, and Carlos A. Romero. 2013. *U.S.–Venezuela Relations since the 1990s: Coping with Midlevel Security Threats*. New York: Routledge.

Crisp, Brian. 2000. *Democratic Institutional Design: The Powers and Incentives of Venezuelan Politicians and Interest Groups*. Stanford: Stanford University Press.

Crisp, Brian F., and Daniel H. Levine. 1998. "Democratizing the Democracy: Crisis and Reform in Venezuela." *Journal of Interamerican Studies and World Affairs* 40 (2): 27–61.

De Moura Castro, Claudio, and Daniel C. Levy. 2000. *Myth, Reality and Reform: Higher Education Policy in Latin America*. Washington, D.C.: Inter-American Development Bank.

Di John, Jonathan. 2004. "The Political Economy of Economic Liberalisation in Venezuela." Working Paper Series 1, London School of Economics.

Domínguez, Jorge I., and Jeanne Giraldo. 1996. "Conclusion: Parties, Institutions, and Market Reforms in Constructing Democracies." In *Constructing Democratic Governance: Latin America and the Caribbean in the 1990s*, edited by J. I. Domínguez and A. F. Lowenthal, 3–41. Baltimore: Johns Hopkins University Press.

Easterly, William. 2001. *The Elusive Quest for Growth*. Cambridge: MIT Press.

————. 2006. *The White Man's Burden: Why the West's Efforts to Aid the Rest Have Done So Much Ill and So Little Good.* New York: Penguin Press.

Ellner, Steve. 1986. "The MAS Party in Venezuela." *Latin American Perspectives* 13 (2): 81–107.

————. 1993. "The Venezuelan Left: From Years of Prosperity to Economic Crisis." In *The Latin American Left: From the Fall of Allende to Perestroika*, edited by Barry Carr and Steve Ellner, 139–54. Boulder: Westview Press.

————. 2001. "The Radical Potential of Chavismo." *Latin American Perspectives* 28 (5): 5–32.

————. 2003. "Introduction: The Search for Explanations." In *Venezuelan Politics in the Chávez Era: Class, Polarization, and Conflict*, edited by Steve Ellner and Daniel Hellinger, 7–25. Boulder: Lynne Rienner.

————. 2008. *Rethinking Venezuelan Politics: Class, Conflict, and the Chávez Phenomenon.* Boulder, Colo.: Lynne Rienner.

Freedom House. 2010. *Freedom in the World, 2010: Erosion of Freedom Intensifies.* Washington, D.C.

Freije, Samuel. 2003. "¿Cómo generar empleos decentes en la Venezuela del siglo XXI?" In *En esta Venezuela: Realidades y nuevos caminos*, edited by Patricia Márquez and Ramón Piñango, 163–85. Caracas: Ediciones IESA.

García-Guadilla, María Pilar. 2002. "Civil Society: Institutionalization, Fragmentation, Autonomy." In *Venezuelan Politics in the Chávez Era: Globalization, Social Polarization, and Political Change*, edited by Steve Ellner and Daniel Hellinger, 179–96. Boulder: Lynne Rienner.

————. 2005. "The Democratization of Democracy and Social Organizations of the Opposition." *Latin American Perspectives* 32 (141): 109–23.

Gates, Leslie C. 2010. *Electing Chávez: The Business of Anti-neoliberal Politics in Venezuela.* Pittsburgh: University of Pittsburgh Press.

Gibbs, Terry. 2006. "Business as Unusual: What the Chávez Era Tells Us about Democracy under Globalization." *Third World Quarterly* 27 (2): 265–79.

Gil Yepes, José Antonio. 2004. "Public Opinion, Political Socialization, and Regime Stabilization." In *The Unraveling of Representative Democracy in Venezuela*, edited by Jennifer L. McCoy and David J. Myers, 231–62. Baltimore: Johns Hopkins University Press.

Green, Duncan. 2003. *Silent Revolution: The Rise and Crisis of Market Economics in Latin America.* New York: Monthly Review Press.

Hagopian, Frances. 2005. "Conclusions: Government Performance, Political Representation, and Public Perceptions of Contemporary Democracy in Latin America." In *The Third Wave of Democratization in Latin America: Advances and Setbacks*, edited by Frances Hagopian and Scott P. Mainwaring, 319–62. Cambridge: Cambridge University Press.

Hawkins, Kirk. 2003. "Populism in Venezuela: The Rise of Chavismo." *Third World Quarterly* 24 (6): 1137–60.

Hellinger, Daniel. 2003. "Political Overview: The Breakdown of Puntofijismo and the Rise of Chavismo." In *Venezuelan Politics in the Chávez Era: Class, Polarization, and Conflict*, edited by Steve Ellner and Daniel Hellinger, 27–54. Boulder: Lynne Rienner.

Hellman, Judith Adler. 1992. "The Study of New Social Movements in Latin America and the Question of Autonomy." *The Making of Social Movements in Latin America*, edited by Arturo Escobar and Sonia E. Alvarez, 52–61. Boulder: Westview Press.

Hillman, Richard S. 2004. "Intellectuals: An Elite Divided." In *The Unraveling of Representative Democracy in Venezuela*, edited by Jennifer L. McCoy and David J. Myers, 115–29. Baltimore: Johns Hopkins University Press.

IISS (International Institute for Strategic Studies). 2000. *The Military Balance, 1999–2000.* London: International Institute for Strategic Studies, 1999.

Inter-American Development Bank. 2005. "The Politics of Policies: Economic and Social Progress in Latin America: 2006 Report." Washington, D.C.

Jones, Mark P., Sebastian Saiegh, Pablo Spiller, and Mariano Tomassi. 2002. "Professional Politicians, Amateur Legislatures: The Consequences of Party-Centered Electoral Rules in a Federal System." *American Journal of Political Science* 46 (3): 656–69.

Katz, Richard S., and Peter Mair, eds. 1994. *How Parties Organize: Change and Adaptation in Party Organizations in Western Democracies*. London: Sage.

Kelly, Janet, and Pedro A. Palma. 2004. "The Syndrome of Economic Decline and the Quest for Change." In *The Unraveling of Representative Democracy in Venezuela*, edited by Jennifer L. McCoy and David J. Myers, 202–30. Baltimore: Johns Hopkins University Press.

Kornblith, Miriam. 2003. "Elecciones y representación en tiempos turbulentos." *En Esta Venezuela: Realidades y Nuevos Caminos*. Edited by Patricia Márquez and Ramón Piñango. Caracas: Instituto de Estudios Superiores de Administración.

Lalander, Rickard O. 2006. "Has Venezuelan Decentralization Survived Chavismo?" *Stockholm Review of Latin American Studies* 1:29–41.

Lander, Edgardo. 2005. "Venezuelan Social Conflict in a Global Context." *Latin American Perspectives* 32 (2): 20–38.

Levine, Daniel H. 1998. "Beyond the Exhaustion of the Model: Survival and Transformation in Venezuela." In *Reinventing Legitimacy: Democracy and Political Change in Venezuela*, edited by D. Canache and M. R. Kulisheck, 187–214. Westport, Conn.: Greenwood Press.

Levine, Daniel H., and Brian F. Crisp. 1999. "Venezuela: The Character, Crisis and Possible Future of Democracy." In *Democracy in Developing Countries: Latin America*, 2nd ed., edited by. Larry Diamond, Juan J. Linz, Seymour Martin Lipset, and Jonathan Hartlyn, 367–428. Boulder, Colo.: Lynne Rienner.

López Obregón, Clara, and Francisco Rodríguez. 2002. "La política fiscal venezolana, 1943–2001." In *Reporte de Coyuntura Anual, 2001*. Caracas: Oficina de Asesoría Económica y Financiera de la Asamblea Nacional.

Martz, John D., and David J. Myers. 1994. "Technological Elites and Political Parties: The Venezuelan Professional Community." *Latin American Research Review* 29 (1): 7–27.

McCoy, Jennifer L. 2004. "From Representative to Participatory Democracy? Regime Transformation in Venezuela." In *The Unraveling of Representative Democracy in Venezuela*, edited by Jennifer L. McCoy and David J. Myers, 263–96. Baltimore: Johns Hopkins University Press.

McCoy, Jennifer L., and Francisco Diez. 2011. *International Mediation in Venezuela*. Washington, D.C.: United States Institute of Peace Press.

Molina, José. 2000. "Comportamiento electoral en Venezuela, 1998–2000: Cambio y continuidad." *Revista Venezolana de Economía y Ciencias Sociales* 6 (3): 45–68.

———. 2004. "The Unraveling of Venezuela's Party System: From Party Rule to Personalistic Politics and Deinstitutionalization." In *The Unraveling of Representative Democracy in Venezuela*, edited by Jennifer L. McCoy and David J. Myers, 152–80. Baltimore: Johns Hopkins University Press.

Monaldi, Francisco, Rosa Amelia González, Richard Obuchi, and Michael Penfold. 2005. *Political Institutions, Policymaking Process, and Policy Outcomes in Venezuela*. Washington, D.C.: Inter-American Development Bank.

Morgan, Jana. 2007. "Partisanship during the Collapse of Venezuela's Party System." *Latin American Research Review* 42 (1): 78–98.

Myers, David J. 2003. "The Institutions of Intelligence in Venezuela: Lessons from 45 Years of Democracy." *Nordic Journal of Latin American and Caribbean Studies* 33 (1): 85–96.

———. 2004. "The Normalization of Punto Fijo Democracy." In *The Unraveling of Representative Democracy in Venezuela*, edited by Jennifer L. McCoy and David D. Myers, 11–32. Baltimore: Johns Hopkins University Press.

———. 2007. "From Thaw to Deluge: Party System Collapse in Venezuela and Peru." *Latin American Politics and Society* 49 (2): 59–86.

Naim, Moisés, and Ramón Piñango, eds. 1984. *El caso Venezuela: Una ilusión de armonía*. Caracas: Instituto de Estudios Superiores de Administración.

Navia, Patricio. 2006. "La izquierda de Lagos vs. la izquierda de Chávez." *Foreign Affairs en español* 6 (2): 75–88.

Ortiz, Nelson. 2004. "Entrepreneurs: Profits without Power?" In *The Unraveling of Venezuelan Democracy*, edited by Jennifer L. McCoy and David Myers, 71–92. Baltimore: Johns Hopkins University Press.

Penfold, Michael. 1999. *Constituent Assembly in Venezuela: First Report.* Atlanta: Carter Center.

———. 2002. "Federalism and Institutional Change in Venezuela." Paper presented at the Annual Meeting of the American Political Science Association, Boston, August 29–September 1.

Power, Timothy J. 2010. "Optimism, Pessimism, and Coalitional Presidentialism: Debating the Institutional Design of Brazilian Democracy." *Bulletin of Latin American Research* 29 (1): 18–33.

Przeworski, Adam. 1991. *Democracy and the Market: Political and Economic Reforms in Eastern Europe and Latin America.* Cambridge: Cambridge University Press.

Przeworski, Adam, Michael E. Alvarez, José Antonio Cheibub, and Fernando Limongi. 2000. *Democracy and Development: Political Institutions and Well-Being in the World, 1950–1990.* Cambridge: Cambridge University Press.

Raile, Eric D., Carlos Pereira, and Timothy J. Power. 2006. "The Presidential Toolbox: Generating Legislative Support in a Multiparty Presidential Regime." Paper presented at the Annual Meeting of the American Political Science Association, Philadelphia, August 31–September 3.

Remmer, Karen. 1991. *Military Rule in Latin America.* Boulder: Westview Press.

———. 2003. "Elections and Economics in Contemporary Latin America." In *Post-stabilization Politics in Latin America: Competition, Transition, Collapse*, edited by Carol Wise and Riordan Roett, 31–55. Washington, D.C.: Brookings Institution Press.

Riutort, Matías, and Ronald Balza Guanipa. 2011. "Salario real, tipo de cambio real y pobreza en Venezuela: 1975–2000." Mimeo, Departamento de Investigaciones Económicas, Instituto de Investigaciones Económicas y Sociales, Universidad Católica Andrés Bello, Caracas.

Roberts, Kenneth. 1998. *Deepening Democracy? The Modern Left and Social Movements in Chile and Peru.* Stanford: Stanford University Press.

———. 2003. "Social Polarization and the Populist Resurgence in Venezuela." In *Venezuelan Politics in the Chávez Era: Class, Polarization, and Conflict*, edited by Steve Ellner and Daniel Hellinger, 55–72. Boulder: Lynne Rienner.

Romero, Carlos. 2006. *Jugando con el globo: La política exterior de Hugo Chávez.* Caracas: Ediciones B.

Salamanca, Luis. 2004. "Civil Society: Late Bloomers." In *The Unraveling of Representative Democracy in Venezuela*, edited by Jennifer L. McCoy and David Myers, 93–114. Baltimore: Johns Hopkins University Press.

Schamis, Héctor E. 2006. "Populism, Socialism, and Democratic Institutions." *Journal of Democracy* 17 (4): 20–34.

Schedler, Andreas. 1996. "Anti-Political-Establishment Parties." *Party Politics* 2 (3): 291–312.

Súmate. 2005. "The State of Democracy in Venezuela." Caracas. http://www.sumate.org/democracia-retroceso/cap6_es_1.htm.

Trinkunas, Harold. 2002. "The Crisis in Venezuelan Civil–Military Relations: From Punto Fijo to the Fifth Republic." *Latin American Research Review* 37 (1): 41–76.

———. 2005. *Crafting Civilian Control of the Military in Venezuela: A Comparative Perspective.* Chapel Hill: University of North Carolina Press.

United Nations Educational, Scientific and Cultural Organization. Various years. *Statistical Yearbook.* Paris.

World Bank. 2001. *Bolivarian Republic of Venezuela: Investing in Human Capital for Growth, Prosperity, and Poverty Reduction. Latin America and the Caribbean Region.* Washington, D.C.

———. 2002. *Globalization, Growth, and Poverty.* Washington, D.C.

Yáñez, Patricia. 2004. "Las inmigraciones del Cono Sur en Venezuela: Década 70–80." In *Las inmigraciones a Venezuela en el siglo XX.* Caracas: Fundación Francisco Herrera Luque.

13 OIL, MACRO VOLATILITY, AND CRIME IN THE DETERMINATION OF BELIEFS IN VENEZUELA

Rafael Di Tella, Javier Donna, and Robert MacCulloch

In this chapter, we use data on political beliefs (broadly, left–right position, meritocracy, and origins of poverty) to discuss Venezuela's economic institutions. Our starting point is the large role attributed to beliefs in determining the economic system and the extent of government intervention (see, for example, Alesina, Glaeser, and Sacerdote 2001). This brings us to the question of what causes changes in beliefs. We briefly discuss and present evidence consistent with the idea that some of the main social and economic forces that affected Venezuela this century may have changed people's rational beliefs. These include a dependence on oil, a history of macroeconomic volatility, the rise in crime, and the rise in a preoccupation with corruption. We end up with a cautionary result: although these results point in the direction of giving a role to real shocks in the determination of beliefs, we test and find that perceptions for different phenomena are sometimes correlated. In particular, the perception of corruption is related to the perception of crime rather than the amount of real corruption actually experienced.

In an important paper, Piketty (1995) showed how beliefs could be central to economic organization. He focused on beliefs concerning the income-generating process and argued that when income was determined by luck, rational agents would be inclined to increase taxes. In contrast, when effort played a large role, rational agents fearing adverse incentive effects would moderate taxes. He then argued that, even if there were one fixed reality, two agents who started with prior beliefs at each end of the spectrum would not necessarily converge as long as agents could not freely find credible information to generalize from their own experience. In fact, he argued that information on how much effort really pays is not easy to observe (given that effort input is not observable), and that eventually agents would settle on some belief about the likely value of these parameters and stop experimenting (a form of bandit problem). Generalizing to countries, he argued that tax choices would reinforce these beliefs: where effort doesn't pay and luck dominates, agents would tend to vote on high taxes and luck would then really dominate. Indeed, the key finding in Piketty's paper is that two different economic systems—one with high taxes and beliefs that luck matters that can be called the French equilibrium, and another with low taxes and a belief that effort pays that can be called an American equilibrium—could arise out of the same underlying reality. Other papers that explore related ideas concern the role of upward mobility (Benabou and Ok 2001), fairness (Alesina and Angeletos 2005b), belief in a just world (Benabou and Tirole 2006), and corruption (Alesina and Angeletos 2005a; Di Tella and MacCulloch 2006). Denzau and North (1994) discuss institutions as "shared mental models" (see also Greif 1994).

A belief-based explanation is attractive given the difficulties that the standard economic model (e.g., Meltzer and Richard 1981) has in explaining the observed patterns of inequality and redistribution across Europe and the United States. Indeed, these models are particularly relevant once one observes the remarkable differences in beliefs across the Atlantic. For instance, Alesina, Glaeser, and Sacerdote (2001) report that 60 percent of Americans—yet only 26 percent of Europeans—believe the poor are lazy, while spending on social welfare in 1995 in the United States was 16 percent of GDP compared to an average of 25 percent for countries in Europe. (See also Lipset and Rokkan 1967; and the evidence in Hochschild 1981; Alesina and La Ferrara 2005; Fong 2004; and Ladd and Bowman 1998.)

Given the centrality of beliefs in economic organization, it seems natural to ask what drives beliefs. Very little evidence (that has a causal interpretation) is available (but see Di Tella, Donna, and MacCulloch 2008 on the connection with crime; and Di Tella, Rafael, Schargrodsky, and Galiani 2007, on the connection with property rights and a windfall gain). One extreme position is to argue that beliefs are cultural norms and are thus immutable. Alternatively, a rational learning process would posit their dependence on economic conditions. The latter hypothesis is particularly interesting in the context of Latin America in general, and Venezuela in particular, given their rather eventful history, with several traumatic and joyous events that may have affected beliefs simply because reality, at least for a while, appeared to have changed. The oil discoveries and the high prices during the 1970s, the macroeconomic crises, and the crime waves are all candidate episodes to be explored.

In this chapter, we take some of the likely forces that may have affected the formation of beliefs in Venezuela, explore their validity using data from a broader sample of countries, and then use the results to see how much of the Venezuelan experience they can explain. In particular, we wish to explain why the economy did so well between 1920 and 1970 yet so poorly after 1970, when the economies of other Latin American countries were growing. Our explanation centers on the increased macroeconomic volatility caused by the oil price shocks in the 1970s that led to a shift toward more leftist economic beliefs. In particular, Venezuelans began to view luck as the predominant determinant of economic success rather than effort. In this sense, the result of Venezuela's "resource curse" may have been a tendency for people to become more left-wing as volatile oil prices ushered in an era of populist and interventionist government policies that hampered the nation's post-1970s economic development.

In the next section, we discuss the role of a history of macroeconomic volatility; after that we explore the role of a country's dependence on oil rents; in the following section, we present further results on the role of corruption and beliefs (along the lines discussed in Di Tella and MacCulloch 2006), while after that we present the correlations between beliefs and having been the victim of crime. The next section studies the correlation between beliefs about a phenomenon (corruption) and beliefs about a second phenomenon (crime) controlling for reality (i.e., the experience with corruption and the experience with crime). After that we discuss the results in the context of Venezuela, while in the final section we offer some concluding comments.

Beliefs and a History of Macro Volatility

In this section, we study the correlation between a country's historical macroeconomic performance and its citizens' average beliefs in a cross-section of countries. We use the average values obtained from the third wave of the World Values Survey to construct our measures of beliefs and the World Bank's World Development Indicators to construct our measures of macro volatility. The basic results are presented in tables 13.1a and 13.1b. All regressions are estimated using OLS for simplicity (similar results are obtained if ordered logits are estimated) and control for income (six categories), gender, and age.[1] Results in columns (1–4) in table 13.1a focus on a general measure of beliefs: ideological self-placement on a 0–10 scale. These regressions are illustrative as a first broad pass at the data, as clearly the answers are provided with some country-specific ideological content. It is still perhaps interesting to note that a history of inflation volatility tilts the survey answers significantly to the left. In order to get some sense of the size of the effect, note that one standard deviation of the history of inflation volatility variable is associated with a decline of right wing-R of 5.8 percent of a standard deviation of this variable [−0.058 = (329.1/2.33)·(−4.1e−04)]. Columns (2–4) in table 13.1a present similar regressions, using history of GDP growth volatility, history of exchange rate volatility, and history of unemployment. The results are consistent (the coefficients are negative) although they are less precisely estimated.

Regressions (5–8) in table 13.1a focus on a more interesting dimension of beliefs, namely, unfair for poor-L, a dummy equal to 1 if the response to the question "Why, in your opinion, are there people in this country who live in need? Here are two opinions: which comes closest to your view? (1) They are poor because of laziness and lack of willpower, or (2) They are poor because society treats them unfairly" is (2) and 0 if the answer is (1). Now the key coefficients are generally positive as expected (the variable is defined so that bigger numbers have a natural interpretation as being left) and significant for both a history of inflation volatility and a history of exchange rate volatility. A history of unemployment volatility is also positive, but only significant at the 15 percent level.

Columns (1–4) in table 13.1b focus on the variable no escape-L (all variable definitions are in the appendix) and reveal that the volatility of inflation and of the exchange rate, as well as the history of unemployment, are correlated with more left-wing beliefs as expected. Columns (5–8) focus on business owner-L. Columns (5–6) are positive and significant, while column (7) is positive but significant only at the 11 percent level.

Beliefs and Oil

We now explore the hypothesis that economic dependence on oil causes the average beliefs in the country to lean toward the left end of the political spectrum. The results are presented in table 13.2, where we now focus on one summary variable of beliefs (ideological self-placement on a 1–10 scale) and regress the average country–year values against several measures of dependence on oil. One improvement over the previous section is that, given that we are no longer interested in historical background, we can exploit the time dimension of the values data and present panel regressions that control for country and year fixed effects. We adopt the convention that data from the WVS for wave 1 is matched to World Development Indicators data from 1981, for wave 2 to 1990, and wave 3 to 1997. All regressions control for age, gender and income of the respondents, although given representative sampling within countries this should not have a

Table 13.1a   How beliefs (general ideology and "poor are lazy") vary with macro volatility: Cross-section, thirty-two countries

Dependent variables	(1) Right wing-R	(2) Right wing-R	(3) Right wing-R	(4) Right wing-R	(5) Unfair for poor-R	(6) Unfair for poor-L	(7) Unfair for poor-L	(8) Unfair for poor-L
History of inflation volatility	−4.1e−04 (1.3e−04)	—	—	—	1.5e−04 (3.9e−05)	—	—	—
History of GDP growth volatility	—	−0.018 (0.034)	—	—	—	−0.006 (0.015)	—	—
History of exchange rate volatility	—	—	−0.033 (0.027)	—	—	—	0.019 (0.007)	—
History of unemployment	—	—	—	−0.017 (0.022)	—	—	—	0.008 (0.005)
R-sq.	0.013	0.010	0.003	0.011	0.018	1e−04	0.011	0.010
Number of groups	32	32	32	32	31	31	31	31
Number of obs.	31,585	31,585	31,585	31,585	27,120	27,120	27,120	27,120

NOTE: Name of dependent variable has L (R) extension if higher numbers mean more left (right). Right wing-R: a categorical variable that is the answer to the question "In politics people talk of the 'left' and of the 'right.' In a scale where '0' is left and '10' is right, where would you place yourself?" Unfair for poor-L: a dummy that is the response to the question "Why, in your opinion, are there people in this country who live in need? Here are two opinions: which comes closest to your view? (1) They are poor because of laziness and lack of willpower, or (2) They are poor because society treats them unfairly." The dummy takes the value 1 if the answer is (2) and 0 if the answer is (1). All regressions are cross-section (third wave) OLS regressions. Standard errors (adjusted for clustering) are in parentheses. The regressions include a set of personal controls that include age, gender and income (which is the respondent's declared income level as captured in the answer to the question "People sometimes describe themselves as belonging to the lower class, the middle class, or the upper class. How would you describe yourself?"). Left-hand variables are constructed using the World Bank's World Development Indicators as follows. History of inflation volatility: average of the absolute value of the inflation (CPI) 1993–1997 (five years before the third wave of the WVS), using annual averages in percent. History of growth volatility: average of the absolute value of the GDP growth 1993–1997 (five years before the third wave of the WVS) using annual averages in percent. History of exchange rate volatility: average of the absolute value of the exchange rate growth 1993–1997 (five years before the third wave of the WVS) calculated using the official exchange rate (LCU per USD, annual average). History of unemployment: average of the absolute value of the unemployment rate 1993–1997 (five years before the third wave of the WVS) using annual averages (percentage of total labor force).

Table 13.1b How beliefs ("escape from poverty" and "ownership of business") vary with macro volatility: Cross-section, thirty-two countries

Dependent variables	(1) No escape-L	(2) No escape-L	(3) No escape-L	(4) No escape-L	(5) Business owner-L	(6) Business owner-L	(7) Business owner-L	(8) Business owner-L
History of inflation volatility	2.2e−04 (5.3e−05)	—	—	—	2.0e−04 (4.4e−05)	—	—	—
History of GDP growth volatility	—	−0.009 (0.022)	—	—	—	0.036 (0.005)	—	—
History of exchange rate volatility	—	—	0.029 (0.010)	—	—	—	0.024 (0.015)	—
History of unemployment	—	—	—	0.016 (0.008)	—	—	—	−8.2e−04 (0.005)
R-sq.	0.024	0.007	0.015	0.023	0.032	0.057	0.014	0.007
Number of groups	32	32	32	32	32	32	32	32
Number of obs.	32,266	32,266	32,266	32,266	29,566	29,566	29,566	29,566

NOTE: Name of dependent variable has L (R) extension if higher numbers mean more left (right). No Eecape-L: a dummy equal to 1 if the answer to the question "In your opinion, do most poor people in this country have a chance of escaping from poverty, or there is very little chance of escaping? (1) They have a chance, or (2) There is very little chance" was category (2) and 0 if it was category (1). Business ownership-L: the response to the World Values question "There is a lot of discussion about how business and industry should be managed. Which of these four statements comes closest to your opinion? (1) The owners should run their business or appoint the managers, (2) The owners and the employees should participate in the selection of managers, (3) The government should be the owner and appoint the managers, (4) The employees should own the business and elect the managers." Business ownership-L was defined as a dummy equals 1 if the answer is category (3) or (4) and 0 if the answer is category (1) or (2). All regressions are cross-section (third wave) OLS regressions. Standard errors (adjusted for clustering) are in parentheses. The regressions include a set of personal controls which include age, gender, and income 1a (which is the respondent's declared income level as captured in the answer to the question "People sometimes describe themselves as belonging to the lower class, the middle class, or the upper class. How would you describe yourself?" Left-hand variables are constructed using the World Bank's World Development Indicators as follows. History of inflation volatility: average of the absolute value of the inflation (CPI) 1993–1997 (five years before the third wave of the WVS), using annual averages in percent. History of growth volatility: average of the absolute value of the GDP growth 1993–1997 (five years before the third wave of the WVS) using annual averages in percent. History of exchange rate volatility: average of the absolute value of the exchange rate growth 1993–1997 (five years before the third wave of the WVS) calculated using the official exchange rate (LCU per USD, annual average). History of unemployment: average of the absolute value of the unemployment rate 1993–1997 (five years before the third wave of the WVS) using annual averages (percentage of total labor force).

Table 13.2   Left-wing beliefs and dependence on oil rents: Panel regressions

Dependent variable: Right wing-R	(1)	(2)	(3)	(4)	(5)	(6)
Fuel exports	−0.010 (0.006)	—	—	—	—	—
Log fuel exports	—	−0.323 (0.092)	—	—	—	—
Ores exports	—	—	−0.065 (0.026)	—	—	—
Log ores exports	—	—	—	−0.466 (0.256)	—	—
Manufacturing exports	—	—	—	—	0.006 (0.004)	—
Log manufacturing exports	—	—	—	—	—	0.211 (0.204)
Adj. R-sq.	0.061	0.062	0.062	0.062	0.060	0.060
Between number of groups	24	24	24	24	24	24
Max number of groups	49	49	49	49	49	49
Number of obs.	79,251	79,251	79,251	79,251	79,251	79,251

NOTE: All regressions are OLS regressions and include country and year dummies. Dependent variable is right wing-R, a categorical variable that is the answer to the question "In politics people talk of the 'left' and of the 'right.' In a scale where '0' is left and '10' is right, where would you place yourself?" and is obtained from the WVS. Fuel exports refers to "fuel exports as percentage of merchandise exports" and is obtained from the World Bank's World Development Indicators. Ores exports refers to "ores and metals exports as percentage of merchandise exports" and is obtained from the World Bank's World Development Indicators. Manufacturing exports refers to "manufactures exports as % of merchandise exports" and is obtained from the World Bank's World Development Indicators. Merchandise exports show the FOB value of goods provided to the rest of the world valued in U.S. dollars. They are classified using the Standard International Trade Classification. In particular, the World Bank figures distinguish between "merchandise exports" and "exports of services." Log variable name refers to the natural log of variable name. All regressions control for age, gender, and income Ia. For income Ia, the respondents declared income level as captured in the question "People sometimes describe themselves as belonging to the lower class, the middle class, or the upper class. How would you describe yourself?" Standard errors on fuel exports, log fuel exports, ores exports, log ores exports, manufacturing exports, and log manufacturing exports adjusted to take account of clustering within countries. Clustered standard errors in parentheses.

large influence in our results.[2] All standard errors are adjusted for clustering at the country level.

Column (1) reports a negative coefficient, significant at the 13 percent level, indicating a tendency to move left when fuel exports (as a percentage of merchandise exports) increase. Column (2) uses logs and reports a somewhat larger and considerably more precise coefficient on the dependence on oil (it is significant at the 1 percent level). In terms of size, one standard deviation of log fuel exports is associated with a decline equal to 4.6 percent of a standard deviation in (right-wing) beliefs.

The rest of the table switches to other measures of income's dependence on luck in the country. Column (3) focuses on ores and metal exports as a percentage of merchandise exports. The coefficient is negative but insignificant. Column (4) uses logs, and finds a negative coefficient significant at the 8 percent level. In terms of size, one standard deviation of log ores exports is associated with a decline equal to 3.5 percent of a standard deviation in beliefs. Columns (5–6) present weaker results (but still with the expected sign) using manufacturing exports and its log.

Beliefs and Corruption

In table 13.3, we explore the relationship between ideological inclination and corruption. When corruption is widespread, the legitimacy of profits and business is called into question and individuals will be attracted to left-wing ideas, particularly in the economic sphere (see Di Tella and MacCulloch 2006). It uses a corruption variable as coded by experts working for Political Risk Services, a private international investment risk service. Introduced into economics by Knack and Keefer (1995), the International Country Risk Guide (ICRG) corruption index has been produced annually since 1982 and intends to capture the extent to which "high government officials are likely to demand special payments," and the extent to which "illegal payments are generally expected throughout lower levels of government" in the form of "bribes connected with import and export licenses, exchange controls, tax assessments, police protection, or loans."

Column (1) in table 13.3 correlates the average ideological inclination in the country with the perceived corruption level, controlling for country and year effects. The coefficient is negative as expected and significant at the 3 percent level. In terms of size, we note that one standard deviation (within) in the ICRG corruption indicator is associated with a decline in a country's ideological inclination, right wing-R, equal to 3.7 percent of a standard deviation (within) of the ideological variable $[-0.037 = 0.42 \cdot (-0.19)/2.15]$. Column (2) shows that the same correlation using logs is weaker, as it is only statistically significant at the 10.5 percent level.

Beliefs and Crime

In table 13.4, we study the connection between crime and beliefs following Di Tella and MacCulloch (2006). Such a connection might be expected when,

Table 13.3 How left-wing beliefs vary with corruption: Panel regressions

Dependent variable: Right wing-R	(1)	(2)
Corruption	−0.190 (0.086)	—
Log corruption	—	−0.262 (0.157)
Adj. R-sq.	0.067	0.061
Between number of groups	25	25
Max number of groups	36	36
Number of obs.	66,144	66,144

NOTE: All regressions are OLS regressions and include country and year dummies. Dependent variable is right wing-R, a categorical variable that is the answer to the question "In politics people talk of the 'left and of the 'right.' In a scale where '0' is left and '10' is right, where would you place yourself?" and is obtained from the WVS. Corruption is obtained the ICRG. See Knack and Keefer 1995. Log corruption refers to the natural log of corruption. All regressions control for age, gender, and income Ia. For income Ia, the respondents declared income level as captured in the question "People sometimes describe themselves as belonging to the lower class, the middle class, or the upper class. How would you describe yourself?" Standard errors on corruption and log corruption adjusted to take account of clustering within countries. Clustered standard errors in parentheses.

for example, agents have incomplete information about the role of effort in the income-generating process, and the observation of crime informs agents about other people's view of how much it pays to work hard (which is probably low, given that they have chosen crime). Indeed, the two equilibriums in the Piketty (1995) model survive only as long as agents cannot observe how much effort others are putting in (and how much income they obtain). This requires that agents cannot reconstruct other people's information set from their choices in the labor market or in the political market, which is a somewhat artificial assumption given that vote outcomes and career choices are well-known. In order to test this hypothesis we need data on people's beliefs and on their view of how much crime there is (or on their experience as victims of crime).

Such data can be found in the Latinobarómetro, an annual public opinion survey of approximately nineteen thousand interviews in eighteen countries in Latin America. Questions of interest rotate, so the number of waves (and thus our sample size) varies considerably depending on the question being studied. It is produced by Latinobarómetro Corporation, an NGO based in Santiago. It has data on a number of attitudinal variables associated with ideological standing (on an economic dimension). From the long list we choose two that are suitable for our purposes. One concerns the fairness of the distribution of income and the other concerns how successful were privatizations. The exact data is fair-L and privatiz-L (see table 13.4 for the exact wording of the questions).

In columns (1–2) of table 13.4, we correlate these beliefs question with perception of crime, the answer to the question "Crime has increased or decreased?"

Table 13.4 How left-wing beliefs vary with crime: Panel regressions

Dependent variables	Latin America							
	(1) Fair-L	(2) Privatiz-L	(3) Fair-L	(4) Privatiz-L	(5) Fair-L	(6) Privatiz-L	(7) Fair-L	(8) Privatiz-L
Perception of crime	−0.283 (0.012)	−0.051 (0.005)	—	—	−0.237 (0.014)	−0.050 (0.005)	—	—
Real crime	—	—	−0.031 (0.009)	−0.011 (0.004)	—	—	−0.022 (0.011)	−0.010 (0.004)
Personal controls I	Yes	Yes	Yes	Yes	No	No	No	No
Personal controls II	No	No	No	No	Yes	Yes	Yes	Yes
Pseudo RSQ	0.082	0.045	0.072	0.044	0.105	0.045	0.099	0.042
Max no. of groups	17	17	17	17	17	17	17	17
Between no. g roups	17	17	17	17	15	17	15	17
Number of obs.	47,283	53,107	47,231	68,738	35,267	51,827	35,181	66,323

NOTE: Name of dependent variable has L (R) extension if higher numbers mean more left (right). All regressions are OLS regressions and include country and year dummies. All variables are obtained from the Latinobarómetro. Standard errors in parentheses. Perception of crime is a dummy that equals 0 if the answer to the question "Crime has increased or decreased?" is "Has increased a lot" and 1 if it is "Has increased a little," "Has stayed the same," "Has fallen a little," or "Has fallen a lot." Real crime is a categorical variable equal to 1 if the answer to the question "Have you or a relative of yours been a victim of an assault, an aggression, or a crime, in the last twelve months?" is "Yes" and 2 if the answer is "No." Personal controls I: age, gender and income Ib. Personal controls II: age, gender, income ib, and city size. Income Ib: the respondents declared income level as capture in the question "The wage or salary you receive and the total family income, does it allow you to satisfactorily cover your needs? In which of these situations are you?" The possible answers are "It is good enough, you can save," "It is just enough, without great difficulties," "It is not enough, you have difficulties," and "It is not enough, you have great difficulties." City size: the size/population of the city where the interview takes place. The two possible categories are 1 if "100,000 or less" and 2 if "capital or more than 100,000." Dependent variables are the answers to the questions:

Columns (1, 3, 5, 7)   Fair-L: Now I'd like you some questions about the problem of poverty, in this country and in other countries: How fair do you think the distribution of income is in this country? The five possible answers are 1. Very fair; 2. Fair; 3. Neither fair nor unfair; 4. Unfair; and 5. Very unfair.

Columns (2, 4, 6, 8)   Privatiz-L: Do you agree or disagree with the following statement: The privatization of public companies has been beneficial to the country. The two possible values are 1. I agree (if the answer to the question is: I completely agree or I agree); and 2. I disagree (if the answer to the question is: I completely disagree or I disagree).

The possible answers are coded such that it takes the value 0 if the answer is "Has increased a lot" and 1 if it is "Has increased a little," "Has stayed the same," "Has fallen a little," or "Has fallen a lot." We collapse the answers into two because, although there are five categorical answers to this question, the overwhelming majority chooses one option. The raw data show that 96,358 individuals selected the answer "Crime has increased a lot," while 14,610 say it has increased somewhat, 8,591 say it has stayed the same, 2,904 say it has dropped somewhat, and 439 say it has dropped a lot. We repeated the analysis using the five categories and all the results remain qualitatively similar. Both coefficients are negative as expected, and significant. Note that this is unlikely to reflect a fixed trait of the respondents because such a fixed characteristic is most likely ideological orientation: right-wing individuals are always complaining that crime is a terrible thing, and they tend to think that the distribution of income is fair. In this case the connection goes the opposite way, so, at least in this regard, it is an underestimate of the true effect. We also include a set of control variables that help ameliorate this concern, including age, gender, and income, as well as year and country fixed effects.

Columns (3–4) move to real crime as an independent variable, namely, whether the respondent (or a relative of the respondent) was a victim of crime over the previous year. Again, both coefficients are negative and comfortably significant. Now the potential confounding effect is not an ideological fixed effect but rather some omitted variable such as income, which determines that you are both the victim of crime and that you hold left-wing views. Columns (5–6) repeat the exercise with a broader set of controls. These include age, gender, dummies for city size, and all the previous explanatory variables, but using a new measure of each respondent's income. A person's declared income level is now captured by the question "The wage or salary you receive and the total family income, does it allow you to satisfactorily cover your needs? In which of these situations are you?" The possible answers are "It is good enough, you can save," "It is just enough, without great difficulties," "It is not enough, you have difficulties," and "It is not enough, you have great difficulties." The results are again supportive of the hypothesis that an experience with crime moved individuals to the left end of the political spectrum. In auxiliary regressions, we included controls for educational attainment, a person's ideological self-placement, and simultaneous controls for both measures of income, and obtained similar results.

Perceptions versus Reality

Having established that perceptions of corruption and crime affect ideological inclination, it is interesting to explore what drives these perceptions. Is it reality, so that people's perception of corruption follows the fact that there is more corruption? Or is it that these perceptions are like "moods" that can be divorced from reality? In a recent paper, Olken (2006) shows that there can be a substantial divorce between reality and perceptions using Indonesian data.

One possible strategy is to evaluate whether the perception of a certain phenomenon is related strongly to the experience of that phenomenon, or the perception of a (presumably unrelated) phenomenon. In table 13.5 we present regressions for perception of corruption on real corruption. The coefficient is positive and significant, suggesting that reality does affect perceptions. Regression (2) includes year fixed effects and the coefficient remains unaffected. Regression (3) shows that when we include the perception and reality of a second phenomenon, crime, the coefficient on real corruption is almost halved and is now statistically insignificant. Interestingly, the coefficient on perception of crime is positive and statistically well defined (while real crime is uncorrelated with perception of corruption). Real crime is included as a reassurance that actual crime is being kept constant (although its inclusion does not affect the conclusions). The size of the coefficient is extremely large, suggesting that the role of perceptions (generally) is important, potentially overwhelming the impact of reality. To get a sense of the relative size, note that one standard deviation increase in real corruption is associated with an increase in perceived corruption equal to less than 1 percent of a standard deviation in that variable [$0.009 = (0.43/0.68) \cdot 0.015$]. In contrast, one standard deviation increase in perception of crime is associated with an increase in perception of corruption equal to 53 percent of a standard deviation [$0.53 = (0.74/0.68) \cdot 0.49$]. Real crime has virtually no effect (just over 1.4 percent in standardized units).

Regressions (5–6) repeat the exercise for Venezuela and reveal that the same phenomenon applies there. This suggests that perceptions of corruption (and of other "bads") are driven not by reality, but rather by some other force. We conjecture that this makes the electorate particularly receptive to "political activists" who supply beliefs, as in Glaeser's (2005) model of hatred.

The Case of Venezuela

We can apply the above results to the case of Venezuela. We first focus on the role of volatility of the economy. High levels of volatility may mean that the connection between effort and reward is lost. This may in turn affect people's (right–left) beliefs about the degree of regulation and taxation that is required for their society. Venezuela lies in the top quarter of the countries in our sample in terms of both

Table 13.5 How perceptions of corruption vary with real corruption, perception of crime, and real crime: Panel regressions

Dependent variable	Latin America				Venezuela	
Perception of corruption	(1)	(2)	(3)	(4)	(5)	(6)
Real corruption	0.028 (0.012)	0.028 (0.012)	0.015 (0.011)	0.015 (0.011)	0.069 (0.064)	0.068 (0.059)
Perception of crime	—	—	0.490 (0.007)	0.490 (0.007)	—	0.660 (0.044)
Real crime	—	—	0.011 (0.010)	0.011 (0.010)	—	−0.028 (0.054)
Year dummy	No	Yes	No	Yes	Year: 2001	Year: 2001
R^2 overall	0.009	0.010	0.217	0.220	0.036	0.211
Number of groups	17	17	17	17	—	—
Number of obs.	17,564	17,564	17,564	17,564	1,037	1,037

NOTE: All regressions are OLS regressions. Dependent variable is perception of corruption, a categorical variable equal to 1 if the answer to the question "Corruption has increased or decreased?" is "Has increased a lot," 2 if it is "Has increased a little," 3 if it is "Has stayed the same," 4 if it is "Has fallen a little," and 5 if it is "Has fallen a lot." Real corruption is a categorical variable equal to 1 if the answer to the question "Have you or a relative of yours been a victim of corruption in the last twelve months?" is "Yes," and 2 if the answer is "No." Perception of crime, a categorical variable, equals 1 if the answer to the question "Crime has increased or decreased?" is "Has increased a lot," 2 if it is "Has increased a little," 3 if it is "Has stayed the same," 4 if it is "Has fallen a little," and 5 if it is "Has fallen a lot." [Real crime is a categorical variable equal to 1 if the answer to the question "Have you or a relative of yours been a victim of an assault, an aggression, or a crime, in the last twelve months?" is "Yes" and 2 if the answer is "No." All regressions control for age, gender, income Ib, and right wing-R. Income Ib: the respondents declared income level as capture in the question "The wage or salary you receive and the total family income, does it allow you to satisfactorily cover your needs? In which of these situations are you?" The possible answers are "It is good enough, you can save," "It is just enough, without great difficulties," "It is not enough, you have difficulties," and "It is not enough, you have great difficulties." Right wing-R is the answer to the World Values question "In politics people talk of the 'left' and of the 'right.' In a scale where '0' is left and '10' is right, where would you place yourself?" Standard errors in parentheses.

inflation and unemployment volatility. An increase in inflation (unemployment) volatility from U.S. to Venezuelan levels explains 6.9 percent (24.8 percent) of the difference in leftist beliefs about the degree to which the poor have been treated unfairly, and 4.3 percent (21.0 percent) of the difference in leftist beliefs about the chances of escaping from poverty between these two nations (see tables 13.1a–b).

Another striking feature of Venezuela is its unusually high dependence on natural resources, in particular oil. To the extent that this country relies on abundant natural resources, becoming wealthy may be more associated with success in capturing rents and belonging to the elite, rather than on working hard in competitive industries. Venezuela has the second highest level of fuel exports as a proportion of total merchandise exports across all the countries in our sample at 78.9 percent (the highest proportion is Nigeria). A high dependence on oil may also be one of the causes of the increased unemployment and inflation volatility discussed above (see Carruth, Hooker, and Oswald 1998). An increase in fuels as a proportion of total merchandise exports from U.S. to Venezuelan levels is predicted to push an individual toward having more leftist beliefs by 1.1 units on the 0–10 right–left scale (see table 13.2).

Turning to corruption, the International Country Risk Guide index places Venezuela in the bottom 13 percent of nations in our sample. An increase in the corruption index from U.S. to Venezuelan levels is predicted to push an individual toward having more leftist beliefs by 0.24 units on the 0–10 right–left scale (see table 13.3). We also noted earlier how higher observed crime rates may lead people to believe that effort exerted in legal labor market activities is not rewarding, thereby affecting their political beliefs. An increase from the lowest to the highest average measures of perception of crime recorded between 1995 and 2001 within Venezuela explains 15.4 percent of the range of leftist values, as measured by fairness of the distribution of income (see table 13.4).

Conclusions

The starting point of this chapter is the fact that the Venezuelan public has become more receptive to left-wing, populist, antimarket rhetoric. This chapter explores why. Our main explanation centers on the increased macroeconomic volatility stemming from the oil price shocks in the 1970s that led Venezuelans to view luck (rather than effort) as the reason behind economic success. Their heavy dependence on oil meant that internationally determined prices became an important driver of the economy, and led to a shift toward more leftist economic beliefs that favored the view that the poor were not to blame for their predicament and therefore should be helped by the government. In other words, the result of Venezuela's "resource curse" may have been a tendency for the people to become more left-wing as volatile oil prices in the 1970s ushered in an era of populist and interventionist policies that hampered the nation's post-1970s economic development.

More specifically, we use anecdotal evidence to focus on four phenomena that appear to be widespread in Venezuela: a history of macro volatility, an economic dependency on oil, a belief that corruption is widespread, and a belief that there has been a crime wave in the country. These four phenomena are theoretically compatible with moving the electorate to the left, because macro volatility and oil dependency mean that luck is important relative to effort in the determination of income, because corruption erodes the legitimacy of business (see, e.g., Di Tella and MacCulloch 2006), and because widespread crime gives us information about how badly other people (criminals) fared in the labor market. The evidence is consistent with the hypothesis that beliefs are correlated with these forces.

Although this all points broadly in the direction of reality being an important factor in the formation of beliefs for some of the factors study (e.g., our data on oil dependency is from actual oil dependency), the data on corruption used in Di Tella and MacCulloch (2006) is based on the perception of corruption. Perceptions may sometimes be divorced from reality, as political players (like Hugo Chávez) can potentially affect the beliefs of the electorate (perhaps by attacking a political group for political gain). In an attempt to shed some light on the relative perception of reality, we run regressions of the perception of corruption on reality (personal experience with corruption) and on the perceptions of another phenomena (the perceptions of how much has crime increased), controlling for reality. We note that the perceptions of corruption are strongly correlated with the perceptions of this second phenomenon (the increase in crime) and have a much weaker connection with the personal experience with corruption or crime (reality).

APPENDIX: DESCRIPTION OF WORLD VALUES SURVEY

World Values Survey and European Values Survey (1981–1984, 1990–1992, 1995–1997)

The Combined World Values Survey is produced by the Institute for Social Research, based in Ann Arbor, Michigan. The series is designed to enable a cross-national comparison of values on a wide variety of norms, and to monitor changes in values and attitudes across the globe. Both national random and quota sampling were used. All the surveys were carried out through face-to-face interviews, with a sampling universe consisting of all adult citizens, aged eighteen and older, across more than sixty nations around the world. The 1981–83 survey covered twenty-two independent countries; the 1990–93 survey covered forty-two independent countries; the 1995–97 survey covered fifty-three independent countries. In total, sixty-four independent countries have been surveyed in at least one wave of this investigation (counting East Germany as an independent country, which it was when first surveyed). These countries include almost 80 percent of the world's population. A fourth wave of surveys was carried out in 1999–2000. The following is the full set of countries and territories covered: Argentina, Armenia, Australia, Austria, Azerbaijan, Bangladesh, Belarus, Belgium, Bosnia–Herzegovina, Brazil, Bulgaria, Canada, Chile, China, Colombia, Croatia, Czech Republic, Denmark, Dominican Republic, East and Unified Germany, Estonia, Finland, France, Georgia, Ghana, Hungary, Iceland, India, Ireland, Italy, Japan, Latvia, Lithuania, Macedonia, Madagascar, Mexico, Moldova, Montenegro, Moscow, The Netherlands, Nigeria, Northern Ireland, Norway, Pakistan, Peru, Philippines, Poland, Portugal, Puerto Rico, Romania, Russia, Serbia, Slovak Republic, Slovenia, South Africa, South Korea, Spain, Sweden, Switzerland, Taiwan, Tambov Oblast, Turkey, Ukraine, Uruguay, United Kingdom, United States of America, and Venezuela.

Latinobarómetro

The Latinobarómetro Survey is an annual public opinion survey of approximately nineteen thousand interviews in eighteen countries in Latin America. Questions of interest rotate, so the number of waves (and thus our sample size) varies considerably depending on the question being studied. It is produced by Latinobarómetro Corporation, an NGO based in Santiago. It surveys development of democracies, economies, and societies; we are particularly interested in a number of attitudinal variables that are associated with ideological standing (on an economic dimension). Just like the WVS, it is designed to enable a cross-national comparison of values and norms on a variety of topics. As far as we can tell, a national random sampling were used, and the surveys were carried out through face-to-face interviews, with a sampling universe consisting of adult citizens, aged eighteen and older. The countries covered are Argentina, Bolivia, Brazil, Chile, Colombia, Costa Rica, Ecuador, El Salvador, Guatemala, Honduras, Mexico, Nicaragua, Panama, Paraguay, Peru, Spain, Uruguay, and Venezuela.

World Development Indicators (World Bank)

WDI Online is a data source on the global economy. It contains statistical data for more than six hundred development indicators and time series data from 1960 to 2004 (selected data for 2005) for more than two hundred countries and eighteen country groups. Data includes social, economic, financial, natural resources, and environmental indicators.

NOTES

1. The controls are chosen to keep constant some basic set of personal characteristics of the respondents that may affect beliefs (although these are country averages, so their influence in this particular case is marginal) without sacrificing sample size.

2. When we add gender as personal control in the regressions of table 13.2, Mexico's observations for the first wave are lost. This might be significant as Mexico is a gross outlier, with the largest reduction in dependence on fuel exports, all concentrated in the first two waves, and the largest decline in right-wing inclinations.

REFERENCES

Alesina, Alberto, and George-Marios Angeletos. 2005a. "Corruption, Inequality, and Fairness." *Journal of Monetary Economics* 52 (7): 1227–44.
————. 2005b. "Fairness and Redistribution." *American Economic Review* 95 (4): 960–80.
Alesina, Alberto, Edward Glaeser, and Bruce Sacerdote. 2001. "Why Doesn't the U.S. Have a European Style Welfare State?" In *Brookings Papers on Economic Activity*, edited by William C. Brainard and George L. Perry, 187–277. Washington, D.C.: Brookings Institution.
Alesina, Alberto, and Eliana La Ferrara. 2005. "Redistribution in the Land of Opportunities." *Journal of Public Economics* 89 (5/6): 897–931.
Benabou, Roland. 2000. "Unequal Societies: Income Distribution and the Social Contract." *American Economic Review* 90 (1): 96–129.
Benabou, Roland, and Efe A. Ok. 2001. "Social Mobility and the Demand for Redistribution: The POUM Hypothesis." *Quarterly Journal of Economics* 116 (2): 447–87.
Benabou, Roland, and Jean Tirole. 2006. "Belief in a Just World and Redistributive Policies." *Quarterly Journal of Economics* 121 (2): 699–746.
Carruth, A., M. Hooker, and A. Oswald. 1998. "Input Prices and Unemployment Equilibria: Theory and Evidence for the United States." *Review of Economics and Statistics* 80 (4): 621–28.
Denzau, A., and D. North. 1994. "Shared Mental Models: Ideologies and Institutions." *Kyklos* 47 (1): 3–31.
Di Tella, Rafael, Javier Donna, and Robert MacCulloch. 2008. "Crime and Beliefs." *Economics Letters* 99 (3): 566–69.
Di Tella, Rafael, and Robert MacCulloch. 2002. "Why Doesn't Capitalism Flow to Poor Countries?" *Brookings Papers on Economic Activity* 40 (Spring): 285–31.
————. 2006. "Corruption and the Demand for Regulating Capitalists." In *The International Handbook in the Economics of Corruption*, edited by Susan Rose-Ackerman, 352–80. Cheltenham, U.K.: Edward Elgar.
Di Tella, Rafael, Ernesto Schargrodsky, and Sebastian Galiani. 2007. "The Formation of Beliefs: Evidence from the Allocation of Titles to Squatters." *Quarterly Journal of Economics* 122 (1): 209–41.
Fong, Christina. 2004. "Which Beliefs Matter for Redistributive Politics? Target-Specific versus General Beliefs about the Causes of Income." Mimeo, Carnegie Mellon University, Pittsburgh.
Geertz, Clifford. 1973. *The Interpretation of Cultures.* New York: Basic Books.
Glaeser, Edward. 2005. "The Political Economy of Hatred." *Quarterly Journal of Economics* 120 (1): 45–86.

Greif, Avner. 1994. "Cultural Beliefs and the Organization of Society: A Historical and Theoretical Reflection on Collectivist and Individualist Societies." *Journal of Political Economy* 102 (5): 912–50.

Hochschild, Jennifer. 1981. *What's Fair? American Beliefs about Distributive Justice.* Cambridge: Harvard University Press.

Knack, Stephen, and Philip Keefer. 1995. "Institutions and Economic Performance: Cross-Country Tests Using Alternative Institutional Measures." *Economics and Politics* 7 (3): 207–27.

Ladd, Everett Carll, and Karlyn Bowman. 1998. *Attitudes towards Economic Inequality.* Washington, D.C.: AEI Press.

Lipset, Seymour Martin, and Stein Rokkan. 1967. "Cleavage Structures, Party Systems, and Voter Alignments: An Introduction." In *Party Systems and Voter Alignments*, edited by Seymour Martin Lipset and Rokkan Stein, 2–8. New York: Free Press.

Meltzer, A., and S. Richard. 1981. "A Rational Theory of the Size of Government." *Journal of Political Economy* 89 (5): 914–27.

Olken, Ben. 2006. "Corruption Perceptions versus Corruption Reality." Working Paper 12428, National Bureau of Economic Research, Cambridge, Mass.

Piketty, Thomas. 1995. "Social Mobility and Redistributive Politics." *Quarterly Journal of Economics* 110 (3): 551–84.

14 UNDERSTANDING THE COLLAPSE: VENEZUELA'S EXPERIENCE IN CROSS-NATIONAL PERSPECTIVE

Ricardo Hausmann and Francisco Rodríguez

During much of the past two decades, it appeared as if there were two distinct alternatives for studying economic growth. One of them was to conduct empirical studies based on the analysis of cross-country data sets, which allowed for the formal testing of hypotheses about the causes of growth. The other was to conduct in-depth studies of a particular country's experience, an avenue that did not allow for formal hypothesis testing but which permitted taking account of the complexities and nuances of particular cases.

There was of course a burgeoning literature on issues as varied as credit and labor markets, sectoral productivity, regional disparities, poverty, inequality, and a number of other topics of special relevance to developing countries. Yet, while this literature provided valuable insights into how developing economies function, attempts to trace them back to aggregate economic performance were scant. Thus two somewhat disconnected literatures emerged: a macro-development literature, which relied heavily on cross-country growth empirics; and a micro-development literature, which concentrated on the study of particular markets within development economics.

This book is an attempt to bring these two literatures together. The fundamental idea of this research project was to test hypotheses about aggregate variables using data available at a lower level of disaggregation than the national one. Doing so allows us to get past the common critique that case studies are just regressions with one data point, while at the same time addressing the legitimate concern that meaningful hypotheses about economic growth may be too dependent on structural and institutional factors to be amenable to testing on cross-national data.

To be fair, this marks a return to an older tradition of studies of economic growth and development. W. W. Rostow's *The Stages of Economic Growth* (1960) and Edward F. Denison's *Why Growth Rates Differ* (1967) are just two examples of work that combined the in-depth exploration of country case studies with the best use of quantitative techniques available at the time in order to test explicit hypotheses about the causes of development. But the key difference between our approach and these older studies has to do with our ability to take advantage of the recent development of microeconomic data sets with detailed information on households and firms. Our approach is strengthened also by appealing to the development of macroeconomic techniques to evaluate time-series behavior (as in chapter 9) and the use of sector-specific cross-national comparisons (as in chapters 1 and 8), as well as the more in-depth exploration of political economy dynamics.

Of course, the method presented is very much a work in progress. Further research is necessary to allow us to systematically understand the relationships between individual-level results and aggregate hypotheses. This is particularly important when the hypotheses being considered involve mechanisms that operate only at the aggregate level (e.g., national learning by doing). Understanding how to combine the results of tests applied to different data sets and using different econometric methodologies is far from an easy question. The relative places of quantitative and qualitative analyses in relationship to one another needs to be sorted out. And we will need to understand how the results of the within-country approach compare to traditional cross-national approaches.

These are questions that we have just started to broach, and which will need to be answered if the method in question is to be applied more generally. The purpose of this chapter is to address one of these questions, namely, the relationship between the results of our approach and the cross-country regression approach. We do this by systematically comparing the results of both methodologies.

The rest of the argument is developed as follows. In the next section we review the results of the chapters in this book and present a schematic representation of our results, contrasting them with those found in the growth literature. The following section then compares our results with those that would have been derived if we had approached these questions through a cross-country regression approach. And in the final section, we conclude our argument.

How Our Results Relate to the Literature

Broadly speaking, the story told by the essays in this book is the following. During the half century before the seventies, Venezuela built a relatively stable economic and political system, which was able to function relatively well given a growing or even stable level of oil rents. The eighties saw Venezuela hit by a double shock: a decline in its export prices and the debt crisis. To a certain extent, these shocks hit most Latin American economies with similar force. But Venezuela fared worse for two reasons. The first is that the decline in export revenues was more pronounced and more long-lasting than in most countries, as it also reflected a long-run decline in per capita oil production. The second is that the Venezuelan economy and polity were not well prepared to handle these negative shocks.

The negative shocks thus set in place a set of reactions that had significant feedback loops. First, since the economy was unable to fill the gap in its export revenues by creating new export industries—a consequence of its lack of export flexibility—the contraction in oil revenues led to a wholesale contraction of the economy's capital stock. At the same time, collapsing oil revenues led to a decline in fiscal revenues, with a consequent costly fiscal adjustment. The fiscal adjustment was heavily biased against long-term investment in public goods, generating adverse productivity effects in the long run.

Venezuela's rigidity was not just in its export sector. Venezuela had built a redistributive system that was heavily reliant on labor market institutions and patronage politics. These performed reasonably well under times of prosperity or even of stagnation, but not under strong negative shocks. As the economy entered a deep recession in the early eighties, labor market rigidities became even more onerous and maintaining, and the patronage structure became even more difficult. When the effect of these restrictions kicked in, the economy contracted even further as employment moved into the lower productivity informal sector and the decline in the power of traditional political parties led to a caving in of the political system.

Admittedly doing injustice to the complexity of the stories presented in each of the chapters, we can set out a schematic representation of the effects of potential forces on the Venezuelan growth collapse. These are presented in the first column of table 14.1, which sets out the key hypotheses presented in the chapters of this book and the conclusions reached in each of these. It is useful to compare the results provided by the chapters of this book with those of the cross-country empirical growth literature. Thus in the fourth column we provide some basic references for each variable from the cross-country growth literature, which we discuss in greater detail below.[1]

Perhaps one of the variables whose effect is most contentiously debated in the growth literature is trade openness. This is natural, as the theory of comparative advantage is one of the essential building blocks of much economic analysis. Views differ markedly on whether trade liberalization leads to growth, or whether

Table 14.1   Effects of potential forces on the Venezuelan growth collapse

Explanatory variable	Chapter	Within-country	Cross-country		Decomposition	
		Result	Relevant literature	BACE	Variable	Effect (percentage of decline)
Trade openness	1, 11	No effect	Frankel and Romer 1999; Rodríguez and Rodrik 2000	Years open, positive and robust	Openness ratio in constant prices (Heston et al. 2007)	6.6(*)
Export flexibility	1	No effect during export growth and stability, adverse effect after negative shocks	Hausmann, Hwang, and Rodrik 2005; Hausmann, Rodríguez, and Wagner 2008; Hidalgo et al. 2007	Not tested	Open forest variable (Hausmann Rodríguez, and Wagner 2008)	17.0
Natural resources	1, 2	Drove economic growth pre-1980: its collapse contributed to stagnation afterward	Sachs and Warner 1995; Rodríguez and Sachs 1999; Lederman and Maloney 2008	Fraction of GDP in mining, positive and robust; primary exports in GDP, negative and not robust	Share of primary exports in GDP (World Bank 2009)	2.6
Infrastructure	3	Significant effect	Easterly and Rebelo 1993; Calderon and Servén 2004	Public investment share, not robust	Road length (World Bank 2010)	(–)
Labor market rigidities	4	Negative effect, particularly after adverse shock	Calderon, Chong, and Leon 2007	Not tested	Number of International Labour Organization conventions (Artecona and Rama 2002)	–2.3
Financial deepening	5	Significant effect—financial collapse impeded the recovery	Levine and Zervos 1998; Demetriades and Law 2004	Not tested	Domestic credit provided by bank sector (World Bank 2010)	14.4
Human capital	6	No effect	Barro 1991; Hanushek and Woessmann 2010	Primary schooling, robust; life expectancy, robust	Average attainment of primary schooling (Barro and Lee 2010)	12.7(***)

Income distribution	7	No effect	Alesina and Rodrik 1994; Banerjee and Duflo 2003	Not tested	Gini index (World Bank 2010)	9.3
International migration	8	Negative effect of changing composition of the labor force	Ortega and Peri 2009; Letouze et al. 2009	Not tested	Migrants as a share of the population (United Nations 2010)	−2.5
Fiscal policy	9	Partial effect—initial overspending crated weak position; posterior adjustment, however, was reasonable	Barro 1991; Easterly and Levine 1997	Government consumption, negative and robust	Government share of real GDP per capita (Heston, Summers, and Aten 2002)	10.4(***)
Institutions	10, 12, 14	Causality mostly runs in other direction—collapse caused institutional implosion. Weakened institutions can explain difficulties in restoring growth.	Acemoglu, Johnson, and Robinson 2001; Rodrik, Subramanian, and Trebbi 2004	Religion dummies, robust	Average expropriation risk (Glaeser et al. 2004)	25.4(**)
Industrial policy	11	Positive effect until mid-1970s; posterior mismatch generated significant efficiency problems	Nunn and Trefler 2008; Estevadeordal and Taylor 2008	Not tested	Skill correlation of tariffs (Nunn and Trefler 2008)	(–)

NOTE: Asterisks denote statistical significance of estimated effect: *** −1 percent, ** −5 percent, * −10 percent. (–) denotes that the variable was not included in the final regression; see text for discussion.

countries that are successful tend to liberalize as a result. The view of the trade optimists is perhaps best represented by the work of Frankel and Romer (1999), who argue that geographically determined trade (which is by nature exogenous) is related to higher income levels. Rodríguez and Rodrik (2000), in contrast, argue that standard measures of trade policies are not associated with growth, and that the Frankel and Romer effect is caused by geographical variables on growth. Despite a plethora of studies, there is little consensus between trade skeptics and trade optimists.

A more recent literature has emphasized that rather than openness per se, what might matter is the type of products exported, the accumulation of productive capabilities these goods require, and the alternative uses of those capabilities. Hausmann, Hwang, and Rodrik (2007) have argued that countries develop by exporting "rich country" goods. Hidalgo and colleagues (2007) have argued that these goods are in a dense portion of the product space—that is, the specialized inputs or capabilities you need in order to produce what you produce are also useful to produce other goods. In contrast, many poor countries can be stuck in sparse regions of this space, making it very difficult to move to alternative products.

The story told by Ricardo Hausmann and Francisco Rodríguez in chapter 1 supports the hypothesis that trade by itself isn't what matters. Measured by its trade-to-GDP ratio, Venezuela's economy has generally been quite open precisely because of its high oil intensity. And although Venezuela's trade policy was protectionist up to the late eighties, it wasn't very different from that of other Latin American nations, and, in fact, Venezuela liberalized trade pretty aggressively from 1989 onward. But the type of product does matter—the authors argue that Venezuela's key problem was that it wasn't able to develop alternative export industries to take the place of oil as export revenues started to decline. Thus the problem was not Venezuela's openness to international trade—it was the form that openness took. In particular, its lack of export flexibility implied that the country lacked the productive capabilities to develop alternative exports at the requisite pace, making the economy vulnerable to external shocks.

Another area of extensive debate in the literature deals with the effect of natural resources on growth. The idea of a "resource curse" has gained significant prominence in academic and policy circles. Some of the first contributions establishing the result in the cross-country evidence and providing some initial explanations were those of Sachs and Warner (1995), Rodríguez and Sachs (1999), and Tornell and Lane (1999). More recent empirical explorations have attempted to provide more exogenous measures of comparative advantage in natural resources and addressed measurement and specification issues in the traditional analysis, and have found a much more ambiguous result (Lederman and Maloney 2008).

Our research finds little support for the idea of a resource curse. In fact, a simple version of the resource curse is demonstrably false for the case of Venezuela before the seventies, a period during which it was the fastest-growing economy in Latin America; one would have to argue that growth would have been even higher in the absence of oil. If anything, Venezuela's experience argues for a positive correlation: as oil revenues expanded before 1980, the economy grew robustly, and as oil revenues collapsed, the economy went downhill. But as Osmel Manzano shows in chapter 2, there was nothing inevitable in the post-1980 collapse in per capita oil production. This collapse was the result of a very costly policy mistake: the strategy of limiting oil production because of concerns about conservation and the need to shift resources into non-oil sectors, leading to a substantial loss in Venezuela's market share. The fact that this mistake was avoidable, as shown by the decisions of similar players in the world oil market, implies that, under a different configuration of policies, Venezuela could have continued to have significant growth in fiscal revenue and could have averted the fiscal and institutional collapse detailed in chapters 9, 10, and 12.

The effect of infrastructure on economic growth has regained attention recently as a number of studies (see in particular Easterly and Serven 2003) have argued that an anti-investment bias characterizing traditional structural-adjustment programs likely generated long-run adverse growth and even fiscal effects. This is a potentially relevant effect in the Venezuelan case as the collapse in oil revenues generated pressure for a massive fiscal adjustment, which was by and large actually carried out, as argued by María Antonia Moreno and Cameron A. Shelton in chapter 9.

In chapter 3, José Pineda and Francisco Rodríguez show that this effect does in fact have significant explanatory power in explaining the collapse. Using a natural experiment from a 1993 law that assigned fiscal revenues to a fund for public investment, the authors are able to estimate the elasticity of manufacturing productivity to changes in public investment. The significant estimated elasticity suggests that the decline in infrastructure investment can actually explain a large part of the decline in productivity.

As economic decline set in, some constraints that were not binding began to have a significant impact on the economy. This was the case of labor market rigidities, which became more stringent over time, partly due to the reaction of policymakers, who tightened restrictions in an attempt to protect formal sector workers from the effects of the crisis, and partly due to inertia—restrictions that were not particularly costly for a relatively prosperous economy became much more onerous as equilibrium wages declined. In chapter 4, Adriana Bermúdez and Omar Bello show that there was a substantial negative employment effect of these growingly stringent restrictions.

This is broadly in line with some of the results from recent cross-national research, although labor market rigidities have been much less studied in the cross-country growth literature than have other variables. Forteza and Rama (1999) studied the effect of labor market rigidities on the success of World Bank adjustment programs, and found that countries with greater labor market rigidities had deeper recessions before the adjustment and weaker recoveries afterward. Calderon, Chong, and Leon (2007) distinguish between enforceable and non-enforceable labor market rigidities and argue that the former have no effect but the latter do. In this case, the results of the within-country analysis based on firm-level data confirm the conclusions of the cross-country research.

Venezuela was also hit by two major credit collapses: one in the late eighties and another one in the mid-1990s. The second one was associated with the 1994 banking crisis, but as Matías Braun points out in chapter 5, the first one was comparable in magnitude. The effect of financial development on growth is, of course, a major source of interest in the cross-country literature, and generally studies have pointed to significant effects (Levine and Zervos 1998; Demetriades and Law 2004). Braun's chapter confirms this hypothesis, but with important nuances and a more detailed explanation of the transmission channels. In particular, the collapse in credit affected more strongly the firms that were more reliant on bank credit, and increased the inefficiency in resource allocation both across and within sectors. It also helps us understand how the credit collapse came about as a result of the fiscal collapse, which increased public sector demand for funds and drove interest rates up.

In some cases, in contrast, the results do not go in the same direction pointed to by cross-country regressions. This is the case with inequality. While some authors point to a negative effect of inequality on growth (Alesina and Rodrik 1994; Persson and Tabellini 1994), others have argued for a positive effect (Forbes 2002), and yet others have argued in favor of a nonlinear effect. Yet Venezuelan inequality does not appear to have had much to do with the growth collapse in Venezuela at all. As argued by Samuel Freije in chapter 7, the fact that Venezuela was a relatively egalitarian country (by Latin American standards) in the seventies and early eighties implies that it is hard to tell a story in which early distributive conflict fueled the decline, especially since the political economy theories often appealed to imply transmission channels that should operate in the medium to long term. Further, Freije actually shows that the increase in inequality is associated with a sustained decline of capital investment, which involved a long-run fall in labor productivity and formal employment. These declines, in turn, are more easily explained as a result of growing inefficiencies coming from labor regulations and a shrinking financial sector, as well as low public goods provision.

Likewise, cross-country growth regressions tend to assign a positive effect to the stock of human capital, although there are differences regarding whether this effect comes mainly from variations in quantity or in quality (e.g., Barro 1991; Hanushek and Woessmann 2010). But the Venezuelan case goes strongly against this hypothesis: schooling in Venezuela was expanding massively during the same period during which growth was collapsing. As Daniel Ortega and Lant Pritchett argue in chapter 6, if we believe that education matters for growth, then the collapse is even more difficult to explain. This argument, which has also been made in the cross-national literature (and which in fact reflects the inconsistency between time-series tests and cross-sectional ones, as discussed by Jones 1995; Pritchett 2001) can be explored in much more detail using intra-country methods, as the authors are able to study the evolution of wage premiums and test alternative stories about the potential contribution of quality decline. Their bottom line, however, is that it is very difficult to construct a story whereby either changes in quantities or quality can be attributed a causal role in the explanation of the decline.

The role of migration in economic growth is somewhat understudied. Some recent papers have taken advantage of bilateral migration flows data in order to obtain reliable estimates of the effect of migration on income. The general conclusion that comes out of these studies is that migration has a neutral effect on income—it does not raise it, nor does it appear to lower it. In other words, the evidence is consistent with the idea that migrants "bring their own jobs" when they migrate into a country, as immigration increases the stock of labor, raises the marginal product of capital, and leads to higher investment (Ortega and Peri 2009; Letouzé et al. 2009). But these studies have not examined in detail how the composition of migration influences these effects. In chapter 8, Dan Levy and Dean Yang show that the effect varies across types of migrants, with European migrants having a neutral effect but Colombian immigrants having an employment-shifting effect, perhaps because of their lower level of human capital. The change in the composition of migration, partly caused by declining economic opportunities and partly by security concerns, could have further contributed to the decline. This is an interesting case in which within-country research can point to hypotheses of broader cross-national applicability: as shown in United Nations Development Programme (2009), a shift that has occurred in migration patterns in the past half century is a significant move in the direction of migration, with many more migrants from developing countries going to developed countries instead of other developing countries. The Levy and Yang results suggest that this shift in the composition of migration may have significant effects on productivity in both source and destination economies.

This chapter opens up an interesting endogenous entrepreneurial dynamic. During the period of high growth and a strong real exchange rate in Venezuela (a price that is key for migrants who are planning to go back home with their savings), before 1980, the country became a magnet for many migrants, but especially for Spaniards, Italians, and Portuguese migrants in the 1940s and 1950s. These migrants had on average the same level of schooling as Venezuelans, but were about six times more likely to be entrepreneurs than were the Venezuelan-born population. With the recovery of Europe and the collapse of the Venezuelan economy, European migration stopped and reversed, starving the economy of an important source of entrepreneurship. This is a hitherto unexplored hypothesis that calls for further research.

In contrast, the effect of fiscal policy on growth has generated a substantial body of research. Some authors point to a negative effect of government consumption on growth (Barro 1991), while others point to an insignificant effect of many fiscal variables (Easterly and Levine 1997). But there is a general consensus that regardless of whether there is a direct effect, the macroeconomic distortions caused by fiscal disequilibriums, such as high inflation and misaligned exchange rates, can have a significant adverse effect on economic growth (Barro 1999). This research has supported the strong emphasis that policy recommendations emerging from international financial institutions have placed on attaining fiscal balance in the context of structural-adjustment programs, often at the expense of other policy objectives. But the story told by María Antonia Moreno and Cameron A. Shelton in chapter 9 goes in a completely different direction. While it may be true that growth could have been worse with greater fiscal disequilibriums, Venezuelan politicians cannot be blamed for failing to carry out the necessary fiscal adjustment—if anything, they may have adjusted too much after the mid-eighties. Failing to realize that the economy was overheated, they continued to spend in 1980–81 during the second oil boom, putting the economy in a weak position when revenues declined starting in 1982.

The wave of cross-national research that started in the 2000s placed much greater emphasis on empirical identification using instrumental variables. Perhaps the one hypothesis that actually emerged strengthened from this second wave of research is that institutions have an effect on economic growth. This is partly due to the ingenious contribution of Acemoglu, Johnson, and Robinson (2001), who used information on mortality rates of European settlers as a source for exogenous variation in current institutions; and partly due to the work of

Rodrik, Subramanian, and Trebbi (2004), who showed that suitably instrumented institutional variables had the greatest explanatory power when measured against all other major hypotheses about the long-run causes of development.

The story told in chapters 10, 12, and 13 is quite different. While those chapters recognize the deterioration in Venezuelan institutions that occurred over the period of study (and which has by now become self-evident), they also find that the causality runs mostly in the other direction. In fact, Venezuela had an admirable set of institutions by Latin American standards in the 1970s—it was precisely those institutions that allowed the country to carry out successive major fiscal adjustments. Institutional channels are perhaps those whose effect on growth operates over the longest run in comparison to other variables, and it is surely the case that the consequent institutional deterioration will have continuing effects. But weak institutions are a result, not a cause, of Venezuela's growth collapse.

Of course, this does not mean that all the policies that came out of these institutions were correct. In fact, chapter 11 identifies how a growing mismatch between the country's industrial policy and its institutional capacity started generating significant efficiency costs in the mid-eighties. Jonathan Di John suggests that perhaps Venezuela had too inclusive a political system to carry out the targeted type of interventions necessary to successfully implement a strategy of picking winners (à la Korea). Di John's results go in a different direction from recent research on industrial policy (Nunn and Trefler 2008; Estevadeordal and Taylor 2008). While this research has concentrated on the structure of protection and whether it benefits particular sectors, Di John's analysis points to the need to study the consistency between political incentives, state capacity, and the successful implementation of industrial policy.

Cross-Country Regression Results and Comparison

How are our results different from those that we would have reached by undertaking a cross-country regression exercise? Broadly speaking, there are two ways in which a traditional growth regression can be used to understand a particular country's performance. One way is by assessing the statistical and economic significance of coefficients in a standard regression. A growth regression is nothing more than a model that is assumed to apply to all countries in the sample, so the magnitude of the estimates of any growth regression will (if one believes in them) tell you what the effect of changes in a particular variable are in your country of interest. This is the way the results of these regressions are most often interpreted— if the regression tells you that variable X is highly significant for growth, this means you should try to improve X in your country in order to increase growth. It also means that if you had made greater efforts to improve X in the past, your growth performance would have been better.

But this may not tell you what the contribution of X was to low growth in your country. X could be highly significant in a growth regression, but may have not varied at all in your country of interest, so it doesn't necessarily explain past changes in growth. That is why a common bridge between cross-country empirics and nation-specific questions relies on carrying out a decomposition based on regression coefficients. Thus, if we estimate the equation

$$\gamma = \alpha_0 + \alpha_1 x_1 + \dots + \alpha_n x_n + \varepsilon, \tag{1}$$

where γ denotes economic growth and $x_1 \dots x_n$ are a set of potential explanatory variables, we can calculate that the difference in growth between country A and country B is given by

$$\gamma_A - \gamma_B = \alpha_1(x_{1A} - x_{1B}) + \dots + \alpha_n(x_{nA} - x_{nB}) + \varepsilon_A - \varepsilon_B. \tag{2}$$

Similarly, one can calculate the difference between growth in country A and growth in the average country in a reference group as

$$\gamma_A - \overline{\gamma} = \alpha_1(x_{1A} - \overline{x}_1) + \dots + \alpha_n(x_{nA} - \overline{x}_n) + \varepsilon_A - \overline{\varepsilon}, \tag{3}$$

where $\overline{x}$ denotes the average of x over all countries in the reference group except country A. The term $\alpha_i(x_{iA} - \overline{x}_i)$ thus denotes the contribution of variable x_i, while $\varepsilon_A - \overline{\varepsilon}$ captures the contribution of unexplained factors.

The last two columns of table 14.1 attempt to answer the question of how our analysis compares to the results of the standard cross-country regression approach. Column 5 starts by comparing against the significance of coefficients in standard analyses. As reference we use Bayesian averaging of classical estimates (BACE), proposed by Sala-i-Martin, Doppelhoffer, and Miller (2004), to identify robust determinants of growth by using a method that essentially evaluates all possible combinations of explanatory variables and examines the robustness of a coefficient's value to changes in the specification.

Of the twelve potential determinants of growth discussed in our project, the BACE estimates of Sala-i-Martin, Doppelhoffer, and Miller omit six. Four of these are variables that have been introduced in the cross-country regression literature in more recent empirical work: export flexibility, international migration, labor rigidities, and industrial policy. The other two variables they do not consider (financial depth and income inequality) may have been dropped from their analysis because of a small number of observations, or because their effects were captured by other variables.[2] Of the six variables in our analysis that they considered, five of them make it into their list of robust variables. This includes years of primary schooling and life expectancy (which are measures of human capital), the years during which the economy is open, the fraction of GDP in mining (which, however, has a different sign from the more conventional measure), the share of primary exports (which is negative yet not robust in their analysis), the share of government consumption (which has a negative effect), and various religion dummies (which can be interpreted as proxies for institutions).

Interestingly, the results of our analysis for the Venezuelan case are almost orthogonal to those of the BACE analysis. Human capital, openness, and institutions play at most a minor role in our explanation of the collapse, while fiscal policy plays a mixed role—contributing negatively in some periods but positively in others. Public investment, which is not robust in the BACE analysis, does play a major role in our explanation. The only variable in which both analyses coincide is natural resources (if we take the measure of mining instead of the primary exports variable as the adequate proxy for this hypothesis).

This comparison, however, may be deemed unfair because of the reasons sketched above—the significance of a coefficient does not tell us much about the role of a variable in explaining a particular experience. To capture this, a decomposition such as the one suggested in equation (3) may be more adequate. Further, any existing growth regression exercise (such as the Sala-i-Martin estimate) is unlikely to consider all the variables outlined in table 14.1, so that strictly speaking the analyses may not be comparable.

Thus, the last column of table 14.1 presents the estimates of the decomposition in equation (3) made based on a regression exercise that considered the same hypotheses as those in the first three columns. In order for the decomposition to be meaningful, we use as a reference group the set of countries that had a similar initial per capita income than Venezuela. Otherwise, the convergence effect would dominate, but this would simply be a reflection of the fact that Venezuela was above its steady state level of income for its given growth determinants. In other words, the best way to display the results may be by showing how much each dimension contributed to Venezuela's inability to maintain the high level of income it attained in the 1970s.

The table lists the variables and estimated effects, expressed as a percentage of the observed difference in annual percentage growth from that of the reference group, 2.3 percent a year. Although a plethora of methods has been used to run growth regressions, we rely on the simplest approach of ordinary least squares on the long-run growth rates, using initial levels for stock variables and period averages for flow variables. Hauk and Wacziarg (2009) show that this method performs reasonably well in contrast to more complex alternatives. A first regression considered all thirteen variables (including the convergence term) but had only thirty-two observations. Thus we dropped the skill correlation measure of industrial policy, which is available for only sixty-three countries, and the roads variable, which is not available for Venezuela. Both of these variables were insignificant in the original specification and are insignificant if added individually to the final specification. We also drop years of schooling, as it is collinear in our sample with life expectancy, the other measure of human capital. This left us with seventy-three observations, not an atypical sample size for growth regressions.

Four potential explanatory variables are significant in the resulting regression: institutions, government consumption, human capital, and openness (the last of these at a 10 percent level of significance). Jointly, these variables explain 55 percent of the variation, with 46 percent explained by variables that are not statistically significant, and another 9 percent of unexplained variation. In terms of magnitude, poor institutions explain almost one quarter of the difference, with export flexibility, financial depth, and human capital explaining around 15 percent each.

Again, the results of this exercise differ strikingly from those found in our analysis. Most important, institutions play no major causal role in our explanation, yet they are assigned a major role in the decomposition exercise. Financial depth and export flexibility have reasonably large magnitudes in our analysis; in the decomposition exercise they are important quantitatively but have large standard errors, so that it is not possible to pinpoint them as statistically significant explanators. The other three statistically significant variables in the decomposition exercise—openness, human capital, and fiscal policy—do not play a major role in our explanation of Venezuela's growth collapse.

Where Do We Go from Here?

The preceding exercise shows that the results of a within-country analysis can be vastly different from those of a cross-country analysis, even when the latter is used to understand the experience of a particular country. This leaves us with a difficult choice. How do we know which of these methods is correct? Should we just ditch cross-country regressions? If not, how do we interpret the fact that they give different results than do within-country analyses?

In our view, the choice of method depends on the purpose of the research. Here the common trade-off between internal and external validity surfaces again.

A within-country analysis has significant internal validity but little external validity; for the cross-country approach, it is the other way around. Thus, if one is seeking to extract general policy lessons for applicability in different countries, the analysis of one country may not be very helpful. What we find might prove true for Venezuela but not for any other country. If we want to understand what the effect of certain variables is on growth in the average developing country, then the information from this analysis is at best only suggestive of the potential channels of influence and causation.

But if we want to understand what happened to a particular country, then we do not need to care about external validity. The fact that our explanation applies only to Venezuela is fine for us, because if what we want to know is why Venezuelan growth collapsed we need internal, not external, validity. Given the severe methodological problems in estimating cross-country regressions, they function as a blunt instrument for analyzing the experience of single country.

The other reason given for relying on cross-country as opposed to within-country experience is that the latter is just econometrics with one data point. We hope to have laid this concern to rest. As this volume has shown, it is perfectly feasible to do within-country analysis with several times the number of data points found in cross-country regressions, because within-country analysis relies on the use of individual and firm-level data sets as well as cross-country data.

We have, however, provided only an initial sketch of the within-country methodology. Much more work is necessary in order to understand the links between different channels of causation, to deal appropriately with external effects, and to capture feedback loops more systematically. These questions form an exciting agenda of research for future empirical growth research.

NOTES

1. We do not attempt to provide a complete survey or even a list of references for these broad literatures, but rather choose a selected and manageable set of studies that we view as representative. Readers interested in a more comprehensive survey should consult Durlauf, Johnson, and Temple 2004.

2. For example, financial depth may be captured by a measure of the degree of capitalism.

REFERENCES

Acemoglu, D., S. Johnson, and J. A. Robinson. 2001. "The Colonial Origins of Comparative Development." *American Economic Review* 91 (5): 1369–401.

Alesina, Alberto, and Dani Rodrik. 1994. "Distributive Politics and Economic Growth." *Quarterly Journal of Economics* 109 (2): 465–90.

Banerjee, A. V., and E. Duflo. 2003. "Inequality and Growth: What Can the Data Say?" *Journal of Economic Growth* 8 (3): 267–99.

Barro, R. 1991. "Economic Growth in a Cross-Section of Countries." *Quarterly Journal of Economics* 106 (2): 407–43.

———. 1999. "Determinants of Economic Growth: Implications of the Global Evidence for Chile." *Cuadernos de Economía* 107:443–78.

Barro, R., and J. W. Lee. 2010. "A New Data Set of Educational Attainment in the World, 1950–2010." Working Paper 15902, National Bureau of Economic Research, Cambridge, Mass.

Calderón, C., A. Chong, and G. Leon. 2007. "Institutional Enforcement, Labor Market Rigidities, and Economic Performance." *Emerging Markets Review* 8 (1): 38–49.

Calderón, C., and L. Servén. 2004. "The Effects of Infrastructure Development on Growth and Income Distribution." Policy Research Working Paper 3401, World Bank, Washington, D.C.

Demetriades, P., and S. Law. 2004. "Finance, Institutions, and Economic Growth." Working Paper 04/5, University of Leicester.

Denison, E. 1967. *Why Growth Rates Differ: Postwar Experience in Nine Western Countries.* Washington, D.C.: Brookings Institution.

Durlauf, Steven N., Paul A. Johnson, and Jonathan R. W. Temple. 2004. "Growth Econometrics." In *Handbook of Economic Growth*, edited by Philippe Aghion and Steven Durlauf, 555–677: Amsterdam: Elsevier.

Easterly, William, and Ross Levine. 1997. "Africa's Growth Tragedy: Policies and Ethnic Divisions." *Quarterly Journal of Economics* 112 (4): 1203–50.

Easterly, W., and S. Rebelo. 1993. "Fiscal Policy and Economic Growth. An Empirical Investigation." *Journal of Monetary Economics* 32 (3): 417–58.

———. 1993. "Marginal Income Tax Rates and Economic Growth in Developing Countries." *European Economic Review* 37 (2/3): 409–17.

Easterly, W., and L. Serven. 2003. *The Limits of Stabilization: Infrastructure, Public Deficits, and Growth in Latin America.* Washington, D.C.: World Bank.

Estevadeordal, A., and A. M. Taylor. 2008. "Is the Washington Consensus Dead? Growth, Openness, and the Great Liberalization." Working Paper 14264, National Bureau of Economic Research, Cambridge, Mass.

Forbes, K. J. A. 2002. "Reassessment of the Relationship between Inequality and Growth." *American Economic Review* 90 (4): 869–87.

Forteza, A., and M. Rama. 1999. "Labor Market 'Rigidity' and the Success of Economic Reforms across More Than One Hundred Countries." Working Paper 2521, World Bank, Washington, D.C.

Frankel, J., and D. Romer. 1999. "Does Trade Cause Growth?" *American Economic Review* 89 (3): 379–99.

Glaeser, E. L., R. La Porta, F. Lopez-de-Silanes, and A. Shleifer. 2004. "Do Institutions Cause Growth?" *Journal of Economic Growth* 9 (3): 271–303.

Hanushek, E. A., and L. Woessmann. 2010. "Education and Economic Growth." In *Economics of Education*, edited by Dominic J. Brewer and Patrick J. McEwan, 60–67. Amsterdam: Elsevier.

Hauk, W. R., and R. Wacziarg. 2009. "A Monte Carlo Study of Growth Regressions." *Journal of Economic Growth* 14 (2): 103–47.

Hausmann, R., J. Hwang, and D. Rodrik. 2007. "What You Export Matters." *Journal of Economic Growth* 12 (1): 1–25.

Hausmann, R., F. Rodríguez, and R. Wagner. 2008. "Growth Collapses." In *Money, Crises, and Transition: Essays in Honor of Guillermo Calvo*, edited by C. Reinhart, A. Velasco, and C. Vegh, 377–428. Cambridge: MIT Press.

Heston, Alan, Robert Summers, and Bettina Aten. 2002. "Penn World Table Version 6.1, Center for International Comparisons at the University of Pennsylvania (CICUP)." http://pwt.econ.upenn.edu/php_site/pwt61_form.php.

Hidalgo, C. A., B. Klinger, A. L. Barabasi, and R. Hausmann. 2007. "The Product Space Conditions the Development of Nations." *Science* 317 (5837): 482–87.

Jones, C. 1995. "R&D-Based Models of Economic Growth." *Journal of Political Economy* 103 (4): 759–84.

Lederman, D., and W. F. Maloney. 2008. "In Search of the Missing Resource Curse." *Economía* 9 (1): 1–56.

Letouzé, E., M. Purser, F. Rodriguez, and M. Cummins. 2009. "Revisiting the Migration–Development Nexus: A Gravity Model Approach." Human Development Research Paper 44, United Nations Development Programme, New York.

Levine, R., and S. Zervos. 1998. "Stock Markets, Banks, and Economic Growth." *American Economic Review* 88 (3): 537–58.

Nunn, N., and D. Trefler. 2008. "The Boundaries of the Multinational Firm: An Empirical Analysis." In *The Organization of Firms in a Global Economy*, edited by E. Helpman, D. Marin, and T. Verdier, 55–83. Cambridge: Harvard University Press.

Ortega, F., and G. Peri. 2009. "The Causes and Effects of International Migrations: Evidence from OECD Countries, 1980–2005." Working Paper 14833, National Bureau of Economic Research, Cambridge, Mass.

Persson, T., and G. Tabellini. 1994. "Is Inequality Harmful for Growth?" *American Economic Review* 84 (3): 600–621.

Pritchett, L. 2001. "Where Has All the Education Gone?" *World Bank Economic Review* 15 (3): 367–91.

Rama, M., and R. Artecona. 2002. "A Database of Labor Market Indicators across Countries." World Bank Development Research Group, Washington, D.C.

Rodriguez, F., and D. Rodrik. 2000. "Trade Policy and Economic Growth: A Skeptic's Guide to the Cross-National Evidence." In *2000 NBER Macroeconomics Annual*, edited by Ben S. Bernanke and Kenneth Rogoff, 261–338. Cambridge, Mass.: National Bureau of Economic Research.

Rodriguez, F., and Jeffrey D. Sachs. 1999. "Why Do Resource Abundant Economies Grow More Slowly?" *Journal of Economic Growth* 4 (3): 277–303.

Rodrik, D., A. Subramanian, and F. Trebbi. 2004. "Institutions Rule: The Primacy of Institutions over Geography and Integration in Economic Development." *Journal of Economic Growth* 9 (2): 131–65.

Rostow, W. W. 1960. *The Stages of Economic Growth: A Non-Communist Manifesto.* Cambridge: Cambridge University Press.

Sachs, J. D., and A. M. Warner. 1995. "Natural Resource Abundance and Economic Growth." Working Paper W5398, National Bureau of Economic Research, Cambridge, Mass.

Sala-i-Martin, X., G. Doppelhofer, and R. I. Miller. 2004. "Determinants of Long-Term Growth: A Bayesian Averaging of Classical Estimates (BACE) Approach." *American Economic Review* 94 (4): 813–35.

Tornell, A., and P. R. Lane. 1999. "The Voracity Effect." *American Economic Review* 85 (1): 22–46.

United Nations. 2010. *Demographic Yearbook, 2009–10.* New York.

United Nations Development Programme. 2009. *Human Development Report, 2009: Overcoming Barriers: Human Mobility and Development.* New York: Palgrave Macmillan.

World Bank. 2009. *World Development Indicators.* Washington D.C.

———. 2010. *World Development Indicators.* Washington D.C.

Contributors

Editors

Ricardo Hausmann is Director of the Center for International Development and Professor of the Practice of Economic Development at Harvard University. Previously, he served as the first Chief Economist of the Inter-American Development Bank (1994–2000), where he created the Research Department. He has served as Minister of Planning of Venezuela (1992–93) and as a member of the Board of the Central Bank of Venezuela. He also served as Chair of the IMF–World Bank Development Committee. He was Professor of Economics at the Instituto de Estudios Superiores de Administracion (1985–91) in Caracas, where he founded the Center for Public Policy.

Francisco Rodríguez is Chief Andean Economist at Bank of America Merrill Lynch. Previously, he served as Head of Research of the Human Development Report Office at the United Nations Development Programme. He has held teaching positions at Wesleyan University, the Instituto de Estudios Superiores de Administración, and the University of Maryland. He has also served as Chief Economist for the Economic and Financial Advisory Office to the National Assembly of Venezuela.

Contributors

Omar Bello is Economic Affairs Officer in the Economic Development Division of CEPAL, ECLAC, United Nations, Santiago.

Adriana Bermúdez is Credit Risk Specialist at a Venezuelan private sector financial institution.

Matías Braun is Director of Strategy and Partner at IM Trust and Professor of Economics and Finance at Universidad Adolfo Ibanez.

Javier Corrales is John E. Kirkpatrick 1951 Professor of Political Science at Amherst College, Amherst, Mass.

Jonathan Di John is a Lecturer in Political Economy at the School of Oriental and African Studies, University of London.

Rafael Di Tella is Joseph C. Wilson Professor of Business Administration at Harvard Business School.

Javier Donna is Assistant Professor of the Department of Economics at The Ohio State University.

Samuel Freije wrote his chapter as Associate Professor of the Department of Economics at the Universidad de las Américas, Puebla, Mexico. Currently he is Senior Economist at the World Bank.

Dan Levy is a Lecturer in Public Policy at the Harvard Kennedy School of Government and a Faculty Affiliate of the Harvard Center for International Development.

Robert MacCulloch is Professor, Economics Chair, and Director of the Doctoral Programme at the Imperial College London.

Osmel Manzano is Principal Economist at the Inter-American Development Bank and Adjunct Professor at Insittuto de Estudios Superiores de Administracion.

Francisco Monaldi is Visiting Professor of Public Policy at the Harvard Kennedy School of Government and Professor and Director of the Center on Energy and the Environment at the Instituto de Estudios Superiores de Administracion, IESA, in Caracas.

María Antonia Moreno is an Associate Professor at Universidad Central de Venezuela.

Daniel Ortega is Senior Economist and Impact Evaluation Coordinator at CAF, Development Bank of Latin America, and adjunct professor at Instituto de Estudios Superiores.

Michael Penfold is Professor and Dean of Research at the Instituto de Estudios Superiores de Administracion in Caracas.

José Pineda is Senior Researcher at the Human Development Report Office of the United Nations Development Programme.

Lant Pritchett is Professor of the Practice of Economic Development at the Harvard Kennedy School of Government and a Faculty Affiliate of the Harvard Center for International Development.

Cameron A. Shelton is an Assistant Professor at Claremont McKenna College.

Dean Yang is Associate Professor in the Department of Economics and the Ford School of Public Policy at the University of Michigan.

Index

Page numbers followed by "f" and "t" refer to figures and tables, respectively; those followed by "n" refer to notes, with note number.

Abiad, Abdul, 163
Abramovitz, Moses, 7
Accíon Democrática. *See* AD
Acemoglu, Daron, 397, 400, 429t, 434
AD (Accíon Democrática)
 and constitution of 1947, 313n14
 and constitution of 1961, 313n14
 decline of, 390
 and El Trienio Adeco, 341–42
 and federalism, loss of influence under, 389–90
 as fundamental party of Venezuela, 343, 365n11
 and institutional closure of Punto Fijo democracy, 378, 381–82
 nonadaptation of, 392–93, 394
 Pérez impeachment and, 304
 Pérez's departure from, 347
 and period of democratic deconsolidation, 298, 299, 300, 301, 302, 315n30, 315n31, 341, 344, 345–46, 347, 349
 and policy process, 294
 political platform of, 341, 347
 political splits within, 344, 345–46, 347
 in Punto Fijo democracy, 294, 295, 342, 343, 372
 radical elements in, 344
 share of votes in lower house, by year, 387f
 technocratic deficits in, 392–93
Adelman, M. A., 62
advanced notice period, and labor costs, 121, 126, 134, 143–44, 152–53n47
Aelo, Oscar H., 375
Agenda Venezuela, 349
Alesina, Alberto, 408, 429t, 431
Allende, Salvador, 391
Álvarez Paz, Oswaldo, 348
Amsden, A., 332, 366n18
Andean Pact, Venezuelan non-oil sector trade and, 31–32, 32f
Arellano, Manuel, 96

Arellano-Bond fixed-effects estimator, in estimation of effect of public capital stock on productivity, 96, 98–100, 99t, 100, 102t, 103
Argentina
 federalism in, 310
 oil production in, 70
 Peronism in, 375
 radical left in, 392
armed forces
 Chávez's control of, 305
 politicization of under Chávez, 307, 308
Aschauer, D. A., 92
Ascher, William, 262, 282n4
BACE. *See* Bayesian averaging of classical estimates
balance of payments crisis (2002), viii, 167
Ball, Laurence, 276
Banco Latino, 168, 348
Banerjee, A. V., 429t
bank credit to private sector
 crowding out by public sector demand, 159, 163, 167–68, 170
 decline of in 1980s–1990s, 167, 167f; anatomy of, 166–68, 167f; causes of, 158–59, 165–66, 167–68, 168–70; depth of, 170, 171f; effect on businesses, 159–60, 178; effect on growth, 158, 160, 174–76, 181t; effect on larger firms, 160, 176–77, 178, 182t; effects of, 171–77, 178, 428t, 432; managers' perception of effects of, 159, 171–74, 172t, 179t, 180t, 183n21; timing of, 164–66, 165f, 171
 vs. GDP in Venezuela: low level of, 158, 160, 161, 161f; timing of break in link between, 164–65, 165f
 levels *vs.* other countries, 160–61, 172
 misapplication of, and growth, effect on, 160, 175–76
 oil GDP and, 165–66
Bank for International Settlements, 162

banking crisis of 1994, management of, and
    sector underdevelopment, 164, 168, 170,
    171f, 380, 432
banking sector. *See also* bank credit to private
    sector; financial system in Venezuela
    bank assets, decline of after 1987, 167, 167f
    and borrower information, suboptimal
        quality of, 158, 163
    and financiers, weak legal protection of,
        158, 163
    high interest rates, causes of, 162–63, 173
    inefficiency of, 158, 162, 177
    low level of concentration in, 162
    overhead costs, 162
    profitability, decline of in late 1980s, 167
    risk of business in factionalized political
        environment and, 358
    size of as proxy for financial development, 157
    small size of *vs.* other countries, 161, 161f, 163
Baptista, A., 211
Barrios, Gonzalo, 315n29
Barro, R., 3, 207, 428t, 429t, 433, 434
Bartelsman, E., 131–32
Batista, Fulgencio, 372
Bayesian averaging of classical estimates
    (BACE), 436–37
Becker, Gary, 2
Bello, Omar D., 16, 130
Bermúdez, A., 115, 117, 119, 126–27, 128,
    145, 151n19
Bernal, Raquel, 117
Betancourt, Rómulo, 313n13, 313n14, 345
big push industrialization. *See also* natural-
    resource-based industrialization (NRBI)
    appropriate institutional and political
        structures: importance of, 330–34;
        Venezuela's failure to maintain, 262–63,
        323, 339–40, 429t, 435
    continued growth, obstacles to, 338
    distinguishing features of in Venezuela *vs.*
        other nations, 339
    diversification of export structure as goal
        of, 337
    Fifth National Plan and, 337
    industry mix in, 263
    periodization of, 335–36, 335t, 338
    as restructuring of patronage system, 346
    and state role, purposeful expansion of,
        337–38, 365n9
    vertical integration as goal of, 337
Bils, Mark, 191, 192
Blanchard, Olivier, 271, 273, 279, 283n16
Bolívar, Simón, 11
Bolivarian revolution, difficulty of analyzing, 11

Bolivarian Revolutionary Movement 200 (MBR-
    200), 349–50, 388, 390
Bolivia, economic growth, vii
Bond, S., 96
bond market in Venezuela, small size of *vs.*
    other countries, 162
bonuses, mandated
    changes in regulations on, 117, 119–20,
        123–24
    and employment, impact on, 133–37, 137t–142t
    indexed *vs.* non-indexed, 123–24
    and labor costs, 120–21, 120f, 123–24
Borjas, George, 239
Botero, J., 116
Braun, Matías, 165, 175
Brazil
    federalism in, 310
    open_forest of, 35, 36f, 42t, 43
    poverty rates in, viii, xiin5
budgetary pressure
    revenue sources and, 229–30, 229t
    and social expenditures, 225–28, 227f
Burgess, Katrina, 402n4
business associations
    and big push industrialization, 331–34
    fragmentation of, in era of political
        deconsolidation, 353
business community
    and financial system collapse, effects of,
        159–60, 178; on larger firms, 160, 176–77,
        178, 182t; managers' perception of, 159,
        171–74, 172t, 179t, 180t, 183n21
    and populist clientelism, impact of, 353, 358
    relations with Chávez administration, 350
    resentment of in late 1990s, 380
    and restructuring of patronage system in
        period of democratic deconsolidation, 346
business owners, impact of economic conditions
    on political beliefs of, 410, 412t
Buxton, Julia, 379
Caballero, R., 127, 152n33
Caldera, Rafael
    and constitution of 1961, 313n14
    departure from COPEI, 347, 348
    and economic collapse, inability to respond
        to, 379
    intelligence warnings about chavistas, failure
        to heed, 388
    and left, rise of, 378, 383
    naturalization of natural gas industry, 64
    and neoliberal reform, 283n9, 349, 379, 380
    oil companies and, 64–65
    presidential terms of, 57t
    and Punto Fijo Pact, 313n13

support of poor voters for, 377
tax policy under, 304
Calderón, César, 93, 428t, 432
calibration-oriented approaches, 16–17
Campíns, Herrera, 380
Canning, D., 92
capital accumulation in non-oil sector, decline
      in, 23–28, 212–13, 232
   and GDP decline, 26–28, 27f
   and labor's share in factoral distribution of
      income, 210–13
   magnitude of, 22t, 23
   measures of, 211–12, 212f
   three-sector model of, 24–28, 27f, 45–46,
      46n6, 47n8
capital investment. *See also* public capital
      stock, non-oil
   decline in: causes of, 208–9; and formal
      employment level, 208, 422–23; and
      increased inequality, 232, 432–33;
      and increased poverty, 232; and labor
      productivity, 94, 97–105, 98t, 99t, 101t,
      102t, 103t, 104t, 106t, 107t, 208, 232, 427,
      431, 432–33; and labor's share of national
      income, 212; as percentage of public
      spending, 351–52, 352t
   effect of external credit constraints on,
      173–76, 180t, 181t
   inefficiency of, and stagnation of
      manufacturing sector, 327–28
   and instability of fiscal revenue, 209
   lower elasticity of in less-developed
      countries, 175–76
   in oil boom period: *vs.* consumption,
      classification of, 271, 282n5; *vs.*
      consumption, impact on GDP, 271–73,
      272t; *vs.* consumption, levels of, 268,
      269f, 270t; immediate investment, as
      problematic, 261–63
   in post boom period, *vs.* consumption,
      impact on GDP, 272, 272t, 427, 434
   private-sector, decline of, and economic
      decline, 212, 380
   public-sector, inefficiency of, and economic
      decline, 327–28, 380
   and redistribution, effects of, 232–33
   social expenditures and, 228
capital investment in oil production
   1960–1973, 77, 77f, 78f
   1989–2003, factors inhibiting, 70–72, 76
   government claim on oil profits and, 56–57,
      56f, 63, 64, 65, 66, 427
   and investment specificity, 56, 84n10
   low levels of in 1990s, 69–70

political factors affecting, 58–59, 62–63, 65, 67
   preservation policies and, 61–62
   production costs and, 62
   and production levels, 55–56, 55f, 64
capital/labor ratio, 1950–2004, 211–12, 212f, 232
Card, David, 239
Cardenas, Mauricio, 117
Catholic Church, El Trienio Adeco and, 341
Causa R, 300, 348, 349, 389, 390
Cecchetti, Stephen G., 276
censoring, duration regressions and, 37
Central Bank Law of 1960, 282n2
Chandler, A., 360
Chávez, Hugo
   abuse of opponents as political tool of, 374,
      398–99
   clientelism as political tool of, 398, 399
   corruption as political tool of, 374, 398
   cronyism as political tool of, 398, 399
   efforts to depose, viii
   election of, 341
   factionalism within support base, 350,
      365n13; Chávez's tools in management of,
      373–74, 377, 396–99, 401
   impunity for supporters as political tool of,
      374, 398, 399
   job discrimination as tool of, 374, 398, 399
   leftward turn of, 396–97
   and manufacturing sector, political
      impotence of, 356
   polarizing radicalism as political tool of, 374,
      396–98, 399, 401
   political platform of, 305, 349, 350
   popularity ratings, viii, 308, 397
   and presidential power, increase of, 296,
      305–6, 307–8, 316n43
   promise to dismantle political system, 305
   rise to power: civic organizations, role
      of, 378; demand side explanations,
      inadequacy of, 374, 377, 381, 394, 399,
      401; economic collapse and, vii, 371,
      372, 374, 377, 394, 400; incorporation
      of left into political mainstream
      and, 381–90; increased influence of
      leftists under federalism and, 389–90;
      institutional closure and, 378–79;
      institutional sheltering of leftists and,
      383–89, 394, 395t, 396, 400; key enabling
      characteristics of Venezuela *vs.* other
      nations, 394–96, 395t; neoliberal
      reforms and, 379–81; nonadaptation of
      mainstream parties and, 390–94, 400;
      oil boom and, viii; social immiseration
      and, 377

Chávez, Hugo (*cont.*)
  and stakes of power, increase of, 286, 296, 306, 307–8
  supporters of, 375, 376t, 399
Chávez administration
  authoritarianism, increase in, 306, 316n45, 317n47
  characterization of, as issue, 371–72
  circumvention of state institutions in, 350
  and crippling of economic growth, 350
  economic policy, vii–x, 307–8, 350
  and growth of government, impact of quality of life, viii
  institutional changes implemented by, 286
  political institutions in: characteristics of, 287, 341; decline of, 291, 305–8, 309, 310, 349–50
  as profound change of regime, 371
  radical left-military alliance in, 371; early supporters of Chávez in military, 375, 376t; exclusionary politics of Punto Fijo regime and, 372–73; grievances of junior officers and, 386–88; military officers in public office, 373, 374t; precedents for in Latin America, 372; sheltering of leftists in military and, 373, 385–89, 394, 395t, 396
  spending, political uses of, ix, 307
  and technical knowledge of legislature, 393–94
chavismo
  appeal of: civic organizations, role of, 378; demand side explanations, inadequacy of, 374, 377, 381, 394, 399, 401; economic collapse and, vii, 371, 372, 374, 377, 394, 400; institutional closure and, 378–79; neoliberal reforms and, 379–81; nonadaptation of mainstream parties and, 390–94, 400; social immiseration and, 377
  definition of, 371
  rise of, exclusionary politics of Punto Fijo democracy and, 372–73
chavistas
  and Constitutional Assembly of 1999, 305
  control of National Assembly, 306, 314n19
  early leadership, backgrounds of, 375, 376t
  intelligence service warnings about, failures to heed, 388
child-care bonus, and labor costs, 123–24, 128–30, 129f
Chile, radical left in, 391–92
Chong, A., 428t, 432

civil society institutions
  increase in number of, 390
  sheltering of far left in, 373, 390, 394
Cleary, Matthew R., 373
Clemente, Lino, 74–75
clientelism as political tool of Chávez, 398, 399
Colombia
  open-forest of, 35, 36f, 42t, 43
  party system in, 309
  poverty rates in, viii, xiin5
Committee for the Political Organization and Independent Election. *See* COPEI
Communist Party
  and constitution of 1961, 313n14
  legalization of, 382
comparative advantage, modeling of, 33–34
Condeferación de Trabajadores de Venezuela (CTV), 343
Congress (National Assembly)
  destabilization of, after federalization, 301, 315n32
  introduction of mixed-member system, 297
  left's influence in, rise of, 382, 387f, 389
  low re-election rate, and decline of technical knowledge, 393
  opposition to Pérez reforms, 303–4
  power of: budget involvement, growth of, 304, 316n37; constitution of 1961 and, 293; increase in after collapse of party system, 301–2, 303
  productivity of, 393
  Senate, elimination of, 305, 308
  stability of, in Punto Fijo democracy, 295, 296f, 314–15nn24–26
Constituent Assembly of 1999, 305, 349, 375, 376t
constitution of 1947, 313n14
constitution of 1961, 293–94, 313n14
  presidential power under, 263, 296, 313n19, 313nn16–17, 343
constitution of 1999
  and electoral system, 316n44
  presidential power under, 296, 305–6, 307–8
  and Senate, elimination of, 305, 308
consumption possibilities frontier, GDP decline after 1979 and, 19–20, 19–21, 21t
Convergencia-LAPI, 299, 348, 390
COPEI (Committee for the Political Organization and Independent Election)
  Caldera's departure from, 347, 348
  and constitution of 1961, 313n14
  decline of, 390
  establishment of, 342
  and federalism, loss of influence under, 389–90

and institutional closure of Punto Fijo
democracy, 378, 381–82
leftist factions of, 382
nonadaptation of, 392–93, 394
and period of democratic deconsolidation,
298, 299, 300, 301, 302, 315n30, 315n31,
341, 346, 349
in Punto Fijo democracy, 294, 295, 372
and Punto Fijo Pact, 342
share of votes in lower house, by year, 387f
technocratic deficits in, 392–93
Coppedge, M., 313n16
COPRE. See Presidential Commission for the
Reform of the State
Corrales, J., 313n14
corruption
as explanation of manufacturing sector
stagnation, 339
levels of vs. other countries, 290f, 291
oil rents and, 288
perception of: impact on political beliefs,
414, 415t, 420, 421; manipulation of by
political activists, 418; vs. reality, 418, 419t
as political tool of Chávez, 374, 398
scandals of 1980s and 1990s: media coverage
of, and collapse of party system, 349; as
tool of political competition, 346
credit risk
increase, as cause of Venezuelan decline, 16
of Venezuela, in 2012, ix
crime, perception of
and perception of corruption, 418, 419t, 421
and political beliefs, 414–17, 416t, 420, 421
Crisp, B., 316n33
cronyism as political tool of Chávez, 398, 399
cross-national data
limitations of, 3
nonparametric growth models and, 4–5
unbundling of, 5
CTV. See Confederación de Trabajadores de
Venezuela
Cuba
radical left-military alliance in, 372
Venezuela foreign policy on, 382
Cuddington, John, 64, 67
CVP. See Venezuela Oil Corporation
decentralization. See also federalism
levels of in Venezuela, 271, 389–90
De Krivoy, Ruth, 164
delayed stabilization theory, 202, 203
Demetriades, P., 428t
democracy
beginning of, 60
consolidation of (1958–1988), 292–97

and export shocks, ability to recover from,
37, 38t–41t
high stakes of power and, 288
oil policy in, 65 (see also preservation policy)
oil revenues and, 293
under Punto Fijo Pact, 293–94, 294–97,
313n13
social spending under, 65
transition to, 292–94
weakening, causes of, x, 286
Democratic Republican Union Party. See URD
Denison, Edward E., 426
Devarajan, S., 92
developmental state theories, on industrial
policy, 330
development experiences, variety in growth
episodes, 16
development strategies. See also big push
industrialization; diversification;
natural-resource-based industrialization
appropriate institutional and political
structures: importance of, 330–34;
Venezuela's failure to maintain, 262–63,
323, 339–40, 429t, 435
changes in over time, 330
developmental state theorists on, 330
free-market views on, 329–30, 334
for oil-exporting countries, theories on, 52
periodization of, 334–38, 335t
protectionism after 1960, 327–29, 336–37,
354, 356
undermining of by populist clientelism, 358,
359–60
Di Tella, Rafael, 414, 421
diversification. See also "sowing of oil" policy
factors suppressing, x
failure to pursue, 1989–2003, 74–75, 76
integration of oil sector, lack of attention to,
60, 65, 74–75, 84–85n19
lack of, oil shock recovery and, x, 44
in non-oil vs. oil-related exports,
effectiveness of, 73–74, 74f, 76
as strategy, value of, 72–74, 76
Doppelhofer, G., 16, 436
downsizing, as response to labor market
regulations, 132
Duflo, E., 429t
Dunning, T., 289
duration regressions, and censoring, 37
Dutch disease. See also resource curse
limited applicability to Venezuela, 323,
325–27
mechanisms of, 324–25
Venezuelan oil industry and, 44

Easterly, William, 1, 92, 397, 428t, 429t, 431, 434
economic collapse after 1979. *See also* GDP
    decline after 1979
    and "capacity to import" problem, 204
    causes of, 15, 380, 427; range of explanations
        for, 1–2; tests for explanations of, 2, 44
    and Chávez's rise to power, vii, 371, 372, 377,
        394, 400
    economic performance in quarter century
        following, 285
    economic performance prior to, 285
    investment decline and, 380
    literature on, 16–17
    magnitude of, 20–21, 21t, 116, 310
    and political institutions, destabilization of,
        297–98, 371, 373
    and political parties, decline of, 378
    relevance of political system to, 359–60
    resource dependence as cause of, 15–16
    and schooling capital: delays in talent
        reallocation and, 188, 202; as despite
        educational gains, 187, 188, 193, 429t, 433;
        links between, 188–89, 193, 201–4; rent
        seeking and, 188–89, 202–4
    second wave of oil boom and, 276
    in Venezuela *vs.* other Latin American
        nations, 427
economic concentration, *vs.* oil richness, for
    select nations, 72–73, 73f
economic conditions
    before 1970s, 1, 15–16, 426–27
    1970–1998: and appeal of Chávez, vii; factors
        affecting, 6, 9; failure to address, as lost
        opportunity, x–xi; parallels to current
        conditions, ix
    after 2004, 285
    current, ix
    cycling of (1972–1994), 264, 265f, 282n3
    as drivers of political beliefs, 409–10, 411t,
        412t, 418–19
    post-boom, hysteresis of, 264, 275
economic policy. *See also* development
    strategies; fiscal policy
    of 1980s–1990s, and financial sector
        development, suppression of, 158, 163–64
    under Chávez, vii–x, 307–8, 350
    decline in quality of, 310
    failures of: as cause of Venezuelan economic
        collapse, 44; as product of poor
        institutional quality, 286
    low credibility of, and underperformance, 286
    mechanisms of: in deconsolidated political
        system (1989–1998), 286, 301–5, 309;
        and economic crisis, inability to

respond effectively to, 304–5; effective,
    characteristics of governments with,
    287–88; in Punto Fijo democracy, 295,
    296–97, 309, 314n21; reversals of 1990s,
    radicality of, 304, 310
    party fragmentation and, 379
    in Punto Fijo democracy, 296–97, 342, 344
    stabilization mechanisms, inability to
        implement, 286
    and veto players, increased number of, 379
    volatility of, 286
economic volatility, impact on political beliefs,
    409–10, 411t, 412t, 418–19, 420, 421
Ecuador, non-oil sector performance, 29
Edmonston, Barry, 239
education. *See also* schooling; universities
    enrollment, expansion of, 384
    spending on, 383–84, 383f
Edwards, Alejandra Cox, 117
Edwards, Sebastian, 117
election(s)
    of 1946, 341
    of 1988, 298
    of 1998, 305, 349, 350
    restrictions on, in constitution of 1961,
        293–94
    separation of presidential and congressional,
        303, 316n34
electoral system
    under Chávez, 306, 316n44
    flux in after 1989, 302
Ellner, S., 346
El Trienio Adeco period, 341–42
employment
    capital investment decline and, 208, 422–23
    informal: 1967–2008, 218–19, 218f, 232;
        expansion of, and Chávez's rise to
        power, 377; and value of conventional
        productive characteristics, 216–18
    labor market regulations and, 131–33, 133–43,
        137t–142t, 428t, 431–32; for blue *vs.* white
        collar workers, 115, 119, 135–43, 138t–139t,
        141t–142t; firm size and, 132–33
    minimum wage laws and, 122–23, 133–36,
        137t–142t
    by state agencies, populist clientelism
        and, 351
Engel, E., 127, 152n33
Esfanhani, H. S., 93
Estevadeordal, A., 429t, 435
European Values Survey, 421–22
exchange rates
    balance of payments crisis of 2002 and, viii
    controls, trade impact of, 32

devaluations following oil booms, 267–68,
274–75, 282n3
foreign exchange rationing, 337
multiple rate regimes, ix, x, 29, 283n9
and non-oil sector performance, 29, 30f
volatility of, impact on political beliefs, 410,
411t, 412t
export industry, alternative
ability to develop: modeling of, 33–34; *open_
forest* and, 33–37
cushioning effect of, 26–28, 27f
and export shocks, recover from, *open_forest*
in, 35, 37–43, 38t–42t
Venezuela's failure to develop: as cause of
slow recovery, x, 43, 44; and growth
collapse, 427, 428t, 430; *open_forest* of
Venezuela *vs.* neighboring countries
and, 35, 36f, 42–43, 42t, 44
exports, oil, as percentage of exports, 51–52
export shocks, ability to recover from, *open_forest*
and, 35, 37–43, 38t–42t
factionalism. *See also* political cooperation
economic effects of, 351–58
literature on, 359
in period of democratic deconsolidation
(1973–1993), 345–47
factorial income distribution, 210–13
Fazzari, Steven M., 173, 176
Federación Venezolana de Cámaras y
Asociaciones de Comercio y Producción
(FEDECAMARAS), 343
federalism
activation of (1989), 297; and political
deconsolidation, 310–11, 348–49; and
political parties, 293, 297, 298, 299–301;
and regional political forces, increased
power of, 299–303, 315n31; and small
opposition parties, increased influence
of, 389–90
restrictions on in constitution of 1961, 293
weakening of under Chávez, 305, 308
Fei, John C. H., 235n22
Fernald, J. G., 92, 97
Fernandez, Aureliano, 72
Fernández, Eduardo, 298
FIDES (Venezuelan Intergovernmental
Decentralization Fund)
creation of, 93, 94–95
effect on productivity, 97–105, 98t. 99t, 101t,
102t, 103t, 104t, 106t, 107t; empirical
results on, 92–93; empirical strategy for
determining, 95–97, 111–12; for large *vs.*
small companies, 100–101; rate of
return on infrastructure development,

105, 113n7; theoretical basis for, 91–92;
theoretical issues in determining, 93
funding formula for, 93–94, 105, 108–11,
112n2, 112n4
impact on state infrastructure spending, 96
power of regional interest and, 304
restrictions on use of funds, 95, 96–97
variations in funding levels, 94
Fifth National Plan, 268, 331, 335, 337
financial system development
banking sector size as proxy for, 157
and growth: detailed country studies, need
for, 158; literature on, 157
measures of, 157, 158
and per capita income: detailed country
studies, need for, 158; literature on,
157; and Venezuelan financial system,
underdevelopment of, 159
stock market size as proxy for, 157
financial system in Venezuela. *See also* banking
sector; stock market
collapse of, 167, 167f; anatomy of, 166–68,
167f; causes of, 158–59, 165–66, 167–68,
168–70; depth of, 170, 171f; effects of,
171–77, 178; and growth, effect on, 158,
160, 174–76, 181t; impact on businesses,
159–60, 178; impact on larger firms, 160,
176–77, 178, 182t; managers' perception
of effects of, 159, 171–74, 172t, 179t, 180t,
183n21; timing of, 164–66, 165f, 171
inefficiency of, 158, 162, 177
low level of development, 158, 159, 160–64,
177, 178; literature on, 163; non-tradable
sectors and, 158, 165, 169; and poor
economic performance, 159, 165; possible
causes of, 160–64
reforms, limited government incentives for, 159
fiscal accounts
budget deficits, in 2012, ix
oil prices and, 274
oil revenue extraction, sustainable, as issue, 262
and patronage, 288
populist clientelism and, 351–52, 352t
since 2000, and fiscal policy, 282n1
spending (*see also* budgetary pressure):
under Chávez, ix, 307; *vs.* social
expenditures (1970–2004), 226, 226f
three phases of, 1958–1999, 259
fiscal accounts, oil boom period (1974–1985)
contraction of non-oil GDP and, 273–74
debt and deficits in, 273–74
oil revenue fluctuations, 260, 267, 267t; and
non-oil GDP, 264, 265f, 282n3
overheating of economy in, 272–73, 276, 277

fiscal accounts (*cont.*)
 spending, 259, 268, 269f; actual effects of,
  266, 270f; continuation of after revenue
  decline, 268–69, 269f, 275; and deficits,
  accumulation of, 269; economic damage
  at sectoral level, 277; expected effects
  of, 264–66; immediate investment of, as
  problematic, 261–63; imprudence of, 277,
  278; and inflation, 273; inter-temporal
  smoothing, lack of, 260, 263–64, 278,
  282n2; investment *vs.* consumption,
  classification of, 271, 282n5; investment *vs.*
  consumption, impact on GDP, 271–73,
  272t; investment *vs.* consumption levels,
  268, 269f, 270t; optimal policy, obstacles
  to implementation of, 260–61; optimal
  policy in response to, 260, 263; political
  pressure for, 277; as poorly managed,
  259–60, 264; and post-boom decline,
  264; responsiveness to revenues, 275; size
  of, 260, 273; as uncontrolled, 297; uses of
  funds, 268
fiscal accounts, post-boom period (1986–1990s)
 crisis, cause of length of, 275, 278, 283n11
 currency devaluations in, 267–68
 declining revenues, adjustments required
  by, 259
 inflation *vs.* debt as policy bind in, 274–76,
  277, 278
 non-oil revenue enhancement measures in,
  275–76
 oil development policy in, 267
 oil prices in, 267, 267t
 oil revenue fluctuations in, 274
 spending: fluctuations in, 259; investment *vs.*
  consumption, impact on GDP, 272,
  272t, 427, 434; lags in reductions, and
  debt increases, 274–76; reductions in,
  269, 269f, 274–76; responsiveness to
  revenues, 275–76, 434
fiscal accounts, pre-boom period (1962–1973)
 increased government consumption in, 282n4
 oil revenues and, 259, 260, 267, 267t
 spending in, responsiveness to revenues, 275
fiscal policy
 critique of, 277–78, 286
 deterioration of in 1990s, 304
 fiscal priority, 225, 226–27, 227f, 228, 229
 and growth, impact on, 429t, 434
 oil boom period (1974–1985): economic
  damage at sectoral level, 277; and
  oil development policy, 267; optimal
  policy, 260, 263; optimal policy,
  obstacles to implementation of, 260–61;

revenue, immediate investment of, as
  problematic, 261–63; size of revenue
  shock and, 260, 273
 post-boom period (1986–1990s): crisis,
  cause of length of, 275, 278, 283n11;
  inflation *vs.* debt as bind in, 274–76, 277,
  278; stabilization programs, 283n9
 pre-boom period (1962–1973), 267
 in Punto Fijo democracy, 296
fiscal revenue
 equation for, 53
 instability of, 260, 267, 267t, 274; adjustments
  required by, 259; and budgetary pressure,
  229–30, 229t; responsiveness of spending
  to, 275–76, 434; and spending on
  economic development, 209
 non-oil revenue enhancement measures,
  275–76
 sources of, 209, 228–29
 and spending, hysteresis in, 268–69, 269f, 275
fiscal revenue, from oil
 1943–2001, 24f
 decline of, 54, 75; and collapse after 1979,
  285; effect on political institutions, x,
  285–86, 288–89, 308, 310–11; and political
  cooperation, decline of, 285–86; and
  presidential power, 303; Venezuelan lack
  of economic diversity and, x
 and democracy, transition to, 293
 evolution, factors affecting, 53–58, 54t
 as exogenous to fiscal policy, 266–67, 282n4
 fluctuations in, 260, 267, 267t, 274;
  adjustments required by, 259; and
  budgetary pressure, 229–30, 229t; and
  non-oil GDP, 264, 265f, 282n3; and
  spending on economic development, 209;
  spending responsiveness to, 275–76, 434
 and GDP per capita, 51, 52
 government claim on oil profits and,
  229–30, 229t
 impact of, effect of political system on, 311
 and nationalization of oil industry, 53–54
 and oil policy alignment with international
  market fundamentals, 51
 as percentage of total revenue, 52
 pre-boom period, 259, 260, 267, 267t
 presidential control of, and government
  spending in Chávez era, 307
 production cuts of 1970s–1980s and, 68
 revenue shock: immediate investment of,
  as problematic, 261–63; optimal policy,
  obstacles to implementation of, 260–61;
  optimal policy in response to, 260, 263;
  size of, 260, 273

and spending, hysteresis in, 268–69, 269f, 275
and spending, responsiveness to, 275
transfers to states from, 304
fiscal system
under Chávez, 307
progressivity of, 224
FIV. *See* Venezuelan Investment Fund
FOGAPE (Fondo de garantías para pequeños
empresarios), 168
Fondo de garantías para pequeños empresarios.
See FOGAPE
Fondo de Inversiones de Venezuela (FIV).
See Venezuelan Investment Fund
food bonus, and labor costs, 123, 124
Forbes, K. J. A., 431
foreign born residents
Colombian: employment, 241, 247–48;
entrepreneurship among, 242, 243f, 434;
history of, 240, 241, 242–43, 244, 245;
impact on employment, 245, 246, 246t,
254–56, 255t, 433–34; source country
shocks and, 251–54, 252t
education levels, 240, 243, 244
entrepreneurship among, 240, 242, 243, 243f,
244, 434
European: countries of origin,
251; employment, 241, 247–48;
entrepreneurship among, 242, 243, 243f,
434; history of, 240, 241, 242–43, 244;
impact on employment, 245–46, 246t,
254–56, 255t, 433–34; number of, 240,
241, 242, 244; source country shocks
and, 251–54, 252t
formal sector decline of
and Chávez's rise to power, 377
increased labor regulation and, 116, 123, 130, 132
Forteza, A., 432
Fourth National Plan, 331
Frankel, J., 428t, 430
free-market reforms
and economic growth, limited evidence of
connection between, 329
lack of as explanation for poor performance, 2
in Latin America, limited success of, 329
Venezuelan level *vs.* other Latin American
nations, 2
free-market views on development, 329–30, 334
Freije, S., 122, 212
Friedberg, Rachel M., 239
G_3, Venezuelan non-oil sector trade and,
31–32, 32f
Gavin, Michael, 271
GDP
balance of payments crisis of 2002 and, viii

vs. bank credit to private sector: low level of,
158, 160, 161, 161f; oil GDP, 165–66; timing
of break in link between, 164–65, 165f
decline, and social unrest, 207
decline after 1960, 207
growth of in 20th century, 1
and inflation, cost of reduction in, 276–77
in oil sector, bank credit to private sector
and, 165–66
volatility of, impact on political beliefs, 410, 411t
GDP decline after 1979, 1
broad disparity in data on, 1–2, 17, 18–21, 18t
and capital accumulation in non-oil sector,
decline in, 26–28, 27f
consumption possibilities frontier and,
19–21, 21t
decline per capita, 15, 20, 21t, 130
decline per worker, 15, 20, 21t, 222, 223f
in non-oil sector, 20–21, 21t, 273–74, 321, 322t;
complete specialization and, 26–28, 27f;
cycling of Venezuelan economy and, 264
in oil sector, 20–21, 21t
production possibilities frontier and, 20
GDP per capita
decline after 1979, 15, 20, 21t, 130
oil fiscal revenue per capita and, 51, 52
oil production per capita and, 55
schooling levels and, 189–90, 189f
and total per capita government spending,
226, 226f
GDP per worker
decline after 1979, 15, 20, 21t, 222, 223f
non-oil sector, non-oil public capital stock
and, 91, 92f
Gini coefficient
for labor earnings, 213–14, 214f
taxes and social expenditures and, 224
Glaeser, Edward, 408, 418
Gomez, Juan C., 72
Gomez, Juan Vincente, 57t, 58–59
González, Wilfredo, 224–25, 229
government. *See also entries under* Chávez; fiscal
administrations, and oil production
eras, 57t
claim on oil profits: and capital investment
levels, 56–57, 56f, 63, 64, 65, 66, 427;
and fiscal revenue fluctuations, 229–30,
229t; under preservation policy, 61, 63,
64, 65; and sustainable extraction, as
problematic, 262
good: definition of, 289; political institutions
and, 289
intervention by, as cause of Venezuelan
decline, 16

governors, direct election of. *See* federalism
Granger causality tests, and credit collapse, 158, 168–69, 179t
La Gran Venezuela project, 337
Great Depression, and oil production, 59
Great Turn (El Gran Viraje), 283n9
growth
    after 2004, 285
    in big push industrialization, obstacles to, 338
    under Chávez, vii, viii
    failure to maintain, number of countries experiencing, 16
    financial system and: collapse, effect of, 158, 160, 174–76, 181t; detailed country studies, need for, 158; literature on, 157
    infrastructure and, 428t, 431
    labor earnings inequality and, 233, 429t, 432–33
    and non-oil sector: importance of, 28; productivity and, 21–23, 22t, 23
    vs. other nations, 1920–1980, 321
    political institutions and, 287, 312n2, 429t, 434–35
    redistribution programs and, 233
    resource abundance and, 16
    strategies, models for design of, 3–4
growth diagnostics, 4
growth empirics, within-country, development of, 3–6
growth regressions, linear, limitations of, 3, 4, 5
growth studies
    combination of cross-country and single-country studies, 425–26
    cross-country *vs.* single-country, 425
    microeconomic data sets and, 426
    single-country microeconomic studies: analytic techniques *vs.* cross-country literature, 435–38; *vs.* cross-country macroeconomic models, 426, 438–39; results *vs.* cross-country literature, 426–35, 428t–429t, 435–38
Gruber, J., 115, 118, 135
Guyana, *open_forest* of, 35, 36f, 42t, 43
Haber, S., 289
Hagopian, Frances, 391, 394
Haltiwanger, J., 131–32
Hanushek, E. A., 428t, 433
Hauk, W. R., 438
Hausmann, Ricardo, 4, 5, 16, 23–28, 34, 37, 130, 203, 428t, 430
health services, erosion of quality in, 228
Heckman, J., 116
Heckscher-Ohlin model, 33

Hellinger, Daniel, 372
Herrera Campíns, Luis, 382
Hidalgo, C., 428t, 430
Hikino, T., 360
Hofman, A., 211
Holtz-Eakin, D., 92
Hubbard, R. Glenn, 173, 176
Hulten, C., 92
human capital, levels of in Venezuela, 322. *See also* schooling
Hunt, Jennifer, 239
Hwang, Jason, 34, 428t, 430
hydrocarbon legislation, before 1943, 59
Hydrocarbons Law of 1943, 59, 60, 65
ICRG. *See* International Country Risk Guide
IEMLC indicator, 128
Immervoll, H., 117, 123
immigration. *See also* foreign-born residents
    changing patterns of, 433–34
    history of, 241
    impact on employment, 429t, 433–34; for Colombian *vs.* European immigrants, 240, 245–46, 246t, 254–56, 255t, 433–34; conventional wisdom on, 240, 244; data set, 242, 249t, 250–51; literature on, 239; modeling of, 244–45, 247–50
    source country shocks and, 251–54, 252t
import controls, ix, x
import substitution
    complexity of big push development *vs.*, 262, 331, 332–33, 335, 358
    as goal of industrialization, 321, 332, 337
    and integration of oil sector into economy, 65
    as political gesture, 352
    populist clientelism and, 358
impunity for supporters, as political tool of Chávez, 374, 398, 399
INCE (Instituto Nacional de Capacitación Educativa), 117, 124
income. *See also* wages
    beliefs about luck *vs.* skill as basis of: corruption and, 414, 415t, 421; crime and, 414–15, 420, 421; economic volatility and, 410, 411t, 418–19, 420, 421; and leftward shift in Venezuela, 409; oil dependence and, 409, 413t, 414, 419–20; and views on taxation policy, 407–8, 418
    financial system development and, 157, 158, 159
    inequality, resentment of, and Chávez's rise to power, 377
income distribution, 209–23
    factorial income distribution, 210–13

labor earnings inequality, 213–19, 214f, 218, 218f, 231; data, gaps in, 214–15, 233, 234n12; decomposition by groups, 215–16, 215f; and economic growth, 233, 429t, 432–33; education level and, 215–18, 215t; productive characteristics and returns and, 216–18, 217t, 234n15

size distribution, 219–20, 235n23

income tax

tax code of 1943, removal of uncertainty, and oil production, 59

volatility of after 1992, 304

indemnity fee, and labor costs, 126, 144

Indonesia

and economic growth, failure to maintain, 16

non-oil sector performance vs. Venezuela, 29–30

industrialization. See also big push industrialization; development strategies; manufacturing sector; natural-resource-based industrialization (NRBI)

appropriate institutional and political structures: importance of, 331–34; Venezuela's failure to maintain, 262–63, 323, 339–40, 429t, 435

capital-intensive nature of, populist clientelism and, 351

as case of late development in long-standing democracy, 321

and Fifth National Plan, 337

import substitution as goal of, 321, 332, 337

laissez-faire perspective on, 329–30

natural-resource-based heavy industry, focus on, 321

and overinvestment, risk of, 332

periodization of stages and strategies, 334–38, 335t

and protectionism, effects of, 327–29, 336–37, 354, 356

as response to oil revenue increase: potential difficulties of, 261–63; projects, 268

as restructuring of patronage system, 346

speed of, as issue, 331

strategy for, similarity to other nations', 321

successful, importance of policy to, 325

inflation

as cause of economic decline, 380

current rate of, ix

and export shocks, ability to recover from, 37, 38t–41t

GDP cost of reduction in, 276–77

oil boom spending and, 273

in post-boom period, management of, 274–76, 278

rate of vs. other countries, 310

volatility of, impact on political beliefs, 409–10, 411t, 412t, 418–19

informal sector

employment in, 1967–2008, 218–19, 218f, 232

expansion of, and Chávez's rise to power, 377

increase in with increased labor regulation, 116, 123, 130, 132

and value of conventional productive characteristics, 216–18

infrastructure

and economic growth, 428t, 431

investment in: oil revenues and, 59–60, 85n34; social expenditures and, 228

Instituto Nacional de Capacitación Educativa. See INCE

Instituto Nacional de Estadística, 211

Instituto Venezolano de los Seguros Sociales, 230

instrumental variables technique, 245, 247, 248–50

Inter-American Development Bank, 287, 291, 292, 292f, 312–13n11, 393

International Country Risk Guide (ICRG), 414, 420

International Monetary Fund (IMF), Pérez's Great Turn and, 283n9

Investment Fund for Macroeconomic Stabilization, 282n2

Iran-Iraq War, and oil dependence, efforts to reduce, 66–67

job competition effect, immigration and, 240, 244, 245, 255

job creation effect, immigration and, 240, 244, 245, 255–56

job discrimination, as political tool of Chávez, 374, 398, 399

job security laws

changes in: and employment, impact on, 133–36, 137t–142t; and labor costs, 126–27, 143–45, 146f–149f

justified vs. unjustified termination and, 144–45, 152–53nn47–51

and labor demand flexibility, 127

Johnson, S., 429t, 434

Jones, C., 433

Jones, L., 332

judiciary

Chávez's control over, 306

increased power of, collapse of party system and, 301

Karl, T., 293

Katz, Richard S., 402n4

Keefer, Philip, 414
Klenow, Peter J., 191, 192
Klingebiel, Daniela, 175
Klinger, Bailey, 34
Knack, Stephen, 414
Kornblith, M., 343
Kroszner, Randy, 175
Kuo, Shirley, 235n22
Kuznets, Simon, 208
labor, share in factoral distribution of income, 210–13, 211f
labor costs
  and economic decline, 364
  labor market regulations and, 115, 116, 117, 119–23, 120f, 123–24, 124–26, 125t, 126–27, 427; child-care bonus mandates and, 128–30, 129f; for large *vs.* small companies, 117, 119, 120–21, 120f, 123, 124, 126–27, 128–30, 129f, 132, 133f; quantification of, 127–30, 129f
labor demand flexibility
  job security costs and, 127
  in Venezuela *vs.* other nations, 127, 151n31, 152n32
labor earnings inequality, 213–19, 214f, 231
  data, gaps in, 214–15
  decomposition by groups, 215–16, 215f
  education level and, 215–18, 215t
  productive characteristics and returns and, 216–18, 217t, 234n15
labor market regulations. *See also* bonuses, mandated; minimum wage; wages, changes in definition of
  burden of *vs.* other countries, 116–17
  changes in: history of, 115, 116, 117, 119–30, 150n1; and resource allocation distortions, 116
  cost of, 116–17
  downsizing as response to, 132
  and increased informality, 116, 123, 130, 132, 143, 427
  and increased labor costs, 115, 116, 117, 119–23, 120f, 123–24, 124–26, 125t, 126–27, 427; child-care bonus mandates and, 128–30, 129f; for large *vs.* small companies, 117, 119, 120–21, 120f, 123, 124, 126–27, 128–30, 129f, 132, 133f; quantification of, 127–30, 129f
  and manufacturing sector employment, 131–33, 133–43, 137t–142t, 428t, 431–32; for blue *vs.* white collar workers, 115, 119, 135–43, 138t–139t, 141t–142t; firm size and, 132–33
labor unions
  activism of, in period of democratic deconsolidation, 345

AD support of, 341
labor costs and, 356
and Punto Fijo democracy, 343, 378
La Causa R, 299
Laeven, Luc, 175
Lagos, Ricardo, 391
Lane, P. R., 430
Larrain, Borja, 175
Latinobarómetro, 415, 422
Law, S., 428t
Law on Immigration and Settlement (1936), 241
LCR, 390
Lederman, Daniel, 72, 428t, 431
leftist-military alliances, history of in Venezuela, 372
leftists. *See also* radical left
  and federalism, increased influence under, 381–90
  incorporation into political mainstream, 381–90
  institutional sheltering of, 373, 383–89, 394, 395t, 396, 400
  military insurgency, 382
  and Punto Fijo Pact, exclusion from, 381–82
  share of votes in lower house, by year, 387f
  size of relative to other groups, 385–86
  subsidization of through cultural programs, 402n3
Leon, G., 428t, 432
Leoni, Raul, 313n14
Letouze, E., 429t, 433
Levine, D., 344
Levine, Ross, 428t, 429t, 434
Levinsohn, J., 101
Levinsohn-Petrin method, 101–2, 103t, 104t
Levitsky, Steve, 402n4
linear growth regressions, limitations of, 3, 4, 5
living standards, decline in pre-Chávez period, vii
Loayza, Norman, 132
local information, in growth diagnostics, 4
Lora, Eduardo, 2
Lusinchi, Jaime, 283n9, 298
MacCulloch, Robert, 414, 421
Macroeconomic Stabilization Fund Law, 282n2
Maignon, T., 343
Mair, Peter, 402n4
Maloney, W. F., 428t, 431
Maloney, William, 72
Mankiw, N. Gregory, 276
manufacturing sector. *See also* export industry, alternative; industrialization; non-oil sector; resource curse
  capital-intensive sectors, productivity *vs.* other sectors and nations, 363t, 364
  competitiveness, factors affecting, 366n18

concentration level, and competitiveness, 328–29
dynamic externalities of, importance of policy to, 325
employment, and labor market regulations, 131–33, 133–43, 137t–142t, 428t, 431–32; for blue vs. white collar workers, 115, 119, 135–43, 138t–139t, 141t–142t; firm size and, 132–33
excess capacity after 1968, 356–57
flexibility, lack of, and growth collapse, 427, 428t, 430
growth: favorable conditions in place for, 322; high levels of, 1920–1970, 321, 322t
job losses, 1991–2003, 131–32
number of firms, reduction of, 353, 354–56, 355t
and oil windfalls: investment of, 325, 326f; potential benefits of, 322
overdiversification in, 353, 357–58, 366n17
plants, decrease in (1975–2003), 131–32
and political climate, as potentially beneficial, 322
political impotence of, as issue, 356
and populist clientelism, impact of, 353–58
productivity growth, low, vs. other countries, 327
proliferation of politically-based licenses and subsidies, 353–54
protectionism, effects of, 327–29, 336–37, 354, 356
research and development, underspending on, 357–58, 366n18
and risk, growth of, 353, 358
and selectivity: importance of, 323, 333, 338; lack of, 339–40, 351, 352–58
stagnation of, 1980–1998, 321, 322t; conventional explanation, limitations of, 338–39; as counterintuitive, 322; distinguishing features of vs. other nations, 339; productivity and, 364; profitability and, 364; as similar to other countries' experience, 359; state protectionism/regulation and, 327–29, 336–37, 354, 356
state disciplining, lack of, 353, 358
state protection/regulation of: after 1960, 336–37; and stagnation, 1980–1998, 327–29
suboptimal scale economies in, 332, 353, 357–58, 365n4
wages, 324, 327
Manzano, Osmel, 71, 72, 74–75, 267
market reforms
ranking of Venezuela vs. other countries in, 291
reversal of in Venezuela, 310

Márquez, G., 116
Martinez, Anibal, 63
Martinez, D., 117, 123
Marx, Karl, 397
MAS (Movimiento al Socialismo)
Caldera administration and, 379
and federalism, increased influence under, 389, 390
founding of, 382
integration into mainstream politics, 382–83, 390
nonadaptation in, 394
and period of democratic deconsolidation, 299, 302, 348, 349
sheltering of by universities, 385
Matos Azócar, Luis Raúl, 383
Mayobre, J., 324
mayors, direct election of. See federalism
MBR-200. See Movimiento Bolivariano Revolucionario-200
Mene Grande oil field, discover of, 58
Merkl, Peter, 16
Mernaldo, V., 289
Mexico
federalism in, 310–11
non-oil sector performance vs. Venezuela, 29–30
open_forest of, 35, 36f
technical experts' role in, 393
Micco, A., 127, 152n33
Middle East crises, and oil dependence, efforts to reduce, 66–67, 66f
military
alliance with radical left in Chávez administration, 371; exclusionary politics of Punto Fijo regime and, 372–73; grievances of junior officers and, 386–88; military officers in public office, 373, 374t; precedents for in Latin America, 372; sheltering of leftists in military and, 373, 385–89, 394, 395t, 396
early supporters of Chávez in, 375, 376t
intelligence institutions, laxity of, 388
size of, 386
spending on, 384f, 385–86, 386f, 387f
military regimes, history of in South America, 372
Miller, R. I., 16, 436
minimum wage, increased number of workers earning, 116, 121, 130
minimum wage laws
changes in, 117, 119–23, 120f; and employment, impact on, 122–23, 133–36, 137t–142t; and increased labor costs, 119–23, 120f, 123–24, 150–51n16
different levels of, 119

minimum wage laws (*cont.*)
  and employment, effect on, efforts in other
    nations to limit, 123
  and increased labor costs, 123
  for large *vs.* small companies, 119,
    120–21, 120f
  literature on, 151n21
  as more binding *vs.* other countries, 121–22,
    122f, 130
Mody, Ashoka, 163
Mommer, Bernard, 53–54
Monaldi, Francisco, 379
Montenegro, Claudio, 117
Moreno, María Antonia, 224–25, 229
Moss, Diana L., 64, 67
Movimiento al Socialismo. *See* MAS
Movimiento Bolivariano Revolucionario-200
    (MBR-200), 349–50, 388, 390
Movimiento de Izquierda Revolucionaria, 382
Movimiento Quinta República. *See* MVR
Munnell, A. H., 92
Murphy, Kevin M., 202
MVR (Movimiento Quinta República)
  early leadership, political/professional
    background of, 375, 376t
  integration into mainstream politics, 390
  and period of democratic deconsolidation,
    299, 301, 302
  rise of, 349–50
Naím, M., 328
nationalization of iron ore industry, 337, 338
nationalization of natural gas industry, 64
nationalization of oil industry, 337, 338
  and capital investment, 56f, 57, 67
  and lessening of restraints of government
    power, 346–47
  and oil fiscal revenue, 53–54
  as restructuring of patronage system, 346
  retreat from in post-boom period, 267
national oil companies, creation of, 66, 68
natural-resource-based industrialization
    (NRBI). *See also* big push
    industrialization
  appropriate institutional and political
    structures: importance of, 330–34;
    Venezuela's failure to maintain, 262–63,
    323, 339–40, 429t, 435
  continued growth, obstacles to, 338
  distinguishing features of in Venezuela *vs.*
    other nations, 339
  diversification of export structure as goal
    of, 337
  and Fifth National Plan, 337
  periodization of, 335–36, 335t, 338

  potential difficulties of, 262–63
  as restructuring of patronage system, 346
  and state role, purposeful expansion of,
    337–38, 365n9
  vertical integration as goal of, 337
neoliberal reforms
  and bureaucracy, efforts to trim, 351,
    379–80
  Caldera and, 283n9, 349, 379, 380
  and chavismo, appeal of, 379–81
  drop in number of firms during, 353
  incomplete implementation of, 379–81
  Pérez and, 283n9, 303–4, 347, 379, 380
  and political instability, 347, 349
  populist clientelism and, 356
Nicaragua, economic decline in, 310
non-oil sector. *See also* export industry,
    alternative; manufacturing sector
  decline in capital accumulation, 23–28, 427;
    and GDP decline, 26–28, 27f; magnitude
    of, 22t, 23; three-sector model of, 24–28,
    27f, 45–46, 46n6, 47n8
  exports decline of under Chávez, vii
  export shocks, ability to recover from, *open_*
    forest and, 35, 37–43, 38t–42t
  GDP decline after 1979, 20–21, 21t, 273–74,
    282n3, 321, 322t; complete specialization
    and, 26–28, 27f; cycling of economy and,
    264, 265f
  importance to Venezuelan growth, 28
  performance since 1980s, 28–33, 29f, 364n1;
    interest rate arbitrage and, 29; market
    participation and, 31, 31f; non-energy-
    intensive sectors within, 28–29, 29f; by
    region, 31–32, 32f
  productivity decline: and growth, 23;
    magnitude of, 21–23
  total factor productivity growth
    decompositions, 21–23, 22t
nonparametric econometrics, in growth
    models, 4–5
non-tariff protections, after 1960, 337
non-tradable sectors
  definition of, 169
  low level of development in financial system
    and, 158, 165, 169
  oil booms and, 324
North Sea oil reserves, discovery of, 67
Norway, oil production in, 70
Nunn, N., 429t, 435
Oficina Central de Estadística e Informátion, 211
oil boom
  and beliefs about luck *vs.* skill as basis of
    income, 409, 419–20

as cause of Venezuelan decline, 16

and currency devaluations, 267–68, 274–75, 282n3

current, political institutions and, 311

and economic destabilization, as similar to other countries' experience, 359

fiscal debt and deficits in, 273–74

fiscal spending in, 259, 268, 269f; actual effects of, 266, 270f; continuation of after revenue decline, 268–69, 269f, 275; and deficits, accumulation of, 269; economic damage at sectoral level, 277; expected effects of, 264–66; immediate investment of, as problematic, 261–63; imprudence of, 277, 278; and inflation, 273; inter-temporal smoothing, lack of, 260, 263–64, 278, 282n2; investment *vs.* consumption, classification of, 271, 282n5; investment *vs.* consumption, impact on GDP, 271–73, 272t; investment *vs.* consumption levels, 268, 269f, 270t; optimal policy, obstacles to implementation of, 260–61; optimal policy in response to, 260, 263; political pressure for, 277; as poorly managed, 259–60, 264; and post-boom decline, 264; responsiveness to revenues, 275; size of, 260, 273; as uncontrolled, 297; uses of funds, 268

global energy use in, 58f

oil development policy in, 267

oil market in, 57t

oil policy in, 59–60, 76

oil production, factors affecting, 58–60

oil revenue fluctuations, 260, 267, 267t; and non-oil GDP, 264, 265f, 273–74, 282n3

overheating of economy in, 272–73, 276, 277

political climate in, 57t, 58–60

and political institutions, decline of, 291, 297

oil companies

capital investment in Venezuela, factors affecting, 62–63, 65, 66

law forbidding removal of assets from Venezuela (1971), 65

reintroduction of after 1991, limited success of, 71–72

oil concession(s)

ending of (1983), 61, 62–63, 65

first, 58

oil demand, growth of in 1960s–1970s, 66, 66f

oil dependence

effect on political institutions, 285–86, 288–89, 312n3

efforts to reduce, 66–67, 66f

impact on economic decline, 15–16, 428t, 430–31

impact on political beliefs, 410–14, 413t, 419–20

and non-oil income redistribution, reduced pressure for, 289

and political institutions, 310

and stakes of power, increase of, 288

and strong institutions, importance of, 286

oil exploration

decline of, in political climate of 1960s, 66

increase in, in 1970s, 67

oil-exporting countries

economic development, theories on, 52

and export industries, ability to develop, 37

and export shocks, ability to recover from, 37, 38t–39t, 42–43

open_forests of, 35–37, 36f

oil fiscal revenue

1943–2001, 24f

decline of, 54, 75; and collapse after 1979, 285; effect on political institutions, x, 285–86, 288–89, 308, 310–11; and political cooperation, decline of, 285–86; and presidential power, 303; Venezuelan lack of economic diversity and, x

and democracy, transition to, 293

evolution, factors affecting, 53–58, 54t

as exogenous to fiscal policy, 266–67, 282n4

fiscal revenue equation, 53

fluctuations in, 260, 267, 267t, 274; adjustments required by, 259; and budgetary pressure, 229–30, 229t; and non-oil GDP, 264, 265f, 282n3; and spending on economic development, 209; spending responsiveness to, 275–76, 434

and GDP per capita, 51, 52

government claim on oil profits and, 229–30, 229t

impact of, effect of political system on, 311

and nationalization of oil industry, 53–54

and oil policy alignment with international market fundamentals, 51

as percentage of total revenue, 52

pre-boom period, 259, 260, 267, 267t

presidential control of, and government spending in Chávez era, 307

production cuts of 1970s–1980s and, 68

revenue shock: immediate investment of, as problematic, 261–63; optimal policy, obstacles to implementation of, 260–61; optimal policy in response to, 260, 263; size of, 260, 273

oil fiscal revenue (*cont.*)
 and spending, hysteresis in, 268–69,
  269f, 275
 and spending, responsiveness to, 275
 transfers to states from, 304
oil market share, Venezuelan losses of 1960s,
 60–65, 61t. 431
oil policy. *See also* preservation policy
 in 1990s, ineffectiveness of, 71–75, 76,
  86n55, 87n56
 alignment with international market
  fundamentals, and fiscal revenue, 51
 and collapse of oil production, 76
 and integration of oil sector, lack of
  attention to, 60, 65, 74–75, 84–85n19
 oil as "temporary" productive sector and, 59
 "opening up" ("apertura") policy, 71
 overview of, 267
 "sowing of oil" policy, 59–60, 65, 69, 268,
  321; critique of, 76, 86n55, 87n56, 431;
  government subsidies and, 75
oil prices
 of 1970s: and energy efficiency measures,
  66–67, 67f; and oil exploration, increase
  in, 67
 in 1980s, decline of, 67–69
 before Chávez, decline of, vii
 in Chávez era, rise of: and growth of
  government, viii; and lost opportunity
  for reform, x–xi; masking of economic
  problems by, vii, viii
 and fiscal accounts, 267, 267t, 274
 for tax purposes, decree fixing (1971), 64
oil production
 1914–1958, 58–60
 1958–1973, 60, 62, 64
 1973–1988, 67–69
 1989–2003, 69–70, 72–73
 capital investment and, 55–56, 55f, 64
 costs, Venezuela *vs.* OPEC nations, 60–61,
  61t, 62
 decline of in 1970s and 80s, 54, 54t, 64,
  67–69, 427, 431
 effort, after 1986, *vs.* other countries, 70
 factors affecting, 70
 fluctuations in, 364n1
 increases after 1986, 69–70
 and intergenerational fiscal burden, 72
 and oil fiscal revenue, 53–58, 54t, 75
 oil policy and, 76, 267
 per capita: and GDP per capita, 55; trends
  in, 54, 54t
 preservation policy and, 61–62
 productivity, vii, 70, 77, 78f, 84n11

oil production periods
 change in international context period
  (1973–1988), 57t, 66–69; and economy,
  efforts to diversify, 69; global energy
  use in, 58t; oil dependence, importing
  nations' efforts to reduce, 66–67, 66f;
  oil market in, 57t; oil policy in, 76; oil
  production declines in, 67–69; political
  climate in, 57t, 66–67
 discovery and boom period (1914–1958),
  57t, 58–60; global energy use in, 58f; oil
  market in, 57t; oil policy in, 59–60, 76;
  oil production, factors affecting, 58–60;
  political climate in, 57t, 58–60
 period after comparative advantage
  (1958–1973), 57t, 60–65; global energy
  use in, 58t; oil market in, 57t; oil policy
  in, 60–61, 62–64, 65, 76; oil production
  costs in, 60, 62; oil production in, 64;
  political climate in, 57t, 64–65
 period of unchanged policy in changing
  international context (1989–2003), 57t;
  capital investment, factors inhibiting,
  70–72, 76; diversification, failure to
  pursue, 74–75, 76; diversification,
  potential benefits of, 72–74, 76; global
  energy use in, 58t; oil market in, 57t;
  oil policy in, 65, 69, 71–75, 76, 86n55,
  87n56; oil production in, 69–70; oil
  production in, factors affecting, 72–73;
  oil production in, *vs.* other countries, 70;
  political climate in, 57t; reintroduction
  of private oil companies, limited success
  of, 71–72
oil profits
 and cycling of Venezuelan economy
  (1972–1994), 264, 265f, 282n3
 decline of: and funding of redistribution
  programs, 209; and non-oil sector
  capital accumulation, 23–28
 distribution of, in Punto Fijo
  democracy, 296
 government claim on: and capital
  investment levels, 56–57, 56f, 63, 64, 65,
  66, 427; and fiscal revenue fluctuations,
  229–30, 229t; under preservation policy,
  61, 63, 64, 65; and sustainable extraction,
  as problematic, 262
 investment of in manufacturing sector, 322,
  325, 326f (*See also* natural-resource-
  based industrialization)
 net, and oil fiscal revenue,
  53–54, 54t
 use in social expenditures, 225

oil-related sectors
   government subsidization of, and
      productivity, 74–75
   growth of, potential benefits of, 74–75, 76
oil reserves
   concerns about, 63–64, 66 (*See also*
      preservation policy)
   increases in in 1970s, 67
oil richness, *vs.* economic concentration, for
   select nations, 72–73, 73f
oil sector. *See also specific topics*
   collapse of 1980s, 51
   and economic rents, 56, 84n11
   and factoral distribution of income, 210
   history of, 58
   and immigration, 241
   importance to Venezuelan economy, 51–52
   periods of production, 57t 57–58;
      importance of considering separately,
      51, 57
   sensitivity to property rights and tax
      regimes, 55
   tax rates, vii, 62, 63t, 64
   and tax revenue, 209
oil sector technology
   improvements of 1970s–1980s, 67
   improvements of late 1950s, 64
oil workers strikes, 1936, 59
Olken, Ben, 418
Olley, Steve, 96
Olley-Pakes semiparametric method, in
   estimation of effect of public capital
   stock on productivity, 96, 100, 101, 101t,
   102t, 103, 111–12
OPEC
   correlation in oil production, 79, 80t–83t
   creation of, 62, 66
   critical reception, 85n26
   market share competition with, 60–65, 61t
   oil production levels *vs.* Venezuela
      (2001), 72
   oil reserves outside, efforts to locate, 67
   oil sector tax rates, 62, 63t
   production quotas: effectiveness of, 68–69;
      and Venezuelan production, 55
   and Venezuela oil development policy, 267
open_forest
   and export industries, ability to develop,
      33–37
   and export shocks, ability to recover from,
      35, 37–43, 38t–42t
   of oil-exporting countries, 35–37, 36f
   of Venezuela *vs.* neighboring countries, 35,
      36f, 42–43, 42t, 44

opponents, abuse of, as political tool of Chávez,
   374, 398–99
Organic Labor Law (1997), 119
   and definition of wages, 121, 150–51n16
   and job security costs, 127
   and payroll taxable wage, 126
Organization of Petroleum Exporting
   Countries. *See* OPEC
Orlando, M., 116
Ortega, F., 429t, 433
Ortiz, Nelson, 380
Oviedo, Ana María, 132
Pagés, C., 116, 117
Pakes, Ariel, 96
Panama, Torrijos regime in, 372
Paravisini, D., 316n33
Parente, Stephen L., 23
Patria para Todos, 299
Patriotic Pole (PP). *See* Polo Patriótico
patronage
   in period of democratic deconsolidation,
      345–46
   in Punto Fijo democracy, and economic
      policy, 344
payroll taxes
   changes in, and labor costs, 124–26, 125t
   types of, 124
PCV, 382, 390
PDVSA (Petróleos de Venezuela)
   autonomy, elimination of, 317n47
   capital investment by, 57, 71
   policies, and fiscal oil revenues, 53, 54
   purchasing policies, and productivity of
      suppliers, 75
Penfold-Becerra, Michael, 348–49, 389–90
Penn World Tables, 16, 19–20
Pérez, Carlos Andrés
   departure from AD, 347
   economic policies of, 345–46
   impeachment of, 84, 347
   and La Gran Venezuela plan, 337
   left's support of, 382
   neoliberal reforms of, 283n9, 303–4, 347,
      379, 380
   and party deconsolidation, 298
   riots after election of, 298–99
   support of poor for, 377
   and técnicos, failure to incorporate, 393
   VAT and, 94
   warnings about chavistas, failure to heed,
      388
Pérez Jiménez, Marcos, 57t, 60, 342,
   343, 388
Peri, G., 429t, 433

period of deconsolidation (1973–1993), political
    factionalism in, and manufacturing
    sector, 339–40
Perotti, Roberto, 271, 273, 279, 281, 283n16
Persson, T., 431
Peru
    and party system, 309
    poverty rates in, viii, xiin5
Petersen, Bruce C., 173, 176
Petkoff, Teodoro, 382, 383
Petrin, A., 101
petrochemical complexes, building of, 60, 65
Petroleos de Venezuela. *See* PDVSA
Petrolia del Tachira, 58
Piketty, Thomas, 407–8, 415
Pineda, J., 115, 118, 133
Pinochet, Augusto, 392
political activists, early supporters of Chávez
    among, 375, 376t
political beliefs
    corruption and, 414, 415t, 420, 421
    crime and, 414–17, 416t, 418, 419t, 420, 421
    economic conditions as drivers of, 408,
        409–10, 411t, 412t, 418–19
    economic volatility and, 409–10, 411t, 412t,
        418, 420, 421
    as immutable cultural norm, 408
    impact of oil dependence on, 410–14, 413t,
        419–20
    influence on views about political system, 407
political climate, and capital investment, 58–59,
    62–63, 65, 67
political cooperation
    Chávez regime and, 286, 287, 306, 307, 308,
        309, 350
    collapse of, economic effects, 339–40,
        351–58
    collapse of party system and, 297–303, 309,
        345–49
    conditions producing, 287–88
    constitution of 1961 and, 293–94
    decline of oil revenues and, 285–86
    levels of *vs.* other countries, 292
    in Punto Fijo democracy, 294–96, 308–9,
        314n23
political economy. *See* democracy; political
    institutions
political forces, regional, increased power of
    under federalism, 298, 299–303, 304,
    315n31
political instability. *See also* political cooperation
    as cause of economic decline, 380
    neoliberal reforms and, 347, 349
    rise of, after decline in oil revenues, 286

political institutions
    in 1990s, characteristics of, 380
    in Chávez era: authoritarianism, increase
        in, 306, 316n45, 317n47; characteristics
        of, 287, 341; circumvention of state
        institutions, 350; and crippling of
        economic growth, 350; decline of, 291,
        305–8, 309, 310, 349–50; presidential
        power, increase of, 296, 305–6, 307–8,
        316n43
    collapse of in pre-Chávez period, vii
    decline of: in 2008 measurement data, 291;
        central factors in, 285–86, 310–11, 435;
        extent of, 309; origin of in 1980s, 291;
        and policy, poor quality of, 286
    decline of oil revenues and, x, 285–86,
        288–89, 308, 310–11
    and economic growth, 287, 312n2, 429t,
        434–35
    as factor in economic collapse, 285
    government control of, limited political
        flexibility due to, x
    measurement of, 289–90
    and oil dependence, effects of, x, 285–86,
        288–89, 308, 312n3
    and oil income, impact of, 311
    perception of, in late 1990s, 305
    in period of democratic deconsolidation:
        characteristics of, 287, 297–305, 309,
        315nn31–32, 340–41; continual flux
        in, 302; distributive conflicts and,
        345–47; and manufacturing sector, poor
        performance of, 339–40; party system,
        collapse of, 347–49; rising factionalism
        in, 345–49
    in pre-democratic period (1928–1948):
        characteristics of, 340; history of, 341–42
    in Punto Fijo democracy: characteristics
        of, 287, 291, 293–97, 340, 342–44; and
        obsession with accommodation, 343;
        politics as driver of economic policy,
        344; and radicals, political costs of
        excluding, 344; social spending in, 343
    and quality of governance, 289
    rankings of *vs.* other countries, 290–92,
        290f, 292f
    reform of, economic conditions and, 311
    relevance of to economic conditions, 359–60
    stability of *vs.* other nations, 290f, 291,
        292, 292f
    stabilization of under Juan Vincente Gomez,
        58–59
    strong, importance in resource-dependent
        nations, 286

political parties
  activation of federalism (1989) and, 293, 297,
    298, 299–301
  Chávez's anti-party platform, 350
  collapse of party system and, 297–305,
    315n30, 315nn31–32, 341, 346, 347–49, 389
  decline in support for: causes of, 286, 378; in
    military, 388–89
  decline of: under Chávez, 305, 306, 309, 350;
    oil revenue declines and, 289; political
    reforms of 1980s–1990s and, 286; and
    rise of populist clientelism, 351
  defunding of, in constitution of 1999, 305,
    306, 350
  and economic collapse, inability to
    respond to, 379
  federalism and, 293–94
  fragmentation of, and economic
    government, 379
  and institutional closure of Punto Fijo
    democracy, 378
  nonadaptation in, 390–94, 400
  and party system under Punto Fijo
    democracy, 293, 313–14n17, 314n20,
    314n22, 315n28, 339, 342
  proliferation of: after activation of
    federalism, 299–301, 341, 348–49; after
    economic collapse, 378
  in Punto Fijo democracy, 294–95, 295f
  representational deficits of, 394
  technocratic deficits of, 392–94, 400
political reforms of late 1980s–early 1990s, and
    party system, weakening of, 286
Political Risk Service, 414
political unrest
  of 1980–1990s, and retreat from Punto Fijo
    democracy, 297, 298–99, 304
  under Chávez, 306, 308, 350
  GDP decline and, 207
Polo Patriótico (PP), 349
populist clientelism
  economic effects of, 351–58
  incompatibility with effective development
    strategies, 358, 359–60
  in period of deconsolidation (1973–1993),
    341, 345; manifestations of, 339; and
    manufacturing sector, poor performance
    of, 339–40
  in Punto Fijo democracy, 343, 344
poverty
  1970s–2000, 208
  1980–2005, 221–22, 221f
  after 2000, 209, 221, 233
  causes of, 209

under Chávez, viii, xiin5
data on, 209, 220–21, 233
decline in, as product of redistribution, 222
and economic growth, 233
growth and inequality components of,
    222, 223t
increase of in 1980s–1990s, causes of, 221–22,
    232, 381
measuring of, 220, 235n26
vs. other nations, viii, xiin5
rise of, and Chávez's rise to power, 377
PP. See Polo Patriótico
Prescott, Edward C., 23
preservation policy
  and capital investment, 61–62
  critique of, 64, 65, 76, 86n55, 87n56, 431
  and growth of oil-related industries,
    suppression of, 75, 86n55, 87n56
  and oil production levels, 61–62
  policies under, 60–61, 65
  in pre-boom period (1962–1973), 267
  rationale for, 63–64
  retreat from in post-boom period, 267
Presidential Commission for the Reform of the
    State (COPRE), 298
presidential power
  Chávez's increase of, 296, 305–6, 307–8,
    316n43
  under constitution of 1961, 293, 296, 313n19,
    313nn16–17, 343
  decline of after federalization, 300, 301, 303
price controls, ix, x
Primero Justicia, 299, 300
Pritchett, Lant, 5, 192, 202, 433
private sector, bank credit to
  crowding out by public sector demand, 159,
    163, 167–68, 170
  decline of in 1980s–1990s, 167, 167f; anatomy
    of, 166–68, 167f; causes of, 158–59,
    165–66, 167–68, 168–70; depth of, 170,
    171f; effect on businesses, 159–60, 178;
    effect on growth, 158, 160, 174–76, 181t;
    effect on larger firms, 160, 176–77, 178,
    182t; effects of, 171–77, 178, 428t, 432;
    managers' perception of effects of, 159,
    171–74, 172t, 179t, 180t, 183n21; timing of,
    164–66, 165f, 171
  vs. GDP in Venezuela: low level of, 158, 160,
    161, 161f; timing of break in link between,
    164–65, 165f
  levels vs. other countries, 160–61, 172
  misapplication of, and growth, 160, 175–76
  oil GDP and, 165–66
private sector investment, decline of, 212, 380

productivity in non-oil sector
  decline of: and growth, 23; lack of
    investment and, 94, 97–105, 98t, 99t,
    101t, 102t, 103t, 104t, 106t, 107t, 208, 232,
    427, 431, 432–33; magnitude of, 21–23,
    130; and poverty, increase of, 222, 232
  as key to growth, 364
  vs. other nations, by time and industry,
    360–64, 361t–363t
productivity in oil-related sectors, low levels of,
  74–75
productivity in oil sector, 77, 78f, 84n11
  after 1986, *vs.* other countries, 70
  decline in, vii
product space density
  and comparative advantage, 34–43, 40t–41t
  of Venezuela *vs.* other Latin American
    nations, 44
profitability
  of banking system, decline of in late 1980s, 167
  of manufacturing sector, *vs.* other nations,
    360–64, 361t–363t
profit bonus, and labor costs, 124
property rights
  current insecurity of, x
  oil sector sensitivity to, 55
Proyecto Carabobo, 300
Proyecto Venezuela, 299, 300, 349
Przeworski, A., 288, 371
public capital stock, non-oil. *See also* capital
    investment
  effect on productivity, 94, 97–105, 98t, 99t,
    101t, 102t, 103t, 104t, 106t, 107t, 431;
    empirical results on, 92–93; empirical
    strategy for determining, 95–97, 111–12;
    estimated non-oil GDP with constant
    capital stock, 105–6, 108f; for large
    vs. small companies, 100–101; rate of
    return on infrastructure development,
    105, 113n7; theoretical basis for, 91–92;
    theoretical issues in determining, 93
  and GDP per worker, 91, 92f
  privatization and, 112n1
public capital stock evolution, formula for, 96
public debt
  in oil boom period, 273–74
  as percentage of government expenditure,
    229t, 230
  in post-boom period, management of,
    274–76, 278
  in Punto Fijo democracy, 296
Puente, Alejandro, 74–75
Puente, J., 304
Puente, José Manuel, 227

Punto Fijo Pact, 313n13
  democracy under, 293–94, 294–97, 342–44
  exclusionary politics of, 381–82
  incorporation of opposition forces into,
    381–90
  and rise of chavismo, 372–73
quality of life in Venezuela, increased size of
    government under Chávez and, viii
Raddatz, Claudio, 165
radicalism
  of Chávez, 396–97, 401
  Chávez's use of as political tool, 374, 396–98,
    399, 401
  of left in Venezuela, ideological non-
    adaptation and, 391–92, 400–401
  origins of, 397
radical left. *See also* leftists
  alliance with military in Chávez
    administration, 371; early supporters
    of Chávez in military, 375, 376t;
    exclusionary politics of Punto Fijo
    regime and, 372–73; grievances of junior
    officers and, 386–88; military officers
    in public office, 373, 374t; precedents
    for in Latin America, 372; sheltering of
    leftists in military and, 373, 385–89, 394,
    395t, 396
  in Latin America: exposure to moderating
    international influences, 391–92;
    as governing party, history of, 372;
    suppression of, 382, 391, 400; Venezuela
    as haven for, 392
  in Venezuela: and federalism, increased
    influence under, 389–90; ideological
    non-adaptation of, 391–92, 400–401;
    incorporation into political mainstream,
    381–90, 400; institutional sheltering of,
    373, 383–89, 394, 395t, 396, 400; political
    platforms of, 390–91; and Punto Fijo
    democracy, 344, 345, 381–82; and rise of
    chavismo, 372–73, 400; subsidization of
    through cultural programs, 402n3
Rajan, R., 169, 174–75
Rama, M., 432
Ramírez, M. T., 93
Rangel, José Vicente, 382
Ranis, Gustav, 235n22
Ravallion, Martin, 227
real-world complexity, incorporation of into
    economic models, 3–6
Rebelo, S., 92, 428t
recall provisions, introduction of, 305, 306
recession of 1978–1984, and fiscal spending
    adjustments, 274

recession of 1989, as cause of financial sector
    underdevelopment, 165, 165f, 170, 171f
redistribution programs, 223–30
    and capital investment levels, 232–33
    data on, 224
    and economic growth, 233
    funding of, oil revenue and, 209
    masking of real economic issues by, ix
    opinions on, beliefs about luck vs. skill as
        basis of income and, 408
    progressivity of, 224
    public's acceptance of, ix
    rationale for, viii–ix
    social expenditures as, 224–25, 225–28, 233
    social security as, 230
    tax structure as, 228–30
referendums, presidential power to call, 305
refining industry, development of, 60, 65
regional political forces, increased power of
    under federalism, 298, 299–303, 304,
    315n31
rent-seeking in Venezuela, as explanation of
    decline, 2, 44
research and development, underspending on,
    357–58, 366n18
resource abundance, and growth rates, 16
resource curse. See also Dutch disease
    and beliefs about luck vs. skill as basis of
        income, 409, 420
    as explanation of Venezuelan decline, 1–2,
        322, 323, 325–27, 428t, 430–31
    literature on, 322
    mechanisms of, 324–25
    oil-exporting countries and, 52
    and political beliefs, 408, 410–14, 413t,
        419–20
    poor policy as component of, 325
    and strong political institutions, importance
        of, 286
resource-rich countries, economic development
    theories on, 52
Restuccia, D., 16, 130
Rey, R. C., 340, 343
Rich, Robert W., 276
right wing, size of relative to other groups, 385–86
Rigobón, Roberto, 23–28, 203
Roberts, Kenneth, 377
Robinson, J. A., 429t, 434
Robinson, James A., 397, 400
Rodríguez, Francisco, 4–5, 16–17, 19, 37, 115, 118,
    130, 133, 428t, 430
Rodríguez, Miguel, 386
Rodrik, Dani, 4, 5, 34, 202, 428t, 429t, 430, 431,
    434–35

Romer, D., 428t, 430
Römer, Henrique Salas, 300
Rostow, W. W., 426
rule of law
    under Chávez, decline of, 306–7
    in Venezuela vs. other countries, 290f, 291
Saavedra, Jaime, 117
Sacerdote, Bruce, 408
Sachs, J. D., 1, 16, 44, 428t, 430
Saénz, Irene, 386
Sakong, I, 332
Sala-i-Martin, X., 16, 207, 436
Saudi Arabia, as OPEC swing producer, 68, 86n39
Scarpetta, S., 131–32
Schamis, Héctor E., 373
schooling
    and economic decline: delays in talent
        reallocation and, 188, 202; as despite
        educational gains, 187, 188, 193, 429t, 433;
        links between, 188–89, 193, 201–4; rent
        seeking and, 188–89, 202–4
    level of: for foreign born residents, 240, 243,
        244; vs. GDP per capita, 189–90, 189f;
        growth vs. other nations, 187, 188, 189,
        189f, 190–91, 190t, 192–93, 204, 433; and
        wage levels, expected vs. actual levels,
        187, 188, 196–97, 196f, 197f, 204; and
        wage premiums, 187–88, 193–97, 194f,
        204, 215–18, 215t; and worker output,
        conventional wisdom on, 187, 188
    quality deterioration, 187, 188, 198, 228;
        timing of vs. economic collapse, 198–200
    school system, expansion of, 195, 195f, 384;
        and quality, impact on, 198
    teacher wage premiums, as proxy for quality,
        198–200, 199f
schooling capital (SK)
    growth, factor accumulation decomposition
        of, 191–92, 205n3
    growth vs. other nations, 187, 188, 189, 189f,
        190–91, 190t, 192–93, 204, 433
    misallocation of, and economic decline,
        201–4, 203f
    schooling quality and, 187–88
Schwab, R. A., 92
SECONSEDE, 388
Seijas, Lizbeth, 224–25, 229
Senate, elimination of in constitition of 1999,
    305, 308
seniority fee, 144
    and employment, impact on, 133–36,
        137t–142t, 143
    and labor costs, 126
Servén, Luis, 93, 132, 428t, 431

Shleifer, Andrei, 202
SIDOR, development of, 335
SK. *See* schooling capital
small opposition forces (SOFs). *See also* radical left
  incorporation into political mainstream,
    381–90
  increased influence of under federalism,
    389–90
  institutional sheltering of, 373, 383–89, 394,
    395t, 396, 400
  rise of, with decline of mainstream parties, 390
Smith, James P., 239
social conflict, as cause of Venezuelan economic
    collapse, 44
social expenditures
  under Chávez, viii
  definition of, 236n41
  factors affecting, 225
  financing of, 209, 233
  and fiscal priority, 225, 226–27, 227f,
    228, 229
  progressivity of, 224
  in Punto Fijo democracy, 343
  quality of social services and, 228
  redistribution function of, 224–25, 225–28
  stability of over time, 226f, 227–28, 227f;
    potential problems masked by, 228
social immiseration, and Chávez's rise to
    power, 377
social inequality
  and economic decline, relationship between,
    207, 208
  and export shocks, ability to recover from,
    37, 38t–41t
  levels of, 207
social security
  funding of, 230, 231t
  and increased labor costs, 124, 125t
  as redistribution program, 230
social services, quality of, as issue, 228
SOFs. *See* small opposition forces
sophistication of economy (*PRODY*), and *open_
    forest*, 34–35, 40t–41t, 42
South Korea, industrialization in, 332
Soviet Union, and economic growth, failure to
    maintain, 16
"sowing of oil" policy, 59–60, 65, 69, 268, 321
  critique of, 76, 86n55, 87n56, 431
  government subsidies and, 75
specialization, as factor in Venezuelan economic
    collapse, 26–28, 27f
specialization traps, 45
Spiller, P., 287, 292
The Stages of Economic Growth (Rostow), 426

stakes of power
  Chávez's increase of, 286, 296, 306, 307–8
  constitution of 1961 and, 293
  definition of, 288
  high, and democratic governance, 288
  and oil income, impact of, 311
  in Punto Fijo democracy, 296, 308–9
standard of living measures, changes in terms of
    trade and, 19–20
state and local government funding. *See*
    FIDES (Venezuelan Intergovernmental
    Decentralization Fund)
stock market
  efficiency of, 163
  market capitalization: and financial system
    collapse, timing of, 164–65, 165f; small
    size of relative to other countries, 161, 163
  size of as proxy for financial development, 157
structural adjustment programs. *See also*
    neoliberal reforms
  of 1990s, limited implementation of, 74
  anti-investment bias in, 431
Subramanian, A., 429t, 434–35
sudden stop, and export shocks, ability to
    recover from, 37, 38t–41t
supply and demand, distortion of by large fiscal
    expenditures, 262–63
Supreme Court
  Chávez's control over, 306
  and Pérez, impeachment of, 304, 347
  support of Chávez's reforms, 305, 306–7
Swaroop, V., 92
Tabellini, G., 431
Taiwan, industrialization in, 332
tariffs
  and development strategies after 1960,
    336–37
  increase in, as populist clientelism, 353
  reduction of in 1990s, 353
Tatom, J. A., 92
taxation. *See also* VAT tax
  decree fixing oil price for tax purposes
    (1971), 64
  income tax law, volatility of after 1992, 304
  oil sector sensitivity to, 55
  opinions on, beliefs about luck *vs.* skill as
    basis of income and, 407–8, 418
  payroll taxes, changes in, 117
  progressivity of, 224, 228–29
  redistribution through, 228–30
  revenue sources, 209
  and social expenditures, 209
  tax breaks for private exploration, in 1990s,
    71, 72

tax rate
    and oil fiscal revenue, 53–54, 54t
    on OPEC member oil sectors, 62, 63t
Taylor, A. M., 429t, 435
technical knowledge
    Chávez regime and, 393–94
    methods of penetration into parties, 393
téchnicos, relationship with politicians, erosion
    of, 393
technocratic deficits of political parties,
    392–94, 400
Terms-of-Trade Adjusted Real DGP per Capita,
    and consumption possibilities frontier,
    19–20
three-sector model (Hausmann and Rigobón),
    24–28, 27f, 45–46, 46n6, 47n8
Tokman, V., 117, 123
Tommasi, M., 287, 292
Torero, Máximo, 117
Tornell, A., 430
Torrijos, Omar, 372
trade policy
    critique of, 286
    import controls, ix, x
    openness of: and growth collapse, 427–30,
    428t; relative openness of Venezuela, 430
transfers to private sector
    complex effects of, 273
    oil boom period (1974–1985): classification
    of vs. government consumption,
    271; impact on GDP vs. government
    consumption, 271–73, 272t; levels of vs.
    consumption, 268, 269f, 270t
Transparency International perception of
    corruption index, 291
transportation, cross-border, Venezuelan
    restrictions on, trade impact of, 31–32
Trebbi, F., 429t, 434–35
Trefler, D., 429t, 435
El Trienio Adeco period, 341–42
twelve apostles, 345–46
unemployment
    1967–2008, 218, 218f
    history of, impact on political beliefs, 410,
    411t, 412t, 418–19
    increase since 1980, 130
Unión Republicana Democrática. See URD
United Nations Development Programme,
    429t, 433
Universidad Central de Venezuela, 385
universities
    early supporters of Chávez in, 375, 376t
    growth of in Punto Fijo democracy,
    383–84

Latin American, purging of leftists
    from, 385
    sheltering of far left in, 373, 383–85, 394,
    395t, 396
University of Oriente, 385
University of Zulia, 385
Un Nuevo Tiempo, 299, 300
Urbaneja, Diego, 59
urbanization, investment in, oil revenues and,
    59–60
URD (Unión Republicana Democrática), 313n14,
    342, 381–82, 387f
Uruguay, radical left in, 392
vacation bonus, and labor costs, 124
VARs (vector auto-regressions), structural, 271,
    273, 278–80
VAT tax
    FIDES and, 93, 94–95
    income generated from, 230
    introduction of, 209, 275, 304
    regional earmarks in, 304
    regressivity of, 224, 228–29
    revenue productivity of, 236n45
Velasco, Andrés, 4
Velásquez, Andrés, 300
Velásquez, Ramón J., 93, 94, 304
Venezuelan Institute of Petrochemicals,
    establishment of, 60
Venezuelan Intergovernmental Decentralization
    Fund. See FIDES
Venezuelan Investment Fund (FIV), 268
Venezuelan Manufacturing Sector Survey
    (VMSS), 115, 118, 130–31, 133–34, 135
Venezuela Oil Corporation (CVP), 62–63
veto players
    Chávez's political tools and, 398
    rise in number of, 379
Viana, H., 357
Villalba, Jóvito, 313n13
Vishny, Robert W., 202
VMSS. See Venezuelan Manufacturing Sector
    Survey (VMSS)
Wacziarg, R., 438
wages. See also labor costs; minimum wage;
    payroll taxes
    and "capacity to import" problem, 204
    changes in definition of, and labor costs,
    120–21, 120f, 144–45, 150–51n16
    data, gaps in, 214–15
    decline since 1980, 116, 130; as despite
    educational gains, 187, 188, 193; and
    poverty rates, 222, 223t, 232; schooling
    premium and, 195; and wage costs, 364
    decomposition by groups, 215–16, 215f

wages (*cont.*)
    decomposition by productive characteristics
        and returns, 216–18, 217t, 234n15
    education premium and, 187–88, 193–97,
        194f, 204, 215–18, 215t; real *vs.* expected
        wage levels, 187, 188, 196–97, 196f,
        197f, 204
    inequality in, 213–19, 214f
    mandated increases in, 119
    vs. other nations, by time and industry, 360,
        361t–363t
Wagner, Rodrigo, 5, 37
Warner, Andrew M., 1, 44, 428t, 430
WBI. *See* World Bank Institute
Why Growth Rates Differ (Denison), 426
"Why Polarize?" (Corrales), 397
within-country growth empirics, development
    of, 3–6
Woessmann, L., 428t, 433

Wooldridge, J., 135
worker output, schooling level and,
        conventional wisdom on, 187, 188
World Bank, 116
    Pérez's Great Turn and, 283n9
    World Development Indicators, 409, 422
World Bank Doing Business Survey, 171–74
World Bank Institute (WBI), governance
        indicators, 290–91, 290f, 312n5
World Development Indicators (World Bank),
        409, 422
Worldscope, 176–77, 182t
World Values Survey, 409, 421–22
Wurgler, Jeffrey, 175
Yom Kippur War, and oil dependence, efforts to
        reduce, 66–67
Zervos, S., 428t
Zingales, I., 169, 174–75
Zou, H., 92